International Business

International Business

Global Competition from a European Perspective

Andrew L. Harrison

Ertuğrul Dalkıran

Ena Elsey

University of Teesside

OXFORD

UNIVERSITY PRESS

Great Clarendon Street, Oxford OX2 6DP

Oxford University Press is a department of the University of Oxford.
It furthers the University's objective of excellence in research, scholarship,
and education by publishing worldwide in

Oxford New York

Athens Auckland Bangkok Bogotá Buenos Aires Calcutta
Cape Town Chennai Dar es Salaam Delhi Florence Hong Kong Istanbul
Karachi Kuala Lumpur Madrid Melbourne Mexico City Mumbai
Nairobi Paris São Paulo Singapore Taipei Tokyo Toronto Warsaw

with associated companies in Berlin Ibadan

Oxford is a registered trade mark of Oxford University Press
in the UK and in certain other countries

Published in the United States
by Oxford University Press Inc., New York

British Library Cataloguing in Publication Data
Data available

Library of Congress Cataloging in Publication Data
Data available
ISBN 0-19-878213-6

1 3 5 7 9 10 8 6 4 2

Typeset by RefineCatch Limited, Bungay, Suffolk
Printed in Great Britain by
The Bath Press
Bath

For Heather, David, and Rachel
For my family
For Derek and my parents

Preface

THIS book addresses one of the major issues affecting our everyday lives: the internationalization, or indeed globalization, of business. Whether as consumers, employees, students of business, or simply as observers of world events, it is difficult to be unaffected by the activities of multinational enterprises and institutions. The book attempts to introduce some order into the study of the complex and often confusing issues of international business. In doing so, the authors aim to make the key issues intelligible to a wide range of readers whilst at the same time capturing the fascination and intellectual challenge of international themes.

The approach used throughout the book is to use sufficient theory from the disciplines underlying international business to elucidate the topics under consideration, without using theory for its own sake. Practical examples are used to illustrate the theory and the aim in each chapter is to explore real issues in international business. Inevitably, some chapters have a larger theoretical content than others because of the nature of the subject matter. In these cases, the ideas developed are applied in subsequent chapters. Many of the issues discussed are topical ones and are therefore unfolding as the reader uses the book, but it is hoped that the analysis developed in the book will serve as a basis for understanding the future course of events as well as for drawing lessons from past events. With this in mind, the reader is well advised to become immersed in international issues with the help of a good newspaper or current affairs journal. To help keep the material in the book up to date, the authors have set up a website, to which analysis of recent developments will be added periodically. Their website address is as follows:

http://www-sss.tees.ac.uk/intbus/

The book is primarily intended to meet the requirements of intermediate or final-year undergraduate students, but it should also be useful for postgraduate students taking a Master's degree in business administration or related disciplines as well as for those studying for professional qualifications in a business field. The wide coverage of the book has been designed to meet the needs of students taking courses in international business, the international business environment, European business, or courses with similar titles. It is hoped that the general reader interested in current affairs may also find the book of value. The book has a strong European as well as international focus, not only because it is written from a European perspective, but also because of the dramatic impact of developments in the European Union and Eastern Europe during the 1990s.

International business has become an academic discipline in its own right in recent years, first in the USA and more recently in Europe and elsewhere. Although a number of topics are common to many international business courses and can be found in different books on the subject, the subject matter of international business is by no means uniform. Indeed, it was the lack of a suitable book covering the topics taught by the present authors which was the primary reason for writing this book. Whilst many of the topics in the book can be found in some form in a number of other books on the subject, there are also topics here which are difficult to find elsewhere. Moreover, the authors have often addressed controversial issues, leaving the reader to draw his/her own conclusions rather than claiming that there is a unique view. Sometimes, it may be clear what the authors' view is on a particular point, but it is hoped that by confronting the difficult issues the reader will be stimulated to agree or disagree.

Each chapter concludes with a learning activity: either a study topic, case study, or group activity. The study topics focus on a topical issue and are designed to encourage discussion. Many of the questions on the study topics have no simple, neat answer. The authors' intention is to raise awareness of the issues and to encourage a questioning approach to the issues concerned. The case studies are based on a company, an industry, or a country. The intention is to draw lessons from experience or to provide a practical application of the ideas developed in the chapter. The group activities encourage a team approach to problem-solving where the generation of ideas or imaginative solutions are required.

A further feature of the book is the research topic, with the theme 'the globalization of business', which is intended to integrate the various topics developed throughout the book. Students can undertake any or all of the tasks contained in the research topic as they progress through the book. Whilst a fuller understanding of globalization will be achieved by completing all the tasks systematically, it is recognized that different courses include different topics and that individual students may have different interests. Any of the tasks may be completed by students working in a group or different tasks may be allocated to different individuals or groups. In this way, the research topic should provide a flexible learning activity.

International business is one of the most intriguing and stimulating aspects of business. It is hoped that, after using the book, the reader will share the authors' enthusiasm for the subject.

University of Teesside   Andrew L. Harrison, Ertuğrul Dalkıran, and Ena Elsey
June 1999

Acknowledgements

THE authors would like to thank Kirsty Burnside, Stephen James, Dr Ian Smith, and Colin Wimpory, all present or former colleagues at the University of Teesside, for their helpful comments on sections of the book; Lynton Bussell, Dr Julian Gough, Joanne Gray, Stephen James, Paul Pye, and Bill Suthers, colleagues in the Economics Subject Group at the University of Teesside, for their frequent support and encouragement; Derek Elsey for his legal expertise; Dennis Bates for his IT skills; the anonymous reviewers, both of the initial proposal and the final draft, for their helpful comments and constructive criticisms; Brendan George, Ruth Marshall, and their colleagues at Oxford University Press for their advice, patience, encouragement, and painstaking efforts in preparing the book for publication; and, last but not least, their long-suffering families for their support, encouragement, and forbearance during the long hours spent writing the book.

The authors would also like to thank the following for permission to reproduce published material: The Free Press, a Division of Simon & Schuster, Inc. and Michael E. Porter (Fig. 13.1); Office for National Statistics (Table 10.2); UNCTAD, Geneva (Table 2.1); and World Trade Organization (Table 8.1).

Notwithstanding the valued contributions of all the above, the authors accept full responsibility for the views expressed in the book and for any remaining errors, omissions, or inaccuracies. Although every effort has been made to ensure the accuracy of the book, to acknowledge copyright material, and to express fair and balanced opinions, the authors would like to apologize if they have inadvertently failed to seek the necessary permission or have caused offence to any individual or organization.

Contents

Preface   vii

Acknowledgements   ix

Research Topic: The Globalization of Business   xvii

List of Figures   xx

List of Tables   xxi

List of Boxes   xxii

Learning Activities   xxiii

Abbreviations   xxv

Part I **International business activities**   1

1 **The Nature of International Business**   3

1.1 Introduction   3

1.2 International business defined   5

1.3 Domestic and international business compared   6

1.4 The importance of international business   7

1.5 Major international business activities   10

1.6 Motives for going international   21

1.7 Summary   24

     Study Topic: UK retailers abroad   25

2 **Multinational Enterprises**   27

2.1 Introduction   27

2.2 The definition of MNEs and scope of their activities   29

2.3 Characteristics of MNEs   30

2.4 Theoretical models of MNEs   35

2.5 The Impact of MNEs on Host Countries   47

2.6 Globalization and MNEs   50

2.7 Summary   51

     Case Study: JCB—the story of a multinational   52

3 **International Market Entry and Organizational Response**   55

3.1 Introduction   55

3.2	International market selection and entry	56
3.3	Human resource management (HRM)	63
3.4	Financing international operations	67
3.5	International logistics	72
3.6	Summary	74
	Group Activity: Finding a new market abroad	75

Part II **The International Environment**   77

4	**The Political, Economic, and Legal Environment**	**79**
4.1	Introduction	79
4.2	Political systems and cultural differences	81
4.3	Economic systems in transition	87
4.4	The legal environment	92
4.5	Summary	98
	Study Topic: China—political control with economic freedom?	99

5	**Culture and Ethics in International Business**	**101**
5.1	Introduction	101
5.2	The nature of culture	102
5.3	The composition of culture	107
5.4	Adjusting to cultural differences	114
5.5	Barriers to effective cultural adjustment	116
5.6	The methodology of cultural assessment	117
5.7	Ethical issues in international business	120
5.8	Summary	123
	Case Study: Cultural differences among South-East Asian managers	124

6	**International Institutions and Global Issues**	**127**
6.1	Introduction	127
6.2	The changing world trade order	128
6.3	Global governance and international institutions	135
6.4	The impact of international business on people and the environment	141
6.5	Summary	144
	Study Topic: The EU banana regime	145

7	**Integration between Countries**	**148**
7.1	Introduction	148
7.2	Levels of integration between countries	149
7.3	Impact of integration between countries	154
7.4	Major regional economic groupings	159
7.5	Regional integration and globalization	166
7.6	Summary	167
	Study Topic: Regional vs. global free trade	168

8	**The World's Major Trading Nations**	**171**
8.1	Introduction	171
8.2	World economic leadership and the triad nations	173
8.3	The major trading nations' role in trade and investment	179
8.4	Doing business in the USA, Western Europe, and Japan	182
8.5	Summary	187
	Case Study: Forging partnerships with Japanese car manufacturers	187

9	**The Emerging Economies**	**191**
9.1	Introduction	191
9.2	The world's emerging economies	192
9.3	Reasons for the rapid growth of the emerging economies	196
9.4	Problems of rapid growth in emerging economies	204
9.5	Persistent problems in the less developed countries	207
9.6	Summary	210
	Study Topic: The emerging economies—opportunity or threat?	211

Part III **International Trade and Investment**   **215**

10	**International Trade and Payments**	**217**
10.1	Introduction	217
10.2	Why do nations trade?	218
10.3	Balance of payments (BoP)	226
10.4	Summary	228
	Study Topic: Trade specialization in the modern world	229

11 Foreign Exchange Markets and Exchange Rate Systems **232**

11.1 Introduction 232

11.2 The nature of exchange rates 233

11.3 The determination of nominal exchange rates 234

11.4 The purchasing power parity theory of exchange rates 238

11.5 The foreign exchange market 239

11.6 Exchange rate systems 241

11.7 The euro 244

11.8 Summary 246

Study Topic: Europe's single currency 247

12 Foreign Direct Investment and Collaborative Strategies **249**

12.1 Introduction 249

12.2 Foreign investment in the global economy 250

12.3 The determinants of FDI 255

12.4 Collaborative strategies 265

12.5 Summary 268

Case Study: Spain's growing attraction as an investment location 269

13 International Competitiveness **272**

13.1 Introduction 272

13.2 The meaning and significance of international competitiveness 273

13.3 Determinants of a firm's international competitiveness 278

13.4 Determinants of a country's competitive environment 282

13.5 Summary 289

Group Activity: Sharpening Philips Electronics' international competitiveness 289

Part IV **The European Union** **293**

14 The Development and Policies of the European Union **295**

14.1 Introduction 295

14.2 The development of the European Union 296

14.3 Major policies of the European Union 305

14.4 The significance of the European Union for business activity 316

14.5 Summary 316

Study Topic: Will enlargement bankrupt the EU? 317

15   The Single European Market   320

15.1   Introduction   320

15.2   Progress towards the Single European Market   321

15.3   The main Single Market measures   326

15.4   Doing business in the Single Market   332

15.5   Summary   334

        Study Topic: Can SMEs survive in the Single European Market?   335

16   European Political and Economic Integration   338

16.1   Introduction   338

16.2   Wider and deeper integration   339

16.3   The Treaty on European Union (Maastricht Treaty): key measures   343

16.4   The implications of economic and political union   349

16.5   Political union and international business   356

16.6   Summary   356

        Case Study: Honeywell Europe—A US firm embraces the euro   357

17   The European Union and International Business   360

17.1   Introduction   360

17.2   'Fortress Europe': true or false?   361

17.3   The EU's relations with the rest of the world   364

17.4   The EU's role in promoting international business   367

17.5   The EU as a world economic leader   370

17.6   Summary   372

        Study Topic: The EU's lagging competitiveness   373

Part V Transition in Eastern Europe   375

18   Economic and Political Challenges for Eastern Europe in 1989   377

18.1   Introduction   377

18.2   Why did communism fail?   379

18.3   The nature of the economic reform programme   384

18.4   Macroeconomic stabilization policies   386

18.5   Problems facing the economic reform programme   389

18.6   Summary   391

        Group Activity: Reforming a state-owned enterprise   392

19 Privatization in Eastern Europe 394

19.1 Introduction 394

19.2 Why privatize? 396

19.3 Method and form of privatization: differences in approach 399

19.4 Privatization and regulation of utilities 409

19.5 Summary 410

Study Topic: Privatization in Poland 412

20 Foreign Direct Investment in Eastern Europe 415

20.1 Introduction 415

20.2 The role of economic reform 416

20.3 The nature and availability of FDI 418

20.4 How can FDI contribute to the development of the economies of Eastern Europe? 420

20.5 The case of the motor vehicle industry 422

20.6 Successes and failures of FDI 426

20.7 Summary 431

Case Study: Skoda's new model 432

21 The Relationship between the European Union and Eastern Europe 435

21.1 Introduction 435

21.2 The changing international political environment 436

21.3 Eastern Europe: the rush for EU membership? 439

21.4 EU Membership: How do Eastern European applicants shape up? 442

21.5 Eastern Europe and EMU 444

21.6 The role of Western assistance in the transition 446

21.7 Summary 448

Study Topic: Is EMU good for Eastern Europe? 450

22 Doing Business in Eastern Europe 454

22.1 Introduction 454

22.2 The successes and failures of the transformation process in Eastern Europe since 1990 455

22.3 The development of Western business culture: The role of entrepreneurship 462

22.4 Limitations to the development of entrepreneurship 465

22.5 Summary 469

Case Study: Western management techniques at Tyumen Oil 471

Glossary 474

Research Project: The Globalization of Business

Introduction

THIS project has three main aims. Firstly, it is designed to increase the reader's awareness of what is perhaps the most important trend in modern international business: the globalization of business activity. Secondly, it serves as a common theme or link between many of the topics covered throughout the book. Thirdly, it should encourage the practice of consulting a wide range of source materials in a subject which is constantly developing in the world around us. The project can be undertaken by students in a directed learning environment or by an independent reader who is dedicated to a systematic study of international business. Guidance is given below on each stage of the project. Using a wide range of published information, from newspapers, journals, books, CDRoms, Internet websites, etc., the reader should gather relevant information as indicated by the questions below. These questions serve as a focus for exploring the issues involved in the globalization of business. Answers to the questions can be presented in a variety of ways, including oral presentations (individual or group), written reports, tutor-led discussion groups or in more formal examination settings.

The meaning of 'Globalization'

WHILST the whole issue should become much clearer by the end of the project, globalization describes the increasing interdependence of business activity throughout the world. Business firms sell their products in 'global' markets, just as though each country's market were part of a single world market, with few barriers to trade and where a single marketing strategy suffices. They acquire their resources in 'global' labour markets, 'global' capital markets, 'global' markets for raw materials and component parts. Some companies are themselves 'global' in that they no longer have a national home base. The world's economies are also becoming more 'global' as events in one country affect the fortunes of another. Of course, this picture of a globalized business world is overstated. Many barriers and differences still exist between countries. The purpose of this project is to examine the extent of globalization and its importance to business decision makers.

Stages of the Project

GATHER relevant information and examples from a variety of sources in order to answer the following questions. Each stage should be attempted at appropriate intervals throughout the course of study.

Stage 1 (to be attempted after Chapter 2)

Have multinational enterprises generally forsaken their national home base to become truly international companies?
   First, you should select an actual multinational enterprise (MNE), then find out (a) the regions or countries of the world where it operates; (b) the modes of entry it uses in different countries; and (c) whether there is evidence of the company having forsaken its home base.

Stage 2 (to be attempted after Chapter 3)

To what extent do international business firms make use of global markets, global resources, etc?
   To answer this question, carry out research to find out (a) whether your chosen MNE sells standardized products in each country or whether it adapts its products to accommodate local circumstances; (b) whether common marketing methods are used in every country; and (c) the extent to which the MNE makes use of the world's resources by locating factories or other facilities abroad or by outsourcing its production to foreign companies, etc.

Stage 3 (to be attempted after Chapter 6)

What barriers still restrict the process of business globalization?
   Focusing on some of the main countries in which your chosen MNE operates, discover (a) the nature of the barriers to trade or investment which exist in these countries; (b) the way in which cultural differences may affect the company's operations; and (c) the extent to which the company is able to overcome these barriers.

Stage 4 (to be attempted after Chapter 7)

How is the proliferation of regional economic groupings affecting the process of globalization?
    For this task you should select a regional economic grouping or trade bloc other than the European Union. Then investigate (a) how this regional grouping has affected trade, investment and other business activity within its borders; and (b) how the activities of foreign companies have been affected by the existence of this regional grouping.

Stage 5 (to be attempted after Chapter 11)

To what extent is international business activity encouraged or inhibited by the exchange rate regime?
    Investigate two or three different currencies which operate under different exchange rate systems. Find out (a) the extent to which these currencies have fluctuated in recent years; (b) the type of exchange rate system in operation; and (c) the impact of currency stability or currency movements on these countries' trade and investment.

Stage 6 (to be attempted after Chapter 17)

In what ways do the existence and policies of the European Union affect the international competitiveness of European companies?
    Consider how the international competitiveness of a particular EU-based company or industry is affected by (a) the single European market; (b) a specific EU policy which is focused on the company or industry concerned; and (c) the external trade policies of the EU.

Stage 7 (to be attempted after Chapter 9 in the case of Asia or Chapter 22 in the case of Eastern Europe)

What impact is globalization having on the emerging economies of Asia or Eastern Europe?
    Select a specific emerging economy in Asia or Eastern Europe. Investigate (a) the extent to which this country has opened its borders to trade and investment; (b) its dependence on foreign MNEs; (c) the way in which its political, economic, and social circumstances have changed in response to international business activity.

List of Figures

1.1	The major activities of multinational enterprises	11
3.1	Stages involved in international market entry	57
4.1	Categorization of 'emerging economies'	90
6.1	Net welfare loss as a result of a tariff or quota	130
7.1	Levels of integration between countries	150
9.1	Growth rates of selected East Asian economies, 1975–96	194
11.1	Determination of the pound sterling exchange rate	237
12.1	Factors involved in the FDI decision	256
13.1	Determinants of national advantage ('Porter's Diamond')	285
14.1	The main institutions of the European Union	301
15.1	The Single European Market project	327
16.1	The three 'pillars' of the European Union	348

List of Tables

1.1	Degree of openness in European Union member states	13
1.2	FDI inward stock in selected countries	14
2.1	The world's top twenty MNEs ranked by foreign assets, 1996	34
7.1	UK trade with the EU	155
7.2	Key data on NAFTA members	163
7.3	Key data on APEC members	165
8.1	Leading exporters and importers in world merchandise trade, 1997	173
10.1	Comparative advantage	220
10.2	Summary of UK balance of payments, 1997	227
11.1	The euro conversion rates	245
12.1	Trends in FDI flows	253
12.2	The EU's top six investment locations	269
13.1	Indicators of international competitiveness in selected countries, 1997	276
14.1	Key data on the USA, European Union, and Japan	296
14.2	Landmarks in the development of the European Union	298
16.1	Applicants for EU membership	340
16.2	The convergence criteria for economic and monetary union	344
19.1	Methods of privatization in Russia and Eastern Europe	399

List of Boxes

1.1	Noddy ventures into Asia	20
2.1	Nissan in north-east England	46
5.1	Christmas comes to Istanbul	105
5.2	Fast-food culture	106
5.3	Unfortunate ambiguities of the English language	108
5.4	Business appointments in Chile	113
5.5	Supermarkets embrace ethical trading	122
7.1	The North American Free Trade Agreement	162
8.1	Fuyo: A Japanese *keiretsu*	178
8.2	South Korea: An emerging economic power	179
8.3	China: An emerging giant	180
8.4	Western Europe's SMEs	185
9.1	Taiwan: Profile of an Asian 'tiger'	201
9.2	Uganda: Struggling to overcome the disastrous years	210
12.1	Ireland: FDI in a European 'tiger economy'	260
12.2	Alliances in the airline industry	267
13.1	Creating a competitive advantage in China	280
13.2	Creating national champions	288
14.1	EU support for small and medium-sized enterprises	310
15.1	Duty-free goods in the Single European Market	330
16.1	EMU convergence: fact and fiction	346
17.1	Competition and change in the motor industry	369
17.2	Airbus—A lesson in European collaboration	371

Learning Activities

Study Topics

Chapter 1	UK retailers abroad	25
Chapter 4	China—political control with economic freedom?	99
Chapter 6	The EU banana regime	145
Chapter 7	Regional versus global free trade	168
Chapter 9	The emerging economies: opportunity or threat?	211
Chapter 10	Trade specialization in the modern world	229
Chapter 11	Europe's single currency	247
Chapter 14	Will enlargement bankrupt the EU?	317
Chapter 15	Can SMEs survive in the Single European Market?	335
Chapter 17	The EU's lagging competitiveness	373
Chapter 19	Privatization in Poland	412
Chapter 21	Is EMU good for Eastern Europe?	450

Case Studies

Chapter 2	JCB—the story of a multinational	52
Chapter 5	Cultural differences among South-East Asian managers	124
Chapter 8	Forging partnerships with Japanese car manufacturers	187
Chapter 12	Spain's growing attraction as an investment location	269
Chapter 16	Honeywell Europe—A US firm embraces the euro	357
Chapter 20	Skoda's new model	432
Chapter 22	Western management techniques at Tyumen Oil	471

Group Activities

Chapter 3   Finding a new market abroad   75

Chapter 13   Sharpening Philips Electronics' international competitiveness   289

Chapter 18   Reforming a state-owned enterprise   392

Abbreviations

ACP	African, Caribbean, and Pacific group of countries
AFTA	ASEAN Free Trade Area
APEC	Asia-Pacific Economic Cooperation
ASEAN	Association of South-East Asian Nations
BPCS	Business Protection Coordination Secretariat (Hungary)
CACM	Central American Common Market
CAP	Common Agricultural Policy
CBI	Confederation of British Industries
CEFTA	Central European Free Trade Area
CFP	Common Fisheries Policy
CIS	Commonwealth of Independent States
CMEA	Council for Mutual Economic Assistance (also known as COMECON)
COMESA	Common Market for East and Southern Africa
COREPER	Comité des représentants permanents
EA	Europe Agreement
EAC	East Africa Cooperation
EAGGF	European Agricultural Guidance and Guarantee Fund
EASDAQ	European Association of Securities Dealers Automated Quotation
EBRD	European Bank for Reconstruction and Development
EC	European Community (prior to November 1993) or European Commission
ECB	European Central Bank
ECJ	European Court of Justice
ECOFIN	Economics and Finance Ministers (of the EU)
ECOWAS	Economic Community of West African States
ECSC	European Coal and Steel Community
ECU	European Currency Unit
EEA	European Economic Area
EEC	European Economic Community
EFTA	European Free Trade Association
EIB	European Investment Bank
EMI	European Monetary Institute
EMS	European Monetary System
EMU	Economic and Monetary Union/European Monetary Union
ERDF	European Regional Development Fund

ERM	Exchange Rate Mechanism
ESF	European Social Fund
ESPRIT	European Strategic Programme for Research and Development in Information Technology
ESCB	European System of Central Banks
EU	European Union
EURATOM	European Atomic Energy Community
FDI	Foreign Direct Investment
FIG	Financial Industrial Group (Russia)
FOREX	Foreign Exchange Market
FSA	Firm-Specific Asset
FTAA	Free Trade Area of the Americas
G7/G8	Group of Seven/Eight (leading industrial nations)
GATS	General Agreement on Trade in Services
GATT	General Agreement on Tariffs and Trade
GDP	Gross Domestic Product
GDR	German Democratic Republic (former East Germany)
GNP	Gross National Product
HIPC	Highly Indebted Poor Country
HRM	Human Resource Management
IBRD	International Bank for Reconstruction and Development (World Bank)
IDA	International Development Association
IFC	International Finance Corporation
IGC	Intergovernmental Conference
ILO	International Labour Organization
IMF	International Monetary Fund
JVA	Joint-Venture Agreement
LAFTA	Latin American Free Trade Area
LAIA	Latin American Integration Association
LDC	Least Developed Country
M&A	Mergers and Acquisitions
MAI	Multilateral Agreement on Investment
MERCOSUR	Mercado Comun del Sur (Common Market of the South)
MITI	Ministry of International Trade and Industry (Japan)
MNE	Multinational Enterprise
NAFTA	North American Free Trade Agreement
NASDAQ	National Association of Securities Dealers Automated Quotation
NATO	North Atlantic Treaty Organization
NEM	New Economic Mechanism (Hungary)

NIC	Newly Industrializing Country
NIF	National Investment Fund (Poland)
NPV	Net Present Value
OECD	Organization for Economic Cooperation and Development
OEEC	Organization for European Economic Cooperation
PHARE	Poland and Hungary: Assistance for Restructuring Economies
POF	Private Ownership Fund (Romania)
PPP	Purchasing Power Parity
PSBR	Public Sector Borrowing Requirement
PTA	Preferential Trade Area
R&D	Research and Development
SACU	Southern African Customs Union
SEM	Single European Market
SIGMA	Support for Improvement in Governance and Management in Central and Eastern Europe
SME	Small and Medium-Sized Enterprise
SOE	State-Owned Enterprise
SOF	State Ownership Fund (Romania)
SPA	State Property Agency (Hungary)
STEP	Sociocultural, Technological, Economic, and Political Environments
SWOT	Strengths, Weaknesses, Opportunities, and Threats
TACIS	Technical Assistance for the Commonwealth of Independent States
TI	Transparency International
TQM	Total Quality Management
TRIPS	Trade-related Aspects of Intellectual Property Rights
UN	United Nations
UNCTAD	United Nations Conference on Trade and Development
UNESCO	United Nations Educational, Scientific, and Cultural Organization
UNHCR	United Nations High Commissioner for Refugees
USSR	Union of Soviet Socialist Republics (former Soviet Union)
VAT	Value-Added Tax
VER	Voluntary Export Restraint
WEU	Western European Union
WHO	World Health Organization
WTO	World Trade Organization

Part I

International Business Activities

1

The Nature of International Business

Objectives

- to outline the main activities involved in international business
- to indicate the significance of international business for individuals, firms, and countries
- to identify the advantages and disadvantages of the main international market entry strategies
- to discuss the reasons why firms go international

1.1 Introduction

I⊤ is hard to imagine a world without international business. Everything that is consumed, everything that is produced, and every financial activity engaged in is affected by international business. Virtually every nation, from the smallest to the largest, has business firms engaged in various types of international business activity. It is through these activities that nations enjoy the benefits of international business by trading in a great variety of goods and services produced around the world and made available locally. An inspection of the local supermarket shelves will reveal a rich variety of imported goods ranging from exotic fruits and vegetables, wines, and cheeses to kitchen utensils and other paraphernalia.

International business is claimed to be as old as the history of mankind itself.[1] Even at the most tribal level, communities found it in their interest to trade, albeit in a very primitive manner and involving the exchange of simple objects mostly for immediate consumption. Citing from the writings of the ancient Greek historian, Herodotus,

Taoka and Beeman give the interesting example of 'silent trade' in which 'deliverers would leave objects in a clearing and then hide. Others would come along and leave articles in exchange for what they took.'[2] Historically, trade was in the form of barter involving the exchange of articles in kind and undertaken as much for social as for economic reasons.

Even though modern trade is conducted in far more advanced forms and for more complex reasons than ever before, the basic human need for trade remains the same. However, unlike ancient times during which trade was devised and undertaken by communities for the benefit of the communities themselves, over 90 per cent of modern trade is undertaken by private firms in pursuit of their own aims and objectives.

The growth of modern trade coincided, to a large extent, with the emergence of the modern nation state and with the consequent formation of national borders. The clear recognition and appreciation of the mutual benefits of free trade (trade without barriers and based on the principle of comparative advantage) provided sufficient incentives for nation states to seek greater opportunities in each others' domestic markets and thus to increase the volume of trade among themselves. Such mutual benefits have been largely responsible for the growth of alliances and regional integration around the world, as evidenced by the establishment of a considerable number of trading areas, such as the European Union (EU) and North American Free Trade Agreement (NAFTA). Over the years, nations have helped to promote trade and international business activities by attempting to create suitable business and investment environments within their borders, not only out of political and strategic necessity but also out of a desire to attract business and foreign investment, often in competition with other nations. For example, the recent spate of liberalization, deregulation, and privatization programmes by governments around the world, in particular by those of the former Soviet republics and Eastern Europe, have given special impetus to the growth of foreign direct investment (FDI).

As a consequence of the endeavours of nation states and international agreements such as GATT and its successor organization, the World Trade Organization (WTO), there has been a steady and impressive growth in both trade and FDI. FDI is a form of investment which entitles the investing firm to equity or ownership rights and concomitant control over its investment in a country other than its own. The following statistics give an idea of the growth in trade and FDI:[3]

- Total GATT membership in 1947 was only twenty-three; by mid-1999 its successor, the WTO, had 135 members; and thirty more countries, including China, had applied for membership.
- The volume of world merchandise exports grew by 9.5 per cent in 1997 while world output grew by 3 per cent despite the negative impact of the Asian financial crisis during the same year.
- In 1997 exports of merchandise and commercial services amounted to $6.6 trillion, with merchandise exports of $5.3 trillion and commercial services of $1.3 trillion.
- The volume of world exports increased sixteen times, exports of manufactures

thirty-one times, world output six times, and manufactured output nine times between 1950 and 1996.

- The stock of FDI was $1 trillion in 1987, $2 trillion in 1993, and about $3.2 trillion in 1996, an increase of over 45 per cent between 1987 and 1996.
- FDI outflow from developed countries was $295 billion and inflow was $208 billion in 1996, with the USA being the largest investor and recipient of FDI. In the same year, developing countries received $129 billion and invested $51 billion, with China being the second largest recipient after the USA.

The growth of modern trade has also been reinforced immensely by the growth and rapid spread of technology. What started as simple improvements in land (trains) and sea transport (steamships) has culminated in a bewildering variety of developments in telecommunications, fast and safe means of transport by land, sea, and air, and products and services ranging from modern aircraft to exotic holidays in all parts of the world. Furthermore, modern trade increasingly involves intermediate products, components used in production processes around the world (cars, computers, and the like), and an array of complex high-technology goods and services. Many of the services which until recently were only available locally, such as financial services, can now be accessed through modern telecommunication systems, even in the remotest parts of the world. Indeed, one is now witnessing the birth of trade through the Internet using the so-called *cyber currency*. Chapters 10 and 12 will further develop the nature of trade, FDI, and related issues.

1.2 International Business Defined

INTERNATIONAL business is any business activity organized and carried out across national borders by business firms in pursuit of their stated aims and objectives. Some international business activities are still being conducted by governments, albeit on an increasingly smaller scale, often in pursuit of political and strategic aims and objectives. However, an overwhelming proportion of international business activities is undertaken by private firms.

International business activities fall into two broad categories: international trade and international investment. International trade takes place when a firm engages in export and/or import of goods and services. International investment takes place when a firm transfers resources to undertake business activities outside its country of origin. The firm's investment activities are carried out in various forms, ranging from investment by its wholly owned subsidiary or in partnership with a local business firm in the form of a joint venture, to a licensed or franchised operation, or a turnkey project (see Section 1.5).

Within the context of these two broad categories of business activity, it is useful to consider international business as an extension of domestic business to other countries. Even the largest multinational enterprises (MNEs) can trace their beginnings to domestic business ventures which, over time, outgrew their domestic market and required their managers to seek business opportunities in other countries (see Section 1.6).

1.3 Domestic and International Business Compared

THE same basic business principles concerning tasks, functions, and processes apply to international business as to domestic business. However, the environment in which domestic and international business firms operate varies considerably and therefore requires an international business firm to alter and modify its business practices country by country. Unlike a domestic business manager, an international manager faces greater difficulties, greater uncertainties, and, more importantly, much greater risks. The tasks of an international business executive are clearly much more challenging.

These difficulties, uncertainties, and risks emanate from differences in the political, economic, and legal environment; in the cultural environment; and in different foreign exchange markets and exchange rate systems. In most cases, these problems manifest themselves as constraints which render the process of decision-making and decision-implementation more difficult (and in some cases, more hazardous) than under domestic circumstances. More importantly, culturally insensitive decisions often result in conflicts which are more difficult (and costly) to resolve without seriously affecting the performance of the firm, its future operations, and the effectiveness of its management. The dynamic nature of constant changes in business, economic, political, and legal environments in the host country adds still more difficulties with which the international business executive must deal on an almost daily basis. More specifically, an international business differs from a domestic business in the following ways:

■ Each country in which the firm operates is culturally different. To be successful, the firm must operate in a culturally sensitive manner and within the constraints of the culturally determined manners, customs, values, and norms of the host country. An international business manager must respect and empathize with cultural differences in all aspects of business and social life, seek to conform and cooperate rather than confront or behave as if operating in his/her own culture.

■ Conducting business across national borders involves the use of different currencies and observing different government rules and regulations limiting the firm's freedom of action; for example, restrictions on the amount of profit to be transferred. Governments practise different exchange rate policies and systems, ranging from daily decrees about the value of the local currency in terms of the world's major currencies to fixed and floating exchange rate systems. These practices add greater risk and uncertainty to the already highly risky and uncertain nature of international financial transactions. To be successful, the firm must develop an appropriate strategy to deal with these differences and the associated problems.

■ The legal environment differs from country to country, requiring firms to show particular sensitivity to laws, rules, and regulations which may affect operations and performance. Disregarding or disobeying the laws of the host country can be very damaging to the finances and the image of the firm. Laws pertaining to joint ownership of assets, for example, are often very complicated, bureaucratic, frustrating, and time-consuming. Legal difficulties are often the source of serious disputes between the host government and the firm, requiring protracted negotiations which may end in failure to invest or to continue with the existing business.

■ Differences in consumer tastes and preferences and demand patterns stemming from cultural differences require the firm to adopt appropriate production, procurement, and marketing strategies to minimize costs and maintain the firm's value. Even in the case of standard global products, certain modifications may be necessary to render the product more acceptable to the consumer in the host culture. For example, the name of the product in the host country's language may be offensive or the packaging may be inappropriate.

■ Different countries possess different factor endowments with different qualities, requiring the firm to formulate and implement suitable product development and logistics strategies consistent with the availability and quality of resources in the host country. Certain skills or supplies may be either unavailable or available in limited quantities and qualities. If unavailable, the firm must either import them or develop local sources of supply. Following its entry into the Soviet market in 1990, McDonald's, one of the first Western fast food firms, experienced serious difficulties in obtaining high-quality local food supplies consistent with its food technology. To meet its high standards in quality, delivery, and production methods, McDonald's had to transfer agricultural technology, equipment, and consultants from other countries with superior technology to work with Soviet farmers. One astonishing outcome was an increase of 100 per cent in potato output alone.[4] It even set up its own dairy farms, cattle farms, food-processing plants, and distribution system.

1.4 The Importance of International Business

THE differences between domestic and international business outlined above are valid reasons for studying international business. In recent years, however, international business has acquired additional importance for host countries in particular and world economies in general as a result of developments in the following areas:

■ Technology

Technological developments are transmitted to every corner of the earth through the practice of international business. This transmission is not only in the form of products and services used every day, but also in the form of modern management, production, marketing, and logistics systems employed by domestic as well as international firms. And thanks to the dramatic developments in communication and information technology, the benefits of such transmissions are shared worldwide. These technological spin-offs are often shared with local partners, suppliers, and educational and training institutions, saving the host country the research and development costs.

■ Competition

Except in the case of acquisition entry, the arrival of an international business firm in the host country, either in partnership with a local firm or on its own, may stimulate domestic competition and lead to increased entrepreneurial challenges, especially in the developing countries. International firms with superior worldwide experience, knowledge, technology, and other relevant resources have the ability to offer goods and services often at lower prices and higher quality. In the short run, domestic firms which cannot compete effectively may be forced to leave the industry. In the long run, however, economies of scale, growth in investment and research and development will result in more efficient techniques in production, management, and marketing.

■ Standardization

One of the major difficulties facing firms, especially in the developing countries, is the lack of universal standards in their basic business functions such as marketing, and, more importantly, in the design and specification of their products. Standardization refers to the adoption of norms and practices generally acceptable in world markets. In some cases, the result is one standard product sold throughout the world using similar selling techniques. Most of these standards originate in the USA and Western Europe and are often used by international business firms as benchmarks in their global business strategies. Common standards enable easier and more effective comparisons to be made by consumers and other interested parties (health and safety authorities, for example).

National and regional differences in consumer tastes, preferences, and interests and in patterns of market demand have diminished as a consequence of advances in technology, telecommunication, transport, and advertising. This has made product standardization an easier option. A further stimulus for greater standardization is provided by the increasing attempts of nation states to integrate their economies and promote the joint prosperity of their citizens. The creation of the European single market is one of the most significant and exciting examples of such attempts. With an enlarged market of over 370 million inhabitants, the European single market offers limitless opportunities and challenges to international firms within and outside the European Union (EU) to market their products with similar characteristics and specifications.

■ The business environment

A business firm operates within its internal and external environment. The internal environment is one over which the firm has considerable control: the firm determines its own internal environmental factors by specifying its corporate mission, organizational structure, recruitment policy, and its relationship with suppliers. The external environment is one over which the firm has little or no control; what little control the firm may have is usually the consequence of its market power or collective action by a representative body such as the Confederation of British Industries (CBI) in Britain. The firm must, therefore, conform to its external environmental factors, whether they be national, international, or global, or suffer the consequences of its failure to do so. For example, changes in health and safety regulations, trade policies, and the legal environment are unavoidable. Nike, one of the world's biggest manufacturers of sports and leisure wear, was forced into cancelling its licensing agreement with one of its Asian licensees suspected of employing child labour.

With the increasing internationalization of business activities, the methods of dealing with internal and external environmental factors tend to become more standardized. The main reason for this development is that domestic firms aspiring to expand internationally often emulate existing international firms in adapting to environmental changes. In other words, international business acts as a conduit for successful business policies and techniques for domestic firms to adopt as a preparation for going international. For example, many US and European firms have adopted Japanese management techniques such as quality circles, the just-in-time system (JIT), and total quality management (TQM) in order to remain competitive in their own as well as in international markets.

■ The political impact of international business

Governments play an important role in the development and promotion of international business activities. They provide a great variety of financial and non-financial incentives to attract FDI into their countries, often in competition with their neighbours. The increasing scale of liberalization of trade and investment, deregulation of domestic industries, and privatization of state-owned enterprises has the attraction of foreign business as one of its primary objectives. These programmes have created immense international business opportunities. The major impact of international business in this area has been the impetus on governments to open up their borders to international trade and investment, standardize their systems and procedures, adopt internationally acceptable values and attitudes, particularly with respect to human rights and child labour, and encourage the development of democratic institutions. For example, in order to qualify for membership of the World Trade Organization (WTO), the Chinese government is having to soften its attitude towards capitalism, undertake a review of and improvements in its human rights record, liberalize its trade and investment policies, and privatize its state enterprises (albeit at a very slow rate).

■ Economic integration and globalization

One of the most fundamental impacts of the process of internationalization since the end of World War II has been the progressive ending of the isolation of national economies. Gradually more and more of the barriers to international trade and investment are being replaced with measures designed to enhance cooperation and coordination among nation states. The need to cooperate and coordinate over wider geographical areas has led to the formation of regional groupings in the form of free trade areas, for example. Attempts to create regional economic integration in which individual economies are merged into a larger economic region have increased significantly over the years in response, among other things, to a rapid increase in the growth of international business activities (see Chapter 7).

International business activities have not only grown but have become much more diverse and complex, putting them far beyond the ability of individual governments to influence or control. One direct result has been the emergence of a new world economic order in which national economies are merging into one global economy, either on an individual basis or, as has recently been the case, in regional groupings. *Globalization* is a dynamic process in which world markets and the production of goods and services become integrated and interdependent. For individual governments, the most compelling reason to integrate their economies with others is being able to take collective measures to maximize the perceived gains and to minimize the perceived costs of globalization.

The rapid emergence of the global economy has also given rise to the need to re-examine the role and effectiveness of the agencies involved in global governance in monitoring global activities and resolving conflicts of interest which may arise; these agencies include the International Monetary Fund (IMF) and United Nations (UN). These issues are discussed further in Chapter 6.

1.5 Major International Business Activities

MULTINATIONAL enterprises (MNEs) are major forces in international business. They concentrate their activities in three main areas: international trade, foreign direct investment (FDI), and a cluster of activities including joint ventures, licensing, and franchising. These activities are discussed in detail in Chapter 2. For now, a brief outline will suffice.

Figure 1.1 The major activities of multinational enterprises

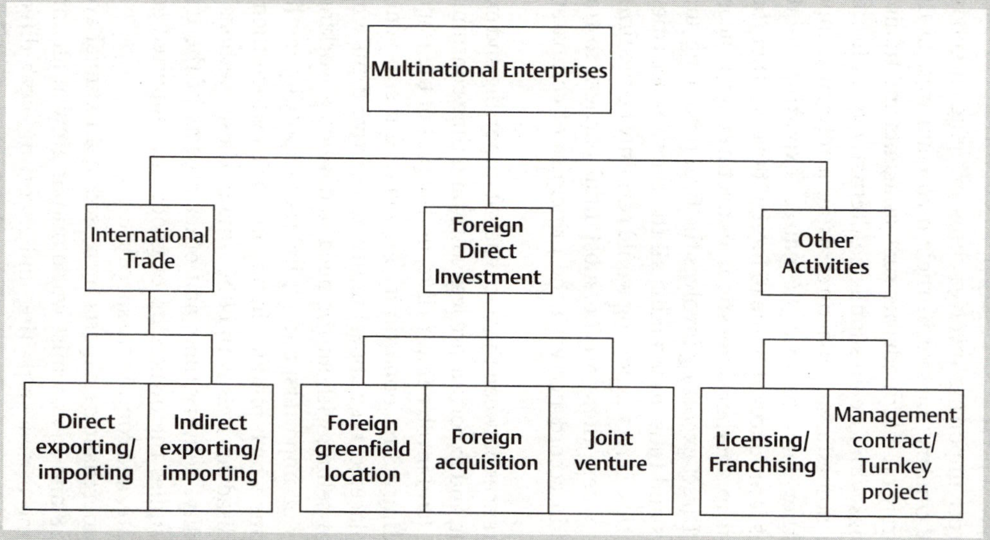

1.5.1 Direct and indirect importing and exporting

Direct importing and exporting are the oldest forms of international trade. Historically, most of this form of trade was undertaken by governments in pursuit of national aims and objectives. At present, over 90 per cent of this sort of trade is undertaken by private firms. Direct importing involves firms bringing in goods and services produced in another country for sale in their own countries. In the case of indirect importing, firms rely on intermediaries such as agents and trading houses to undertake all the dealings with foreign suppliers. Alternatively, indirect importing may be in the form of a domestic manufacturer using a foreign component as an input imported by another domestic firm. In indirect exporting the domestic firm sells goods and services it produces at home to foreign buyers either through intermediaries or by selling it to another domestic manufacturer who incorporates them into goods for export. Direct exporting involves the firm producing and selling directly to foreign customers and thus undertaking all the relevant activities itself without the use of intermediaries. Direct exporting would certainly be the firm's preferred option in circumstances where there are no substantial barriers to trade, in which case trade takes place in accordance with the principles of comparative advantage (see Chapter 10).

The main differences between the two types of importing and exporting are that (a) indirect importing and exporting are less costly and time-consuming; (b) they require less commitment (and involve fewer risks) on the part of the importing or exporting firm, thus providing a first opportunity for many firms to venture into the international marketplace; (c) they appeal mostly to reactive firms which are more interested in buying or selling without the need to develop a working relationship with foreign exporters or importers; and (d) indirect exporting methods are frequently used by small firms which produce inputs for MNEs which then export them overseas. The major disadvantages with either one of these methods are that firms lose control over quality, delivery time, and other aspects of the transaction once the foreign buyer assumes the ownership of goods and imported goods may arrive in poor condition, late, and contrary to specifications.

In real terms, merchandise exports increased at an annual average rate of 6 per cent between 1948 and 1997, whilst world output grew at an annual rate of 3.8 per cent over the same period. Importing and exporting, both direct and indirect, are therefore very important activities in the study of international business. In the first place, they provide very useful data to help understand the impact of international business on national economies. One way of measuring this impact is to calculate the *degree of openness* of national economies to international trade. Openness is defined as the ratio of nominal visible trade (exports plus imports) to nominal output. Table 1.1 illustrates the degree of openness in the European Union (EU) member states. One of the obvious advantages of international trade is that any deficiency between domestic output and demand can be met through imports and an output surplus can be exported.

Table 1.1 Degree of openness in European Union member states (%)

Country	1996	Country	1996
Austria	72.6	Ireland	118.3
Belgium/Luxembourg	138.6	Italy	39.9
Denmark	78.0	Netherlands	104.3
Finland	74.0	Portugal	44.0
France	46.9	Spain	38.4
Germany	56.6	Sweden	88.2
Greece	30.2	United Kingdom	49.6

Source: Author's calculations based on *Statistical Yearbook of the UN Economic Commission for Europe, 1998.*

Countries' dependence on each other for trade has increased considerably in recent years. It is interesting to observe in Table 1.1 that smaller countries like Ireland sometimes have a greater degree of openness than larger countries. Belgium and Luxembourg (which are treated as one for trade purposes) and the Netherlands also have a high degree of openness, reflecting their traditional importance as trading nations. Exports provide incomes for countries to pay for their imports: the greater the value of exports, the greater is the ability of countries to import. This two-way process ensures the benefits of free trade are spread worldwide through international business. According to estimates by the WTO, the ratio of world trade to world output increased by 7.5 percentage points (from 15 to 22.5 per cent) between 1974 and 1995. Invisible trade, which includes trade in services, has also become an important element in international business activity. World exports of commercial services amounted to $1,310 billion in 1997.

The second reason why data on exports and imports are important is that they indicate the types of activity undertaken and strategy developed by international business firms in pursuit of their aims and objectives. It is, therefore, no coincidence that over 70 per cent of the world's trade is within the so-called *triad* countries including the EU, North America, and Japan. We also find nearly 80 per cent of foreign direct investment flows taking place between and within the triad markets. Data on world exports and imports provide a picture of the concentration of international business activities, the geographical distribution of international trade, practical information about trading opportunities, and an indication of the degree of interdependence among the world's trading nations.

1.5.2 Foreign direct investment (FDI)

FDI is a form of equity investment which gives the investing firm control over its assets, property, and subsidiaries in the host country. It inevitably involves transfer of resources, mostly in the form of capital, to enable the firm to undertake its business

Table 1.2 FDI inward stock in selected countries				
($m. and percentage increase, 1980–97)				
Host region/economy	1980	1990	1997	1980–97
France	22,617	86,845	174,152	670
Germany	36,630	111,232	137,731	276
Japan	3,270	9,850	33,164	914
United Kingdom	63,014	203,907	274,369	335
United States	83,046	394,911	720,793	768
Developed countries	371,917	1,377,609	2,349,442	532
Developing countries	108,068	357,815	1,043,666	866
World	479,985	1,736,326	3,455,509	620

Source: World Investment Report, 1998, UNCTAD.

activities. The most important characteristic of FDI is that it demonstrates the firm's commitment to its future and the future of the host country. FDI would be the preferred option in cases where trade barriers prevent a firm from exploiting its comparative advantage through direct exporting. This preference for the FDI option has been given a significant boost during the past decade by the liberalization of FDI policies by governments throughout the world. The global stock of FDI has gone up from $480 billion in 1980 to more than $3.4 trillion in 1997. This phenomenal growth in FDI stock reflects the increasing propensity of firms of all sizes to invest in other countries, especially in the developing countries since the 1990s. Table 1.2 gives some idea of the scale of FDI stock worldwide.

The motivations for FDI range from a desire to have manufacturing facilities in countries with market growth potential and the existence of relevant factor endowments to the need to diversify production and marketing activities in order to take advantage of different trade cycles and opportunities in other countries. Trade and investment liberalization and the increasing scale of globalization has expanded opportunities for international firms to locate production facilities and to produce final or intermediate products for customers in the host country as well as in third countries located within a reasonable distance. The linkage between production locations and markets in other countries is provided through exports, a process which has become increasingly easier thanks to trade liberalization. The existence of this linkage enables firms to organize their activities vertically (involving production at different stages) at production sites, and horizontally (producing similar products) at market locations. FDI aimed at the creation of this linkage is especially suitable for natural resource-based firms, such as oil and other mineral-producing companies.

The discussion so far may have implied that the majority of FDI is undertaken solely for the purposes of establishing greenfield site production units in other countries. However, in recent years FDI activity has focused on mergers and acquisitions (M&As), both domestic and cross-border. Domestic M&As are mainly horizontal ones and involve at least one international firm or its subsidiary. One of the reasons for horizontal M&As may be to increase the firm's concentration of market power with serious implications for consumer welfare and the efficiency of resource allocation. The motivations for cross-border M&As are more varied and require case-by-case analysis to establish their rationale. The following scenarios are suggested by UNCTAD:[5]

- Export-linked M&A in which the exporting firm from country A merges with the firm in country B to which it exports.
- The firm from country A merges with the parent companies of two foreign subsidiaries or affiliates in country B.
- Joint ventures between rival MNEs.
- Acquisition of a major firm in a host country, such as the acquisition of Rolls-Royce cars of Britain by Volkswagen of Germany.
- M&As where the main reason might be to curtail competition, existing or potential.

Whatever the real motivation, whether reactive or proactive, the major concern with cross-border M&As is the real or potential threat to reduce competition in the host country's domestic economy. These and other related issues are developed further in Chapters 2 and 10.

1.5.3 Licensing

Licensing is a form of market entry involving two firms, the licenser and the licensee, in which the licenser agrees to sell to the licensee the right to use the licenser's intellectual property for a specified period of time in return for an agreed fee or royalty. The licenser's intellectual property is the firm's intangible assets developed over time at considerable research and development costs. These assets include technical know-how, brand names, patents, trade marks, copyrights, exclusive trade or intimate market knowledge, experience, and expertise.

The amount of royalty involved depends on the market value of the intellectual property and, most importantly, on the assessment of future profits the licensee expects to generate. Clearly, well-known brand names such as Levi, Nike, Budweiser, and Ford are likely to demand higher royalties than relatively less well-known brand names. In economic theory, these royalties are economic rents or monopoly profits which the licenser receives in exchange for the use of its intellectual property.

The transfer of intangible assets to the licensee is usually accompanied by the flow of technical advice and other supporting services to ensure the success of the venture. This arrangement is particularly suitable in the case of the transfer of high-technology products and services or manufacturing processes where the licensee may lack the necessary expertise.

As with all other market entry modes, licensing has certain advantages and disadvantages. The main advantages to the licenser may be outlined as follows:

- The relatively low cost of licensing as most of the initial costs of developing the new market and associated risks are assumed by the licensee. In this way, the licenser is provided with a first valuable step for entering a new and, perhaps, unknown market before it commits itself to other forms of market entry, such as establishing a manufacturing facility, which would require investment and present greater risks.

■ In cases where the licenser lacks the necessary intimate knowledge of the market or where entry carries a certain amount of risk due, for example, to political instability in the host country, licensing may provide an attractive alternative.

■ Licensing also provides easier access to markets where entry may be made difficult and risky by protectionist barriers such as tariffs, quotas, special technical requirements, or cultural barriers (as typified by Japanese markets).

■ Licensing is an attractive way of activating a firm's dormant intellectual property or diversifying its uses without the firm giving up its core activities. For example, a firm may possess intellectual property with limited potential in its own domestic market but which, through licensing, can be developed with greater success in foreign markets. Or the firm may opt for a special form of licensing known as 'trademark licensing'. In this arrangement, firms with well-known brand names, such as Coca-Cola, Nike, and Sony, or famous sports clubs grant the right to the licensee to use their names or logos on its own products. For example, many textile manufacturers produce T-shirts and other leisure-wear items bearing the brand names and logos of famous products, pop and sports stars. This type of licensing has become a substantial source of additional revenue for many firms throughout the world.

Attractive as licensing may sound, it has, nevertheless, certain disadvantages for the licenser which may be listed as follows:

■ Whenever a licenser grants the right to a licensee to use its intellectual property, it incurs an opportunity cost (the cost of alternatives forgone) of developing the market itself, albeit at a financial cost to itself. This is particularly true in cases where the licenser may be barred from entering the market in which the licensee is operating and thus prevented from exploiting the secondary market opportunities. For example, Ford may not sell cars in markets in which the licensee is granted exclusive operating rights.

■ The licenser's share in the profits is limited to an agreed amount of royalties, unless a special clause is included in the agreement for adjustments to be made in the case of excess profits.

■ The licenser may have limited rights in the control of the use of its intellectual property. For example, any damage by the licensee to the licenser's brand image through an ill-conceived advertising campaign or to the quality of its product through poor quality control, neglect, or lack of proper care will reverberate on the licenser's reputation and possibly adversely affect its sales in other countries.

■ Despite careful wording of licensing agreements, there is always the possibility that the licensee will employ (in some cases, clandestinely) the licenser's intellectual property rights for its benefit and ultimately emerge as its main rival. In the use of processing or design technology, the licensee may choose to use this technology to enhance its own reputation at the expense of the licenser. In countries where intellectual property rights are not strictly observed, the licensee may continue using the licenser's technology, even after the licensing agreement has been terminated, to produce goods and services in direct competition with the licenser. Especially in the case of multiple licensees, additional difficulties may be encountered in determining which licenser's intellectual property rights are infringed and how.

Most licensing agreements are subject to the licensee's local laws, rules, and regulations and in the case of disagreements, for example, over the employment of child labour, it may be very difficult, if not impossible, for the licenser to defend its rights in the country of the licensee. Intellectual rights are enforced differently in different countries and this may create bitterness between the licensee and the licenser which may be difficult to overcome.

One particular negative aspect of licensing is the issue of technological dependency which is of special relevance to developing countries. Even though developing countries gain direct access to valuable technology, they may become dependent on the continued transfer of new and modern technology to maintain the momentum of their economic development efforts.

1.5.4 Franchising

Franchising is a form of licensing arrangement whereby the franchiser (the owner of intellectual property) agrees to allow the franchisee (the firm being allowed) to use the franchiser's intellectual property, such as a trademark, brand name, marketing technique, or particular business system, to undertake a business activity in a manner specified by the franchiser in return for a fee. To ensure the success of this arrangement, the franchiser also agrees to provide support services such as standard staff training programmes and facilities (for example, McDonald's Hamburger University), marketing and management techniques, quality control, and other forms of logistics support. In addition to the basic franchising fee, the franchiser may receive additional payments for the support services it provides.

Franchising has been growing in popularity throughout the world as a means of making global brand names and popular products and services available locally, mostly through retail outlets or shopping centres. Its relative popularity may be largely due to (a) its highly prescriptive nature where all operational aspects of the business, including contractual terms and obligations, have been already prescribed by the franchiser; (b) the relatively high rate of success achieved by franchisees who own the business and are given a specific geographical territory in which to operate; and (c) growing global demand for standard products and services largely due to the worldwide convergence of consumer tastes and preferences.

Most of the examples of franchising are found in service industries, such as fast-food restaurants (McDonald's, Pizza Hut, Burger King), the hospitality industry (Hilton Hotels, Travelodge, Hospitality Inns), rental services (Budget and Avis car rental, tool hire), car parts supplies, and convenience chain stores.

The main advantages of franchising as a method of market entry are that:

- The franchisee enters a business to produce goods and services for which there is a well-established demand (for example, Body Shop products) supported by an effective and efficient operating system. A high degree of standardization employed means instant recognizability of the product and associated services (the big 'M' of McDonald's, for instance), although some of these standards may have to be modified to suit local conditions. In essence, the franchisee is implementing a proven concept in product and service (for example, fast food) requiring a limited amount of innovativeness on the franchisee's part.

- The franchisee is given an opportunity to enter a growth industry with lucrative profit potential without incurring the initial costs of product and market development.

- The host country benefits from being chosen by some of the world's most respected firms as the location for their global expansion and experiences very little foreign exchange loss as most of the developmental and operational costs are incurred in the country employing local resources. For example, advertisements by the international hotel chain Intercontinental list the names of cities and countries in which it is operating, often with a very complimentary description of each city and country as destinations for pleasure or business.

Major disadvantages of franchising are that:

- In essence, the franchisee is implementing a proven product and service concept and helping the franchiser to extend its reputation and geographical boundaries.

- Unless the product or the service involved is of such reputation and recognizability that success is more or less guaranteed, the franchisee may be taking risks in introducing a product or service with little rewards at the end.

- In some countries, franchising agreements may not be easily implemented or legally enforced.

- Franchising is seen as a substitute for internal R&D since the product is already developed outside the host country.

1.5.5 Management contracts

Some firms have as their basic competitive advantage proven management techniques and expertise which they may wish to share with other firms or authorities in other countries. A management contract is a type of licensing agreement between the firm and another firm (privately or state owned) whereby the contracting firm makes available its managerial expertise and a part of its management personnel in training local managers for the efficient operation of a project in return for an agreed fee. The contract is for a specified period of up to three or five years, depending on the size and volume of the project. For example, the British Airports Authority (BAA) signed a management contract with the Atlanta, Georgia, Airport Authority to (a) modernize the existing airport and all its facilities to current modern standards and (b) train local managers and technical staff to assume full responsibility for the running of the airport.

For the firm receiving the management expertise, the basic advantage of a management contract is that it obtains readily available managerial expertise for the efficient operation of the business and training for its key personnel. In addition, the firm may find it easier to obtain the necessary financing for the project from financial institutions as the reputation of the contracting firm may provide the confidence required. The main disadvantage is that the firm may develop overdependency on the contracting firm's technology and lose control over essential aspects of its business.

The main advantage to the contracting firm is that a management contract provides an opportunity for the firm to exploit its valuable managerial skills and resources worldwide. It considerably lowers the risks involved because the firm can exercise greater control over the project. Where management contracts are undertaken in highly industrialized regions like the European Union, the firm gains valuable experience and reputation which it can use to further its competitive advantage. The main disadvantage is that in transferring its skills and resources the firm may end up creating a potential competitor and thus limit its opportunities for future contracts.

1.5.6 Turnkey projects

A turnkey project is a term used to describe an agreement under which a firm, either on its own or in a consortium with other firms, undertakes to design, build, equip, and train personnel to operate an entire production or service facility before turning it over (that is, handing over 'the key') to its owner, which may be a private company or the government of the host country. One of the most successful forms of this type of arrangement is the 'build, operate, and transfer' (BOT) model, particularly appropriate for development projects in developing countries. For example, a group of Western energy and construction firms have been awarded contracts by the Turkish government to build, operate, and transfer power stations to meet Turkey's ever-increasing electricity demand. Other projects may include airports, dams, railways, and similar infrastructure projects, some of which may be financed by foreign governments as part of their development aid programmes and by international institutions such as the World Bank.

Turnkey projects often involve highly specialized exports of industry-specific services and the transfer of technology, the sort of specific input which the host country may lack. Payment for these projects is either in cash or in a special form of arrangement known as 'countertrade' which involves the exchange of goods and services.

Advantages of turnkey projects for the firm include:

- The opportunity for the firm to exploit its special technical know-how.
- Projects involving firms in a consortium enable the firms to benefit from the collective pooling of financial resources and experience.
- The main advantage for host countries is that turnkey projects provide a more suitable and speedy alternative way of building their capital infrastructure and enable them to take advantage of financial aid and low-cost project finance provided by foreign governments and international agencies.

Disadvantages of turnkey projects for the firm can be listed as follows:

- The relatively short-term nature of most of the turnkey projects and the fact that they involve governments mean the firm(s) will not be able to form long-term relationships with the host country but success in one country may lead to contracts being awarded by other countries.
- The technology the firm transfers may actually benefit the local firms which may later turn out to be the firm's chief rivals in similar projects.
- When a firm transfers its technology and other resources, it is in fact transferring a part of its competitive advantage from which no long-term benefit may be forthcoming.

Box 1.1 Noddy Ventures into Asia

The Enid Blyton company, which owns the rights to books such as *Noddy*, the *Famous Five*, and the *Secret Seven*, announced its intention to establish a new operation in Hong Kong in June 1998. Its parent company, Chorion, also now owns Agatha Christie's novels and some of the associated film rights. The company has been exporting its products to Asia for some time but the new strategy should enable it to exploit the potential of its products in this region more fully. The products are sold in about forty countries worldwide and the company plans to develop Enid Blyton's works as an international brand.

Some of Blyton's books are already popular in countries like Japan, but the company now hopes to develop other aspects of the market. In particular, it wants to produce a number of new television series based on *Noddy* and other books, using local actors. This will be part of a strategy to promote the brand and thus to maximize its market potential. Having a base in Hong Kong should enable the company to take account of the cultural differences in Asia and be more closely involved in product development. Hong Kong will also serve as a platform for its activities in China as a whole and in the neighbouring countries of India, Japan, the Philippines, Singapore, South Korea, and also Australia and New Zealand. Adapted from D. Parsley, 'Noddy's Asian Adventure', *Sunday Times*, 7 June 1998.

1.6 Motives for Going International

SECTION 1.5 (above) has shown that there are various methods of entering foreign markets, from the simplest and least costly (indirect importing and exporting) to one which is complex and risky and requires a great deal of commitment (FDI). However, the basic question still remains: why do firms want to internationalize their operations? What do they hope to achieve by going international? This section offers some answers by considering the key elements of the internationalization process which 'describes the sequence in which a firm evolves from a domestic organization, serving a relatively homogeneous home market, to becoming an active exporter, and subsequently an international corporation serving a large number of diverse multinational and cultural markets.'[6]

Clearly, the internationalization process is initiated from many different motives. It is not simply a matter of wishing to go international and achieving success over a short period. The process of internationalization requires the following five basic ingredients if the firm is to be successful:

- A well-developed and clearly articulated mission which reflects a serious commitment to international business activities.
- The ability to identify and adjust rapidly to consumer needs and opportunities in international markets using products which clearly reflect the firm's competitive advantage.
- The ability to understand consumer behaviour in different cultures and to evaluate the nature of changes taking place.
- The ability to develop and maintain high-quality products which can withstand competition from their nearest rivals in domestic as well as overseas markets.
- A programme of serious and effective business research to identify international markets and their requirements.

Within the context of these ingredients for success in the internationalization process, it would be useful to consider the dichotomy between a *reactive firm* and a *proactive firm*. A reactive firm is a passive firm: following rather than leading, responding to opportunities rather than actively seeking them, avoiding risk rather than taking risk, content with the *status quo* rather than actively seeking ways to change it, inward- rather than forward-looking, more concerned with the present than planning and investing for the future. In short, a reactive firm is defensive in character and its actions reflect management's response to changes in the firm's external environment and pressures from its competitors. In contrast, a proactive firm is always initiating and creating new products to stay ahead of rivals, always seeking new challenges rather than being content with what has so far been achieved, is aggressive and more prone to take risks, investing for the future to take on its rivals. It is often the case that the more proactive the firm, the more likely it is to succeed in international business.

The internationalization process demonstrates a proactive firm at its best. In some instances much of the firm's FDI activity may be a reactive response to competitors' moves, basically a defensive strategy to discourage entry into the industry, to increase market concentration, or to undertake M&As in order to deny rivals access to valuable assets. The process starts with the firm having a product which clearly reflects its competitive advantage over its rivals, both in home and international markets, often as a leader in its field. Its competitive advantage may be its superior design capability, the skills of its workforce, the unique talents of its management or marketing team, or simply its ability to do things better or more efficiently than its competitors. In short, to be successful in international markets, the firm must first be successful in its own domestic market. It is this success in its domestic market which often propels the firm to go international.

It has been shown, in the discussion in Section 1.5, that the firm uses its firm-specific intangible assets to enter foreign markets. Clearly, its products and brand name developed within the firm over many years need to be fully exploited if the firm is not only to recover its initial research and development costs but also earn sufficient profits to satisfy its shareholders and fund future investment. So, the profit motive is the most compelling proactive motive. In cases where the domestic market is either too small or too saturated, the firm may have no real alternative but to seek markets overseas. The key difference between a reactive and a proactive firm is that a proactive firm does not wait until its domestic market is saturated, demand is showing signs of decline, or it is forced to take action before it actively seeks opportunities abroad by undertaking continuous market research and acting upon its findings. These and other related issues are the subject of Chapter 13. The following summary contains the major motives for going international:

■ To avoid protectionist barriers

Governments erect various forms of barrier to entry in their domestic markets by foreign firms. These barriers include some of the most common measures such as tariffs and quotas as well as rules and regulations to protect specific industries and markets. These measures make imports less attractive and more costly. Therefore, it behoves the firm to establish export bases or production facilities in host countries in order to avoid these protectionist measures.

■ To access international markets

As a consequence of the increasing convergence of consumer tastes and preferences and demand patterns in general, firms find it necessary to establish international customer bases in foreign countries from which to serve the needs of existing as well as potential customers. The firm is thus able to expand its market internationally at a lower cost than by exporting from the home base. A firm with a declining home market may be able to tap into foreign markets and extend the life cycle of its product. As the experience of many US, Japanese, and Korean MNEs demonstrates, EU member states offer many location-specific advantages to these firms to enable them to gain access to its single market with over 370 million inhabitants.

■ To access sources of specific inputs

Countries are endowed with different natural and acquired resources which offer international firms yet another set of location-specific advantages, ranging from relatively low-cost labour, raw materials, land for large-scale operations, and suitable climate to specific technical skills and knowledge which can only be accessed by establishing operations on location. Even if the firm's home country has similar resources, it may still be advantageous for the firm to locate facilities in another country for additional low-cost resources such as finance.

■ To follow competition

With an increasing number of firms going international, other firms feel compelled to follow their competitors into markets which may later be denied to them. In oligopolistic industries (those dominated by a few firms making interdependent decisions), it is normal to expect several firms to establish operations in a given country within a short time. The main reason is that any particular change in the internal and external business environment affecting one firm will affect the others at about the same time and, given their interdependence on each other for decision-making, will induce a similar response. For example, the liberalization of trade and investment in China produced almost an instant response by the world's most dominant car producers to establish a presence in one of the world's biggest potential markets. An associated motive might be to create *synergy* which would result from combining benefits from one location with those of another, especially in cases where the firm is able to combine its own managerial competence with the intimate knowledge and expertise of the local personnel in order to overcome cultural difficulties.

■ To seek opportunities

International business firms are often characterized as opportunity seekers; that is, seeking to take advantage of any event or development worldwide which is likely to have a positive impact on their marketing and resource acquisition strategies. This particular attribute is especially relevant to reactive firms. One major source of such an impact has been the creation of the European single market which helped to create one of the world's largest markets by integrating the individual member states' markets into one. Consequently, many distinct opportunities have been created for international business firms to undertake market-seeking and production-seeking investments.

■ To take advantage of incentives on offer

Governments throughout the world offer a variety of incentives to attract international firms, especially reactive firms. These incentives range from direct financial assistance to defray part of the initial costs of operations to indirect financial schemes such as favourable corporate tax rates. All these incentives help companies to maximize their after-tax profits and thus provide additional funds to invest either in the host country, home country, or in other countries.

■ To create economies of scale

In cases where the domestic market may be too small for efficient production, the firm may want to expand into world markets to create economies of scale (falling costs per unit produced as the scale of production is increased). Entry into overseas markets increases total sales and therefore justifies larger-scale operations in production, marketing, and transport.

■ To protect the domestic market

In essence this is a defensive (reactive) motive whereby the firm initiates an offensive into the competitor's home market in order to protect its own domestic market. Such an offensive may have the effect of putting pressure on the competitor to reconsider its move or, depending on the strength of the offensive, abandon it completely.

Each and every one of these motives must be carefully assessed by the firm contemplating internationalization of its activities in terms of its inherent capabilities and ability to respond to worldwide opportunities. Clearly, no firm could be motivated to go international by one particular factor; rather a host of interrelated factors will have a cumulative impact on its decision—including those of a subjective nature, such as Henry Ford's original decision to locate his first overseas production unit in England because it was the birthplace of his parents. Similarly, the decision by a Turkish graduate to establish a production facility in Scotland reflected the fact that he felt comfortable operating in the British business culture in which he had studied. Moreover, each motive will have different merits and demerits depending on whether the firm is reactive or proactive.

In this context, the 'SWOT model' (strengths, weaknesses, opportunities, and threats) can be employed to enable the firm to formulate and answer specific questions about the process of going international. As the model suggests, all these questions relate to the firm's internal environment (that is, its strengths and weaknesses) and its external environment (the opportunities and threats it is likely to face by going international). Its strengths and weaknesses must be thoroughly examined in relation to existing as well as potential rivals in the markets it plans to enter. Similarly, opportunities and threats must also be carefully evaluated with these rivals in mind. This model and related issues will be discussed in greater detail in the chapters that follow.

1.7 Summary

INTERNATIONAL business has probably existed throughout history in one form or another, but it has become more important in recent times. International business exposes firms to a variety of situations and risks they do not face in the domestic environment. The two main types of cross-border activity are trade and investment. Trade involves exporting or importing at a distance, whereas investment requires a firm to transfer resources outside its home country. 'Globalization' of the world's economies and business activities is increasing the interdependence of nations, bringing technology, competition, and standardized products to every corner of the world. Strategies to enter foreign markets include exporting and importing, foreign direct investment, licensing, franchising, management contracts, and turnkey projects. Each of these is appropriate in different circumstances and brings different risks and benefits. Firms go international to seek new opportunities, to gain efficiencies, to avoid trade barriers, and for various other reasons. Their motives may be classified as reactive or proactive, but in either case careful preparation is needed before venturing abroad.

Review Questions

1 Why is international business becoming more important?

2 What kind of risks are involved in international business that are not involved in domestic business?

3 If a firm has exported goods to a particular country for several years, what factors should it consider before deciding to produce its goods in that country instead?

4 Why might a firm consider granting a licence or franchise to a foreign firm rather than engaging in foreign direct investment itself?

5 Are proactive firms likely to be more successful in international business than reactive firms?

Study Topic: UK retailers abroad

Unlike firms in a number of other industries, UK retailers have been relatively slow to move abroad. In the UK, as elsewhere, many retailers have grown considerably during the post-war years, with large increases in the number of branches as well as in floor area and sales volume. However, this growth has not generally been matched by foreign expansion. Relatively few retailers have ventured abroad and those who have done so have taken a number of years to build up their foreign business. During the 1980s, companies like Marks & Spencer and Dixons bought US retailers in their respective industries (clothing and electrical goods), but these purchases turned out to be less profitable than expected. Retailers found that foreign markets were not as similar as they had imagined, even when the language was basically the same. Success has often eluded them because of differences in consumer tastes, the intensity of competition, or the difficulty in finding a suitable location. Despite these problems, internationalization of their activities can bring economies of scale in sourcing, buying, and distribution. During the 1990s, more retailers have been expanding abroad, particularly into the emerging markets of Eastern Europe and Asia. Consumer tastes are apparently converging and new ideas travel more easily across borders. Retailers are also preparing their foreign ventures more carefully and using new entry strategies like franchising to avoid the high costs and other risks of foreign direct investment.

Study topic questions

1 Why do you think UK retailers have generally been cautious about venturing abroad until recently?

2 In what ways do you think retailing is likely to differ in different countries? Does this apply equally to all types of retailing?

3 What potential benefits to retailers may arise when they venture abroad?

4 Do you agree that consumer tastes are converging internationally? If so, why? Does this apply to some products and not to others?

5 Why do you think some retailers prefer to franchise their foreign outlets rather than to own them directly?

Notes

1 See e.g. S. O. Monye, *The International Business Blueprint* (Blackwell, 1997) ch. 1; and J. H. Taggart and M. C. McDermott, *The Essence of International Business* (Prentice-Hall, 1993), ch. 1.

2 G. M. Taoka, and D. R. Beeman, *International Business: Environments, Institutions and Operations* (Harper Collins, 1991), 3.

3 Main source: *World Investment Report* (UNCTAD, 1997).

4 See Video Case: 'A Taste of the West' in M. R. Czinkota, I. A. Ronkainen, and M. H. Moffett, *International Business* (Dryden Press, 1999), 307–9.

5 *World Investment Report* (UNCTAD, 1997), 157.

6 E. P. Hibbert, *International Business: Strategy & Operations* (Macmillan, 1997), 34.

Recommended Reading

- Czinkota, M. R., Ronkainen, I. A., and Moffett, M. H., *International Business* (Dryden Press, 1999).

- Daniels, J. D., and Radebaugh, L. H., *International Business: Environments and Operations (Addison-Wesley, 1995).*

- Dawes, B., *International Business: A European Perspective* (Stanley Thornes, 1996).

- Hill, C. W. L., *Global Business Today* (McGraw-Hill, 1998).

- Meier, G. M., *The International Environment of Business* (Oxford University Press, 1998).

2

Multinational Enterprises

Objectives

- to identify the chief characteristics of multinational enterprises (MNEs) and the scope of their activities
- to determine the significance of MNEs for the development of international business
- to analyse the contribution of theoretical explanations of the activities of MNEs
- to evaluate the impact of MNEs on the host countries in which they operate
- to discuss the role of MNEs in the process of globalization

2.1 Introduction

MULTINATIONAL enterprises (MNEs) are the key feature of international business. They dominate the world's trade and investment activities by producing most of the well-known products we consume and undertaking significant amounts of foreign direct investment (FDI) in host countries. The world's most famous brands, such as Levi, Nike, Gillette, Coca-Cola, and Microsoft, are the standard names for the products they represent in markets throughout the world. The size and range of their operations significantly influence the development and growth of the world economy. They are often viewed as agents responsible for the changing world economic, political, and social order. It is this aspect of MNEs that provides the most compelling rationale for studying their nature.

MNEs are not a recent phenomenon but have their roots in the history of mankind. Until the end of World War I, their activities were primarily resource-oriented; that is, they attempted to secure sources of raw materials to ensure uninterrupted production in their home countries. By employing vertical integration (bringing under one management the successive stages of production and distribution) they were also able to maintain markets for their output. In the period between the wars, MNEs concentrated their operations on obtaining valuable exploration rights from host governments to explore and extract raw materials. In return, MNEs made a positive contribution to economic developments in their host countries by providing expertise and capital for social and infrastructural investment projects. It must be remembered that during this period most of the industrial economies were experiencing a serious economic depression and the governments involved had neither the resources nor the expertise to provide the much needed development of health, education, and road and rail transport systems. Many European countries, for example, were suffering an acute shortage of capital funds and changed their status from being creditors to debtors as a result of the devastating effects of World War I.

This was also the era that witnessed the exploration for oil in the Middle East, gold and other precious stones in Africa, and industrial minerals in various parts of the world. Transfers of capital funds, technology, management and marketing skills formed the basis of their success in their working relationships with host governments.

However, since the end of World War II, it is the speed of their expansion and proliferation which has made MNEs the subject of intense academic interest and research, especially MNEs of US origin. During this period, they continued deepening their vertical integration to exploit comparative advantages by using their firm-specific assets (FSAs). In addition, they increased their efforts to exploit markets abroad by means of licensing and franchising agreements. In recent years, this rapid expansion and proliferation has been extended to include the service industries such as banking and other financial services, telecommunications, public utilities, and transport. The growth of MNE activity in banking and other financial services was particularly robust following the ending of the International Monetary Fund (IMF) fixed exchange rate system in the early 1970s which resulted, among other things, in the liberalization of global capital markets. The collapse of the communist regimes, especially in Eastern Europe, the end of isolationism in countries like China, and the introduction of more market-oriented systems have provided MNEs with immense opportunities to expand into countries which had hitherto remained closed to them for so long.

In this chapter we are concerned with the characteristics of MNEs, the scope of their activities, their modes of operation, their role in the global economy and business, and their impact on host economies.

2.2 The Definition of MNEs and Scope of Their Activities

THERE is no generally accepted definition of an MNE. This is due largely to differences in the interpretation and use of the word 'multinational' and also in the evaluation of the characteristics of MNEs as international and global firms, the nature of their operations, types of ownership, structure of management, and geographical diversification. There are so many firms which claim to be 'multinational' and so many different types of firm that any given definition is bound to be incomplete and imprecise, if not at times confusing. In the main, academics and organizations such as the United Nations (UN) and the Organization for Economic Cooperation and Development (OECD) define MNEs in a way which reflects their concern about the impact MNEs have on the world trade and investment environment. The UN regards MNEs as 'transnational corporations' which are 'enterprises which own or control production or service facilities outside the country in which they are based'.[1] Here the emphasis is on the ownership, control, and multinationality of their production with centralized managerial control of the business based in the firm's home country.

Dicken uses the term 'transnational corporation' (TNC) 'because it is a more general, less restrictive, term' and defines it by using the ownership criterion, that is, the amount of control the MNE has over its assets and activities in at least two countries in addition to its own.[2] He cites the definition of a TNC given by Cowling and Sugden as a justification for his preference: 'A transnational is the means of coordinating production from one centre of strategic decision making when this coordination takes a firm across national boundaries.'[3]

In an effort to highlight their structural and operational characteristics, Weekly and Aggarwal employ the term 'multinational corporation' and define it as 'a group of business units located in different countries, whose operations are coordinated by a management "control center" that makes decisions on the basis of global profit opportunities and objectives.'[4] In this context, the structural characteristics refer to the way in which the firm integrates its overseas operations with the parent company and include the number of overseas subsidiaries or affiliates, the amount of overseas earnings, the managerial style and practices the firm employs in its relationship with subsidiaries, and its management culture. The operational characteristics refer to the way in which the firm conducts its activities, the type of ownership and control it exercises, and the nature of the relationship between its subsidiaries and affiliates.

Many academics, however, prefer to use the term 'multinational enterprise' simply because not every multinational firm is a 'corporation' and the term 'enterprise' has a greater and more useful application in the analysis of international business since it includes firms which may be owned privately or by the state, or whose ownership may be a mixture of the two. Caves defines it as 'an enterprise that controls and manages production establishments located in at least two countries'.[5] Rugman, Lecraw, and Booth opt for the same definition but add the F/T ratio (where F = foreign operations and T = total operations) to provide a useful quantitative approach to measuring an MNE's overseas commitments.[6] Dunning, on the other hand, emphasizes the foreign direct investment element in his definition,[7] whilst Hood and Young stress the control and management of an MNE's 'income-generating assets in more than one country'.[8]

In this book an MNE is defined as an enterprise which extends its business activities into more than two countries with the aim of responding to worldwide opportunities for the most efficient employment of its firm-specific assets, including its production and service facilities and knowledge, either on its own or in partnership with other firms, in pursuit of clearly defined aims and objectives.

2.3 Characteristics of MNEs

As previously stated, MNEs have gone through various stages of evolution and in this process they have acquired some important common characteristics. It is difficult to determine the stage at which a domestic firm becomes an MNE. However, by studying the individual characteristics of a given MNE, one might be able to discern certain key developments in its history leading to its becoming an MNE. For example, Zander and Zander tell us how the Swedish MNE, Alfa Laval AB, took the first step towards becoming an MNE by applying for a US patent in 1883 for its cream separator technology so that it could take advantage of the huge market potential in the USA.[9] In addition, these characteristics are used not only to distinguish one MNE from another but also to evaluate the nature of their operations and their impact on host countries' economies. The characteristics of MNEs are divided into two general categories: quantitative and qualitative.

2.3.1 Quantitative characteristics of MNEs

■ **Size**

Not all MNEs are giant firms with absolute control over their activities and with strong influence over their rivals. However, quite a number of the world's MNEs are large corporate entities with substantial financial and technological resources which they use to gain power and influence in the markets in which they operate. Some MNEs have more resources and generate more income than their host countries. For example, General Electric, the world's largest MNE ranked by foreign assets, had total assets of $272 billion and worldwide sales of $79 billion in 1996. According to UN estimates, the world's MNE population includes 'some 40,000 parent firms and some 250,000 foreign affiliates'.[10] Nine MNEs dominate the world's motor manufacturing industry and the recent spate of mergers (such as the $92 billion merger between Daimler-Benz of Germany and Chrysler of the United States) is likely to lead to further consolidation in this global industry. According to UN figures, over 500 of the world's largest MNEs produce more than one-half of the world's output and account for 80 per cent of its FDI by value.

There are also many other MNEs which are not as well known and readily recognizable as, say, Fiat and Unilever, but which have immense impact on the quantity and quality of goods and services produced around the world. The majority of big MNEs are located in the advanced economies, the USA, UK, Germany, France, Japan, Sweden, and Italy. An interesting development, however, has been the recent increase in the number and world rankings of MNEs in developing countries such as Argentina, Brazil, the countries of South-East Asia, Israel, South Africa, and Turkey.

■ Geographical diversity

The number of countries in which MNEs operate varies enormously, depending on the product range, competition, and marketing requirements. As we have seen, many academics believe an MNE must operate in at least two countries, in addition to its own, if it is to be classified as an MNE. Harvard Business School considers six or more to be the norm. Before World War II, MNEs concentrated their activities in extractive industries such as minerals, oil, and natural gas and some of these MNEs emerged later as the world's largest oil companies like BP, Exxon, Mobil, and Shell. These extractive activities required firms to locate their operations at or near the source of raw materials. For example, BP, having discovered large reserves of oil in the Beaufort Sea, established one of the most modern and sophisticated oil production sites in one of the world's most inhospitable regions and built an 8,000 mile pipe-line system to carry the crude oil to the ice-free Port of Valdez in Southern Alaska.

During the 1920s and 1930s opportunities in many of their other trade and investment activities were limited because of the severity of the world depression and the increasing propensity of governments to resort to protectionism to protect their domestic industries and markets against competitive devaluations. Since the end of World War II, MNEs have become increasingly more active (and more powerful) in manufacturing and related activities requiring them to be close not only to raw materials and other inputs but also, more importantly, to their major markets. This led inevitably to further expansion in the number of locations in which to base their production and marketing operations. Technological advances in telecommunications, transport, and information systems provided a further impetus for their growth by helping them to create almost a 'borderless' world of business.

■ Networking

One distinct advantage of geographical diversity is that it enables MNEs to engage in interfirm (as opposed to international) trade whereby they supply components (SKF, the Swedish ball-bearing manufacturer, supplying ball-bearings to car manufacturers), equipment (Caterpillar supplying excavators to construction firms,) and raw or semi-finished materials (Odebrecht, a relatively small Brazilian MNE supplying chemicals) to other manufacturers. To be able to undertake inter-firm trade, the MNE would have to locate near its major customers, or at least be at arm's length, to benefit fully from the locational advantages. Another advantage is that it provides scope for intra-firm or intra-group trade which takes place between the MNE's subsidiaries or affiliates. In this way, the parent company is able to create a series of networks to take advantage of locational opportunities—an arrangement similar to the creation of an internal market within the firm.

■ Revenue

This characteristic reflects another aspect of an MNE's geographical diversity by highlighting the geographical distribution of its sales and revenue. There is no consensus of opinion as to what proportion of the firm's total revenue should be generated outside its home country before it can be classified as an MNE. However, any percentage above 25 per cent seems to be the norm. Using the ICI Group as an example, it is noted that 79 per cent of its turnover was generated outside the UK in 1995. Overseas sales contributed over 50 per cent to British Steel's revenue in 1997. In the case of Japanese MNEs, this percentage is often higher than 50 per cent, denoting a heavier reliance by these firms on their overseas operations as their main source of revenue. Sony, the Japanese consumer electronics group, earned more than 20 per cent of its total revenue from East Asian markets alone through exports and joint ventures. A significant proportion of foreign earnings results from the activities of MNEs' overseas subsidiaries and affiliates, including the royalties earned through licensing and franchising agreements.

■ Ownership

Ownership characteristics are uniquely an important quantitative and qualitative attribute of MNEs and constitute one of the most important means by which MNEs are distinguished from one another. The primary aim of ownership is for the firm to acquire the right to exercise control over decision-making in key operational areas and proprietary scrutiny over its firm-specific (or ownership-specific) assets in use in overseas locations. The amount of control an MNE is able to exercise depends on the mix of ownership which is in turn determined by the method of entry. In the case of wholly owned subsidiaries, which the firm may have either established itself or acquired through cross-border acquisitions or mergers, the MNE has complete control over all strategic and operational aspects of its subsidiaries. In a joint venture, the ownership is shared between the MNE and the local partner on an agreed basis and subject to periodic review. Japanese firms in general insist upon majority control in their joint ventures. In an arrangement where the MNE provides most of the capital in the form of FDI and basic inputs such as technology, one would expect the MNE to assume the majority of the ownership and control of the business, subject to any host government rules and regulations governing the ownership of domestic firms and assets.

Alternatively, the MNE may want to undertake portfolio or indirect investment by buying equity shares in a foreign company, perhaps as a prelude to eventual merger or takeover. Portfolio investments are an alternative means for the MNE to spread risks over a range of financial assets (which may include bonds and other interest-bearing instruments as well as equity shares), providing the firm with future income or capital gains, as opposed to entrepreneurial income, but with no control.

The ownership characteristic has three connotations: first, it relates to the question of 'who owns whom' and the percentage of ownership (spread of ownership); second, which countries own what percentage of the world's MNEs, bearing in mind that MNEs may shift their headquarters from country to country for strategic reasons (geographical distribution of MNEs); and third, the ownership of intangible firm-specific assets which MNEs can employ as the main source of competitive advantage in the process of their internationalization (ownership advantages). This book is concerned with the third meaning of the ownership characteristic which is developed further in Section 2.4.

2.3.2 Qualitative characteristics of MNEs

■ Management philosophy

The key qualitative distinguishing feature of an MNE is the management attitude and commitment exemplified by its behaviour. According to Perlmutter, firms' management philosophies can be identified as being either ethnocentric, polycentric, or geocentric.[11] Ethnocentric MNEs are oriented towards domestic markets and cannot therefore be regarded as true MNEs unless their domestic market forms an integral part of their worldwide operations. A polycentric MNE is oriented towards foreign markets which are loosely connected to the firm without an integrative system. Finally, a geocentric (or regiocentric) MNE views world markets from a global perspective; that is, it strives to integrate its world markets and resource acquisitions as part of its global strategy to serve customers wherever they may be, acquiring the best-quality resources at the lowest cost. Clearly, the definition given above describes an MNE as a geocentric enterprise with a fully integrated global business system, centralized management of strategic planning and decision-making, and a clearly articulated global perspective in all its operations.

Differences in management philosophy, vision, and practice are also reflected in the way an MNE develops and maintains its intra- and extra-firm relationships with its rivals and stakeholders (anyone who benefits or incurs costs directly or indirectly from the firm's actions or inactions: employees, customers, shareholders, managers, and members of the community). It is the quality of its corporate strategy and its implementation, along with the ability and speed with which the management deals with a wide range of business environmental factors in different cultures, which often distinguishes one MNE from another and gives it its distinct managerial superiority over its rivals.

Table 2.1 The world's top 20 MNEs ranked by foreign assets, 1996

($bn. and number of employees)

Rank	Corporation	Economy	Industry	Assets: foreign	Total	Sales: foreign	Total	Employment: foreign	Total
1	General Electric	US	Electronics	82.8	272.4	21.1	79.2	84,000	239,000
2	Shell	UK/Neth.	Petroleum	82.1	124.1	71.1	128.3	79,000	101,000
3	Ford	US	Automotive	79.1	258.0	65.8	147.0	—[b]	371,702
4	Exxon	US	Petroleum	55.6	95.5	102.0	117.0	—[b]	79,000
5	General Motors	US	Automotive	55.4	222.1	50.0	158.0	221,313	647,000
6	IBM	US	Computers	41.4	81.1	46.6	75.9	121,655	240,615
7	Toyota	Japan	Automotive	39.2	113.4	51.7	109.3	34,837	150,736
8	Volkswagen	Germany	Automotive	—[a]	60.8	41.0	64.4	123,042	260,811
9	Mitsubishi	Japan	Diversified	—[a]	77.9	50.2	127.4	3,819	8,794
10	Mobil	US	Petroleum	31.3	46.4	53.1	80.4	22,900	43,000
11	Nestlé	Switzerland	Food	30.9	34.0	42.0	42.8	206,125	212,687
12	ABB	Switz/Swed.	Electrical Equip.	—[a]	30.9	32.9	33.8	203,541	214,894
13	Elf Aquitaine	France	Petroleum	29.3	47.5	26.6	44.8	41,600	85,400
14	Bayer	Germany	Chemicals	29.1	32.0	25.8	31.4	94,375	142,200
15	Hoechst	Germany	Chemicals	28.0	35.5	18.4	33.8	93,708	147,862
16	Nissan	Japan	Automotive	27.0	58.1	29.2	53.8	—[b]	135,331
17	Fiat	Italy	Automotive	26.9	70.6	19.8	51.3	90,390	237,865
18	Unilever	UK/Neth.	Food	26.4	31.0	45.0	52.2	273,000	304,000
19	Daimler-Benz	Germany	Automotive	—[a]	65.7	44.4	70.6	67,208	290,029
20	Philips	Netherlands	Electronics	24.5	31.7	38.9	40.9	216,000	262,500

[a] Data unavailable. Estimated on the basis of the ratio of foreign to total sales and foreign to total assets.
[b] Data unavailable.
Source: World Investment Report, 1998, UNCTAD, table II.1, p. 36. Reproduced with permission.

▪ Operational structure

Another chief qualitative characteristic of an MNE is the way in which it organizes its production activities. Three types of MNE can be identified: a vertically integrated MNE, a horizontally integrated MNE, and a diversified MNE (a conglomerate). A vertically integrated MNE is a multi-plant or multi-facility firm that organizes successive stages of production in different locations to produce intermediate inputs for subsidiaries, affiliates, or other firms. In general, vertically integrated MNEs tend to be industrial firms supplying a variety of manufactured, processed, or assembled goods. For example, a petroleum firm explores for oil in many parts of the world, transports it to its refineries where crude oil is processed, and supplies various petroleum outputs to retail outlets. A horizontally integrated MNE produces the same or similar products in its worldwide production units. These MNEs are usually found in retail industries operating retail outlets on high streets or in shopping centres. For example, Marks & Spencer is a highly successful food and clothing retailer with shops in many different countries. In the case of a diversified MNE or conglomerate, the firm operates a chain of production units in many parts of the world which are neither vertically nor horizontally linked to one another but operate as semi-independent subsidiaries or affiliates. These diversified MNEs are basically risk-averters engaging in different, unrelated business activities in order to spread risks. This diversification can be either geographical or product-based or both. In either case, the firm is seeking to develop a low-risk portfolio with growth potential. For example, Cadbury Schweppes is a highly diversified food conglomerate with extensive international operations in confectionery products and soft drinks.

By integrating their operations, MNEs are able to create economies of scope (the cost of producing two distinct goods or services within the same firm is lower than producing them in two separate firms) and economies of scale (falling unit costs of a common good or service as the volume, or scale, of output increases). Moreover, they are also able to reduce risks by consolidating production activities (vertical and horizontal integration) and by spreading risks over a wide range of activities (conglomerates).

2.4 Theoretical Models of MNEs

WHY should any firm leave the relatively cosy domestic business environment and go multinational unless forced to do so, as in the case of MNEs attempting to escape a depressed home market or to seek lower-cost production sites abroad? What motivates a firm to expose itself to the plethora of difficulties, risks, and uncertainties discussed in Chapter 1? What determines its behaviour in the international business environment, given that it will have to compete against the host country's domestic firms as well as international rivals? How does it determine which method of entry to choose and why? The aim of this section is to attempt to answer these and other relevant questions, mostly using economic principles developed over a number of years to explain the behaviour of the firm. A variety of approaches offer different perspectives on the internationalization process and reflect academic interests in the increasing importance of MNEs and the diversity of their activities.

2.4.1 The profit motive approach

The maximization of profit is one of the major assumptions in economic analysis about the behaviour of the firm operating under various forms of competition. The profit is defined as the difference between the firm's total revenue (TR) and its total cost (TC), where total revenue is equal to the price at which a given commodity sells multiplied by the quantity sold at that price. Total cost is equal to the total opportunity cost the firm incurs in undertaking a particular type of economic activity. To maximize its profit, the firm would have to maximize the difference between its TR and TC by either (a) minimizing TC (that is, by maximizing the efficiency of resources used) with TR remaining the same or by (b) maximizing TR with TC remaining constant. The firm's ability to maximize TR is determined by the type of competitive environment in which it operates. In the case of perfect competition, the firm faces a given price (that is, it faces a horizontal or perfectly price-elastic demand curve) for its homogeneous product and therefore changes in its TR are determined entirely by the quantity demanded at that given price. Clearly, the only other alternative the firm has in maximizing its profit is to minimize its TC.

In the case of pure monopoly, the main difference is that the firm faces a downward-sloping demand curve with varying price elasticities so that its TR depends on the price it charges and the quantity it sells at that price. A pure monopolist is a single seller of a unique product which is the sole source of the firm's monopoly power. However, no matter how powerful the monopolist is, it cannot control both the price and the quantity demanded at the same time. It can fix its price and let the market determine the quantity demanded, or fix the quantity produced and let the market determine the price. So the monopolist will set a price or produce a quantity which will maximize its profits, other things being equal. Alternatively, as in the case of perfect competition, the monopolist can minimize its TC, assuming perfect competition in factor markets.

The two forms of competition described above are the two extreme ends of the competition spectrum. In the real world, however, neither exists in its pure form. In between there are other forms of competition which explain more realistically the type of competition an MNE faces in international markets. Most of these markets are dominated by a few giant MNEs (for example, tyre manufacturing, cars and trucks, steel and aluminium) and are characterized as oligopolistic, a form of competition in which no *a priori* outcome is possible as it depends on a host of pertinent factors, including interdependence among rivals. Under monopolistic competition many firms are competing with each other on the basis of differentiated, non-homogeneous products, each firm exercising an amount of monopolistic influence determined by the degree of success in its product differentiation.

Whatever the form of competition, the profit motive approach predicts that an MNE will enter markets where it can earn greater amounts of profit than in its existing markets. Furthermore, it will locate its production facilities in countries where lower-cost resources enable it to minimize its TC. Given that MNEs operate in a world of oligopolistic and monopolistic competition, their ability to maximize profit by minimizing costs or maximizing revenues depends significantly on a wide range of other business environmental factors.

Before moving on to the next approach, two points need to be made. First, profit-maximization is a theoretical behavioural assumption which may not always hold true, as MNEs have other, perhaps even more important, motives for their activities. Nevertheless, the profit motive approach serves as a very useful theoretical framework, albeit an extreme one, with which to compare the effectiveness of other explanations. What is important, however, is the prediction that as long as an MNE generates sufficient profit, it will tend to continue its operations in existing markets unless conditions dictate otherwise. Likewise, if it expects greater potential profits in the future, it will tend to expand its involvement in these markets in line with its overall strategy. Secondly, profit is not the only measure of success in international markets; other criteria, such as market share, sales revenue maximization, and customer satisfaction, may be more important indicators of future performance and provide more valid reasons for continued presence in markets.

2.4.2 The market imperfections/failures approach

One important conclusion from the above discussion is that MNEs engage in international business activities on the basis of their differentiated products. Product differentiation is a deliberate attempt by the MNE to render its product characteristics sufficiently different in the minds of consumers from those of its rivals, that is, to make the product as non-homogeneous as possible. To differentiate a product successfully requires the firm to possess certain technological advantages in the design and production process coupled with equally important marketing and organizational skills and talents, not to mention a considerable amount of financial strength. The differentiated features could be real, and tangible (for example, the design and style of a car or furniture) or perceived (the extent to which consumers are made to think the product is different, even though generically it may be the same). An essential corollary of product differentiation is that, having differentiated its product, an MNE needs to advertise it extensively on a global basis to sustain the consumer allegiance and attract new consumers to its products. Even in the case of a standardized product which the firm produces and markets such as Hilton Hotels or Pepsi Cola, advertising is an immensely important function of the firm's global marketing strategy.

The word 'deliberate' in the given definition of product differentiation needs to be explored further to illustrate the meaning of the market imperfection. The fact that it is a deliberate act implies that the firm is trying to capture a particular segment of the market or to increase its market share. The mere existence of market segmentation, through the use of product differentiation, indicates market imperfections or failures. So the whole of a given market, with all its segments, becomes an area of competitive activity with many firms competing for a relative market share. A comparison with the criteria for perfect competition will reveal one major source of market imperfection; namely, restricted entry. Entry into the market is difficult and risky because the incumbent firms may have already differentiated their products successfully and built up, as a result of their success, a formidable market lead and consumer allegiance that would put the new entrant at a considerable disadvantage. Consequently, the new entrant would either be forced to leave the market—as in the case of PepsiCo having to close down its Pepsi Cola operations in South Africa due to the overwhelming success and dominance by its nearest rival, Coca-Cola—or to rethink and devise a new entry strategy, such as a market-sharing agreement or strategic alliance, and try again later. This happened in the case of Apple Computers in the USA in the early 1990s.

One important point needs to be emphasized. MNEs undertake extensive market research in their home market or in a chosen market to estimate the potential success of their differentiated product. One of the significant advantages US MNEs have over their rivals is the sheer size of the US domestic market, with the world's most discerning consumers enabling US firms to achieve considerable economies of scale compared to, say, European firms. If the product is a proven success, then it is marketed in the rest of world; in other words, success in domestic markets often breeds success in international markets. To be successful in domestic markets, firms must be able to compete effectively, innovate to stay ahead of rivals (by continuing to differentiate their products), respond effectively in all areas of business activity, and finally, to do all these things with greater speed than their rivals. The only way to repeat domestic success in international markets is to excel in all these areas.

A moment's reflection upon the contents of the paragraph above will identify the areas of distinct competitive advantage which the firm must have and utilize effectively in order to be successful: a well-developed product (preferably one with an established brand name), reflecting clearly the firm's technological superiority over its rivals; financial resources to undertake extensive market research; a large, competitive domestic market; and the ability to innovate and upgrade with speed. Each and every one of these advantages provides the firm with a unique opportunity to earn an economic rent (or monopoly profit) as a reward for its success.

What determines (a) whether the firm has the ability and competence to undertake successful product differentiation, (b) whether it can be sure of success, and (c) whether it can maintain and further exploit its acquired competitive advantage? The answers to these questions lie in the firm's ownership of intangible firm-specific assets (FSAs). It is the quantity and, more importantly, the quality of these assets, deliberately, intensively, and effectively utilized, that is the main (perhaps even the only) source of the firm's distinctive competitive advantage in the process of internationalization.

The main reason for concentrating on product differentiation as a source of market imperfections is that it epitomizes the total impact of the firm's FSAs. The original research by Hymer was first to draw attention to the firm's FSAs as the source of its distinctive competitive advantage when extending its business activities overseas.[12] These FSAs are regarded as distinct in the sense that they would be superior to those enjoyed by local firms and thereby create a market imperfection for the MNE to exploit. According to Hymer, a firm with such distinctive FSAs possesses market power. That in turn makes it possible for the firm to act in collusion with other firms in oligopolistic competition. What is implied here is that a firm with valuable FSAs has, at least, the potential to determine the outcomes in collusive negotiations, whether they relate to market-sharing agreements, pricing agreements, or agreements which prevent or eliminate competition. Furthermore, such a power can also be used in negotiations involving mergers or acquisitions, again giving the firm a distinct advantage over other interested firms. It is equally plausible that a firm with very distinctive FSAs may be the least likely to share these assets with other firm(s) through collusive agreements.

Each and every one of the FSAs is seen as a source of monopoly power and hence the cause of market imperfections. As *The Economist* puts it, 'multinationals are not exploiters of purity but rather creatures of market imperfections or failures' and further 'the modern multinational is thus a creature of imperfection, organising itself to adjust to market flaws and, indeed, to create such flaws.'[13]

In general, there are two major sources of market imperfections (failures): natural barriers to entry and man-made or artificial barriers to entry. Natural barriers are inherent in market structures. For example, in the global publishing business British and American firms have a natural advantage in having English as their native language, an advantage not enjoyed by their non-English speaking rivals. This natural advantage acts as a natural barrier to any possible entry into the global publishing industry because, given the substantial size of the global market, English-language firms have the ability to create both internal and external economies of scale and as a result develop a very distinctive cost and price competitiveness.

Man-made barriers are created deliberately to discourage or even prohibit entry. For example, government protectionist policies (tariffs, quotas, local content requirements, a variety of exchange rate policies, etc.) are designed to protect domestic industries against potential foreign entry. Clearly, these measures provide unfair advantages for the protected industries and thus cause distortions in the flow of free trade. More importantly, protectionist policies create market imperfections and engender opportunities for MNEs. One way of overcoming these man-made barriers to entry is for the MNE to establish a production site or an export base in these countries through FDI. This is seen by many observers as one of the major causes of the influx of FDI into Britain and other European Union countries by American, Japanese, and Korean MNEs to take advantage of the creation of the European single market.

Thanks to the worldwide liberalization of trade and the efforts of the General Agreement on Tariffs and Trade (GATT) and World Trade Organization (WTO) to promote global free trade, these protectionist policies are disappearing fast, but there are still sufficient residues of market imperfections to make any attempt at entry worthwhile (see Chapter 6). Product differentiation is a good example of man-made barriers to entry as it gives the incumbent firm a considerable competitive advantage and poses a formidable barrier to entry. Another example of a man-made barrier is the amount of advertising expenditure by the incumbent firm to ward off potential entry by rivals.

The market imperfections model offers a varied approach which explains the firm's motives for engaging in international business activities under monopolistic and oligopolistic market structures. One of the main sources of the relatively large volume of transatlantic FDI is the oligopolistic rivalry between American and European MNEs in which each firm tries to be the first mover into potential markets, a move which may also be regarded as an attempt to deter entry by rival firms. It also provides a clear rationale for vertical and horizontal integration and diversification into portfolio investment. However, it concentrates too heavily on the FDI option and omits the potential for alliances and other forms of close cooperation between international firms.

2.4.3 The internalization approach

Repeated references have been made in this and the previous chapter to the existence of a firm's FSAs which, when efficiently and effectively employed, contribute to the firm's success in domestic and international markets. Let us now examine briefly the nature of the most important FSAs.

■ Technology

The most common type of FSA is the technological advantage developed over time. This technological advantage is equivalent to superior knowledge (technical know-how) and is the ability the firm possesses to produce goods more efficiently or to produce them at least as efficiently as other firms but with better quality and distinctive features with consumer appeal. Once developed, tested in the market, and proven successful, this asset provides the firm with a continuous flow of revenue. Technology as an asset can take several forms which are specific to the firm. It could be a particular production process such as the floating glass technology developed by the Pilkington Glass Company and used throughout the world under licence. Or it could be a particular design such as the Dyson 'bagless' vacuum cleaner which has been so successful in capturing market shares from its nearest domestic and international rivals like Electrolux and Hoover. The firm is now planning distribution networks and production under licence in a number of countries.

■ Marketing technique

Every firm has a marketing technique but some firms are better at it than others. A firm may employ it with a certain amount of flair and success in promoting its product in such a way that consumers can easily distinguish it from its rivals (see product differentiation discussed earlier). The product's style may be so unique and attractive that the product virtually sells itself, as in the case of Dyson's bagless vacuum cleaner. Another example is the Disney Corporation's success in selling $25 billion worth of Disney merchandise in 1997. This could be attributed largely to the much envied skills and talents of its marketing team. In short, marketing technique is simply the ability of the firm to satisfy a consumer demand in a unique and attractive manner as part of its global marketing strategy.

■ Intellectual property

This intangible asset comes in the form of patents, trademarks, and brand names and is often an important source of competitive advantage and income for the MNE. These assets are the results of extensive research, significant amounts of investment in terms of manpower and capital, and a great deal of managerial competence, skill, and vision. The names of Kodak, Walkman, Benetton, Microsoft, Lego, to name but a few, have now come to represent not just products but generic terms used to describe items in their class. For example, the term 'Walkman', a brand name belonging to Sony, is used to refer to transistor radios which can be carried around with the greatest ease, even though the 'Walkman' bought may be made by Philips or Hitachi.

■ Ability to upgrade and innovate

This involves both existing and future products. Such an ability takes years to develop and requires profound commitment to maintain. Porter emphasizes also the need for speed in employing this ability.[14] A car manufacturer, for example, that has not introduced a new model which incorporates the most recent technological advances in all aspects of design, safety, comfort, fuel efficiency, and so on, is bound to lose its market share. This 'planned obsolescence' is a deliberate attempt to beat the rivals in the survival-of-the-fittest race. An innovative firm is able to secure markets to enable it to reap the rewards of investment in R&D in the future.

■ Management style and competence

These intangible assets have many dimensions which require much broader treatment than is possible in this book. However, it is possible to list some of the important management skills as part of the firm's FSAs. First, the management style must reflect clearly the firm's vision as an international organization based on a structure which is flexible and varied enough to cope with diverse and complex international business issues. Second, relationships between subsidiaries and affiliates and head office must be managed in a way that promotes and maintains synergy (joint efforts and joint benefits) and learning at all levels of the organization. Third, competence is essential in developing and implementing strategies for change in the global business environment; this includes skills in identifying and taking advantage of opportunities to upgrade and innovate and to respond to technological developments. Finally, the firm's management must provide effective leadership in promoting and maintaining unity of purpose and motivation across borders, with emphasis on quality, trust, and respect for individual talents and aspirations.

The market imperfections approach helps one to understand which firms in which industries will internationalize their activities and assumes that all FSAs are marketable and can be valued using the external market mechanism. But not all FSAs are marketable nor can they be priced by the external market mechanism alone (as opposed to administrative pricing used internally by the firm). Take knowledge as an example: it is in the nature of knowledge that, once developed and passed on to the subsidiaries and affiliates, it becomes a public good (a good whose consumption by one does not exclude its being consumed by others) which subsidiaries and affiliates can share at no extra cost to the parent firm. But other firms in the industry would have to pay to use this knowledge or incur costs in developing it themselves. The research and development costs of knowledge as an intangible asset form an effective barrier to entry and constitute an important source of market imperfections.

The existence of these assets and the associated difficulties concerning their marketability and pricing provide the essence of the internalization approach. It is an integral part of the market imperfections explanation inasmuch as both approaches take the quantity and quality of FSAs as their main concern. The key difference is that the internalization approach concentrates on imperfections in intermediate product markets (products used as inputs) rather than on consumer product markets (products for final consumption).

This approach is also referred to as the transactions approach in recognition of the original work by Ronald Coase who, in the first instance, analysed the circumstances under which private parties could voluntarily negotiate the efficient outcome of conflicts arising out of the problem of externalities, or the spillover effects of productive activities.[15] The most important condition is the existence of private property rights which give their owners the right to protect their intellectual property as well as to negotiate voluntarily for their use by others or their disposal. Coase's analysis provides the basic framework within which one can evaluate the alternatives available to a multi-plant MNE for the use of its FSAs and the exchange of its property rights using the external market mechanism to obtain the most effective outcome in the first instance.

The basic question in this context is: how does the firm utilize these assets? There are basically three options available to the firm: (a) it can use its FSAs to produce at home and export abroad (assuming free trade or insubstantial barriers to trade); (b) it can undertake FDI to establish subsidiaries abroad; or (c) in cases where internalization is not a prime objective, it can license their use by other firms in return for royalties. The relative merits and demerits of exporting and FDI have already been discussed in detail (see Section 1.5); here, concentration will be on the third option. If it were to license other firms to use them, the firm would face the additional problem of transaction costs. These costs may arise out of time spent on negotiations—it took the McDonald Corporation twelve years to negotiate the terms of entry for its first Moscow restaurant with the Soviet government—or time spent on determining the amount of royalty, the contractual obligations of the parties, the costs of coordination between the licenser, the licensee, and other parties, and protection against dissipation of the licenser's rights. Costs may also be incurred through circumstances beyond the control of the licensing firm; for example, host governments may insist on certain conditions being satisfied before the deal goes ahead, such as the amount of taxes to be paid and the exchange rate on the basis of which the royalty will be paid. There will always be transaction costs but how efficient are these costs relative to the costs of the other two options: exporting and FDI?

According to the internalization approach, the MNE will internalize the use of its FSAs and all the relevant activities wherever and whenever it is more cost-efficient to do so by using an internal pricing mechanism rather than the external market mechanism. Internalization means that the firm bears the costs and receives the benefits by retaining the ownership of its FSAs within the firm. The firm choosing internalization as an option is not likely to use licensing, especially in cases where FSA security is of paramount importance. The internalization approach focuses on imperfections in intermediate product markets rather than on final product markets. The advantages of internalization to the firm are numerous.

- First, the MNE is able to retain direct control over its FSAs rather than sharing them with a licensee. The MNE thus avoids the risk of dissipation of its ownership rights, especially those pertaining to its technology or knowledge.

- Second, internalization provides opportunities for internal economies of scope (falling per unit costs as the degree of utilization of the firm's existing productive capacity is increased) and economies of scale (benefits of increasing the scale of operations over time by adding additional capacity). These benefits could be obtained through the vertical integration of its production processes so that the whole production system becomes interlinked. For example, an oil company like Shell has developed a fully vertically integrated production system in which oil is discovered, brought to the surface, and transported to the refinery where it is processed into various final products which are then delivered to its own retail outlets. An interesting aspect of vertical integration is that production units may be located in different countries because of locational advantages, with the parent company retaining the overall administrative control. Consequently, the market for an intermediate product is internalized in a vertically integrated firm. Economies of scope and scale can also be realized through horizontal integration; in this case, an MNE internalizes the markets for its intangible assets. Despite the apparent attractions, however, diseconomies of scale can easily put the firm at a disadvantage by making it too big and unmanageable.

- A third possible advantage of internalization is that an MNE may be able to exercise more effective and efficient internal coordination of its activities throughout its network of subsidiaries as part of a global management strategy. Assuming this coordination is effective and efficient (which may not always be the case), the MNE is able to minimize transaction costs.

- A fourth advantage is that the firm may be able to secure a continuous and reliable source of raw materials and components to ensure an uninterrupted flow of production. The firm reduces the associated risks and increases the efficiency of its operations. This is the basic rationale for an oil firm like Shell to engage in backward vertical integration. It minimizes the risks of interruption in the constant flow of crude oil to its refineries. Integration, whether vertical, horizontal, or both, gives the firm a distinct advantage over its rivals and may, indeed, be interpreted as an attempt to curtail competition by denying other firms access to these sources and markets.

■ Finally, vertical and horizontal integration offer an MNE the necessary flexibility to service customer needs in increasingly fragmented markets, especially in advanced economies. MNEs are facing increasing pressure to respond to changes in the nature of markets and developments in technology. One way to cope with this pressure is for MNEs 'to think globally but act locally' through changes in their strategy and structure so that their subsidiaries and affiliates are able to embody the characteristics of local demand in their operations. This is particularly the case for car and truck manufacturers. Even though every car manufacturer endeavours to create a global car, such as Ford's Mondeo, modifications are made to suit local customer needs and government requirements.

One of the chief merits of the internalization model is its emphasis on the control the firm exercises over its operations. Because the firm's FSAs are internalized, rather than licensed to others, the firm is able to use them in the best manner possible and benefit from the experience and knowledge gained. The internal market which is thus created becomes an integral part of the firm. The firm also benefits from its increased ability to produce and distribute goods and services using this experience and knowledge. In addition to this comparative advantage, the firm is able to create an effective network of subsidiaries and affiliates through the process of integration.

Despite these advantages, this model shares the same basic weakness as the other approaches presented above; namely, it is only a partial analysis based on the existing FSAs. Secondly, it assumes that the parent company has the power to exercise effective control over its FSAs at all times, but this may not necessarily be so as subsidiaries and affiliates may perform at different levels and under different local conditions. Thirdly, if the firm is too successful in integrating its operations and creating an effective network of associated firms, then the parent company may use its effective power to restrict competition. Fourthly, it suffers from being too general as it applies to both domestic and international firms and treats internationalization as a special case. Finally, as in all other explanations, it assumes an almost total absence of external constraints, especially with respect to government rules and regulations such as competition legislation.

2.4.4 Dunning's eclectic paradigm

Dunning's eclectic paradigm is a synthesis of various approaches based on theories of the firm, international trade, location, and industrial organization.[16] Its basic aim is to offer a combined explanation of the major factors which determine the location of international production through FDI. These factors are categorized as three conditions which must be satisfied if the decision to locate in a particular host country is to be successful. These three conditions are: ownership or firm-specific advantages, advantages derived from internalization, and location-specific advantages. The first two advantages have already been discussed earlier in some detail in this chapter. Here, emphasis will be on location-specific, or host country-specific, advantages.

Location-specific advantages provide the MNE with a unique opportunity to combine its FSAs with the host country's specific factor endowments. These factor endowments consist of natural advantages (suitable climate, proximity to markets, availability of raw materials and minerals) and the availability of relatively low-cost inputs, especially labour. Factor endowments also include acquired advantages such as highly skilled human resources, research, educational and training facilities, modern and efficient infrastructure, and related supporting industries which create externalities for the firm to enjoy. Location-specific advantages enable the firm to make the most efficient use of its FSAs (ownership advantages) at a particular foreign site. According to the eclectic paradigm, however unique the firm's FSAs might be, they need to be combined with natural and acquired advantages that the host country can offer. For example, to explore for oil in the Beaufort Sea would require an oil company to use its firm-specific advantages, especially its accumulated technical know-how, to extract oil in the most efficient manner possible, in full cognizance of climatic, logistical, and ecological conditions. To exploit this natural resource, the company would have to undertake an appropriate amount of FDI on the site. To give another example, MNEs establish production units in countries with low-cost inputs such as labour. Given the relative immobility of labour, it makes sense for the firm to go where it can take advantage of this cheap labour when a labour-intensive production process is involved.

One further important implication of the eclectic paradigm is that, as well as using low-cost locations, MNEs establish a presence in areas where there are clusters of closely related firms supplying anything from the smallest component to high-quality services. Such a high concentration of related industries, talents, and skills, linked in a network of information and knowledge, helps to create an important source of externalities or spillover effects. However, in some cases, the arrival of a foreign investor acts as a magnet to bring component suppliers and supporting services to the area (see Box 2.1).

One attraction of the eclectic paradigm is that it offers a combined explanation not only for why firms choose FDI as an option but also why they choose to locate in a particular country. It is a unified approach which incorporates both the ownership and internalization advantages and which views FDI as an effective conduit through which the firm spreads its operations across national borders and extends the use of its FSAs through internalization. There are, however, several limitations to the eclectic model:

- One serious limitation is that it assumes that all firms will adopt the same strategies in their international production.
- It also assumes that firms will respond in similar ways to country-specific advantages and characteristics.

> **Box 2.1** Nissan in North-East England
>
> Nissan's decision to locate its car manufacturing plant in Sunderland, North-East England, seems to suggest that MNEs can sometimes attract clusters of specialist firms to their vicinity. Until the arrival of Nissan, the North-East of England had no tradition of car manufacturing. Despite this, the company's decision was taken after a thorough evalua-tion of all the relevant locational advantages the area offers. Initially, incentives were offered by local and central government, but these were also available elsewhere and, in any case, they are mainly of short-term benefit. Other advantages included: the existence of a good communications and transport infrastructure, including ports to bring in supplies and ship out exports; the availability of a highly skilled and well-disciplined labour force; high-quality research and educational and training facilities provided by the region's colleges and universities; and the existence of a cluster of related industrial firms ranging from specialist transport companies to financial service providers.
>
> But Nissan's presence has been largely responsible for attracting high-quality compo-nent manufacturers and related service providers into the area. Japanese manufacturing companies need a close network of suppliers to meet their just-in-time production requirements. These firms must be close geographically but must also have a close working relationship with the purchasing company to ensure that components are made to the correct specifications and quality standards. Whilst this network of component suppliers had to be developed after Nissan's arrival, the location offered a combination of incentives and natural and acquired endowments which gave Nissan a unique locational advantage.

- It omits the policy issues connected with location-specific factors. Governments formulate and implement certain policies to attract FDI across their borders and offer incentives which may, on balance, outweigh the natural advantages which the country in question may lack. Furthermore, governments adopt protectionist measures that may either discourage or, if the predictions of the market imperfec-tions model are correct, encourage entry. In either case, the firm's FDI decisions will have to take into account the possible effect of these measures.

- What may matter more to MNEs is not the existing but rather the potential advan-tages the host country may develop over time. This means greater emphasis needs to be placed upon the host country's ability to acquire and create comparative locational advantages over time.

- Recent experience with fluctuating exchange rates and attempts by governments to stabilize the external value of their currencies suggest strongly the need to include foreign exchange rates and other related international financial considerations in FDI decisions.

- The model emphasizes the need for advantages to be specific to the firm. However, the recent spate of strategic alliances among the world's airlines suggests that firms may benefit from a combination of ownership, internalization, and locational advantages jointly by cooperating and coordinating parts of their operational strategies.

■ Finally, the eclectic paradigm is a more relevant explanation of greenfield operations than it is of mergers or acquisitions. The latter have been a preferred option for MNEs in recent years as they provide internal control of operations and offer already available technologies or, in the case of cars, a range of existing models with a certain amount of consumer allegiance.

2.5 The Impact of MNEs on Host Countries

THROUGHOUT their history, MNEs have had what might best be described as a love–hate relationship with their host governments. They are loved as agents of much needed change, as channels of FDI with many benefits for the local economy, and as allies of governments trying to come to terms with the difficult tasks of economic development. But at times they are also feared for being selfish and greedy organizations, too concerned about the size of their profits rather than the interests of the country in which they operate. They are admired and in many ways emulated by their rivals for the ease with which they exercise power and influence, harness worldwide resources, and, in the process, amass huge amounts of wealth that dwarf the economies of many of their host countries in the Third World. They are also admired and envied for the skills and talents they employ in their operations, for being inventive and innovative, and for the success they achieve despite all the odds in world markets.

At the theoretical level, most of the criticisms of MNEs stem from their monopolistic and oligopolistic behaviour which has been one of the most widely researched and debated topics of our time. Some of these debates have resulted in outright condemnation of MNEs as agents of 'modern imperialism' or neocolonialism.[17] Yet others have regarded them as the inevitable outcome of the development of modern trade and investment activities around the globe, aided and abetted by government policies and technological advances in all areas of human endeavour.[18]

The impact of MNEs can be positive or negative or both depending on the country and industry in which they operate. The positive impacts may be summarized as follows:

■ Transfer of technology in the form of technical know-how, managerial skills, and marketing techniques result in externalities or spillover benefits that permeate local firms and even government departments. Local firms benefit also from the network of alliances and suppliers of MNEs, resulting in improvements in productivity.

■ In the case of developing countries, the transfer of technical know-how and managerial skills is instrumental in improving the quality of indigenous labour, management, and education and training systems. This improvement enables developing countries to catch up ultimately with the economic development of industrialized countries. This was particularly important in the rapid development of the economies of Taiwan, South Korea, and Hong Kong, which are now classified as some of the fastest-growing newly industrialized countries with huge export capacity.

■ MNEs also bring in much needed capital into host countries (or raise capital locally if interest rates are favourable) and, especially in the case of developing countries, usher in necessary reforms and the modernization of financial services and institutions, thus helping to increase the productivity of capital.

■ The extension of MNEs' global production into host countries often contributes directly to incomes and employment and indirectly to regional and sectoral development and improvement.

■ One of the most effective ways to reduce the monopoly power of indigenous firms, stimulate domestic competition and at the same time encourage the growth of entrepreneurship is to attract MNEs into the country, provided MNE entry is not through mergers and acquisitions which may have the opposite effects. This is one of the basic ideas behind the privatization and deregulation programmes being undertaken by governments worldwide.

■ Potential entry by MNEs often prods host governments into liberalizing their trade and investment policies by lowering or removing barriers to free trade and investment. The resultant increase in trade and investment enhances world prosperity.

■ MNEs may also make a positive contribution to the host country's trade balance by producing goods that used to be imported (import substitution) and which can even be exported (reversal of the direction of trade) and, to its capital account, through FDI. Consequently, the host country's balance of payments improves.

■ Finally, MNEs make important contributions to the quality of goods produced and consumed locally and, by producing standard products, MNEs help contribute to the convergence of global consumer tastes and preferences. This may be regarded as an advantage in bringing different cultures closer, as well as helping MNEs to reduce their marketing costs.

The negative impacts of MNEs on host countries may be summarized as follows:

■ The presence of MNEs is sometimes regarded as a sinister threat to the sovereignty of the host country. This is a particularly valid argument in the case of developing countries which are often seen as being vulnerable to MNEs' worldwide power and influence. Their economic development programmes are often dominated by the conditions formulated by MNEs for the inflow of FDI. MNE subsidiaries are seen as implementing the decisions made by the headquarters of the parent company that may bear no relation to the needs and aspirations of the host country. In this context, they are often accused of neocolonialism.

■ The technology transferred by an MNE may be of an inferior type or ill-suited to the needs of the host country. For example, production methods based on modern and sophisticated technology (for which the host country may not have suitably qualified manpower and supporting industries) may require a capital-intensive production system which may not create as many jobs as the host government had hoped. An important implication of the transfer of modern technology is that the MNE may end up dominating the industry by using its technological advantage as an effective barrier to entry by domestic and other international firms.

- The question of industrial dominance is particularly relevant in the case of an MNE using its unique ownership advantages to obtain concessions from the host government. For example, in the early stages of the development of the computer industry, computer firms would often insist on exclusive rights to produce or supply only their own brands, and to provide their own materials and replacement parts. They also insisted on products being serviced only by their own or authorized technicians; in other words, they excluded local supply firms. One major concern about this dominance is that MNEs may use their power and influence to interfere in the host government's economic and political policies for their own interest.

- The cultural impact of an MNE is a very controversial topic and one that arouses national indignation about the presence of MNEs and the practices they adopt in host countries. By introducing new technology and work practices and challenging management philosophies, MNEs transmit cultural change into the host country. For example, McDonald's arrival in Moscow in the early 1990s heralded a completely new concept in the food industry, the hitherto unheard-of treatment of Russian consumers with politeness and professionalism, the complete overhaul of marketing and logistic systems and, most importantly, it significantly altered the eating habits of Moscovites. Whether some or all of these changes are welcomed only time will tell, but already there seems to be some resentment, especially by the older generation, of the cultural intrusion by McDonald's.

- There is also the danger that FDI by MNEs may crowd out domestic investment and thus lead to capital outflow in countries where such outflows may endanger the long-term growth prospects of the country involved.

- In some cases, mergers and acquisitions by MNEs may stifle domestic competition and discourage entrepreneurship.

- The positive balance of payments effects may fail to materialize if the MNE produces for the host country's domestic market only.

- The impact on local suppliers may sometimes be limited if the firm is vertically integrated, producing most of the parts and components itself.

- The transfer of modern technology may result in technological dependency by the host country, a fall in R&D and employment, and tied imports.

- In cases where the MNE employs its own centralized marketing, employment of local white-collar workers may fall giving rise to 'the branch plant syndrome'.

2.6 Globalization and MNEs

ONE of the most fundamental developments in the world economy today is the steady progress towards globalization, a dynamic process in which the world's economies are seen to be merging into one immense global economy. Globalization and related issues will be developed in detail in Chapter 6. In this section the aim is to give a brief summary of the role played by MNEs in the globalization process.

As has been seen, MNEs play a vital role in linking worldwide markets, sources of raw materials, and components and, in doing so, the economies of the countries in which they operate. An increasing number of MNEs are now seeing themselves as global firms, as opposed to being just multinational firms, adding one more distinguishing feature to their already colourful list of characteristics. The major difference between a localized MNE and a global MNE is the development and implementation of a global strategy which aims to integrate markets and resource acquisition on a global basis. This strategy is usually based on a homogeneous, standard product which is produced and marketed worldwide, often employing a centralized marketing strategy. A global MNE sees itself as operating in any market where the potential for its product may exist and acquiring resources wherever they may be available. In other words, a global MNE is a truly geocentric firm.

The following developments have given a further impetus to the globalization of MNEs' operations:

■ Worldwide convergence of consumer tastes and preferences and other demand patterns has made the production and marketing of standard products and services much easier and less costly.

■ The ease with which the firm's ownership advantages can be spread globally has increased appreciably following recent trends in the liberalization of trade and investment worldwide.

■ Enormous advances in transport and communication technologies have made it easier for parent companies to exercise effective control over their subsidiaries and affiliates operating globally.

■ The development of strategies based on global profit potential by the world's major MNEs has intensified the search for global markets and resource acquisition.

It must be noted that globalization is not limited to consumer products alone but includes intermediate and industrial goods and services as well as supplies of raw materials and components.

2.7 Summary

MULTINATIONAL enterprises (MNEs) may be defined in different ways but generally they operate in more than two countries, taking advantage of worldwide opportunities and resources in pursuit of their aims and objectives. They may be identified by quantitative characteristics such as size, geographical diversity or interfirm trade, or by qualitative characteristics such as their management philosophy or operational structure. Various theoretical models have been used to explain the behaviour of MNEs. The main ones are: (a) the profit motives approach, where MNEs are viewed as firms seeking opportunities for profitable expansion abroad; (b) the market imperfections/failures approach, where MNEs use their firm-specific assets to differentiate their products from rivals and exploit the monopoly power that differentiation brings; (c) the internalization approach, which considers the advantages arising from FDI and other forms of expansion which 'internalize' the benefits within the firm; and (d) Dunning's eclectic paradigm, where the growth of MNEs is seen as resulting from a combination of ownership-specific advantages, internalization, and location-specific advantages. MNEs have a variety of effects on their host countries, some of which are beneficial to their economic development while others create problems or restrict their development. Whatever their impact on particular countries, MNEs are major contributors to the process of globalization in the modern world.

Review Questions

1 In what ways can MNEs be defined and why do different organizations and authors define them in different ways?

2 By what characteristics can MNEs be distinguished from domestic firms?

3 To what extent do theoretical models of MNE behaviour help us to understand the reasons for their development? What are the limitations of each of the theoretical approaches?

4 Why are MNEs sometimes criticized for their activities in host countries, particularly in the Third World? Are these criticisms justified?

5 In what circumstances might MNEs be described as 'global companies'?

Case Study: JCB—The Story of a Multinational

In 1945, Joe Bamford started his business in a rented lock-up garage in Uttoxeter, England. Today, J. C. Bamford Excavators (JCB) is the world's fifth biggest producer of construction equipment in terms of unit sales and 'JCB' has become the generic name for earth-moving equipment. Whilst still a relatively small family-owned business, the company is the largest UK producer of construction equipment and has 40 per cent of the European market for 'backhoe loaders'. Its share of the total European market for construction equipment is currently about 16 per cent, though the company's aim is to increase this share to 35–40 per cent.

In the early years, its founder struggled to raise even modest amounts of capital, but this experience has taught the company to manage its finances carefully and to keep its debt to a minimum. In building up his successful business, Joe Bamford made use of his family background in agricultural machinery which dates back to 1871. The company has remained in this specialized product area and has continually ploughed back profit into product development. Its expansion, both domestically and abroad, has come almost entirely from organic growth and the company has resisted the pressure to go public, as many of its rivals in the industry have done.

In addition to careful financial management, JCB has developed a reputation for product design and marketing flair. A particular aim in product design has been to keep the number of machine parts to a minimum. This helps to keep down costs compared with competitor products. In the marketing field, the company has achieved considerable success in creating the impression of a much larger company. Some of its advertising campaigns have also been memorable, such as the choreographed routine featuring 'JCB Dancing Diggers' as a testimony to the power and versatility of their machines. The company's combination of attractive marketing and sophisticated engineering skills has proved to be a unique asset.

Although generally preferring home-based production, JCB has always been export-oriented. But while its UK competitors were often exporting to Britain's traditional markets in the Commonwealth countries, JCB chose France and other European markets for its exports. This was not so much because of a far-sighted desire to be part of the Single European Market, but rather because continental Europe was a less costly export destination. Now, however, the company regards Western Europe as its home market and 65 per cent of its sales are in Europe, including the UK.

The company still regards its family ownership and small-firm management approach as an asset. Although growing in size, JCB is still smaller than its two main rivals: the US firm Caterpillar and Komatsu of Japan. JCB's key advantage is its less bureaucratic style of management. This enables it to make quicker decisions and be more responsive to market opportunities. The company now has sufficient size to increase its bargaining power with suppliers but without losing the personal touch. It also has sufficient financial resources to pursue its ambition of increasing its share of the European market, especially in Germany which accounts for about 40 per cent of the European market. This ambition was boosted in 1991 when the company formed a joint venture with Sumitomo Construction Machinery of Japan. JCB also hopes to expand in Asian markets. Whilst not typical of multinationals generally, JCB's story illustrates many of the features of MNEs discussed in this chapter. (Adapted from A. Baxter, 'A Simple Story of Success', *Financial Times*, 23 Oct. 1995.)

Case study questions

1 Identify JCB's chief characteristics as an MNE and explain briefly how these characteristics have been developed over the fifty years or more of its existence.

2 Identify JCB's major firm-specific assets (FSAs) and explain how these FSAs have helped the company to achieve the fifth position in the world's construction equipment market.

3 Comment on the company's management philosophy and show how it differs from another MNE with which you are familiar.

4 How likely do you think it is that the company will achieve its ambition of increasing its European market share to 35–40 per cent?

Notes

1 United Nations, *The Multinational Corporation in World Development* (1973), 23.

2 P. Dicken, *Global Shift: The Internationalisation of Economic Activity* (Paul Chapman Publishing, 1992), 47–8.

3 Ibid.

4 J. K. Weekly and A. Aggarwal, *International Business: Operating in the Global Economy* (Holt, Rinehart & Winston, 1987), 311.

5 R. E. Caves, *Multinational Enterprise and Economic Analysis* (Cambridge University Press, 1982), 1.

6 A. M. Rugman, D. J. Lecraw, and L. D. Booth, *International Business: Firm and Environment* (McGraw-Hill International Edition, 1985), 7–8.

7 J. H. Dunning, *International Production and the Multinational Enterprise* (Allen & Unwin, 1981), 3.

8 N. Hood and S. Young, *The Economics of Multinational Enterprise* (Longman, 1990), 3.

9 I. Zander and U. Zander, 'The Oscillating Multinational Firm: Alfa Laval in the Period 1890–1990' in *The Nature of the International Firm, Nordic Contributions to International Business Research* (Handelshojskolens Forlag, Copenhagen, 1997), 89–115.

10 *Yearbook of the United Nations* (1995), 974.

11 H. V. Perlmutter, 'The Tortuous Evolution of the Multinational Corporation' *Columbia Journal of World Business*, 4 (1969), 9–18.

12 S. Hymer 'The International Operations of National Firms: A Study of Direct Investment', doctoral dissertation, MIT (1960).

13 *The Economist Survey*, 'Multinationals: Back in Fashion', 27 Mar. 1993, 9–10.

14 M. E. Porter, *The Competitive Advantage of Nations* (Free Press, 1998).

15 R. H. Coase, 'The Nature of the Firm', *Economica*, 4 Nov. 1937.

16 J. H. Dunning, *Multinational Enterprises and the Global Economy* (Addison-Wesley, 1993).

17 See e.g. H. Radice, (ed.), *International Firms and Modern Imperialism* (Penguin Books, 1975).

18 See e.g. *The Economist Surveys* 'Multinationals: Back in Fashion' 27 Mar. 1993 and 'Big is Back', 24 June 1995.

Recommended Reading

■ Caves, R. E., *Multinational Enterprise and Economic Analysis* (Cambridge University Press, 1996).

■ Buckley, P. J., and Ghauri, P. N., *The Internationalisation of the Firm: A Reader* (Harcourt Brace Jovanovich, 1993).

■ Dunning, J. H., *Multinational Enterprises and the Global Economy* (Addison-Wesley, 1993).

■ Rugman, A. M., *The Theory of Multinational Enterprises: The Selected Scientific Papers*, 1 (Edward Elgar, 1996).

■ Rugman, A. M., *Multinational Enterprises and Trade Policy: The Selected Scientific Papers*, 2 (Edward Elgar, 1996).

3

International Market Entry and Organizational Response

Objectives

- to identify strategies for international market selection and entry
- to outline the organizational changes necessary to enable a firm to internationalize its activities
- to examine the role played by human resource management, finance, and logistics in the efficient operation of international activities
- to discuss the organizational difficulties facing firms operating abroad and the policies necessary to overcome these difficulties

3.1 Introduction

THE decision to enter foreign markets is normally taken after considering a wide variety of factors. A firm may be proactive in seeking opportunities in foreign markets or reactive in responding to slow growth or other problems in the home market. The firm's stage of development may be a determining factor. The decision will also take account of the firm's access to finance, the actions of competitors, the appropriateness of different entry strategies, and many other factors. When contemplating international expansion, a firm has to align its international strategy with its objectives and evaluate both its own strengths and weaknesses and the opportunities and risks of operating abroad. It then has to select a suitable market and determine an appropriate marketing strategy.

The nature of a company changes fundamentally once the decision is taken to expand its operations into the international sphere. A company's organizational structure and operations need to be adapted and developed to support its international activities. The recruitment, selection, and training of its managers and workforce have to reflect its needs at the international level. The financing of international activities is more complex than the financing of domestic operations. International operations are associated with a higher degree of risk; this risk increases as a result of geographical distance and cultural diversity and the company must also take into account problems which may arise from a country's political and economic situation. A further important consideration is the planning and management of a company's operations from materials sourcing to the distribution of the finished product; in international business this process is known as 'international logistics'. In various ways, therefore, the organization and management of a company must respond to the needs of its international operations.

3.2 International Market Selection and Entry

IN the first part of this chapter we consider the procedures involved in going international. Initially, a company needs a clear sense of direction to motivate its management and workforce and to drive its international strategy. This is usually described as its 'mission'. Next, the company has to evaluate its strengths and weaknesses and the environment in which it operates—the opportunities available at home and abroad, the strength of competition, and the risks of operating in different markets. Having carried out a thorough evaluation of its present situation, the company is then ready to set specific objectives and a corporate strategy for its international expansion. This is followed by the painstaking task of evaluating potential markets and making a final selection. Before entering a foreign market, a detailed marketing strategy must be drawn up, indicating the broad approach to product or service marketing, the choice of entry mode, and the desired marketing mix. These steps are summarized in Figure 3.1. Of course, the process of international market entry is not always carefully and meticulously planned. A firm is sometimes swept along by events or seizes a fleeting opportunity without forward planning. For most firms, however, it is generally wise to plan ahead as mistakes can be costly.

Figure 3.1 Stages involved in international market entry

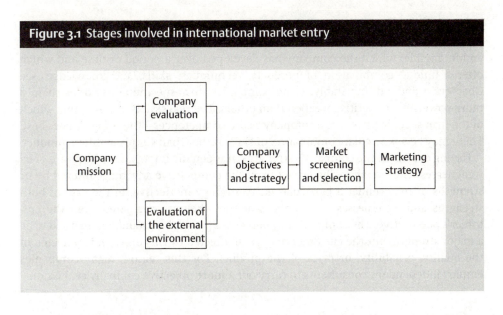

3.2.1 Company mission

Many organizations now have a written mission statement. This is sometimes a fairly bland statement of the organization's overall purpose and values but, in the case of a business firm, it should ideally give an indication of the firm's intentions with regard to the scale and extent of its operations, its competitive and product positioning, and its policies towards stakeholders (customers, suppliers, employees, shareholders, and financial institutions). Whether a firm has a formal mission statement is less important than that it has a broadly understood policy in each of these areas. What is more, its mission should pervade all levels of the organization and also be evident to customers, suppliers, and other outside organizations. It should not be the exclusive preserve of management. For firms contemplating international market entry, a clear sense of purpose is essential in helping to focus their choice of market, mode of entry, and entire marketing strategy.

3.2.2 Company evaluation

Two important steps should precede the formal planning of an international expansion strategy: company evaluation and evaluation of the external environment. This combined stage is often described as 'SWOT analysis' (strengths, weaknesses, opportunities, threats). The important point is that a company's strengths and weaknesses and the opportunities and threats it faces in the external environment should be analysed and evaluated after careful research. Identifying each of the SWOT elements is simply the first step. In terms of the company's strengths and weaknesses, it is essential to ascertain its firm-specific assets—those assets, both tangible and intangible, which the company has developed over a period of time and which offer a unique combination of products, techniques, skills, and knowledge (see Chapters 2 and 13). Inevitably, some companies' firm-specific assets offer them a more powerful competitive weapon than others. The real skill is in discerning which of the firm-specific assets are a company's core competences—the things it does best. These may be a particular combination of skills rather than simply a unique product.

Having evaluated the company's strengths, it is equally important to be aware of its weaknesses. These may easily detract from the competitive advantage offered by its strengths or may render a particular entry strategy ineffective. In the case of both strengths and weaknesses, it is important that they are evaluated from the customer's perspective. The company may perceive a particular production method to be a major strength, but the customer may be unaffected by this unless it is reflected in the quality, reliability, or price of the product. For this reason, many companies employ independent consultants to carry out a more objective company evaluation.

3.2.3 Evaluation of the external environment

The external environment in which a firm operates is sometimes seen in terms of opportunities and threats. One method of analysing these opportunities and threats is to use 'STEP factor analysis' (the sociocultural, technological, economic, and political environments). This approach provides a useful checklist of factors, the analysis of which forms much of the subject matter of this book (see Chapter 4 in particular). As with SWOT analysis, however, it is important to analyse and evaluate the impact of these environments on the company's probability of success in international markets. The sociocultural and political environments require careful investigation in unfamiliar countries. Cultural sensitivity and political stability are often regarded as prerequisites for business success. Technology is an underlying factor in the process of innovation and change in the modern business environment. It may affect production, distribution, and marketing, as well as the way in which demand patterns change and the ability of a firm to communicate with customers, suppliers, and subsidiaries around the world. The economic environment also has far-reaching implications. This refers to the impact of economic growth and recession, inflation, exchange rates, taxation, interest rates, and, most importantly, competition. A full analysis of competition provides a vital indication of a firm's competitive strengths relative to its rivals. It may also provide a picture of its competitors' strengths, weaknesses, and market shares in different parts of the world—an important factor in determining a firm's own international strategy.

3.2.4 Company objectives and strategy

Once a company and its operating environment have been evaluated and its core competences have been identified, the company is in a position to set clear objectives for its international expansion strategy. The objectives indicate 'what' the company aims to achieve: its targets in terms of markets, market share, level of investment, expected rate of return, etc. The strategy indicates 'how' it proposes to achieve these objectives. An international strategy of this kind should set out in broad terms how the company intends to compete in foreign markets. Primarily, it is a competitive strategy with specific reference to a country or region, though the country or countries concerned still have to be investigated in depth. Its international strategy must also take account of the organizational requirements needed to support the venture. Some of the more important requirements are discussed later in this chapter.

The nature of a company's international strategy will depend on the company's size, resources, competitive strengths, previous international experience, and a number of other factors. Several major MNEs have developed global strategies where they view the world as their market place and their resource base. Decisions on location, sourcing, product specification, marketing, and distribution are part of a global plan. Smaller firms, or those with less international experience, are wiser to adopt a more limited strategy which proceeds in stages, allowing time for feedback and reflection at each stage. Even a global strategy will normally have to reflect local conditions, however, and all international strategies should be constantly reviewed in the light of research and experience.

3.2.5 Market screening and selection

The selection of foreign markets requires careful screening of the country or countries under consideration, an investigation into the market potential for a company's product (or product type if the product is not currently available in the selected country), and, finally, identification of the target market segment.

■ Country screening

The country screening process is designed to assess the general suitability of the countries under investigation. Countries which offer an unsuitable or difficult business environment will be eliminated at this stage. Country screening is based on factors such as (a) the general political and economic situation, (b) risk factors, (c) general product data, and (d) cultural assessment. The political situation can be assessed by examining the type of political system and the degree of political stability in a country. The economic situation gives an indication of the general suitability, size, and growth rate of the national market; data would include population, age structure, national income, the economic growth rate, income per capita, the volume of external trade, output of relevant products, and similar figures. Risk factors might include the risk of late or non-payment, poor industrial infrastructure, civil unrest, or antagonistic government policies, for example. General product data give an idea of the standard of living in a country; data might include the number of passenger vehicles, telephones, or television sets per 1,000 people, or similar wealth indicators. Cultural assessment gives an indication of the cultural impact of particular types of product; this requires research to determine the acceptability of a product with respect to religious beliefs, customs, attitudes, political views, and other cultural characteristics. This screening process enables the company to narrow down its choice of country before undertaking further investigation.

■ Estimating market potential

The potential demand for a product may be estimated on the basis of (a) sales of similar products in the country under investigation or in countries with similar characteristics; (b) surveys of consumer demand for similar products; (c) input–output analysis, where demand is forecast from growth trends in industries for which the product is an input (for example, the demand for steel depends on growth in the motor-manufacturing, construction, and other steel-consuming industries); or (d) indices which incorporate data on the factors which affect the demand for the product (for example, the demand for motor cars may depend on population size, disposable income, savings, availability of personal finance, etc.). In these ways, it is possible to estimate demand patterns, the share of income spent on particular goods, and the way in which demand for these goods responds to growth in related industries or in the economy as a whole. It is also necessary to analyse competition, market structure, supply networks, and distribution channels. Existing or potential competition can be estimated in terms of the number and size of firms, their competitive strengths and probable reactions to a market entrant. Market structure is determined by the ease of market entry and the ability to operate freely inside the market; entry and market freedom would be hindered by import restrictions and internal regulatory barriers (product rules, advertising restrictions, testing procedures, etc.). The absence of adequate supply networks and distribution channels would present major difficulties and may require the company to establish an extensive support operation. This information provides a more detailed picture, enabling the company to reach a firm choice of country.

■ Identifying the target market (segmentation)

Armed with a wealth of data on the selected country or countries, it is now necessary to segment the market. Segmentation involves breaking down the market into groups with particular characteristics. These characteristics may include geographical location, age group, gender, income level, social group, occupation, education, and a number of other factors. Ideally, the company should try to identify the group most likely to buy its product as accurately as possible, though it should be noted that individuals who share the same characteristics in terms of occupation, income, and social group, for example, may have markedly different characteristics in other respects. These differences may relate to life style, religion, attitudes, and other factors. The choice of market segment will depend not only on the company's product but also on its priorities as indicated by its objectives and international strategy. An ambitious strategy will require larger market segments, though 'large' may relate to any characteristic, not necessarily to geographical area. The more accurately the target market is identified, the more carefully the marketing strategy can be tailored to the particular characteristics of the market.

3.2.6 Marketing strategy

The marketing strategy incorporates the various methods and techniques used to enter the chosen market segment. This includes the mode of entry, the identification of demand, the elements of the marketing mix, the customer relationship, and mechanisms for continual feedback and improvement. Some of the more important considerations affecting the marketing strategy are now considered in turn:

■ Mode of entry

Market entry may be effected in a variety of ways. These include direct or indirect exporting, foreign direct investment (FDI), licensing, franchising, management contracts, and other strategies. Some of these modes of entry incorporate further variants; for example, FDI may include a greenfield operation, a merger or acquisition, or a joint venture. Detailed discussion of these modes of entry and their respective merits can be found in Chapters 1 and 12. The choice of entry mode depends on factors such as the need for ownership and control, the level of financial commitment, the importance of market proximity, the time frame involved, the nature of the product or service, and a number of other factors. In all cases, the mode of entry should be appropriate for the company and country concerned, taking account of the company's objectives and strengths and weaknesses and the country's cultural and other characteristics. It is also worth noting that, for many small and medium-sized enterprises, the choice of an effective local distributor is often critical in achieving success in foreign markets.[1]

■ Identifying consumer demand

Consumer demand can be identified either on the basis of previous experience or through market research. Market research is generally a more scientific approach, providing quantifiable responses from potential consumers and/or detailed information from other sources. There is also a cultural dimension to the approach adopted: whilst American companies are likely to conduct formal market research, Japanese companies are more likely to base their marketing strategy on their knowledge of existing and potential customers and to gauge the reaction to a product after it has been launched.[2]

■ Choosing the marketing mix

Conventional analysis of the marketing mix focuses on *product*, *price*, *promotion*, and *place*—the 'four Ps'. In international marketing, a more complex range of issues has to be addressed, but these elements still provide a framework for developing an appropriate international marketing mix. The product itself will normally have been sold in the domestic market already, but the key question is whether a standard product can be sold internationally or to what extent it should be adapted to meet local requirements. Standardization is common for office and industrial equipment, computers, and certain consumer products like toys or breakfast cereals. Even here, however, some adaptation may be needed to reflect differences in language, business procedures, or consumer taste. Many other products are subject to considerable local variation; Nestlé, for example, had 560 brands in 1995, but 250 were unique to individual countries and only nineteen were marketed in over 50 per cent of the countries in which Nestlé operates.[3]

Similar issues affect the pricing decision. The main options are as follows: price may be standardized across international markets; a dual pricing policy may be adopted, with one price for the domestic market and one for export markets—generally a lower price reflecting the marginal cost of the exported goods without an apportionment of product development costs; or a market-differentiated price may be used, reflecting the different conditions in each market. Transfer prices for goods sold to different branches of the same MNE also need to be considered; these will reflect the internal policies of the company concerned and may, in some cases, be designed to minimize the company's international tax liability. Price is, in any case, a sensitive issue in international markets, as claims of 'dumping' and unfair competition may arise if export prices are lower than domestic prices. Promotion presents particular problems where different languages, cultures, laws, and advertising media are concerned. 'Place' refers to transport and distribution. Methods of transport and channels of distribution may well have to be adapted to the situation in a foreign market. Indeed, the complexity of international transport and distribution may necessitate careful logistical planning.

■ Relationship marketing in international markets

The conventional marketing-mix approach is more appropriate to the marketing of consumer goods than it is to services or industrial marketing. It tends to be associated with a short-term view of customers as one-off consumers of a product and with the idea that the marketer's task is to persuade people to make a transaction on the basis of the product's features, price, and attractiveness at a particular place and time. This approach, sometimes called *transaction marketing*, may be contrasted with a *relationship-marketing* approach.[4] Relationship marketing is concerned with the building up of long-term customer relationships which are mutually beneficial. The seller gains more lasting benefits from repeat orders but may also be able to establish more effective feedback mechanisms from a closer knowledge of the customer. The customer feels more valued by the seller and is better able to influence the development of the product or service to satisfy his/her own requirements. It is clear that these are important factors when the product is an expensive piece of industrial equipment which has to meet a corporate customer's specific requirements. They are also important to consumers of specialized services; complex legal advice is not sought purely on the basis of promotion or price. Even for consumer goods a long-term relationship approach may be preferable, especially where the customer is a corporate distributor of the product. In international business, relationship marketing may help a company to establish a firmer foothold and to gain more intimate knowledge of a market over a period of time, though by its very nature it is not a substitute for an initial market entry strategy. It may also prove invaluable in a culture where long-term relationships are of paramount importance.

■ The 'innovation loop'

Whether a relationship-marketing or more conventional marketing-mix approach is used, it is important for all companies to engage in continual innovation. Companies should establish mechanisms for the flow of information between the customer and themselves. With modern technology it is easier to monitor information on the type of purchases made by customers through bar-code scanners and customer loyalty schemes and to target Internet advertising to specific market segments, for example. These facilities may also be one of the benefits of a relationship-marketing strategy. Continual feedback and innovation, both of product and customer service, enables a company to stay ahead of its competitors and, where appropriate, to provide a complete customer solution rather than simply a product. The process of feedback leading to innovation, then to consumption and further feedback and innovation may be described as the 'innovation loop'.

3.3 Human Resource Management (HRM)

3.3.1 An international strategy for HRM

A company which decides to expand its activities abroad will need to review the skills and training levels of its staff to ensure that it can fully meet the challenges which it will encounter abroad. It is essential that personnel dealing with international operations are not only knowledgeable about the political and economic situation, currency risks, and the operational level of the business abroad, but also the business culture of the host country and the difficulties which this may pose for a company undertaking investment there for the first time. Management of human resources at an international level differs from that at a domestic level for a range of important reasons.

First, firms will face different labour market conditions and a different range of labour costs. They will have to make a decision about the optimum labour mix in terms of skill levels and whether the manufacturing process or the nature of the product needs to be adapted to take into account the different conditions in the labour market. Second, companies need to decide whether it will be necessary to move managers and key shop-floor workers from the parent company to the host country in order to overcome skill shortages. Difficulties with geographical labour immobility will need to be considered when assessing the willingness of workers to move abroad. In recent years, companies operating in Eastern Europe, notably, Volkswagen in the Czech Republic, have moved managers from the parent company to work abroad for fixed terms. When local managers are competent to take over the responsibility of running the enterprise, many MNEs have operated the popular policy of 'putting the locals in charge'.

The third problem relates to the different management styles encountered from country to country and this may mean that managers from the host country encounter resistance, but it may also benefit both countries as companies transfer good management practices from one country to another. The fourth problem concerns the difficulty of controlling a business which is conducted at a long distance, and an important element of control must necessarily be implemented through the personnel function. Despite the problem of host country resistance, MNEs must exert control over their subsidiaries by placing senior managers from the home country into key positions within their foreign operations. This is the most effective method of ensuring that the objects of the parent company are being fulfilled with controls being enforced over the production process, product quality, the labour force, and the quality of raw materials and spare parts being produced by secondary industries.

3.3.2 Management recruitment, selection, and training

MNEs tend to recruit prospective managers through university careers services, and if successful, candidates join a company as graduate trainees. The new recruits are put through rigorous training programmes and are expected to work within the company in the home country for a number of years in order to gain experience of the methods of organization and the business culture of the company. As a result of the information held by the personnel department on the experience of managers working within the home company, prospective candidates may be identified for selection for work in a foreign subsidiary. Many companies operate a minimum age for eligibility for foreign transfer and it is highly unusual for companies to recruit candidates from among university graduate applicants. Most MNEs operate very strict selection processes and investigations will include information on the candidate's adaptive capabilities for foreign transfer, for example, level of adaptation to a previous domestic transfer, his/her linguistic capabilities, and the results of tests administered by the company to ascertain an individual's match with different environments, and his/her willingness to change certain basic attitudes.

Indeed, some companies are increasingly including a candidate's spouse or partner in this selection procedure, since the stress of adapting to a new environment can be greater for the partner than for the transferred manager. There is still a tendency for the transferred spouse to be the female partner of the relationship and she may have had to decide to give up her career and relinquish family and social relationships in the home country. A company must ascertain whether the partner is adaptable enough to weather the stress of having to rebuild her life in a new environment. However, there has been some anecdotal evidence from companies in recent years which suggests that in the case of couples in dual income households, the female partner is increasingly unwilling to give up her career in favour of advancement for her partner. This has produced a shortage of managers available from the home country for transfer abroad and MNEs are having to rely on local managers from the host country to fill this shortfall. In the USA, a consortium of thirty-eight companies has been established to try to find jobs with a company in the group for spouses whose partners are moving abroad.

Some MNEs operate a policy of maintaining a pool of highly trained international specialists who move from one foreign operation to another and may never work in their home country. Although business schools in universities are offering high-level management training, there is no real consensus about what managers need to know to make them effective internationally. In many cases, companies provide managers with in-house training which not only deals with information about the nature of the companies' international operations abroad but will also include language training and orientation programmes. In some respects, firms have been criticized for concentrating on providing transferees and their families simply with an informational briefing on the host country prior to transfer (which could include details about housing, climate, health conditions, taxes, etc.), rather than providing full training on the host country's cultural background.

3.3.3 Employment strategies

When planning its international employment strategy a company must take into consideration the quality of the workforce in the home country in order to assess the feasibility of employing local labour. The main reason for the use of expatriate labour is the desire to transfer skills from the home country operation. However, it must be considered that host country nationals may be more adaptable to the cultural conditions than expatriates and also they may be resentful of foreign nationals entering the country to take what are perceived as local jobs.

Another consideration which must be taken into account by the home country is the level of compensation to be offered to home country nationals working abroad. In other words, how much will it cost MNEs to undertake international labour transfers in order to service their operations abroad. If the expatriate worker is being transferred to a country with a higher cost of living then financial compensation for this will need to be built into the salary package. Other adjustments will need to be made if the level of taxation is higher in the host country. In addition, most employees will not accept a transfer abroad unless enhanced job status forms part of the transfer package. In most cases, job promotion also means salary enhancement and this will increase the value of the compensation package.

In addition to compensation packages relating to salary, companies may also decide to provide expatriate workers with 'hardship allowances' to cover the costs of adjusting to a new culture and social circumstances. These may involve the employment of domestic help or having to send children to school away from home, possibly abroad. In some countries, where there is danger from political unrest or possible attack from terrorist groups, the company may have to provide expatriate employees and their families with security guards or a secure environment around their work and living quarters. 'Fringe benefits' may also include a company car, subsidized housing, and profit-sharing. It may also be beneficial to arrange part payment of salary in the home country in order to avoid host country taxes, where these are relatively high. To encourage employees to transfer to inhospitable countries, companies have tended to offer tax-free high salaries on fixed-term contracts. But the payment of hardship allowances is being increasingly phased out for staff who are transferred to international capitals where living and working conditions are regarded as equal to those in major cities elsewhere in the developed world. The calculation of compensation packages is an extremely complex issue, and not only varies from company to company, but also depends upon the prevailing conditions in the host country, the type of job, and the distribution of salaries within the corporate hierarchy.

3.3.4 Labour relations and labour standards

MNEs will be bound by the traditions and regulations concerning collective bargaining in labour relations in the host country. The situation may differ substantially to labour bargaining procedures which are familiar in the home country. MNEs can play an important role in influencing the future development of labour relations and collective bargaining procedures in the host country. Generally, in Europe, collective bargaining takes place between the employer and several trade unions which establish wages and conditions for an entire industry. The influence of Japanese MNEs in Western Europe in recent years has seen collective bargaining take place between the Japanese employer and a single industrial trade union representing all trades within the industry, so assisting in breaking down the restrictive practices in employment which were particularly prevalent in British industry in the 1960s and 1970s. As far as the Japanese approach is concerned, the increased mobility between labour and management has helped to break down social divisions within the workplace.

However, in many Western countries, especially the USA and the UK, there has been a tradition of adversarial relationships between the management and the workforce, perhaps partly as a result of the lack of mobility between labour and management. Another factor influencing labour relations is the fear of unemployment. Until recently, in Japan, most key workers were guaranteed jobs for life and this is said to remove a major problem confronting many trade unions in Western countries— concern about job security. Guaranteed lifetime employment is said to increase workers' morale and foster a commitment to remain in the company, so reducing the problem of labour turnover.

The successes achieved by the Japanese in fostering a sense of worker participation in the form of factory production and quality teams has also led the way for Western companies to introduce elements of worker participation into their own organizations. In countries like Germany, some companies operate a process called co-determination, whereby workers are allocated places on supervisory boards to assist in the communication and transfer of information between workers and management. In the UK, large companies have traditionally operated a system of workers' councils which also allow workers a say in the management of the business by allocating them places on such a representative body.

The use of worker participation in the fostering of good labour relations is probably unique to the major industrialized countries. There are many countries in which workers have few or no rights. In the past, MNEs have been criticized for exploiting this situation in countries with poor labour bargaining procedures in an attempt to reduce their operating costs. However, in recent years, MNEs have been subject to greater scrutiny from the media, shareholders, and investors, and it is now in their own interests to comply with international labour standards and also standards on health and safety, rather than rely upon local standards.

3.4 Financing International Operations

3.4.1 International financial management and risk

Financial management is concerned with the decisions taken by a firm which relate to cash flows. There can be three elements present in a firm's cash flows, depending upon the level and nature of its business activities. Cash flow may simply represent the sales revenue which a firm receives from the sale of its products; it may constitute the capital it raises on foreign and domestic capital markets to finance its current activities or support its plans for expansion; or it may involve the funds held by the firm as a hedge against possible fluctuations in international exchange rates and interest rates.

The difficulties facing a firm become more complicated when it takes the decision to expand its activities into international markets. The promotion and marketing of a good product is not sufficient to ensure success in foreign markets and the firm must demonstrate an ability to gain access to capital in different countries in order to finance its operations and future expansion plans. The level of financial risk is greater in the international environment where a firm must take into account different laws, different market conditions, and different levels of interest and exchange rates. A notable benefit for firms operating in the EU which should arise from the advent of the single currency and membership of EMU is that international financial risks should fall due to the stability of exchange and interest rates between countries operating in the system. It may attract new FDI into the EU from outside the area, but countries which choose to remain outside EMU in the early years may lose new investment opportunities offered by foreign firms.

The firm must consider all aspects of international financial management when taking the decision to invest abroad. First, a firm needs to consider the financial feasibility of the investment (also known as capital budgeting). Second, a firm must assess the balance of debt capital and equity capital which will be required for the funding of the investment (i.e. the capital structure). Third, the firm must consider methods of raising long-term capital and its sources. Finally, a firm will need to determine the method of managing its cash flow during the period of the investment. In assessing the risks faced by a firm when embarking upon international activities, difficulties associated with fluctuations in exchange rates are probably the most serious problem to resolve.

The two main problems associated with currency risks are exchange rate fluctuations and inflation (the latter often being a sign of a weak currency). Although it should be recognized that inflation is present in all economies, very high inflation rates can have an important effect on the strategies employed by firms in this situation. Inflation can erode the value of the financial assets of a firm, whereas financial liabilities can become worth less, but this benefit can be eroded on outstanding loans if a government charges high interest rates in order to tackle inflation. In countries suffering from hyperinflation, the difficulties are often exacerbated by the imposition of price controls by the government. A firm operating under these conditions may have to circumvent the price control regulations by making changes to product size and packaging in order to reflect the price rises which are taking place in the economy.

In the absence of fixed exchange rate systems in most areas of the world, MNEs are faced with high currency risks, such as the substantial exchange rate fluctuations suffered in South-East Asia during the 1997/8 financial crisis. Problems with exchange rate fluctuations can result in three different types of exposure for companies. First, *translation exposure* involves the conversion of all foreign currency financial statements into the currency of the parent company (e.g. £ sterling for UK companies, $ for US companies and, increasingly, euros for German companies after 1 January 1999). This means that exposed accounts are translated at the current rate of exchange and may gain or lose depending on currency fluctuations on international financial markets.

Second, *transaction exposure* occurs where a sales or purchase transaction has been undertaken in a foreign currency and so accounts receivable or payable must be settled by the company eventually. Third, *economic exposure* arises from the risks associated with the cost of labour and raw materials, the location of investments, and the pricing of the product itself. Fluctuations in exchange rates will affect the prices of these variables and may encourage firms to move the site of operation away from countries with overvalued exchange rates. Some companies like Toyota have argued that the UK is in danger from capital flight by failing to join the single currency in the first stage.

3.4.2 Sources of finance for international business

There are three main financial instruments which are available to provide finance for MNEs: loans, bonds, and equity. These are all available through the international capital markets or through the domestic capital market.

■ Loan markets

Short-term and long-term finance can be obtained from both local or domestic capital markets. An advantage to a firm using local markets is that host governments may offer MNEs loan capital at attractive rates of interest. In other words, interest rate subsidies may be available in addition to other grants to attract new FDI into a country. In general, large companies obtain their finance through the international capital market (also known as the eurocurrency market).

Eurocurrency is the term given to any currency which is deposited in a bank account outside its country of origin. For example, if £s sterling are deposited in banks in Germany or the USA, they become known as Europounds. In the same way, US dollars deposited in banks in the UK become Eurodollars.

Generally, Eurocurrency markets deal in short-term loans and deposits of a maturity of one year or less, although it is possible for firms to borrow for longer periods (in this case the loan becomes known as Eurocredit). The majority of transactions in this market are between banks themselves with firms making up only about 20 per cent of the business. Individual firms have to gain access to Eurocurrency funds through banks as they are prohibited from borrowing from the market directly. Since Eurocurrency markets are unregulated, loans do not have to be supported by reserves and this enables deposit takers to charge lower rates of interest.

■ Bonds

Bonds can be issued through individuals or syndicates. They are long-term securities, usually with a maturity period of between four and ten years. The most common forms of bond which are most frequently traded are fixed rate bonds, floating bonds, and equity option bonds. All are subject to interest which is paid during the period of their issue and all types can be traded in secondary markets. The most common of the three types is the fixed rate bond which provides a fixed rate of interest, payable annually. The floating rate bond pays a variable rate of interest which is usually adjusted on a six-monthly basis. The equity option bond offers the flexibility of paying interest in the current period but allowing the holder to convert the bond into a shareholding in the company at a later date. Domestic bonds are issued through domestic bond markets by residents of that country, but international bonds allow companies to gain access to capital provided by foreign investors.

■ Equity financing

This involves issuing shares through the domestic stock exchange although companies can apply to obtain a listing on a foreign stock exchange if domestic capital markets are considered too small to meet the demands of large MNEs.

■ The venture capital market

Some high-risk activities undertaken by a firm may preclude it borrowing capital through the sources which have been considered above. These activities may include the development of a new product or entry into a new market which may constitute high risks. Venture capital is often provided by companies established for the purpose, but in recent years banks and insurance companies have entered the market to supply this form of finance. Finance for high-risk ventures and lesser known companies is also provided by 'over-the-counter' equity markets, such as NASDAQ (National Association of Securities Dealers Automated Quotation) in the USA or Europe's fledgling equivalent, EASDAQ. The recipients of venture capital are usually small companies which are involved in developing a new product and are unable to obtain finance through mainstream channels.

■ Export financing

In the case of firms which are specifically concentrating on exporting products into foreign markets, financial services are available to those companies in the form of letters of credit, bills of exchange, factoring, and forfaiting.

A letter of credit is issued by a bank and guarantees payment to the exporter at a specified time, generally, thirty, sixty, or ninety days, on behalf of the importer. A bill of exchange is issued by the exporter's bank which orders the importer or the importer's bank to pay a specified sum on a specific day. Factoring can be undertaken by banks as well as by specialist factoring houses. A factor will undertake to purchase an exporter's outstanding accounts at a discount. It is the factor who then receives payment from the importer. The main advantage of factoring is that it can be used by a small firm to improve cash flow. Forfaiting has been used extensively for transactions with Eastern European countries and other emerging markets where there is a high risk of the exporter not receiving payment for goods offered for sale. In the case of forfaiting, the importer is allowed to pay in stages. The issuing bank also takes out a guarantee of payment with the government bank in the importer country.

3.4.3 Investment decisions

In order to properly evaluate the expected returns from a potential investment, the company must compare the net present value (NPV) or internal rate of return of an activity abroad with that of its other investments and also of others available in the host country. It is necessary for the firm to determine whether the net present value of an investment is positive or negative by discounting the net cash flows in the future by the average cost of capital for the firm (the average of debt and equity costs). The reason for discounting is to take into account that the firm is being charged interest on the capital it has borrowed. This capital could have been used for alternative investment and so by discounting future cash flows the opportunity cost of the income from the capital forgone can be taken into account. If NPV is positive, then the investment is worthwhile, but if NPV is negative, then the cash flows which are expected to result from a particular investment are not sufficient to provide a reasonable rate of return.

3.4.4 International accounting and taxation

The additional risks which are involved when a firm decides to undertake international activities have been discussed earlier in this chapter. The objective of the international accounting function is to ensure that managers possess full information about the company's capability of meeting the additional risks it encounters in the global market place. Although accounting principles and practices vary from country to country, there has been a development towards standardization across countries in recent years. This is a logical step given the move towards European economic and monetary union, but it must also be considered to be one of convenience given the large number of firms now involved in global business activities. At the same time, a convergence of tax systems between countries has been occurring with the tax policies of governments becoming increasingly similar.

Nevertheless, accounting principles and practices vary according to measurement and disclosure between countries, that is, with respect to the valuation of assets and the methods of presenting information and results in financial documents. Countries like the UK and the USA adopt more open policies about the nature and extent of information entering the public domain, while countries such as Switzerland, Germany, and Japan tend to have less disclosure. Some countries, like Germany for example, whose companies are largely bank-funded, utilize more conservative methods when valuing assets than others in order to reduce their tax liability and so increase cash reserves for paying off bank loans. On the other hand, US companies emphasize profits in their financial statements in order to attract investors.

Most countries usually adopt either the residential approach or a territorial approach to international taxation. The residential approach taxes the income of its citizens from foreign investments regardless of where the income is earned, whereas the territorial approach taxes all income earned within its territorial jurisdiction regardless of the country of residency of investors. In practice, most countries find it beneficial to use a combination of these approaches where domestic companies can be taxed according to the residential approach, and the territorial approach can be applied to non-resident investors within their territorial jurisdiction.

3.5 International Logistics

IN order to remain competitive, MNEs must pay full regard to international logistics. This means that they must formulate and coordinate a strategy to manage the flows of materials into and out of the international organization. The concept covers all systems which control the movement of all products at all stages of manufacture and also the logistics of establishing relationships with customers and suppliers. The use of such systems for the efficient movement of all materials into and out of the organization will ensure that the company develops important competitive advantages. Technological advances have enabled firms to improve their communication systems and order processing facilities. These will be important areas where firms can seek further cost savings over the next few years, given that many companies have already achieved all possible cost reductions in the financing and production function.

3.5.1 International transport and distribution

Transportation is an important element of any system of international logistics. An efficient transport and distribution system determines how quickly the goods are received by the customer. In most industrialized countries a well-developed infrastructure exists but in developing countries distribution within the internal market may be limited by poor road networks and poor availability of motorized transport. It is the role of the international logistics manager employed by an MNE to investigate the costs and benefits of locating and operating in a particular country. One mode of transport may be appropriate in one country but may prove more costly or unreliable in another.

Cost is a major factor when a company selects a particular mode of international transport. For example, although air freight is undoubtedly more costly than transport overland, it possesses the advantage of rapidity for a firm which may be entering the market for the first time and wants to avoid having to invest in warehousing or distribution centres. In addition, air freight can be cost-effective for high-priced items where the additional cost can be absorbed into the price of the product more easily.

In addition, non-economic factors are also important and should be taken into account, for example, whether a country's transportation system is subject to government subsidies. There may be preferential policies in force whereby pressure is put on firms involved in government contracts to use national flag carriers, even though these may prove to be more costly.

3.5.2 Documentation, procedures, and legal requirements

The international logistics manager must be aware of all the different types of import/export documentation which are required for each country and a company must comply with all the local regulations and law on this. The types of document required will depend upon the type of product being sold and its country of destination. However, the vast range of documents required can deter firms from selling goods abroad and can act as a barrier to international trade. Some firms use freight forwarders who specialize in handling all export documentation. The EU has tried to simplify and eliminate the red tape and bureaucracy in order to encourage trade between member states. It has been estimated that nearly 200 customs forms were eliminated after the introduction of the Single Administrative Document in 1988.

The International Chamber of Commerce has defined Incoterms which are internationally accepted terms and conditions of sale. These terms lay down the rules relating to what is and what is not accepted in the sale and when ownership passes from the seller to the buyer. In addition, customs duty must be paid on the goods at the point of entry into the country and this will depend upon the type of goods, their country of origin, and their value. It may be possible for companies to limit their liability to payment of duty by applying for refunds on goods which are to be used as raw materials for finished products which may later be exported. Another method of deferring liability for customs duty is for the company to store its goods in bonded warehouses until the goods are sent for sale or are used as raw materials in the manufacturing process.

3.5.3 Managing international logistics

Generally, it is more efficient for an MNE to organize its international logistics department centrally so that the main organization in the home country can retain control over these activities on a centralized basis. However, the system will break down if the central department fails to maintain constant contact with local staff in the host country. A centralized system may not be appropriate if the firm is engaged in activities on a global basis with subsidiaries in a number of countries. Where the many international markets are of a diverse nature, a policy of total centralization could fail to take into account local needs. If subsidiaries are allocated a budget centre and are given responsibility for meeting their own logistic needs, this may take into account local market conditions, but the disadvantage may be that individual subsidiaries are unable to extract the lowest rates from transportation carriers. However, another possibility is for large MNEs to outsource its logistics requirements to another company specializing in this field. Whilst there may well be some cost advantages associated with this strategy, problems may occur when control over this important aspect of a firm's organization is lost.

3.6 Summary

INTERNATIONAL market entry requires consideration of a wide range of factors. A company must have a clear mission and its intentions and values must be reflected in its international strategy. Before an international strategy is worked out, a company must evaluate both its own strengths and weaknesses and the opportunities and threats of the external environment. Its international strategy must also be based on a clear set of objectives. Before selecting a target market, a country screening process and preliminary assessment of consumer demand should be undertaken. A detailed marketing strategy can then be drawn up. Since MNEs have established increasingly sophisticated networks of subsidiaries in a wide range of different countries in the last twenty or thirty years, it has become essential for international firms to develop adequate support systems to ensure the successful marketing of their product range, effective hiring of personnel, efficient international financial management, and cost-effective international logistics. If a company successfully implements strategies in these areas to establish and develop policy, it can expect to be able to achieve a competitive advantage in the global market place.

Review Questions

1 What is involved in the processes of 'company evaluation' and 'evaluation of the external environment' prior to international market entry?

2 What factors must be taken into account when designing the 'marketing mix' for international market entry? In what sense might 'relationship marketing' be preferable to 'transaction marketing' in foreign markets?

3 What factors must be taken into account when recruiting and selecting managers for a foreign venture?

4 What are the main sources of finance for a company's international operations? What additional financial risks are involved in international operations?

5 What is involved in 'international logistics' and why is its effective management crucial to the success of a company's international operations?

Group Activity: Finding a New Market Abroad

Working in groups of three or four, select a product or service that you are considering marketing in one of the following countries: Australia, Brazil, China, Germany, Japan, Poland, Russia, USA, South Africa, Thailand.

Having chosen a product or service, each group should select *one* of the above countries as a potential market and produce a brief report or presentation on the suitability of the country as a market for your product or service. Each group should gather information on its chosen country. Possible sources of information include: *The Economist* (especially country reports), *Financial Times* (especially periodic country surveys), Government Trade Department, Internet websites for individual countries or international organizations (UN, UNCTAD, OECD, IMF, World Bank, etc.). Each group should choose a different country where possible. The report should comment on the suitability of the country based on the following factors: (1) general political and economic situation; (2) risk factors; (3) general product data; (4) cultural assessment; (5) market potential; (6) any other country-specific factors; and (7) an outline marketing strategy.

Notes

1 For a discussion of this issue see, e.g. T. Ambler, 'How SMEs enter foreign markets', *Financial Times Mastering Marketing*, Part 10: International Marketing (16 Nov. 1998).

2 A. Sahay, 'Finding the right international mix', *Financial Times Mastering Marketing*, Part 10: International Marketing (16 Nov. 1998).

3 Ibid.

4 See e.g. M. Christopher, A. Payne, and D. Ballantyne, *Relationship Marketing* (Butterworth Heinemann, 1994) or C. Gronroos, 'From marketing mix to relationship marketing: towards a paradigm shift in marketing', *Asia-Australia Marketing Journal* (1994), 2 (1).

Recommended Reading

■ Bennett, R., *International Marketing* (Kogan Page, 1998).

■ Demirag, I., *Financial Management for International Business* (McGraw-Hill, 1994).

■ Flaherty, M. T., *Global Operations Management* (McGraw-Hill, 1996).

■ Hill, C. W. L., *Global Business Today* (McGraw-Hill, 1998).

■ Meier, G.M., *The International Environment of Business* (Oxford University Press, 1998).

■ Nugent, N., and O'Donnell, R., *The European Business Environment* (Macmillan, 1994).

■ Terpstra, V., and Sarathy, R., *International Marketing* (Dryden, 1994).

Part II

The International Environment

4

The Political, Economic, and Legal Environment

Objectives

- to identify the factors which affect international business activity
- to assess the impact of political, economic, and legal factors in influencing the extent and location of international business
- to discuss the impact of different political and economic systems and their effect on international business
- to identify the important world political and economic events since the 1970s and their impact on the activities of international firms

4.1 Introduction

THE increasingly global nature of business activities in recent years and the need to respond to the challenges of the emerging markets, the Single European Market, and the move towards EU enlargement, means that all firms should be aware of the changing nature of the business environment. In this chapter, problems arising from the business environment are discussed. Particular emphasis is placed on the changing nature of the political, economic, and legal culture which make up the characteristics of the global economy in which many firms now compete. However, from Europe's point of view it was the late 1980s which saw the move towards the introduction of the Single European Market and the break-up of the former Eastern bloc. It became obvious that the EU's move towards greater integration had its mirror image in the East with the disintegration of the Communist bloc. The destruction of the old

East–West divide meant that in the 1990s firms could seek to establish new links with other countries in order to take advantage of early entry into the newly emerging markets.

However, the extent to which firms take advantage of international opportunities will depend on their present structure and outlook. It is the multinationals which are already well established in Europe which will normally be in a good position to seek further expansion. In many ways, the advent of the single market may force other 'less mobile' firms into internationalizing their activities. For example, in order to be able to compete in the single market, even SMEs in Europe, not normally needing to internationalize their activities, may be forced to do so to ensure their survival in the long term. Since the business environment is an extremely important factor for all firms entering new markets, an environmental audit can identify the potential threats or opportunities which are likely to be faced by them. Of course, the key to a firm's success when entering a new market is how far can it adjust its strategy to cope with the new environmental conditions.

The most common form of environmental audit is undertaken by STEP factor (or PEST) analysis, which focuses on the sociocultural, technological, economic, and political factors that might affect a firm seeking to operate in a new market. Political factors will inevitably have a very important effect on the business environment, not only in terms of the political nature of the government in power, but they will also influence the legal situation faced by a company entering a new market since it is the role of the government to pass laws which can have an important influence on the operations of a company trading there. The activities of firms can be directly affected by changes in company laws, health and safety legislation, environmental regulations, employment law, competition law, and the law of intellectual property. For firms operating in the EU this is further complicated by European legislation which may operate alongside, or even supersede, national legislation governing a particular area of activity.

Social factors which need to be taken into account relate to the effects of changes in social mobility and changes or differences in cultural attitudes. These factors are of paramount importance to companies when deciding upon the nature of the product to be introduced into a particular market and also when selecting the form of marketing technique appropriate for the promotion of the product. For example, a recent phenomenon common to the countries of Western Europe is the ageing population, with a greater proportion of people in the over sixty age group than ever before. The prospect of more people living longer has meant that companies have had to tailor their products to attract older consumers, many with higher disposable retirement incomes than were enjoyed by their parents' generation. Consequently, a plethora of travel companies are offering holidays specifically targeted to the interests of the over fifty-fives, and in the UK a number of construction companies have undertaken high-quality retirement housing developments to attract the affluent 'grey consumer'.

In general, it is often economic factors which are most important for firms considering expanding their operations abroad. It may be that the poor economic performance of the home economy persuades firms to seek expanding markets elsewhere. Since predictions of the expected performance of national economies are published by government agencies, firms can make an assessment of the situation by ascertaining how inflation, interest rates, wage rates, and exchange rates are expected to fluctuate. The nature of government policy is also very important—a complete *volte face* on economic policy by a new government recently elected to power may create uncertainty and discourage investment from abroad. In addition, the government's attitude towards regional policy and the availability of subsidies to foreign firms, either from the national government or from the EU, may also prove to be an important factor influencing foreign investment. Indeed, this proved to be the case when the UK government secured investment by Nissan in 1985 resulting in the construction of the greenfield production plant at Washington, near Sunderland.

Finally, technological factors are probably the least important consideration to most firms since technology is available on a worldwide basis and is unlikely to vary significantly from country to country. However, where there is a technology gap between countries or regions, as has been seen in Russia and Eastern Europe after 1990, Western companies have been willing to import technology and this has itself proved to be one of the major benefits of FDI for these countries. Indeed, it could be argued that the large Western MNEs are themselves responsible for the development of modern technology with the heavy investment made by them in research and development (R&D). It is essential for these companies to be at the forefront of R&D if they are to continue to enjoy a competitive advantage.

4.2 Political Systems and Cultural Differences

4.2.1 Political systems and ideology

It could be argued that the single most important event since the end of World War II was the fall of communism in Eastern Europe in 1989. For a period of nearly fifty years after 1945 the world political environment had been characterized by political polarization with the division between East and West precipitated by the onset of the Cold War. These rivalries failed to erupt into another worldwide conflict but did become visible in secondary disputes played out on the Third World stage from as early as the 1950s until the 1980s. The need by the countries of Eastern Europe to establish new political alignments after 1989 coincided with the relaunch of the EU after the countries of Western Europe emerged from a long period of economic and political turbulence at the end of the 1980s.

During the 1970s and 1980s many countries in Western Europe had been hit by deep recessions caused by the Middle Eastern oil crises. This also contributed to the decline in manufacturing industries in regions which could no longer compete with cheap imports of motor vehicles and electronic goods from Japan and goods from the newly emerging economies of South-East Asia. Regional economic imbalances within the UK and the countries of southern Europe, with their rising rates of unemployment, were one of the consequences of this decline. New industries in the service sector using modern technologies tended to gravitate to areas of Europe like West Germany and the South of France. Governments were unable to raise tax revenue from struggling firms who were laying off workers and from workers who were either low paid or had already joined the dole queue. Increasing burdens placed on government expenditure to support welfare benefits for the unemployed meant that other important areas of government expenditure, like health and education programmes, suffered.

The direct result of these developments was the emergence of social unrest which manifested itself in resentment of minority racial groups in the UK, France, and West Germany. In addition, the continued threat from terrorist groups like the IRA, the Red Brigades, and the Basque separatist movement, ETA, meant that the capitals of Western Europe lived under threat of terrorist bomb attack, although in all of these cases, the causes of such actions were far more complex than merely Western Europe's inability to cope with recession. Although the threat to Europe from many of its indigenous terrorist groups has diminished recently, the European political order is still under threat from a complicated network of terrorist groups based in the Middle East.

The 1970s was generally a period of government by parties on the Left in Europe, but by the 1980s this situation had been reversed in many countries in Northern Europe. The electorate in the UK was the first to vote a new right-wing government into power, represented by Margaret Thatcher's Conservative Party which had, during a period in opposition in the 1970s, acquired a new political ideology with its origins in monetarist economics and the belief that by controlling the money supply, the problem of inflation would become a thing of the past. The high interest rate policies pursued by the government in their failing attempts to control the supply of money in the early 1980s led to deep recession with unemployment rising to levels which were unprecedented in the post-war period. Dissatisfaction with government policy led to social unrest in several inner cities with associated racial divisions manifesting themselves in street rioting, notably in Toxteth, Liverpool, and in Brixton, South London.

Despite these problems, it was the 'Falklands War factor' which ensured the victory of the Conservative Government in the 1983 elections. Towards the end of the 1980s, the government managed to increase its popularity by pursuing a vigorous programme of privatization which ensured an increase in the number of small shareholders. The government had also increased private property ownership by its policy of selling off the local authorities' housing stock. In addition, the government had been able to reduce direct taxation and pay off part of the national debt from the proceeds of privatization. The combination of these factors, along with the boom in the private housing market (fuelled by low interest rates) and the consumer spending boom (also the result of interest rate policies and easy credit), meant that by the 1987 general election, the 'feel-good factor' was high and ensured a third election victory for the Conservative Party.

After its 1987 defeat, the Labour Party was forced to reinvent itself as a party of the Centre emphasizing its social democratic principles. The days of the Far Left masquerading as part of the mainstream party were numbered as the leadership faced up to the fact that it had to present new policies and attract alternative support if it were to have any chance of re-election in the future. This was very much the pattern in the rest of Europe at that time. Where socialist parties did remain in power, as in the case of Italy, there were attempts to decentralize economic control and allow market forces to prevail in some sectors. Other countries, like Spain, experimented with limited privatization, notably with the sale of the car manufacturer SEAT to the German car giant VW. By the end of the 1980s, the once powerful communists in Italy and France were becoming discredited due to increasing evidence of the crumbling of communist ideologies in Eastern Europe.

Consequently, the 1990s has continued to be a decade where European governments have emphasized the sovereignty of the market in their approach to economic policy. This has been mirrored in the relaunch of the EU and the movement towards greater economic and political integration in the West. In Eastern Europe the prevailing Western European ideology has been an important factor in shaping the pattern of both political and economic reform during its transition to market economies. However, a crisis in market economics occurred as a result of the problems which hit the economies of South-East Asia and Russia in 1997–8, although it is questionable whether Russia ever managed to achieve anything approaching a market economy in its attempts to reform after 1991.

4.2.2 Political culture

An important feature of the political culture in Western Europe over the last decade or so is that despite widespread acceptance of the orthodox thinking on the role of markets, the opportunity remained for new political groups to gain influence. This has been particularly the case in the area of environmental issues and the rise of the Green Party in Germany. By the end of the 1980s the German Greens had forty-two Members of Parliament and 15.6 per cent of the vote. The Greens' success in the October 1998 elections is the culmination of a period which has seen the party develop from an association of student radicals in the 1960s and 1970s to an accepted mainstream political party which will take an important role in the German coalition government under the leadership of Chancellor Gerhardt Schröder. In addition, the Greens have enjoyed successes in other countries, especially Switzerland, Italy, Austria, Belgium, and Finland. Despite successes in the European parliamentary elections by the Greens, the Green Party in the UK has been unable to shake off its 'anorak' image in recent years. The cause of the Greens is not helped by the fact that the mainstream political parties have also been promoting policies relating to environmental issues.

Another new development in Europe in the 1980s and 1990s has been the emergence of parties from the Far Right, their cause being fuelled by the increasing number of immigrants coming into Europe from Asia, North Africa, and also from Eastern Europe. The response to the growing number of immigrants from former French colonies in Africa has been the increasing support received by the Far Right which has resulted in notable election victories in the National and European parliaments by the National Front led by Jean-Marie Le Pen.

The new migration of workers from Eastern Europe was made possible by the revolutions of 1989, but by the summer of 1990 it was apparent that nothing very much had changed and that politicians of the old regime remained in office but were by that time trading under the new social-democratic flag. Furthermore, the rise of nationalism in countries like Yugoslavia and the re-emergence of traditional groups in search of their national identities, saw the start of a bloody civil war which has yet to achieve an effective resolution.

Problems relating to the costs of German reunification and the support given by the West to the reform programme in Eastern Europe were factors which contributed to the recession in Europe in the early 1990s. This meant that although reunification had fuelled the desire of the East Europeans to return to what they regarded as their rightful place in Europe, it also meant that the countries of Western Europe were not well placed to meet the financial challenges of EU enlargement and greater economic and political integration. As a result, the EU membership aspirations of the reformers were placed on the back burner when some countries were granted associate membership status under the Europe Agreements in 1992 in what turned out to be a failed attempt at appeasement by EU member countries.

4.2.3 Political decisions and business risk

International companies normally endeavour to conduct their business in countries where there is a stable political environment. Managers operating within a country will need to assess the degree of political risk and monitor the changing political situation regularly. Generally, countries with an established tradition of parliamentary democracy will present the lowest level of political risk to companies conducting business there. Obviously, a high level of risk occurs in countries which do not have that tradition and political instability may result in a government being overturned as a result of a popular uprising. The nature of the political risk has changed as a result of the fall of communism in Eastern Europe in 1989: the difficulties which Western companies encountered when trying to operate within the straitjacket of central planning have disappeared but have been replaced with new political and economic uncertainties resulting from the inability of some countries to sustain real market reform.

Until recently, in South-East Asia, strong government with little evidence of democracy can itself be seen as advantageous to foreign investment where political risk is assessed as being low and the future of the government is stable. However, the 1997–8 economic crisis in South-East Asia can itself produce political risk when governments become unpopular due to their inability to reverse the economic collapse. Some economists predict that the Asian financial crisis will lead to a global recession on a scale which will not have been seen since the end of World War II. In the long run, the collapse of the financial markets in South-East Asia and the financial crisis in Russia will mean that companies are likely to switch investments away from these areas and search for countries with lower political and economic risks.

Other forms of political risk may arise from terrorist activities which may be targeted against the property or personnel of large Western companies. In recent years, US companies operating in the Middle East have faced high levels of political risk and have been subject to attack from terrorist groups. In some cases, terrorists will resort to kidnapping executives in order to obtain funds for their cause by making ransom demands.

International firms can reduce the incidence of political risk by ensuring that they become fully integrated into the country where their operation is based. In some cases, the citizens of the host country have complained that they feel exploited by the activities of foreign investors. A foreign company can overcome this by offering employment to local people and by supporting local charitable organizations. In addition, by establishing joint ventures with local companies, foreign firms can demonstrate their willingness to share their expertise and profits with local people.

It is now possible for foreign companies to take out insurance against the losses which may occur from high political risk. Risk insurance can cover currency inconvertibility (the inability to convert profits out of the local currency); expropriation insurance (the loss of an investment due to expropriation, confiscation, or nationalization of a foreign firm's assets due to the activities of the host government); and political violence insurance (the loss of company assets due to war, revolution, terrorism, sabotage, etc.). This type of insurance will only cover actual loss and not loss of profits, but in the future it may be an important factor which persuades a company to undertake investment abroad.

4.2.4 International relations and global institutions

The development of regional economic groupings on a global scale has had an important influence on the structure and pattern of world trade and investment. It could be argued that until the collapse of the economies in South-East Asia, the world economy was dominated by three major markets: Japan and South-East Asia; North America (the USA and Canada); and Western Europe. These are sometimes known as the Triad nations. Economic groupings such as ASEAN or NAFTA have established their own trading areas in order to eliminate trade barriers between members but retain the option of erecting trade barriers for non-members. GATT, now under the auspices of the World Trade Organization, was the first of the international trading agreements to be established at the Bretton Woods conference in 1944, along with major international financial institutions like the World Bank and IMF.

The IMF was established to facilitate international trade by encouraging member countries to set 'managed' exchange rates, but to avoid using foreign exchange controls which restrict the supply of foreign currencies necessary to undertake international trade and investment. The IMF was concerned with establishing exchange rate stability in order to promote world trade, while the objective of the World Bank was to provide a vehicle for lending to war-damaged countries in the immediate post-war period so the reconstruction of the economic infrastructure could take place. However, by the 1960s the focus of its assistance had changed and the World Bank had turned its attention towards supporting the economic development of Third World countries in Africa, Asia, the Middle East, and South America. The IMF also now focuses much more on economic development and on providing support for countries in financial difficulties (see Chapter 6).

The difficulties facing the World Bank, the IMF, and the World Trade Organization in the 1990s relate to questions about the continued feasibility of their existence given the significant changes which have occurred in the world economic environment during the last two decades. The effects of the recent collapse of the financial markets in South-East Asia were quickly felt in the financial markets in other parts of the world. Since only 5 per cent of finance available on a global basis is directly involved with the promotion of trade in goods and services, the question arises whether the institutions established under the Bretton Woods Agreement actually remain relevant today. Although the time may be right for wide-ranging reform of the international financial institutions, the G7 group of leading industrialized countries have no model of international finance upon which to base policies to promote reform. However, in recent years, policies promoting deregulation have been implemented at the cost of open financial markets with the accompanying problem facing countries of establishing domestic economic and monetary policies which are independent of world markets. This is an increasingly difficult objective to achieve. Domestic interest rate policies may also put pressure on capital flows into, and out of, the domestic economy, and will affect the rate of exchange of the domestic currency. This may lead to pressure on government policy-makers to restrict capital flows in order to stabilize the rate of exchange of the domestic currency. This is the problem which has to be resolved by members of the EU and has defined their approach towards further integration since the Maastricht Treaty.

At the end of 1998 the group of Commonwealth Finance Ministers called for countries such as Russia to be allowed to suspend debt repayments during an economic crisis without triggering default mechanisms. It was also suggested that regulators from foreign countries should be required to review financial regulation in any country, so that US and French regulators, for example, could make checks on the UK's financial markets. Although this would constitute a move to undermine a country's national sovereignty, such considerations may become less important in the face of growing difficulties caused by the global nature of international finance in the twenty-first century. It is argued that when a country's currency is under pressure, as has recently been the case in Russia and Brazil, the last thing these countries need is relatively small-scale assistance from the IMF on condition that they adopt self-defeating austerity measures. They need a central bank to act as a lender of last resort when any individual economy is under speculative pressure. A new world central bank seems to be the answer to the problem of the global financial crises which have occurred at the end of the twentieth century, with the acknowledgement that the USA can no longer be allowed to organize the world financial system to promote its own interests.

4.3 Economic Systems in Transition

4.3.1 Market economies and planned economies

The political division between East and West which dominated international relations throughout the post-war period was reinforced by the economic divisions created by communism and capitalism. Central control through a centralized political authority represented by the Communist Party in a one-party state was supported by a high degree of central control over the economy through an economic planning mechanism. The planning of all productive resources was controlled by state institutions through the publication of annual and five-year plans. Production was traditionally concentrated in the hands of large state-owned monopolies largely in the extractive, defence, and machine tool industries. The development of a manufacturing sector was largely neglected by the communists after 1945.

In a centrally planned economy it was the state planning authority which took key production decisions and this accounted for the poor assortment of consumer goods being produced in Eastern Europe until after 1990. The central planning system was devoid of all the incentives of the market mechanism where resources are allocated according to consumer preferences. Since the profit motive was also absent, central planning stifled all aspects of entrepreneurial activity. Given that the main measure of success was the fulfilment of production quotas laid down in the plan, there were no incentives for enterprises to over fulfil their quota, given the danger of having the quota increased in the next planning period. Consequently, enterprises had no incentive to introduce new or improved technology to enhance the quality or quantity of their output, and they certainly felt no urge to engage in the process of new product development. In other words, state enterprises were caught in a straitjacket within the planning process itself. They were dependent upon fulfilling the plan for their survival (and for the payment of workers' bonuses), so setting their own targets to improve the production process would hardly have been compatible with the operation of a system which depended upon strict central control.

It was the economic stagnation caused by the strictures imposed by the central planning system which provoked countries like Poland and Hungary to attempt to reorientate their economies towards the market during the 1980s. Since foreign trade had been largely undertaken in the form of 'countertrade' (the barter of goods between countries) with other countries in the Soviet bloc, the new policy pursued by Poland and Hungary in the 1980s of seeking out export markets in Western Europe and allowing their enterprises to be exposed to competition provided by Western firms, was seen to be a dramatic break with the past. After 1985, with the introduction of *perestroika* and *glasnost*, the Soviet Union, under the new General Secretary, Mikhail Gorbachev, indicated a new preoccupation with improving technology and modernizing its industrial base, as well as trying to improve the standard of living for its citizens. At the same time, the People's Republic of China was also engaged in an ongoing programme of reform specifically designed to modernize its economy and establish its own MNEs. As with the reforms in Eastern Europe in the 1980s, China was keen to encourage FDI.

4.3.2 Economies in transition

The fall of the Berlin Wall in 1989 brought unprecedented challenges for the development of Europe and for the move towards the global economy itself. For the first time in nearly fifty years the countries of Eastern Europe were able to abandon the strictures of central planning and make the transition to market economies. This will undoubtedly change the face of Europe in the twenty-first century since the countries of Eastern Europe are currently pursuing their claims for full EU membership. If the EU with its current fifteen member countries is to welcome countries from the former Communist bloc, then a future membership amounting to, possibly, twenty-five countries will inevitably produce fundamental changes to the political and economic face of Europe.

The transition process itself has not been without its difficulties. The move from a highly centralized economic and political system to a market economy with the development of democratic political institutions cannot be expected to be achieved overnight, but in practice a very rapid pace of reform was instituted by most countries in the region. The progress which had been achieved in the first two years was unprecedented. By 1992 the Communist empire had ceased to exist, with democratic governments replacing the communist parties, East Germany had been reunified with West Germany, and Hungary, Czechoslovakia, and Poland had all been accepted as associate members of the EU. Indeed, by 1992 the Soviet Union itself had disappeared with its former republics declaring their independence, but loosely realigned in the Commonwealth of Independent States (CIS).

The collapse of the Soviet Union also meant that the trading relationships established between the former communist countries disintegrated and the role of the Council for Mutual Economic Assistance (CMEA), the Soviet-dominated trading bloc which regulated trade between the USSR and its satellites, became redundant. With the collapse of intra-East European trade, the countries of the region started to look towards Western Europe and the EU to establish new trade links. As far as the domestic economies were concerned, the anti-inflationary policies imposed by the governments of the region meant that high interest rates and tight monetary policy measures plunged the economies of Eastern Europe into recession. Extensive programmes of privatization were introduced and the accompanying attempts at restructuring former SOEs and the increasing incidence of bankruptcies signalled an increase in unemployment. Far from achieving rising living standards, most citizens in Eastern Europe had seen their living standards plummet by 1993 and the rising popular discontent with the reforms meant that the communist parties in many countries gained support in the 1993 elections.

The 'shock therapy' approach to economic reform is not without its critics. Nevertheless, progress made by some countries has been significant with Poland being the first country in the region to register positive rates of economic growth by the end of 1993. However, it should be noted that limited reforms in Poland began with the old regime in the early 1980s in response to the demands of the increasingly popular free trade union, Solidarity. Important problems remain even in countries which are leading the economic reform progress in the region, notably, high inflation, rising unemployment, chronic budget deficits, and slow privatization with the selling off of large industrial enterprises having reached a virtual standstill in some countries. Perhaps the most notable failure of all countries attempting to reform has been Russia, but Ukraine and Belarus are also states which are poised on the brink of economic collapse. Whilst problems arising from political instability have caused the implementation of a feasible economic reform programme in Russia to be delayed, the neo-Stalinist regime in power in Belarus has returned the economy to central control and imposed the political monopoly of the Communist Party upon all aspects of government.

As a result of the serious economic problems facing Russia and its neighbours in the CIS at the end of 1998, it is difficult to believe that the countries of the former Soviet Union will be able to catch up with the more successful countries of Eastern Europe in the near future. President Yeltsin's government has failed to introduce a sustainable reform programme since the mechanism of central planning coupled with central government control collapsed in 1991 and was not replaced with a viable alternative. Existing state institutions are unable to carry out the functions of government—for example, tax collection agencies have failed to collect taxes from firms and individuals, the government conducts tight monetary policy by raising interest rates to 150 per cent and failing to pay wages and salaries to public sector workers. Since the collapse of state control and the demoralization of the security service, the activities of criminal organizations have proceeded unchecked. In Russia, important sectors of the economy have fallen into the hands of organized crime as a result of the disastrous share distribution programme during privatization. Free share vouchers were sold on by ordinary citizens prior to privatization and found their way on to the black market where they were bought up by criminals and then exchanged legally for legitimate shares. Some privatized companies have been used subsequently for the purposes of money laundering—a mechanism through which the profits from activities such as drugs, arms dealing, and prostitution, can be channelled. In addition, profits arising from legitimate business activities are also being invested in foreign banks outside Russia by entrepreneurs who are worried about increasing signs of instability, but who are creating serious shortages of funds for legitimate investment in capital projects. The future development of the private sector in Russia is now at risk as a result of the wholesale export of capital.

4.3.3 Emerging economies

Although the countries of Eastern Europe whose economies are in transition can also be described as 'emerging economies', a second group of countries, often known as 'newly industrialized countries', notably comprising countries from South-East Asia and Latin America, also qualify under this definition. The International Finance Corporation defines 'emerging economies' or 'newly industrialized countries' as those which have low or middle per capita incomes. This approach seeks to divide the world's economies into three categories: the first group comprises the advanced industrial economies of Western Europe and North America; the second group is the 'emerging countries' or 'developing countries' comprising a wide range of economies in four groups spread across four continents (see Figure 4.1). In the third category are less developed countries with very low per capita incomes and predominantly agrarian economies.

This definition of 'emerging markets' based on income is normally used by financial analysts when advising foreign investors, whereas the World Bank classification would identify some countries in the J. P. Morgan groupings as 'less developed'. In any case, from 1995 some analysts began to describe the 'emerging economies' as 'submerging' since the stock exchanges in South-East Asia have suffered losses resulting

Figure 4.1 Categorization of 'emerging economies'

Africa

Algeria, Côte d'Ivoire, Morocco, Nigeria, South Africa, Zimbabwe

Asia

China and Hong Kong, India, Indonesia, South Korea, Malaysia, Philippines, Singapore, Taiwan, Thailand, Vietnam

Europe

Bulgaria, Czech Republic, Greece, Hungary, Poland, Portugal, Russia, Slovenia, Turkey

Latin America

Argentina, Bolivia, Brazil, Chile, Colombia, Costa Rica, Dominican Republic, Ecuador, Jamaica, Mexico, Panama, Paraguay, Peru, Uruguay, Venezuela

Source: J. P. Morgan, NY, 1995.

from too heavy a reliance on foreign investment. This problem has gradually worsened, culminating in the collapse of the South-East Asian emerging markets in 1997 when large Western institutional lenders called in their loans.

Before the collapse of the emerging economies of South-East Asia, the benefits of investment in the region were twofold. The opportunity for high returns from financial investments was immense, but emerging markets also provided foreign firms with new marketing opportunities for selling a wide range of consumer goods or providing infrastructural investment. The criteria for investment in emerging markets has been confidence in the high level of returns that investments will produce. Any fall in confidence among investors, for whatever reason, will signal a massive withdrawal of funds as soon as the market becomes jittery. It is not surprising that the crisis in South-East Asian markets in 1997 quickly became catastrophic given the level of foreign investor involvement in those economies. These events underline the problems which will continue to arise from the increasing globalization of the economic activities of both governments and firms. In other words, the greater the degree of economic integration on a global scale, the more difficult it will be for individual economies to shield themselves from recession or from other difficulties which originate in other regions of the world.

4.3.4 **Economic interdependence and the global economy**

In much the same way as international business has become dominated by a small group of large MNEs, the new global order is now characterized by the emergence of a relatively small number of major trading blocs. For example, in the USA the high degree of integration between individual states has allowed it to remain at the forefront of world trade and investment for a long time. It could also be argued that economic integration as enjoyed by the USA has contributed to the greater competitiveness of US companies over their European rivals. The greater degree of integration in the US market allows for economies of scale to be achieved and the availability of more investment resources. The benefits of economic integration have proved attractive to European countries in recent years, and the development of the Single European Market has been an attempt to borrow the model of US economic integration and so try to achieve access to wider market opportunities, promote efficiency, and strengthen the position of Europe in the face of competition from other leading trading blocs.

The global economy is now dominated by the Triad markets. Aggressive competition undertaken by one group of countries will be countered by another group which sees itself as under attack. For example, in the face of increased economic integration in Europe after 1992, the USA and Japan made moves to retaliate by threatening the imposition of renewed protection against European imports. This was further fuelled by rumours from Brussels that EU firms would themselves be offered short-term protection from external competition in an attempt to encourage firms to strengthen their position in the new European market. The UK had been vehemently opposed to protectionist policies and the idea of a policy of protectionism emanating from Brussels went against national policies. Although the UK government was keen to put forward its own opinion on external trade protectionism, including the view that it allows industries to avoid adjusting to the challenges of international competition and new technologies, the other side of the argument is that such exposure to competition has left industries in the UK unable to compete, with subsequent problems of bankruptcy.

Ironically, it is the Japanese experience that leads to the conclusion that their success story in world trade partly lies in strict protectionist policies which were pursued in the early years of economic development. Policies involving import substitution meant that Japan could take time to develop domestic industries to produce goods which had been previously imported. Although in recent years Japan has pursued more liberal trade policies and has tried to use competition from foreign industries, particularly in pharmaceuticals and chemicals, to stimulate innovation and product development in their own, problems remain in the Japanese market, especially caused by cultural factors, which produce difficulties for foreign investors entering the market.

The accusations of the Americans and the Japanese that Brussels was intent upon creating a 'Fortress Europe' after the introduction of the Single European Market in 1992 are not entirely unfounded. The Japanese felt that new regulations relating to the common external tariff were directed towards restricting their high-technology exports to the EU. The European Commission faces a dilemma when implementing external protectionist policies: on the one hand, it is flying in the face of the principles laid down by GATT in the late 1980s on dumping and rules of origin, but the other difficulty relates to the fact that EU members themselves are by no means in agreement on whether protectionist policies should triumph over the promotion of 'free market' principles.

4.4 The Legal Environment

4.4.1 Different legal systems

The different legal systems operating in the various member countries of the EU offer another example of cultural diversity. The law exists to provide formal guidelines and rules to govern the behaviour of individuals and organizations. Failure to comply with the law means that penalties will be inflicted by the courts depending on the seriousness of the offence. Given the specific individuality of all members' legal systems within the EU, harmonization throughout the Union will be very difficult to achieve. Cultural diversity is also apparent from the increasingly litigious nature of some countries like the USA, whilst in countries like Japan, recourse to the law is frowned upon except in extreme circumstances since it means that the parties have failed to find a compromise, which is against Japanese tradition and results in loss of face.

Although the law changes over time, it may only do so over a long time-period and may lag behind important cultural changes which are taking place in a country. In many cases, it is not cultural changes which lead the way for changes in the law, but ambiguities in the law itself which are challenged in the courts. It may be that in the long term harmonization of EU law is achievable since countries are already used to making alterations or introducing new laws which reflect changes in cultural attitudes. The citizens of a country may oppose the introduction of a new national law and, as EU law is now increasingly taking precedence over national law, member governments should expect greater public opposition to what may be viewed as an erosion of national legal sovereignty in the future. On the other hand, member governments should also reconcile themselves to a greater number of their citizens seeking ultimate legal redress in the European Court of Justice (ECJ) and this may assist the process of legal harmonization by forcing national governments to address issues arising from cases which are taken to the ECJ.

Generally, the system of law in use worldwide can be classified into 'common law' and 'statute law'. Common law is based on tradition and customs, and it depends on precedent rather than on written rules and statutes. The English legal system is traditionally based on common law with legal rules and principles becoming codified through practice over many centuries. On the other hand, statute law is based on a comprehensive set of written rules which became law by being passed by national parliaments and provides a much more rigid legal system than one which is based largely on common law. In recent years, and with the aim of trying to overcome the shortcomings of both classifications, many countries have established a body of legal rules which apply specifically to commercial practice. The objective is to assist firms to engage in international business activities and many countries have introduced laws which govern, for example, the use of tariffs and quotas, intellectual property rights, employment rights, etc.

4.4.2 Trade and investment restrictions

The increasing tendency towards economic integration among groups of countries to create customs unions and trading blocs is discussed at greater length in Chapter 7. This development has meant that the EU has been criticized by countries from outside Europe (especially the USA and Japan) for the stance taken over the Single European Market with its discriminatory external tariff policy, giving rise to the accusation that the EU is intent upon creating a 'Fortress Europe'. In fact, in the period before 1992 there was evidence that the EU was pursuing a more stringent policy on 'dumping' and 'rules of origin'.

Different definitions of 'dumping' exist and the term generally refers to the exporting of goods at prices below the cost of production, or alternatively, it can mean the practice of charging different prices in separate markets without the price variations being supported by difference in costs. The two definitions are different: the first refers to prices which are set below cost, and the second refers to prices which are lower than those in other markets, notably, the domestic market. Although charging prices below cost does imply anti-competitive behaviour, there may be valid reasons why firms need to charge different prices in different markets. It may not be possible for a firm to charge a 'global price' because market conditions will necessarily differ from country to country due to different costs of the factors of production, differing price elasticities in foreign markets, etc.

The EU's anti-dumping law in its external trade policy was specifically aimed at preventing anti-competitive behaviour through unfair pricing, but undoubtedly it can also be viewed as a potential weapon to protect EU industries from competition from imports from the rest of the world. In practice, if it can be proved that an EU company is being damaged by competition from a foreign firm and also that the foreign firm is selling goods at a price which is either below that charged on the domestic market or below the cost of production plus a reasonable mark-up under WTO rules, then the European Commission can force the firm to increase its price or, alternatively, pay import duties on its goods. There have been accusations by firms that the EU is abusing its power by using the laws for protectionist reasons rather than to increase competition. Abuse of anti-dumping legislation by the EU may mean that EU firms are subject to retaliatory action by foreign governments who resent their own national companies being subject to restrictions in the EU. In the past, it has meant that complaints against the pricing activities of foreign firms reflect an inability of some EU firms to compete in the face of the lower prices of imported goods rather than foreign firms actually being in breach of the anti-dumping regulations.

The difficulties in complying with regulations relating to 'rules of origin' involve the different definitions of *origin*, especially where several of the raw materials or components of a product originate from a country other than that of its manufacture. A definition of origin was introduced by the EU in 1968 as being the country where the product underwent its last major transformation. Even this was fraught with difficulties so more specific rulings were established on an industry-to-industry basis which include regulations relating to 'local content', i.e. materials and components which are derived solely from local manufactures. For example, in the case of radios and televisions 35–40 per cent of their value must be added in the EU for them to be considered European, whereas up to 90 per cent of the value of Japanese cars must be added in the EU for them to be of European origin.[1]

Policies which impose local content rules are often said to restrict trade (that is, imports) as they force non-EU firms to locate in the EU. However, the benefits to the EU of increasing inward investment can be substantial and involve increased employment opportunities (especially in depressed regions), and the transfer of technology and labour skills. A contrasting argument is that in the long term such a strategy could strengthen the position of foreign investors by allowing them to become more competitive within the EU.

4.4.3 Property rights in international business

The role of international law is to assist in the conduct of international business. Although no enforceable body of international law exists, certain treaties and agreements relating to the activities of business organizations are respected by a number of countries. Intellectual property law protects an individual or firm's right to an invention, design, patent, or trade mark, and also provides copyright protection for literary, musical, artistic, and dramatic works (including photography, films, video and sound recording, and broadcasts). At present, these types of intellectual property are not governed entirely by any international treaty and national laws differ to the extent that rights granted by patent, trade mark, or copyright in one country may offer no protection under the law in another country. However, some international agreements do exist to enable firms to submit applications for international patents, trade marks, or copyrights under a country's existing intellectual property law, and for national copyrights to be recognized in signatory countries.

In the EU national laws relating to intellectual property rights have the potential for restricting trade between member states. In recent years, some progress has been made in creating EU-wide schemes for patents, trade marks, designs, and copyright. Indeed, two important issues which EU members have been addressing recently relate to the control of counterfeit goods, and also the operation of the Internet and access to information by individuals and organizations. Firstly, complaints from companies have prompted the EU to tighten the 1994 Regulation which sought to clamp down on counterfeit goods circulating within the European Single Market. Amendments will broaden the inspection-and-seizure powers of customs authorities by allowing them to suspend customs operations for suspected counterfeit and pirated goods that violate intellectual property rights.[2]

The second issue relates to the implications of intellectual property rights for the use of the Internet which permits users to produce numerous temporary or permanent copies during a transmission. An organization called 'The Ad Hoc Alliance for a Digital Future' is supporting legislation that would provide strong protection for rights holders and argues that the EU should avoid exposing network operators and Internet service providers to legal claims relating to copyright infringement by their customers.[3]

4.4.4 Contracts and product liability

If a dispute arises between two contracting firms in two different countries, a problem occurs relating to which country's laws are to be used and in which country the dispute is to be settled. Often, a clause will have been inserted into the contract which lays down which country's law is to be used and in which courts the dispute will be settled. However, if such a clause is absent from the original contract the parties in dispute will have to agree to either follow the laws of the country in which the agreement was made or follow the laws of the country in which the agreement was to be fulfilled. The potential for long disputes between companies to settle this issue is enormous, but the parties could apply for arbitration, where an independent third party intervenes to resolve the issue.

Prior to 1985 the EU approach to product liability tended to be one of piecemeal directives and legislation in member states relating to specific products with reliance on local consumer, sale of goods, and tortious liability laws to deal with any defective product claims which fell outside the legislation directed at the specific products. By 1985 it was apparent that this approach had allowed significant divergences between the consumer protection laws of individual member states, with potential for the distortion of competition between member states. If the liabilities of industry varied in severity from state to state, this could increase industrial costs in some states, and thus hamper the free movement of goods in the EU. Furthermore, it was apparent that the rights of consumers to be protected from and to seek compensation for injury caused by defective and harmful products varied considerably from state to state, and in some cases such rights were virtually non-existent.

In order to resolve this divergence, the European Commission produced Council Directive (EEC) 85/374 on the Approximation of Laws, Regulations and Administrative Provisions of Member States Concerning Liability for Defective Products. The purpose of the Directive was to lay down a fundamental legislative framework of essential broad safety and other mandatory requirements relating to the generality of products, rather than detailed regulations for specific products. The aim of the Directive was to provide a high level of safety for consumers with adequate enforcement measures. Although the purpose of the Directive was to cover all products, primary agricultural products and game were excluded. The Directive required member states to pass national laws necessary to comply with the Directive within three years of the date of notification of the Directive and so the UK government passed the Consumer Protection Act 1987 to fulfil this requirement. The Directive also provides that, except in certain limited circumstances, the producer of a product is liable to compensate any person injured by his/her defective products.

In addition to the civil rights of action introduced by member states to comply with the 1985 Directive, many member states (including the UK) went further and provided for criminal sanctions if products failed to meet 'the general safety requirement' (Section 10 of the UK Consumer Protection Act 1987). Again, the Commission found that some states had established legislation imposing a high level of obligation and protection to individuals throughout the EU so that competition became distorted within the internal market. As a result, the Council Directive (EEC) 92/59 on General Product Safety was passed. The purpose of this Directive is to ensure that products placed on the market are safe. The effects of the 1985 Product Liability Directive are primarily remedial, whereas the aim of the 1992 Product Safety Directive is to require a high level of preventative measures to be put in place in member states to ensure product safety. Article 3 lays down the general safety requirement that producers must ensure that all products placed on the market are safe. However, producers may be able to discharge this duty by advising consumers of any risks inherent in the product through its normal or forseeable use, and advising consumers of any precautions which need to be taken, especially if the risks are not obvious. This may involve the producer withdrawing the product from sale if necessary. An example of this occurred when Safeway and Asda withdrew their own brand canned tomatoes from supermarket shelves in December 1998 in response to reports of nausea suffered by consumers and attributed to excessive levels of tin used by canning firms in Italy to line the inside of the cans.

4.4.5 Employment rights and social insurance

A collection of documents which became known as the 'Social Charter' have become embodied in the 'Social Chapter' of the Maastricht Treaty, and aim to cover all aspects of the EU's social policy which have an impact on companies. Social policy in the EU encompasses equality of opportunity, health and safety, employment law, social protection and social security, poverty, and the role of the disabled. The Charter was signed at the Madrid Summit in 1989 by eleven of the member states with the UK being the only country not to comply. At the Madrid Summit the UK Prime Minister, Margaret Thatcher, argued that the Charter would place an unacceptable burden on companies resulting in reduced employment opportunities and reduced competition. These arguments were based on the UK government's (and ostensibly Mrs Thatcher's) views on the workings of the free market as the key to reducing unemployment. It was argued that the introduction of minimum wages and contracts of employment which limited working hours, would increase government intervention to an unacceptable level. However, an important argument in favour of the Social Charter, put forward notably by France and Germany, is that the single market would be disrupted by the continued existence of vast differences in health and safety provisions, social insurance, and employment legislation between member countries. It is argued that companies could exploit the situation by moving to areas of the EU where the costs of employment are lower. However, since the election of the Labour Party into government in May 1997, UK has now adopted the Social Charter and begun to implement its requirements.

It may prove very difficult to implement the Social Charter throughout the EU's current fifteen member states. It is the responsibility of individual member states to implement the provisions of the Charter through appropriate legislation. In many EU countries employer–employee relations are already subject to regulation through government legislation. Traditionally, this has not been the case in the UK where such relationships have largely been established through negotiation. It may be that as the UK has now 'opted-in' to the Charter, employers and trade unions will resent further interference from central government. It is argued that an important and significant benefit of the implementation of the Social Charter is the achievement of full worker participation based on the promotion of equal opportunities. In the long term, this should increase worker satisfaction and raise productivity levels, while promoting an improvement in industrial relations. If workers are given more freedom to determine the nature of their working lives, then this must also enhance democracy within the context of Europe itself.

4.5 Summary

SINCE the late 1980s firms have had to adapt to a much more rapidly changing business environment. This has been caused not only by national government policy, but also by the introduction of the Single European Market after 1992, the economic and political challenges caused by the fall of communism after 1989, and the increasing globalization of business through better telecommunications and improved technology. In the rapidly changing business environment in the approach to the new millennium, firms cannot rely upon historical information relating to economic trends as they could in the past, but instead, they have to be able to predict future trends and be in readiness to adapt their organization quickly if they are to survive in what promises to be the increasingly global business environment of the twenty-first century.

Review Questions

1 What factors do firms need to take into account when deciding to internationalize their activities?

2 What have been the political and economic consequences for international firms of the ending of the Cold War?

3 In what ways have the risks of doing business in Russia and Eastern Europe changed since the fall of communism?

4 What have been the opportunities and risks for investors in the emerging economies of South-East Asia in recent years?

5 How will the requirement on member governments to adopt EU laws affect the future investment decisions of MNEs?

Study Topic: China—Political Control with Economic Freedom?

Since the late 1970s, Chinese governments have been gradually opening up their economy to private enterprise whilst retaining firm political control of Chinese society. Despite some relaxation of its centralized control, the Chinese Communist Party still dominates political and economic affairs. During this period, however, market forces have been allowed to operate in a growing number of economic sectors and some of China's state enterprises have been privatized. China is now becoming a major trading nation and there has been a huge influx of foreign direct investment during the 1990s.

China's experiment with market economics has produced high growth rates during much of this period, but its communist leadership has sometimes been reluctant to relinquish control of the economy. When threatened by the Asian financial crisis in the late 1990s, China reintroduced restrictions in some sectors of the economy. Its sweeping reform of state enterprises, proposed in 1998, was slowed down in 1999. Price controls were placed on the sale of foreign pharmaceutical products, approval was required for shipping freight charges, telecommunication equipment manufacturers were forced to 'buy local', and the export quotas of some foreign investors were transferred to Chinese firms.[4] China also continues to be sensitive about Western pressure on human rights issues. Any attempt on the part of foreign governments to link human rights with trade or investment is met with a firm response. Chinese governments will not be bullied into relaxing their political grip, even if it means slowing down economic reform or delaying China's proposed membership of the World Trade Organization.

Study topic questions

1 Is it feasible for a country like China to combine strict political control with a modern market economy?

2 What further economic reforms are likely to be necessary if China is to become an open market economy?

3 What sort of problems do Western MNEs face when investing in China? How might they overcome some of these problems?

4 Why do you think China resorted to price, local content, and export controls when threatened by the Asian financial crisis? What would be the effect of these restrictions?

5 Are Western governments right to link human rights issues with trade and investment in their relations with China?

Notes

1 R. Welford, and K. Prescott, *European Business* (Pitman, 1996), 439.

2 EU Initiative: *An Advance Briefing from Brussels* (May 1998), 8.

3 Ibid. (Jan./Feb. 1998), 11.

4 S. Fidler and J. Kynge, 'Clinton's China policy runs into trouble on Capitol Hill', *Financial Times*, 25 Jan. 1999.

Recommended Reading

■ Czinkota, M. R., Ronkainen, I. A., Moffett, M. H., and Moynihan, E. O., *Global Business* (Dryden, 1998).

■ Daniels, J. D., and Radebaugh, L. H., *International Business: Environments and Operations* (Addison-Wesley, 1995).

■ Welford, R., and K. Prescott, *European Business* (Pitman, 1996).

■ Nugent, N., and R. O'Donnell, *The European Business Environment* (Macmillan, 1994).

■ Harris, N., *European Business* (Macmillan, 1996).

5

Culture and Ethics in International Business

Objectives

- to emphasize the importance of cultural awareness in international business
- to identify the nature, characteristics, and key elements of culture
- to examine how international business firms can adjust to cultural differences and assess the impact of a host country's culture
- to discuss some of the ethical dilemmas faced in international business

5.1 Introduction

WHEN an international firm crosses national borders to undertake business activities, it may also cross cultural borders. With increasing international cooperation to promote trade and investment opportunities and the formation of trading blocs, crossing national borders for business purposes has been made progressively easier and mutually advantageous for both MNEs and host countries. However, the same cannot be said about cultural borders. In spite of impressive improvements in transport, telecommunication, and information systems, cultural differences between nations remain intact and represent one of the challenging tasks facing international business managers. Consumer behavioural patterns, tastes, and preferences have recently shown a tendency to converge, largely thanks to the global spread of standard brand names, the role played by global marketing activities, and technological innovations. But deep differences in values and attitudes, customs, manners, and basic cultural structures have hardly changed. Therefore the magnitude of cultural issues confronting an international business manager is as great as it has ever been.

In Chapter 2 we emphasized the crucial role played by firm-specific assets (FSAs) in determining the firm's internationalization process. Within the context of culture, experience and intimate host-country knowledge are unique FSAs which determine what Dunning refers to as the 'culture related' comparative advantage of the firm.[1] These FSAs are useful in helping to reduce the transaction costs (market imperfections) when internalized by the firm. This is particularly true in the case of such complex and diverse cultures as those of Japan and Saudi Arabia, where experience in knowing how to conduct business and intimate knowledge of cultural nuances help to expedite business transactions and reduce associated costs. Turkish construction companies presently concentrate their business activities in Islamic countries and the Turkic republics of Central Asia with which Turkey shares broadly similar religious beliefs and other cultural practices. One observes also the rapid development of looser strategic alliances and intra- and inter-firm relationships where MNEs give greater autonomy to local subsidiaries and affiliates in an effort to minimize the adverse impact of cultural differences.

The aim of this chapter is to explore the nature of culture, its basic elements and its impact on the performance of international business firms.

5.2 The Nature of Culture

THE basic aim of any business activity, whether domestic or international, is to satisfy human wants and needs. People around the world share the same basic wants and needs, but the manner in which they try to fulfil these wants and needs and the order in which they rank them vary significantly, even between individual members of the same society. Perhaps the most important determinant of consumer behaviour is culture. Innovative and sophisticated marketing research techniques may be required to identify the basic characteristics of consumer demand and monitor changes over time. In satisfying these wants and needs, the firm must demonstrate clear *cultural awareness* (being formally and informally knowledgeable) and *cultural sensitivity* (being consciously or unconsciously responsive, caring, empathizing) when operating in the host culture. The firm's activities must be based on an *interactive culture*; that is, culture that reflects the realities of operating in different cultures and one in which the firm clearly demonstrates its ability to adjust and adapt. Any failure to demonstrate either or both of these cultural competences would seriously threaten the future of the firm.

5.2.1 The definition of culture

Culture is a very broad and complex concept which is difficult to define in simple terms. There is, however, a generally accepted view that it consists of a complex set of learned, shared, and interrelated behavioural patterns which distinguish one society from another. These behavioural patterns reflect common values, attitudes, customs, manners, beliefs, practices, language, aesthetics, and education. The primary source of these behavioural patterns is, of course, parents and members of vertically and horizontally extended families. As one gets older, one acquires knowledge and experience and develops common methods of thinking through education, training, and association with others. This acquired knowledge, experience, and thinking in turn generate other types of social behaviour and life styles which are often reinforced through social pressure. The roles assigned to families and educational institutions are themselves the product of the prevailing culture.

Hofstede views culture as a 'collective programming of the mind'.[2] This results in members of a particular community sharing common beliefs and ways of thinking. This mental programming manifests itself in the national patterns of behaviour adopted by individual members of a community. Mental programming may also be thought of as providing guidelines to understand the cultures of other nations, the implication being that unless one understands and appreciates one's own culture one would not be able to appreciate and understand the cultures of others.

With emphasis on human resource management, Hofstede expands his definition of culture by identifying the 'category of people' as consisting of 'a nation, region, or ethnic group (national, etc. culture), women versus men (gender culture), old versus young (age group and generation culture), a social class, a profession or occupation (occupational culture), a type of business, a work organization or a part of it (organizational culture), or even a family.'[3]

One of the practical uses of Hofstede's view of culture is that it provides a theoretical basis to evaluate existing cultural patterns and to monitor cultural changes. More specifically, it offers a valuable framework to analyse the process of *enculturation*—how individuals are introduced to and inculcated into a particular culture, learning how to do 'things' in the correct and appropriate manner—and *acculturation*—a process of learning how to live and work in a culture other than one's own through adjustment and adaptation. Thus, an international manager is under constant pressure to fit into a 'new' culture and maintain a healthy balance between his/her own culture and that of the host country, often acting as an ambassador between these two cultures.

5.2.2 The characteristics of culture

However defined, culture has certain generic characteristics that are important in understanding the key relationships between a specific culture and an international business firm and its organization. These characteristics may be outlined as follows:

■ Culture is acquired, not inherited

Every aspect of a given culture reflects learned behaviour acquired through a lifelong learning process and transmitted from one generation to the next. Each generation passes on to the next a set of rules and behavioural norms which identify an individual as a member of society. Much of this cultural conditioning may be a subtle process of inculcation in which the individual goes through a collective learning process with other members of the same society.

■ Culture is shared

Culture is the source of bonds that provide unity and continuity in a given society. Every member of a given culture shares with other members a common set of beliefs, values, attitudes, norms, rules, and behavioural patterns. Individuals relate to one another in terms of these common traits which identify them as members of a given society. One can thus speak of French culture, German culture, Arabic culture, etc. when wishing to refer to a nation or group of nations sharing and feeling a sense of belonging to a common culture.

■ Culture is all-pervasive

Individuals in a specific culture behave in a manner consistent with that culture but without actually being conscious of the impact of their culture on their behaviour. An individual's behaviour is demonstrated spontaneously when faced with a given stimulus and without any forethought. An individual's behaviour reveals, in a complex (and often perplexing) manner, the totality of cultural influences acquired throughout life. To understand the nature of an individual's behaviour, one must first understand his/her culture.

■ Culture is total and interrelated

An individual's behaviour cannot be studied on the basis of just a few cultural elements because all elements of culture interact in determining that behaviour. Culture provides the whole behavioural context and therefore must be examined as a fully integrated phenomenon. For example, education cannot be studied without examining it as an integral part of religion, social structure, language, the political system, etc.

■ Culture is adaptive

Even cultures change in the face of forces that affect the way societies live and work. Advances in technology, communication, information systems, and other fields have made it possible for consumers around the world to modify their consumption habits and behavioural norms. We now live in the 'Coca-Cola', 'Levi' culture. Tastes and preferences among all age groups are changing thanks to the global advertising of standard or near-standard products. Even the staunchest cultures, for example the Chinese, seem to be bending before the inexorable external forces of change. As time goes on, members of a given culture live, learn, and adapt. Cultural change may, therefore, be either imposed by external forces or be willingly embraced, in which case members of a specific culture may adapt certain behavioural patterns in order to become a part of the 'wider world' (see Boxes 5.1 and 5.2).

■ Culture is the source of inspiration and orientation

Culture provides the basic guidelines to the way in which members of a society react to changes in circumstances. It is generally assumed that individuals in a given culture react in the same predictable manner to an external stimulus. This is an important consideration in formulating marketing and recruitment strategies. For example, in a materialistic culture, one would expect consumers to react in the same way to a promotion in which they are promised attractive rewards if they respond

---

Box 5.1 Christmas Comes to Istanbul

Turkey is predominantly an Islamic country and over 95 per cent of the population of its capital city, Istanbul, is Muslim. Like other major cities, Istanbul has also been influenced by the cultures of the many foreigners who visit the city. Products and advertising images from Europe and America, in particular, have brought Western habits and values to the city and attitudes towards dress and alcohol have become more liberal. Istanbul still retains much of its distinctive character, but this exchange of cultures has created a contrasting back-cloth of cultures.

This contrast is particularly apparent at Christmas. Since the mid-1980s, the Christian celebration of Christmas has increasingly become a part of the Turkish way of life—not Christian beliefs, that is, but a view of Christmas as the season of goodwill with many of its commercial trappings. The people of Istanbul are now used to seeing Christmas trees, Christmas decorations, and images of Santa Claus in their streets and shops. Christmas gifts are exchanged, on New Year's Eve rather than 25 December, and Christmas carols can be heard in shops and cafés. Although there are no crib scenes of Jesus in the manger, the casual observer might be forgiven for thinking that Christmas is as much a part of life in Istanbul as it is in London or New York. (Adapted from 'Strange, That's Santa in the Seat of Sultans!', New York Times, 21 Dec. 1996, as it appears in M. R. Czinkota, I. A. Ronkainen, M. H. Moffett and E. O. Moynihan, *Global Business* (Dryden, 1998), 277.)

Box 5.2 Fast-Food Culture

Global sales of hamburgers, pizzas, breakfast cereals, and other fast food products have surged in recent years. Even more specialized tastes in ethnic fast food from China and Thailand are now being catered for. People everywhere are leading busier lives and are demanding convenience foods. More frequent foreign travel is exposing people to different cultures and their tastes in food. Young people, in particular, tend to be influenced by the internationalization of eating habits. The USA still leads the world in fast food consumption, with twenty-five burger and eleven pizza outlets per 100,000 people. The comparable figures for Japan, in second place, are five burger and two pizza outlets per 100,000 people. Even in France, Spain, and other European countries where people have traditionally enjoyed more leisurely lunch breaks, fast food is taking off rapidly.

However, despite these international trends in fast food consumption, people in different countries often expect their food to reflect something of their own culture. Thus, for example, McDonald's restaurants in France offer a wide selection of salads, in Italy there are pasta dishes. Pizza parlours in Japan provide a variety of seafood and seaweed toppings to cater for local taste. Health-conscious consumers also require fast food which respects their beliefs and preferences. This means different things to consumers in different parts of the world. Europeans may avoid eating red meat or prefer organic products while, to the Japanese, healthy eating may mean food which is enhanced with minerals and vitamins. In this way, fast food culture is spreading across the world, but each country retains elements of its own individual culture. (Adapted from J. Willman, ' "Fast food" spreads amid changing lifestyles', *Financial Times*, 27 Mar. 1998.)

to a questionnaire or telephone call-in or would-be employees to respond more positively to a promise of bonuses.

The cultural characteristics explained above should serve as important reminders to an international manager that, when operating in a different culture, he/she must avoid using the *self-reference criterion*—conscious or unconscious use of his/her own culture in assessing the impact of management decisions and actions. *Cross-cultural literacy* is one way of avoiding the use of the self-reference criterion. As the term 'cross-cultural literacy' implies, this involves accumulating personal experience of conducting business and working abroad. Every manager is an 'innocent abroad' when he/she travels abroad for the first time. What is important, however, is how this gained experience is utilized and built upon. There are many sources of such experience: intimate knowledge provided by universities, consultancy organizations, other experts in the field and, of course, a plethora of books on 'how to do business in——'. For example, Farnham Castle Centre for International Briefing in Farnham, Surrey, is one such source of learning on how to adjust to working and living in new and different cultures.[4]

However effective the preparation for working abroad might be, culture cannot be learned thoroughly at a distance. One must live in it in order to understand it. The process of acculturation clearly must start with some form of basic cross-cultural literacy. Adaptation to a new culture and modification of behavioural norms compatible with a given culture, however, require on-the-spot experience. This is one reason for EU student-exchange programmes like SOCRATES.

5.3 The Composition of Culture

Culture is a very complex and multi-faceted concept comprising many elements. All these elements have evolved over time, sometimes through revolutionary and sometimes peaceful means, and are themselves the product of a number of factors affecting a society. They interact in a complex manner to determine the totality of a given culture. The elements of culture provide the basis on which comparisons can be made between cultures and used to assess the likely impact of culture and cultural changes on international business organizations. To understand any culture in depth, therefore, would require close examination of each of these elements. To examine fully each of these elements would necessitate treatment far beyond the scope of this book. Perforce, the discussion of elements of culture will be limited to those which are considered influential on international business practice.

5.3.1 Language

Language is the most obvious key element of any culture in terms of which one can differentiate between cultures. It provides one of the most important underpinnings in the socialization of peoples. It is the primary means of communication, both verbal, written, and non-verbal body language, to transmit information, concepts, and ideas between individuals. Verbal communication around the world makes use of over 3,000 languages and 10,000 distinct dialects. Each country with its unique language has in turn many dialects within its borders. Indeed, some such dialects are sometimes mutually unintelligible.

A clear understanding and effective use of language is essential for the success of any international business practice. It helps to determine success in the following ways:

- It provides a clearer understanding of a given situation. Having the ability to communicate in the host language enables an international manager to conduct business directly with his/her hosts without the need for an interpreter. There is no need for a third person to explain the situation or what is being discussed. Thus, the manager is able to size up the situation instantly and act accordingly. This obviously saves time and adds spontaneity to social intercourse.

- Language establishes one of the most effective and flattering bridges to local people. To speak the host's language means having direct access to hosts who are more

> **Box 5.3** Unfortunate Ambiguities of the English Language
>
> A European Commission investigation, reported in the *Wall Street Journal*, identified a number of misuses of English which have appeared in hotels and other businesses around the world. Here is a selection:
>
> To guests in a Japanese hotel: 'You are invited to take advantage of the chambermaid'.
> At a Paris hotel: 'Please leave your values at the front desk'.
> At an Acapulco hotel: 'The manager has personally passed all the water served here'.
> Visitors to a Budapest zoo were asked not to 'feed the animals. If you have any suitable food, give it to the guard on duty'.
> And at a Copenhagen airline office: we 'take your bags and send them in all directions'.
> (Adapted from 'English as she is worst spoke', *Sunday Times*, 22 Nov. 1992.)

willing and delighted to communicate openly in their own language. In many instances, this is how friendships develop and prosper, as in most cultures speaking the host's language is one of the most flattering ways to pay compliments to the host culture and those who belong to it.

- Even the most competent interpreter could have difficulty conveying hidden, implied meanings of words and nuances, phrases, or slang. Speaking directly with the host in his/her language gives the speaker a feel for the emotions and significance with which the host communicates.

- Language, properly and effectively learned and practised, provides one of the most practical means of understanding another culture. When learning a foreign language, one is not just acquiring a means of communication but also developing a deeper understanding and appreciation of the host's history, politics, social life, and other cultural aspects.

- Learning a language, understanding all the nuances and clichés, and enjoying ways of socializing with a host are some of the most practical and rewarding experiences for an international manager. It builds confidence and earns the respect and admiration of local people. In short, they help to make a manager more effective.

The alternative to communicating in the host's language is to rely on translations and interpretations, but these can be inaccurate and achieve the opposite of the intended purpose, as Box 5.3 illustrates.

5.3.2 Education

In its broadest sense, education is the lifelong process of learning through which members of a society acquire knowledge and develop skills, ideas, values, norms, and attitudes which they share with other members of society. In the formal sense, education refers to a period of study in schools and universities for self-development and enhancement of career prospects. Not all education takes place in the classroom, however. In some societies education takes place at home under the tutelage of parents and other members of the family and is used mainly for transmitting skills, ideas, and attitudes. Both types of education are pivotal to the formation of attitudes and development of social skills. Not all cultures value both types of education equally. For example, in some countries females are excluded from any form of formal education and only males are given this opportunity. By contrast, in other societies both sexes are, in principle, treated equally in terms of educational opportunities and attainments.

Education is used by all societies not only to strengthen existing cultures but also to prepare the society for a desired change. For example, Maoism in the People's Republic of China was designed to create a culture based on communist ideology. In many countries around the world, universities are offering courses in business and management based on the idea of capitalism. In this way, education is seen as the main agent of cultural change laying down the foundation for the acquisition of new behavioural norms, knowledge, and experience.

Differences in education, especially those relating to the quality of education, are important sources of information, particularly in the field of international marketing. The type and quality of education often indicate the type of products and services that can be offered in a specific country. One important source of such information is the United Nations Educational, Scientific, and Cultural Organization (UNESCO) which publishes annual data on literacy rates and other social indicators. Such data can be used by an international marketing executive to glean information about the tastes and preferences of consumers, their behaviour, and the level of economic development in different countries.

According to Terpstra and Sarathy, international marketing activities by MNEs also contribute to a country's educational process by introducing new products, informing and 'educating consumers about their use and benefits', and providing technical training for before- and after-sales activities.[5] They further argue that a marketing strategy in a given culture depends on the following considerations:[6]

■ The level of literacy and educational attainment often determines the nature of advertising and packaging. For example, the colour yellow has a special religious significance in Thailand and anything packaged in yellow is bound to be spurned by consumers. In countries with low literacy rates, graphic illustrations and simple instructions may be used to transmit information to existing and potential customers. This is particularly true in the case of health and safety and high-technology products.

■ Separation of the sexes may require different approaches when advertising products. For example, any advertising or packaging about men's toiletries with sexual connotations may be considered offensive in Saudi Arabia but received with interest and amusement in Italy. Such activities would, therefore, have to be modified to suit local tastes. An English businessman informs *Financial Times* readers that when advertising in Saudi Arabia 'You can't even show someone washing her hair because it's a presupposition that she hasn't got any clothes on.'[7]

- The quality of market research and the availability and usage of marketing information are directly related to the quality and level of education and training of the key members of the marketing department of the firm. Where no such educational and training facilities exist in the host country, the MNE may have to provide on-the-job training which may be time-consuming and costly.

- Effective and efficient operation of distribution systems requires suitably qualified personnel to complete the cycle of consumer satisfaction.

- The availability and quality of marketing activities depend on the the way the country's educational system prepares students for careers in marketing and provides additional training opportunies.

Clearly, the level of education and its quality affect all aspects of international business.

5.3.3 Religion

Religion is often regarded as the mirror image of a country's culture. It is the bedrock of all the shared beliefs, ideas, behavioural norms, motivations, and actions. It is the most important element in understanding the human environment of business and all related activities and therefore it is essential for an international manager not only to understand how people in different cultures behave but also why. In Iran, for example, the entire economic, political, legal, and social systems are based on the teachings of the Koran and any deviations are severely punished and offenders ostracized. One might disagree with the Iranian government's actions but as outsiders there is nothing one can do to change their attitudes and norms; they must simply be respected for what they are. Religious beliefs and practices are often the major source of frustration and misunderstanding for an international manager and may ultimately lead to job dissatisfaction, loss of interest, low morale, and business failure. Ignorance of and disrespect for religious differences have a very high price.

Religion is of extreme importance strategically and operationally for an MNE. Strategically, an MNE manager has to take into account how religion will help to shape the future of the host country as religion is often the source of political, economic, and social stability or instability. The religious problems in Algeria, for example, have all but stopped any progress towards the attainment of political, economic, and social goals, with horrendous loss of life and civil liberties. Similarly, fundamentalism in Egypt, Turkey, and Pakistan are considered to be major sources of concern not only in the countries involved but also for the regions in which they are located. Furthermore, the formulation of strategy will have to take full cognizance of possible external forces impacting on the development of cultural values in years ahead.

Operationally, the MNE has to consider the practical implications of deeply held religious beliefs and practices. These aspects of religion influence many of their day-to-day decisions and activities: how to conduct business, what the opening and closing hours are, whether business may be conducted on Sundays or on other religious days, whether productivity can be increased without offending religious attitudes, whether both sexes can be employed on equal terms, whether members of different religions or sects can be employed at the same facility, dress codes, how much time should be allowed for daily prayers and other events of religious significance. Disputes arising out of religious differences often impose serious constraints on the ability of an international manager to manage effectively. Problems in Northern Ireland, Israel, and Algeria have served as constant reminders of such constraints.

5.3.4 Social structure and institutions

Social structure is the basic framework within which individuals relate to one another. It is also the social hierarchy which determines the role of individuals in society. It refers to a society's social organization based on a variety of systems which govern all aspects of socially acceptable norms of behaviour. Social systems include a wide variety of attitudes and acceptable forms of relationship among family members, friends, and relatives, in courting and marriage rituals, class structure, and respect for the national flag and other symbols. An MNE has to recognize these established systems and operate within their confines, always being alert to any changes which may affect its activities. The scope of this book does not allow for full discussion of all these systems; instead, it concentrates on those of direct relevance to an MNE.

■ Values and attitudes

Values are a shared set of beliefs or creeds, convictions and ideologies, or a set of 'isms'. Values represent the very essence of any culture and society and form the context within which individual norms of behaviour or attitudes are rooted, reasoned, and, if necessary, defended. Values manifest themselves in the form of attitudes which are opinions or ways of thinking reflected in an individual's behaviour. Attitudes include opinions about individual freedom, democracy, truth and honesty, the role of the sexes, justice, marriage, love, and sex. Readers will notice that each one of these concepts carries a certain amount of emotion and therefore makes objective analysis of values and attitudes almost impossible. Despite this handicap, a brief consideration will be given, below, to some of the key attitudes which have a direct impact on the performance of international business firms.

■ Attitudes towards work

Work is the main source of most individuals' income and material wealth in any society. As a source of income, work is the means by which individuals satisfy their basic needs for food, clothing, and shelter. As a source of wealth, work is the occupation enabling individuals to accumulate material possessions over time. However viewed, societies differ in their attitudes towards 'work' in a way that distinguishes them from other societies and forms the basis of the so-called 'work ethic'. In most industrialized societies in which work is better organized and institutions established to provide some sense of job security, workers may be unwilling to put in more effort than the normal hours of work and instead favour more time for leisure. In some other societies, people may feel lucky enough to have a job, so that they would be willing to condone conditions which their counterparts in industrialized societies would regard as being atrocious. An international business firm has to devise a system of compensation and reward for extra effort for its employees congruous with the prevailing attitudes to work in the host culture.

■ Attitudes towards business

In capitalist systems an individual views a business basically as a profit-making organization producing goods and services in response to market demand. In most Islamic social systems, business is part of an all-important personal relationship which exists to provide goods and services based on mutual trust and respect. Business firms are viewed as providing not only a commercial but also a social service for their customers, with shops and offices often serving as venues for social intercourse. Some business practices, such as charging interest on the amount of money owed might be condemned as usury in some Islamic countries but viewed as being perfectly normal in other countries. Attitudes towards profit-making and business in general are an important part of the decision of an MNE to expand into a particular country.

■ Attitudes towards material possessions

People in most of the industrialized nations, especially the USA, are regarded as members of the so-called 'affluent society' or the 'acquisitive society'. These terms are often used to describe the basic motivating factors in the behaviour of individuals in such societies. Material wealth is often viewed as evidence of individual success and achievement and receives social approval. It is a sort of 'material culture' based on investment, technology, innovation, and a constant quest for increased productivity and efficiency. The quantity and quality of wealth often determine an individual's social status. In a Buddhist society, on the other hand, material possessions are spurned in favour of *nirvana*, a never-ending search for spiritual perfection characterized by asceticism and belief in reincarnation, with individuals striving to lead a life devoid of many ordinary items of convenience and comfort taken for granted in other societies. Between these two extremes, there are other differing attitudes towards wealth, depending on religion and other elements of culture. An international business firm operating in an acquisitive society may have to offer job security, career enhancement opportunites, participation in decision-making at the workplace, and environmentally acceptable working conditions instead of monetary incentives which would be considered more desirable in other societies.

■ Attitudes towards time and the future

One of the major sources of misunderstanding and at times embarrassment arises out of the concept of time. In most Western and capitalist societies time denotes punctuality, precision, and routine in scheduling business activities. Every business activity is timed in terms of hours, minutes, days, months, and years. Long-term strategic plans are prepared to ensure targets are met on time. Time seems to control every aspect of human endeavour. Pay and productivity are measured in terms of the time it takes to complete a given task. To waste time is to waste money. Punctuality, for example, is one of the most important virtues everyone involved in business activities is expected to have. Being late for a meeting or appointment is not only considered rude but also offensive. But in other cultures, punctuality is treated with such a laxity that time seems to have no meaning. For example, Box 5.4 illustrates how American Airline's monthly publication *American Way* informs its readers about business appointments in Chile.

Associated with the concept of time is how individuals in different cultures view the future. In many Western cultures, the basic view is that people can influence and even control the future. Educational systems offer a variety of training and self-development courses to help individuals to alter their lives and search for a better and more secure future. Thus, one can prepare oneself for the future through self-development and thus be in a position to determine the desired future. However, in Islamic countries and also in some Western religious groups, such as Calvinists, the view of the future is fatalistic or predetermined: individuals are born with a pre-determined future they are powerless to change or modify. This attitude often manifests itself in an almost total absence of forward business planning, with each day taken as it comes. What is not finished today can be continued tomorrow.

■ Manners and customs

Manners are appropriate patterns of social behaviour which members of a society display in their daily lives. Customs are what individual members are expected to observe in given circumstances. Manners are very much part of an individual's character whereas customs are what society collectively expects its members to do. What is appropriate and inappropriate differs from culture to culture. In Middle Eastern

---

Box 5.4 Business Appointments in Chile

■ 'Be punctual at meetings. Do not be offended, however, if your counterpart is up to thirty minutes late. On the other hand, everyone is expected to arrive at social functions late. Be about fifteen minutes late to a dinner and thirty minutes late to a party.

■ 'Make appointments about two weeks in advance of your arrival and reconfirm them when you get there. A popular time for vacations is January and February (summer holidays). This is not the time to try to do business in Chile.' Source: 'Doing Business in Chile', *American Way*, American Airlines, July 1997.

cultures men greet each other by kissing on each cheek or walk arm in arm, acts which may be inappropriate in some Western cultures. Jumping one's place in the queue in Britain is an unacceptable norm of behaviour but in some other cultures the idea of queuing may be non-existent. Table manners vary from culture to culture, ranging from precise placement of eating implements to using fingers instead. Understanding manners and customs is particularly important during discussions and negotiations. Bodily expressions may contradict what is being said or implied. Observing manners and respecting customs are essential ingredients of successful negotiations in Far and Near Eastern cultures.

5.4 Adjusting to Cultural Differences

THROUGHOUT this chapter, we have emphasized the need for international business firms to show special sensitivity towards cultural differences and willingness and ability to adapt to such differences if they are to survive in countries where they operate. There are no easy rules for success and no easy answers to the problems an international business manager is likely to face. The safest way for an international business firm to ensure success is to understand the nature of the host culture and operate within appropriate behavioural patterns and local cultural constraints. No firm has the right to expect changes to be made in the local culture to suit its needs and expectations. An international manager has to bear in mind at all times that local people often expect higher standards of behaviour and tolerate far less deviation from local manners and customs from foreign companies than from native firms.

One of the surest ways to ensure a measure of success in different cultures is to create a *cultural awareness* programme. There is no one particular formula for such a programme as each firm must assess its own cultural environment and design a programme of cultural awareness to suit its own needs. This programme may include anything from learning about table manners to considerations to be given in decision-making situations. Whatever the nature of such a programme and its contents, its basic aim must be to improve continuously the cultural awareness and sensitivity of everyone working for the firm. Only through the success of such a programme can the firm ensure success in adapting to cultural differences in the host country.

But what should the firm adapt to? In an interesting article, Lee suggests three general categories of adaptation: product, individual, and institutional.[8] He argues the degree of a firm's success in cultural adaptation can range from zero success (total failure) to comprehensive success. To be successful, adaptation must enable the firm to achieve its aims and objectives at the least cost possible and without serious problems arising out of cultural conflicts and disagreements.

5.4.1 Product adaptation

Readers who have studied marketing may recall the '4-Ps' in formulating marketing strategies: product, price, place, and promotion. The success of an international business firm may depend almost entirely on its ability to differentiate its product (see Chapter 2) in such a way that it captures a particular niche in the market. Within the context of culture, differentiation also means adapting the product to suit cultural differences in the host culture by modifying its characteristics. In general, a firm has four basic alternative approaches in reaching its international customers: (a) selling the same product in all countries in which it operates (standard products like Coca-Cola, Pepsi Cola, Levi jeans, Rolex watches); (b) modifying it to suit cultural differences in every country or even regions in the same country (for example, Coca-Cola changing the name of its Diet Coke to Coke Light in Japan because the word 'diet' has a disagreeable connotation); (c) creating a new global product which eventually becomes a world standard (as in the case of the Ford Mondeo and Boeing 777 aircraft); and (d) designing a new product for each foreign market (for example, Microsoft packages for different languages).

The cheapest option is the first one but it reflects cultural *naïveté* on the part of the firm and often fails if the firm wants to establish a presence in another culture. However, this option may suit a reactive firm which undertakes direct exporting with a unique product with few substitutes (very limited competition). The exporting firm in this case would expect the importing firm to assume full responsibility for cultural differences at no cost to the exporting firm. Alternatively, the firm may opt for the franchising option.

Of the three remaining options each may require the targeting of specific potential markets and product adaptation may prove too costly. Which option will ultimately be adopted by a firm will depend on a range of factors, including host government rules and regulations (for example, health and safety rules), the intensity of local competition, cultural differences as reflected in different consumer behavioural norms, differences in product usage (for example, in the case of baby medicines and other pharmaceutical products), and differences in climatic conditions. With increasing competition both in home and international markets, international firms are becoming culturally more aware and sensitive to their customers' needs and variations in foreign demand for their products.

5.4.2 Individual adjustment

The process of individual adjustment starts with basic cultural training at home and continues in the host culture. Training should be provided for all personnel and their families going on international assignments. For the international manager and family going abroad, a new adventure begins in a cultural environment which may be very different from their own. The manager and family will face daily challenges, excitement, frustrations, uncertainty, and anxiety. The degree of success with which they respond to these feelings and emotions and their ability to handle them effectively will depend on the success of their initial training and, more importantly, on their skills, stamina, linguistic and communicative competence, intelligence, level of interest in and knowledge of the host culture, and their ability to empathize with members of the host culture. A successful manager is one who communicates in the host's language, behaves in an appropriate manner, observing all the local manners and customs, and relates to everyone in a manner which enables the local people to accept him/her as one of them.

5.4.3 Institutional adaptation

A culturally aware and sensitive international firm will adopt an appropriate organizational structure and policies to fit into the host culture. An organizational structure in one culture may be totally inappropriate in another. Human resource management practices will have to be modified to take into account the differences in remuneration, employment, promotion, and training methods. In Islamic countries, for instance, work scheduling would have to allow sufficient time and provision of suitable facilities for employees to pray at certain times of the day. Recruitment policies would have to recognize class and ethnic distinctions in order to avoid causing offence to employees and customers from different class and ethnic backgrounds.

5.5 Barriers to Effective Cultural Adjustment

No matter how effective the cultural adjustment and adaptation programme may be, there will always be some barriers, individual or institutional, which prevent that programme from being completely successful. Summarized below are some of these barriers which may impede progress in cultural adjustment and adaptation.

5.5.1 Cultural illiteracy

Being ill-informed is one of the greatest sources of potential failure facing an international firm. Ignorance about values, manners and customs, and appropriate norms of behaviour will not only be resented by the firm's hosts but will also be the source of conflicts. One of the most effective ways of overcoming this danger is to employ local people to act as guides and advisers in coming to terms with the specifics of the host culture. Another way is to ensure that managers are well trained in the art of tactfulness and diplomacy and given plenty of opportunity to experience living and working in different cultures.

5.5.2 Ethnocentrism

An ethnocentric manager views his own culture or ethnic group as being superior to others. He evaluates the host culture from his own perpective and approaches it with a condescending or even contemptuous attitude. Everything his hosts do seems illogical, inferior, and ineffective. This sort of attitude displayed by American executives and government representatives till about the 1970s earned them the unenviable title of 'the ugly American'. The best way to combat ethnocentrism is to encourage empathy at all levels of the firm.

5.5.3 Limited cultural adaptability

An international manager who has limited cultural adaptability is one who is not able to transform his/her behavioural norms into those consistent with and acceptable to local people. He/she lacks empathy and always resorts to his/her own way of thinking and behaviour instead of acquiring local habits and responses. He/she is unable to relate to local people and feels isolated, preferring the company of those from his/her own culture. He/she lacks tolerance and understanding of those in the new culture, often viewing hosts with bias and prejudice. In short, he/she lacks cultural empathy and adaptability and thus deprives the firm he/she manages of culture-related competitiveness.

5.6 The Methodology of Cultural Assessment

GIVEN the enormous impact culture has on the international firm's performance and the effectiveness of its managers, a basic framework is needed to evaluate cultural differences and similarities. As one would expect, there are various models which focus on different aspects of culture and provide a variety of approaches to the assessment of cultural differences and similarities. Some models are far more complex, whilst others concentrate on purely sociological aspects of culture. One model which gained considerable acceptance in international business studies and research is Hofstede's cultural dimensions model which offers a comprehensive assessment of how culture relates to international business management. This model was developed using a worldwide survey of values and attitudes of some 100,000 employees of MNEs operating in over seventy countries.

According to Hofstede, there are four basic cultural dimensions ('four universal values') which can be used to identify the chief characteristics of a national culture and explain differences in management styles and practices.[9] These four universals can be explained briefly as follows:

5.6.1 Power distance

This refers to the level of acceptance and tolerance for the unequal distribution of power and the relationship which exists between those with power and those without it. Of course, there are inequalities in every society simply because no two individuals are endowed with the same physical and intellectual capacities. The level of acceptance and tolerance of these inequalities varies from society to society. According to Hofstede, there are two types of power distance culture: *high-power distance culture* (in which power and authority are accepted and obeyed without question) and *low-power distance culture* (in which power and authority are less acceptable and tolerated and in which institutions exist to distribute power and authority more equally). Many Latin American and Asian countries are characterized as being high-power distance cultures whilst those in North America and Europe are classified as low-power distance cultures.

In high-power distance cultures, the manager or the owner wields autocratic power. He alone makes decisions and his subordinates must obey them or face the consequences. When the boss is not around, business decisions are held in abeyance simply because there is no one else with authority to make any decision. Teamwork and power-sharing are regarded as anathema and are never practised. In contrast, in low-power distance cultures, organizational structure is based on teamwork in which every member is treated more equally. Managers have far less power and fewer subordinates reporting to them. Decision-making is much more democratic and based on a high degree of interdependence and consultation among members of staff.

5.6.2 Individualism

This refers to the extent to which individuals in a society have the freedom to pursue their own interests and those of their families without interference from those in authority. An individual not only enjoys personal freedom but also accepts responsibility for his actions. He/she alone determines the type of relationship he/she wants to develop and maintain with other individuals in society. In an individualistic society individual achievement is prized as much as the personal freedom to take advantage of opportunities for self-improvement and career enhancement and to maintain self-sufficiency. In contrast, in a collectivist society, an individual is bound by decisions made collectively for the benefit of the society, group, or tribe as a whole. Relationships between individuals are prescribed to ensure social homogeneity, harmony, and collective prosperity. No individual is more important than the society itself and none is singled out for special attention and merit. Every member is required to look after the interests of the collective. The whole idea of collectivism is based on the view that unity is strength to be shared equally.

5.6.3 Uncertainty avoidance

This refers to the extent to which individuals in a society avoid risks and ambiguous situations and seek security by creating institutions and common beliefs. It focuses on how individuals deal with the unfamiliar and unknown environment. The degree to which individuals accept, tolerate, and agree to cope with uncertainty varies from society to society. In countries with a high degree of uncertainty avoidance, individuals seek to minimize risks by developing systems and methods to deal with uncertainty and ambiguity. Hofstede regarded Greece, Japan, Korea, Turkey, Uruguay, Portugal, and Chile as having a high degree of uncertainty and ambiguity avoidance. In these countries there is greater emphasis on a clear set of rules prescribing actions and methods to deal with uncertain and ambiguous situations. In business organizations, individual employees tend to rely more heavily on strong managerial leadership and guidance to combat anxiety and stress. Decisions relating to security and peace of mind are often the result of collective decision-making.

   In low uncertainty-avoidance countries, such as Britain, USA, Australia, New Zealand, and Canada (countries that share the same common language), there is far less emphasis on structured and collective methods of uncertainty and ambiguity avoidance. Individuals and especially managers are encouraged, and indeed expected, to take risks in decision-making and exercise greater self-reliance in dealing with risky and ambiguous situations.

5.6.4 Masculinity vs. femininity

This cultural dimension considers the importance of masculine values in a given society. The most dominant masculine values include achievement, material posses- sions, assertiveness, success, money, individualism, and ambition. The sort of values which the Marlborough cigarette advertisements seem to imply. Feminine values, on the other hand, signify caring, helping, more interest in environmental issues, quality of life, and family values. Countries with high masculine values have clearly defined roles for both sexes, with masculine values dominating all aspects of relationships between the sexes. These countries with high masculinity (low femininity) include Italy, Austria, Switzerland, Japan, Venezuela, and Mexico. Countries with low masculinity (high femininity) include the Nordic countries, the Netherlands, and Chile.

The four universals described above can be used to characterize cultural differences in managerial approaches and form the basis of international business practices in different countries. For example, in countries with high masculinity, assertiveness in negotiations would be more valued, with each side on the negotiation table trying to dominate the other side to achieve the best outcome. Each side views the other side as a rival. A salesman would be more anxious to 'close the deal' rather than worry about the feelings of his customers. In high femininity countries greater emphasis is placed on personal relationships and each negotiator is viewed as an equal partner. A salesperson would be more patient in ensuring customer satisfaction and more sensitive to their needs.

5.7 Ethical Issues in International Business

ETHICS is about beliefs as to what is right and wrong based on the elements of culture, especially family and religious influences, the laws of a country, social and peer pressures, our own experiences and observations. In other words, it is all about moral principles. One way in which our beliefs are manifested is the manner in which our responsibilities are discharged to other members of society and the way in which we observe appropriate norms of behaviour. One of the most interesting and controversial topics in international business has been the way in which international firms respond to their corporate social responsibilities and their stakeholders, especially to their employees, customers, and the host government. There is often an ethical dilemma facing an international firm when it tries to respond to its corporate social responsibilities. This section considers two ethical issues which have direct relevance to international business.

5.7.1 Bribery and corruption

Bribery is a deliberate attempt to persuade someone (usually in a position of power and authority) to act improperly in favour of the briber by offering money or gifts or any other material gain. Bribery has been at the root of corruption in many countries. Corruption has been defined by the World Bank as 'the abuse of public office for private gain'.[10] The issue of bribery is controversial mainly because it depends on how it is defined and practised. In some Middle Eastern countries, it would be perfectly acceptable to give a gift to an official or host as a token of appreciation for the time and consideration given. In Britain and the USA, however, such an act might be construed as an attempt to bribe for personal gain and might therefore be considered unlawful. The EU is in the process of legislating against any attempt by EU firms to offer bribes to their customers, wherever they may be. There are stories about dictators taking their share of any business deals made with foreign companies as a bribe in return for a promise of favourable treatment for the firm concerned. The greater the value of a contract, such as a huge defence contract, the greater is the temptation to bribe in order to clinch the deal.

As *The Economist* points out, bribery may be *malign* or *benign*.[11] A benign bribe is one which would benefit an economy by expediting and simplifying procedures, reducing bureaucracy, and reducing or eliminating unnecessary costs, thereby reducing prices and improving society's welfare. Malign bribery does the opposite and, in addition, leads to widespread corruption and a decline in public morals. So, should an international firm offer a bribe to gain an unfair advantage over its rivals, bearing in mind that the firm offering the bribe may not necessarily be the one offering the best deal the host country can afford? The answer obviously depends on the definition and practice of bribery adopted and observed in different cultures and on the laws of an MNE's home country.

5.7.2 Work practices and worker remuneration

One of the main reasons for international firms to invest in production facilities abroad is to take advantage of the availability of relatively cheap labour in order to remain competitive in international markets. Indeed, they are actively encouraged to do so by host governments. The ethical dilemma facing an international firm is what type of technology it should employ in the host country. Inappropriate technology, especially in a Third World country, may fail to make sufficient use of the host country's resources and increase its technology-dependence. Employing capital-intensive instead of labour-intensive methods of production may be cost-effective for the firm but fail to create many jobs in the host country. One way out of this dilemma might be to bring in the appropriate technology which would create employment. However, increasing global competition might force the firm to employ the most cost-effective technology and production methods to remain competitive.

Because of the cultural differences explained thus far, one might expect an international firm to vary its work practices to suit the local culture and avoid ethnocentrism. But does this mean the firm should abandon its well-founded and efficient work practices developed at home for the sake of 'doing the right thing' in the host country? For example, should Britain have denied Japanese firms the right to insist on single-union representation on the shop floor in Britain? What if the country in question is so desperate to attract foreign investment to help develop its economy that it is prepared to waive the usual health and safety regulations and workers' rights? Should an MNE succumb to such an attraction? What happens if host-country work practices conflict with the firm's home practices? In many Western countries there are child labour laws preventing firms from employing children under a minimum age. But in other countries, like India, Indonesia, and Thailand, there are few such laws and firms are free to employ children as young as 6 or 7. Should an MNE take advantage of the laxity of these rules and regulations or abide by its own ethical values?

MNEs are often criticized for exploiting workers in Third World countries. This criticism is particularly forceful in the case of MNEs paying unskilled or semi-skilled women workers wages well below those in their own countries. MNEs argue that they create job opportunities for women who would otherwise remain dependent and continue their traditional subservient roles in society.

Many MNEs adhere to their own strict business ethics no matter where they operate. They insist that their licensees, franchisees, and other affiliates fulfil strict contractual obligations by observing minimum standards concerning working conditions, minimum age and wages of their employees, and health and safety regulations. This means that MNEs assume increasing responsibility not only for their own actions and business practices but also those of their suppliers. Levi and Nike, for example, guarantee their products to be manufactured by their foreign contractors under conditions acceptable to their global customers. International business firms have come under increasing pressure from various groups and agencies of global governance, such as the World Trade Organization (WTO) and International Labour Organization (ILO), to observe and maintain acceptable standards of working practices and pay, and assume greater moral responsibility for their subcontractors, as Box 5.5 illustrates.

Box 5.5 Supermarkets Embrace Ethical Trading

Christian Aid has been lobbying British supermarket chains to adopt 'ethical' trading policies towards their suppliers in the developing world. The charity has urged the industry to agree common standards which insist on minimum conditions for workers involved in their supply chains. Whilst not wanting consumers to boycott particular supermarkets, Christian Aid wants consumers to be able to buy goods which are not the product of worker exploitation. Several supermarkets have now introduced an ethical trading policy, including seven of the top ten supermarket chains. Tesco, Safeway, and Sainsbury head the list. It will take some time for their ethical trading policies to have a significant effect on the lives of ordinary people in the worst-affected countries, but Mike Taylor, Director of Christian Aid, regards these policies as a step in the right direction. Adapted from A. Bellos, 'Supermarkets toe ethical trading line', *Guardian*, 27 Oct. 1997.

5.8 Summary

Iɴ this chapter we stress the importance of cultural awareness in international business. Although foreign travel and the activities of MNEs have brought about an exchange of cultures between countries, culture is still one of the most important factors an MNE has to take into account when operating in a host country. Culture is a broad and complex concept, but it is usually defined as a set of learned, shared, and interrelated behavioural patterns which distinguish one society from another. The main elements of culture include language, education, religion, and social structure and institutions. Social structure encompasses the values, attitudes, manners, and customs of a society. These cultural differences require some degree of cultural adjustment on the part of international business firms. An MNE can make the necessary adjustment through product adaptation, cultural training, and changes to its organizational structure, provided it is convinced of the need for cultural adjustment. The chapter provides a basic framework for assessing the impact of different cultures. Finally, we discuss some of the ethical issues faced in international business and the cultural origins of differences in approach to these issues. Two important issues are used to illustrate the ethical dilemmas that can arise: bribery and corruption, and work practices.

Review Questions

1 In what sense can culture be described as a 'collective programming of the mind' (Hofstede)?

2 If culture is all-pervasive, acquired through lifelong learning, and transmitted from one generation to the next, in what ways may it also be 'adaptive'?

3 In what ways does an understanding of (a) language, (b) education, (c) religion, and (d) social structure help an MNE to overcome cultural difficulties in a host country?

4 How can an MNE adapt its product and organizational structure to adjust to cultural differences in a host country?

5 Should an MNE apply consistent ethical standards in each host country? What ethical dilemmas may have to be faced if it pursues this approach?

Case Study: Cultural Differences among South-East Asian Managers

The cultural characteristics of the countries of South-East Asia are not as similar as an outsider might imagine. Most of the countries of this region belong to ASEAN, the Association of South-East Asian Nations. ASEAN's economic aim is to create a free trade area and agreement has been reached on tariff reductions to below 5 per cent by 2003. This should encourage their own and foreign companies to trade freely within the region. A large volume of foreign direct investment has already established a Western and Japanese presence in a number of South-East Asian countries.

Foreign, and particularly American, culture now influences business practices in the region. US-style business schools educate South-East Asian managers and many of their young people study at Western universities. But, in other respects, Western managers doing business in South-East Asia find few similarities in culture and management styles. As a general rule, there is an expectation that representatives of foreign companies will behave courteously towards their hosts. Visible signs of frustration at the formalities of business etiquette or the slow pace of business will simply not be tolerated and will probably result in wasted effort on the part of the Western executive. However, whereas in Singapore or Malaysia straight-talking is generally acceptable after the initial formalities, this is unlikely to be the case in Indonesia or Thailand. Indonesians expect foreign executives to act out elaborate rituals of etiquette as a precondition for establishing a good working relationship.

In Singapore there is a highly disciplined and organized approach to business, not unlike the Japanese approach. In the Philippines, a more relaxed approach is taken. Democracy, the country's American colonial past, and widespread use of the English language mean that Filipinos are generally more Westernized and less reserved than many of their neighbours. Business people in Singapore are likely to be transparent in their business dealings as tax evasion, for example, results in severe penalties. In some parts of the region business corruption is more common. Singaporeans have fewer long-standing national traditions, however, and family ties are weaker than in many countries in the region. In Thailand and Indonesia, extended family responsibilities are much stronger and Western managers find it difficult to extract undivided loyalty from their employees in these countries. In the Philippines, local managers may expect to take time off for family and other social commitments, causing frustration for their Western employers. Japanese companies often try to build a 'patriarchal aura' around their chief excutives when operating in the region in order to establish loyalty to the company rather than to local clan leaders.

Western companies operating in Thailand have found that local workers are submissive and reluctant to ask questions or to suggest improvements. It is therefore difficult to obtain feedback from those with local knowledge. This problem also occurs in Indonesia, whereas Filipinos are more likely to speak out.

There are also significant political and religious differences in the region. Democracy is well established in the Philippines but more restricted in Malaysia and Indonesia.

Authoritarian leaders still hold sway in several countries. Newer members of ASEAN range from Vietnam, with its communist regime, to Burma (now Myanmar), with its military dictatorship. The region's religions are also varied, including Islam, Buddhism, Christianity, and animism. Several countries have a less homogeneous population than might be imagined. Malaysia, for example, has significant Chinese and Indian minorities as well as its native Malay people. In particular, tensions arise between the region's indigenous ethnic groups and people of Chinese origin. Chinese people are often successful in business, but local rules in Malaysia and Indonesia restrict their activities through the *bumiputra* (or local partner) system. There is therefore no unique Malaysian or Indonesian way of doing business and Western companies, in all instances, need to be well advised when negotiating the cultural complexities of South-East Asia. (Adapted from E. Luce, 'S. E. Asia: singularly different', *Financial Times*, 4 Dec. 1995.)

Case study questions

1 How do you account for the fact that each of the South-East Asian countries retains its own distinctive business practices despite the invasion of Western culture?

2 American business executives have a reputation for 'straight talking'. To what extent should they modify this approach when faced with what they perceive to be time-wasting formalities in South-East Asia?

3 If 'corrupt' business practices are the norm in some countries, how would you advise a foreign company unused to these practices to respond?

4 Given that workers in Thailand are apparently submissive and reluctant to ask questions, what problems might this cause for a foreign company located in Thailand, and how might the company overcome this difficulty?

5 What cultural differences might a foreign company with plants in Singapore, the Philippines, and Malaysia encounter in each of these countries?

Notes

1 J. H. Dunning, *The Globalisation of Business* (Routledge, 1993), ch. 1.

2 G. H. Hofstede, *Culture's Consequences: International Differences in Work-Related Values* (Sage, 1980).

3 G. H. Hofstede, 'The Business of International Business is Culture', *International Business Review* (1995), 3 (1), 1–14; repr. in T. Jackson, *Cross-Cultural Management* (Butterworth-Heinemann, 1995), 150–63.

4 See J. Hutton, *The World of International Manager* (Philip Allan, 1988), ch. 6.

5 V. Terpstra, and R. Sarathy, *International Marketing* (Dryden, 1997), ch. 4.

6 Ibid. 127–8.

7 V. Mallet, 'Doing Business in Saudi Arabia', *Financial Times* (9 Nov. 1990), 24.

8 J. A. Lee, 'Cultural Analysis in Overseas Operations', *Harvard Business Review* (Mar.-Apr. 1966), 106–14.

9 G. H. Hofstede, *Culture's Consequences*.

10 Quoted in M. Wolf, 'Corruption in the Spotlight', *Financial Times* (16 Sept. 1997).

11 *The Economist*, 'Bribonomics' (19 Mar. 1994), 94.

Recommended Reading

■ Hampden-Turner, C., and Trompenaars, F., *The Seven Cultures of Capitalism (Piatkus, 1994).*

■ Hickson, J. D., and Pugh, S. D. *Management Worldwide: The Impact of Societal Culture on Organisations Around the Globe* (Penguin Books, 1995).

■ Randlesome, C., Brierley, W., Bruton, K., Gordon, C., and King, P., *Business Cultures in Europe* (Butterworth-Heinemann, 1993).

■ Wartick, S. L., and Wood, D. J., *International Business and Society* (Blackwell, 1998).

6

International Institutions and Global Issues

Objectives

- to outline the nature of the world trade order
- to examine the case for global free trade and the reasons for the persistence of trade barriers
- to discuss issues concerning trade relations between countries
- to evaluate the role of international institutions and their impact on international business
- to discuss the social implications of international business

6.1 Introduction

AFTER a period of decline during the two world wars and the intervening Great Depression of the 1930s, international business activity has, in some respects, only just returned to the level seen at the beginning of the twentieth century. Merchandise trade between the major industrialized nations was about the same as a proportion of gross domestic product in the mid-1990s as it had been before 1914. International labour mobility was, in fact, greater in the late nineteenth and early twentieth centuries than it is today. This was also true of foreign direct investment as a proportion of GDP for some of the leading industrial nations. Indeed, some writers have claimed that globalization is not a new phenomenon.[1] The nature of business activity, however, has changed in a number of ways. In particular, the number of large multinational enterprises has increased significantly. The goods and services traded and the direction of trade flows have also changed. Perhaps the greatest changes have occurred in methods of doing business, the use of technology, innovations in communication, and developments in financial and other services.

The growing interdependence of the world's economies has brought with it the need for international institutions which can coordinate and regulate the activities of governments and MNEs. After numerous attempts to remove trade restrictions under the General Agreement on Tariffs and Trade (GATT), the World Trade Organization (WTO) was set up in 1995 to provide a more systematic oversight of trade and investment. Some of these institutions, like the United Nations, arose out of a desire for the peaceful resolution of political conflict after two world wars or, in the case of the International Monetary Fund (IMF), the need to provide a stable financial system for world trade. Other institutions were established in response to specific events, like the European Bank for Reconstruction and Development (EBRD) which has played a role in the transformation of Eastern Europe.

Discussion of these institutions requires an understanding of the nature of the world trading environment and of the implications of trade and investment for the companies and countries involved. Inevitably, the arguments for free trade or for intervention by international bodies raise a number of controversial and often global issues. Some of these issues will be considered in this chapter.

6.2 The Changing World Trade Order

6.2.1 The case for free trade

One of the most compelling explanations for the rapid growth of the world economy during the late nineteenth and early twentieth centuries is the policy of free trade or laissez-faire pursued by the major trading nations at that time. The years which followed brought the wartime disruption of normal trade flows and the declining industrial output and protectionism of the interwar depression. A number of factors may account for the post-World War II recovery in world economic activity but, once again, it has been accompanied by moves towards the liberalization of trade and capital flows. Most of the mature industrialized nations and some of the newly emerging industrial nations have removed foreign exchange and investment controls, allowing greater freedom of capital movement and encouraging the growth of international financial markets. Several rounds of GATT negotiations have gradually persuaded governments to reduce tariffs and sometimes other barriers to trade during the post-war years. Another important development which is currently in progress is the growth of *electronic commerce*. The buying and selling of goods and services through the Internet is already breaking down many of the conventional barriers to trade between national markets (see Section 6.2.3).

Although progress towards free trade has not been smooth since World War II, the 1980s and 1990s have witnessed trade liberalization with renewed zeal among a surprisingly broad group of countries. The seven-year Uruguay Round produced a significant, if tortuously negotiated, reduction in tariffs between its member nations. It is not difficult to see why large trading nations favour free trade for their goods. However, some of the developing countries, like the members of ASEAN, are also keen supporters of free trade and even China, with its record of trade restrictions, has been actively seeking membership of the WTO during the late 1990s. Why then are so many countries, rich, poor, and emerging, trying to create multilateral free trade?

Clearly, every exporter would like to have free access to foreign markets. But multilateral free trade involves a two-way process for each country. In any case, the promotion of exports rather than international trade generally (a common practice) exposes the myopia of mercantilism (see Chapter 10). To determine the benefits of free trade we need to consider each of the following:

- the welfare gains from the removal of tariffs, quotas, and export subsidies;
- the merits of international competition;
- theories of international trade; and
- political difficulties which may arise from protectionism.

Tariffs not only increase the price of imports, they also restrict the supply of a good available to domestic consumers and allow the domestic price to rise. The higher domestic price encourages increased production by higher-cost domestic firms and protects inefficient firms from foreign competition. This is illustrated in Figure 6.1. The tariff allows the domestic price (p_d) to be above the world price (p_w) and restricts the flow of imports to qt_2-qd_2 (that is, total output minus domestic output at price p_d). As a result, domestic producers gain additional sales revenue equal to area A (the aim of the tariff policy) and the domestic government gains the tariff revenue shown by area C. Unfortunately, the consumer is the main loser. Certainly, the importer loses sales, but this is nothing in comparison with the consumer's loss. The consumer loses areas A, B, C, and D (known as a loss of *consumer surplus* when compared to the situation without the tariff). When the balance of gains and losses is worked out, areas B and D, previously part of the consumer surplus, have now disappeared completely. This is known as the *deadweight loss* or *welfare loss* from the tariff. It means that the country as a whole has lost out.

Quotas control the quantity rather than the price of imports but their impact is similar to tariffs. By restricting the supply of a good, they raise its price. This can also be illustrated in Figure 6.1 except that now, whereas the consumer's loss is the same, there is an unexpected gainer: area C represents a gain for the importer because of the higher price their product now commands. Studies of the US government's imposition of a quota on Japanese car imports in 1981 suggest that, whilst jobs in the US car industry were protected in the short term, the cost to the consumer in terms of higher prices and the adverse impact on the US car industry's international competitiveness made the policy difficult to justify.[2]

Even an export subsidy may have perverse effects. It provides a boost for exporters by reducing their prices in foreign markets but does little to encourage more efficient

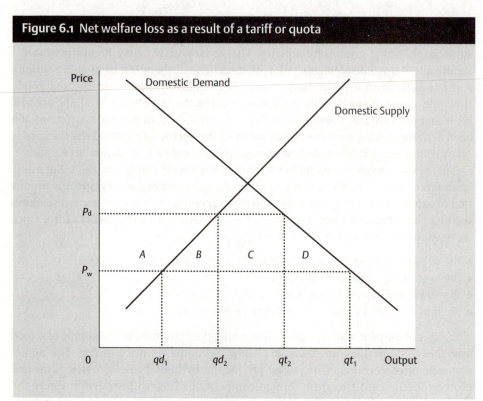

Figure 6.1 Net welfare loss as a result of a tariff or quota

production and is likely to distort production decisions and trade flows between countries where prices fail to reflect true competitive advantage.

Exposure to international competition is a second line of argument. Openness to trade acts as a spur to efficiency, innovation, and international competitiveness generally (see Chapter 13). The theoretical case for competition is powerful. The simple model of *perfect competition* leads to the conclusion that competitive firms allocate society's resources and use their own inputs efficiently. They also charge a price which maximizes the consumer surplus.[3] This is essentially a static view of competition, but a similar conclusion can be drawn from alternative views of competition. A more radical view comes from writers of the Austrian School of Economics, among others, who see competition as a dynamic process of entrepreneurial discovery, innovation, the creation of new firms and products, and the elimination of old. Here, competitive market forces provide the stimulus for proactive firms to seize opportunities for profitable investment. Efficient, innovative firms prosper and consumers benefit from new and better products or services. Government regulation of market entry in the form of import controls is likely to obstruct the refining process of competition.[4] Evidence from Eastern Europe and some of the 'tiger' economies of South-East Asia suggests that, although initially painful, openness to international competition gradually brings about this refining process, creating a more streamlined but internationally competitive industry.

Theories of international trade are developed in Chapter 10. Traditional theories argue that when each country's producers specialize in goods in whose production they enjoy a *comparative advantage*, resources are allocated efficiently and international trade results in all countries being collectively better off. A comparative advantage may arise from the fact that different goods require different factor-proportions (Heckscher–Ohlin Theory). Thus, countries with a relative abundance of land will offer a relatively low-cost location for producers of land-intensive goods. Free trade allows all countries to take advantage of specialized production in a perfectly competitive environment. In the modern world, specialization often stems from acquired rather than natural comparative advantage and competition is more likely to be imperfect. Recent theories of international trade view the reasons for specialization in terms of historical accident, national characteristics and tastes, developments in technology, the benefits of internal and external economies of scale, or as a response to changing markets, for example. In each case, however, free trade generally facilitates the full exploitation of these advantages.

Even where some form of trade protection can be justified (see Section 6.2.2), such policies may not be politically desirable. Import controls by one country may well provoke retaliation by another. A series of tit-for-tat retaliations will lead to a breakdown of international free trade. This has sometimes happened during the years following a GATT Round and is one of the reasons for granting the WTO powers to enforce trade agreements. A further political argument is that special interest groups may lobby governments to impose tariffs which serve their own, but no one else's, interests. A Western European steel producer, for example, may argue a persuasive case for anti-dumping tariffs against East European steel exporters. A Western European car manufacturer, who buys large quantities of steel, may take a different view.

6.2.2 Tariff and non-tariff barriers to trade

Tariffs (or import duties) are one of the oldest forms of trade protection. They are usually *ad valorem tariffs*, i.e. a percentage added to the value of the goods imported. They bring in revenue for governments though generally they are more important as a means of protecting a domestic industry than as a source of revenue. Although a wide variety of tariffs are still used by most countries, the average level of tariffs in industrial countries is now down to about 4 per cent.[5] This is largely the result of successive GATT Rounds, but also because many countries have made free trade agreements with their neighbours. Tariffs between European Union members, for example, were long since removed. Possible justifications for the use of tariffs will be considered below.

Non-tariff barriers are a more important form of trade restriction in the modern world. These may be quantifiable barriers such as import quotas, which restrict the value or volume of a particular good which may be imported from specified countries. Quotas are often used to restrict the access of prolific or low-cost foreign producers but may also allow preferential access to a particular country's products.

Sometimes, access is granted subject to a country-of-origin or local-content require-ment; thus, an EU agreement with Israel in 1995 allows quota access to certain Israeli products provided they originate within the state of Israel. Restricted access may also take the form of voluntary export restraints (VERs). A number of EU countries have used VERs to restrict the entry of Japanese cars and electronic goods, though restric-tions on car imports should be phased out by 1999. VERs have the political advantage that they are imposed with the agreement of the exporting country.

Variations in domestic tax rates on goods in neighbouring countries, whilst not strictly trade barriers, may distort trade flows between countries. Large differences in rates of excise duty on alcohol and other goods are known to distort trade between EU countries, for example, encouraging the importation of goods solely for the purpose of avoiding excise duty (see Chapter 15). Export subsidies, discussed briefly above, or export credit subsidies may cause similar trade distortions.

Many non-tariff barriers are less obvious but are often very difficult for an exporter to overcome. These include cultural differences, product standards and testing pro-cedures, national public procurement policies, environmental and labour market regulation, restrictive distribution systems, and a plethora of bureaucratic regula-tions. The implications of culture for international business are examined in Chapter 5. Some of the other barriers are discussed in a European context in Chapter 15. The Japanese market also provides an example; its highly prescriptive product standards, lengthy and costly product-testing procedures and seemingly impermeable networks of companies (*keiretsu*) make market entry difficult for even the best-prepared com-panies (see Chapter 8). Japan is by no means an isolated example of such barriers, of course.

Clearly, there are numerous barriers which prevent free trade in practice. Whether they can be justified is another matter. Product standards, for example, may be vital for health and safety or to facilitate product compatibility. Ideally, standards would be internationally agreed but this would be a mammoth task. Environmental standards may well be worthwhile on a unilateral basis in order to protect the domestic environment or to put pressure on other countries to take similar action. Some people would go further in encouraging the WTO and other agencies to link environmental or labour standards to trade rules, thus forcing countries with lower standards, and MNEs which operate in them, to raise their standards if they wish to participate in international trade. Sometimes, however, standards are overly restrict-ive for no real purpose. They may have developed piecemeal over a number of years or even have been deliberately designed to keep imports out.

Much has been written about the case for tariffs and quotas. Specific arguments can be used in support of the protection of an infant industry or an industry experi-encing genuine but temporary difficulties. Members of the Mercosur trading area responded to the turmoil in world financial markets and its associated effects on their economies in November 1997 by raising their external tariff from an average of 12 to 15 per cent. Such tariffs are commonly used to protect declining or struggling industries, such as European textile manufacturing, rather than infant industries. There has also been an increase in the use of anti-dumping duties. Genuine dumping (selling goods below cost price in a foreign market) is difficult to prove but, like export subsidies, it may distort trade and inflict damage on the recipient country's producers. In some cases, however, anti-dumping duties may simply be an excuse for unfair trade protection.

In general, the case for tariffs and quotas rests on the existence of market failure. Given the many distortions and imperfections in real world markets, some of the benefits of trade do not materialize for particular countries or producers. Tariffs and similar barriers are therefore an attempt to correct an instance of market failure where a country or firm would otherwise be disadvantaged. Thus, Caribbean banana growers have received privileged access to EU markets as members of the ACP group of countries, under the Lomé Agreement, to the chagrin of Latin American and other producers. Free trade for all banana growers may seem preferable, but this could destroy some of the Caribbean economies (see Study Topic at the end of this chapter). Similarly, an industry struggling to become established may benefit from import protection. Two points should be noted, however. First, the protective policy is more likely to be effective if it is directed specifically at the distortion to be corrected, otherwise the policy itself may cause a further distortion. Second, the policy should be the best method of solving the problem. Many countries and industries experience problems, but these may stem from a variety of causes: overdependence on particular products, inadequate capital markets, infrastructure deficiencies, labour shortages, inflexible labour markets, or lack of information about export opportunities. None of these problems will be solved by import protection; tariffs are more likely to obscure the real problems by offering a false sense of security.

Government attempts to protect or promote specific industries are sometimes referred to as *strategic trade policy*. The apparent success of Japan and other East Asian countries in supporting strategic industries adds strength to the case for such policies. This issue is discussed further in Chapters 8 and 9 in relation to Japan and the 'tiger' economies and in Chapter 17 in the European context. It is probably fair to say that evidence on the success of strategic trade policy is mixed.

6.2.3 International trade in the 'information age'

At a time when there is greater access to information, via computers and the Internet, it is perhaps not surprising that business is increasingly being conducted by electronic means. As the Internet is not confined within national boundaries, it is becoming a medium for international trade as well as for domestic business. Electronic commerce, or e-commerce as it is known, is beginning to revolutionize the way firms do business. Essentially, e-commerce consists of two types of transaction: first, transactions where the Internet simply allows the seller to advertise and the purchaser to browse, place an order, and make payment, after which the goods are delivered by conventional means; second, transactions where the goods are delivered or the service is provided 'on-line' and then downloaded by the purchaser.

An increasing variety of goods and services are being bought and sold in this way. Among the pioneers of e-commerce were the banks, dealers in stocks and shares, and booksellers like Amazon. Rapidly, mainstream firms have been joining the specialist on-line traders, fearing a loss of business as more and more consumers link up to the Internet and recognize the convenience of buying goods via their computer. Whilst many areas of business and international trade remain predominantly off-line, this situation is unlikely to persist long into the twenty-first century.

E-commerce has potentially far-reaching implications for international trade. Given the ease with which business can be conducted across national frontiers, many of the traditional barriers to trade are likely to diminish. No doubt governments and other organizations will try to regulate these markets and impose restrictions to protect their domestic industries or consumers, often with good intentions. However, their task will be more difficult than it has been in the past, and the nature of these barriers may change as the regulators become more sophisticated in handling electronic trade. A good example of the way in which national markets are being opened up to international competition is in bookselling. Countries like Britain, which until the late 1990s had a resale price maintenance agreement restricting price competition in the book trade (the Net Book Agreement), will soon find such restrictions difficult to defend when books can so easily be bought on the international market. Certainly, technology is forcing the pace of liberalization in many hitherto protected markets.

6.2.4 Managing trade relations between countries

The above discussion has highlighted the importance of trade between countries on the one hand and the prevalence of trade barriers, especially in conventional trade, on the other. The desire to promote freer trade has led to international cooperation through GATT and the WTO. Other agencies like the IMF were set up to help finance the post-war growth of international trade. There has also been a recognition that some countries experience more of the benefits of trade than others. Thus the World Bank and some of the agencies of the United Nations were established to promote the development of the world's poorer countries. Groups of countries with common interests have also been formed to coordinate their economic policies or to encourage trade links between them.

The extent to which international institutions should influence international business activity is a matter of some debate. Clearly, their influence represents a form of public sector intervention. Perhaps trade and investment should be left to individual companies and market forces. National governments have a mixed record in promoting successful businesses. The record of international agencies in sorting out problems is scarcely better. Yet, the creation of free trade requires multilateral agreement and, with all such agreements, there is a temptation for individual countries to break the rules when it suits their interests whilst enjoying the benefits of general free trade at the same time. A clear set of rules is therefore required as well as a means of enforcing these rules. This is the role of the international agency.

A further compelling argument for international cooperation arises from a desire to encourage 'best practice' among trading nations. Thus, if local or multinational companies take advantage of poor labour standards or lax environmental regulations, there is a case for international pressure to improve standards. Trade agreements may be made conditional upon agreed minimum standards. Trade sanctions such as those imposed on Iraq during and after the Gulf War or US sanctions under the Helms–Burton Act[6] against individual companies which invest in Cuba are examples of trade rules which attempt to put pressure on countries whose political regimes are perceived to be undesirable. These, and other issues, are now considered in the remainder of this chapter.

6.3 Global Governance and International Institutions

6.3.1 Global governance and the global economy

The use of international institutions to manage global activities and resolve global problems is sometimes known as *global governance*. One of the main reasons for the growing demand for global governance is the increasing globalization of business activity. As more countries become involved in trade, investment, and other forms of international business, the world economy becomes more integrated. It has long been known that stock market fluctuations in the major industrialized countries set off a chain reaction throughout the industrialized world. Similar stock market turbulence in the emerging economies of South-East Asia in 1997 surprised many by the speed with which it affected both the developing and the industrialized nations. Booms and recessions in the real economies of these countries are also becoming more synchronized, not least because of the global activities of MNEs.

Another reason for the increasing emphasis on global governance seems to be a belief that, in the modern world, global problems should be capable of global solution. If there are trade distortions or problems resulting from foreign investment or if companies and countries pursue undesirable practices, there should be an internationally agreed way of resolving these issues. These pressures face the United Nations or Nato when they intervene in countries where there is human deprivation or military conflict. Indeed, there is also increasing pressure on MNEs to take account of the global impact of their activities.

As well as the growing importance of international institutions, there has also been a proliferation in the number of regional groupings of countries. Regional integration is often primarily for trade reasons, but these trading areas tend to link their members politically and in other ways. It is sometimes argued that regional integration hinders the process of global integration and the work of international institutions because it favours some nations at the expense of others. It also allows powerful trade blocs to influence the outcome of international deliberations, though this was always the case with powerful trading nations. This issue is discussed further in Chapter 7. In order to consider the way in which global governance is developing, we now examine the role of individual institutions in more detail.

6.3.2 The United Nations and its influence in world affairs

The United Nations (UN) arose out of a desire for world peace at the end of World War II. It came into being in 1945, though the League of Nations had been an earlier, largely unsuccessful attempt to secure peace after World War I. UN membership has grown from fifty countries in 1945 to more than 180 today. Although the UN's foremost aim is to maintain world peace and security, it also acts as an umbrella organization for numerous economic, social, cultural, and humanitarian agencies. Included among these are the United Nations Educational, Scientific, and Cultural Organization (UNESCO), which promotes international cooperation through education, research, and other avenues; the United Nations High Commissioner for Refugees (UNHCR), which has been active in the former Yugoslavia, war-torn regions of Africa, and elsewhere; the World Health Organization (WHO); the International Monetary Fund (IMF) and World Bank; the International Labour Organization (ILO); and the United Nations Conference on Trade and Development (UNCTAD). The International Court of Justice, based in The Hague, is also a UN institution.

Much of the work of the UN and its agencies has only indirect relevance to international business. At times it has been overly influenced by the vested interests of powerful countries or embroiled in regional disputes between warring factions. Perhaps its most important work is done through the activities of its many agencies rather than through the UN General Assembly acting as a whole, though MNEs attach great importance to political stability when deciding where to invest.

In some areas, however, the UN does provide a forum for the promotion of international business issues. The work of its financial institutions and the General Agreement on Tariffs and Trade (GATT), negotiated under the auspices of the UN but now under the control of a separate institution (the WTO), are discussed below. These all play an important role in the international business environment. Another important activity has been UN support for *sustainable development*, which is often understood to mean economic growth which is consistent with the protection of the environment. In particular, the 1992 United Nations Conference on the Environment and Development in Rio de Janeiro (known as the 'Earth Summit') led to a number of commitments by individual countries to tackle environmental problems.

The role of UNCTAD is also worthy of special attention. UNCTAD first met in 1964 and it represents an attempt by the developing countries (sometimes known as the Group of 77 or G77) to establish a New International Economic Order. Exasperation at what they saw as bias towards the industrialized world under GATT, the IMF, and the World Bank led these nations to call for a new approach to development policy. Basically, they wanted to reduce their dependency on the developed countries and to promote their own economic growth. In order to achieve this they have pursued a number of objectives: favourable access to developed country markets; price stabilization policies for commodities produced by developing countries; regulation of the investment activities of MNEs; improved arrangements for technology transfer to developing countries; an easing of the burden of foreign debt; increased foreign aid from developed countries; and institutional changes to give developing countries more influence in UN organizations. Some of these measures have been achieved, to an extent, but often outside the UN framework.

6.3.3 The International Monetary Fund and World Bank

The International Monetary Fund (IMF) and World Bank were set up as a result of the 1944 Bretton Woods Agreement. Although UN institutions, they are in practice fairly autonomous. The IMF was created to help provide a stable financial environment for international trade. It did this by establishing a system of fixed exchange rates, with member currencies being pegged to the US dollar which was in turn valued against gold, and by providing loans to member countries facing short-term balance of payments problems. The system of fixed exchange rates operated until 1971, after which many countries moved to floating exchange rates. Member countries provide the IMF's reserves through a quota system. Each member's quota, which is partly in gold but increasingly in the form of currency, depends on the size of its economy. Members then have *drawing rights* to borrow foreign currencies from the fund. This facility has been extended by the periodic allocation of *special drawing rights*, which allow member countries to borrow additional sums.

The period of fixed exchange rates and IMF financing arrangements coincided with a period of rapid growth in international trade during the 1950s and 1960s. This was interrupted by a more turbulent period during the 1970s, with inflation, economic stagnation, exchange rate volatility, and growing balance of payments problems for several leading industrial nations. Developing countries were also pressing the case for international support for their own balance of payments and debt problems. This combination of factors led the IMF to redirect its attention during the years that followed.

Since the 1980s the IMF has been increasingly providing longer-term loans, especially to developing countries, and has been helping with debt problems resulting from a wider range of financial difficulties. Normally, these loans are made as part of an agreed *structural adjustment programme*, requiring a recipient country to adopt a set of stabilization policies. These policies are based on the IMF's free market approach to economic policy and usually include macroeconomic stabilization (strict budgetary and monetary policies) and the liberalization of external trade and internal goods, financial, and labour markets. Financial crises in Mexico (1995) and East Asia (1997–8) have brought about a series of large financial rescue packages from the IMF. The conditions attached to IMF loans are sometimes seen as too harsh or too market-oriented, bearing in mind the difficult circumstances of many developing countries. In the case of South Korea (1997), the biggest IMF financing facility to date, the IMF's insistence on strict monetary policy and financial liberalization has been criticized as inappropriate for a country where excessive lending has been a problem but inflation has not. The view that the IMF is a political organ of the major economic powers, especially the USA, has also been revived by the South-East Asian nations, some of which see the IMF's remedies as unsuited to their economies (see Chapter 8 on the 'East Asian Model'). However, IMF approval has also become an important signal to other public and private investors in regions like Eastern Europe and Latin America.

The International Bank for Reconstruction and Development (IBRD), generally known as the World Bank, was initially set up to help with European reconstruction after World War II. In practice, it has been more active in providing loans for infrastructure development projects. It raises funds from its members and from international financial markets and operates in partnership with private investors. Much of the World Bank's work has been in developing countries and its attention has turned more to the general problems of these countries, especially the relief of poverty and debt, since the 1970s. The World Bank Group also operates through its specialist agencies, including the International Development Association (IDA), which provides long-term subsidized loans to very poor countries, and the International Finance Corporation (IFC), which supports private businesses in developing countries. In some respects, the work of the World Bank and the IMF have become less distinct in recent years. The IMF, in particular, has now taken on a major role in sorting out financial problems and promoting economic restructuring in the developing world.

6.3.4 The EBRD and other regional development banks

Some institutions have a specifically regional focus, like the European Bank for Reconstruction and Development (EBRD). The EBRD was established in 1991 to aid the economic transformation of Eastern Europe and the former Soviet Union. Its capital was initially provided by its fifty-eight country and two institutional shareholders, which include the USA, Japan, and the countries of Western and Eastern Europe, as well as the European Union and the European Investment Bank. The EU has a major stake in the EBRD, including the appointment of its president, but the EBRD is not an EU institution. The EBRD has been involved in the financing of numerous projects in Eastern Europe, through loans and equity finance, and it normally operates in partnership with other investors where conventional sources of finance are unavailable. Although project finance has been its major activity, including environmental and energy efficiency schemes, the EBRD is increasingly investing in trade-enhancing activities in the private sector and its purview is also moving further eastwards into more high-risk regions of the former Soviet Union. Its role in Eastern Europe is discussed further in Chapter 21.

Similar publicly funded banks operate in other developing regions. The Asian Development Bank, set up in 1966, promotes the development of infrastructure and capital markets in Asian countries. For example, it has been involved in arranging loans to help countries like Thailand cope with its debt problems during the 1997–8 financial crisis in East Asia. Its development fund channels grants and soft loans from developed countries, as well as from economically stronger Asian countries, into development projects and the relief of poverty in the region. The bank's annual development outlook also provides a useful survey of the economic prospects of Asian countries. The African Development Bank is engaged in similar activities, bringing together the interests of African countries and aid from its partner countries outside Africa in an attempt to bring relief to this struggling continent. The Inter-American Development Bank, active in Latin America, is a further example.

6.3.5 GATT and the World Trade Organization

The General Agreement on Tariffs and Trade (GATT) has been responsible for a series of reductions in tariffs between trading nations during the post-war period. The first GATT Conference was held in 1947 and, since then, there have been eight rounds of multilateral negotiations on reductions in tariffs and other trade barriers, culminating with the Uruguay Round which was concluded in December 1993. Its contracting parties were initially the major industrialized nations, but its membership has increased to include the (now former) communist countries of Eastern Europe as well as many of the developing countries. GATT established some important trade principles: in particular, the commitment to international free trade, the most favoured nation principle, and the principle of reciprocity. The most favoured nation principle means that countries agree to treat all GATT members in the same way as they treat their most favoured trading partner—the principle of non-discrimination. Reciprocity implies that reductions in trade barriers should be made equally by all participating countries—a balanced move towards free trade.

In practice, whilst GATT has been remarkably successful in reducing tariffs, some of its principles have been weakened by a number of exceptions and by the use of non-tariff barriers. Groups of countries have often favoured preferential trading agreements, especially where the products of developing countries are involved. In general, agricultural and textile products have presented the most difficult problems though these issues were at least addressed for the first time during the Uruguay Round. Perhaps the main success of the Uruguay Round was the agreement by the USA and the EU to reduce tariffs on goods by an average of 50 per cent. GATT has also provided support for countries in dispute over trade barriers, though the lack of a formal machinery for resolving these disputes has limited its effectiveness.

In order to overcome this problem and to create a more permanent forum for trade negotiations, the World Trade Organization (WTO) came into operation in January 1995. The WTO has now taken over responsibility for future GATT negotiations, the next round being due to start in the year 2000. More importantly, the WTO is likely to provide more effective monitoring of the implementation of GATT agreements. It also operates a formal appeals procedure for the settlement of trade disputes. The decisions of the appeals panel are normally binding on member states. This has led some critics to complain about the over-legalization of trade disputes and has led to claims, notably from within the USA and the EU, that the WTO is overstepping its authority. These are, in the main, the very countries which have most successfully used the WTO disputes procedure to their advantage, however.

The other major area where the WTO has extended its influence is in the service sector, an area neglected under GATT. As manufacturing has been overtaken by services in its share of output in most of the developed countries, services are becoming more and more important. However, international trade in services, whilst significant in some sectors, is generally less developed than trade in goods. One of the reasons for this is the wide range of barriers which restrict trade in services. The General Agreement on Trade in Services (GATS) and also the agreement on Trade-Related Aspects of Intellectual Property Rights (TRIPS) were concluded under the Uruguay Round. GATS provides a framework for detailed agreements on specific services in the future. Since then, the WTO has turned its attention, in particular, to the liberalization of world telecommunications and financial services. An agreement on telecommunications was reached in February 1997. Under this agreement the USA, the EU, and Japan, the three biggest operators, are to open their markets to foreign (and domestic) competition from 1998. Many other countries, including some Latin American and Eastern European countries, have agreed to work towards the liberalization of telecommunications over a longer period. As this is one of the more monopolistic markets, these measures are likely to have a significant effect on foreign investment and the international structure of the telecommunications industry.

6.3.6 Other multinational organizations

A number of other multinational organizations attempt to coordinate the activities of groups of countries. Among the more important is the Organization for Economic Cooperation and Development (OECD). The Paris-based OECD was formed in 1961 as the successor to the Organization for European Economic Cooperation (OEEC), which had been set up to coordinate aid for post-war reconstruction under the Marshall Plan. The OECD now has twenty-nine members and includes most of the major industrialized nations, including the recent addition of Poland, the Czech Republic, and Hungary. One of its primary purposes is to coordinate aid to the developing countries, but the OECD also encourages general economic policy coordination between its members. A recent example is its attempt to broker a Multilateral Agreement on Investment (MAI) which would lay down rules for foreign investment between its member countries. Its annual surveys of members' economies are widely used as a guide to their economic performance.

Nations have often felt the need to cooperate with like-minded countries. The Group of 7 (G7) consists of the world's most powerful economies: Canada, France, Germany, Italy, Japan, the UK, and the USA. Russia has also been invited to attend the group but has not yet been admitted as a full member; the term G8 is sometimes used to describe the larger group. G7 provides a forum for the discussion of economic policy (notably monetary and trade policy coordination), but the group has also debated the reform of international institutions and the impact of globalization as well as non-economic issues like Middle Eastern conflict or the Chernbobyl nuclear power station disaster. At times, the group has been criticized for being inward-looking though, individually, its members are the main aid donors as well as the major trading nations.

Some multinational organizations are confined to particular regions. Examples of these are the Organization of African Unity, the Arab League, the Organization of American States, the Association of South-East Asian Nations (ASEAN), the Nordic Council, and the Council of Europe; this latter body is a forum for political stability in Europe and is a larger group than and distinct from the EU. Some organizations are military alliances such as the North Atlantic Treaty Organization (NATO), which now includes some of the former communist states in Eastern Europe, and the now defunct Warsaw Treaty Organization (known as the Warsaw Pact) in the former Soviet bloc. Others are groups of producers with common interests like the Organization of Petroleum Exporting Countries (OPEC). OPEC is a group of oil-exporting nations, predominantly based in the Middle East, though it also has members in Africa and Latin America. In the 1970s and early 1980s OPEC's output-fixing cartel had a major impact on world oil prices and the economies of many of the industrialized nations, though in more recent times its influence has been less dramatic.

6.4 The Impact of International Business on People and the Environment

6.4.1 Social implications of international business

Trade and investment and other international business activities clearly affect the economies of all but a few of the world's nations. They also have a political impact and are influenced by political decisions. The above discussion of global governance and the role of international institutions illustrates some of the ways in which politics and economics intertwine. We now turn our attention briefly to the social impact of international business.

The volume and variety of goods and services available to consumers around the world is testimony to the influence of international business firms. Further evidence is provided by the speed with which technology and other innovations spread from country to country. Consumers and producers are also exposed to foreign cultural influences; consumers in the Far East respond to Western images when they buy Coca-Cola or Levi jeans, just as European or American producers learn Total Quality Management (TQM) from the Japanese. International business has many effects on the way people live and work.

International business also affects the gross national product (GNP) of nations. The leading trading and investing nations, like the USA, Japan, or Germany, tend to have large GNPs and relatively affluent populations. The gains are not evenly spread, however. Indeed, it may be argued that some producers and countries gain at the expense of others. Certainly, the resources of many of the developing countries were exploited by their colonial masters in the past, not always to their mutual benefit. Today, MNEs are sometimes criticized for exploiting cheap labour and other resources in the poorer regions of the world. Whether these regions remain poor because of, or in spite of, the activities of MNEs is an open question. What is beyond dispute is that people in many of the world's poorer nations suffer from disease and malnutrition. They also work long hours in unhealthy conditions for very low rates of pay. The issue is perhaps the extent to which MNEs, and organizations responsible for monitoring their activities, should actively seek to alleviate poverty and its associated problems.

Other issues of social concern include the ethics of business transactions, respect for culture and national heritage, and the protection of the environment. Business ethics and culture are discussed in Chapter 5. Further discussion of the plight of poor countries and of how some developing countries emerge as successful industrial nations appears in Chapter 9. Here, we will focus on two specific issues: labour standards and the environment.

6.4.2 International labour standards and 'social dumping'

Labour is one of the resources which MNEs take advantage of when locating abroad. Popular opinion regards cheap labour as the main attraction for companies investing in Asia, Latin America, or Eastern Europe. When a plant is closed in a high-wage country and transferred to a low-wage country, this is sometimes described as *social dumping*. This argument is often overstated. Certainly, it is very attractive for German companies to move production to the Czech Republic where labour costs are much lower just over the border. It may even help to explain, though to a lesser extent, why Japanese or South Korean companies sometimes choose to locate in the UK rather than Germany. If it were the major reason for locating abroad, however, there would be a flood of companies moving into Chad and Laos or other low-wage countries.

Clearly, political and economic stability, the availability of high-quality resources, and market opportunities are also important (see Chapter 12).

The question remains, however: should MNEs simply take advantage of cheap labour and poor working conditions or should they try to do something about them? There are two main lines of argument here. First, there are those who emphasize the ethical case. MNEs should as far as possible apply the same rules when employing workers in low-wage countries as they do in their home countries. Thus, unsafe working conditions and child labour are no more acceptable in Asia than they are in Western Europe. This argument has also been applied to European companies which obtain supplies from developing countries. Few, however, would argue that wage equality is feasible since the payment of European wages would distort labour markets and harm local businesses in low-wage countries. The second argument is that the presence of MNEs in developing countries and the participation of developing countries in international trade will, over a period of time, raise living standards and working conditions more effectively than any attempt to impose Western standards on these countries. Here, the economic growth and rising real wages of emerging economies like South Korea over the last thirty or more years are cited as examples.

This debate is encapsulated in some of the deliberations of the UN, the WTO, and other international organizations. The WTO, for example, has been urged by some of its members to incorporate a *social clause* into its trade and investment rules. This would require companies to comply with agreed minimum labour standards and may apply to local companies as well as MNEs. Companies or countries which refused to abide by these rules would face sanctions. There are, of course, those who disagree with the use of such tactics.[6] There is a tendency for rich countries to want to impose 'Western' standards on developing countries—those which are already finding it difficult to compete. The implication of this criticism is that Western countries are only interested in imposing standards when they know they are on safe ground and when it is to their competitive advantage. It may also be argued that free trade is a more effective way of integrating poorer countries into the world economy, allowing them to gain an advantage from their low-cost production. Shunning their products merely isolates them, whereas trade participation exposes them to peer pressure from their trading partners. Pressure for improved standards through MNEs may offer more scope for action than direct pressure on the countries concerned.

6.4.3 International business and the protection of the environment

Resource depletion, pollution, and other forms of environmental damage have been one of the consequences of the growth of international business. Indeed, it is sometimes argued that the reckless misuse of the environment allowed the major industrial nations to achieve their economic success at much lower cost than would otherwise have been the case. In effect, the failure to take account of the *externalities* of production led to the wasteful use of scarce resources and allowed producers to make a competitive gain by not incorporating the social or environmental cost of production into their prices. Consumers also benefited from these lower prices.

Towards the end of the twentieth century, greater attention has been paid to the environmental consequences of business activity. This issue was debated at great length at the UN Conference on Climate Change in Kyoto in 1997. If the scientific predictions are correct, then countries and companies have a responsibility to take action. This involves changing production methods and consumption patterns, energy efficiency, the use of renewable energy sources, and the adoption of environmental measures such as pollution taxes or tradable pollution permits. Pollution permits allow 'clean' firms to sell their permits to 'dirty' ones; restrictions on the number of new permits issued enable the authorities to limit total pollution while leaving the market to put pressure on the worst polluters. Whilst all countries have a part to play in protecting the environment, the case for the major industrial nations to take a lead, especially on reducing greenhouse gas emissions, is compelling. Other problems, like the destruction of rain forests, occur mainly in the developing countries, though the industrial nations are often their main customers.

There is now growing awareness of the need for MNEs and the institutions of global governance to become more active in protecting the environment. Many of the leading companies carry out environmental audits of their activities and are becoming increasingly aware of their responsibilities in this area. However, companies based in countries where environmental controls are well developed tend to be more committed than those from countries with lax regulations. This suggests that governments and international institutions have an important role to play. It is also worth noting that, while the developed world is concerned about climate change and the ozone layer, for many developing countries the lack of clean water and sanitation are more pressing environmental problems.[7]

6.5 Summary

THE world trade order since World War II has been characterized by a gradual reduction in tariff barriers, especially between the industrialized nations. Greater openness to trade has resulted in a vast increase in world exports and imports. There is a strong theoretical and practical case for free trade and the economic benefits it brings. However, despite these arguments, governments have frequently resorted to the use of non-tariff barriers in the belief that trade protection is sometimes in their interests. This view is probably mistaken more often than it is correct, not least because trade relations between countries may suffer when barriers are erected. There has been an increasing tendency during the post-war years for the institutions of global governance to become involved in managing the world trade order and resolving disputes. These institutions include the UN, IMF, World Bank, and WTO.

Finally, we discuss some of the social implications of international business, focusing in particular on the responsibility of MNEs and global institutions for improving labour standards and protecting the environment.

Review Questions

1 How do you account for the vast increase in world trade since World War II?

2 What are the main arguments in favour of free trade? What types of trade barrier prevent free trade?

3 How have the roles of the IMF and World Bank changed in recent years?

4 In what ways does the WTO differ from what happened under GATT?

5 To what extent can MNEs influence labour standards or environmental protection policies in their host countries?

Study Topic: The EU Banana Regime

The EU has a preferential trading agreement with the African, Caribbean, and Pacific (ACP) group of countries. In theory, preferential trading agreements contravene GATT's most favoured nation principle, but as they generally favour developing countries, they are often regarded as acceptable. This does not mean that they are always non-controversial. Preferential access to EU markets for Caribbean banana growers has been the subject of a long-running WTO dispute. Some of the Latin American countries have been successful in arguing that their own banana growers have been unfairly treated by the EU banana regime. They have been supported in this action by the USA, some of whose companies own Latin American banana plantations and distribute their bananas. Where some developing countries receive preference over others, the issue is not straightforward.

The favoured treatment of ACP countries may be explained by their historic links as former colonies of Britain and France. The Latin American countries, on the other hand, have close links with the USA. The fact that two of the more recent EU members, Spain and Portugal, also have a shared history with Latin America, illustrates the complex geopolitics which affects trading relationships both in the wider world and even within the EU. For the WTO, the issue has more to do with free trade and equal treatment between countries. Some of the tiny Caribbean countries, which are heavily dependent on banana exports, see the issue as one of survival. In the long run there is also the problem of their overdependence on a single product, which may be perpetuated by the favourable banana regime. In practice, the regime also provides much more income for the large companies involved in the distribution of bananas, courtesy of high European banana prices, than it does for the poor Caribbean producers.

The WTO ruled that the EU is unfairly discriminating against the Latin American producers and their US distributors. The EU responded by removing the licensing system for banana imports in order to allow easier access to its markets, whilst retaining a separate import quota on Latin American bananas and a duty-free quota for Caribbean and other ACP producers. The ACP quota now forces each country to compete for its share of the quota. This compromise gives the less efficient ACP producers a breathing space to diversify out of banana production, but the Americans see it as not going far enough. Without waiting for a WTO ruling on the EU concessions, the US government expressed its dissatisfaction by threatening to impose punitive duties on a wide range of EU goods. Whilst the USA claimed the EU was not complying with the original WTO ruling against it, the EU claimed the USA was 'jumping the gun' by threatening trade sanctions before the WTO had considered the revised EU proposal. Other countries then began to support one side or the other, spurred on by their political sympathies or economic interests.

Subsequently, the WTO again ruled against the EU. At the time of writing, the EU is searching for a way of satisfying the US and Latin American complainants, whilst minimizing the adverse impact on the Caribbean banana growers. Whatever the final outcome, the issue has brought the USA and the EU to the brink of a trade war and may undermine the trade disputes procedure of the WTO. The new world trade order has come under threat because the world's two major economic powers seem unable to avoid slipping on a 'banana skin'.

Study topic questions

1 Is the EU justified, in principle, in offering preferential access to its markets to its former colonies in the ACP group of countries?

2 If the EU abandons its ACP banana agreement, what are likely to be the consequences for the Caribbean banana-producing countries?

3 Do you consider that the proposed EU concessions would have been an acceptable compromise?

4 Why do you think the US government threatened to impose punitive import duties on EU goods without waiting for a WTO ruling on the EU compromise proposal?

5 What are the implications of this dispute for the world trade order and the WTO?

Notes

1 See e.g. P. Hirst and G. Thompson, *Globalization in Question*, (Blackwell, 1996).

2 See R. S. Pindyck and D. L. Rubinfeld, *Microeconomics* (Prentice Hall, 1998), 607–8.

3 There is a wealth of good introductory economics textbooks which explain the theory of perfect competition. See e.g. D. Begg, S. Fischer, and R. Dornbusch, *Economics* (McGraw-Hill, 1997).

4 See e.g. F. A. Hayek, *The Road to Serfdom* (London, Routledge, 1944).

5 'Schools Brief: Trade Winds', *The Economist* (8 Nov. 1997), 124–5.

6 The Cuban Liberty and Democratic Solidarity Act, known as the Helms–Burton Act, was introduced in the USA in 1996. It builds on thirty-five years of US sanctions against Cuba which have attempted to put pressure on the country to abandon its one-party communism. Under the Act, sanctions can be placed on foreign companies which invest in assets expropriated by the Cuban regime. The law has been the subject of criticism in Europe and elsewhere. Similar US restrictions apply to foreign investors in the energy industries of Iran and Libya under the Iran–Libya Sanctions Act (also known as the D'Amato Act).

7 See e.g. J. Bhagwati, Free Trade, 'Fairness' and the New Protectionism, IEA Occasional Paper 96 (Institute of Economic Affairs, 1995).

8 See *The Economist*, 'A Survey of Development and the Environment' (21 Mar. 1998).

Recommended Reading

■ Brenton, P., Scott, H., and Sin, P., *International Trade: A European Text* (Oxford University Press, 1997).

■ Jepma, C., *International Trade: A Business Perspective* (Longman, 1996).

■ Kreinin, M. E., *International Economics: A Policy Approach* (Dryden, 1998).

■ Krugman, P. R., and Obstfeld, M., *Internatiotial Economics: Theory and Policy* (Addison-Wesley, 1997).

■ Rengger, N. J., with Campbell, J., *Treaties and Alliances of the World* (Catermill International, 1995).

■ Whittaker, D. J., *United Nations in Action* (UCL Press, 1995).

7

Integration between Countries

Objectives

- to identify the various types of economic and political integration between countries
- to analyse the impact of economic integration on trade, industrial activity, and the countries concerned
- to discuss the development and significance of the major regional economic groupings in different parts of the world
- to consider the link between regional integration and globalization

7.1 Introduction

INTEGRATION between countries is an important feature of the international business environment. International integration may be either political or economic. Political integration is where countries pool their sovereignty to some degree. Economic integration involves links between the economies of a group of countries. These are often known as trade blocs or, more formally, regional economic groupings. The various forms of integration are the subject of this chapter. In practice, economic integration tends to produce some degree of political integration as well, though not necessarily full political union.

Whilst some regional economic groupings are well established, there has been a proliferation of such groupings in recent years. Many countries regard economic cooperation as in their long-term interests and they are anxious not to be excluded from these trade blocs. The European Union, for example, has no shortage of would-be members, especially from countries in Eastern Europe. In South-East Asia, even communist Vietnam and Burma, with its military dictatorship, have recently been admitted to the ASEAN Free Trade Area (AFTA).

These trading areas and their policies have a major impact on the activities of international business firms. We therefore need to examine the various forms of integration and to consider how firms respond to integration. A brief summary of the main levels of integration between countries is shown in Figure 7.1. We also consider whether regional integration should be seen as a stepping stone towards global free trade or whether, as some people argue, it is hindering the process of global integration by creating distortions between intra- and inter-regional trade.

7.2 Levels of Integration between Countries

7.2.1 Preferential trading agreement

A preferential trading agreement is the loosest form of economic integration. It is where a group of countries have a formal agreement to allow each other's goods to be traded on preferential terms. This usually means that reduced tariffs are in operation between these countries or that special quotas allow preferential access for their goods. Some writers regard a preferential trading agreement as merely a trading arrangement between countries rather than integration. Certainly, such an agreement lacks the more formal institutional arrangements that tend to accompany other forms of integration. Often they are agreements between developed and developing countries and are designed primarily to support the latter countries' economic development. However, they may involve a degree of integration in that they increase the link between the products of one country and the markets of another.

A good example of a preferential trading agreement is the Lomé Agreement between the African, Caribbean, and Pacific (ACP) group of countries and the European Union. Like many preferential trading agreements, this agreement mainly covers agricultural products which are the main exports of the ACP countries. The EU also has a number of individual preferential trading agreements with other countries in the Middle East, Latin America, and elsewhere. Indeed, such agreements are commonplace throughout the world.

7.2.2 Free trade area

A free trade area is usually a permanent arrangement between neighbouring countries. It involves the complete removal of tariffs on goods traded between the

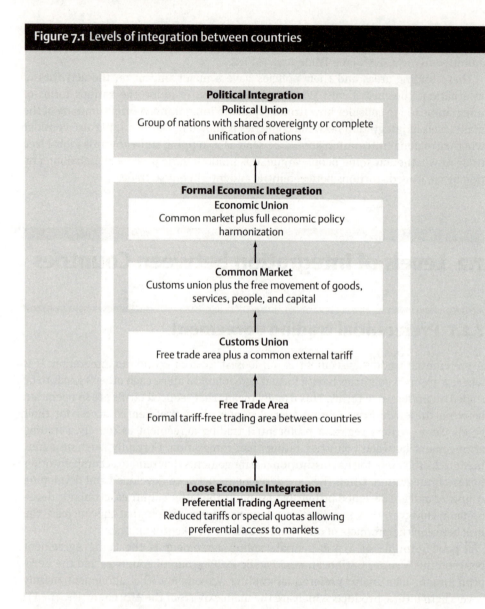

Figure 7.1 Levels of integration between countries

Political Integration
Political Union
Group of nations with shared sovereignty or complete unification of nations

Formal Economic Integration
Economic Union
Common market plus full economic policy harmonization

Common Market
Customs union plus the free movement of goods, services, people, and capital

Customs Union
Free trade area plus a common external tariff

Free Trade Area
Formal tariff-free trading area between countries

Loose Economic Integration
Preferential Trading Agreement
Reduced tariffs or special quotas allowing preferential access to markets

members of the free trade area. In general, it does not apply to agriculture and fishing or to services, though in practice the precise arrangements will vary from one free trade area to another. Member countries are free to levy their own external tariff on goods from outside the free trade area. Each member thus retains autonomy over trade with external countries and there is little need for formal institutions and policies other than to maintain the internal tariff-free area. The main difficulty faced by these countries, however, is that goods from outside the area will tend to find the easiest point of entry, that is, where the external tariff is lowest, and can then cross any of the internal borders without incurring further tariffs. This practice will distort patterns of trade between the member countries and will, in effect, circumvent the external tariff sovereignty of the members with higher tariffs. To overcome this problem, the members of the free trade area usually resort to controls on the country of origin for goods crossing their internal frontiers. This involves extensive border checks and other procedures.

The removal of tariffs is likely to offer net welfare benefits for the countries involved, though there may also be a lengthy adjustment process for their firms and industries. This issue is discussed in Chapter 6. Tariffs are one of the more obvious barriers to trade between countries and one of the easiest to remove. It is for this reason that a free trade area is often regarded as a fairly basic level of integration. It may also be regarded as a first step towards deeper forms of integration. Free trade areas are quite common in practice. The North American Free Trade Agreement (NAFTA) is one of the best-known examples. Others include the European Free Trade Association (EFTA) and the ASEAN Free Trade Area (AFTA). In some cases a complete free trade area has not yet been achieved, in others there are aspects which go beyond a free trade area. The EU has a higher level of integration which incorporates a free trade area but which has progressed well beyond the simple removal of tariffs. These and other examples are discussed more extensively later in this chapter.

7.2.3 Customs union

As noted above, the main problem with free trade areas is that goods from non-member countries may circumvent the external tariff barriers of individual members and then circulate freely within the free trade area. A customs union avoids this problem by the members agreeing to a common external tariff for each type of product. Thus, for the external producer, the tariff barrier is the same no matter which point of entry is used. Internal country-of-origin procedures are therefore no longer required. The issue which now arises, however, concerns the ownership of the external tariff revenues. This may be resolved by treating these revenues as the common property of the customs union. This of course requires a higher degree of political cooperation than is necessary within a free trade area. Agreement is needed on the level of the common external tariff and on the administration of the tariff revenues.

As the level of integration increases, it becomes harder to find examples which match each of the textbook models exactly. In the EU a customs union was established among the original six members by the late 1960s. This has since been extended, after phasing-in periods, to each of the new EU member states. The EU also agreed to form a customs union with Turkey in 1995. Once again, integration within the EU has progressed beyond that of a customs union. Elsewhere, one of the best examples is Mercosur in South America. Although the Mercosur countries do not yet have a common external tariff on all products (or indeed a complete free trade area), they have made rapid progress towards establishing a customs union since the formation of Mercosur in 1991.

In view of the unifying effect of the common external tariff, together with the internal free trade area, a customs union may be seen as a more comprehensive form of integration than a simple free trade area. As a result, customs unions have received more attention from integration theorists and researchers. One of the earliest formal attempts to analyse the advantages and disadvantages of a customs union was made by Jacob Viner.[1] A brief discussion of Viner's analysis appears later in this chapter. More recent developments in the analysis of customs unions and other forms of integration are also explored.

7.2.4 Common market

Although the term 'common market' was widely used to describe the European Union in its early years, it is in fact a technical term used in integration theory. A common market is a customs union where internal non-tariff barriers have also been removed. In theory, this allows goods, services, people, and capital to move freely across internal frontiers. The existence of a common market implies that the internal market, comprising all the member nations, is 'common' to all firms trading within it; the removal of all internal barriers, both tariff and non-tariff, allows all firms access to the entire internal market. Non-tariff barriers are often much more of an obstruction to trade than tariff barriers because they are less visible and more difficult to overcome. Trade in goods may be obstructed by differences in product standards or testing procedures, customs formalities, transport restrictions, and a wide variety of other regulations. Some of these non-tariff barriers are discussed in Chapter 6, but they are considered more extensively in the EU context in Chapter 15.

Trade in services and the free movement of people and capital are also important here. The ability of banks and insurance companies to offer their services across national borders is often restricted by different regulations governing their activities. Similarly, customs procedures and, more especially, work permit requirements and the failure to recognize qualifications may be a barrier to the free movement of people in general and of labour in particular. The movement of capital (and thus the ability to invest abroad) is often obstructed by exchange control regulations and investment restrictions, imposed either by the home or the foreign country. The removal of non-tariff barriers to trade is sometimes described as *trade liberalization*.

Some of the more ambitious regional economic groupings are striving to become a common market. The Central American Common Market (CACM) and Mercosur (whose name is an acronym for Common Market of the South) are both working towards this goal, though it would be inaccurate to suggest that they have achieved it. The EU, on the other hand, provides a good example of a trading area which has systematically set about achieving a common market. Whereas a customs union was put in place by the founder members during the EU's first decade, the Single European Market (SEM) Project was designed to remove non-tariff barriers by the end of 1992. In other words, the EU set about creating a true common or single market. The term 'single market' or 'internal market' was chosen in preference to 'common market' because the latter term was already in common use and would have failed to capture the imagination of the European public. The fact was, however, that the common market envisaged by the Treaty of Rome was still far from complete by the mid-1980s and a new impetus was needed. The SEM project is still not complete, but great strides have been made towards this end since the late 1980s.

7.2.5 Economic union

The most complete form of economic integration between countries is called an economic union. This involves a common market and also the harmonization of economic policies, in particular monetary union and the coordination of fiscal policies. Monetary union means there is a fixed exchange rate system between the member countries, perhaps even a single or common currency, and central control over interest rates and other instruments of monetary policy. Fiscal policy coordination includes the harmonization of tax rates, especially VAT, excise duties and other taxes on goods, and some degree of control over government budgets and budget deficits. There is also likely to be coordination of other economic policies such as regional, industrial, and agricultural policies. Economic union ties its members' economies closely together so that, in effect, they function as a single economy.

Clearly, central coordination of economic policy requires a high level of cooperation between the member governments, central banks, and other institutions. A number of transnational coordinating institutions will also exist. Thus, in terms of policy making, there will be a high degree of political integration as well as economic integration, though in areas like defence and foreign policy the member countries may still act independently. Countries which achieve economic union will normally have graduated from lower to higher levels of integration, though such progression is not an inevitable process. Many regional economic groupings remain as free trade areas or customs unions. Indeed, political resistance is often the main obstacle to deeper or higher levels of integration.

Once again, the EU provides a useful illustration, though it has not yet attained full economic union. Whereas the SEM Project was an attempt to create a common market, the Treaty on European Union or Maastricht Treaty is taking the EU towards economic union (and, in some respects, also political union). Certainly, monetary union is a key element in this process for most EU member states. Economic union in the wider sense may take a little longer to achieve. It is rare for large groups of independent countries to achieve full economic union though currency unions and other forms of economic policy cooperation are more common.

7.2.6 Political union

Whilst some degree of political integration often accompanies economic integration, political union implies more formal political links between countries. A limited form of political union may exist where two or more countries share common decision-making bodies and have common policies. In its fullest sense, it involves the unification of previously separate nations. The (re-)unification of East and West Germany in 1990 is an example of complete political union, after years of separation following the post-war settlement and Soviet domination of Eastern Europe. Indeed, the formation of the Soviet Union itself brought political union between its various republics, though in this case integration was less universally popular.

In the context of the European Union, the terms 'United States of Europe' or 'Federal Europe' have sometimes been used to describe a vision of an economically and politically integrated Europe. In practice, it is more likely to mean a federation of states sharing common policies and institutions rather than political union with a single supranational government. *Federalism*, in this context, describes a system where central political institutions have some degree of authority over the affairs of independent nation states. This is sometimes contrasted with *functionalism*, where economic and social cooperation between countries gradually leads towards political integration. Shared policies in the EU already include aspects of policing, immigration, and foreign policy, as well as economic policy, and may even be extended to issues such as defence in the future. Unfortunately, discussion of these issues is often clouded by misunderstanding and prejudice and terms like 'federal' are used emotively and with conflicting meanings. A more extensive analysis of integration in the EU appears in Chapter 16.

7.3 Impact of Integration between Countries

7.3.1 Trade creation, diversion, and suppression

International economic integration may have a number of identifiable effects on trade flows between the countries involved. 'Trade' here is simply shorthand for 'international trade'. The analysis of these trade flows was first developed by Jacob Viner in the context of customs unions.[2] When tariffs, or indeed other barriers, are removed between the members of a trading area, new opportunities for trade are created. This is because exports can now be sold or imports bought more cheaply or more easily inside the trading area. The efficient exporter can sell surplus goods abroad and the importer, instead of producing the goods inefficiently at home, can reallocate resources to more efficient production. The adjustment process may, of course, cause short-term problems in the importing country but, in the long run, both countries will benefit from *trade creation*.

Trade diversion occurs when trade is diverted from countries outside the trading area to countries inside. This results from the removal of tariffs and other barriers in the trading area, making it cheaper or easier to export to or import from these countries. External countries will find it especially difficult to retain their export markets if the common external tariff is higher than the previous importing country's tariff. In such a case trade diversion may not be beneficial as trade may be diverted from a more efficient producer outside the trading area to a less efficient one inside. Generally, there will be gainers and losers from trade diversion—the net gain or loss will depend on the particular circumstances.

Trade suppression is less likely to occur as a result of a new trading area, unless the common external tariff is high and there is no exporter within the trading area who is efficient enough to replace an efficient external producer. In these circumstances, trade which previously occurred would now be suppressed. Trade suppression leads to a loss of welfare in the countries concerned.

A brief look at the UK's trading position before and after joining the European Union in 1973 shows that some combination of trade creation and trade diversion has occurred vis-à-vis its trading partners in the EU (see Table 7.1). A detailed analysis of changes in UK trade flows would be necessary to establish the balance between trade creation and trade diversion and, in the latter case, to determine whether net welfare has been enhanced. Generally, it can be said that the lower the common external tariff, the more likely it is that there will be net benefits from the creation of a regional trading area. This is even more likely to be the case if there is external as well as internal trade liberalization in addition to tariff reductions. These provisos help to explain why there has been much outside concern about the dangers of 'Fortress Europe' (a perception that the EU has high external barriers) or the apparent protectionist tendencies of Mercosur, for example. With some exceptions, the EU is in reality becoming less of a fortress than it used to be, however. The EU's external relations are discussed in some detail in Chapter 17.

7.3.2 Prices and competition

The removal of trade barriers has both consumption and production effects. The production effects, in terms of producers inside or outside the trading area, are described in the previous section. The consumption effects are on prices and consumer choice. When trade barriers come down consumers can buy goods more

Table 7.1 UK Trade with the EU				
	1972		1997	
	£m.	% of total	£m.	% of total
UK exports to EU14	332	40.9	96,126	55.5
UK imports from EU14	393	42.3	101,037	53.4
Source: Economic Trends (HMSO, December 1973, and Office for National Statistics, Feb. 1999).				

cheaply. This applies not just to tariffs, where price is directly affected, but also to non-tariff barriers like customs formalities which raise the cost of selling goods across borders. In a customs union prices of goods sold between member states will generally fall though, where trade from external countries is diverted or suppressed, prices may actually rise if internal producers have higher costs. Similar arguments apply to consumer choice. Trade creation increases the availability of goods, but trade diversion may simply replace some goods with others or even reduce consumer choice if external tariffs are high.

Perhaps a more important issue concerns competition. By removing barriers between national markets, trading areas create competition. Generally speaking, the larger the trading area and the higher the level of integration (thus the greater the elimination of barriers), the more competition will be created. Competition brings numerous benefits, especially for consumers. These benefits include lower prices, more choice, and better value for money. It is sometimes argued that excessive price competition forces producers to cut costs by eliminating variety or reducing quality, but there are many examples of competition extending the variety of products available with a wide spectrum of prices and quality. Moreover, competition also stimulates innovation, not only in the products themselves but also in the channels of distribution, methods of payment, customer care, and so on. Reorganization and other changes in the European motor industry illustrate many of these benefits (see Box 17.1).

The removal of barriers or gradual liberalization of markets such as telecommunications or airways in the EU and elsewhere is leading to similar competitive changes. Competition can be painful for firms which are inefficient or unresponsive to change. It may make some firms vulnerable to takeovers or force them into alliances to acquire complementary skills. It also weakens the market power of firms whose dominance comes from legal protection rather than commercial success. These painful changes may sometimes disorientate consumers but often produce long-term benefits.

7.3.3 Economies of scale and other static effects

Firms which operate in relatively closed national markets are sometimes unable to expand to their minimum efficient scale. They are constrained by the size of the domestic market. This is particularly true in the case of utility industries such as transport and telecommunications. It may also apply to their supply industries: for example, manufacturers of railway rolling stock or telecommunications equipment may be favoured suppliers to their national utility operators but may find access to foreign markets more difficult. This issue was highlighted by the Cecchini Report on the Single European Market; the report contrasted the highly fragmented European market for telecommunications equipment which had eleven separate suppliers with that of the USA, a similar-sized market, with only four suppliers.[3] The implication here is that Europe's small, protected suppliers cannot achieve full economies of scale and are therefore less efficient (have higher long-run average costs) than their US counterparts.

These economies of scale apply to the costs of production associated with the size of a plant or factory. Doubling the size of a factory does not necessarily double the costs of production, so the unit cost of production falls. This kind of economy of scale is less of a problem for large MNEs which have already achieved these advantages by locating production around the world. Indeed, the existence of trade barriers may encourage MNEs to locate production within a country rather than suffer export barriers. However, when Nissan located a large new plant in the north-east of England, the opportunity to sell its cars in the larger European market was clearly a factor determining the size of plant. The concept of economies of scale can also be applied to the size of a firm as a whole. Thus, when viewing the EU as a single market, a firm may centralize some of its administrative, accounting, marketing, or research and development activities. This will enable the firm to reduce its overall costs per unit sold. 'Plant' and 'firm' economies of scale are known as *internal economies of scale*.

External economies of scale may also arise in an integrated trading area. These occur when large numbers of firms locate in particular regions in order to take advantage of the facilities available. Indeed, specialist suppliers, consultancies, and other agencies are often attracted to areas where there is a convergence of firms in a particular industry. The removal of barriers increases the mobility of firms in seeking out these locations and has the effect of improving their productivity.

Improved *factor productivity* is one of the main benefits which arise when firms relocate all or part of their operations into a region where labour, capital, and other factors of production can be more productively employed. An example of this was the decision of Hoover to relocate its production of vacuum cleaners from Dijon to Glasgow in 1993, apparently to reduce the cost and increase the flexibility of its workforce.

Actions by companies to achieve economies of scale or improved factor productivity may be described as *static effects of integration*. This means that they produce once-for-all gains for these firms. When a firm increases its scale of operations, any cost reductions will benefit the firm and also its customers, if prices are reduced or extra profits reinvested, for as long as the firm continues on this scale. The effect is static in the sense that costs fall initially when scale is increased, then remain at this level; they do not fall continuously. Other static effects include cost reductions which result from the removal of tariffs and border controls, the simplification of export and import documentation, the harmonization of product standards, and the elimination of other trade barriers. A number of studies have attempted to measure the static effects of integration. Perhaps the most comprehensive study of EU integration was a European Commission investigation into the probable effects of the Single European Market, the results of which are summarized in the Cecchini Report.[4] The findings of this study are discussed in Chapter 15.

7.3.4 Dynamic effects of integration

Dynamic effects are more difficult to quantify. This term describes the continuous pressure for change which is a feature of an integrated competitive environment. Market forces act as a spur to improvements in efficiency, increases in investment, and continual innovation. A new product or process may create a competitive advantage for a time, but before long a competitor will introduce something better. The search for success is ongoing. The need to innovate promotes investment in new technology, new methods of production and distribution, and product design. This investment has a *multiplier effect* on the level of economic activity generally and stimulates further increases in production, income, and demand. Competition also increases the necessity to be efficient. Not only do competitive companies try to minimize their costs of production, they also seek to maximize the effectiveness or productivity of their resources by reducing *X-inefficiency*—the failure to use a resource, especially labour, to its maximum potential.

In a general sense, the dynamic effect of integration is that it brings about a more efficient allocation of resources throughout the trading area, promoting the growth of some businesses and the decline of others, the development of new technology and products, and the elimination of old. This process is creating a large-scale restructuring of industries and firms in the EU, with relocation of industry and many cross-border mergers and alliances. Clearly, it can be a painful process, but it is one which generally improves the competitiveness of European companies and produces choice, new products, and lower prices for consumers.

7.3.5 The politics of integration

Whether integration results from a desire to increase trade or from more overt political motives, there are often political implications for the member countries and their trading partners. Regional economic groupings may have increased bargaining power when participating in international forums such as the International Monetary Fund or World Trade Organization. For example, the EU is achieving growing recognition when it acts on behalf of its members in trade negotiations or, perhaps less successfully, when it pursues a common foreign policy. NAFTA is also a powerful trade bloc, though the USA is inevitably dominant here. Similarly, if APEC is successful in achieving its ambitious free trade area, this will potentially become a huge power bloc in trade and other negotiations. It should be remembered, however, that viewed from the perspective of a developing country, the most powerful trade blocs tend to increase the already dominant role of the industrialized nations.

In a different sense, a trade bloc may create a political link between independent nations. This may seem unlikely at present in such a diverse group as APEC, but some would argue that the EU has contributed towards peace in Europe since the disastrous world wars of the first half of the twentieth century. Arguably, it has promoted greater understanding of neighbouring European nations. Even the frequent disputes over EU policy are infinitely preferable to what went before. More specifically, governments in some European countries have seen further economic integration as the route to a political union which will strengthen the relationships between countries. The checks and balances of political union may also weaken the influence, though not necessarily reduce the activities, of groups and parties on the political extremes.

7.4 Major Regional Economic Groupings

IN recent years a large number of regional economic groupings or trade blocs have been established. These exist in all the main regions of the world. The number of regional trade agreements rose from under twenty-five in 1990 to over ninety in 1998.[5] These range from huge regional trade blocs like APEC or the EU to loose arrangements between groups of small countries. Some of the main regional economic groupings are discussed in this section.

7.4.1 Integration in Western Europe

After the Great Depression of the interwar years and the destruction caused by World War II, there was a great desire for some form of cooperation or integration in Europe during the late 1940s and early 1950s. The post-war division of Europe also increased the perceived threat from the Soviet Union now that its influence had been extended throughout Eastern Europe. Various free trade agreements and customs unions had existed between individual European countries during the nineteenth and early twentieth centuries. However, the post-war years brought more ambitious attempts at integration. The Organization for European Economic Cooperation (OEEC), formed in response to the US Marshall Aid plan in 1948, was an early attempt at cooperation between Europe's devastated economies. The Council of Europe, established in 1949, also brought some of the European governments together to promote common ideals and principles. The Council of Europe still exists today, with an expanded membership, and its major achievements include the Convention on the Protection of Human Rights, the European Commission of Human Rights, and the European Court of Human Rights.

During the 1950s a more formal process of integration began between France, Germany, Italy, and the Benelux nations (Belgium, the Netherlands, and Luxembourg). This led to the formation of the European Economic Community (now European Union) in 1958. From its inception, the EU has had ambitious goals for the creation of a common market and 'an ever closer union among the European peoples'.[6] Other members of the OEEC decided to form a looser free trade area and in 1960 the European Free Trade Association (EFTA) was formed. EFTA's founder members were Austria, Denmark, Norway, Portugal, Sweden, Switzerland, and the UK, later joined by Finland, Iceland, and Liechtenstein. Six of its members have subsequently joined the EU, leaving only Iceland, Liechtenstein, Norway, and Switzerland. EFTA is mainly concerned with free trade for industrial goods between its members. There is no common external tariff and decisions are generally made on the basis of unanimity at the intergovernmental level.

The European Union has followed a very different course. Because of its importance in international business, and for European companies in particular, the EU is extensively examined in Chapters 14 to 17. After successive expansions, the EU now has fifteen member states. These include Austria, Belgium, Denmark, Finland, France, Germany, Greece, Ireland, Italy, Luxembourg, the Netherlands, Portugal, Spain, Sweden, and the UK. The EU achieved a customs union among its original members by 1968 and has since made considerable progress towards a common market. The common market initiative, whilst always an objective under the Treaty of Rome, the EU's founding treaty, had made only piecemeal progress until the Single European Market Project gave it a new impetus in 1985. The EU has also achieved a fledgling monetary union among the majority of its members. Monetary union is a key element of economic union. The first steps towards monetary union were taken after the Werner Report in 1970, but a single European currency and integrated monetary policy only came into effect among eleven of its member nations in 1999.

The single market between EU members now also extends to three of the remaining four EFTA countries. This eighteen-member Single European Market is known as the European Economic Area (EEA). The agreement covers the free movement of goods, services, people, and capital but excludes agriculture and fishing. It came into effect, after a short delay, in 1995. Only Switzerland, among EFTA members, rejected membership of the EEA after a national referendum. The EEA not only opens the single market to the three EFTA members but also extends EU jurisdiction to these countries in policy areas such as competition, company law, consumer protection, social policy, education, and the environment. Under EU association agreements (the 'Europe Agreements'), a number of Eastern European countries are also working towards trade liberalization with the EU, as well as modelling their laws on EU legislation. These countries have applied for EU membership and are likely to become members during the early years of the twenty-first century. After a faltering start and numerous setbacks along the way, European integration has become both wider and deeper during the years since 1945.

7.4.2 Eastern Europe and the Former Soviet Union

Under the period of Soviet domination of Eastern Europe (1945–89), trade and other forms of economic cooperation in this region were developed through the Council for Mutual Economic Assistance (CMEA), also known as COMECON, which was established in 1949. COMECON was intended to promote economic regeneration in the countries of Eastern Europe which had been denied access to Marshall Aid and membership of OEEC by the Soviet Union. Its founder members were Bulgaria, Czechoslovakia, Hungary, Poland, Romania, and the Soviet Union (USSR). These were joined by the German Democratic Republic (East Germany) in 1950 and later by countries sympathetic to the Soviet model of communism further afield, including Mongolia, Cuba, and Vietnam. Albania also became a member but withdrew in 1961 to pursue a more independent course as a non-aligned nation. COMECON led to close economic and political ties between these countries, including the central planning of key industries, but it was always dominated by the Soviet Union. It was disbanded in 1991 after the collapse of the Soviet empire in Eastern Europe.

During the 1990s the former communist centrally planned countries of this region moved broadly in two directions. With the exception of the three Baltic Republics (Estonia, Latvia, and Lithuania), the remaining twelve ex-Soviet republics formed a loose federation known as the Commonwealth of Independent States (CIS) in 1991. Its members are Armenia, Azerbaijan, Belarus, Georgia, Kazakhstan, Kyrgyzstan, Moldova, Russia, Tajikistan, Turkmenistan, Ukraine, and Uzbekistan. The CIS exists to coordinate foreign, defence, and economic policies within this group though it is inevitably dominated by Russia. Despite agreements on the control of nuclear weapons and decisions by some members to re-establish the link between their currencies and the Russian rouble, further cooperation remains limited because of fears of continued Russian dominance.

The three Baltic Republics and the Central European group of nations have generally favoured closer links with Western Europe and the EU. In particular, Hungary, Poland, and the Czech and Slovak Republics (formerly Czechoslovakia) signed the Visegrad Agreement in 1991. The 'Visegrad states' have now been joined by Romania, Bulgaria, and Slovenia, one of the former Yugoslav republics, in re-establishing trade links. These states have affirmed their desire for integration within the EU and in 1993 they inaugurated the Central European Free Trade Area (CEFTA) as a preparation for EU membership. While most trade in industrial goods is already tariff-free, progress on agricultural trade has been slower. The free movement of services and capital is also on the agenda. In view of the historic developments in this region since the late 1980s, Chapters 18–22 offer an extensive analysis of market transition in Eastern Europe and its implications for international business.

7.4.3 Regional integration in the Americas

The USA and Canada have traded extensively with each other for many years and trade barriers between them have generally been low. They are, in fact, each other's largest trading partner. However, the US–Canada Free Trade Agreement only came into effect as recently as 1989. The agreement was to eliminate tariffs by 1 January 1999 and some non-tariff barriers have also been reduced, including trade in financial services and foreign investment restrictions. This free trade area was then extended to include Mexico when the North American Free Trade Agreement (NAFTA) came into effect in 1994. Although in economic terms the inclusion of Mexico is less significant than the earlier US–Canada agreement, NAFTA has become more important because it now encompasses the whole of North America. With the exception of APEC, which has yet to materialize in any coherent sense, NAFTA is the largest regional economic grouping in the world (see Table 7.2). The formation of NAFTA has also been quite controversial, especially in the USA (see Box 7.1).

The countries of Latin America have also made various attempts at integration. The Latin American Free Trade Area (LAFTA), formed among all the countries of South America as well as Mexico in 1960, was an ambitious attempt to create a free trade area. LAFTA, which was reorganized as the Latin American Integration Association (LAIA) in 1980, has had only limited success in expanding trade between its members. At present, there are two main regional economic groupings in South America: the Andean Pact and Mercosur. The Andean Pact, formed by some of LAFTA's members in 1969, is based in the north-western region of the subcontinent. It includes Bolivia, Colombia, Ecuador, Peru, and Venezuela and its aim is to achieve a common market.

Box 7.1 The North American Free Trade Agreement

As well as being the world's largest trading area, NAFTA is unusual in that it combines two of the world's major trading nations with a large developing nation. Clearly, geographically, there is a strong logic to this trading area. Indeed, the USA is by far Mexico's main export market and Mexico is one of the USA's main trading partners. Canada's trade with Mexico is much smaller. However, many Americans fear that Mexico's low-wage economy will attract investment from the USA, with a resulting loss of employment when US companies relocate. Business migration to Mexico's border region is certainly an issue of concern—the so-called *maquiladora* industries or assembly plants which are attracted by tax benefits, low costs, and lax regulations. Despite these fears and a US trade deficit with Mexico, trade between the USA, Canada, and Mexico has increased substantially since NAFTA's formation in 1994 and US investment in Mexico is still small compared to US domestic investment.

The main objective of NAFTA is the elimination of tariffs on most products within ten years and, on certain agricultural and other sensitive products, within fifteen years. The agreement also extends to a wider range of non-tariff barriers than the US–Canada agreement which preceded it. These include most services, public procurement, foreign investment, intellectual property rights, and environmental measures. In this respect, NAFTA goes well beyond the scope of a simple free trade area, but it is not a customs union. Members are free to set their own external tariffs and rules of origin have been put in place requiring a minimum 50 per cent local content for cross-border trade in most products. This provision, which is common in free trade areas, restricts the ability of foreign companies to trade freely once they are inside NAFTA, unless their products are largely manufactured and sourced locally.

Table 7.2 Key data on NAFTA members

	Population millions (July 1998 est.)	Gross domestic product[a] $US bn. (1997 est.)	Gross domestic product[a] per cap. $US (1997 est.)
Canada	30.7	658	21,700
Mexico	98.6	695	7,700
USA	270.3	8,083	30,200

[a] GDP figures are estimated on a purchasing power parity basis.
Source: CIA World Factbook, 1998.

A recent but in many ways more important and more rapidly developing group is Mercosur (Mercado Comun del Sur or Common Market of the South). Mercosur began operating in 1991 and has already achieved free trade and a common external tariff on many goods. It aims to have completed its free trade area by the year 2000 and its customs union by 2006. Its members include Brazil and Argentina, the region's two largest countries, and also Paraguay and Uruguay, with Bolivia and Chile as associate members; Bolivia and Chile have agreed to join Mercosur's free trade area but not its customs union. Chile is also regarded as a possible future member of NAFTA. As a high tariff group of countries, Mercosur has made remarkable progress in removing tariff barriers, though its relatively high external tariffs have attracted criticism among the developed nations as well as encouraging huge inward investment in industries like motor manufacturing where trade barriers have been particularly high. The region's underdeveloped infrastructure, inflation-prone economies, and the lack of an institutional framework to oversee progress towards a common market may hold back Mercosur's future development. Despite these problems, trade between its four members increased by an average of 27 per cent a year between 1990 and 1995.[7]

Groups of smaller nations have formed trade blocs in Central America and the Caribbean. The Central American Common Market (CACM), including Costa Rica, Guatemala, Honduras, El Salvador, Nicaragua (and Panama as a looser member), has achieved some tariff reductions and the removal of other trade barriers. Progress tends to be slow and uncoordinated, but even this is a step forward for an often inward-looking region which has suffered armed conflict and natural disasters in recent years. Fourteen English-speaking Caribbean and neighbouring countries belong to the Caribbean Community (Caricom).[8] Caricom is reducing internal tariffs and has now established a common external tariff. Fearing a loss of markets in the USA and Canada after Mexico's entry into NAFTA, Caricom has also accelerated its preparations for the creation of a common market. Measures already taken include the convertibility of its member currencies and the deregulation of air transport, though integration is difficult in this dispersed group of tiny nations.

Discussions have also been held between various regional groups in the Americas to form wider free trade areas. The most ambitious of these is the agreement to establish a Free Trade Area of the Americas (FTAA) by 2005. If the reality matches the enthusiasm of some of its participants, the FTAA will incorporate all the countries of the hemisphere except Cuba into a single trading area. Two other significant possibilities are free trade areas between the USA and the EU (the so-called New Transatlantic Marketplace) and between Mercosur and the EU. Unlike the other two initiatives, a US–EU trading area combines countries at similar stages of development, but in practice each of these proposals is likely be difficult to implement.

7.4.4 Asia and the Pacific Rim

The most prominent regional grouping in Asia is the Association of South-East Asian Nations (ASEAN). Established with the support of the USA in 1967, ASEAN now includes most of the countries of South-East Asia. The original five members, Indonesia, Malaysia, Philippines, Singapore, and Thailand, have been joined by Brunei (1984), Vietnam (1995), and by Burma[9] and Laos (1997). Cambodia was to have joined at the same time as Burma and Laos, but the country's rehabilitation after the 'killing fields' of Pol Pot and the Khmer Rouge (1975 and 1978) now appears to be in doubt. Despite Cambodia's absence, the inclusion of Vietnam, with its communist regime, and Burma, with its military dictatorship, is a significant development. Burma's entry, in particular, met with opposition from the USA and the EU over the issue of human rights.

The significance of this grouping is not limited to its varied membership, however. Not only does it encompass almost the whole of South-East Asia, with a population of around 483 millions in 1996, it also contains several of the so-called Asian 'tiger economies' (most of which have suffered in the Asian financial crisis). Its member nations lie close to the sea lanes between Europe and China and Japan, and ASEAN is sometimes seen as a political counterweight to China's dominance in the region. Despite their political, economic, and cultural diversity, these countries are close neighbours. They recognize their mutual need to promote the region's development, whilst generally preferring to respect each other's independence in internal politics. The group's members have agreed to reduce tariffs on most goods to below 5 per cent by 2003 (with ten-year phasing-in periods for the newer members). The ASEAN Free Trade Area (AFTA) has already contributed towards an increase in intra-ASEAN trade from $27 billion in 1990 to more than $70 billion in 1996.[10]

Perhaps the most intriguing regional grouping is Asia-Pacific Economic Cooperation (APEC), which has members on both sides of the Pacific Basin. This is a much looser economic grouping but it is unique for the variety of its members, the huge differences in their economies and stage of development, and for the juxtaposition of almost every type of system along the political spectrum (see Table 7.3). Its eighteen members were joined by Peru, Russia, and Vietnam in November 1998. In the 1991 Seoul Declaration, APEC members agreed to work towards liberalization of the flow of goods, services, capital, and technology. They later firmed up this commitment by agreeing to free trade among their industrialized members by 2010 and among their developing ones by 2020. In practice, the actions of APEC's members have not yet

Table 7.3 Key data on APEC members

	Population millions (July 1998 est.)	Gross domestic product[a] $US bn. (1997 est.)	Gross domestic product[a] per cap. $US (1997 est.)
Australia	18.6	394	21,400
Brunei	0.3	5	18,000
Canada	30.7	658	21,700
Chile	14.8	169	11,600
China	1,236.9	4,250	3,460
Hong Kong, China	6.7	175	26,800
Indonesia	212.9	960	4,600
Japan	125.9	3,080	24,500
Malaysia	20.9	227	11,100
Mexico	98.6	694	7,700
New Zealand	3.6	63	17,700
Papua New Guinea	4.6	12	2,650
Philippines	77.7	244	3,200
Singapore	3.5	85	24,600
South Korea	46.4	631	13,700
Taiwan	21.9	308	14,200
Thailand	60.0	525	8,800
USA	270.3	8,083	30,200

[a] GDP figures are estimated on a purchasing power parity basis.

Source: CIA World Factbook, 1998.

matched their ambitions and some of its members have done little more than reaffirm their existing commitments under GATT. Potentially, however, this group could have far-reaching implications for trade and investment around the Pacific Rim.

7.4.5 Africa and the Middle East

Economic development in Africa and the Middle East has generally lagged behind development in Asia and Latin America. The countries of North Africa and the Middle East belong to various groupings with common political, religious, or economic affiliations but attempts to create formal trade links in this region have been limited. The region's development was the subject of the Middle East and North Africa economic summit, held in October 1995, but more tangible progress was made at the EU–Mediterranean conference the following month. The Barcelona Declaration, as it is known, produced an agreement between the EU and twelve of its southern-rim Mediterranean neighbours to work towards a 'Euro-Med' free trade area in non-agricultural products by 2010, together with aid and other measures to promote economic growth in the region (see Chapter 17 for further comment on this agreement). While many of these nations have a shared Muslim heritage, they are diverse countries often divided by regional conflict or torn by internal strife.

On the face of things, other parts of Africa have been more successful in creating regional economic groupings. Many of these trade blocs have had limited success, however. Among the more lasting examples of regional cooperation have been the Southern African Customs Union (SACU) and the fourteen-member CFA Franc Zone (a currency union with the French franc),[11] both of which are remnants of a colonial past. The Economic Community of West African States (ECOWAS), formed in 1975, includes all sixteen countries of West Africa and has removed a number of trade barriers in preparation for an eventual customs union. The Preferential Trade Area (PTA) of twenty Southern and East African states was set up in 1984 to promote economic cooperation and trade liberalization. In 1993 members of the PTA established the Common Market for East and Southern Africa (COMESA) with more ambitious aims for a common market by 2000. Kenya, Tanzania, and Uganda (all members of the PTA and COMESA) took this a step further in 1996 by establishing East Africa Cooperation (EAC) to promote further economic integration and cooperation in key economic projects. Despite numerous integration initiatives in Africa, progress has often been held back by political instability and the huge economic and social problems facing this continent. Relatively little foreign direct investment has been attracted into its trading areas, though there are signs of progress in a few African countries (see Chapter 9).

7.5 Regional Integration and Globalization

IT is clear from several of the above examples that regional economic groupings tend to promote increased trade between their members. They also have implications for competition, the organization of industries and firms, and for investment flows between members, among other things. What is less clear is the extent to which they promote or inhibit trade and investment between their members and the rest of the world. Some critics claim that these trading areas favour internal trade at the expense of external trade. This trade diversion encourages inefficient production and specialization where there is only an artificial comparative advantage. Trade blocs are second best to the ideal solution of global free trade. Indeed, the 'theory of the second best' suggests that partial or regional free trade may not be a good alternative to complete free trade.[12] Thus, the critics claim, the creation of regional trading areas restricts the growth of world trade and hinders the World Trade Organization in its efforts to promote global free trade.

Certainly, there is growing evidence that these trading areas attract inward investment. One explanation for this is that companies are trying to circumvent external trade barriers. These barriers may be high tariffs, as in the case of Mercosur or on certain products entering the EU, they may be quotas or voluntary export restraints such as those on Japanese motor and electronic imports into the EU, but they may also include a wide range of restrictions on the operation of services, the local content of products, and many other aspects of trade. Another reason for the growth of inward investment is that companies recognize the opportunities offered by a large internal market and see a number of advantages in being established within the market. Access to local design and marketing skills, familiarity with the local culture, and having a local presence are all important in opening up market opportunities.

Clearly, if regional economic groupings erect high external barriers, they are likely to hinder and distort trade. Barriers are sometimes subtle and difficult to detect. There is therefore a need to encourage greater transparency and openness to external trade. Alternatively, it may be argued that trade blocs act as a stepping stone to global free trade. Fifty years' experience of GATT suggests that complete free trade can, at best, only be achieved in a piecemeal way. Some trading areas have achieved much more rapid progress within their own region. It is also common for trade blocs to expand and take in new members and to explore links with neighbouring or more distant trade blocs; examples of both these trends are given above. It may be the case therefore that, if protectionist tendencies can be restrained, regional economic groupings are a useful step in the direction of trade liberalization. Politically, they can sometimes marshal more bargaining power than their individual members, but even this can be beneficial if they use it to support open trade policies.

7.6 **Summary**

THERE has been a proliferation of regional economic groupings or trade blocs around the world in recent years. They have therefore become an important part of the international business environment. Regional integration can exist at various different levels. A preferential trading agreement is a loose kind of economic integration, usually between developed and developing countries. Levels of formal economic integration include a free trade area (where internal tariffs are removed), a customs union (which also has a common external tariff), a common market (where non-tariff barriers to the free movement of goods, services, people, and capital are removed), and an economic union (involving the harmonization of fiscal, monetary, and other economic policies). Some element of political integration tends to accompany economic integration, but political union involves common policy-making and shared political institutions or, in its complete form, the unification of independent nations. Economic integration can have a number of effects. These include trade creation and diversion, price reductions and increased competition, the opportunity for greater economies of scale, and the dynamic effects on efficiency, investment, and innovation. Economic integration may also lead to closer political integration. Important regional groupings, which have achieved various levels of integration, include the EU, NAFTA, APEC, ASEAN, and Mercosur. Whilst it is clear that these regional groupings have stimulated trade and other economic activity within their trading areas, there is less agreement on whether they are beneficial for global free trade.

Review Questions

1 What is the difference between a free trade area, a customs union, a common market, and an economic union? Which of these terms most closely describes the EU?

2 What is meant by trade creation and trade diversion? What other static effects may result from economic integration?

3 What is meant by the dynamic effects of economic integration?

4 What are the major regional economic groupings in North and South America and how do they differ in terms of the level of integration reached?

5 What type of integration is APEC working towards? What difficulties will have to be surmounted before its aims can be achieved?

Study Topic: Regional vs. Global Free Trade

The formation of a trade bloc frequently raises fears of protectionism against outsiders. This was certainly the case when the EU set about establishing its single market during the mid-1980s. Indeed, claims of 'Fortress Europe' sometimes ring true when individual member states argue for import protection or anti-dumping tariffs or resort to their own trade-restricting tactics. Similar claims have been made about Mercosur's ambitious trading area in Latin America, perhaps with more justification as Mercosur's external tariffs are quite high. In the case of NAFTA, the main criticisms have come from within, from those who claim that US firms will migrate to Mexico in search of lower labour costs. The Pacific Rim's embrionic trading area, APEC, is perhaps too diverse to be seen as an imminent threat to outsiders, but even here Europeans have expressed fears of being left out as the USA formalizes its links with the Asia-Pacific region.

There is certainly evidence to indicate that trading areas have numerous economic effects. These include trade creation and diversion, increased efficiency from economies of scale and industrial relocation, industrial consolidation in the form of mergers and acquisitions, and a number of other effects. Many of these effects are beneficial for consumers and society's economic welfare. Whether they help to promote world trade generally as they expand their membership and exercise their collective economic influence or whether they tend to be inward-looking and protectionist is a more open question. Indeed, some would argue that trading areas between unequal partners, with different economies and different policies, are not always beneficial for their own members. In practice, however, there is little sign of slowdown in the growth of regional economic groupings.

Study topic discussion questions

1 Why do the members of regional economic groupings sometimes have a tendency to be protectionist towards outsiders? Is protectionism in their own economic interests?

2 Have the developing countries of Mercosur more grounds for protecting their external frontiers than the developed countries of the EU?

3 Some Americans fear the adverse effect of NAFTA on their domestic employment. Do you think these fears are justified?

4 Are the Europeans right to fear being left out of the Asia-Pacific region?

5 Do you regard regional economic groupings as a stepping stone or a hindrance to global free trade?

Notes

1 J. Viner, 'The customs union issue' (1950), in R. Robson, (ed.), *International Economic Integration* (Penguin, 1972), 31–47.

2 Ibid.

3 P. Cecchini, *The European Challenge: 1992: The Benefit of a Single Market* (Wildwood House, Aldershot, 1988).

4 Ibid.

5 'Trade: GATT at 50', *The Economist* (16 May 1998).

6 Preamble to the Treaty of Rome.

7 *Financial Times Survey: Mercosur* (4 Feb. 1997).

8 Caricom includes Antigua and Barbuda, Bahamas, Barbados, Dominica, Granada, Jamaica, Monserrat, Trinidad and Tobago, St Kitts-Nevis, St Lucia, St Vincent and the Grenadines, and also the South American states of Guyana and Surinam and the Central American state of Belize.

9 Burma is now officially known as Myanmar.

10 'Asean agrees to Burma's membership', *Financial Times* (2 June 1997).

11 The members of the CFA (Communauté Financière Africaine) Franc Zone are: Benin, Burkina Faso, Cameroon, Central African Republic, Chad, Comoros, Congo, Côte d'Ivoire, Gabon, Equatorial Guinea, Mali, Niger, Senegal, and Togo.

12 R. Lipsey, and K. Lancaster, 'The General Theory of Second Best', *Review of Economic Studies* (1956), 24: 11–32.

Recommended Reading

- Lanjouw, G. J., *International Trade Institutions* (Longman, 1995).
- Nevin, E., *The Economics of Europe* (Macmillan, 1990).
- Robson, P., *The Economics of International Integration* (Routledge, 1998).

Also, for up to date information on the major regional economic groupings, consult websites such as the following:

EU: http://europa.eu.int/

NAFTA: http://www.nafta.net/

ASEAN: http://www.aseansec.org/

APEC: http://www.apecsec.org.sg/

Mercosur: http://www.mercosur.org/

8

The World's Major Trading Nations

Objectives

- to indicate the relative size and significance of the world's major trading nations
- to discuss the roles played by the USA, the European Union, and Japan in the world economy
- to identify newly emerging trading nations
- to determine the impact of the activities of the major trading nations on world trade and investment and on the developing countries
- to consider the advantages and disadvantages of doing business in the USA, Western Europe, and Japan

8.1 Introduction

THE modern international business environment is dominated by a relatively small number of nations. These nations' governments take a lead in international organizations and their companies are responsible for a large share of international trade and investment. The size of a country's economic activity can be measured in various ways. Most commonly, countries are ranked according to their national income or their share of world trade (see Table 8.1). Another indicator might be the level of foreign direct investment (FDI) undertaken by their home-based MNEs; this measure is considered further in Chapter 12. Surveys of the national origin of the world's largest companies[1] or the world's largest banks,[2] for example, provide further indications of a country's economic influence.

A glance at the international trade figures in Table 8.1 reveals the predominance of

North America, Japan, and Western Europe. The USA clearly emerges as the world's largest trading nation. Germany and Japan come in second and third place. France, the UK, and Italy also rank among the leading economies, as do some of the smaller European nations. These nations are, among others, the main industrialized or developed economies. They are also, despite the inclusion of Japan, sometimes described as the 'West', a description which reflects their allegiance to open market capitalism as well their antagonism towards communism during the Cold War years. It is interesting to note, however, that these countries have now been joined by South Korea, an emerging industrial power, and by China, a vast developing country with a strict communist regime and an emerging market sector. Before the recent turmoil in Asian financial markets, the World Bank estimated, on the basis of previous growth trends, that Asia would be the home of four of the world's five leading economies by the year 2020.[3] What is clear, historically, is that the relative economic (and political) position of countries changes over time.

There are various reasons for studying these major trading nations. Firstly, their MNEs tend to dominate trade and investment and are the power behind many economic developments around the world. The growth of the major economies may be attributed to many factors, including the activities of innumerable small and medium-sized enterprises as well as large corporations. However, the vast increase in international trade since World War II and the waves of FDI flowing into South-East Asia, Latin America, and Eastern Europe during the 1990s are, in no small part, a consequence of the activities of the world's major companies. Secondly, the governments of the major trading nations tend to have a powerful influence over international policy through bodies like the UN, IMF, and G7 (see Chapter 6). This begs the question as to whether they influence policy for good or bad. Certainly, Western free market thinking has become the predominant force behind the main policies of the IMF, World Bank, and WTO. It may also be argued that this influence, as well as the activities of Western MNEs, has allowed Western culture to permeate many parts of the world. Thirdly, we may ask why these countries and their companies have come to dominate international business. The answer to this question will enable us to identify some of the factors which lead to economic success and to evaluate the prospects of newly emerging economic powers. By studying the major trading nations we hope to shed light on these issues and also to consider the practical implications of doing business in these countries.

Table 8.1 Leading exporters and importers in world merchandise trade, 1997

($bn. and percentage)

Rank	Exporters	Value	Share	Rank	Importers	Value	Share
1	USA	688.7	12.6	1	USA	899.0	16.0
2	Germany	511.7	9.4	2	Germany	441.5	7.8
3	Japan	421.1	7.7	3	Japan	338.8	6.0
4	France	289.5	5.3	4	UK	308.2	5.5
5	UK	281.6	5.2	5	France	268.4	4.8
6	Italy	238.2	4.4	6	Hong Kong[b]	213.3	3.8
7	Canada	214.4	3.9	7	Italy	208.1	3.7
8	Netherlands	193.8	3.5	8	Canada	200.9	3.6
9	Hong Kong[a]	188.2	3.4	9	Netherlands	177.2	3.1
10	China	182.7	3.3	10	Belgium-Lux	155.8	2.8
11	Belgium-Lux.	168.2	3.1	11	Rep. of Korea	144.6	2.6
12	Rep. of Korea	136.2	2.5	12	China	142.4	2.5

[a] Includes re-exports.
[b] Includes imports for re-export.

Source: World Trade Organization Annual Report 1998, *International Trade Statistics*, table 1.5, reproduced with permission of the World Trade Organization.

8.2 World Economic Leadership and the Triad Nations

8.2.1 The triad or trade triangle

In recent years international trade, investment, and finance has been dominated by North America, Western Europe, and Japan. These three groups of countries are sometimes viewed as representing the points of a triangle, figuratively if not geographically. The terms 'trade triangle' or 'triad' have therefore been used to describe them. A similar approach has been taken by the Trilateral Commission in the USA, a body set up in 1973 to secure a partnership between these three groups of nations with the objective of promoting Western capitalism and a stable world order based on Western economic values. The term 'trilateralism' has also been used in this context. The triad nations represent the dominant world economic order. The USA, of course, represents dominance in political and military affairs as well, but the world order in these spheres contains a different balance of players. However, since the triad nations are the world's largest economies, they are also important as potential markets and locations for investment as well as engines of the world economy.

A closer look at the major triad nations will help us to understand the reasons for their pre-eminence in international economic activity. In general terms, they share a free market view of the world, but the degree of openness of their economies varies considerably, as do their economic institutions, history, and culture. There is now a growing awareness that the performance of an economy is influenced by these factors, as well as by the role played by government, the legal framework, and the incentive structures provided by property rights and other market mechanisms.[4] The following discussion of individual countries or regions will highlight both the similarities and the differences between the triad nations. It will also focus on some of the newer economic powers and consider whether the world economic order is changing.

8.2.2 US leadership in the world economy

US hegemony in international affairs has been reaffirmed since the collapse of the Soviet Union in 1991. The USA joined the ranks of the great powers, at first through industrial success, during the nineteenth century. However, its position as one of the two great powers, alongside the Soviet Union, was consolidated at the end of World War II as France, Germany, and Japan emerged with their economies in ruins. Britain, although still influential in world affairs, had already seen its influence diminishing. The Soviet Union always carried more influence because of its military strength and its political control in Eastern Europe than for the economic performance of its industries. The events in Eastern Europe and the former Soviet Union since 1989 have left the USA alone as a world power, though Japan and Germany have re-emerged as powerful economies and China is often seen as an emerging, if unpredictable, political force. Russia may also re-emerge as a great power if it can return to political and economic stability.

Whether US political hegemony will continue is a matter of debate, but its companies consistently dominate international business. Their numerical superiority is beyond dispute. Seventeen of the world's fifty largest companies had their home base in the USA in 1998.[5] Their superiority has also extended to labour productivity and profitability, two key measures of industrial performance. US companies have outperformed their Japanese and German counterparts in reducing unit labour costs since the late 1980s and in increasing their return on capital employed since 1970.[6] Companies like Coca-Cola, McDonald's, Ford, Boeing, and Microsoft have become household names around the world.

The USA has not only the world's largest single economy but also the most competitive internal market. Its economy has been built on the free market principle, with relatively less government intervention than most other national markets. Whilst non-intervention has not always precluded a tendency towards defensive import protection, the USA is regarded as having one of the most flexible internal markets. It has also been a supporter of multilateral free trade through GATT and the WTO. The US economy has been described as the prime example of the so-called Anglo-Saxon model. Other examples include the British economy, especially since 1979, and the New Zealand economy since 1984. The Anglo-Saxon model represents a free market or laissez-faire economy where government economic intervention is confined largely to cautious fiscal and monetary policy and where individual freedoms take priority over collective action; this view of society is sometimes described as liberalism. However, liberalism in the Anglo-Saxon model balances individual freedom against individual moral responsibility and stresses the importance of property rights in establishing the ground rules of the market system. Society tends to be 'atomistic'—organized predominantly around individuals, the non-extended family, and other groups of individuals with common interests. The model is often characterized by policies of privatization, deregulation, labour market flexibility, and by independence and competition between firms and other economic agents.

The Anglo-Saxon model, or more particularly its US version, has been in the ascendant during the 1980s and 1990s, dominating the aid policies of the IMF and World Bank and the trade policies of the WTO. It has also influenced many of the debates on EU economic policy, especially the arguments for flexible labour markets in an integrated European economy.

8.2.3 An emerging world role for the European Union

The EU contains six of the world's twelve largest trading nations: Germany, France, the UK, Italy, the Netherlands, and Belgium. Four of these countries are also members of G7 and two of them (France and the UK) are permanent members of the UN security council. Whilst membership of the UN security council reflects a historical rather than a current position of world influence, some of the EU's individual members clearly still carry considerable economic weight. The sum total of their individual influence has generally outweighed the EU's collective influence, however.

Companies based in the EU represented ten of the world's fifty largest companies in 1998. Whilst not generally rivalling the pre-eminence of the leading US companies, firms like Shell, BP, Volkswagen, Unilever, and Siemens are achieving something approaching a global presence. Whereas US companies dominate a wide range of industries, European strengths lie more particularly in industries such as petrochemicals, pharmaceuticals, banking, and, despite European fears of Japanese dominance, in motor manufacturing. European countries also have strengths in scientific research and innovation. In a survey of the average number of worldwide citations for scientific papers between 1981 and 1990, seven European countries ranked among the top eight countries, with Switzerland (a non-EU member) and Sweden coming first and second.[7] The USA came third, but Japan, with its high-technology industries, ranked fifteenth. By contrast, Japan and the USA have been more successful in the commercial development of innovations.

The reasons for Europe's relatively weaker industrial performance, despite its reputation for creativity, are complex and the subject of much debate. However, compared with the USA and Japan, Europe contains a group of separate nation states, each with its own distinctive culture, institutions, and industrial structure. An attempt is made in Sections 8.4.2 and 8.4.3 below to analyse these cultural and economic differences in terms of a European model, though no single model fully captures this diversity. Yet, as the EU has increased in size and become more politically and economically integrated, its influence in world trade issues has increased. Foreign investors also see the EU as an attractive location. The Single European Market has acted as a magnet for FDI from North America and East Asia in particular. The EU's influence has not yet translated into much success in foreign policy issues, but the reasons for this are discussed in Chapter 17.

8.2.4 The Rise of Japan

Japan had become an economic power by the beginning of the twentieth century, but its more recent resurgence as one of the world's two or three leading economies has been a post-World War II phenomenon. More than any other country, Japan is dependent upon a liberal world trade order. This is because Japan has to import most of its raw materials and relies on foreign markets for the sale of its industrial products. Recognizing this dependence, Japanese governments have encouraged exporters and channelled resources into particular industries which have export potential—industries like motor manufacturing, electronics, and computing. On the other hand, they have also adopted more restrictive policies towards imports and foreign investment, favouring imports of necessary raw materials but not competitor products, allowing inward investment but discouraging foreign control of Japanese companies. Import barriers are not, as often supposed, the result of excessive tariffs but rather a consequence of the plethora of regulations, testing procedures, and complex distribution systems in Japan. These restrictions and procedures are faced by Japanese companies as well as foreign ones but the Japanese are used to dealing with them and their companies are an integral part of the complex network of distribution.

Japanese governments have tended to adopt supportive policies towards their industry. In particular, the Ministry of International Trade and Industry (MITI) has helped to shape the country's industrial structure, by directing resources, overseeing the distribution of credit, and promoting networks of companies, in order to maximize the country's advantage in international trade. Partly as a result of this policy and also because of Japanese success in creating high-quality technological products, Japan has become not only a major trading nation but also one of the main direct investors in the USA, Western Europe, China, and the South-East Asian region. Companies like Toyota, Mitsubishi, Fuji, Yamaha, and Sony have become established international names. The company networks (or *keiretsu*) for which Japan is famous, link manufacturing, distribution, and finance companies to their mutual advantage (see Box 8.1). Japanese society is characterized by close relationships between government and industry, between companies, and between management and labour. Traditionally, large Japanese companies have provided lifetime employment for their more valued employees in return for lifetime loyalty. Job mobility between companies is much less common than in North America or Western Europe. Many workers do not have lifetime employment, however, including those who work in the large number of small and medium-sized firms throughout the Japanese economy.

These characteristics of Japanese society and the Japanese economy describe what might be called the Japanese or East Asian model. The latter term may be preferable given that it also offers a reasonable model for South Korea and other countries of the region. The East Asian model incorporates a liberal view of international trade and free enterprise, but also represents a more authoritarian, close-knit, and highly regulated view of society where the collective good supersedes individual freedom. Japanese companies typically establish clusters of suppliers when they set up plants abroad; this practice also enables them to keep close checks on the quality of supplies and to facilitate their just-in-time approach to production, keeping stock levels of parts, work-in-progress, and finished goods to a minimum. Their emphasis on quality in all aspects of production is typified by the Japanese concept of *kaizen*, the practice of involving all employees in the search for continuous improvement. This pursuit of quality, increasingly copied by American and European companies, has become known as *total quality management*. Despite their hierarchical structure, Japanese companies encourage a more participative and consensus approach to management than their American and European counterparts.

Japan has enjoyed enormous industrial success during the post-war years, though this success has not been matched by commensurate political influence. Japan is a major participant in G7/G8 and the OECD but its influence in international organizations generally has not reflected its economic strength. This may result partly from a lack of self-confidence after wartime defeat, a period of post-war American occupation, and the loss of its empire in East Asia. It may also reflect a natural sense of isolation. Japan is geographically as well as culturally isolated from the other industrial powers and is also separated from its main markets and sources of raw materials. However, as the biggest investor in the neighbouring countries of South-East Asia, Japan is now being encouraged to play a leadership role in the region's development. Despite Japan's seemingly inexorable rise as an industrial nation, the Asian financial crisis of the late 1990s has cast some doubt on the country's economic stability and on some of the policies adopted by the Japanese government. In particular, several of Japan's leading financial institutions appear to be unstable, with large portfolios of loans which are commercially imprudent. This may represent the down-side of Japan's reliance on close relationships between government and companies; this issue is discussed further in Chapter 9 in relation to the Asian financial crisis as a whole.

8.2.5 The emergence of new economic powers

A number of countries have experienced rapid economic development in recent years, especially in the South-East Asian region. Some, like Hong Kong (now under Chinese sovereignty), and Singapore, have well-developed industrial sectors but are

Box 8.1 Fuyo: A Japanese *Keiretsu*

The Japanese economy is dominated by a number of large industrial groupings or networks, known as *keiretsu*. Fuyo is one of six horizontal *keiretsu*, where companies from various industries are centred on a bank. The others are Dai Ichi Kangyo, Mitsui, Mitsubishi, Sanwa, and Sumitomo. Fuyo has twenty-seven member companies, including Fuji Bank, Nissan Motor, Nippon Paper, NKK (iron and steel), Hitachi, Canon (electrical/electronics), and Marubeni (trading). Some of its members are large multi-national companies in their own right. The *keiretsu* are the successors to Japan's pre-war *zaibatsu*—huge powerful conglomerates—though Fuyo is a looser grouping than some of the others, based on a few smaller *zaibatsu*. There are also thirty-nine vertical *keiretsu* such as Toyota, formed around industrial groups and their subsidiaries. In some industries, a convoy system operated, cutting across the *keiretsu*; for example, major Japanese motor companies like Toyota, Nissan, and Honda expanded abroad in step with each other, with similar techniques and product ranges.

   Keiretsu are mutual support groups with interlocking shareholdings, providing low-cost finance, protected markets, and other forms of cooperation between their members. Their existence has also allowed governments to implement their industrial policies through cooperative channels, but has made market entry by foreign firms more difficult. The *keiretsu* fell victim to the Asian financial crisis and problems in the Japanese economy during the late 1990s. Many of Fuyo's members are laden with debts, including Fuji Bank, its core member; and another member, Yamaichi Securities, has been allowed to go bankrupt. What were once close relationships are now becoming looser as the financial crisis and the competitive global market close in.

too small to translate their industrial success into economic power. For example, Hong Kong is a major trading nation but about 85 per cent of its exports in 1997 were goods which had been imported and then re-exported. Others, like Malaysia or Indonesia, have the potential to become major industrial nations but are still in the process of economic development. India's economy has also recorded high rates of growth. These countries are discussed more extensively in Chapter 9. However, two new economic powers appear to be emerging: South Korea and China. Both countries ranked among the top twelve trading nations in 1997.

Box 8.2 South Korea: An Emerging Economic Power

South Korea has been following in Japan's economic footsteps since the 1960s. Samsung, Hyundai, Daewoo, and other leading Korean companies can be found among the major investors in the USA, the UK, and other parts of Europe. Daewoo was the largest single investor in Eastern Europe during the 1990s. The South Korean government started to invest heavily in the country's infrastructure from the mid-1960s and began to promote export industries and encourage foreign investors. Like Japan, Korea's experience combines private enterprise with active government intervention, supported by a high standard of education and close relationships between government, financial institutions, and industry.

A particular feature of the Korean economy is the dominant position occupied by the industrial conglomerates or *chaebol*—huge companies with subsidiaries in numerous industries. Some of these *chaebol* dominate Korea's overseas investment as well as its domestic economy.[8] A more extensive analysis of the rapid economic development of Asia's 'tiger economies' appears in Chapter 9. What is intriguing about South Korea is that an annual growth rate of about 8 per cent was sustained over a period approaching thirty-five years. Indeed, in 1996, South Korea's income per capita crossed the line between 'middle-income' and 'high-income' countries in the World Bank's classification system (and Korea was subsequently accepted as a member of the OECD).

8.3 The Major Trading Nations' Role in Trade and Investment

8.3.1 Patterns of trade and investment

The twelve leading trading nations were responsible for 64.3 per cent of world exports and 62.2 per cent of world imports in 1997 (see Table 8.1). In fact, almost half of total world trade was accounted for by the G7 nations (48.5 per cent of exports and 47.4 per cent of imports). These figures illustrate the importance of the major trading nations in the world trading system. Indeed, world trade as a whole has played a large part in the development of the post-war world economy. The newly industrializing economies, however, are now joining the ranks of the trading nations, not only in the export of their traditional products but increasingly in manufactured goods. By 1995, 86.9 per cent of the combined exports of Brazil, Mexico, Hong Kong, Singapore, South Korea, and Taiwan consisted of manufactured goods, for example. The major and emerging trading nations are based predominantly in the Americas, Europe, and,

> **Box 8.3** China: An Emerging Giant
>
> China fits an altogether different mould from South Korea. Since the late 1970s, and particularly under the leadership of Deng Xiaoping (the leading figure in the Chinese Communist Party, 1978–97), the Chinese government has pursued a two-track policy. The Communist Party has retained political control, whilst at the same time gradually opening up the economy to market forces. Initially, a degree of private enterprise was encouraged in agriculture. This was then extended to other sectors during the 1980s and 1990s. The government has supported the growth of export industries and allowed joint ventures and other forms of foreign investment in selected industries, especially in the designated 'special economic zones' in the eastern and south-eastern provinces of China. State enterprises are being privatized, shareholding systems and stock markets are being developed, financial markets are being deregulated, and state banks commercialized, allowing them to perform a more active role in company financing. Centralized state control is gradually being replaced by local autonomy.
>
> This combination of political control and market reform brought about a 10 per cent average annual growth rate in the Chinese economy between 1980 and 1995, with growth reaching almost 13 per cent at its peak. Chinese exports and imports increased from $10 billion and $11 billion in 1978 to $183 billion and $142 billion respectively in 1997. This remarkable economic progress has not been without its problems, but it has encouraged governments and business people to take China seriously as an emerging economic power.

increasingly, in Asia. Trade is, in various ways, increasing the interdependence of nations and regions and is one of the main factors contributing towards the globalization of the world economy.

The major trading nations, or rather their companies, are also the leading overseas investors. The USA, UK, Germany, France, and Japan led the field in terms of outward foreign direct investment in 1997, with US companies investing just over twice as much as their nearest rivals. The Netherlands, Spain, and other Western European countries are also major overseas investors. Whilst the level of FDI generally fluctuates more than trade from year to year, these nations have tended to be the main instigators of world FDI activity in recent years. The USA is also the largest recipient of FDI though China, and to a lesser extent Asia as a whole, has seen a huge increase in FDI inflows during the 1990s. Foreign direct investment is discussed at length in Chapter 12.

8.3.2 Implications for developing nations

The dominance of the triad nations in world economic activity clearly has an impact on the developing nations. The G7 nations, in particular the USA, have a major influence on the policy agenda of international institutions like the UN, IMF, World Bank, and WTO. Even if they do not instigate policy, they are expected to take a lead in its implementation. Thus, for example, at the Rio Earth Summit in 1992 and the Kyoto Conference on Climate Change in 1997, the USA and other industrialized nations were expected to show leadership in agreeing to reductions in greenhouse gas emissions—perhaps with some justification as they are also among the major polluters.

The triad nations also take advantage of the developing nations as a market for their products and a location for their investment. Companies from the rich nations generally have a competitive advantage in terms of productivity and technology, while the developing countries offer a low-cost environment and, in some cases, an expanding market. Low-cost production is also one of the developing countries' key advantages when selling to the industrialized nations.

It is sometimes argued that free trade benefits rich countries more than poor ones—that the WTO's free trade agenda is a conspiracy against the developing countries. To the extent that the rich countries have bigger economies and more export trade, there is some truth in this claim. Yet, poor countries also need to trade. If they are dependent on a few basic commodities, as many of them are, the only way they can pay for imports of necessities, energy, or machinery is to export their surplus production. Tariffs in the rich countries simply make their task more difficult. Tariffs in the poorer countries provide a competitive shield in a few sectors but also increase the cost of imported goods for their struggling population and the cost of inputs for their struggling industries. China, South Korea, Hong Kong, Singapore, and Taiwan are all examples of countries whose economic development has benefited from greater openness to trade. Whilst this trade has not always been free, it may be argued that trade barriers are beginning to act as a brake on future development in some of these countries. This issue is discussed further in Chapter 9.

FDI also offers mutual benefits, providing much-needed capital, technology, and skills for the recipient, production and marketing opportunities for the investor. But does the investor gain more from FDI than the recipient, especially where the latter is a developing country with little influence over the investor and whose political institutions, culture, workers, or environment are being compromised? This is a more complex question.

On the face of things, large multinational investors often appear to have little loyalty to their host countries, sometimes exert undue pressure on the host government, and ride roughshod over the host country's culture, labour force, or environment. This scenario applies in varying degrees, however, and sometimes not at all. Loyalty may depend on the multinational's business culture, which will vary from one company to another. Anglo-Saxon business culture is more likely to place company performance ahead of loyalty either to the home or the host country, though even here company policy varies considerably.

The extent to which a company uses its economic power to influence the political process also has a cultural dimension. Business links with government or government officials are commonplace in many countries. Once again, home and host countries may receive similar treatment, though clearly small countries may be more vulnerable to pressure than larger ones. Even where an investor is culturally sensitive, foreign investment is bound to influence the culture of the host country—both in terms of business practices and also through the product itself. China, or the countries of Eastern Europe, will never be the same again after the FDI invasion of the 1990s. Whether they will change for the better or the worse is a matter of opinion. They will certainly be different from their recent past, but will they be any less Chinese, Russian, or Polish? The impact of FDI on the host country's labour force and environment are discussed in Chapter 6. Whatever the merits of these arguments, developing countries often depend on FDI for their economic development.

8.4 Doing Business in the USA, Western Europe, and Japan

8.4.1 The USA: opportunities and threats in a competitive market

The USA is without doubt the most competitive national market in the world. In value terms, it is also the largest national market. The US economy is about twice the size of the Chinese economy, two and a half times the size of Japan's, and nearly five times that of Germany, measured on a purchasing-power parity basis. It also has the third largest population of any country, after China and India, and has a high national income per capita. These factors make the USA a much sought-after market. It consistently attracts more FDI than any other country and imports large quantities of goods of all kinds. Despite these attributes, however, the US market is not an easy one to enter. NAFTA is gradually creating free trade between the USA, Canada, and Mexico, but companies from outside this area may only trade freely within NAFTA if they observe a 50 per cent minimum local-content requirement. However, the main difficulties in entering the US market relate more to the business environment than to trade barriers.

US companies are very competitive and US consumers very demanding. Companies venturing into this market must therefore be efficient, productive, and responsive. Whilst the US population originates from many other regions of the world, the US economy has developed its own unique features. Even British companies, which share the Anglo-Saxon culture and the English language, often find the US market less similar than they had imagined. Whilst sales volumes may be large, the intensity of competition means that profit margins are often small. Mergers between European and US firms can be problematic because of differences in management style and business practices.

Americans are known for their directness, their defence of liberty and open democratic government, a strong sense of national identity, and their belief in America's destiny as an arbiter of world affairs. They are also an entrepreneurial nation, with many small and medium-sized businesses as well as large multinationals. Their business executives have a reputation for their hard-headed, professional approach and they are likely to be business school graduates. Socially, they are hospitable and have an easy manner but prefer to keep work and leisure separate.

Despite a number of common American traits, however, it may be a mistake to regard the USA as a homogeneous market. Many of the barriers which still separate EU countries are absent in the USA, but each of the different US regions has its own distinctive characteristics. Ethnic mix, language, culture, religion, social structure, and income levels vary considerably across the country. The USA is perhaps the most racially mixed country in the world. African Americans, Hispanic Americans, Irish Americans, and communities of Indians, Japanese, Chinese, Filipinos, and numerous other groups have each brought something of their culture and aspirations to modern America. From New England to New Mexico, Mississippi to Minnesota, or the Carolinas to California there are vast differences the foreign company must take into account. Even the huge distances across the country may present logistical problems. Despite these difficulties, the USA imported 16.0 per cent of the world's traded goods and received $90.7 billion of foreign direct investment in 1997. Clearly, many companies have been able to overcome the difficulties.

8.4.2 Western Europe: cultural and economic diversity

The Western European economy has become highly integrated through years of trade and investment and, more recently, through the expansion and policies of the European Union. Yet, the region has a much more overt cultural diversity than the USA. In fact, a Western European or, for that matter, a European, identity is difficult to define. During the Cold War years, Western Europe encompassed the area to the west of the Iron Curtain. The distinction between east and west, or indeed central Europe, is now less clear. Even the geographical boundary of Europe to the east has been a matter of some debate.

Western Europe, however defined, contains a variety of nation states, each different in size, culture, language, and other characteristics. Some observers speak of a European model to describe the political and economic systems in Western Europe.[9] At best, this description is an approximation and applies more closely to the northern countries of Western Europe than to the Mediterranean countries in the south. The European model is often applied to Germany, Austria, Switzerland, Belgium, the Netherlands, the Scandinavian countries and, perhaps less accurately, to France. The model is based on consensus politics and the concept of a social market economy. The desire for consensus is illustrated by the generally successful political coalitions which govern many of these countries or by the way in which industrial policy involves government, industry, and trade unions in decision-making.

The social market economy can be contrasted with the free market economy. While the latter is a laissez-faire system, leaving the economy largely to market forces, the social market involves more active government intervention. In particular, high levels of taxation are used to pay for social policy—health, education, housing, pensions, unemployment benefits, and other forms of social insurance. Social provision is generally much higher in Germany, the Netherlands, and the Scandinavian countries than it is in the USA or UK, for example. Equally, although there is some concern about the high cost of social protection, there is still a general consensus on its desirability in these countries. From a business perspective, the high social cost of employing labour increases production costs, though high productivity offsets these costs to some extent.

Clearly, the European model simplifies the picture in these countries. The Scandinavians have tended to favour high rates of taxation with correspondingly high levels of social provision. They have also invested heavily in education and research— providing the underpinning for industrial innovation as well as achieving social objectives. Political consensus has also been a cornerstone of social and industrial policy. The so-called 'negotiated economy' involves a continual dialogue between the public sector, business, institutional investors, trade unions, and other interested groups. The Scandinavian model is a term sometimes used to describe these distinctive features.

Germany seems to characterize the mainstream European model, though here again there are many distinctive features. Germany has a devolved or federal system of government. Its *Bundesländer* (federal states) have considerable powers and its major institutions, including the Bundesbank (the German central bank), have clearly defined roles, independent of government. Germany has a highly developed social security system and places a strong emphasis on education and vocational training. A particular feature of German industrial relations is the participation of workers in company decision-making under the policy of co-determination or *Mitbestimmung*. The Dutch and Belgians have generally followed a similar path, though since the mid-1980s Dutch governments have adopted austerity measures aimed at reducing their large public sector. Belgium and the Netherlands are also among the most open economies in the world, reflecting their historical dependence on trade.

France has the second biggest economy in the EU, after Germany, and the Franco-German alliance provides one of the central political pillars of the EU. However, the French and German political and economic systems are less similar than might at first appear. France has a more centralized system of government and its president has considerable powers. There are also closer links between public administrators and industrialists than is the case in other European countries. French governments have generally favoured a more active role in economic development—known as indicative economic planning or *dirigisme*.

The southern states of the EU are more difficult to characterize. Italy has one of the EU's advanced economies, in contrast to its succession of unstable coalition governments. Spain has achieved some success in restructuring its economy since its return to democracy in 1978. Along with Portugal and Greece, Spain is one of the EU's less

Box 8.4 Western Europe's SMEs

Large multinational enterprises (MNEs) are often the dominant players in international business. This fact should not obscure the important role played by small and medium-sized enterprises (SMEs). SMEs employ most of the working population in most countries of the world, though their share of output is normally smaller. They also form a major part of the supply chain to MNEs and some of them export a large proportion of their output, often in specialized markets. Even in Western Europe's industrialized economies, SMEs frequently predominate in agriculture, construction, a number of manufacturing industries, and especially in the service sector.

SMEs are common in all the Western European countries. The term SME is usually understood to mean firms with fewer than 500 employees, though EU enterprise policy uses 250 employees as the cut-off point. In Spain, Portugal, Greece, and Ireland, industrial development has until recently been largely based on SMEs, with the exception of certain industries such as steel, shipping, shipbuilding, and paper and pulp processing. These countries now play host to a number of foreign MNEs, but SMEs are still the most important source of employment. In Scandinavia, manufacturing industries are generally dominated by SMEs, though there has been a shift from small to medium-sized firms in recent years. Denmark, for example, has become more internationally oriented during the 1990s, but many of its companies are still small by international standards. Despite lacking size, Danish companies have gained a reputation for their niche products.

Unexpectedly, the share of manufacturing employment in SMEs in both Britain and France increased during the 1980s. This may be partly explained by favourable government policies and partly by a decline in employment in large manufacturing companies. Even in Germany, where a number of large companies have achieved international prominence, small and medium-sized companies (known as the *Mittelstand*) play an important role in many industries.

However, perhaps the most intriguing example of large-scale employment in SMEs in Western Europe is Italy. Even at the height of Italy's post-war industrial development, the growth of small firms, especially those with fewer than fifty employees, outstripped the growth of larger firms. Many of these small firms are in traditional, less technologically advanced industries or are suppliers or subcontractors to larger firms, but a particular feature is the integrated systems of small firms sharing external economies of scale which can be found in most of Italy's industrial regions.[10] In a variety of ways therefore, SMEs contribute a great deal to the economies of Western Europe.

developed countries. Despite numerous differences, the southern economies tend to have large agricultural sectors, a preponderance of small and medium-sized firms, and high levels of government support for industry. However the Western European economies are categorized, they have nevertheless become a huge market for industrial and consumer goods. EU integration and global competition are also putting pressure on European governments to privatize and deregulate their economies, control their government expenditure, and reduce the non-wage costs of labour.

8.4.3 Japan: assessing the complexities of Japanese business and markets

Japan is a country of contrasts. Its economic growth rate has been higher than any other industrialized nation since the 1950s. It has achieved industrial prowess in computers, electronics, robotics, and other advanced technologies. Several of the world's largest banks are Japanese. Its management practices have been copied by many leading MNEs. The Japanese workforce is highly educated and motivated. Its people have a high savings rate and its companies invest far more in research and development and take a longer-term perspective than their American or European counterparts. The post-war 'Japanese economic miracle' has been admired and analysed by industrialized and industrializing nations alike. Yet, Japan has few natural resources and an ageing population. Its rigid economic system enabled the authorities to direct resources into priority industries but it is becoming a constraint now that the economy has slowed down. A number of economic weaknesses have also become evident during the 1990s. Its banks have grown too big on the strength of large high-risk lending. Financial market supervision is weak. Other industries, such as agriculture and retailing, are inefficient and lag far behind the high-performing sectors.

This contrasting picture presents an enigma for the would-be foreign exporter or investor. On the one hand, Japan has a large high-income economy, a highly sophisticated consumer market, and a skilled workforce. On the other hand, its plethora of regulations, complex testing procedures, and intricate distribution networks make its markets difficult to enter. Although Japanese companies are major investors abroad, inward foreign direct investment into Japan is tiny by comparison with the USA or the UK.[11] Foreign companies have to do careful research and may incur heavy additional costs when venturing into Japan, though Japanese consumers have acquired a taste for quality foreign goods.

Japan suffered a severe economic recession during the 1990s, exacerbated by the Asian financial crisis of the late 1990s. Its economic expansion had seemed unstoppable in the 1980s. The Japanese government is now trying to tackle some of the problems discussed above. The US and EU authorities, as well as the WTO and other organizations, are putting pressure on Japan to deregulate its economy and to become more open to international competition. However, Japan's belief in a combination of market capitalism and government intervention is deep-rooted in its history and culture. Whilst substantial economic reform may be needed, Japanese commitment to enterprise and the systematic pursuit of its objectives may yet enable it to resume its expansion path. For many foreign companies, Japan is still a largely untapped market.

8.5 Summary

World trade is dominated by a relatively few countries. These countries are the so-called triad nations of North America, Western Europe, and Japan. The USA in particular has the most powerful economy and has now assumed political leadership in international affairs. The European Union countries rival the USA in economic terms, but this strength has not yet been translated into commensurate political influence. Some of the Asian countries are now beginning to emerge as major trading nations, especially China and South Korea. The model of economic success varies in the different regions of the world. The USA has achieved considerable success with the Anglo-Saxon free market model, whereas Japan's economic power has been built on the close relationships within the East Asian model. On the other hand, the European social market model has served many of the Northern European countries well. The characteristics of these models also have a bearing on the ease with which foreign firms can enter their markets. The major trading nations have a significant impact on world trade and investment and have implications for the development of the world's poorer nations.

Review Questions

1 In what ways do the major trading nations influence the world economy and the policies of international institutions?

2 What are the main distinguishing features of the Anglo-Saxon, European, and East Asian models?

3 How would you account for the emergence of China as an economic power?

4 Does the dominance of the industrialized nations in world trade suggest that free trade is generally against the interests of the developing countries?

5 What important differences would an American business executive discover when first venturing into Japan?

Case Study: Forging Partnerships with Japanese Car Manufacturers

During the late 1990s the world motor manufacturing industry was engaged in a process of industrial consolidation. Takeovers and mergers such as BMW-Rover, Daimler-Chrysler, and Ford-Volvo were becoming increasingly common. For a number of years, the industry has been developing a network of strategic alliances, but the links are now becoming more formalized. Japanese manufacturers have participated in these alliances along with their US and European counterparts and have sometimes allowed foreign partners to take a minority shareholding under a joint-venture agreement. Until recently, however, it has been difficult to imagine a foreign company gaining a controlling interest in a Japanese company. Japanese car manufacturers were, in any case, regarded as among the industry leaders with their pioneering management and production methods and advanced productivity.

The economic slowdown and financial crisis in Japan has forced Japanese companies and the Japanese government to contemplate more lasting partnerships with foreign firms. In early 1999, the president of Mitsubishi motors announced the company's intention to seek a foreign partner on the basis of a full merger if necessary. At the same time, Nissan, Japan's second biggest motor manufacturer after Toyota, agreed an arrangement with Renault whereby the French company took a 37 per cent stake in Nissan. The two companies will share development costs and save on common purchasing but Renault does not have overall control. Both Mitsubishi and Nissan have been experiencing financial difficulties at home, with debts of around Y2,000 billion ($17.54 billion) and Y2,500 billion ($21.9 billion) respectively in February 1999, despite having successful car plants abroad. Foreign partnerships will enable them to combine their resources in developing expensive new technology and, in the case of Mitsubishi in particular, to help with company restructuring. Whether a foreign firm could be expected to take on their debt burdens as well is another question.

Why would an American or European car manufacturer want to form a partnership with a Japanese firm? There are two important reasons for wanting to do so. First, some of the major Japanese manufacturers have established an enviable reputation as technologically advanced producers with a global presence. Second, such a partnership would allow greater access to the difficult Japanese market. Nissan, for example, is the world's fifth largest car manufacturer with advanced production plants in the USA, Europe, and elsewhere and with a 20 per cent share of the Japanese market.

A number of American and European car manufacturers have already taken on board some of the production and management methods they have learned from Japanese companies. However, importing Japanese methods into a foreign company is not the same as working alongside a Japanese company, as the foreign company will have adapted the Japanese approach to suit its own internal needs and organizational culture. For Japanese firms, their production methods and management style tie in with the Japanese collective culture and elaborate network of close-knit relationships. Both Mitsubishi and Nissan, along with most other large Japanese companies, are key members of keiretsu—the Mitsubishi keiretsu, whose main lender is the Bank of Tokyo-Mitsubishi, and the Fuyo keiretsu, which includes Nissan and is headed by Fuji Bank. Moreover, Mitsubishi Heavy Industries owns nearly 30 per cent of Mitsubishi Motors, so the motor manufacturing arm is not an independent enterprise.

Foreign firms may clearly have much to gain from working with Japanese partners in their global operations. Whether such a partnership will enable them to negotiate the intricacies of the Japanese market and to marry the two cultures successfully is a more difficult question. Main sources: A. Harney, 'Mitsubishi seeks a foreign partner' and A. Barber, 'Schrempp promises decision on Nissan', *Financial Times* (16 Feb. 1999).

Case study questions

1 Why do you think Mitsubishi and Nissan now appear to have accepted the need for a merger or joint venture with a foreign car manufacturer?

2 Do you agree that the two suggested reasons for foreign firms to form a partnership with a Japanese car manufacturer provide a sufficient justification for Renault's decision to link up with Nissan?

3 What are the distinctive management and production methods employed by Japanese companies?

4 How are management styles likely to differ between US, European, and Japanese firms? How might conflicts of style be resolved?

5 Although a partnership between a foreign and a Japanese firm will allow easier access to the Japanese market, what problems is the foreign firm likely to face when attempting to use its normal marketing methods in Japan?

Notes

1 See e.g. the *Fortune Global 500* or the *Financial Times 500*.

2 *The Banker* (July 1998) lists three US banks, three Japanese banks, and one bank from each of France, Germany, the Netherlands, and the UK among the world's ten largest banks ranked by 'tier-one capital' (the core capital base of equity, retained earnings, and disclosed reserves).

3 The World Bank estimated, on the basis of pre-Asian financial crisis growth rates, that the five largest economies in 2020 would be (ranked from the largest) China, USA, Japan, India, and Indonesia.

4 See e.g. D. C. North, *Institutions, Institutional Change and Economic Performance* (Cambridge University Press, 1990).

5 *Fortune Global 500* (1998).

6 'Testing times for America', *Financial Times* (6 July 1998).

7 'Innovation: the machinery of growth', *The Economist* (11 Jan. 1992).

8 South Korea's five leading *chaebol* are Hyundai, Samsung, Daewoo, LG, and SK. There are about fifty-five *chaebol* in total and their sales represent about 50% of South Korea's GNP.

9 In an interesting and controversial book, Michel Albert describes the European model as the 'Rhine model': M. Albert, *Capitalism against Capitalism* (Whurr, 1993), trans. from the original French edition (Editions du Seuil, 1991).

10 See F. Somers, *European Community Economies: A Comparative Study* (Pitman 1994), 110–12.

11 In 1997, the USA received $90.7bn of FDI, the UK received $36.9bn, while Japan only received $3.2bn.

Recommended Reading

- Albert, M., *Capitalism against Capitalism* (Whurr, 1993), translated from the original French edn. (Editions du Seuil, 1991).
- Francks, P., *Japanese Economic Development: Theory and Practice* (Routledge, 1992).
- Hampden-Turner, C., and Trompenaars, F., *The Seven Cultures of Capitalism* (Piatkus, 1994).
- Schnitzer, M. C., *Comparative Economic Systems* (South-Western, 1994).
- Somers, F., *European Community Economies: A Comparative Study* (Pitman, 1994).
- Todaro, M. P., *Economic Development* (Addison-Wesley, 1997).

9

The Emerging Economies

Objectives

- to identify the emerging economies: the regions and countries where rapid economic development is occurring
- to examine the contribution of theories of economic development to an understanding of the growth of the emerging economies
- to identify the key determinants of the success of the emerging economies
- to analyse the problems of rapid economic growth and, in particular, the causes of the Asian financial crisis of the late 1990s
- to determine the reasons why some countries remain poor

9.1 Introduction

A remarkable feature of the world economy in the 1980s and 1990s has been the growth of the so-called 'tiger economies' of South-East Asia. These developing countries have undergone rapid industrialization and the annual growth rates of their economies have sometimes reached double figures. This expansion has not been confined to South-East Asia. Several other Asian and Latin American countries have also experienced high rates of economic growth. The speed with which some of these countries have been transforming their economies has been unprecedented in recent history. This has elicited a mixture of responses from the industrialized nations. Whilst clearly being impressed, many Western observers have also expressed fears about the competitive threat from East Asian exporters. Some have even speculated about a coming 'Asian century', replacing the American dominance of the twentieth century. Certainly, there have been many attempts to explain the reasons for the success of these emerging economies.

Then, in the second half of 1997, the Asian financial crisis began to emerge. Most of the 'tiger economies' slowed down significantly in 1998. Almost immediately, a chorus of critics were questioning the basis of their economic success and describing their 'economic miracle' as illusory. Whilst it is difficult to take a balanced view of these events as they are taking place, this chapter attempts to analyse the reasons for the rapid development of the emerging economies and also to point to possible explanations for the recent setback. The causes and consequences of economic development are among the most intriguing issues in international business. We also attempt to explain why some developing countries lag behind.

Throughout this chapter we use the term 'emerging economies' to describe the countries concerned. Clearly, they are 'developing countries', but they are developing at a faster rate than many of the world's other developing countries. A more common term for the fast developers is 'newly industrializing countries' (NICs), but this term does not seem to convey the significance of their emergence from economic backwaters to the mainstream of trade, investment, and the international economy. Nor could it be applied to the countries of Eastern Europe, which were already industrialized. 'Emerging' does not, of course, imply that most of these countries have fully emerged as major players on the world stage, rather that they have taken significant steps along that road. We begin by identifying the regions and countries where the emerging economies can be found.

9.2 The World's Emerging Economies

9.2.1 China and the 'tiger economies' of East Asia

East Asia, and South-East Asia in particular, has produced the most dramatic examples of these emerging economies. Table 9.1 illustrates the growth rates of the best-performing economies in this region. Hong Kong, Singapore, South Korea, and Taiwan, following in Japan's footsteps as the East Asian 'tiger economies', were achieving impressive growth rates by the 1980s or earlier. These were joined by China, Indonesia, Malaysia, and Thailand by the early 1990s. The fact that some of them have enjoyed sustained periods of high growth over a relatively long period suggests that their development has a firm basis, though this issue has been the subject of much debate. It is also the case that four of the economies worst affected by the Asian financial crisis (Thailand, South Korea, Indonesia, and Malaysia) are among this group.

These countries have all achieved some degree of rapid industrialization (sometimes in technological industries); they have achieved rapid expansion of overseas trade (especially within ASEAN); they have attracted large amounts of foreign investment (portfolio and direct investment); and, until the Asian financial crisis, they had generally had good records in maintaining macroeconomic stability.

9.2.2 Latin America

Emerging economies can also be found in Latin America. The situation in this region is rather different from that in East Asia, but some of the same trends can be observed, albeit with less dramatic growth rates. Economic gains were made during the 1960s and 1970s, based mainly on export revenues from commodities like oil or coffee. These gains were then reversed during the 1980s. This was a period of financial turmoil in much of Latin America. Foreign debts incurred when commodity prices were high crippled many of these economies when the terms of trade moved against them. Inflation was rampant (reaching around 1,000 per cent in Argentina) and currencies collapsed.

Since the late 1980s, however, there has been a move towards greater democracy and economic reform, especially in Mexico, Argentina, Chile, Brazil, Uruguay, and Peru. Industrialization has been slower in Latin America than in East Asia and has been more inward looking, tending to promote industry through high tariffs and import substitution rather than by creating export industries. Argentina and Brazil have attracted large amounts of foreign direct investment, creating a new foreign-owned motor manufacturing industry in Brazil, for instance. Several Latin American countries have also been actively privatizing their state industries and liberalizing their economies during the 1990s, something which is only now beginning in East Asia.

9.2.3 Eastern Europe

Because of the historic changes which have been occurring in Eastern Europe during the 1990s, this region is given extensive treatment in Chapters 18–22. However, Eastern Europe's new democracies may also be described as emerging economies. The difference here is that they are emerging from communist central planning rather than from pre-industrialization. Many Eastern European countries in fact were highly industrialized, though they have been undergoing vast privatization and other economic reform programmes. Heavy manufacturing industries dominated their economies, geared towards the markets of their neighbours in Comecon. With the exception of key industries such as defence, many of their state enterprises used out-of-date technology. Most of their enterprises were over-manned and inefficient.

By the mid-1990s, several of these countries were achieving quite high rates of economic growth. Poland's GDP was the first to recover its 1989 level, after a period of severe economic decline in the early 1990s, but most of the CEFTA members and Baltic Republics were recording annual growth rates between 4 and 10 per cent by

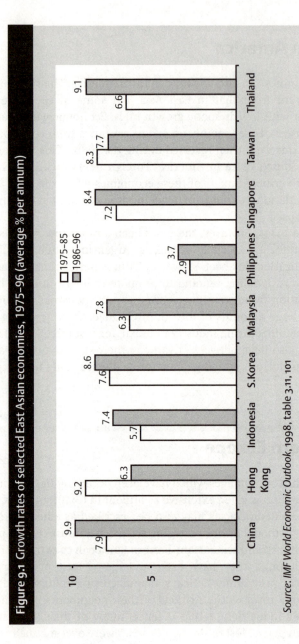

Figure 9.1 Growth rates of selected East Asian economies, 1975–96 (average % per annum)

Source: IMF World Economic Outlook, 1998, table 3.11, 101

1996 or 1997. The fast-track reform economies have been Hungary, Poland, the Czech Republic, Slovakia, and Estonia; Slovenia has also been progressing steadily. Like their Asian and Latin American counterparts, they attracted a large volume of foreign direct investment during the 1990s.

9.2.4 India and other emerging economies

A few other countries may be considered as emerging economies, mainly for their economic potential or for the steps they are taking towards economic reform. India, in particular, should be singled out. India is the world's fifth biggest economy, if its GDP is measured by the purchasing power of its domestic currency (the purchasing power parity method), but this reflects its size as the country with the world's second largest population rather than its economic performance. India is a country of contrasts. It has a large industrial sector, a pool of highly skilled labour with expertise in satellite technology, software design, and other advanced fields, and has achieved an annual growth rate as high as 7 per cent during the 1990s. On the other hand, the majority of the population are employed in subsistence agriculture and the economy remained relatively closed until recently. India has begun to move away from its state-directed policy of self-sufficiency and import substitution towards a more liberalized, export-led economy during the 1990s.

Turkey might also be considered. The country faces political and social difficulties, but its economic growth rate has accelerated during the 1990s. Participation in a customs union with the EU is a sign of its desire to join the mainstream market economies, though full EU membership seems unlikely in the near future. Other parts of the world offer only tentative examples. Although African growth rates have been rising during the 1990s, they are rising from an extremely low base and signs of economic reform have been patchy. Foreign investment in Africa has been minimal by comparison with Asia or Latin America. Protectionism is rife and the industrial infrastructure is generally poor. South Africa has the potential for renewed growth if it can rebuild itself after the apartheid years. Uganda has been attracting attention because of its ambitious economic reform programme, but these are early days. Some of the Middle Eastern and North African countries have also shown signs of economic development but the lack of political stability, either internal or external, has been a perennial constraint. Others became oil-rich when OPEC was in control of the world oil market, but they have not generally managed to develop their non-oil sectors to the same extent.

9.3 Reasons for the rapid growth of the emerging economies

9.3.1 Theories of economic development

There is no single theory which fully explains why some countries have more developed economies than others. In this section, we consider four of the main theoretical approaches which have been advanced since World War II. Each of them has been influenced by a particular ideological perspective, is the product of a particular period of recent history, or has been developed as a response to earlier ideas. They all attempt to explain the different development patterns that can be seen around the world, but there is no generally accepted 'complete theory of development'.

■ Theories of the stages of economic development

The most prominent theory to view a country's development as a series of stages is Rostow's 'Stages of Economic Development'.[1] Rostow was an economic historian who argued that countries go through five stages of economic development: the traditional society; the preconditions for take-off into self-sustaining growth; the take-off; the drive to maturity; and the age of high mass consumption. The traditional society describes not only a subsistence-level agrarian society, but also a closed, self-sufficient community with fatalistic beliefs in its inability to change its traditional ways or improve its economic well-being. The preconditions for take-off are perhaps the most interesting feature of this theory from an economic development perspective. At this stage there is a cultural or philosophical change from fatalism and determinism towards entrepreneurship and the taking of risks. Machinery begins to replace simple labour-intensive production methods, trade with other societies emerges, and business organizations are formed. The take-off stage involves investment in key manufacturing industries, increased mechanization and social migration to the towns; this stage describes what is often known as an 'industrial revolution'. During the drive to maturity a country develops new technology and produces ever more sophisticated products. The culmination is the age of high mass consumption, where living standards are high and consumer durables and services take over as the main sectors of an economy.

Rostow's stages of development should be seen as an attempt to generalize from historical experience. There are two main criticisms of the theory. First, it compares countries at different stages of development without clearly establishing the reasons for their development. Second, it is essentially based on the experience of the developed countries and takes no account of the different cultures, institutions, and political systems of countries in different parts of the world or of the interdependence of countries. Adherents of this theory tend to argue that investment is the key to take-off. The need for investment means that a country either has to save a proportion of its income or to attract aid or private capital from abroad. What causes a society to become less deterministic and more entrepreneurial is less clear.

Other theorists, whilst still focusing on the stages of development, have concentrated on the factors involved in the development process.[2] They have identified the importance of factors such as a country's endowment of resources (both human and physical), the availability of capital and technology, changing patterns of consumer demand, government policies, the external trade environment, and the decline in population growth and family size. These factors are said to determine the pattern of economic and institutional change in a particular country and hence the course of development in that country. Like Rostow, however, these theorists argue that there are identifiable patterns of growth which are broadly similar in different countries.

■ Dependency theory

Dependency theory focuses on the developing countries' dependence on the rich countries.[3] Some of its proponents approach the issue from a Marxist perspective. Others simply look for ways of enabling the poorer nations to become politically and economically independent. Many of the world's developing countries were formerly under the sovereignty of a colonial power. Often they were dependent economically as well as politically. Even when they gain independence, economic ties with their former colonial masters may be difficult to break and industries which were developed under colonial rule may have benefited the needs of the colonial power more than their own. This culture of dependency is believed to hold back their development. Indeed, some advocates of this view argue that conventional economic growth is not the desirable path for developing countries to follow. Dependence may also stem from the nature of the world political and economic order, dominated as it is by the powerful nations, or from reliance on multinational companies or foreign advisers.

Dependency theory tends to focus on two solutions to these problems. First, it advocates policies to alter the balance of power between the rich and poor countries, through bodies like UNCTAD or by increasing the representation of developing countries at the UN, IMF, or World Bank. Second, it argues for domestic political, social, and institutional reforms, including direct government action to promote or (in extreme cases) to control economic development. Dependency theory has been quite persuasive in explaining why many countries remain underdeveloped, but it offers only limited insights for the 'tiger economies'. Certainly, these countries have made extensive use of government intervention, but this approach has been only one of several possible explanations for their rapid development.

■ The neoclassical revival

The 1980s saw a revival of neoclassical free market economics. Writers such as Deepak Lal and Jagdish Bhagwati have argued that competitive markets, the absence of government intervention, and the promotion of free trade are the best prescription for economic efficiency and growth.[4] This leads them to advocate privatization, market deregulation and the liberalization of foreign trade and investment. These policies have become the predominant view of the IMF, World Bank, and WTO in recent years. Several countries in Latin America, including Chile, Argentina, and Peru, have been adopting these policies with some success. Isolated examples can also be found in Africa—notably in Uganda, which has been courageously reforming its economy along free market lines. Whether they apply equally to the Asian 'tiger economies' is more debatable. Certainly, these countries have taken advantage of the more liberal international trading environment, but they also have highly regulated economies and active government intervention. However, the Asian financial crisis has arguably highlighted some of the deficiencies of their inflexible economies.

The debate between the free marketeers and the interventionists is sometimes heated. The former argue that the principles of efficient resource allocation are universal, that government intervention is frequently counter-productive, and that the problems of developing countries stem either from their own economic mismanagement or from the misguided policies of well-meaning external agencies. The latter take the view that, while free markets may be efficient, they do not solve the problem of poverty, reflect the different structures or institutions of each developing country, or take account of actual conditions which frequently preclude the simple application of free market principles. For example, consumers in African society are often dispersed, inarticulate, and at the mercy of producers. These countries often have a poor industrial infrastructure, limited educational provision, unstable or corrupt political systems, and legal institutions which provide little protection for private property. Cultural norms and belief systems may also make free market activities difficult to implement. In reality, neither free market reforms nor government intervention can guarantee to resolve these problems, but each approach may offer some useful insights.

■ Endogenous growth theory

Traditional theories of economic growth tend to focus on the importance of savings and investment and on the introduction of technology into the developing economies. Technology is usually seen as an exogenous factor, determined by developments outside the country concerned. By contrast, endogenous growth theory attempts to explain the importance of internal factors within an economy.[5] These factors help to explain why countries develop at different rates. It is argued that long-term growth is created not simply by the existence of free market forces, but also by investment in the infrastructure and in knowledge-intensive activities such as education, research and development, and new technologies. Since this kind of investment creates external economies of scale, beyond the benefits which would be received by a private investor, the theory is sometimes used to justify public sector involvement. However, endogenous growth theory has its roots in the neoclassical tradition. Thus, it might be argued that a combination of market forces and long-term public and private sector investment is required. This combination of factors should set in motion the dynamic forces which lead to efficiency, innovation, and economic growth.

Endogenous growth theory is less well developed than some of the earlier theories but it offers some interesting insights which can be applied to the 'tiger economies'. However, despite its intuitive appeal, empirical support has been less forthcoming.[6] As an attempt to explain the dynamic processes which stimulate long-term growth, the theory adds to our understanding of economic development. Its weaknesses are that it understates the importance of short-term factors, which may influence growth at a particular time, and that it takes little account of cultural and institutional differences between countries. It also revives the issue of government intervention. Some of its adherents emphasize the role of government or concerted international action in promoting the required investment in education and research and development. Others remain closer to their neoclassical roots in endorsing the benefits of trade and domestic liberalization as spurs to endogenous growth.

9.3.2 Factor endowment and cultural values

Perhaps one of the oldest ideas about the causes of economic development is that the size and quality of a country's natural resources determine its rate of economic progress. Thus, countries with large amounts of arable land, mineral resources, a favourable climate, or a strategic geographical location might be expected to have highly developed economies. Sometimes this is the case. The USA and Canada both have large productive agricultural sectors which exploit their vast open spaces. Norway has made good use of its North Sea oil reserves, Spain of its favourable climate, and Hong Kong of its strategic location at the hub of the Asia Pacific region. But there are many examples of countries which remain underdeveloped in spite of natural advantages: Nigeria and several other OPEC members have rich oil deposits but remain poor; Ukraine has high-quality coal, iron ore, oil, and chemical raw materials but its post-Soviet economy has virtually collapsed; Turkey occupies a key strategic location between Europe, Asia, and the Middle East but, despite recent progress, it has been unable to maintain its historic importance in political and economic terms. Japan, on the other hand, has few natural resources apart from its people but is one of the most developed countries in the world.

This is not to say that natural resources are unimportant. Rather, it is the way in which a country develops its resources that matters. Indeed, a country's ability to acquire or accumulate resources (including financial and intellectual capital) may be more important than whether its resources occur naturally. Industrial success requires a combination of raw materials, technology, and human skills. Thus, a country's factor endowments may be said to include the innate qualities of its people, its standards of education and training, the attributes of its culture and values, its capital stock and level of technological knowledge, as well as factors such as raw materials, land, climate, and location.

From this wider perspective, it is possible to argue that Japan and the East Asian 'tiger economies' initially overcame a shortage of natural resources by acquiring raw materials, technology, and skills from abroad. More recently, they have improved the quality of their factor endowments by concentrating on education, the quality of their workforce and work practices, and on investment in research and development. East Asian culture may also be a significant factor. Japanese workers have a strong sense of pride in their work, for example, and this is supported or enforced by the close-knit, authoritarian structures of Japanese society. The emphasis on education, particularly mathematical and technological education, may also have cultural roots in countries like Japan, Singapore, South Korea, and Taiwan. The influence of these factors is the subject of much debate. The case of Taiwan, one of the most dynamic of the 'tiger economies', is explored in Box 9.1.

It should be noted, however, that some of the 'tiger economies' may have simply made intensive use of resources in order to expand production. Krugman argues that their economic growth has resulted mainly from the use of large quantities of factor inputs rather than from productivity growth.[7] This intensive resource use has only been made possible by massive government investment, government-supported bank lending, or through the mutual support of company networks like the Japanese *keiretsu*. Without increases in efficiency, continued economic growth in these countries will be constrained by the availability of resources and by the law of diminishing returns. If this view is accepted, the East Asian model does not appear to provide a sound basis for long-term development.

9.3.3 Domestic savings and foreign investment

Theories of economic development often recognize the importance of savings and investment. It is also interesting to note that most of the East Asian 'tiger economies' have high savings ratios, sometimes as high as 40–45 per cent of GDP. This compares with very low savings ratios in many of the world's poorer countries. Savings represent a willingness to forgo present consumption in favour of investment in future production capacity and future consumption. In some cases people may save because there are few goods to buy or because consumer credit is scarce, as in Eastern Europe during the Soviet era. In East Asia, the high level of savings may be explained as a cultural phenomenon or as a consequence of official encouragement in the form of tax and other incentives. Nevertheless, these savings provide large funds for investment.

During the 1990s another source of investment funds grew rapidly: foreign direct investment. Whilst not new in historical terms, FDI inflows into some of the emerging economies have greatly increased during this period (see Table 12.1). FDI alone cannot account for the rapid development of an entire economy unless it dominates the country concerned. Nor is there any guarantee that it will spread its benefits to the rest of an economy; for example, there is evidence to suggest that the large volume of FDI going into Hungary is creating a two-tier economy of struggling domestic firms and strong export-oriented foreign investors. However, FDI does provide much-needed capital, as well as employment, technology, expertise, and other benefits. Whether FDI is a major instigator of economic growth or is simply attracted by

Box 9.1 Taiwan: Profile of an Asian 'Tiger'

Taiwan offers an interesting example of East Asian economic development. In many ways, the country is similar to the other 'tiger economies': it has achieved a persistently high rate of economic growth, has used active industrial policy to promote exports and key technological industries, and has achieved high levels of savings and investment. In other respects there are differences, however. Although Taiwan was beginning to experience the impact of the Asian financial crisis by the end of 1998, mainly through a loss of Asian export markets, its financial system has been remarkably resilient. The government has been liberalizing financial markets only gradually; this appears to have kept the inflows and outflows of capital at lower levels than elsewhere. The ratio of loan to equity capital is generally lower in most Taiwanese companies than it is in South Korea, for example.

Taiwan also has a unique political backgound. It broke away from direct Chinese rule in 1949 when members of the defeated nationalist army fled to the island to escape the communist forces. Since then, Taiwan has forged its own way as a capitalist economy, though China still claims sovereignty over the island. Taiwan has enjoyed US friendship and economic support, in contrast to China, though the formerly strained Sino-US relations are now beginning to improve. Taiwan has introduced a democratic system of government, unlike many of its neighbours, and has nurtured a thriving enterprise culture. It has also understood the advantages of attracting foreign investment and know-how when trying to develop its high-tech industries.

favourable political and economic developments is a more open question. Perhaps FDI is not so much attracted by economic growth as by economic potential. This potential, in turn, is demonstrated by conditions and by government policies which are seen as conducive to business success.

9.3.4 Trade liberalization and market reform

Liberalization, either of external trade or domestic markets, is often regarded as one of the main determinants of economic development. This has become the established view in IMF, World Bank, and WTO circles. It is also the view of many business people in the West. It is, of course, based on the neoclassical free market view discussed in Section 9.3.1 above. It is also supported by less orthodox views such as those of the Austrian School of Economics[8] or the theory of contestable markets.[9] Economists of the Austrian School focus on the dynamic process of competition rather than the neoclassical concept of equilibrium. They believe that genuinely free markets (unhindered by regulations or trade restrictions) encourage entrepreneurship, innovation, and economic growth. Government intervention, they contend, is more likely to distort market forces and stifle innovation and growth. Contestable markets theory arrives at a similar conclusion on the merits of free markets via the theory of market entry barriers. A contestable market is one where there is absolute freedom of entry and costless exit. Import restrictions and entry regulations prevent freedom of entry. Excessive product or production regulations in a particular country may also impose sunk costs on a foreign entrant, thus deterring entry; sunk costs are costs incurred on entering a market which are irrecoverable when leaving the market—these costs may discourage a foreign firm from entering a country when it already faces higher risks than domestic firms.

This powerful array of theoretical support for free markets cannot easily be dismissed. In practice, the USA provides the best example of a free market economy; size alone cannot explain its economic dominance. Similarly, countries around the world which have been liberalizing their economies—the UK, New Zealand, Chile, India, and others—have generally experienced improvements in their economic performance as a consequence. The East Asian 'tiger economies' have also benefited from their exposure to international trade, though the encouragement of exports has not always been matched by a corresponding liberalization of imports. Experience suggests that market liberalization is a necessary condition for the efficient operation of a market economy. Whether it can be applied in a country which lacks the basic institutional and economic infrastructure is a more open question; this issue is considered in Box 9.2 in relation to Uganda. In itself, liberalization is unlikely to provide a sufficient condition for economic development.

9.3.5 Macroeconomic stability

A comparison between Latin America, Eastern Europe, and East Asia indicates the importance of achieving macroeconomic stability. The economies of Argentina, Brazil, and other Latin American countries, which experienced severe economic problems during the 1980s, clearly illustrate the need to control inflation and large public debts. Similarly, experience of the transition process in Eastern Europe during the 1990s suggests that macroeconomic stabilization is a prerequisite for successful recovery; Poland soon learned the importance of reducing inflation and public debt, after the inflationary side effects of its 'shock therapy' in the early 1990s and its legacy of foreign indebtedness from the latter years of communism. By contrast, the East Asian 'tiger economies' have generally maintained a tight grip on inflation, though their recent experience of financial turbulence suggests that company and bank indebtedness has grown out of control.

The theoretical case for macroeconomic stability hinges on the debate between the Keynesians and monetarists. This debate raged fiercely during the 1970s and 1980s. Keynesians advocate demand management to restore a full employment level of output, accepting the need for deficit budgets as an active short-run policy instrument. Monetarists stress the need to control the money supply in line with economic growth and the importance of balanced budgets over the economic cycle. They argue that reflationary policies are unable to move an economy from its natural (or non-accelerating inflation) rate of unemployment in the long-run. In some respects, the difference between them is overstated. Keynesians see demand management as a short-term expedient and also advocate policies to control inflation, though they disagree on the impact of monetary policy.

Whatever the merits of this debate, the 1990s have witnessed a more general acceptance of the importance of 'sound money' and 'prudent fiscal management'. Monetary discipline is necessary in order to keep inflation low and to maintain exchange rate stability. Fiscal prudence helps governments to avoid the inflationary consequences of printing money and the burden of excessive debt and high long-;term interest rates. It also increases the scope for reducing taxes. Together, these measures help to promote business, consumer, and investor confidence. Whilst not in themselves promoting economic development, they may be seen as a necessary prerequisite. This discussion leaves open the question as to whether judicious government policy should be used to stimulate business growth within an overall framework of macroeconomic stability—an issue which is explored in the next section.

9.3.6 Government industrial policy

Selective industrial policy has played a key role in the economies of Japan, South Korea, Singapore, Taiwan, and other East Asian countries—though less so in Hong Kong. In the West, industrial intervention is often in the form of subsidies, tax concessions, or regional incentives. In East Asia, intervention has been altogether more intrusive. In Japan, for example, government agencies have close links with specific industries. During the post-war years, Japan has successively promoted shipbuilding, steel, motor manufacturing, electronics, computers, and other high-tech industries. It has done this through tax incentives, government-sponsored research, the setting of strict industrial standards (which make foreign incursions difficult), restrictive patenting rules, low-interest and preferred loans, and numerous other devices. The existence of *keiretsu* has enabled governments to influence lending between banks and companies belonging to the same network. The need for consensus in Japanese society has also made it easier for governments to implement this type of industrial policy.

Similar policy objectives have been adopted in South Korea and Taiwan. In Korea, intervention has been even more overt than in Japan. Governments have imposed import restrictions to protect key industries and have chosen particular *chaebol* to produce required products. Hyundai, for instance, was selected to be the country's sole car producer in the early 1980s. Other favoured companies were later allowed to rejoin them. Taiwan initially used a policy of import substitution to promote light manufacturing, then turned its attention towards heavier industries including electronics. State-owned banks and research institutes have enabled Taiwanese governments to direct resources into its preferred industries. Other strategies have included the encouragement of joint ventures with foreign companies in key technological industries. Each of these countries has placed particular emphasis on exports.

It is beyond dispute that the East Asian 'tiger economies' have achieved some success in promoting particular industries through government intervention. The Japanese car and electronics industries have gained a worldwide reputation, as have several other high-tech industries. Their consumers have also had to pay a high price for industrial protection. Import barriers and highly regulated markets mean that competition is restricted. A lack of competition means that prices are high; internal air fares in Japan, for example, are well above those in the USA or Europe. It also allows inefficiencies to remain, in distribution and financial services if not in industrial production. Some of these inefficiencies have begun to surface during the Asian financial crisis.

9.4 Problems of Rapid Growth in Emerging Economies

9.4.1 The Asian financial crisis

The Asian financial crisis has brought about a re-examination of some of the issues discussed above. The crisis started in mid-1997 in Thailand, then spread rapidly to South Korea, Indonesia, Malaysia, the Philippines, Japan, and other East Asian countries, as well as to countries beyond Asia. Although the severity and scale of the crisis was unusual, such problems are not unique. Financial crises requiring bank bail-outs have been relatively common in recent years, notably in Israel (1977–83), Argentina, Chile, and Uruguay (in the early 1980s), Mexico (1995), and even, though on a smaller scale, in the Scandinavian countries (in the late 1980s and early 1990s). Nor is it unusual for rapidly developing countries to experience economic problems. The gradual opening up of China's huge planned economy, for example, has created problems of inflation and macroeconomic management and exposed the weaknesses of an inadequate financial infrastructure.

Yet the Asian financial crisis has been so severe that its impact has disturbed the world economy as a whole. Not only have large financial institutions suffered, but the rapid depreciation of East Asian exchange rates and the sudden downturn in their economies have resulted in the collapse of East Asian markets and the possibility of a global recession. Ordinary people in countries like Indonesia have also suffered economic and social hardship. These problems have led to much debate about the causes of the crisis. In broad terms, the main culprits have been seen as either the international financial system or failures within the East Asian countries themselves.

The trigger for the crisis was a loss of confidence among international investors and lending institutions. Suddenly, what had seemed a worthwhile risk in these high-performing economies became a cause for concern when Thailand's currency collapsed or a Korean bank was unable to honour its debts. This loss of confidence led to a rapid outflow of capital from the affected countries as investors sought to minimize their losses and banks to recover their loans. The result was a shortage of liquidity in domestic financial markets. Banks became insolvent, investment projects were halted, and industrial firms got into difficulties. These problems were exacerbated by the close links between banks and other firms within Korea's *chaebol*. Before long, their economies were slowing down and their currencies depreciated further. Many foreign banks and portfolio investors also incurred losses and bad debts, as well as companies which traded or had direct investments in the region. The loss of confidence in these emerging markets soon became infectious. It was not long before investors in Russia and some of the weaker Latin American economies grew nervous. It is not difficult, therefore, to see why the world economy as a whole has been affected by the Asian financial crisis.

The key question is whether the East Asian economies were growing too rapidly and have structural weaknesses in their economies or whether the international financial system or Western banks and investors are to blame. Certainly, there are concerns about the rapid globalization of business and financial markets. Capital can now move freely between the world's financial centres or to finance direct investment in the emerging economies. Whilst many developed countries have reasonably well-regulated financial markets, emerging markets often fall somewhere between tight state control and unregulated free market capitalism. International markets are even more difficult to regulate. When huge capital movements are combined with lax controls in high-risk financial markets, the dangers become clear. In some ways, the 'tiger economies' had become victims of their own success. They had become too attractive to the world's investors and lending institutions. Given that these countries already attracted high levels of domestic savings, they had become awash with capital. This enabled them to invest in major infrastructure projects as well as more speculative ventures. The world's banks and multinational companies willingly shared complicity in this process.

The IMF and World Bank have also been criticized. On the one hand, they are expected to (and generally do) bail out countries in financial crisis or provide guarantees which encourage other institutions to do the same. The expectation that they will intervene in this way encourages private sector banks to lend money to emerging countries and may also create a sense of security in the borrowing countries. This practice may encourage excessive amounts of high-risk lending—an example of what is known as *moral hazard*. On the other hand, the multinational lending institutions have been criticized for imposing overly strict or inappropriate conditions on the countries they help—especially involving liberalization and other market reforms.

Of course, investors would be less likely to lose confidence if they regarded the emerging markets as a secure long-term investment. The fact that they lost confidence suggests that this was not the case. In the next section we consider the weaknesses in the East Asian economies which may have precipitated this loss of confidence.

9.4.2 The 'tiger economies': a flawed economic miracle?

The proximate cause of the Asian financial crisis was a shortage of foreign exchange reserves in Thailand and the collapse of its currency, the baht. This highlighted the difficulties of trying to peg an exchange rate in an emerging economy when major currencies like the US dollar and the Japanese yen were themselves fluctuating in a turbulent international environment. However, the underlying causes are more deep-rooted. The nature of the East Asian socio-economic model may itself be part of the problem. Before we explore this problem, we should recognize an important caveat: the existence of inherent weaknesses in the East Asian model, or in the policies of its governments, should not be taken to mean that the model has no strengths. It does, however, mean that we need to be more circumspect in evaluating the lessons from the East Asian 'economic miracle'.

The close links within company networks and between government and industry, which played an important part in East Asian industrial success during the growth years, may have contributed to their present problems. Banks within Japanese *keiretsu* or Korean *chaebol* understandably provided preferential loans to their fellow group members. These loans were often encouraged by government policy. Many of the loans were 'soft loans' at low rates of interest or loans to high-risk borrowers. Banks also loaned or invested surplus funds abroad. The financial crisis has now left many of these banks on the verge of insolvency with large portfolios of insecure loans and bad debts. These practices have encouraged their domestic companies to become overreliant on loan capital. They have also distorted company investment decisions, making it easy for them to expand production capacity and to invest in commercially unsound ventures. Korea's *chaebol* have invested in a diverse range of industries where there is no apparent synergy and in which they have little previous experience. Recent estimates suggest that Japanese non-financial companies have collectively achieved a rate of return on equity capital which has been below the cost of capital during the 1990s.[10] In other words, the value of Japanese companies has been falling during this period.

Government industrial policy may also be part of the problem. Governments have been distorting resource decisions by promoting the expansion of particular industries. Vast amounts of resources have facilitated huge increases in production capacity. This capacity has created a number of large, apparently successful industries, but there has been a high price. Even in Japan, the most successful of these economies, the returns on investment have been falling for some years. In some of the other 'tiger economies', where resource inputs may not have been accompanied by the same rate of productivity improvements, the situation is worse.

Clearly, these underlying problems existed before the onset of the Asian financial crisis. The crisis has simply brought them out into the open. In fact, the Japanese economy has been slowing down or in recession throughout most of the 1990s. This may be a natural process after years of high growth, but it may also suggest that the above problems have been emerging for some time.

Signs of change are now appearing in Japan: foreign companies are beginning to play a more active role in what were formerly arm's-length joint ventures; share option schemes are becoming more common, encouraging the pursuit of share value rather than sales and expansion; management positions are becoming less secure; and some of the *keiretsu*, which have been the backbone of Japanese industry, are beginning to loosen control over their members (see Box 9.1). In South Korea, financial sector and other market reforms are being introduced by the government and some of its *chaebol* are beginning to restructure and focus more on their core activities. The need for these changes has surprised many people, both within Asia and in the wider world. The East Asian model had apparently provided the economic and social structure for rapid industrialization and the creation of global companies. Many Western companies have learned valuable lessons from Japanese production methods. Perhaps the necessary reforms will help the East Asian economies to return to more sustainable, if less dramatic, growth. Only time will tell.

9.5 Persistent Problems in the Less Developed Countries

9.5.1 Why do some countries remain poor?

About half the world's nations had a per capita GDP of US$3000 or less in 1996. In fact, the United Nations has identified the forty-eight least developed countries (LDCs) as having an average per capita GDP of about US$230 and a total population of over 600 million.[11] Nearly two-thirds of these LDCs are in Africa. The two decades before 1995 had been a period of almost continuous economic decline in sub-Saharan Africa. Since 1995 Africa's economic growth rate has been positive, at around 3–4 per cent per annum, partly fuelled by higher commodity export prices. The Asian financial crisis was beginning to affect these growth rates by 1998, but there are at least some signs that Africa's struggling economies may have more growth potential than is commonly recognized. Unfortunately, these countries still face massive economic, social, and political problems.

Some of the reasons for their poor performance are not difficult to identify. Many of them have had ruthless and corrupt governments, more interested in amassing power and personal wealth than in the development of their countries. Some have been torn apart by civil strife or wars with neighbouring countries. Climates are sometimes inhospitable. The limited infrastructure they once had has often been destroyed or allowed to deteriorate through lack of investment. Inefficient administrative agencies make normal business activities difficult. Numerous social problems—poor health and education, the prevalence of AIDS and other diseases, malnutrition and famine—all add to these problems. In many cases, these countries were poorly served by their colonial masters and development assistance from the rich countries has left them heavily indebted. They remain on the periphery of the world trading environment.

Yet, the existence of similar problems has not prevented some of the emerging nations from making an economic breakthrough. We therefore need to focus our attention on the core economic problems that seem to hold back development. UNCTAD and a number of pressure groups have been lobbying for the cancellation or reduction of foreign debt. This is a huge problem and there is clearly a case for action to be taken on this front. The external debt of the forty countries classified by the World Bank as highly indebted poor countries (HIPCs) rose from $55 billion in 1980 to $206 billion in 1996. But these figures suggest that the increase in debt has accompanied the problem, and perhaps exacerbated it, rather than been the root cause of the problem. Elimination of the debt problem may relieve the financial burden on the poorest nations and help their governments to finance essential public expenditure, but it is unlikely, in itself, to be the catalyst for economic development. Essentially, two factors seem to be lacking. First, many African and other least developed countries lack the basic market institutions and mechanisms required for efficient economic activity. At a fundamental level, these include the establishment of legitimate government, the maintenance of law and order, the protection of private property rights, and the existence of independent economic agents; at a higher level, well-functioning goods, capital, and labour markets are also required. Second, indigenous entrepreneurs are needed in order to facilitate the development of a dynamic market economy. This may require a fundamental cultural change in inward-looking societies still dominated by ruling élites and feudal practices.

9.5.2 How can poor countries be helped?

Ultimately, the world's poor countries need to participate more fully in international trade and the global economy. Otherwise, they will remain underdeveloped and dependent on the rich countries for aid. As one might expect, there are divergent views on how this can be achieved. Most observers agree that peace, stable democracy, and observance of the rule of law would be a good starting point. Beyond this, there are two broad camps: those who argue that free trade and market liberalization are the answer, following the example of the industrialized countries, and those who believe that active government intervention and concerted international action are required. The former view has prevailed in the policies of the IMF and is sometimes characterized as the 'Washington consensus'. The latter view is perhaps most closely represented by UNCTAD, the UN body which speaks on behalf of the developing countries.

Critics of the Washington consensus claim that market liberalization is, at best, a means and not an end. The consensus has stressed the importance of financial liberalization, for example, without recognizing the parallel need for market regulation or has advocated privatization without ensuring that competition is possible. Furthermore, it is argued that the conditions for free markets simply do not exist in some countries. On the other hand, the interventionist view is criticized for having too much faith in the ability of governments and institutions to resolve the problem. In some cases governments have been one of the main causes of the problem; even their best intentions result in wasteful schemes and inefficient state sectors.

Given this lack of a general consensus on how to resolve the problem of under-development, any policy prescriptions are inevitably a matter of debate. There is growing support for the view that some measure of debt relief is required. Otherwise, governments in the poorest countries must use their limited budgets mainly to repay debt—not only normal debt repayments but also arrears of debt on which they have previously defaulted. This situation leaves them locked into a circle of debt. It is also clear that external funds are needed to provide for essential investment. Ideally, private investors should be encouraged to build factories or form joint ventures in these countries. In practice, this is only likely to happen if the conditions are favourable. Thus, the IMF and World Bank, together with regional investment banks, play a vital role.

The question then becomes: what sort of conditions should the lending institutions impose on the governments concerned? Macroeconomic stabilization and market liberalization alone may be too harsh. Governments need to be encouraged to implement the reforms necessary for markets to operate effectively. These will include reforms to the system of public administration, the creation of regulated financial markets, laws governing trade and commerce, and the protection of property rights, among other things. Selective measures may also be needed to encourage small businesses and entrepreneurial skills, perhaps even to promote or protect important or developing industries in the short term. Help will also be needed in tackling social problems and in improving education and training. However, experience suggests that internationally competitive companies and industries will only prosper in the long term if competitive home markets constantly keep them on their toes. Governments then have the job of deciding how to use this wealth to improve the welfare of society as a whole. Box 9.2 explains how Uganda has approached this problem and illustrates some of the dilemmas facing policy-makers.

Box 9.2 Uganda: Struggling to Overcome the Disastrous Years

Uganda is one of the forty-eight LDCs with a per capita GDP of under US$240. A period of healthy economic growth followed independence in 1962, but by the mid-1970s the economy was starting to collapse. President Idi Amin turned Uganda inward, expelled its Asian community (many of whom were successful in business), and presided over armed conflict and economic disintegration. By 1986, GDP per capita had fallen to 57 per cent of its 1970 level. Although some attempts at reform were made after Amin's fall in 1982, it was not until 1987 that a serious reform programme was started under President Museveni.

Under this programme Uganda obtained aid from the IMF, World Bank, and International Development Association. The IMF's structural adjustment facility was agreed in return for structural reforms. These reforms included tight budgetary and monetary control, privatization of the country's inefficient state enterprises, and measures to promote external and internal market liberalization. The introduction of banking facilities and cash activities into rural areas also helped to bring Uganda's large informal sector into the formal economy. The reforms helped to encourage foreign companies like Shell, Unilever, and PepsiCo to return to Uganda. As a result, the Ugandan economy grew by 5.7 per cent per annum from 1989 to 1996, rising to 7 per cent between 1995 and 1997. Despite this improvement, GDP per capita was still lower in 1995 than in 1970 and Uganda is now much more heavily indebted. Key social indicators such as life expectancy and the infant mortality rate have also deteriorated. Ordinary Ugandans have not yet experienced much benefit from the reforms. But Uganda is recovering from a period of political, economic, and social disaster; the economic reform programme is only the beginning of an uphill struggle.

9.6 Summary

A remarkable feature of the 1980s and 1990s, and earlier in some cases, has been the rapid economic development of the world's emerging economies. These economies are predominantly in Asia, Latin America, and Eastern Europe, the most striking examples being the 'tiger economies' of South-East Asia. Explanations for this phenomenon can be found either in the theories of economic development or by examining the key features of these economies: factor endowments and culture, high levels of saving and investment, economic reform programmes, macroeconomic stability, and government industrial policy. Despite their success, a number of the emerging economies experienced severe economic problems during the Asian financial crisis of the late 1990s. This crisis may be explained by overexpansion and a lack of regulation in the world financial system or by the existence of structural weaknesses in some of the emerging economies. Notwithstanding the ups and downs of the emerging economies, some countries, especially in sub-Saharan Africa, remain persistently poor. Even here, however, there are some tentative signs of economic development.

Review Questions

1 Which of the countries of Asia and Latin America have experienced high rates of economic growth during the 1980s and/or 1990s?

2 To what extent does endogenous growth theory provide a more useful explanation for the growth of the emerging economies than Rostow's 'stages of economic development'?

3 What features of the emerging economies appear to have contributed to their rapid economic development?

4 What appear to be the main causes of the Asian financial crisis of the late 1990s?

5 Why do some countries continue to remain poor?

Study Topic: The Emerging Economies: Opportunity or Threat?

Do the emerging economies represent an opportunity or a threat to the industrialized nations? In one sense, the opportunity to capture new markets in the Asian 'tiger economies' turned into a threat as the Asian financial crisis deepened and newly captured markets disappeared. More commonly, the threat is seen in terms of competition from low-cost producers. A number of MNEs have responded to this threat by establishing their own production plants in low-cost countries or by outsourcing production to companies located there. Other Western companies have concentrated on products where they still have a competitive advantage through superior productivity or more specialized technology.

Clearly, a period of rapid economic development brings considerable change throughout the global economy. Companies and industries experience a process of adjustment, some survive by becoming better at what they do or by moving into new markets, some are taken over or go out of business. It is worth remembering, however, that countries and their consumers as a whole generally benefit from international trade—imports as well as exports—and, of course, companies are themselves consumers of components and raw materials as well as suppliers of products. When viewed from a developing-country perspective, the odds are clearly stacked against the low-cost producers: low production costs are their main competitive advantage—in most other respects they see themselves as being at a disadvantage.

Study topic questions

1 Enumerate the main opportunities and threats of the emerging economies to a Western firm.

2 Is the establishment of production facilities in a low-cost country a desirable way for a Western firm to reduce the competitive threat from the emerging economies?

3 Are 'superior productivity and more specialized technology' likely to provide a continuing competitive advantage for Western firms?

4 In what sense do 'consumers as a whole generally benefit from international trade—imports as well as exports'?

5 Are the emerging economies justified if they claim that the 'odds are clearly stacked against [them]'?

Notes

1 W. W. Rostow, *The Stages of Economic Growth: A Non-Communist Manifesto* (Cambridge University Press, London, 1960).

2 See e.g. H. B. Chenery, *Structural Change and Development Policy* (Johns Hopkins University Press, Baltimore, 1979).

3 See e.g. T. C. Lewellen, *Dependency and Development: An Introduction to the Third World* (Bergin and Garvey, Wesport, Conn. 1995).

4 See e.g. D. Lal, *The Poverty of Development Economics* (Harvard University Press, Cambridge, Mass. 1985).

5 See the symposium 'New growth theory', *Journal of Economic Perspectives*, 8, (Winter 1994), 3–72.

6 Ibid.

7 P. R. Krugman, 'The myth of Asia's miracle', *Foreign Affairs*, 73 (6): 62–78.

8 See e.g. F. A. Hayek, *The Road to Serfdom*, (London, Routledge, 1944).

9 The primary source on contestable markets theory is W. J. Baumol, J. L. Panzar, and R. D. Willig, *Contestable Markets: An Uprising in the Theory of Industry Structure* (Harcourt Brace Jovanovich, 1982).

10 P. Abrahams, 'Japan's ray of hope', *Financial Times* (6 May 1998).

11 UNCTAD *Trade and Development Report*, 1998: The Least Developed Countries.

Recommended Reading

- Lingle, C., *The Rise and Decline of the Asian Century* (Asia 2000, 1997).
- Meier, G. M., *The International Environment of Business* (Oxford University Press, 1998).
- Poulson, B. W., *Economic Development: Private and Public Choice* (West, 1994).
- Schnitzer, M. C., *Comparative Economic Systems* (South-Western, 1994).
- Todaro, M. P., *Economic Development* (Addison-Wesley, 1997).

Part III

International Trade and Investment

10

International Trade and Payments

Objectives

- to indicate why the study of international trade is important
- to outline and evaluate the relevance of classical theories of international trade
- to discuss the contribution of modern explanations of international trade
- to identify the components of a country's balance of payments and evaluate its significance for the country concerned

10.1 Introduction

BEFORE an international business activity can take place, a country has to have a commodity to exchange with other nations. There must somehow be a basis for international trade in goods and services. Firms resident in a particular country engage in international business activities in accordance with the pattern of international trade established over time and peculiar to that country. As international trade is a two-way process of exchange, it must be mutually beneficial to both sides or no trade would be possible.

The term 'international trade' describes the flow of goods and services between nations and the type of transactions, especially those relating to payment for goods and services, which must accompany it if traded goods and services are to satisfy human wants. The variety of goods and services traded is so vast and the nature of accompanying transactions so wide-ranging that it requires a special branch of economics to study international trade in depth. In addition, there are other reasons for understanding the nature of international trade, including the fact that (a) international factor mobility, especially that of labour, is relatively low compared to factor mobility within a given country; (b) most countries have their own national currency whose international value changes over time, requiring governments to take the necessary steps to maintain the stability of their currencies; and (c) countries engage in a variety of protectionist measures to control the flow of international trade in pursuit of national objectives.

As in the case of domestic firms, international firms also operate in two basic markets: real markets and money or financial markets. In real markets, they engage in activities involving the exchange of goods and services, including the recruitment of labour and management personnel. In money or financial markets, they engage in activities which involve payments and the provision of capital. As is shown in Chapter 1, basic business functions and processes remain the same when the firm engages in these two markets except that, in the case of international firms, these engagements involve greater difficulties, risks, and uncertainties.

International trade can have both direct and indirect effects on business firms. Firms operating in domestic markets may be subject to indirect effects through the potential threat of foreign competition, forcing them to take the necessary measures to protect their markets, in some cases with the help of their governments. Direct effects involve firms that are active in international business. For example, any increase in international competition or changes in the commercial policies of host countries will have direct effects on their operations, requiring them to develop strategies to maintain their market share and to minimize the adverse effect of policy changes in the host country.

The purpose of this chapter is to provide a brief survey of the explanations of international trade and a country's balance of payments. Why do nations trade and what determines the volume and geographical distribution of a country's trade? What is the balance of payments and what is its composition?

10.2 Why Do Nations Trade?

THERE are two basic categories of explanation for why nations trade: classical and modern. Classical trade theories are concerned mainly with the demonstration of the benefits of free trade, that is trade without barriers. They are also referred to as 'country-based theories' of trade as they try to explain how countries rather than firms trade internationally. The first two classical theories—absolute advantage and comparative advantage—were the outcome of the opposition to mercantilism, a very nationalistic approach to trade which focuses on the need for governments to promote exports and restrict imports in order to improve the economic well-being of the country. The third classical approach to trade, the Heckscher–Ohlin factor endowments theory, is in essence a refinement of the first two classical theories concerned mainly with the sources of a country's comparative advantage.

10.2.1 Classical explanations of trade

■ The theory of absolute advantage

In his much acclaimed book the *Wealth of Nations*, published in 1776, Adam Smith (1723–90) argued that international trade should be based on cost differences and not on nationalistic policies to promote exports at the expense of imports.[1] Furthermore, mercantilist policies led to inefficient use of a nation's resources by forcing the country to export goods which it produced without any cost advantage and to stifle imports which other countries could produce more efficiently. In consequence, countries following the basic tenets of mercantilism were forcing their economies to produce inefficiently and, by restricting imports, considerably reducing consumer choice at home.

In a model based on the assumptions of two countries, two commodities, no transport cost, immobility of factors between countries and constant returns to scale (constant costs where a given increase in inputs yields a proportionate increase in output), Adam Smith showed that trade between two countries would be mutually beneficial if each country specialized (that is, if it devoted all its resources) in the production of the commodity in which it had an absolute advantage. The resulting surplus from this specialization could then be exchanged for a commodity in whose production it had an absolute disadvantage. The absolute advantage could be due to the combination of suitable factors of production, favourable climate, good fertile soil, and other natural endowments. In this way each trading nation uses its resources with greater efficiency, leading to an overall increase in the output of the two commodities. If every nation did the same with respect to other commodities, then the total world output would increase and trade would flourish, spreading mutual benefits worldwide. Thus, in the words of Adam Smith,

> It is the maxim of every prudent master of a family never to attempt to make at home what it will cost him more to make than to buy. If a foreign country can supply us with a commodity cheaper than we ourselves can make it, better buy it of them with some part of the produce of our own industry employed in a way in which we have some advantage.'[2]

■ The theory of comparative advantage

The main criticism of the theory of absolute advantage is the assumption that each country specializes in the production of one commodity. What if a country has an absolute advantage in two or more commodities? Which one of these commodities would the country produce? Furthermore, suppose that a country had no absolute advantage in any commodity. Does this mean there can be no basis for international trade?

Answers to these questions were provided by the theory of comparative advantage developed by David Ricardo (1772–1823) in his book *The Principles of Political Economy and Taxation* published in 1817.[3] According to Ricardo, a basis for trade exists whenever and wherever relative (comparative) costs differ between countries. Using the same basic model of two countries and two commodities, he argued that a country with an absolute advantage in the production of two goods could still benefit from trade by specializing in the production of that commodity in which it had a comparative advantage; that is, in which its absolute advantage is greatest or its absolute disadvantage least. It could then export the surplus of this commodity in exchange for imports produced by other countries with respective comparative cost advantages. What is being argued here is that it is relative efficiencies that matter and that differences in these relative efficiencies could lead to mutually beneficial trade, an increase in world output, and greater prosperity to be enjoyed by all trading countries.

At this point it would be useful to review briefly the concept of *opportunity cost*. The opportunity cost of one extra unit of commodity X is the amount of commodity Y which must be sacrificed or given up in order to obtain this extra unit of X. Thus, a country which can produce X with the least opportunity cost should specialize in its production and export it in exchange for Y in whose production its opportunity cost would be greater.

The argument so far is illustrated numerically in Table 10.1. Country A has an absolute advantage in the production of both X and Y, with varying degrees of efficiency for each commodity. Country A is 2.5 times as efficient as country B in the production of X but only 2 times as efficient in the production of Y. Alternatively stated, for country A the opportunity cost of X in terms of Y (Y_A/X_A) is 0.4; that is, for each extra unit of X, 0.4 units of Y must be sacrificed. Similarly, the opportunity cost of Y in terms of X (X_A/Y_A) is 2.5; that is, for each unit of Y, 2.5 units of X must be given up. Opportunity costs for country B can be calculated using the same method. As country A is comparatively more efficient (has the lower opportunity cost) in the production of X, it should specialize in the production of X and export it in exchange for Y in whose production country A's relative efficiency is lower (opportunity cost higher). Thus, according to the theory of comparative advantage, specialization and exchange will benefit both countries as long as their trade is based on cost differentials. Alternatively, comparative advantage arises from differences in the productivity of resources employed. As labour was assumed to be the only factor of production, differences in productivity were in fact differences in labour productivity.

Despite its elegance and simple explanation of trade, the law of comparative advantage suffers from a number of limitations. Its main drawback is that it is based on the unrealistic and simplistic assumptions of two countries producing only two goods. No reference is made to the possibility of dynamic effects of trade as it is assumed that

Table 10.1 Comparative advantage (output per unit of labour)

	Country A	Country B
Commodity X	10	4
Commodity Y	4	2

each country possesses a fixed stock of resources whose efficiency remains constant as trade takes place. To be mutually beneficial, trade should lead, over time, to such dynamic effects as growth in the stock of resources and greater efficiency in their use through research and development and economies of scale. The theory is also based on the relative productivity of entire industries and takes no account of the differences between individual firms. It does, however, provide a basic rationale for the mutual benefits of trade, which has important implications for the trade policies of national governments and the World Trade Organization alike.

■ Heckscher–Ohlin theory of factor endowments (1933)[4]

The H–O theory of factor endowments (also known as factor proportions theory) was an attempt to refine the law of comparative advantage by emphasizing differences in factor endowments as the source of comparative advantage. This theory is still based on one of the assumptions of the classical models, namely, two countries. However, it includes some additional assumptions which make the theory more realistic. First, capital was added to labour as a factor of production. Second, countries were assumed to have different factor endowments and commodities produced with different factor intensities. This means that countries with relatively more abundant labour tended to use labour more intensively whilst countries with relatively more abundant capital tended to use capital more intensively. Thus, goods produced in China, a country with a huge amount of labour, reflect labour intensity whilst machinery produced in, say, Germany reflects capital intensity in factor usage. Third, whatever the factor intensity, both countries employed the same production technology, so that capital-abundant countries produced capital-intensive goods and labour-abundant countries produced labour-intensive goods.

The basic prediction of the H–O theory is that a country with a relative abundance of labour would be able to produce labour-intensive commodities at lower cost and export these commodities in exchange for capital-intensive commodities from capital-rich countries. How is factor abundance related to lower costs? A capital-abundant country will employ capital-intensive methods of production with a higher capital-to-labour ratio than the labour-abundant country. Assuming the same demand conditions in both countries, the prices of capital in the capital-abundant country and of labour in the labour-abundant country will be relatively lower. Capital-intensive commodities in the capital-abundant country will be produced at lower cost and give the country a comparative advantage in these commodities. By the same token, labour-intensive commodities in the labour-abundant country will be produced at lower cost and give the country a comparative advantage in these commodities. Thus, countries will export commodities that make intensive use of those factors with which they are well endowed and import goods that make intensive use of those factors which are relatively scarce.

10.2.2 Modern explanations of trade

Unlike classical explanations which are mainly concerned with trade between nations, modern explanations use firm-based approaches to explain how firms trade. They focus on the process through which firms develop comparative advantages over time so that they can compete effectively with their rivals. Thus, modern theories of trade ask why is it that some firms are more successful in exporting than others.

An important aspect of modern theories is the removal of the assumption of constant returns to scale and its replacement with increasing returns to scale. Increasing returns to scale give rise to the concept of *economies of scale* whereby a given percentage increase in inputs results in a greater percentage increase in output. That is, as we increase the scale of production, costs per unit of output (average costs) diminish. This implies increasing productivity of the factors of production. This increased productivity, combined with the firm's specific assets, such as its superior technical know-how, management and marketing techniques, enables the firm to derive further advantages from internal economies of scale.

In addition to these *internal economies of scale*, firms may also benefit from *external economies of scale* by operating in close proximity to each other in a cluster of related firms and industries supplying materials and services. Whereas internal economies of scale are related directly to the scale of a firm's operations, external economies of scale arise from the size and structure of the industry. The closer the cooperation and the sharing of common expertise, the greater the benefits to individual firms making up the industry. This is particularly true in the case of the motor and aircraft manufacturing industries in which an individual manufacturer relies heavily on its interaction with other firms to create a highly competitive critical mass. Each firm, small, medium, or large, specializes in a particular product or service and thus contributes the direct benefits of its own comparative advantage to this critical mass. The consequence is a highly interactive and interdependent cluster of firms that enjoy joint benefits and provide one of the most effective barriers to entry to foreign firms, which may resort to FDI to take advantage of this location-specific shared advantage.

■ Product life-cycle theory

In an important paper published in 1966, Vernon advanced the hypothesis that new products experience a series of stages or phases in their development and their comparative advantage varies from one stage to the next as they go through their life cycle.[5] Vernon's observations were based largely on products developed and produced in the USA and are therefore an attempt to explain US trade patterns in terms of the life-cycle of the products exported by the USA. Vernon identified the following four stages of a product's life cycle:

Stage 1: Introduction. The new product is introduced requiring a great deal of highly skilled labour input and investment through research and development. Following its innovation, the new product is produced employing capital-intensive production methods reflecting the relatively rich capital endowment of the innovating country. Product innovation is in response to an observed need by potential customers in the domestic market where it is first introduced using a variety of marketing techniques. The very novelty of this new product, developed with the use of highly firm-specific assets, gives its innovator a certain amount of monopoly power with rising profits. If the new product is successful in the market of the innovating country, the product is then exported.

Stage 2: Growth. At this stage exports continue to rise as foreign demand grows. The continued success of the product inevitably attracts more competition by the firm's local and international rivals who respond with similar products in an effort to protect their market segments. Increased competition in turn forces the innovating firm to increase the capital intensity of production to maintain its comparative cost advantage. It is at this stage that the firm starts the search for alternative production sites in countries with low-input costs, such as relatively cheap labour. This is the beginning of the firm's FDI activities. Profits stabilize.

Stage 3: Maturity. Exports from the innovating country begin to decline as the firm's rivals begin to catch up with the success of the innovating firm. In an effort to reduce costs and remain competitive, the product is standardized to make its production more flexible and relatively cheaper using largely low-skilled labour in labour-rich countries. Production at home continues but with much higher capital intensity, especially if the product is given a new lease of life by upgrading. Increased price competitiveness forces the firm to discount the price to maintain its market share. Production in low-cost countries is stepped up using subcontractors. With the maturity of the firm's comparative advantage, monopoly profits begin to decline as its initial technological advantage is eroded by rival firms with superior technology and a better product.

Stage 4: Decline. At this stage the product becomes completely standardized in its manufacture. Production is concentrated in the lowest-wage countries using unskilled labour with vital parts and components shipped from the home country. Home production may have reached its end and, quite possibly, what used to be exported from the innovating country may now be imported. Foreign prices continue to fall, reducing the product's profitability still further.

The product life-cycle approach can be applied to a variety of products such as synthetic fibres, electronic goods, radio and television, pocket calculators, and computers. One of the advantages of this theory is its flexibility in explaining not only why trade takes place but also why FDI replaces trade. However, as with many other theories, it is only a partial explanation. Innovation can take place not only in relatively capital-rich countries but also in countries with relatively high income and large domestic markets. Large domestic markets provide great incentives and opportunities to innovators and investors. Capital-intensity may in fact be human capital-intensity with highly skilled and scientifically trained labour, designers, scientists, researchers, engineers, and technicians accounting for the majority of the value chain from the innovation to the decline of the product. All these considerations indicate clearly why countries like the USA and Japan lead the world in the innovation and exporting of high-technology products.

■ Human skills

One of the implications of the product life-cycle theory is that countries which invest heavily into human capital will emerge with relatively abundant human skills, providing the country with an important source of comparative advantage as suggested by Hecksher–Ohlin theory. Investment in human capital takes many forms but is mainly in education and training, health and safety, and facilities to supply a continuous flow of highly educated and trained personnel and skilled labour. It is not just the quantity but also the quality of this type of investment which gives countries certain comparative advantages. Thus, countries with a relative abundance of human skills, made possible by heavy investment in human capital, will provide incentives and opportunities for firms to innovate new products for export. By tracing the skills development of a particular country, it is possible to provide some explanation for its trade patterns.

■ Income similarities theory

Linder (1961) considers the role incomes play in determining the demand patterns and volume of trade between countries with a similar level of economic development and factor endowments.[6] It is argued that in countries with relatively high levels of income and discerning consumer tastes, such as the USA, it pays the innovators of new and high-technology products to concentrate their efforts on capturing the domestic market. Once the domestic market has been saturated, firms seek markets in countries with similar incomes and tastes. The consequent pattern of trade is similar to that of domestic sales, with similar products and service requirements since similarity in income levels often leads to similarity in tastes and preferences. This is particularly true in the case of luxury goods such as expensive cars, watches, computers, computer games, and the like. Thus, by targeting these countries, firms are able to create economies of scale and the basis for further comparative advantage.

■ Intra-industry trade

The income similarities theory can be used to explain the nature of trade in similar products between countries known as intra-industry trade. However similar the traded products may seem, in reality they are highly differentiated products whose individual attributes appeal differently to different groups of consumers. Britain exports Jaguar cars to Germany but at the same time imports Mercedes cars from Germany because, even though both cars may be generically similar, Jaguar and Mercedes are highly differentiated products. As there is demand in both countries for both products, both will be imported and exported simultaneously to satisfy this demand. There is a wide range of different but highly substitutable products, each with brand allegiance, being traded between countries throughout the world.

What makes intra-industry trade possible? First, consumers in each country prefer a wide choice of brands, ranging from beer to textiles to pharmaceuticals, giving international firms wider markets. Second, as each manufacturer specializes in the production of a highly differentiated product with brand allegiance, it is able to benefit from economies of scale as foreign demand grows. Third, economies of scale enable firms to absorb transport costs to remain competitive in world markets.

■ Porter's competitive advantage

A survey of the world's trading countries reveals that some countries are more successful in exporting than others. It also shows that even countries with natural endowments giving them an inherent absolute advantage sometimes fail to exploit their absolute advantage to the full, whilst others, even those with less of an absolute advantage, excel. What accounts for these differences? How do countries and their firms and industries develop and maintain their distinct competitive advantages?

Porter argues that the existing international trade theories provide only a partial explanation and suggests that answers to these questions may be found in the way the countries and firms develop strategies to maintain and enhance their productivity and competitiveness over time.[7] According to Porter, countries possess very few natural resources or factor endowments that are inherited but instead create competitive advantage through sustained effort in investment and capital formation. It is not just the quantity of investment but its quality that really matters. Relative factor abundance is no guarantee that countries will compete successfully in world markets. Indeed, even countries with little or no factor endowment may find it necessary to establish key industries by providing incentives to stimulate innovation, investing in the country's infrastructure, and establishing institutions for education and training to create a skilled labour supply. Governments can do a great deal to create the right business environment and investment climate to encourage firms to specialize and ultimately become world leaders. The Dutch experience in reclaiming land from the North Sea to increase the size of the land is a good illustration of Porter's view of how countries can overcome their lack of factor endowment and turn it into a distinct advantage through sheer determination and creativeness. The result is that the Dutch are now major suppliers of fruit and vegetables and world leaders in the cut-flowers industry.

Porter identifies four broad determinants of a country's international competitiveness or competitive advantage:

- *Factor endowments*: Natural resources provide a country with an initial competitive advantage but ultimately it is the quality of its advanced factors which determine and enhance its competitive advantage.

- *Demand conditions*: The nature and structure of the domestic industry, the intensity of domestic competition, the size and composition of the home market, and the existence of consumers who consistently demand high-quality products and services underpin the ability of a country's firms and industries to compete with the best in the world through product innovation and upgrading.

- *Related and supporting industries*: A firm that is operating within the critical mass created by these industries enhances its competitive advantage through close working relationships, joint research and problem-solving, close proximity, and sharing of knowledge and experience.

■ *Firm strategy, structure, and rivalry*: The ability of firms to create and sustain international competitiveness is either enhanced or hindered by the way in which firms are owned, managed, and formulate their competitive strategy. According to Porter, firms with sound and creative management styles, facing the intensity and vigour of domestic competition, will be successful by continually striving to reduce costs and undertaking research and development to stay ahead of their rivals.

These four determinants, collectively rather than individually, create the conditions to enable countries and firms to compete with the best in the world. Porter's view of competitive advantage is developed further in Chapter 13.

10.3 Balance of Payments (BoP)

A country's economy is said to be open when the country trades with other countries. The degree of 'openness', usually measured by the ratio of its exports and imports to its gross domestic product (GDP), indicates the extent of the country's dependence on trade to sustain its economic performance and standard of living. This dependence on or linkage with the rest of the world's economies is through two broad flows of economic activities: real flows (trade in goods and services) and money flows (financial transactions to pay for goods and services and to purchase assets).

The balance of payments may be defined as the official record of all transactions between residents of one country and residents of the rest of the world (RoW) over a given period of time, usually a year. It is a flow statement, similar to a cash flow statement of a firm, keeping a record of all international transactions between a country and the RoW. Any transaction which gives rise to a payment to be made to a country's residents is entered as a credit item in that country's BoP and any transaction which results in a payment to be made to a resident of the RoW is entered as a debit item. Thus, flows of payments to residents of the UK, for example, are credit (plus) items while payment outflows from the UK are debit (minus) items. UK exports of machinery, receipt of gifts from the RoW, deposits by foreigners in a UK bank, or the purchase of assets by foreigners, are all credit items. By the same token, imports of cars into the UK, the purchase of assets in the RoW by UK residents, and holidays abroad are all debit items.

As Table 10.2 illustrates, there are two basic accounts in the balance of payments: the *current account* and the *capital and financial account* (often known simply as the capital account). The current account shows flows of goods, services, and transfer payments between the UK and the RoW. There are two sub-accounts within the current account: *visible trade* and *invisibles*. Visible trade includes exports and imports of goods and the resulting balance is referred to as the *trade balance*. If exports exceed imports, there is a *trade surplus* and if imports exceed exports, there is a *trade deficit*. Invisibles include imports and exports of services, such as tourism, shipping, banking, professional services, and transfer payments. Transfer payments include

Table 10.2 Summary of UK balance of payments, 1997 (£m.)

Current Account		
Visible trade		
Exports		171,798
Imports		183,590
Trade balance		−11,792
Invisibles		
Net trade in services	11,160	
Net income	12,168	
Net current transfers	−3,530	
Invisible balance		19,798
Current account balance		8,006
Capital and Financial Account		
Capital account balance		262
Net direct investment	−13,087	
Net portfolio investment	−22,368	
Net other investment	24,986	
Changes in official reserves	2,357	
Financial account balance		−8,112
Net errors and omissions		−156
Capital and financial account balance		−8,006

Source: UK Balance of Payments, Office for National Statistics, Crown copyright 1999. Reproduced with permission.

payments between individual residents (the so-called *net property income from abroad*, consisting of interest, profit, and dividends, and *compensation of employees*) and between governments (grants and aid to foreign governments and contributions to overseas institutions such as budgetary contributions to the EU). The resulting invisible balance plus the visible trade balance make up the *current account balance*.

The capital and financial account of the balance of payments shows transactions in financial assets between a country and the RoW. In any given year, UK residents purchase real assets (holiday homes, plant, and equipment, etc.) or paper assets (financial assets in the form of shares in companies, government bonds, and the like) abroad. Likewise, residents of the RoW purchase similar assets in the UK. The capital account records migrants' transfers, EU fixed capital transfers (under the regional development and agricultural guidance funds), and the cancellation of debt. The financial account records payments to UK residents for investments in the UK and payments by UK residents for investments overseas. Investments include direct investment, portfolio investment, and other investment (trade credit, loans, currency transactions, and transfers of deposits). As in the case of current account entries, payments into the UK are credited and payments out of the UK are debited.

An important aspect of the capital and financial account is that a current account surplus is always matched by a capital and financial account deficit and a current account deficit with a capital and financial account surplus. Just as in the case of a firm, any deficits in current transactions are financed either by borrowing, by selling assets, or by drawing on reserves. The opposite is true in the case of a surplus in current receipts, in which case the surplus is either loaned out, used to purchase foreign assets, or used to build up the country's currency reserves. The final entry in the financial account relates to *official financing*. The main function of this entry is to ensure that the balance of payments always balances. That is, if there is an overall deficit in the balance of payments, the accommodating balance is a credit, so that the sum of all the entries in the balance of payments is always zero. The opposite is true in the case of a surplus in the balance of payments. As the name 'official financing' suggests, this entry shows the role a country's central bank plays in ensuring this accommodating balance. Suppose there is a balance of payments deficit. The central bank finances this deficit on behalf of the government by running down its official reserves of foreign currency. And in the case of a surplus, the central bank adds to its official reserves. Thus, changes in the overall balance of payments position are reflected in changes in the size of official reserves. This aspect of official financing is developed further in the next chapter.

Balance of payments statistics are very difficult to obtain and forecast. For one thing, not every payment into and out of a country is properly accounted for. In an ideal world every resident entering and leaving a country should declare accurately the value of items brought in and taken out. But this is not an ideal world and many items go unnoticed and undeclared. Much of the value of foreign investment in and out of a country is extremely difficult to measure. Many contraband items such as drugs are smuggled in without being declared even though it is common knowledge that the drugs trade exists. Consequently, it is very seldom that the BoP balance is obtained through accurate figures. Therefore, a statistical device known as the *balancing item* is used to account for net errors and omissions and bring about the necessary statistical adjustment.

10.4 Summary

'**INTERNATIONAL** trade' describes the flow of goods and services and accompanying payments between countries. It has a major impact on the firms and countries which engage in it. A number of theories have been proposed to explain why nations trade. These theories can broadly be classified under two headings: classical and modern. Classical theories are mainly country-based and concern the use of natural resources. These include Adam Smith's theory of absolute advantage, Ricardo's theory of comparative advantage, and the Hecksher–Ohlin factor proportions theory. Modern theories focus more on firms or the resources a country develops through investment in education and technology. They attempt to explain why intra-industry trade occurs or why some industries and countries appear to be more successful in trade than others. Payment flows, investment, and other financial transactions between countries are recorded in the balance of payments. The balance of payments consists of a current account, which records visible exports and imports and invisible trade in services and related items, and a capital account, which records investment and other transactions in financial assets. When official financing is included, the capital account deficit (surplus) should equal the current account surplus (deficit).

Review Questions

1 Explain the difference between 'absolute advantage' and 'comparative advantage'.

2 To what extent do the theory of comparative advantage and Hecksher–Ohlin theory contribute to our understanding of the reasons for and the benefits of international trade?

3 To which type of industries and countries might product life-cycle theory be applicable?

4 How does Porter's theory of competitive advantage explain why some industries and countries appear to be more successful in trade than others?

5 Which items make up the current account of a country's balance of payments? Why should the current account balance equal the capital and financial account balance?

Study Topic: Trade Specialization in the Modern World

Why is it that some countries seem to produce more successful trading companies than others? Why is the USA home to world leaders in computers and computer software, aircraft manufacture, mass-market car manufacture, soft drinks, fast food, and numerous other industries? Or, for that matter, why are Boeing and Microsoft both based in Seattle, in the north-western corner of the USA, rather than in another part of the country? Why are the Japanese good at making cameras, the Germans at making upmarket cars, or the Swiss at making watches and clocks? Why are the major financial centres of the world in places like New York, Tokyo, London, and Zurich? Why do Americans and Western Europeans buy Japanese cars when they produce large numbers of cars themselves?

Traditional theories explain trade specialization in terms of absolute or comparative advantage. They argue that natural resource endowments are important, as well as relative production efficiencies in different industries and countries. The question is: to what extent do these theories provide an answer to the questions above? Does the USA have a comparative advantage in producing computers or Japan in producing cameras? And if so, is it a natural or an acquired comparative advantage? Or is it simply these countries' good fortune that they are the home of a number of successful companies like IBM or Canon? Perhaps it is the companies themselves which have created their own advantages.

Modern theories suggest a variety of other explanations for these trade patterns, focusing on the way in which countries or companies develop their resources and skills or on the competitive environment in which companies and industries operate. It may be that traditional and modern theories each provide part of the answer to the above questions, or simply that a company's location is sometimes an accident of history.

Study Topic Questions

1 Why do you think the USA has become the most successful trading nation?

2 Why do you think the Japanese are good at making cameras, the Germans at making upmarket cars and other types of precision engineering, and the Swiss at making watches and clocks?

3 Why do you think giant companies like Boeing and Microsoft retain their operating base in the place where they originated?

4 To what extent, if any, is the theory of comparative advantage still relevant to the above questions?

5 Which of the modern theories of international trade seem to offer the most perceptive answer to these questions?

Notes

1 Adam Smith, *An Inquiry into the Nature and Causes of the Wealth of Nations*, Great Books (Encyclopaedia Britannica, 1952), vol. 39; first published in 1776.

2 Ibid., bk. 4, Pt. 2, 194.

3 David Ricardo, *The Principles of Political Economy and Taxation*, edited by R. M. Hartwell, (Pelican Classics, 1971); first published in 1817.

4 Bertil Ohlin, *Interregional and International Trade* (Harvard University Press, 1933).

5 Raymond Vernon, 'International Investments and International Trade in the Product Life-Cycle', *Quarterly Journal of Economics* (May 1966), 190–207.

6 S. B. Linder, *An Essay on Trade and Transformation* (John Wiley, New York, 1961).

7 M. E. Porter, *The Competitive Advantage of Nations* (Free Press, 1998); first published in 1990.

Recommended Reading

- Bhagwati, J. N., Panagariya, A., and Srinivasan, T. N., *Lectures on International Trade* (MIT Press, 1998).

- Brenton, P., Scott, H., and Sin, P., *International Trade: A European Text* (Oxford University Press, 1997).

- Carbaugh, R., *International Economics* (South-Western, 1999).

- Jepma, C., *International Trade: A Business Perspective* (Longman, 1996).

- Kreinin, M. E., *International Economics: A Policy Approach* (Dryden, 1998).

- Krugman, P. R., and Obstfeld, M., *International Economics: Theory and Policy* (Addison-Wesley, 1997).

11

Foreign Exchange Markets and Exchange Rate Systems

Objectives

- to distinguish between nominal, effective, and real exchange rates
- to explain the operation of the foreign exchange market
- to outline the purchasing power parity theory of exchange rates
- to compare and contrast different types of exchange rate system
- to relate the different types of exchange rate system to the single European currency

11.1 Introduction

ONE of the main features of international business is that transactions involve the use of different national currencies whose values fluctuate frequently, adding yet another source of risk and uncertainty to a firm's operations. International business managers must be prepared to use whatever measures are available to them to protect the value of cash flows in the face of these fluctuating currencies, or face operating losses. What makes the task of minimizing exchange rate risks so difficult is that, unlike selling goods and services over which the firm may have more effective control, exchange rate fluctuations are completely beyond the firm's control or influence. Wrong or ill-timed strategies to deal with exchange rate fluctuations can seriously affect an international business firm's ability to conduct business, or even to remain in business. On the other hand, firms with experience and foresight may be able to turn these risks to their advantage and even make a certain amount of profit through foreign exchange gains.

The purpose of this chapter is to consider four aspects of foreign exchange that are important to international business: the nature of exchange rates, the determination of exchange rates, foreign exchange markets, and exchange rate systems.

11.2 The Nature of Exchange Rates

FOREIGN exchange is any financial instrument which enables firms or individuals to make payments from one national currency to the currency of another country. Banks and similar institutions are the most active facilitators in the use of such an instrument. Using the most advanced means of communication at their disposal, they effect the transfer of currencies in a matter of seconds. At its simplest level, such an exchange of currencies is undertaken by individuals who offer their own national currencies in exchange for another currency, as in the case of going abroad for holidays.

There are three types of exchange rate, each with its own definition and usefulness. The commonest type is the *nominal* or *bilateral* exchange rate which is used daily to pay for internationally traded goods and services. It expresses the value of one national currency in terms of another; alternatively, it is the rate at which one unit of a given national currency will exchange for a foreign currency. Thus defined, the exchange rate of the pound sterling is the price of one unit of the £ expressed in terms of, say, the US dollar ($), the Deutsche Mark (DM), or the euro. Using the DM as an example, this exchange rate can be expressed as either the number of units of the DM which can be purchased with one unit of the £ i.e. 1£ = DM,2.81 (= DM/£), or the number of units of the £ needed to purchase one unit of the DM, i.e. DM1 = £0.356 (=£/DM). A UK resident can obtain DM2.81 worth of German goods and services with one unit of the £ and a German can expect to purchase only 36p worth of British goods and services with one unit of the DM.

Although very useful in indicating the daily value of a given currency for transaction purposes, nominal exchange rates offer very limited information about the value of one currency in relation to other currencies. Countries that trade with many other countries use many different currencies to pay for goods and services. Therefore, an indication of how much one unit of a given national currency can buy in international markets is useful. A measure of a national currency's international value in terms of a given basket of other national currencies is provided by the *effective exchange rate*. In the case of the £, this rate is often referred to as the *sterling trade-weighted index* ('sterling index' for short) and calculated as follows:

$$EER_£ = (DM/£ \times W_G) + ($/£ \times W_{US}) + (FF/£ \times W_{Fr}) + \dots \text{etc.}$$

Thus, the international value of the £ is expressed as the average of the nominal exchange rates included in the 'basket', each multiplied by a given weight (W_G, W_{US}, W_{Fr}, etc.), indicating the relative importance of each country in Britain's international trade. The effective exchange rate is then normally expressed as an index. In the last week of December 1998 the sterling index stood at 101.00, with the highest for the year at 108.90.[1] This means that, at the end of 1998, the UK bought 1p more of imports for each £'s worth of exports than it had done in the base year (1990 = 100). This represented a small appreciation of the £ against the currencies of the countries making up the 'basket'.

Nominal exchange rates are of limited use in indicating competitiveness in the countries they represent. A measure of international competitiveness is given by the *real exchange rate*. International competitiveness indicates a country's competitive advantage in relation to other trading nations. In particular, it refers to the relative competitiveness of its industries and firms, their ability to gain market shares both in domestic and international markets. One of the major determinants of the international competitiveness of a country is its inflation rate as compared to the inflation rates of its trading partners. It is no surprise, therefore, to see in the following formula the relative inflation rate playing the key role in determining the real exchange rate. For example, the pound sterling's real exchange rate with respect to the DM is expressed as:

$$RER_£ = (£ \text{ price of UK goods})/(DM \text{ price of German goods}) \quad (DM/£),$$

that is, the ratio of the UK price level to that of Germany, multiplied by the nominal exchange rate between the DM and the £. Whenever the UK inflation rate goes up, assuming the German inflation rate and the nominal exchange rate remain the same, Germans pay more for UK goods. However, this situation cannot be expected to last long because German consumers would find alternative, cheaper sources of the same goods and, in consequence, British firms would lose their German market share. Ultimately, a higher inflation rate in the UK would lead to a fall in the demand for sterling by Germans and would be compensated by a consequent fall in the exchange rate for sterling against the DM.

11.3 The Determination of Nominal Exchange Rates

IN the definition given above, an exchange rate was defined as the price of one national currency in terms of another. As an exchange rate is a price, it can therefore be determined in the same way as the price of any other commodity. The price of any commodity is determined through the interaction between the demand for and the supply of the commodity in question. One word of caution, however: there is a need to be clear about the meaning of the demand for and supply of a particular currency.

11.3.1 The demand for a currency

Taking the pound sterling and the DM as an example, the demand for the pound is the need for Germans to convert their DMs into £s to pay for British goods, services, and assets—both direct (FDI) or indirect (portfolio) investment—that Germans wish to purchase. Likewise, demand for the DM is the need by Britons to convert their £s into DMs to pay for German goods, services, and assets that they wish to purchase. A quick review of the balance of payments section of Chapter 10 will reveal the sources of demand for both currencies. Under the current account, the demand for UK exports of goods and services and, under the capital and financial account, the demand for UK-owned assets will give rise to demand for the pound sterling. Demand for the pound sterling is a derived demand: anyone wishing to buy something produced in Britain will have to pay for it in pounds sterling. The same reasoning applies equally to the DM from British purchasers' point of view. Whenever a UK resident wishes to purchase German goods, services, and assets, he/she is expressing a demand for DMs to pay for these purchases. Therefore, the demand for DMs is derived from the demand for German goods, services, and assets by UK residents.

Another important source of demand for the pound sterling is the need for foreign governments to maintain foreign exchange reserves, a form of official savings. These reserves are used to pay for official transactions and to intervene in foreign exchange markets to support the exchange rate for their own currencies under a fixed or managed floating exchange rate system. These reserves normally consist of the major foreign currencies used in international trade and financial transactions. Reserve currencies are often referred to as 'hard currencies' because they are easily convertible into other currencies and relatively stable over time. They include the US$, Japanese yen, DM, and sterling. Thus, if a foreign government wanted to reduce its holdings of US$ but increase its holdings of sterling, the result would be an increase in the demand for sterling and reduction in the demand for the US$.

The total demand for sterling is, therefore, the sum of the demand for pounds to purchase UK goods and services and short-term and long-term UK assets, and the demand arising from the need for foreign governments to add sterling to their official reserves. Every international transaction shown on a country's balance of payments will give rise to a foreign exchange transaction in the foreign exchange market and thus will influence the exchange rate of a currency.

Whatever the sources of demand for sterling (or for any other currency), the basic law of demand will apply. Other things being equal, the higher the price of sterling, the lower will be the quantity demanded of sterling, and vice versa. Thus, there is an inverse relationship between the price and the quantity demanded of a currency; this means the demand curve for sterling and any other currency is downward-sloping from left to right, that is, a negatively sloped curve when it is plotted against the price of another currency.

To summarize, the demand for any currency will be generally determined by: (a) its exchange rate; (b) the price of goods and services in the country it represents; (c) the prices of competing goods and services produced by other countries; (d) the income of consumers; and (e) in the case of portfolio investment, relative interest rates and investors' expectations about future developments.

11.3.2 The supply of a currency

The sources of supply of a given currency are exactly the opposite of the demand for another currency. The supply of pounds is the amount offered by UK residents to be converted into DMs to purchase German goods, services, and assets. To demand DMs, UK residents must supply pounds, just as Germans must supply DMs to obtain pounds. Whenever a foreign currency is demanded, domestic currency must be offered to pay for it. It is, therefore, convenient to speak in terms of the demand for and the supply of pounds or the demand for and the supply of DMs, instead of both, as a demand for DMs implies a supply of pounds and a demand for pounds implies a supply of DMs.

Unlike the demand for pounds, the supply curve of pounds slopes upwards (positively) when plotted against the DM price of pounds, indicating a positive relationship between the quantity of pounds demanded and its DM price. Other things being equal, the lower the DM price of pounds, the greater the quantity of UK goods, services, assets, and hence of pounds demanded by Germans; and the higher the DM price of pounds, the lower will be the quantity of German goods, services, assets, and hence of DMs demanded by UK residents.

To summarize, the supply of any currency will generally be determined by the same factors as those determining the demand for any currency.

11.3.3 The equilibrium exchange rate

Figure 11.1 illustrates the relationship between the demand for and the supply of pounds in the market for foreign exchange, expressing the price of pounds in DMs. The vertical axis measures the price of the pound sterling (its exchange rate) in terms of DMs and the horizontal axis measures the quantity of pounds. The demand curve for pounds, representing the total number of transactions resulting in receipts of DM by UK residents, slopes negatively downwards, indicating the inverse relationship between the price and quantity demanded of pounds. The supply curve, representing the total number of transactions giving rise to payments of DM by UK residents,

Figure 11.1 Determination of the pound sterling exchange rate

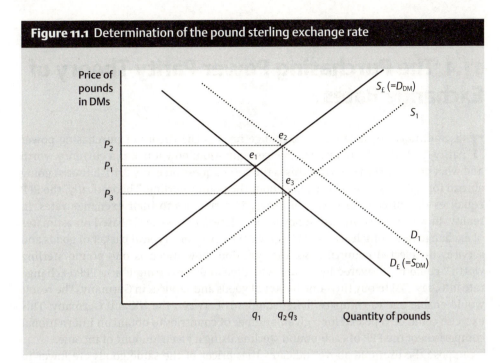

slopes positively upwards, indicating the positive relationship between the price and quantity supplied of pounds. The intersection between the demand for and supply of pounds (e_1) indicates the point of equilibrium, that is, the equilibrium rate of exchange. As long as the demand and supply of pounds remain the same, this equilibrium rate will prevail and the quantity demanded will be q_1.

But what happens if the demand and supply conditions do not remain the same? Suppose the German demand for British goods increases, shifting the demand curve for pounds to D_1. With the supply of pounds remaining the same, the equilibrium exchange rate will now move to e_2, with the quantity demanded of pounds moving from q_1 to q_2. The result is an *appreciation* of the pound sterling against the DM, as more DMs will be required to purchase one pound's worth of British goods. If, on the other hand, British demand for German goods were to increase, the supply curve of pounds would shift to S_1 and, with the demand curve for pounds remaining as $D_£$, the equilibrium exchange rate would move to e_3 and the quantity of pounds supplied to q_3. The result is a *depreciation* of the pound sterling, as more pounds will be required to purchase a given amount of German goods.

11.4 The Purchasing Power Parity Theory of Exchange Rates

THE traditional explanation of exchange rates is the theory of purchasing power parity (PPP). It seeks to answer the basic question: how much is a currency worth and what determines its worth? This is the sort of question every British tourist going abroad for holidays would be asking about the pound sterling. Theoretically, the PPP equalizes the purchasing power of different currencies to their exchange rates. In reality, however, the purchasing power of different currencies is based on estimates of exchange rates which are used to equate the prices of a typical basket of goods and services in selected countries. So, the question 'how much is one pound sterling worth?' could be answered by taking, say, £100 and converting it at a PPP exchange rate into, say, DM to buy the same basket of goods and services in Germany. The result would enable one to compare living standards between the UK and Germany. This exercise could be repeated for a given number of countries to obtain an international comparison of the PPP of each pound sterling using a given amount of income.

Suppose the example above indicates that prices of the same goods are lower in Germany than in the UK. It would be profitable for UK importers to import these goods from Germany where they are cheaper and sell them in the UK where they are relatively dearer (disregarding transport costs). This practice, known as 'goods arbitrage', brings about an equalization of prices in both the UK and Germany and the result is 'one price' with respect to each commodity in the basket. Once this price equalization is complete, goods arbitrage will cease, as it would be pointless to engage in importing goods whose prices are the same in both countries.

An interesting example of this law of one price is provided by *The Economist* which has been publishing the McDonald's Big Mac index every year since 1986. To apply the law of one price to actual prices in a given number of countries, a standard product which is identical in quality and content in every country is selected. McDonald's Big Mac seems to fulfil the requirements of such a homogeneous product admirably. Using a list of seventy-nine countries, *The Economist* compares Big Mac prices to see if an exchange rate is under or overvalued with respect to its long-term equilibrium rate. That is, the Big Mac index compares the actual exchange rate with the rate implied by the PPP of a given currency. For example, on 1 November 1997 *The Economist* gave the prices of a Big Mac in the USA and China as $2.53 and 9.70 yuan respectively.[2] By comparing the ratio of these prices, the PPP implied exchange rate can be calculated as follows:

9.70 yuan/$2.53 = 3.8340 yuan/$.

Thus, according to the PPP theory, the exchange rate between the Chinese yuan and the US dollar should be $1= 3.8340 yuan based on the comparison of Big Mac prices. But the actual exchange rate between the $ and the yuan on that day was in fact 8.310 yuan/$; this would indicate that the yuan was undervalued by 0.5386 or nearly 54 per cent.[3]

Using the example above, the following formula is used to calculate the PPP exchange rate:

$P_C = E_{\text{yuan}/\$}\ P_{\text{US}}$, which can be rearranged to give

$E_{\text{yuan}/\$} = P_C / P_{\text{US}}$.

Whilst it offers an interesting and useful indication of divergences between actual and implied exchange rates, the PPP theory suffers from some serious shortcomings. First, it applies only to tradable goods and not every good is tradable. The Big Mac is sold only domestically and not traded internationally. Second, economy-wide price and expenditure data used in calculating PPPs are unlikely to be appropriate for each country in question and in some countries may be very difficult to obtain. Third, domestic prices can differ because of the existence of trade barriers and/or differences in rates of tax, for example, value added tax (VAT) rates. Fourth, it is difficult to assemble a representative basket of goods and services for each country because of differences in tastes, preferences, and buying habits due to cultural differences. As long as these shortcomings exist, it is very difficult to obtain the truly representative exchange rates implied by PPP theory.

11.5 The Foreign Exchange Market

A market is an area of activity which facilitates negotiation between buyers and sellers in the exchange of a well-defined commodity. Foreign currencies are a homogeneous commodity: a pound sterling is a pound sterling no matter where or how it is traded. In the case of the foreign exchange market (forex) for pounds, buyers are those who need pounds in exchange for their own currencies and sellers are those who possess pounds which they want to convert into foreign currencies for reasons explained in Section 11.3. The basic function of the foreign exchange market for pounds is to provide facilities for foreign exchange transactions between buyers and sellers of pounds and to enable them to negotiate the price (exchange rate) at which one pound can be converted into other currencies. As with any other market, this function of the foreign exchange market can be analysed by using the basic laws of demand and supply as explained in Section 11.3.

There is not a single location for the foreign exchange market. Foreign exchange transactions are carried out over the telephone or on computers which link national foreign exchange markets around the world. The main participants are central banks, which buy and sell foreign currencies to maintain a desirable level of foreign reserves, and commercial banks, which engage in interbank transactions on behalf of their clients (that is, between banks in the UK and in other countries). Approximately

90 per cent of total trading in the London foreign exchange market is in the form of interbank foreign exchange transactions.

Other functions of the foreign exchange market include the provision of facilities for *spot* and *forward* transactions. Transactions in the *spot market* involve currencies for immediate delivery, usually within two working days. The spot rate is the commonest exchange rate quoted daily in all papers and by electronic means. The *forward market* is the market for foreign exchange for delivery and payment on a specified future date, usually in one month or three months, at today's spot rate. This market provides its participants with *hedging*, which means taking an offsetting position in the foreign exchange market to eliminate exposure to foreign exchange risk. Unless fixed in value, as is the case under a fixed exchange rate system, exchange rates are subject to fluctuations. With each fluctuation, the exchange rate of a foreign currency changes, requiring its holder to take the necessary measures to protect the value of its stock of foreign currencies.

For example, suppose a British exporter sold £1 million worth of goods to an Australian importer. In order to avoid any currency losses as a result of fluctuations, the British exporter might insist on immediate payment. In this case, the Australian firm would instruct its bank (which is usually an international bank with world-wide branches) to debit its account with AUS\$2.6270 million (at the spot rate £1 = AUS\$2.6270) and credit the British firm's account with £1 million (assuming no transaction costs for the sake of simplicity). However, the majority of international trade involves payments some time in the future. Suppose, the British firm allows the Australian firm to pay at the end of one month. There is no guarantee that at the end of one month the British firm will get its £1 million because of possible changes in the AUS\$ and £ exchange rate. It would, therefore, be in the interest of the British firm to sell forward AUS\$2.6270 million for delivery at the end of one month at today's spot rate. To do this, it enters into a forward contract with a financial intermediary (usually a commercial bank) which now assumes the foreign exchange risk for a commission. The financial intermediary in turn sells forward the £1 million's worth of AUS\$ to any firm which expects to make payment by the same amount to an Australian firm at some future date. Thus, as a consequence of this hedging, the British firm has eliminated its exposure risk because it knows how much it will receive for its AUS\$ at the end of one month (minus fees and commission charges) and no matter what happens to the exchange rate, the forward rate will remain the same.

By providing facilities for hedging, the foreign exchange market performs two more important functions. By arranging for payments to be made in the future, it provides credit facilities for international business firms. Secondly, the forward market is used for reducing exchange risks as shown in the example above.

11.6 Exchange Rate Systems

An exchange rate system reflects the nature of the exchange rate policy a country adopts in determining its currency's exchange rate. At one extreme, the policy may be to allow market forces to operate freely in determining exchange rates or, at the other extreme, the policy may be to intervene actively in foreign exchange markets to maintain the exchange rate at a particular, desired level.

11.6.1 Flexible exchange rate systems

Under a *flexible exchange rate system*, the monetary authorities of a country, represented by its central bank, allow market forces to determine the exchange rate for their currency. In other words, the currency is allowed to float in order to find its own rate in a freely competitive foreign exchange market. The alternative name for this system is a *floating exchange rate system*. The monetary authorities do not intervene at all in order to influence the conditions of supply and demand which operate exactly as illustrated in Figure 11.1. Whenever the price of the pound is above its equilibrium value, Germans will demand less pounds than the quantity supplied. This excess supply of pounds will result in a fall in the price of pounds, fewer pounds will be supplied and a greater quantity of pounds will be demanded. This process of automatic downward adjustment will continue until once again the equilibrium price of the pound is re-established. Exactly the opposite will occur whenever the price of the pound is below its equilibrium value. Thus, under a flexible exchange rate system, appreciation and depreciation of a currency are the spontaneous consequences of changes in the conditions of supply and demand, with the authorities playing no part in the process.

The main advantages of the flexible exchange rate system are as follows: (a) because of the automatic exchange rate adjustment, there is also an automatic adjustment in the actual current and capital transactions; (b) there is no need for the monetary authorities to maintain stocks of foreign monetary reserves with which to peg the value of the currency; and (c) the equilibrium exchange rate represents the true value of the currency at a particular time, as it is determined through the interactions of supply and demand. The main disadvantages are as follows: (a) as the exchange rate fluctuates in accordance with the laws of supply and demand, holders of the currency have no way of knowing in advance what the actual exchange rate will be, although this uncertainty may be reduced by the use of forward exchange markets; (b) there is no guarantee that market forces will generate an exchange rate appropriate for the prevailing economic conditions; (c) in cases of intense speculation against a currency, governments may not be able to avoid intervention to prevent such speculative activities from damaging the economy; and (d) freely fluctuating exchange rates may reduce the effectiveness of domestic economic policies, for example, depreciation may lead to a rise in the cost of imports and consequently in the inflation rate.

11.6.2 Fixed exchange rate systems

Under a *fixed exchange rate system*, the exchange rate can only fluctuate within specified bands around an official *par value*. These bands are necessary as it would be technically impossible to maintain a completely fixed exchange rate without some built-in flexibility and an unlimited stock of foreign exchange reserves. It is the responsibility of the country's central bank to peg the exchange rate to prevent unwanted and undesirable deviations from its par value by intervening in the foreign exchange markets. As long as the exchange rate remains within the specified bands, no intervention by the central bank would be necessary. To be able to intervene in the foreign exchange markets, the central bank must maintain a sufficient stock of foreign exchange reserves, consisting of the world's major foreign currencies such as the US dollar, DM, French franc, yen, and gold. The manner in which this intervention takes place may be summarized as follows.

Suppose the official par value of the pound in terms of the DM is £1 = DM3 with a band of + or − 5 per cent within which the exchange rate would be allowed to fluctuate. This would give an upper limit of DM3.15 and a lower limit of DM2.85. If the actual exchange rate begins to move towards its upper limit, the country's central bank would intervene in the foreign exchange market by selling pounds in exchange for foreign currencies which are added to its stock of foreign exchange reserves. If, on the other hand, the actual exchange rate moves towards its lower limit, then the central bank would intervene by buying pounds and paying for them out of its stock of foreign currencies. So, movements towards the upper limit of DM3.15 would increase the central bank's stock of foreign currency reserves and movements towards the lower limit of DM2.85 would reduce it.

A country's foreign exchange reserves are not limitless. No central bank can allow foreign exchange reserve losses to continue indefinitely, any more than it can keep on adding to its reserves. In cases where an exchange rate persistently threatens to exceed its upper or lower limit, a change in the official par value may be required. The currency is said to be *revalued* when its par value is increased and *devalued* when it is reduced. Revaluations and devaluations are characteristics of fixed exchange rate systems and are designed to give central banks and governments time to remedy the underlying causes of a currency's undesirable performance in the foreign exchange markets.

The main advantages of a fixed exchange rate system are: first, it removes uncertainty about the future value of a currency. Unless the currency's par value is changed suddenly, foreign exchange transactions are based on the existing par value and fluctuations within the specified bands. In this way, international trade and business activities are easier and international credit is safer. Second, it imposes a discipline on governments to pursue economic policies consistent with their exchange rate policy. Its disadvantages include (a) the need for central banks to maintain large stocks of foreign exchange reserves; (b) a country's balance of payments is prevented from automatic adjustment as under a flexible exchange rate system, forcing governments to use deflationary or reflationary policies to remedy balance of payments problems; (c) the maintenance of a fixed exchange rate system requires close international cooperation in agreeing on policies for economic growth and price stability, but such an agreement may not always be attainable as different governments have different political and economic objectives; and (d) changes in domestic interest rates may lead to pressure for the exchange rate to change, which may in turn disrupt the government's overall economic policy.

11.6.3 Managed exchange rate systems

A *managed exchange rate system* is a compromise system attempting to combine the best of the two extreme systems explained above and, at the same time, avoiding their disadvantages. It is basically a floating exchange rate system under which the central bank intervenes in the foreign exchange market in anticipation of unwarranted or undesirable changes in the exchange rate. If the country's currency is weakening in the foreign exchange markets, the central bank attempts to support the currency by buying the currency (selling foreign currencies). If the currency is strengthening, then the central bank sells the domestic currency (buys foreign currencies). Thus, the central bank *manages* the supply of the domestic currency in such a way as to stabilize its value at a particular level consistent with the government's overall economic policy. This system is sometimes known as a *managed float* or *dirty float* (as opposed to a 'clean float' where there is no intervention by the authorities).

16.6.4 Target zones

Target zones are a modified version of the flexible exchange rate system in which the central banks of major currencies engage in strategic market intervention to maintain their respective exchange rates within the agreed target zones or bands, with clearly indicated upper and lower limits. The main purpose of such an arrangement would be to bring stability to the world's major economies by limiting the amount by which each major currency (the US dollar, yen, and now the euro) can fluctuate against each other. The agreed target zones would be changed periodically to take into account global events and developments such as the Asian financial crisis of the late 1990s, causing volatility and misalignments. A variety of economic indicators, such as comparative inflation rates, international competitiveness, the amount of capital flows, and interest rates, would be used to determine the actual target zones.

Proponents of this system envisage the establishment of target zones as a formal exchange rate regime based on the dollar, the euro, and the yen as the core currencies. The stability of these currencies, which account for the great majority of payments in world trade, would in turn ensure the stability of the global economy, promote trade, encourage investment, and increase world prosperity.

The European Monetary System's Exchange Rate Mechanism (ERM) provides a good example of the way in which a target zone system operates. Under the ERM, each member currency was given a central value with an agreed percentage target zone, originally + or − 2.25 per cent for most of the member currencies and later increased to 15 per cent for all except the DM/Dutch guilder exchange rate (which remained at 2.25 per cent). To ensure the currencies remained within their target zones, close monetary policy coordination between member countries' central banks was required, especially the coordination of interventions in foreign exchange markets. A system like the ERM is also known as a *crawling peg* or *adjustable peg* exchange rate system.

To be successful, the target zones system would require close coordination by central banks on a global basis, with an international governance agency, such as the International Monetary Fund (IMF) acting as the coordinator and arbiter in the case of disagreements among members. However, in the face of uncertainties surrounding the global flows of capital, it would be very difficult to determine the actual target zones and to defend them at all costs. In addition, a larger stock of foreign exchange reserves would be needed to fend off any speculative attacks on the currencies concerned. Furthermore, close policy coordination and the linking of exchange rates would also require close coordination of domestic economic policies, a condition which participating countries would be reluctant to accept for fear of losing domestic policy sovereignty. Finally, setting target zones may tend to exacerbate business cycles by depriving economies of the self-adjustment mechanism. For example, during a recession an exchange rate tends to fall, which would require the raising of interest rates to keep the currency within its target zones. The rise in interest rates would worsen the economic slowdown requiring more potent measures to halt it.

11.7 The Euro

O^N 1 January 1999 a new currency called the euro came into being with the participation of eleven members of the European Union (EU). The UK, Denmark, and Sweden opted out and Greece was unable to qualify at that time. The introduction of the euro is the culmination of long-term efforts to create monetary union within the EU. If successful, the euro will enhance the efficiency of the Single European Market and will act as a step towards complete economic union in the EU. It is seen as the logical extension of the single market. The issue of the euro is discussed in detail in Chapter 16. At this point, a brief outline of its chief characteristics as an intra-EU fixed exchange rate system will be given.

The euro is designed as the future single currency to be used, ultimately, by all

Table 11.1 The euro conversion rates

National currency	1 euro equals	National currency	1 euro equals
Austrian schilling	13.7603	Irish pound	0.787564
Belgian franc	40.33990	Italian lira	1936.27000
Deutsche Mark	1.95583	Luxembourg franc	40.3399
Dutch guilder	2.20371	Portuguese escudo	200.482
Finnish markka	5.94573	Spanish peseta	166.38600
French franc	6.55957		

Source: European Central Bank.

members in place of their own currencies. Until 2002, the euro is being used as the common denominator to express the fixed exchange rate of each of the eleven national currencies and, increasingly, as a working currency. Table 11.1 indicates the fixed conversion rates as agreed in December 1998.

The European Central Bank (ECB) has been vested with the responsibility of implementing a single monetary policy with the agreement of the eleven participating members. The ECB is independent of national governments and its primary statutory responsibility is to 'maintain price stability' in the EU. With the ceding of their primary responsibilities to the ECB, national central banks have thus become a part of the European System of Central Banks, with the governor of each member central bank sitting on the ECB council responsible for formulating its monetary policies.

In January 2002, euro notes and coins will be introduced and in July 2002 all national currencies of the participating member states will be replaced by the euro, which will then become a true single currency. In the meantime, it will be used alongside the national currencies, enabling individual consumers and firms to pay either in their national currencies or in euros.

Even though the euro operates on the basis of a fixed exchange rate system within the EU, it floats against other major currencies. Since, even at the outset, it serves a market of nearly 290 million consumers, the euro is already considered as one of the three major world currencies alongside the US dollar and the Japanese yen. It will thus provide a much needed addition to the present level of international liquidity. Its early performance in the international foreign exchange markets, as represented by its bilateral exchange rate against the US dollar, was rather mixed. After a promising and almost euphoric start, which saw it reach the rate of $1.16, it fell to around $1.12 in February 1999.[4] Its future international value will be determined largely by the performance of the eleven participating member states and their ability to adhere to the EMU stability pact.

The euro is viewed as an instrument of Economic and Monetary Union (EMU), which itself has a political dimension. Once completed successfully, EMU may ultimately lead to a greater degree of political union. In the meantime, every decision affecting the performance of the euro and related issues will have a political ring to it.

11.8 Summary

THE most commonly quoted type of exchange rate is the nominal or bilateral exchange rate. This gives an indication of the rate at which one currency can be exchanged for another at a particular time. The nominal rate is determined by the supply and demand for the currencies concerned on the foreign exchange market. The supply and demand for a currency is derived from the supply and demand for a country's goods, services, and assets. The effective exchange rate values a currency in terms of a 'basket' of other currencies, weighted according to the proportion of the country's trade accounted for by each currency in the basket. The real exchange rate takes account of the relative inflation rates in two countries as well as the nominal exchange rate of their currencies. In theory, a nominal exchange rate should reflect the purchasing power parity of two currencies, that is, the amount of each currency required to buy the same basket of goods in each country; for various reasons, this is not always the case in practice.

Currencies have a spot rate at a particular time, but can also be bought at a forward rate—a rate which enables a trader to avoid currency fluctuations over a specified time. Countries adopt a variety of exchange rate systems. These range from a flexible or floating exchange rate system, where exchange rates are determined entirely by market forces, to a fixed exchange rate system, where the authorities maintain the rate within prescribed limits. Some currencies also operate within a managed system, which allows the central bank to intervene when necessary. Others operate within a target range. This was the case with the EU Exchange Rate Mechanism but the euro, whilst fixing its member currencies, also floats against the world's other convertible currencies.

Review Questions

1 How is the nominal exchange rate between two currencies determined?

2 What is meant by an effective exchange rate and why is it sometimes used in preference to the nominal exchange rate?

3 Why do nominal exchange rates not always reflect the purchasing power parity of the currencies involved?

4 What is the difference between a spot rate and a forward exchange rate? Why do traders sometimes make forward exchange contracts?

5 To what extent does a crawling peg exchange rate system overcome the disadvantages of both a fixed and a floating exchange rate system?

Study Topic: Europe's Single Currency

On 1 January 1999, eleven EU member states embarked on what was perhaps the most ambitious project in the EU's history: monetary union with its single European currency, the euro. Prior to 1999, most of the EU national currencies belonged to the Exchange Rate Mechanism (ERM). The ERM was a crawling peg exchange rate system where each member currency was allowed to fluctuate within agreed margins. After the foreign exchange market turbulence of 1992 and 1993, the fluctuation margins were increased, for most countries, from + or − 2.25 per cent to 15 per cent. This effectively took away the incentive for currency speculators to play one ERM currency off against another, as the member currencies rarely approached their limits and the authorities were therefore unlikely to be under pressure to intervene. What had been a narrow target zone, however, now became virtually a managed floating exchange rate system. The arrival of the euro has changed all that. National exchange rates within the euro zone are now permanently fixed to each other and to the euro and national currencies will be replaced by the euro by July 2002.

This raises the question: are permanently fixed exchange rates within the euro zone preferable to a crawling peg system or managed float or to the more freely floating system in which the pound sterling operates, for example? Fixed rates offer a number of advantages, especially when transaction costs are eventually eliminated as the euro replaces the national currencies. If the euro zone or wider EU is seen as an 'optimum currency area'—an area whose member countries enjoy close trade links and mobility of the factors of production (especially labour and capital)—then the euro may be seen as a logical and beneficial extension of the integration the EU has already achieved with its Single European Market. On the other hand, flexible exchange rates offer a self-adjusting mechanism to correct a balance of payments problem and boost a country's flagging competitiveness. Of course, the euro floats against the rest of the world's convertible currencies. This should allow external flexibility whilst hopefully providing a more stable currency than its smaller constituent currencies. However, its success will depend not only on the performance of its member economies, but also on the degree of convergence between these economies and on the flexibility of their labour and other factor markets.

Study Topic Questions

1 In what circumstances might a crawling peg exchange rate system like the ERM become a target for currency speculators?

2 In what ways, if any, might a single European currency be preferable to a simple fixed exchange rate system between the existing EU member currencies?

3 Do you think there is sufficient similarity, trade, and factor mobility between the euro zone countries to describe them as an 'optimum currency area'?

4 Would the loss of exchange rate flexibility be a major problem for a country like the UK if it adopted the euro?

5 What do the euro zone countries need to do in order to improve the internal flexibility of their economies?

Notes

1 *Sunday Times* Business News (27 Dec. 1998), 3.

2 *The Economist* (1 Nov. 1997), 113.

3 CHINA'S UNIT OF CURRENCY IS THE RMB YUAN, ALSO KNOWN AS THE RENMINBI.

4 A. BEATTIE, 'THE EUROPEAN ECONOMY', *Financial Times* (26 Feb. 1999), 6.

Recommended Reading

- El-Agraa, A. M., *The European Union: History, Institutions, Economics and Policies* (Prentice Hall, 1998).

- Ethier, W., *Modern International Economics* (Norton, 1995).

- Hansen, J. D., and Nielsen, J. U-M., *An Economic Analysis of the EU* (McGraw-Hill, 1997).

- Jepma, C., J., Jager, H., and Kamphuis, E., *Introduction to International Economics* (Longman, 1996).

- Kreinin, M. E., *International Economics: A Policy Approach* (Dryden, 1998).

- Robson, P, *The Economics of International Integration* (Routledge, 1998).

12

Foreign Direct Investment and Collaborative Strategies

Objectives

- to distinguish between types of foreign investment
- to indicate global trends in foreign direct investment (FDI) and the impact of FDI flows on home and host countries
- to analyse the determinants of FDI
- to evaluate the usefulness of theoretical explanations of FDI
- to contrast FDI with joint-venture agreements, strategic alliances, and other collaborative strategies

12.1 Introduction

MULTINATIONAL enterprises (MNEs) use a variety of strategies to enter foreign markets: exporting, foreign direct investment, licensing, franchising, and a number of other methods. These are discussed at length in Chapter 1. Historically, the two most important entry strategies have been exporting and foreign direct investment (FDI). Although FDI is not a new phenomenon, there has been a marked increase in FDI since the 1980s. Total world inflows of FDI in 1997 amounted to US$400 billion, seven times their value in 1980. Most of the investing companies are based in the industrialized countries, and most of their investment goes into other industrialized countries, but increasingly FDI is also flowing into the developing regions of the world. During the 1990s there has been a large influx of FDI into Asia, Latin America, and Eastern Europe.

In this chapter we explore these global trends in FDI and examine the reasons for the growth in FDI. We consider the impact of FDI on both the home and the host country's economy, as well as its implications for the global economy. We also discuss joint ventures and other collaborative agreements between companies. Each of these strategies raises complex and controversial issues. Some countries welcome inward investment, while others cautiously protect their domestic industries. Collaborative agreements help companies to develop their research, production, and markets, but they raise competition issues. These and related issues are developed in this chapter.

12.2 Foreign Investment in the Global Economy

12.2.1 Portfolio investment

Before considering the implications of foreign investment, it is important to distinguish between two forms of investment: portfolio investment and direct investment. Portfolio investment involves the acquisition of stocks and shares, financial deposits, and other financial assets in order to earn a return on surplus funds. In the international arena huge amounts of portfolio investment flow between the world's stock markets and other financial centres. Investors purchase shares on foreign stock markets or hold currency deposits at foreign banks, transferring large sums of 'hot money' across frontiers as investor confidence or interest rates rise and fall. Derivatives markets are now responsible for a vast increase in these capital flows. Derivatives are contracts which are 'derived' from underlying assets such as currencies, commodities, or equities. A derivatives contract may be for the purchase of currency at an agreed price on a future date (a forward exchange contract), for the purchase of a commodity at an agreed price on a future date (a futures contract), or it may grant an option to sell an amount of shares at a fixed price within a specified time (a share option). These contracts, and numerous similar variants, provide one of the parties with insurance or a 'hedge' against fluctuations in the price of the asset; the other party bears the risk in return for a 'premium' on the asset price.

In each case portfolio investors are searching for a profitable use for their surplus funds, either in the form of interest and dividends or when their financial assets are sold at a higher price. Portfolio investors may be financial institutions and brokers, institutional investors like insurance companies or pension funds, industrial and commercial companies, or individuals. Their investments are often sensitive to economic fluctuations or perceived weaknesses in an economy and, when there is turmoil in world markets, movements of portfolio investment may precipitate financial crashes such as the Asian financial crisis of the late 1990s. These investment flows tend to respond quickly when confidence is damaged, but their movements often reflect underlying strengths and weaknesses in economies and their institutions. Whilst the activities of portfolio investors are sometimes criticized as wasteful speculation, their funds also help to provide capital and a variety of financial services and their activities send important market signals.

12.2.2 Direct investment

Direct investment is fundamentally different. The European Commission defines foreign direct investment (FDI) as 'the establishment or acquisition of income-generating assets in a foreign country over which the investing firm has control.'[1] FDI may include the building of a new plant on a greenfield (or brownfield) site as well as a takeover or merger. 'Control' would normally imply not only the ownership of shares in an operation but also some degree of management control. This may include a joint venture, especially where the company in question has a majority shareholding, as in the case of Volkswagen in its joint venture with Skoda; Volkswagen has a 70 per cent shareholding and management control of Skoda. However, there is no generally agreed definition of 'control'. The IMF uses the term 'significant degree of influence', which may imply a stake of less than 50 per cent.[2]

FDI involves a strategic decision on the part of a company. It is usually, though not necessarily, regarded as a long-term commitment on the part of the investing firm. It represents an expansion strategy or a new strategic direction rather than simply an outlet for surplus funds. Its basic purpose is of course to generate a financial return, like portfolio investment, but the means of doing so and the implications for the company and the host country are quite different. A company which builds a major new plant abroad may not be able to sell the plant at an acceptable price if the investment is a failure. Nor can the company easily recover its investment in the training of its foreign workforce, for example. FDI is therefore the most complete form of market entry strategy and the one which involves the highest risks, but it enables the investor to retain control over its foreign operations.

12.2.3 The measurement of FDI

FDI is normally measured in value terms. Estimates of its value are based on the expenditure of foreign companies on new plant and equipment or the purchase of shares in an acquired foreign company. This approach raises numerous problems. International comparisons of FDI are only possible if a common currency is used. The

US dollar usually fulfils this role, but where exchange rates fluctuate wildly, as with the Russian rouble during the 1990s, for example, the value of FDI may change substantially as the currency's dollar value changes. Each country has its own methods of calculating FDI and the reliability of national data collection may also vary. Ideally, it would be preferable to calculate the volume rather than the value of FDI, since a dollar spent in one country or on one project may not produce the same level of investment as a dollar spent elsewhere. In other words, the marginal productivity of investment may vary. An estimate of the volume of FDI would have to take account of the efficiency with which investment expenditure generates productive assets in each case. Volume would indicate the quantity of FDI, measured in terms of factory-floor area or some similar measure. Such calculations are clearly problematic and it would be difficult to find a single unit of measurement for all types of FDI.

Further problems arise when considering exactly what to include in an estimate of FDI. When the German electronics company, Siemens, built a new state-of-the-art factory on a greenfield site near Newcastle in north-east England in the mid-1990s, Siemens's expenditure on the project was clearly FDI, though the project's value also included UK government grants. If the company has subsequently reinvested profit earned by its UK operation, it is less clear whether this should be classed as FDI. The profit is an asset of a German company but the funds have not been directly transferred from Germany. Even additional funds invested by the German parent company may not be recorded as FDI unless information on the use of this capital is readily available. The company may also have a significant influence over some of its smaller suppliers or subcontractors, perhaps even a minority shareholding. These activities could be treated as FDI, but it is unlikely in practice. In 1998, Siemens announced its intention to withdraw its operations from Newcastle. The sale of its UK plant might be regarded as negative FDI if it is sold to a British firm or as having a neutral effect on the FDI stock if sold to a foreign firm, though in both cases the investment and employment would remain.

The composition of FDI also varies between countries. Inward FDI in the UK, for instance, includes a large number of takeovers since UK takeover rules are relatively relaxed. In the US civil aviation industry, foreign ownership is restricted to 25 per cent, but this level of investment would still be classed as FDI. China opened its retail sector to foreign joint ventures in 1992, provided the Chinese partners held 50 per cent shareholdings; in practice, provincial and local authorities relaxed these rules, allowing majority foreign ownership and management control, but the central government decided to clamp down on foreign retail ownership in 1998. Such changes of policy must be taken into account when evaluating long-term FDI trends in China. These difficulties cast doubt on the reliability or comparability of FDI data, but FDI in its various forms is, nevertheless, an extremely important international business activity.

12.2.4 Global trends in FDI

The vast increase in FDI since the late 1980s has been a prominent feature of the globalization of the world economy. In some respects, the recent process of globalization has unique characteristics. This is particularly true of the revolution in computing and information technology. But the present level of FDI is not unique from a historical perspective. It has been estimated that FDI was approximately 9 per cent of world output in 1913, about the same proportion as it was in the mid-1990s.[3] Of course, the actual amount of FDI and world output were much higher in the 1990s, but 1913 was the culmination of a period of trade liberalization, industrial expansion, and empire building by the major industrial nations.

The period covering the two world wars and the interwar Great Depression was one of falling FDI. The level of FDI has gradually recovered during the post-war years, with the rate of increase accelerating during the last decade or more. Table 12.1 illustrates the recent trends. The increase in the total value of FDI is particularly marked. Whereas the developed countries still do most of the investing and receive most of the investment, the proportion of total FDI going into the developing countries, especially into Asia and Latin America, has been increasing significantly. The flow of FDI into Eastern Europe has also been increasing, though generally on a smaller scale and from a much lower base. It is worth noting that companies from some of the developing countries are now themselves becoming significant outward investors.

The dominant investing country is the USA, with outward FDI of $115 billion in 1997. The UK, Japan, Germany, and France are the other leading investors. The USA is also the main destination for FDI, receiving $91 billion in 1997, followed by China, the UK, and France. While these countries now generally head the lists of investing and recipient countries, it should be noted that a large multinational takeover or other one-off investment may distort the figures in a particular year, so FDI figures tend to vary over time. The cumulative stock of FDI over a period of time is a better indication of long-term trends than the flow of FDI in a particular year. Up to 1997, the USA had

Table 12.1 Trends in FDI flows ($bn.)

	1985	1997
Inward FDI		
Developed countries	43.1	233.1
Developing countries	13.7	144.9
Central/Eastern Europe	–	19.1
Outward FDI		
Developed countries	52.5	359.2
Developing countries	1.2	59.7
Central/Eastern Europe	–	0.3

Source: World Investment Reports, UNCTAD.

received a cumulative FDI stock of $721 billion, well ahead of the UK ($274 billion) and China ($217 billion).

A vibrant economy and high corporate profitability continue to make the USA the most attractive location for FDI. Whilst this investment comes from all over the world, the EU countries are the biggest investors in the USA, with Germany, the Netherlands, France, and the UK heading the list in 1997. Several EU countries are major outward investors and about half of this investment goes outside the EU. EU countries, especially Germany and Austria, are now the most important source of FDI in Eastern Europe. The main inward investors into the EU were the USA, Switzerland, Japan, and Norway in 1997. Asian countries receive about two-thirds of all FDI going into developing countries and about half of Asia's share goes into China alone. Japan has long been the largest investor in Asia, though investment from China and Hong Kong (predominantly the latter) is now at a similar level. In Latin America, Brazil is the major destination for FDI, followed by Mexico, and the USA the main investor. Investment in Africa is still much lower than in the other main regions of the world, with South Africa and Nigeria receiving just over 40 per cent of this investment in 1997.

12.2.5 The impact of FDI for global and national economies

FDI has grown more rapidly than either trade or world output since the mid-1980s. It has contributed greatly towards the globalization of business and the interdependence of the world's economies. On the one hand, since the major investing firms are based in the developed countries, FDI has helped these countries to consolidate their dominant influence over the world economy and the international trade and financial institutions. On the other hand, FDI has probably enabled the emerging economies to develop more rapidly than would otherwise have been possible. Some of the emerging economies are now also producing major foreign investors of their own.

The investor's home country gains certain advantages from having home-based MNEs. These companies repatriate profits and some of their international reputation rubs off on their country of origin. Smaller domestic firms may be their suppliers and this helps to give these firms a measure of international experience. MNEs are also taking their operations abroad, closing down plants at home or depriving their home country of new investment. This sometimes leads to charges that they are unpatriotic and some countries, particularly in the developing world, prevent or restrict their companies from investing scarce funds abroad. It is likely, however, that outward FDI has net benefits for the home country in the long term as, like international trade, FDI generally helps to expand the world economy.

Host countries are sometimes more fearful of the effects of FDI. They may see inward FDI as evidence of a loss of control of their economy. Smaller or weaker countries, in particular, often try to retain control over their domestic industry. Even larger ones do this to protect what they regard as strategic industries. Inward FDI, of course, brings capital, skills, and technology. It also provides employment and may help to develop key resources and aid regional regeneration. More importantly, FDI has been a major factor in the development of some of the emerging economies. Countries like Taiwan, for a number of years, or China, more recently, have recognized the contribution of FDI to the development of specific industries. Countries generally are now beginning to realize that FDI can bring substantial benefits.

12.3 The Determinants of FDI

EXCEPT in a few cases, it is unlikely that foreign direct investment will be determined by a single factor. In most cases, a potential investor will consider a wide range of factors before taking such an important step. Some of these are broad overarching factors which indicate the overall desirability of investing abroad or the general suitability of a particular country. Other factors are more specific to the needs of a particular company, like the need to gain access to resources and markets or to reduce costs. These factors are considered in turn below and are summarized in Figure 12.1.

12.3.1 Overarching factors in the FDI decision

■ General motives

Ultimately, companies engage in FDI in order to increase their profitability. They select investment projects which offer the prospect of increased net returns. To this extent the reasons for FDI are similar to those for portfolio investment. However, FDI also offers opportunities to expand the company or to change the focus of its activities. It can develop its business through diversifying into new products, extending the life of an existing product, or specializing in its core activities. FDI may enable the company to gain a competitive advantage over its rivals by reducing costs or by being the first to enter a developing market ('first-mover advantage'). In a broad sense, it allows a company to extend its business interests or 'business empire' and achieve market power and a world reputation. Some MNEs have recently been turning themselves into 'global companies' with a presence in all the world's major markets and regions. FDI enables them to do this whilst retaining control of their operations.

■ The business environment and business culture

The business environment is a broad term which encompasses the framework of government policies discussed below, as well as the general political and economic

Figure 12.1 Factors involved in the FDI decision

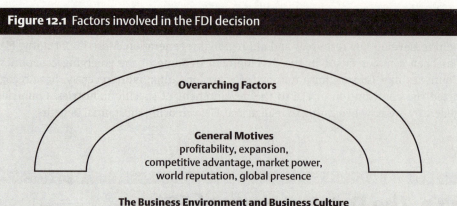

Overarching Factors

General Motives
profitability, expansion,
competitive advantage, market power,
world reputation, global presence

The Business Environment and Business Culture
stable political & economic environment, absence of 'nuisance costs'
(bureaucracy & corruption), quality of life; business culture: procedures,
relationships & networks, preference for similar or familiar culture

Supportive Government Policies
macroeconomic stability, market liberalization, low corporate taxation,
currency convertibility, ownership & profit regulations, good
education & training, efficient infrastructure, financial incentives

A Country's Stock of 'Created Assets'
tangible assets: infrastructure, distribution networks;
intangible assets: skills, technology, innovation, intellectual
property, organizational relationships, business culture

Specific Factors

Access to Resources
where large quantities of resources are needed,
where specialized resources are immobile, where
resources are core business, e.g. mining & petroleum

Market Advantages
access to large & growing markets, regional export base, SME supply chains,
benefits of local labour & supplies, local knowledge and acceptance,
supports 'relationship marketing', competitive advantage

Cost Reduction
international competitiveness, low-cost raw materials, energy & labour,
external economies of scale, financial incentives, low taxation &
non-wage labour costs, reduced transport costs, internalized operations

Overcoming trade barriers
natural barriers: culture & language; trade barriers: tariffs, quotas
& non-tariff barriers, barriers can be circumvented or overcome by FDI

environment. Above all, investors like a stable political environment. This is probably more important than whether a country is in the upturn or downturn of its economic cycle, since investors are more concerned about an economy's future potential than its present state. But political stability is crucial. Wars and civil unrest are an obvious case where loss of life or destruction of property may result. Turbulent changes of government may also lead to volatility in the business environment, leading to the nationalization or confiscation of foreign assets. It is noticeable that FDI into Northern Ireland appears to have been directly affected by the relative probabilities of peace or continued civil unrest during the twists and turns of the 'peace process'. On the other hand, whereas portfolio investors have been fleeing from Asia in the wake of the financial crisis, direct investors seem to be more content to bide their time.

In many countries, businesses are hampered by bureaucratic procedures and by corruption. In a number of African countries customs and other public officials are often so poorly paid that they rely on bribes to supplement their income. In Russia and some of its neighbouring states, the breakdown of law and order, loss of jobs and income, and the availability of large quantities of arms has made 'mafia' activity commonplace. MNE's operating in several parts of the world find it necessary to use 'slush funds' to bribe public officials in order to obtain contracts. Bureaucracy and corruption represent the 'nuisance costs' of doing business in the countries concerned and may act as a negative factor in the FDI decision. These factors, and also the general quality of life in a particular city or country, affect the willingness of company personnel to work abroad.

The term 'business culture' describes the ways in which people conduct business and attitudes towards various types of business activity in a particular country. Business culture is greatly influenced by the general culture and traditions of a country. This subject is discussed at length in Chapter 5. At one level, a foreign firm has to take account of the practical details of the host country's business procedures: forms of address and greeting, use of language and body movements, dress codes, methods of conducting business, and so on. At another level, there are the complexities of business relationships and networks which reflect the patterns of society as a whole. Whilst it is possible for a foreign investor to adapt to these cultural differences, mistakes can easily be made and inadequate preparation can lead to frustration and even the failure of a project.

In order to avoid these pitfalls some MNEs adopt a cautious approach to FDI, particularly in the early stages of internationalization, venturing initially into countries which have a similar or familiar business culture. Thus, British companies venture into the USA, with its Anglo-Saxon culture, or into France, with its different but familiar culture, and Spanish and Portuguese companies are major investors in Latin America. In practice, business cultures sometimes turn out to be less familiar than expected and numerous other factors may influence these investment decisions.

■ Supportive government policies

It is often argued that potential foreign investors are attracted by financial incentives or tax concessions from the host government. Indeed, governments seem to compete with each other to provide the largest incentives. Sometimes this happens within the European Union when investors are enticed by regional funds from a common European budget as well as by individual government schemes. It may even happen within a single country when competing regional agencies outbid each other to attract a prestigious investor. Whilst these efforts may confirm the importance of FDI to the host country, it is doubtful whether a long term cost-benefit analysis would indicate net benefits in each individual case. This is because, where a firm is attracted by incentives which are not complemented by a generally favourable investment climate, the firm is less likely to stay for the long term. Competing incentives may simply create an 'incentive merry-go-round', leaving redundant workers and other resources in its wake (see Chapter 6 on 'social dumping').

Clearly, governments do resort to these short-term strategies and investors are sometimes attracted by them. If they are used sparingly to help overcome the inherited disadvantage of a decaying industrial infrastructure or a legacy of redundant skills in a particular region, government financial support may be justified. If they distort investment location by encouraging firms to make inappropriate short-term decisions, they are more difficult to justify.

Much more important are government policies which provide a supportive business environment. These include macroeconomic stability and market liberalization. Macroeconomic stability helps to ensure low inflation, low interest rates, and a stable exchange rate. Inflation raises production costs and puts pressure on a firm either to raise its prices or to reduce its profit margins. It also makes it difficult to estimate the price of a long-term contract. High interest rates increase the cost of capital. Exchange rate instability increases a firm's foreign exchange exposure and a falling currency may severely reduce the value of repatriated profits. Market liberalization allows the foreign investor to enter markets, make flexible use of resources, and have the freedom to make its own decisions. The 'Anglo-Saxon' economies (especially the USA) are often cited as examples of countries with flexible labour markets and deregulated markets generally (see Section 8.2.2). Privatization often accompanies market liberalization and this provides an opportunity for the foreign investor to acquire an established enterprise and its markets.

Supportive government policies may include low corporate taxation (in general, as well as 'tax holidays' for foreign investors) and policies such as tax credits to encourage research and investment in technology, for example. The convertibility of currencies and regulations on foreign ownership or the repatriation of profits are also important. Investors may be attracted by policies which promote high standards of education and training and create an efficient industrial infrastructure through public investment, privatization, or deregulation. Increasingly, governments around the world are realizing the importance of creating a policy environment which is attractive to foreign investors. As more countries adopt such policies, investors will of course become more demanding. This may again stimulate competition between governments to attract FDI. If this competition encourages them to provide the best environment for business, this will benefit domestic as well as foreign firms. In practice, there is still some way to go in many countries.

■ A country's stock of 'created assets'

UNCTAD uses the term 'created assets' to describe a wide range of assets which a country has developed over time.[4] They have been 'created' by human endeavour and by the supportive actions of firms, governments, and other organizations. Some of these assets are tangible such as a country's industrial infrastructure or distribution networks. Others are knowledge-based and are therefore intangible. These include labour and managerial skills, the level of technological knowledge, the capacity for innovation, the stock of intellectual property (patents, trade marks, etc.), and relationships between governments, companies, universities, and other organizations. The business culture in a country and its people's attitude towards wealth creation may also be regarded as intangible 'created assets'.

These created assets are now generally more important in many industries than the availability of natural resources. Thus, a country with few natural resources may still be an attractive location for FDI, provided it offers a favourable environment in other respects. Japan could offer an attractive location for FDI with respect to some of its created assets, despite its lack of raw materials. Its skilled labour and stock of technological knowledge are key assets, but unfortunately its business relationships and culture have in some respects become liabilities, both for its own companies and also for foreign investors (see Sections 8.2.4, 8.4.3, and 9.4.2). FDI into Japan, therefore, has been consistently low for a major industrialized nation, even before its recent financial problems. Some firms may look for specific created assets like skilled labour or technology but, in general, created assets help to provide a broadly favourable business climate in a host country. These assets do not simply create a sympathetic business climate, they help to provide the combination of factors a multinational enterprise needs in order to be internationally competitive.

12.3.2 Specific factors in the FDI decision

■ Access to resources

Historically, many industries were located close to raw materials or sources of energy, especially iron ore and coal. In the modern world of fast, low-cost transport, readily available power supplies, and less reliance on bulk raw materials, investment decisions are less likely to be influenced by these factors. For many firms, the availability of resources is no longer a limiting factor in their location decisions. In a few industries, access to resources is still crucial, however. This is clearly the case in the extractive industries such as mining and petroleum. A significant proportion of the FDI in the less developed countries is in these industries, particularly in Africa and the Central Asian republics of Azerbaijan and Kazakhstan. In general, the location of resources may affect FDI decisions where raw materials, energy, or labour are required in large quantities, where specialized resources are immobile, or where access to resources is a company's core business.

Box 12.1 Ireland: FDI in a European 'Tiger Economy'

The Republic of Ireland has a population of just 3.7 million and is situated on the periphery of the European Union. Yet, during the 1990s its economy recorded an average annual growth rate of about 6 per cent, reaching 10.4 per cent in 1995 and 9.5 in 1997. This was the highest growth rate in the EU and one of the highest rates among the OECD countries. Ireland's per capita GDP is now rising rapidly and is soon likely to exceed that of the United Kingdom. This has led some observers to liken the Irish economy to the Asian 'tiger economies'. Moreover, Ireland has achieved this economic performance whilst reducing its budget deficit and public debt and maintaining low inflation—aided by a series of wage agreements between workers and management. Its economic success has been accompanied, and to an extent caused, by large inflows of FDI. Foreign investment has not been predominantly in Ireland's traditional industries, it has been in electronics, computers, health care, financial services, and other high-technology sectors. US invest-ment in information technology has been a particular feature, making Ireland the second largest exporter of computer software after the USA.

So how has Ireland managed to attract FDI on this scale and in these industries? First, even before it started to comply with the Maastricht Treaty's convergence criteria for monetary union, the Irish government was adopting policies of macroeconomic stabili-zation. The Irish economy has close links with the UK, but it also has an open economy, with exports and imports accounting for a high proportion of its GDP. Ireland has a growing and well-educated workforce, enabling foreign investors to recruit people with the required skills. It has received large amounts of EU funding, especially from the Cohesion Fund and other structural funds. These funds, amounting to about 2.5 per cent of Ireland's GDP in recent years, have helped to improve the country's industrial infra-structure.

US investors have received encouragement from the US administration and the Irish Industrial Development Authority has been active not only in attracting foreign investors but also in setting up support services for them. If this were not enough, Ireland also has a corporate tax rate of 10 per cent (due to rise to 12.5 per cent in 2003), which is particularly attractive to companies in sunrise industries keen to maximize their slender profit margins. Ireland's experience illustrates many of the factors which determine FDI. In the longer term, when some of the support policies recede, it should be possible to see whether Ireland provides the right kind of environment to persuade its foreign investors to stay. (Main source: *Financial Times Survey*: Ireland, 22 Sept. 1998.)

■ Market advantages

As access to resources has diminished in importance, access to markets has become more important. Many of the markets in developed countries have been growing more slowly in recent years and some markets may be approaching saturation. Foreign markets, especially in rapidly developing countries, therefore provide an opportunity for further expansion. The size and growth rates of these markets are likely to attract FDI. A foreign location may also act as an export base for other markets in the region. Proximity to markets is not just of benefit to large MNEs. Small and medium-sized enterprises (SMEs) are often suppliers to large companies and may need to follow their customers abroad. FDI into Eastern Europe, for instance, has included large numbers of SMEs which make up the supply chains of their larger customers.

There are a number of advantages in being located close to the market. FDI within a target market enables the investor to employ a local workforce and to use local suppliers. This gives the firm access to local knowledge and understanding of the local culture. It may also help the firm to gain acceptance of its product if it is seen as belonging to the local community and making a positive contribution to the local economy. This will of course depend on how the firm conducts itself.

The present emphasis on 'relationship marketing' (discussed in Chapter 3) may also increase the desirability of being close to the market. The development of long-term relationships with customers, building up a picture of their requirements and preferences, helps the supplier to focus its marketing more effectively on its customer profile. This reduces the cost of marketing and some of the transaction costs involved in selling the product and improves the effectiveness of a company's marketing effort. Proximity to the market may not be essential but it is likely to make this process easier. It may also offer competitive advantages. A company may gain 'first mover advantages' by entering a market before its competitors or may attempt to catch up by following the competition. In both cases, the company will be able to respond more quickly if it is close to the market.

■ Cost reduction

MNEs sometimes transfer all or part of a production process to low-cost countries in order to reduce their overall production costs and improve their international competitiveness. This is likely to occur where large amounts of basic raw materials, energy, or labour are required in the production process. Hourly labour costs in Asia (excluding Japan), including both the wage and non-wage costs of labour, are only about 5 per cent of labour costs in Germany, for example, though German productivity helps to reduce the gap in terms of unit labour costs. It is less likely that a company would seek a low-cost location for access to specialist skills, management expertise, advanced technology, or other high value-adding assets. A firm may, of course, achieve a cost reduction by taking advantage of external economies of scale in a country where clusters of highly skilled labour or technical support are in abundance; the influx of South Korean investment into Western Europe during the 1990s may, in part, reflect this motivation.

Cost motives are clearly an important factor in the FDI decisions of many companies. Despite this, MNEs still collectively employ the majority of their workforce in the high-cost industrialized countries, which suggests either that other factors are considered more important or that unit costs can be controlled without the need to locate in low-cost countries. These costs are sometimes reduced for investors by financial inducements in the form of government grants or tax concessions.

Similarly, low corporate tax rates and low employers' social security contributions may act as a cost incentive. Proximity to markets or raw materials may also help to reduce transport costs. FDI offers a unique advantage in that the management of a company's international operations is internalized, thus reducing the transaction costs which would arise between separate companies.

■ Overcoming trade barriers

Finally, companies have to contend with innumerable barriers when attempting to enter foreign markets. Some of these are natural barriers like culture or language. These can be overcome by being learned, but real understanding is easier to achieve through FDI and the employment of local workers than at arm's length through trade. Other barriers are man-made trade barriers such as tariffs, quotas, and a plethora of non-tariff barriers like product standards and testing procedures. These barriers are discussed in Chapter 6. Tariffs and quotas can be circumvented by FDI in the country concerned. Some of the non-tariff barriers still have to be complied with, but compliance is easier when production is locally based and the company has access to local officials. The USA and a number of European countries have imposed quotas or agreed voluntary export restraints on Japanese goods, especially motor vehicles and electronic goods. In practice, Japanese companies have been able to overcome the restrictions by investing in these countries. A company like Toyota can now sell its cars freely from factories in Britain or France to other EU countries.

12.3.3 Theoretical explanations for FDI

Writers on FDI have tried to formalize the reasons for FDI by developing or applying theoretical explanations. Some of these ideas are derived from the theories of international trade, investment, or marketing. Each of them contributes towards our understanding of the underlying reasons for FDI or offers an explanation for a particular kind of FDI, but there is no complete theory of FDI.

■ Traditional theories of international trade and investment

In traditional theories of international trade, countries specialize in producing goods in whose production they have a comparative advantage. This enables them to use their resources of land or labour in the most productive way and to export their surplus production. Other goods are then imported from countries that can produce them relatively efficiently. If all countries exploit their comparative advantages—and all countries are comparatively (though not necessarily absolutely) better at producing something—international trade will benefit the world as a whole. The basic theory of comparative advantage was later adapted in the Heckscher–Ohlin Model.[5] Heckscher and Ohlin argue that comparative advantage stems from differences in natural factor endowments. Where land or labour are in plentiful supply, their cost will generally be lower. Not only will a country with abundant or productive resources develop its own industries which use these resources, it will also attract foreign firms. Thus, these theories offer an explanation for FDI as well as for international trade.

In its basic form, traditional theory helps to explain why resource-intensive activities, like extractive industries, agriculture, and even tourism, are attracted to particular countries or regions. If comparative advantage stems from acquired or created assets as well as natural resources, these theories can also be applied to firms in other industries which are in search of specific labour skills, technology, and other sophisticated assets. In a broad sense, traditional theory provides an underlying explanation for FDI, but it does not capture the variety of factors which affect FDI decisions in practice.

■ Capital arbitrage theory

Arbitrage in capital markets is the process by which financial assets are bought at a lower price in one market and sold at a higher price in another. Alternatively, funds may be borrowed at a lower interest rate and loaned to someone else at a higher rate. The arbitrageur does this, of course, to make a profit but the effect of arbitrage is to equalize prices or interest rates between markets, provided there is completely free movement of capital. As long as there are price or interest rate differences between markets, capital will be attracted to the markets where it can earn the highest return.

This theory has been applied to flows of foreign investment. It is easy to see its applicability to portfolio investment as this type of investment is often very sensitive to international movements in interest rates and other factors. It is less readily applicable to FDI, which responds to long-term rather than short-term factors. However, in a general sense, any investment will be attracted to locations where there is a prospect of a higher return. In the case of FDI, the profitability of an investment is often influenced by a combination of factors, so capital arbitrage theory only offers a rather general explanation.

■ Product life-cycle theory

Vernon's theory of the product life cycle is sometimes applied to FDI.[6] Vernon argued, on the basis of empirical research, that a new product would initially be manufactured, say, in the USA, then as the US market developed, opportunities for exporting to other advanced countries would arise. When the US market reached maturity, these other markets would have grown large enough to justify investment in production plants in those countries. As these markets mature, production would become more standardized and price competition would become more intense. Producers would then look for lower-cost locations for production, probably in developing countries. This theory helps to explain why products once manufactured in developed countries are in due course made at lower cost in developing countries and then exported to the original producing countries. For example, a number of European textile machinery manufacturers, who formerly supplied the European textile industry, now have their main markets in Asia where most of the low-cost textile producers are based.

In a more limited way, companies have sometimes extended the life of their product by licensing its production in a less developed country. This was the case when Rover arranged for its obsolescent Maestro range of vehicles to be produced under licence in Bulgaria in the mid-1990s. But herein lies one of the problems with this theory. It does not explain why a firm should engage in FDI rather than licensing or even exporting from its home base, for example. Labour costs may be lower in the developing country but economies of scale could be achieved by concentrating production in an established plant at home. Product life-cycle theory helps to explain why some products follow a particular pattern of production and FDI. It does not explain why some products are first produced in developing countries or why similar products sometimes appear simultaneously in different countries.

■ Dunning's eclectic theory of FDI

The eclectic theory of FDI brings together a number of explanations for FDI which can be classified either as ownership-specific advantages (O), location-specific advantages (L), or internalization advantages (I).[7] For this reason it is also known as the OLI paradigm. Ownership-specific advantages arise because FDI allows a company to retain ownership of its foreign subsidiaries (though FDI may involve control without full ownership). Ownership enables it to enjoy exclusive use of patents, technology, research, management, supply chains, financial sources, and marketing techniques. These factors enable it to obtain economies of scale at the level of the firm as a whole (not necessarily at the plant level). Location-specific advantages relate more closely to the traditional theories of FDI. Location provides access to raw materials, low-cost labour, and markets. It may also help a firm to avoid trade barriers and other government restrictions.

Internalization advantages arise because FDI allows a firm to remain or become integrated. Horizontal integration exists where a takeover or internal expansion extends a firm's main activities abroad. Vertical integration extends its activities to operations at different stages of production, such as the control of suppliers or distributors. In both cases, integration enables a firm to 'internalize' its operations within the group and therefore to reduce the transaction costs that would otherwise arise between two independent firms. Careful use of transfer pricing between the various divisions now becomes possible, enabling a firm to manage its resources and overall tax liability. Vertical integration permits a greater degree of control over supply, production, and markets. Internalization may also help a firm to retain the benefits of skilled labour and technology within the organization.

The eclectic theory of FDI provides a wide range of possible explanations for FDI, suggesting that investors are motivated by a combination of these factors. The theory is probably realistic, but it does not offer guidance on which factors are likely to be the important ones in particular circumstances.

12.4 Collaborative Strategies

WE now turn to a group of strategies which involve collaboration between independent firms. These include joint-venture agreements, where two or more firms hold an equity stake, and various other types of cooperation agreement where there is no equity participation. The latter may be of two types: first, there are buyer–seller agreements—those which involve either the purchase of supplies or services through a subcontracting or exclusive supply agreement, or agreements to supply specified services through licensing, franchising, management contracts, and turnkey projects. Second, there are strategic alliances. A number of these strategies are discussed in Chapter 1. Here, we concentrate on joint-venture agreements and strategic alliances.

12.4.1 Joint-venture agreements (JVAs)

A joint-venture agreement (JVA) may be described as an agreement where two or more firms hold equity capital in a venture over which they each have some degree of control. The venture may be a separate operation set up by the shareholding companies or one of the companies may hold shares in the other(s). A JVA lies somewhere between a merger at one end of the spectrum and a strategic alliance at the other. When a merger takes place two or more independent firms join to become a single legal entity. Under a JVA the firms retain their separate legal status though one firm may, in some instances, have a majority shareholding in the other. A strategic alliance is a looser type of arrangement which does not normally involve the holding of equity.

It has been common for JVAs to be used by companies from developing countries as initial entry strategies to gain access to markets or natural resources in developed countries. Even large Japanese companies have used this type of strategy. For example, in 1983 Toyota set up its first manufacturing operation in the USA as a 50/50 joint venture with General Motors. As a short-term strategy, JVAs help to reduce the risks of complete FDI. More recently, JVAs have been seen as a valid long-term entry strategy in their own right. Companies from developed capital-exporting countries are now using JVAs as an alternative form of entry when seeking complementary assets in high technology as well as traditional industries. In such cases each partner brings different but complementary resources, markets, and skills to the joint venture.

JVAs are sometimes used where governments want the benefits of technology, skills, and other assets of foreign companies without losing complete ownership and control. In Asia, Taiwan has used this strategy to good effect when developing its technology industries. JVAs have been encouraged in selected industries in China for similar reasons. Some of the Eastern European governments during the 1990s have also favoured joint ventures in preference to full FDI, but more for ownership reasons than to develop strategic industries. In this case, large-scale privatization has created many opportunities for foreign ownership and joint ventures. Volkswagen's joint venture with the Czech state enterprise, Skoda, which has seen VW's shareholding rise to 70 per cent, brings German capital and expertise in return for established plants, a low-cost well-educated workforce, and an embryonic market. The Czech government has also retained the Skoda name and gained a revitalized car manufacturer. The VW-Skoda joint venture has experienced some of the disagreements which are common in this type of arrangement. JVAs, by their very nature, require their consenting parties to have common objectives and these can change over time.

12.4.2 Strategic alliances

A strategic alliance is a non-equity cooperation agreement between two or more firms which is intended to promote their joint competitive advantage. Strategic alliances generally involve cooperation in one or more of three areas: production, research and development, and marketing. Firms may lack the necessary resources for a project or may want to share the risks with a firm engaged in similar or complementary activities. Alliances in the motor manufacturing industry are commonly of this type. An alliance may also enable firms to gain market access, sometimes denied by government restrictions, or to share the benefits of each other's markets. This type of alliance is prevalent in the airline industry.

An interesting illustration of the pros and cons of alliances is the case of the Rolls-Royce motor company. Rolls-Royce entered into an alliance with BMW, whereby BMW supplied vehicle engines to Rolls-Royce prior to the sale of the latter's business to Volkswagen in 1998. The alliance between Rolls-Royce and BMW enabled Rolls-Royce to develop a new generation of engines to meet modern efficiency and environmental requirements whilst allowing BMW to move further into the luxury car market with the prestigious Rolls-Royce company. BMW was outbid by Volkswagen when the Rolls-Royce business was sold by its parent company, Vickers, but BMW used its close links with Rolls-Royce Aerospace, the owner of the Rolls-Royce brand name, to gain the long-term right to use the name from the year 2003, leaving Volkswagen with the Rolls-Royce production plant but only the Bentley name. This example illustrates not only the research, production, and marketing benefits of an alliance, but also indicates the ease with which the partners can end the alliance when it suits them.

Despite the precariousness of many strategic alliances, their popularity has been increasing in recent years. An alliance allows its partners to speed up the processes of innovation and market expansion. The time saved can often provide significant strategic advantages over rivals. Indeed, as more firms form alliances, those which do not are more likely to be left behind. There is, of course, a competition issue with strategic alliances. Firms which cooperate, especially in the market place, are less

Box 12.2 Alliances in the Airline Industry

There are estimated to be about 500 airline alliances around the world. Many of these are between international airlines and regional or local airlines. There are also a number of links between major international airlines. The four largest of these alliances are Star Alliance (United Airlines of the US, Lufthansa of Germany, Scandinavian Airlines System (SAS), Air Canada, Varig of Brazil, Thai Airlines, Air New Zealand, and Ansett Australia), Oneworld (British Airways, American Airlines, Cathay Pacific of Hong Kong, Canadian Airlines, and Quantas of Australia, joined by Iberia of Spain and Finnair during 1999), Wings (KLM of the Netherlands, Continental Airlines of the US, and Alitalia), and an alliance between Delta Air Lines of the US, Swissair, Austrian Airlines, and Sabena of Belgium. The Oneworld alliance was formed after its two leading members, British Airways and American Airlines, became impatient with the US, UK, and EU competition authorities for failing to approve their proposed transatlantic link-up unless they were willing to give up large numbers of airport slots.

Alliances enable airlines to code-share (selling tickets to destinations served by their alliance partners), cooperate on fares, share each other's frequent flyer schemes and airport lounges, share information, purchase airport services jointly, and coordinate aircraft use. Oneworld is at present unable to code share or cooperate on fares as they have not yet received regulatory approval. Cooperation of this kind can bring benefits to passengers from cost savings and the convenience of through-tickets, extended frequent flyer schemes, shared information and other facilities. However, airline alliances increase the market power of the major airlines, which they may use to raise fares or keep smaller airlines out of the market. Alliances are often fragile, lasting only a short time, though recent evidence suggests that airlines are beginning to settle down with their preferred partners. Although alliances are generally a loose arrangement, equity stakes are sometimes involved and the management of airline alliances is becoming more formal. In the airline industry, alliances provide evidence of worldwide industry consolidation as global competition intensifies. (Adapted from M. Skapinker, 'Airline tie-ups show their staying power', *Financial Times*, 25 Jan. 1999 and M. Skapinker, 'Take-off for five-airline alliance', *Financial Times*, 26 Jan. 1999.)

likely to compete. Competition between alliances replaces competition between individual firms. The consumer and smaller non-aligned rivals face the increased risk of collusive anti-competitive behaviour. On the other hand, cooperation which leads to worthwhile innovation, including improvements in product or service quality and the spread of technology, is a positive feature of strategic alliances.

12.4.3 The choice between FDI and collaborative strategies

In principle, firms will choose between FDI and various types of collaborative agreement on the basis of a trade-off between the desire to control their operations and the desire to minimize resource usage. In both cases, they will have particular strategic objectives which may be attainable by different means. The degree of risk involved and the suitability of potential partners will be key factors in the decision. FDI involves a large capital outlay and is only likely to produce substantial returns over a long period. Collaborative strategies are less permanent but can produce quicker returns. In general, joint ventures and strategic alliances work better where the partners have complementary rather than similar assets. Complementarity offers them greater potential competitive advantages.

12.5 Summary

THE flow of investment between countries has increased dramatically in recent years. Foreign investment is of two types: portfolio investment and direct investment. Foreign direct investment (FDI) has played a major part in the globalization of the world economy and the development of many individual economies. The decision to invest abroad is influenced by overarching factors such as a firm's desire to take advantage of opportunities for profit, the business and cultural environment, the existence of supportive government policies, and a country's stock of 'created assets'. Specific factors, such as access to resources and markets and opportunities for reducing costs or avoiding trade barriers, may also be taken into account. Theoretical explanations attempt to provide a more inclusive rationale for FDI; these include traditional explanations based on the theory of comparative advantage and Hecksher-Ohlin theory, capital arbitrage theory, product life-cycle theory, and Dunning's eclectic theory. As an alternative to full FDI, some firms choose to develop collaborative strategies, including joint-venture agreements and various forms of strategic alliance.

Review Questions

1 What is the difference between foreign portfolio investment and foreign direct investment?

2 Why is it difficult to measure FDI?

3 What are the main determinants of FDI? How important are the actions of governments in influencing the FDI decision?

4 Compare and contrast the relative merits of the theory of comparative advantage and Dunning's eclectic theory (the OLI paradigm) as explanations for FDI.

5 Why do firms sometimes prefer joint-venture agreements and strategic alliances to full FDI?

Case Study: Spain's Growing Attraction as an Investment Location

In a recent survey of 500 senior European business executives, Spain was the only country to have two of its cities, Barcelona and Madrid, ranked among the top ten European business locations. Spain as a country was also ranked second only to Germany as an emerging location for manufacturing investment. These findings seem to be supported by the trends in inward FDI stock shown in Table 12.2. Although Spain still trails behind the top five FDI destinations in the EU, the rate of increase in its FDI stock has only been matched by Belgium and Luxembourg, the two countries at the administrative centre of the EU.

Despite its location on the geographical periphery of the EU, Spain has one of the lower inflation rates and higher growth rates in the EU. The Spanish political system is more stable than it used to be and its government has also been promoting privatization, deregulation, and other market reforms. Spain is one of the EU's less developed countries, but this means that it now offers an expanding market for a wide range of industrial and consumer goods and services. It is also a founder member of the euro zone, offering price transparency at the same time as lower land rental and labour costs than the other leading investment locations. Madrid, its capital, is the largest urban concentration in Southern Europe and is at the heart of the Iberian

Table 12.2 The EU's top six investment locations (FDI inward stock)

	1997 ($m.)	1980–97 % increase
Belgium and Luxembourg	143.1	1,859
France	174.2	670
Germany	137.7	276
Netherlands	127.9	568
Spain	110.6	2,051
United Kingdom	274.4	335

Source: World Investment Report, 1998, UNCTAD, Annexe table B3, 373.

peninsula, midway between Lisbon and Barcelona. It therefore makes a suitable location to coordinate marketing and distribution for the entire region.

A particular feature of the Spanish economy is its close links with Latin America. Spain is the biggest European investor in Latin America and a Spanish business location is seen as a springboard to investment in that region. This is particularly attractive at a time when the EU is trying to strengthen its trade links with Latin America through the creation of an EU–Mercosur free trade area.

The major problem for investors in Spain has traditionally been the poor quality of Spain's transport and communication infrastructure. Although still relatively less well developed than in the other main EU investment locations, Spain's infrastructure is now improving markedly, helped in no small measure by the EU cohesion fund. Major investment projects include the expansion of the motorway network, a high-speed rail link between Madrid and Barcelona, and expansion of Madrid's Barajas airport. In addition to its growing attractions, Spain also offers one of Europe's more attractive climates and was the world's second most visited tourist destination after France in 1998.[8] (Adapted from T. Burns, 'Two hits in the top 10', *Financial Times: Business Locations in Europe*, 2 Nov. 1998.)

Case Study Questions

1 In what ways has the business environment in Spain become more attractive to foreign investors in recent years?

2 What attractions does the Spanish market offer to foreign investors in comparison with Germany or France, for example?

3 Are land and labour costs in Spain likely to be a major factor in attracting foreign investors? Against what other factors do lower costs have to be balanced?

4 In what ways are Spain's close links with Latin America likely to make Spain a 'springboard' for further investment in Latin America?

5 Apart from the problems with Spain's transport and communication infrastructure, what other problems might a foreign investor encounter when locating in Spain?

Notes

1 *Panorama of European Industry*, European Commission (1991).

2 *IMF Balance of Payments Manual* (Washington: IMF 1993), 5th edn.

3 P. Hirst and G. Thompson, *Globalization in Question* (Blackwell, 1996).

4 UNCTAD *World Investment Report: Trends and Determinants* (1998).

5 B. Ohlin, *Interregional and International Trade* (Harvard University Press: Cambridge, Mass., 1933).

6 R. Vernon, (1966), 'International Investments and International Trade in the Product Life-Cycle', *Quarterly Journal of Economics* (May 1966), 190–207.

7 See J. H. Dunning, *Multinational Enterprises and the Global Economy* (Addison-Wesley, 1993).

8 'Top tourism destinations', 1998, *The Economist* (20 Feb. 1999), 132.

Recommended Reading

■ Buckley, P. J., *Foreign Direct Investment and Multinational Enterprises* (Macmillan, 1995).

■ —— and Ghauri, P. N., *The Internationalisation of the Firm: A Reader* (Harcourt Brace Jovanovich, 1993).

■ Caves, R. E., *Multinational Enterprise and Economic Analysis* (Cambridge University Press, 1996).

■ Culpan, R. (ed.), *Multinational Strategic Alliances* (International Business Press, 1993).

■ Dunning, J. H., *Multinational Enterprises and the Global Economy* (Addison-Wesley, 1993).

13

International Competitiveness

Objectives

- to explain the meaning and significance of international competitiveness
- to discuss the measurement of international competitiveness and make comparisons between the major trading nations
- to determine the factors which affect a firm's international competitiveness
- to determine the factors which affect a country's competitive environment

13.1 Introduction

THE issue of international competitiveness has become the focus of much attention in recent years. Companies are increasingly aware that they have to be internationally competitive not only when they venture abroad but also because they face international competition in their home market. Even small firms in the supply chain of larger firms may have to fight off foreign competition. As markets become more open to global competition, competitiveness may well be the key to survival. In this chapter, we examine what is meant by international competitiveness and discuss the factors that are likely to influence a firm's competitiveness. Some of these factors are under the direct control of the firm, some can be managed by strategic planning, others are outside the firm's control.

Countries or governments may also be able to influence the international competitiveness of their firms. For example, the economic conditions prevailing in a particular country or aspects of its culture may have a bearing on competitiveness.

Governments may also achieve this effect by creating a favourable economic, legal, and regulatory environment or, in some cases, by more active intervention. Because national characteristics and government policy help to create the conditions for competitiveness, countries themselves are often described as being internationally competitive. However, this is a misleading notion since countries do not actually compete in business. More properly, national attributes should be described as factors which affect the competitiveness of a country's firms. In fact, some of these factors apply to all firms located in a particular country, regardless of a firm's country of origin. The extent to which countries and governments help their firms to be internationally competitive is an important issue. This and related issues are explored more fully in the remainder of this chapter.

13.2 The Meaning and Significance of International Competitiveness

13.2.1 A firm's international competitiveness

International competitiveness can be defined as the ability of a firm to compete in international markets. Competitiveness is a relative term which can only be interpreted in relation to a firm's competitors—it has no absolute value. Thus, firm 'A' may be more competitive than firm 'B' but less competitive than firm 'C'. Competitiveness is often measured in terms of price, unit production cost, or labour productivity relative to a firm's competitors. Some indicator of product quality could also be used, but measures of this kind are more difficult to quantify. Ultimately, superior competitiveness should lead to an improvement in market share, profit, or some other measure of successful performance, though firms do not always translate their competitiveness into improved performance. Competitiveness should not be confused with the level of competition in a market. The existence of international competition may act as a spur to competitiveness, but it will not in itself make a firm internationally competitive. Some firms will, for various reasons, fail to respond to the competition and either leave the market or be taken over by more successful firms.

All a firm's activities should ideally contribute towards the achievement of its objectives. If the ultimate objective is to maximize profit or at least to make what economists call 'supernormal profit' (profit over and above what could be earned from the next best alternative use of capital), then a firm has to organize its activities in such a way that this objective is met. Every part of its operations should be fine-tuned and dovetailed into the corporate effort: management and organizational structure, production, plant location, product quality, marketing, distribution, customer service, recruitment and training, financial planning, stock control, information systems, research and development, and all its other activities.

Kay speaks of the creation of 'added value' rather than supernormal profit: 'the ability to sustain a positive margin between input costs and output value.'[1] In this sense, firms are adding value to their capital investment—achieving whatever return their competitive advantages and market conditions will allow. By raising the quality of its product, controlling its price, reducing delivery times, or providing a higher level of customer service, a firm is able to improve its competitiveness and create more added value. In difficult economic conditions, even the most competitive firms may struggle to add much value to their business, but competitiveness will certainly improve their chances of survival. A firm's competitiveness therefore depends on its ability to create value, to reduce the cost of creating value, and to respond effectively to changes in its external environment.

13.2.2 A country's international competitiveness

A number of writers and organizations refer to the international competitiveness of a nation, that is, the ability of a country to increase its share of world output, world exports, or some other measure of economic performance. Thus, for example, the World Economic Forum, which meets each year in Davos, Switzerland, produces an annual World Competitiveness Report, ranking countries according to various 'competitiveness' criteria. While this may not be its intention, the report appears to suggest that countries can themselves be internationally competitive. Since it is companies rather than countries which compete in international markets, this is clearly not the case. This point is developed more extensively by Krugman.[2] It may be that the 'international competitiveness of nations' is simply shorthand for the way in which nations contribute towards the international competitiveness of their firms. Certainly, there are distinctive ways in which the business environment, government policies, and national culture of a particular country can be beneficial or detrimental to a firm's competitiveness. A firm may even take some of its national characteristics with it when it ventures abroad. Foreign firms may also benefit from the environment in their host country and some of their own cultural attributes may be absorbed by the host country's domestic firms. Thus, for example, Japanese total quality management and other techniques have now been copied by American and European firms.

In fact, this transfer of competitive advantage from country to country illustrates one of the reasons why the idea of a country's international competitiveness is not only misleading but also potentially harmful. The idea helps to foster the view that an increase in exports, leading to a larger share of world markets, should be a country's prime objective. It is then only a small step to the mistaken notion that imports should be discouraged, perhaps through import controls. An elementary knowledge of the theory of international trade (see Chapter 10) reveals that this 'mercantilist' view will only lead to a reduction in world trade and in the world's economic welfare.

It is important to remember that trade as a whole is beneficial, not exports alone. The fact that MNEs transfer aspects of their culture to host countries and their firms, and also take advantage of the host country's culture and environment, helps to confirm the view that the benefits of trade are not confined to the exporting country. Later in this chapter, we discuss the extent to which a country can influence the competitiveness of its firms but, in an increasingly global environment, national characteristics are only one of several determinants of international competitiveness. Companies often create their own competitive advantages and these are exploited through their global operations.

13.2.3 Measurement and comparisons of international competitiveness

For an individual firm, the measurement of international competitiveness is quite complex since it depends on a number of qualitative and sometimes intangible factors as well as quantifiable ones. Certainly, a firm can compare its prices with those of its competitors if their products are sufficiently similar, though price also reflects differences in quality and product specification. The more differentiated a product, the less useful is price as a measure of competitiveness. Relative wage rates in different firms may provide a superficial comparison, but unit labour costs are a more useful indicator as they reflect productivity differences between firms. Alternatively, a straightforward measure of labour productivity may be appropriate: gross output or net output (value added) per unit of labour (for example, per labour hour). It should be noted, however, that both unit labour costs and output per labour hour may vary with the complexity of the product, not just with productivity. On the other hand, for manufacturers producing a comparable product, such measures are often considered to be a reliable indicator of competitiveness. This is the case in the volume car industry, for instance, where the production plants of Japanese manufacturers like Nissan are regarded as the most productive in Europe.

Despite the caveat about the international competitiveness of nations in Section 13.2.2, it may sometimes be useful to consider national indicators to provide a broad picture of the factors affecting the competitiveness of firms in general. The following economic indicators are commonly used:

- consumer price indices, comparing rates of retail price inflation;
- producer price indices, giving an indication of the price of manufactured goods at the factory gate;
- indices of export and import prices, which combine price and exchange rate changes to indicate the price of goods to a foreign or domestic buyer;
- earnings indices, comparing changes in wage rates and other income from employment;
- indices of unit labour costs, where total labour cost (including wage costs and non-wage labour costs) are divided by total units produced in a given time period; and

■ exchange rate indices, for example, nominal exchange rates valued against a trade-weighted basket of currencies (effective exchange rates) or in terms of relative inflation rates (real exchange rates).

Some of these indices are illustrated in Table 13.1 for six of the G7 leading industrial nations. Each of the measures gives a quantifiable indication of the general way in which prices or costs of production are affecting the international competitiveness of firms operating in different countries. For an individual firm, they provide only a crude and incomplete indication of competitiveness. For firms in general, they provide a broad view of changes in the relative competitiveness of firms based in the countries under comparison. They do not explain why some firms are more successful than their compatriots in international competition, nor why firms from Germany or Japan have been consistently more successful than firms from numerous countries with lower prices, lower labour costs, and weaker currencies over prolonged periods of time. Each measure provides a part of the overall picture. In highly price-sensitive markets, these factors may make the crucial difference between gaining and losing orders. Where reputation, quality, product specification, reliability, and similar attributes distinguish one producer or product from another, the market may tolerate price differences to a greater extent. Some firms will specialize and find a market niche which enables them to exploit their firm-specific assets. In this way, they may be able to overcome the competitive disadvantage of price. Location and sourcing close to the market may also enable them to avoid the problem of an unfavourable exchange rate.

Movements in exchange rates are perhaps the most common comparator used for international competitiveness at the macroeconomic level. Although in practice nominal exchange rates are often used for this purpose, real exchange rates (taking account of relative inflation rates) should ideally be used. Large fluctuations sometimes occur between floating exchange rates and these may cause significant variations in export and import prices over a short period. During the Asian financial crisis of the late 1990s, for example, the Indonesian rupiah suffered an 80 per cent depreciation against the US dollar. This clearly had an enormous effect on trade between

Table 13.1 Indicators of international competitiveness in selected countries, 1997 (1985 = 100)

	Consumer prices	Producer prices	Earnings	Unit labour costs	Real exchange rate
France	134.2	105.2	149.0	n.a.	102.2
Germany	131.5	108.2	164.8	103.1	104.7
Italy	178.2	146.6	181.6	148.7	102.7
Japan	117.4	91.0	139.7	110.0	111.5
UK	166.5	151.5	215.8	144.4	108.5
USA	149.2	125.9	138.0	103.7	79.1

Source: 'International economic indicators: prices and competitiveness', *Financial Times* (26 Jan. 1999).

Indonesia and Western nations. More modest but nevertheless significant currency depreciations occurred in both Italy and the UK after they left the Exchange Rate Mechanism in 1992. In the case of Italy, there was little adverse effect on domestic inflation following the depreciation and export competitiveness showed a sustained improvement; imports slowed down in response to the falling lira, the trade balance improved significantly, and this provided a stimulus to economic growth.[3] In Britain, on the other hand, the value of imports rose to match the increase in exports, leaving the trade deficit virtually unchanged; in fact, it appears that some exporters took advantage of the weaker pound by allowing their prices to drift upwards, giving them larger short-term profits but little improvement in competitiveness. The elasticities of demand for exports and imports are also important factors here.

As a short-term expedient, exchange rate depreciation may clearly offer a competitive advantage to exporters. In the longer term, sustained improvements in competitiveness require continuous macroeconomic stability and constant vigilance on the part of individual firms. Long-term depreciation of a currency, as in the case of the pound sterling against the dollar during sustained periods since the early 1970s (and in earler devaluations in 1949 and 1967), appears to offer little long-term competitive advantage. Similarly, for most Japanese firms the continual appreciation of the yen between 1973 and 1995 had little effect on their international competitiveness. This is probably accounted for by the fact that, for most of this period, the yen/dollar exchange rate remained close to the purchasing power parity of the two currencies (indicated by the relative inflation rates in each country, that is, the amount of each currency required to purchase the same basket of goods). Higher productivity in Japan's key export industries appears to have been the underlying reason for the steady and sustainable appreciation of the yen against the dollar. Only when Japan's domestic motor and electronic goods manufacturers—its former star performers—began to lose their comparative advantage to makers of higher-value and higher-technology products during the 1990s was there some 'hollowing out' of Japanese industry as a result of the high yen.[4] In the main, therefore, if an exchange rate reflects the purchasing power parity of two currencies and this in turn is determined by the superior productivity of key export industries in one of the countries, long-term appreciation or depreciation of exchange rates should have little effect on the international competitiveness of export industries in either country.

13.3 Determinants of a Firm's International Competitiveness

13.3.1 Firm-specific assets and core competences

Each firm has a variety of assets, some of which are unique to itself. In some firms these assets are highly specific and well developed, in others they are less distinctive or underutilized. Whilst some of these assets are tangible, some of the more import-ant ones are intangible. They have often been developed through skill, effort, and experience over a number of years, though personnel with particular skills may be brought into the firm or another firm may be acquired for its firm-specific assets (FSAs). Firms which nurture and refine their FSAs gradually develop core com-petences in the things they do best. These core competences can then be exploited to their competitive advantage in international markets. Further discussion of the importance of FSAs to MNEs can be found in Chapter 2. FSAs which potentially have a significant influence on a firm's international competitiveness are as follows:

■ Technology and technological know-how: the use of technology, when combined with a knowledge of its potential applications, contributes to product innovation and hence to competitiveness based on a superior or differentiated product rather than price; technology, as measured by the level of R&D expenditure and by the number of patents filed, appears to contribute to the competitiveness of firms in a number of manufacturing industries.[5]

■ Marketing techniques: successful marketing depends not only on the choice of appropriate methods, but also on intimate knowledge of the product and market, and the ability to learn from previous experience; these qualities rely on know-ledge and abilities which are specific to the firm.

■ Intellectual property: patents, copyright, and trade marks provide a degree of pro-tection for a firm's products and reputation; these can be exploited to the firm's competitive advantage in international markets.

■ The ability to upgrade and innovate: innovation requires a creative imagination, design skills, an understanding of what the consumer wants, and a corporate cul-ture which encourages the generation of ideas as well as technology and technical ability; most innovation is incremental rather than fundamental—refinements of existing products or new applications of existing technology—but this process may be essential to create or retain a competitive advantage.

■ Management style and competence: unity of purpose, the ability to motivate, and flexibility in the face of changing circumstances are crucial in maintaining a com-petitive position; no single style of management suits all firms in all circum-stances, but it should be able to facilitate these requirements.

When using these and other FSAs a firm is able to differentiate its product or service from its competitors. The more specific and developed its FSAs, the more distinctive will be its activities in international markets. There are many fast-food outlets throughout the world, but McDonald's have achieved their competitive advantage by offering a particular blend of products, service, and restaurant design; even management training is supported by the company's 'Hamburger University' in the USA. In a very different market, Microsoft has established its competitive lead, not because it was the first to develop each of its product features, but because it offers a package of products which are 'user friendly' and its operating system provides a platform for a wide range of compatible software; its success reflects its own specific combination of marketing, design, and production skills, among other things. Similar examples of competitive success can be found in many industries, each using their own specific blend of FSAs. They may not be good at everything, but they are good at what they do—these are their core competences.

13.3.2 Reputation

A firm which makes good use of its core competences is likely to develop a particular reputation over a period of time. In the case of large MNEs, an international reputation will have been established with the aid of successful marketing and public relations. No amount of publicity alone will establish a lasting reputation if the firm does not have a product or service to match, but it helps to increase product or company recognition on the part of the consumer and to convince the consumer that the company believes in what it does. Reputation may apply to a brand or trade mark, a product or range of products, a standard or type of service, a type of sales outlet, a company name, or a method of doing business. Names such as McDonald's, Burger King, or Pizza Hut represent particular types of restaurant, range of products, and standard of service. Heinz and Kellogg are brand (and company) names which indicate market leaders in their respective fields. Coca-Cola and Pepsi Cola have achieved perhaps the widest international recognition among consumers and are immediately associated with a particular soft drink. Ikea suggests a range of modern, uncomplicated household furniture of distinctive design, while Microsoft is what we expect when we switch on a personal computer.

A good reputation takes time to establish but can be quickly damaged when things go wrong. As a source of competitive advantage, however, it is often worth more than any amount of advertising, since it immediately differentiates a product. Even a new product will carry a certain amount of recognition and gain more rapid acceptance if it carries a well-known label. The essential characteristics of a brand, which help to distinguish it from its rivals, are sometimes described as 'brand DNA'. An international reputation is particularly useful when entering a new foreign market as it helps to break down any resistance there may be to foreign products. Even the market entrant's country of origin may carry a certain reputation. Thus, for example, the

Box 13.1 Creating a Competitive Advantage in China

Many MNEs have ventured into China during the last few years. Its population of 1.2 billion and its growing economy have made it look the world's most attractive emerging market. But there are plenty of stories of disappointment: the white goods manufacturer, Whirlpool, machinery manufacturer, Caterpillar (both from the USA), and the French car manufacturer, Peugeot, have all had to scale down their operations in the face of difficult market conditions; Kimberley-Clark, the US paper products maker, has been involved in a legal battle. Many foreign investors have formed joint ventures with the Chinese to help them enter this difficult trading environment. Bureaucratic procedures have to be overcome, distribution is often difficult in this large and varied market, and the number of people who could afford to buy many of these products is much smaller than China's massive population would suggest.

American Standard is one firm which appears to have succeeded where others have failed, however. The company makes baths, wash basins, toilets, and other bathroom fittings. It now has seven manufacturing plants in different parts of China, six of which are joint ventures. Apart from one joint venture set up in 1984, it had mainly exported its products to China from plants and distributors in the USA, South Korea, Hong Kong, and South-East Asia until the early 1990s, but meeting the precise requirements of the Chinese market had proved difficult without local production facilities. At first, American Standard entered the top end of the market, supplying bathroom fitments to five-star hotels. Even now, there is a limited market for standard Western-style toilets, but the company has adapted its product design to fit in the space previously occupied by China's 'squat' toilets. It has also produced a superior squat toilet for the Chinese market. Its joint ventures have proved something of a handicap as local managers and facilities are often unsuitable, but the company has now increased its financial stake in these ventures to about 55 per cent from its original 30 per cent. On the other hand, local wholesalers have been essential in organizing product distribution. The company has also faced problems trying to protect its intellectual property against manufacturers of fake products and many cheap alternatives are on offer at the lower end of the market.

None of American Standard's actions in the Chinese market involves unique strategies, but the company has used its specific assets to good effect. These include a flexible management approach, the ability to recognize a niche market, production facilities which can respond to China's varied markets, imaginative product design and adaptation, and a willingness to use good local distributors when its own knowledge of the market is lacking. Its efforts to establish a competitive position in the Chinese market will have to continue, of course. Sustained international competitiveness requires continual innovation and careful nurturing of competitive advantages. (Adapted from J. Harding, 'Plumbed in to success', *Financial Times,* 20 Mar. 1998.)

British electrical goods retailer, Curry's, uses the Japanese-sounding name 'Matsui' for its own brand. Having established a strong reputation, it is in the interests of a firm to exploit its reputation as a source of competitive advantage. Reputation can then be used to increase brand recognition through an increasing range of products, whether the organization be the Disney Corporation or Manchester United Football Club.

13.3.3 Continual innovation

The ability to innovate may be a firm-specific asset but, in many markets, innovation is a prerequisite for international competitiveness. This is particularly the case in large competitive markets such as the USA or the Single European Market, and in markets where global products are sold. It applies to many manufactured products, but especially to specialized or high-specification products like computers, pharmaceutical products, or motor vehicles. It also applies increasingly to services like banking, insurance, and telecomunications where technology and new services are revolutionizing these industries. Innovation is often measured by the level of R&D expenditure as a percentage of sales. This is an input measure of innovation and therefore measures innovative effort rather than actual innovation. Patents provide an output measure of innovation, but the reliability of this measure will vary depending on the proportion of innovations which are patented in different industries and different countries. Innovation, it should be remembered, includes incremental improvements to existing products or services and new applications of existing technology. Few innovations are fundamentally new. Nevertheless, despite the measurement problems, continual innovation of one kind or another may be essential if a firm is to sustain, enhance, or create a competitive advantage.

13.3.4 A firm's architecture

'Architecture', in this context, describes the culture of an organization. This is not simply the sum total of an organization's firm-specific assets, it is a unifying corporate ethos which underpins all its activities and relationships. A firm's architecture can, of course, be identified by the things it does and the way it is organized. First of all, it should be distinguished from the skills and attributes of the individuals who make up the firm. Thus, if a particular company chairman is a flamboyant entrepreneur, a university professor is an expert in a specialized field, or a footballer is exceptionally talented, these characteristics do not necessarily say anything about the architecture of the company, the university, or the football club. Each may have some influence on the fortunes and reputation of their organization, but they will not in themselves create a successful organization. There are many examples of star football players being bought by struggling clubs, but consistent success generally requires a team approach. It also requires an organizational culture which motivates and creates unity of purpose.

A firm's architecture incorporates its procedures and knowledge base, its cooperative ethic, its commitment to quality, its organizational relationships, and its sense of purpose as an organization. All its routines and procedures will be influenced by the corporate culture; for example, the chain of authority and division of responsibilities, methods of internal and external communication, and the degree of formality or informality in its procedures all have a bearing on its architecture. Its knowledge base will depend on the way in which it recruits, trains, and promotes its staff and also on its cooperative ethic. A firm's cooperative ethic is the extent to which its procedures and work practices allow for flexible response and the sharing of information. Its commitment to quality may be a token adherence to established procedures or it may pervade the entire corporate culture. Organizational relationships refer to the relationships between employer and employee, between employees doing different jobs, and between the firm and its customers, suppliers, and other external organizations. The way in which many of these issues are dealt with will determine the firm's sense of purpose; unity of purpose clearly requires a strong cooperative ethic and good relationships both inside and outside the firm.

Architecture is often implicit rather than explicit. It does not depend on a plethora of written procedures and mission statements. No amount of documentation can in itself change a firm's architecture. Rather, it can be seen in a firm's recruitment and promotion practices, the rate of staff turnover, the volume of customer complaints, the number of faulty goods produced, the way in which market research feeds back into product design, and its working relationships with suppliers and other external organizations. Japanese companies typically have an architecture which is influenced by close relationships and a strong co-operative ethic; this involves relationships with government as well as other members of the *keiretsu*. A company like Marks & Spencer also has a reputation for its corporate culture which is not simply about its product range or the presence of its distinctive stores in the high street; its architecture is described by an expectation about quality, its practice of exchanging goods without question, and its reputation for staff training and internal promotion. Its reputation for management cohesion was recently tarnished by a boardroom battle for succession, but this is unlikely to change the overall architecture of the company. A firm's architecture is a vital part of its competitive advantage, especially when the firm is extending its operations abroad.[6]

13.4 Determinants of a Country's Competitive Environment

IN Section 13.2.2, we discuss some of the difficulties with the notion of the international competitiveness of nations. Here, we focus on the extent to which the characteristics, culture, and environment of a country, or the policies of its government can influence the international competitiveness of its firms.

13.4.1 National characteristics and culture

In Chapter 8 we consider in some detail how the Anglo-Saxon, European, and East Asian models influence the political, economic, and cultural environment of the countries concerned. In broad terms, US companies operate in a free market economy where individual freedom and choice are paramount, German companies operate in a social market economy where consensus decision-making prevails, and Japanese companies operate in a close-knit environment of complex interrelationships. Despite the gulf between these apparently conflicting models, each seems to have produced its share of economic success. What perhaps can be said is that each of the models has its particular strengths and weaknesses. Resources may be allocated more efficiently in the Anglo-Saxon economies and their companies, but long-term planning and relationships are sometimes lacking. Consensus in the European model may be helpful in supporting unity of purpose, but it can also lead to inflexibility and increased costs. East Asian networks provide mutual support and focused industrial development, but have created unsound financial systems and inflexible business conditions. It seems that each model offers an approach which is in harmony with its culture. Certainly, it is doubtful whether one can simply transplant the Anglo-Saxon model to East Asia or vice versa. This does not, of course, mean that American firms cannot learn from Japanese firms or that Japanese firms operating abroad do not absorb some of the host country's culture and business practices.

Another way to think of national characteristics is to consider the resources and attributes a country or its people possess or what they appear to be good at. Traditionally, countries with rich natural resources were thought to have important natural advantages. This may still be regarded as true for countries like Saudi Arabia or Kuwait which have plentiful supplies of oil. Yet, these countries have not generally turned their natural resources into a competitive advantage in other industries. It seems that attributes like entrepreneurial skills, the qualities and skills of the workforce, and an ability to adapt to changing conditions are more likely to offer a competitive advantage. Thus, for example, North America, the UK, and a number of other countries offer the advantage of English, probably the world's most widely used language, but news media, publishers, and others who rely on the English language also need the skills and foresight to exploit this advantage. Some countries have achieved a reputation for having specialist skills in particular industries: the Swiss are good at making watches and clocks, the Japanese at making cameras and electronic goods. Some have important financial centres: New York, Tokyo, London, and Zurich, for example. These specialisms may reflect the skills or interests of the local people or may be a spin-off from other business activities. However, having developed an area of expertise, a country often attracts more firms who take advantage of the skills, support services, and other external economies of scale on offer.

National culture may also help to create particular competitive advantages. It is probably no accident that US firms dominate many international markets. The American culture of individualism and entrepreneurship promotes competition and the taking of business risks. Japan's collectivist culture has spawned large high-productivity companies in selected industries, surrounded by an integrated support network. Asian 'tiger economies' like South Korea and Singapore, as well as Japan, have a well-educated labour force because their culture places a high value on education. Germany's highly structured vocational training system, reflecting its disciplined pursuit of high standards, provides the skills needed by its precision manufacturers. Britain's tradition of trade and exploration may help to explain why its companies are among the world's leading outward investors. Each of these cultural traits provides the basis for a specific competitive strength. Religious beliefs and social systems may also help to create a particular business environment. A strict Islamic culture, for example, is conducive to a cooperative and disciplined business framework rather than open, competitive capitalism. The Indian caste system and the British class system promote hierarchical business structures where managers have the freedom to manage with little worker participation. These characteristics can sometimes be a disadvantage as well as an advantage but, in one way or another, national culture can influence the competitive environment.

13.4.2 The economic environment

A country's economic environment may be an important source of competitive advantage. If international competitiveness is defined in a narrow quantitative sense, prices and costs of production become the key determinants of a firm's competitiveness. At a national level, prices and costs are affected by the rate of inflation and the exchange rate. A persistently higher inflation rate clearly puts domestic firms at a competitive disadvantage. Short-term exchange rate movements may have either a positive or negative effect on competitiveness. In the longer term, as argued in Section 13.2.3, exchange rates are less likely to affect competitiveness unless the actual rate is consistently out of line with the purchasing power parity of the currencies concerned. In political and business discussion, the exchange rate is often regarded as being synonymous with international competitiveness. In reality, it is only one of many factors which should be included in the equation.

Arguably the most important economic determinant of competitiveness at the national or international level is the existence of healthy competition. This includes both the home market and the external trading environment (free trade). Competition in the domestic economy may result from policies of privatization and deregulation and other ways in which competition is encouraged. At the external trade level, competition depends on the trade policies of individual governments and on the efforts of the World Trade Organization. Regional groupings like the EU and NAFTA are also creating the conditions for trade liberalization within their own region. The EU has gone further than any other grouping in opening up domestic markets to international competition.

13.4.3 'Porter's Diamond'

In a major research study covering ten countries, Porter set out to discover why some countries seem to produce more successful industries than others.[7] Porter identified four determinants of national advantage (known as 'Porter's Diamond') which individually and jointly provide the conditions for international competitiveness:

■ **Factor endowments**

Early theories of international trade focused on natural resources, but Porter distinguishes between 'basic factors' and 'advanced factors'. Basic factors include natural resources, climate, and the general skills of the labour force. Advanced factors include sophisticated communication systems, highly skilled labour, and specialist support services; these are the most important factors for competitive advantage.

Figure 13.1 Determinants of national advantage ('Porter's Diamond')

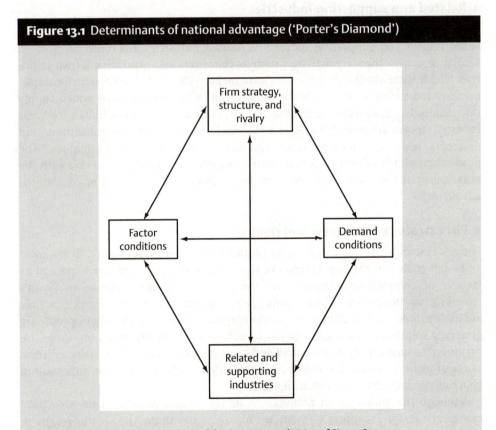

Source: Reprinted with the permission of the Free Press, a division of Simon & Schuster Inc., from *The Competitive Advantage of Nations* by Michael E. Porter Copyright 1990 by Michael E. Porter

Unlike traditional theory, Porter argues that these factors are not simply inherited but are developed through investment, especially in the case of advanced factors.

■ Demand conditions

The nature of demand in a firm's home market was found to be another significant factor in determining national advantage. The type of goods demanded in the home market and the expectations of consumers were found to be particularly important. When faced by demanding home consumers who expect innovative products, firms become sensitive to consumer demands and develop a culture of innovation which keeps them ahead of their foreign rivals. A large, growing home market may then create the conditions for economies of scale and technological development which help to promote an advanced competitive industry. If developments in a country's home market become well known abroad, foreigners will begin to demand these same products and the country's competitive advantage will spread to international markets.

■ Related and supporting industries

Porter emphasizes the importance of having internationally competitive, locally based related and supporting industries. Related industries are those involved in similar or complementary activities such as chemicals and printing ink (two industries which share similar processes in Germany) or VCRs and videotape (two complementary industries in South Korea).[8] Supporting industries are those which supply raw materials, components, and other inputs. For example, in the Italian footwear industry, footwear manufacturers liaise closely with leather manufacturers and designers, learning from each other and sharing new ideas and techniques.[9] The physical proximity of these internationally competitive industries, together with the other parts of the 'diamond', seems to be an important determinant of national advantage.

■ Firm strategy, structure, and rivalry

Porter's research also indicated the importance of harmony between a firm's strategies and goals and the organization of firms in industries on the one hand and its sources of competitive advantage on the other. Thus, for example, in Japan's close-knit, authoritarian culture firms are organized in networks, work practices are highly integrated, and there are strong corporate goals. In Italy, where people are generally sceptical of authority and family networks are strong, many industries are organized around family-owned small and medium-sized firms which make a diverse range of niche products. Intense domestic rivalry was also found to be important in spurring the industry to innovate and upgrade.

   Although the 'diamond' of national advantage focuses mainly on the structural characteristics of a country's resources, markets, and industries, Porter's view of these factors is dynamic rather than static. Whereas traditional theories were based on natural resource endowments, Porter emphasizes the importance of investment in advanced factors and the constant pressure to innovate. Porter also argues that 'chance' and the actions of governments play a role in determining the course of events in a particular industry or country, but that the function of government should be to influence the four determinants described above, not to determine competitive advantage directly.

13.4.4 Can governments create international competitiveness?

Basically, governments are able to influence international competitiveness in one of four ways. First, they can opt for a 'competitive devaluation' of their currency. This may be a formal policy decision to devalue a fixed exchange rate, a decision to reduce interest rates under a floating regime, or simply a decision not to intervene to prevent a currency depreciation when its market value is under pressure. In view of the discussion in Section 13.2.3, a 'competitive devaluation' is only likely to offer a competitive advantage in the short-run unless the exchange rate is out of line with its purchasing power parity in the longer term.

The second approach is for governments to create the right kind of environment for business to flourish. Modern consensus suggests that this requires macroeconomic stabilization (low inflation, stready economic growth, a balanced budget over the economic cycle, and balance of payments equilibrium); competitive market conditions (policies to remove barriers to competition, deregulate markets, and create a thriving private sector); and effective incentive mechanisms (low direct taxation, low interest rates to encourage industrial investment, flexible labour markets, performance-related pay, and similar incentives). Consensus in this context is based on the ascendancy of free market economics, which pervades the major international lending and trade organizations. The leftward shift in Western European politics during the late 1990s might suggest the need for some revision of this view, but in practice there is still broad agreement on the economic rationale for, if not always the social desirability of, the current market consensus. By creating a stable and competitive economic environment, governments are providing the preconditions for international competitiveness, but individual firms are responsible for the way they respond.

The third way is for governments to be more active in developing the transport and communication infrastructure, the financial system, the education and training system, and the support for research and development. This approach is not necessarily incompatible with the creation of a stable, competitive environment. In Germany and the Scandinavian countries in particular, considerable emphasis is placed on investment in education, vocational training, and research. This effort is not generally directed towards specific outcomes, but rather it provides the basic underpinning for a highly educated and skilled workforce, and for the development of advanced scientific and technological knowledge.

The fourth approach involves active intervention in a particular industry or firm.

Sometimes this type of policy is known as 'picking winners'. Examples of active industrial policy range from the French tradition of indicative economic planning or dirigisme to the various degrees of government support and direction in East Asia (see Chapters 8 and 9). This issue is discussed in Box 13.2. Whether this type of active policy intervention actually creates 'winners' is a matter of some debate.

Box 13.2 Creating National Champions

Many governments have from time to time focused their attention on specific industries or firms. Often this attention has turned to industries in long-term decline like coal, textiles, or shipbuilding, or to companies in financial difficulties like the former British Leyland, France's Crédit Lyonnais, or some of Europe's struggling national airlines (Air France, Iberia, Al Italia, etc.). In some countries, attention has been focused on 'sunrise' rather than 'sunset' industries. Europe's success in this area has been patchy; its success stories have tended to come not from firms which have been nurtured by government support but from those that have broken free from it, such as British Airways or Volkswagen. Lessons from Japanese experience, however, have tended to suggest that Europe is missing out. Japanese, Korean, Taiwanese, and other East Asian governments have not simply supported their favoured industries financially, they have actively directed resources into these industries and used all manner of devices to promote their development.

Of course, most countries have their 'national champions': Boeing (US), Germany's Daimler-Benz (now Daimler-Chrysler), Glaxo-Welcome (UK), Hyundai (S. Korea), Nestlé (Switzerland), Nokia (Finland), Renault (France), Skoda (Czech Rep.), Toyota (Japan), Volvo (Sweden), to name but a few. Sometimes national champions are taken over by a foreign firm or form a joint venture so that nationality becomes blurred. Sometimes they are 'national' but not really 'champions'. But there is still a feeling that any nation worth its salt ought to have a stake in one or more strong national competitors. It is just a question of which is the best way to achieve this. During the 1980s, there was a growing consensus in favour of the Japanese approach. Certainly, many of its manufacturing exporters have been remarkably successful. Slowdown, recession, and financial crisis in the Japanese economy has cast some doubt on this wisdom during the 1990s. Despite problems at home, companies like Toyota, Nissan, and Sony are still successful abroad, but the Japanese have paid a high price for this success. A more promising approach may be for governments to create 'opportunities [for their firms] to exploit competitive advantages' by opening up competition, encouraging 'supportive relationships between firms', creating 'collective knowledge bases', and through technical and managerial training.[10] Even if governments follow this approach, there is no guarantee that they will retain all the benefits of their efforts. In a global business environment, the international spillover effects are often significant.

13.5 Summary

A firm's international competitiveness is its ability to compete in international markets, often measured in terms of price, unit production cost, or labour productivity relative to its competitors. Whilst countries do not actually compete, a country's business environment or government policies may influence the international competitiveness of firms operating within it and its culture may be influential when its firms operate abroad. International competitiveness in its broader sense is often measured in terms of export and import prices, exchange rates, and similar variables. A firm's international competitiveness is not simply determined by quantitative factors such as price and production costs but also by the quality of its firm-specific assets, its reputation, its ability to innovate, and its 'architecture'. A country's competitive environment is influenced by its national characteristics and culture, its economic environment, and by the policies of its government. Porter argues that a country can provide a competitive environment for its firms and industries if four key determinants are in place: factor endowments; market conditions; related and supporting industries; and firm strategy, structure, and rivalry.

Group Activity: Sharpening Philips Electronics' International Competitiveness

About the company. Philips Electronics is Europe's largest consumer electronics group. It is a world leader in the manufacture of colour picture tubes, shavers, lighting, and a number of other electronic products. It ranked twentieth, by foreign assets, in UNCTAD's top 100 MNEs in 1996, but fell from 102nd position in 1997 to 201st position in 1998 in the FT500 world's largest companies by market capitalization. This reduction in size reflects the policy of Philips's new president, who initiated the closure of one-third of the company's factories over a four-year period and the sale of investments in Grundig and PolyGram, in car audio equipment and cable television, and the music and film industry respectively. Philips's profit has held up, despite weak global markets, but the company is attempting to get rid of its poor-performing businesses and to concentrate on its core activities. The company president, Cor Boonstra, sees enormous potential in its main electronics markets.

Philips's success in Europe has not yet been matched by comparable success in the US market. A joint venture with Lucent Technologies, a large US company, only lasted a year after delays with semi-conductor design. This joint-venture was intended to help Philips enter the US market for mobile phone handsets, but the two companies were apparently less compatible than envisaged and the failed venture cost Philips Dutch fl1 billion. For the moment, Philips has shelved its attempt to challenge Nokia, Motorola, and Ericsson, the market leaders in the US mobile phone market. At present, US brand awareness of Philips's products is limited and the company expects it to take ten to twenty years to establish a strong reputation in the USA.

As an initial step towards redressing its earlier failure in the mobile phone market, Philips has now bought ATL Ultrasound, a US manufacturer of diagnostic imaging equipment. ATL Ultrasound is seen as a company with a world reputation, good management, and an innovative product with unrealized potential. Philips's president has identified medical equipment as one of the areas he wants the company to specialize in, along with semiconductors and lighting. Semiconductors and other electronic components underpin the company's activities in the field of television-related digital products.

Philips has always been based in the Netherlands, though its management was recently moved from Eindhoven to the larger, cosmopolitan city of Amsterdam in order to attract high-quality international personnel. Its presidents have traditionally been selected from managers who have spent most of their career with the company. Cor Boonstra is an exception, though the company has still chosen a Dutchman. Boonstra initiated Philips's first global advertising campaign shortly after his arrival and authorized a 30 per cent increase in the company's US media budget in 1998. The president also encourages openness on the part of his staff, though he generally remains cautious in his approach to the company's takeover strategy, preferring to invest in companies which offer their own distictive strengths rather than simply market access. (Adapted from G. Cramb, 'Trying to make it better', FT Interview: Cor Boonstra, *Financial Times*, 4 November 1998.)

Group activity

Working in groups of three or four, discuss *one* of the following questions, drawing on additional information sources where necessary. Each group should choose a different question and then, in turn, present its findings to the other groups.

1 What are Philips's firm-specific assets and core competences? Is the company doing the right things to capitalize on its core competences? If not, what should it do?

2 On what factors is Philips's reputation in the US market likely to depend? How can the company establish a strong reputation?

3 Philips's attempt to establish itself in the US mobile phone market was apparently unsuccessful. What does this experience tell us about the right and wrong way to enter a new product market? How can Philips improve its innovation strategy in the highly innovative electronics industry?

4 How would you describe Philips's 'architecture'? Does its present architecture serve the company well? If not, what changes should be made?

5 Philips is a Dutch company trying to establish itself in the US market. What do its forays into the US market tell us about the company's international competitiveness vis-à-vis the companies operating in the US? How might the company change its strategies to improve its international competitiveness?

Notes

1 J. Kay, *The Business of Economics* (Oxford University Press, 1996), 58.

2 P. R. Krugman, 'Making sense of the competitiveness debate', *Oxford Review of Economic Policy* (1996), 12(3): 17–25.

3 See R. Dornbusch, 'The effectiveness of exchange-rate changes', *Oxford Review of Economic Policy* (1996), 12(3): 26–38.

4 For a fuller discussion of this issue, see M. Yoshitomi, 'On the changing international competitiveness of Japanese manufacturing since 1985', *Oxford Review of Economic Policy* (1996), 12(3): 61–73.

5 See J. Fagerberg, 'Technology and competitiveness', *Oxford Review of Economic Policy* (1996), 12(3): table 3, 47.

6 A fuller discussion of this topic can be found in J. Kay, *Foundations of Corporate Success* (Oxford University Press, 1993), esp. ch. 5.

7 M. E. Porter, *The Competitive Advantage of Nations* (Free Press, 1998), first published in 1990.

8 Ibid., table 3-1, 105.

9 Ibid., 100–5.

10 J. Kay, *Business of Economics*, 79–80.

Recommended Reading

■ Kay, J., *Foundations of Corporate Success* (Oxford University Press, 1993). *Oxford Review of Economic Policy* (1996), 12(3): International Competitiveness.

■ Porter, M. E., *The Competitive Advantage of Nations* (Free Press, 1998).

■ —— *Competitive Advantage: Creating and Sustaining Superior Performance* (Free Press, 1998).

Part IV

The European Union

14

The Development and Policies of the European Union

Objectives

- to outline the origins and aims of the European Union
- to describe the functions and policy-making processes of the main EU institutions
- to outline the key EU policies which affect the operation of business organizations
- to identify the main issues arising out of these EU policies

14.1 Introduction

THE European Union (EU) is probably the most highly developed example of polit-ical and economic integration between a group of consenting, independent nations in the modern world. Its fifteen member states encompass the majority of the land area and population of Western Europe. The EU's gradual enlargement means that its population now greatly exceeds that of the United States and Japan, the other Triad nations, and its combined GDP is now approaching that of the USA (see Table 14.1). Individually, the EU nations account for about 40 per cent of world exports and six of these countries rank among the world's ten leading exporting nations (see Table 8.1). The EU contains several of the world's major industrialized countries, though some of its members are still relatively less developed.

Since the signing of the EU's founding treaty, the Treaty of Rome, in 1957, the EU

Table 14.1 Key data on the USA, European Union, and Japan°

	Population millions (July 1998 est.)	Gross Domestic Product[a] ($USbn.) (1997 est.)
USA	270.3	8,083
European Union	373.7	7,700
Japan	125.9	3,080

[a] GDP figures are estimated on a purchasing power parity basis.

Source: CIA World Factbook, 1998

has been engaged in deeper integration as well as enlargement. After initially creating a customs union, the EU has now achieved something approaching a common or single market among all its members (and beyond) and has recently introduced a fledgling monetary union between eleven of its members. The EU has also been establishing formal links with countries and trade blocs beyond its borders. These issues are the subject of this and the following three chapters. In this chapter we briefly outline how the EU has developed and consider the implications of its main economic and business policies.

14.2 The Development of the European Union

14.2.1 The origins and aims of the European Union

The twentieth century witnessed the two most devastating wars in history. Both world wars had their origins and centre of gravity in Europe. Against this background, it is not surprising that there were several attempts during the late 1940s and early 1950s to create unity between the European nations. Some of the earlier attempts resulted in the creation of bodies such as the Council of Europe in 1949 and the Western European Union (WEU) in 1955. The Council of Europe is a pan-European intergovernmental organization concerned with the protection of human rights, the promotion of democracy and related issues. The WEU involves security cooperation between the countries of Western Europe. Both organizations still exist today.

However, such organizations have never satisfied the desire of many European leaders for closer integration within Europe.

The first real step towards the creation of what we now call the European Union was taken in 1950 with the proposals contained in the Schuman Plan. Robert Schuman, then French foreign minister, put forward a plan for the integration of the European coal and steel industries overseen by a supranational authority. The architect of the plan was in fact Jean Monnet, who had been in charge of the reconstruction of the French economy after the war. The coal and steel industries were seen as the main engine of economic recovery at that time and they had also been the industrial powerhouses which had driven the war effort. This was regarded as a major step towards integration and the prevention of future wars in Europe and the Schuman Plan resulted in the establishment of the European Coal and Steel Community (ECSC) under the Treaty of Paris in 1951. For this reason, Schuman and Monnet are often described as the founding fathers of the EU.

The fact that the first concrete step on the road to European integration was the creation of an economic community should not be taken to mean that the EU has been essentially an economic project. From the very beginning, economic integration was always seen as a means to achieving political union, especially within the developing Franco-German alliance and the Benelux nations. After all, it was the political aspirations of independent nation states which had led Europe to war. By establishing ECSC, the founding member states had therefore set in motion the integration process which has developed into the present-day EU. The six members of ECSC, and subsequently the founder members of the European Economic Community, were France, Germany, Italy, and the Benelux nations—Belgium, the Netherlands, and Luxembourg—known as 'the six'.

During the 1950s 'the six' realized their ambitions to go beyond the coal and steel industries. At Rome in 1957 they established the European Economic Community (EEC) and also the European Atomic Energy Community (Euratom), which was intended to coordinate the peaceful development of nuclear energy. The EEC was the basis of the present EU and the three communities—EEC, ECSC, and Euratom were later brought together under a single structure of authority. The main aims of the EEC were essentially twofold: first, 'to establish the foundations of an ever-closer union among the European peoples';[1] second, to establish a common market and closer economic cooperation between member countries. Even at this stage, it was envisaged that economic cooperation would include the gradual approximation of national economic policies, the balanced regional development of the community as a whole, and closer relations between member states. A number of more specific objectives are also contained in the Treaty of Rome, such as the establishment of a common agricultural policy and a commitment to free and fair competition. These objectives are now enshrined in the policy framework of the EU and some of them are discussed later in this chapter.

Table 14.2 Landmarks in the development of the European Union

1951	Treaty of Paris established the European Coal and Steel Community (ECSC) between 'the six' (Belgium, France, Germany, Italy, Luxembourg, and the Netherlands); ECSC came into operation in July 1952.
1957	Treaty of Rome established the European Economic Community (EEC) and, under a separate treaty, the European Atomic Energy Community (Euratom).
1958	(January) EEC and Euratom came into operation.
1965	Merger Treaty to unify the EEC, ECSC, and Euratom under a single executive; the unified Council of Ministers and Commission came into effect in 1967.
1968	Removal of EEC internal tariffs and establishment of a common external tariff.
1970	Werner Report on Economic and Monetary Union; Davignon Report on European Political Cooperation.
1972	Introduction of the 'Snake in the tunnel', an early form of exchange rate mechanism.
1973	Accession of Denmark, Ireland, and the UK to the European Community.
1979	Introduction of the European Monetary System (EMS) and its Exchange Rate Mechanism (ERM).
1981	Accession of Greece to the European Community.
1984	Establishment of a free trade area between the European Community and EFTA.
1985	Agreement on the creation of a Single European Market by December 1992; withdrawal of Greenland, formerly an integral part of Denmark, from the European Community after a referendum.
1986	Accession of Spain and Portugal to the European Community; Single European Act 1986, coming into effect in July 1987.
1989	Delors Report on three-stage progression to EMU; Social Charter agreed.
1990	(October) Former East Germany became part of the European Community as a result of German unification.
1992	Treaty on European Union (Maastricht Treaty), came into effect November 1993; the European Community, together with intergovernmental cooperation, became known as the European Union (EU); completion date for Single European Market (31 December).
1994	European Economic Area (EEA) between the EU and EFTA (excluding Switzerland) came into effect, established by a treaty signed in Oporto in 1992.
1995	Accession of Austria, Finland, and Sweden to the EU.
1997	Treaty of Amsterdam.
1999	(January) Introduction of the single european currency (the euro) during the transition period 1999–2002; participating countries are Austria, Belgium, Finland, France, Germany, Ireland, Italy, Luxembourg, Netherlands, Portugal, and Spain.

14.2.2 The European Union in historical perspective

Whilst some Western European leaders wanted close political and economic integration, others preferred looser cooperation. By 1958, the European Economic Community was in operation, but in 1960 a second group of countries established the European Free Trade Association (EFTA). EFTA was not so much a rival organization, it was simply intended to be a free trade area without the aspirations of deeper integration. Although EFTA still exists, several of its members have subsequently joined the EU and its four remaining members—Iceland, Liechtenstein, Norway, and Switzerland—are a disparate group with little geographical cohesion. Indeed, three of the EFTA members joined the European Economic Area (EEA) in 1994 to form a wider single market with the EU, leaving only Switzerland whose electorate had rejected membership of the EEA in a referendum.

In its early years, the EEC set about establishing its key institutions and policies. Its four main institutions, and those of Euratom, were already modelled on the institutions of ECSC: the Council of Ministers, the Commission (known as the High Authority in ECSC), the Assembly (later called the European Parliament), and the Court of Justice. The Assembly and Court of Justice of ECSC were used for all three communities from 1958, but a unified Council of Ministers and Commission were not introduced until 1967 as a result of the 1965 Merger Treaty.

The 1960s were also an active period on the economic front. The two major economic policy developments during this period were the creation of a customs union and a common agricultural policy (CAP). This was a difficult period of transition for the six EEC members, but internal tariffs had been removed and a common external tariff set by 1968. Similarly, it took until the late 1960s before a common policy for agriculture had been established. However, agriculture was a major industry, employing large numbers of people, and even today the CAP accounts for a larger proportion of the EU budget than any other policy. In some ways, the CAP is also a microcosm of the Single European Market, representing an early attempt to create a genuinely common market for agricultural products.

The accession of Denmark, Ireland, and the UK to the Community in 1973 was the first in a series of enlargements. Norway was to have joined them but pulled out after a referendum. Further expansion has taken place with the accession of Greece (1981), Spain and Portugal (1986), and Austria, Finland and Sweden (1995). Even before the first enlargement, the Community was pressing ahead with political and economic integration. The profile of political integration was raised by the publication of the Davignon Report in 1970. The report initiated the first formal attempt at foreign policy cooperation (known as European Political Cooperation) though, as today, this was carried out at an intergovernmental level rather than through the Community institutions. Since the Maastricht Treaty, cooperation on foreign and security policy and on home affairs have become two of the main 'pillars' of the EU, but the EU has some way to go before it can present a united front on these policy areas.

Also in 1970, the Werner Report set the scene for eventual economic and monetary union (EMU). The report initially led to the introduction of the 'Snake' in 1971 and the 'Snake in the tunnel' in 1972—arrangements for the management of exchange rates between European currencies. These early attempts at exchange rate management were largely unsuccessful because of US dollar instability and the collapse of the Bretton Woods dollar-based exchange rate system. The subsequent world oil crisis and world recession of the mid-1970s added to these problems. Community governments had originally intended to move towards a single currency by 1980 but world economic events disrupted these ambitious plans. However, a second and more successful attempt at currency management began with the introduction of the European Monetary System in 1979. The EMU project was later revived by the Delors Report in 1989 and set in motion by the Maastricht Treaty of 1992. These issues are discussed at greater length in Chapter 16.

Undoubtedly the two most important EU achievements of recent years have been the single internal market project and progress towards economic and monetary union. The creation of a single market was of course one of the original aims set out in the Treaty of Rome. At that time the term 'common market' was used. This is the term used in integration theory, but a new term was needed in 1985 in order to capture the public imagination when the single market initiative was launched. Although progress had been made in achieving a customs union, steps towards a genuine common or single market had been taken in a slow and piecemeal fashion. The 1985 decision to aim for completion of the single market by the end of 1992, supported by the extension of majority voting introduced by the Single European Act, was therefore critical. Although the single market is still incomplete, the project was given an enormous boost by this initiative. The EMU project is in many ways even more ambitious, not only for its economic implications but also as a step towards political union. In creating a single currency and working towards greater policy harmonization, the EU is venturing into uncharted territory for a large group of independent nations. Further enlargement to include the transitional economies of Eastern Europe presents another major challenge.

14.2.3 The institutions and policy-making processes of the European Union

The basic institutional structure of the EU was laid down in the Treaties of Paris and Rome and later confirmed by the Merger Treaty. The four main institutions were the Council of Ministers, Commission, Parliament, and Court of Justice. A Court of Auditors was later established, with responsibility for ensuring financial control of EU institutions and policies. Each of these institutions was given clearly defined powers and responsibilities, though some of their powers have been extended by subsequent legislation, especially in the case of the European Parliament. As the Community developed, heads of government began to meet periodically as a European Council outside the main framework of the Community institutions. Another important institution is the European Central Bank, set up in June 1998 in preparation for the introduction of the single currency.

Law-making in the EU is generally carried out through regulations or directives. Regulations are binding throughout the EU and are used mainly to implement policies which have already been agreed. Directives are more common, requiring national authorities to incorporate measures into their own legal systems. Following the Single European Act, for example, a large number of directives were approved paving the way for the single market. Regulations and directives are either approved by the Council of Ministers on the recommendation of the Commission or, increasingly, are agreed by the Council of Ministers and the Parliament through the co-decision procedure. The Commission also has powers to make decisions or rulings on specific issues arising under an agreed policy, such as the block exemptions granted to motor manufacturers and other industries under the competition rules (see Section 14.3.5 below).

There has often been tension between conflicting ideas about the scope of EU competence and the policy-making process. In some respects, the EU's institutional framework reflects the federal ambitions of its founders. Federalism implies a formal structure of authority with a clear division of responsibility between different levels. On the other hand, functionalists prefer practical cooperation in well-defined areas with minimal need for institutional structures. In practice, EU competence has gradually been extended to new policy areas as its members have felt it necessary and the powers of its institutions have been modified to facilitate these changes. The establishment of the European Central Bank, with its clearly defined powers, reflects a federal approach but its operation of monetary policy and the way it interacts with the other EU institutions will no doubt develop in a functionalist way over time. Intergovernmentalism has also reappeared as an important element of EU decision making. After playing a major role in the establishment of the EU, intergovernmental cooperation has always had a significant influence on the EU's development, but its role has now been formalized by the Single European Act and Maastricht Treaty.

■ The Council of the European Union

The Council of the European Union, or Council of Ministers as it is commonly known, is the chief decision-making body of the EU in its normal policy-making role. It is

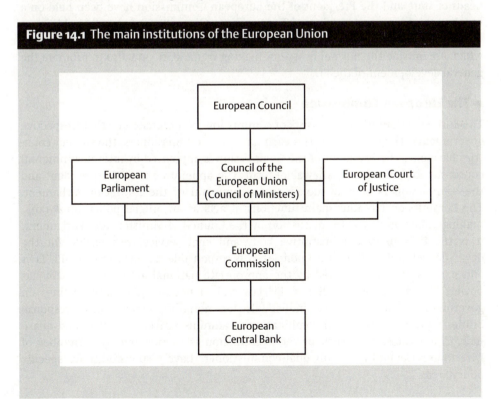

Figure 14.1 The main institutions of the European Union

made up of ministers from each of the member governments. The minister concerned varies depending on the subject under discussion. The two most important Councils are the Foreign Affairs Council and the Council of Economics and Finance Ministers (known as Ecofin). The presidency of the Council of Ministers rotates between the member governments at six-monthly intervals. On matters relating to taxation, the free movement of people, amendments to the Treaties, and the accession of new member states, voting must be unanimous. In most other areas, voting is on the basis of a qualified majority. Under the Maastricht and Amsterdam Treaties, provision is also made for co-decision making between the Council of Ministers and the European Parliament. The Council of Ministers is supported by COREPER (Comité des représentants permanents), consisting of the permanent representatives or ambassadors of the member states who prepare much of the groundwork for the ministerial meetings. The Council is also advised by the influential Economic and Social Committee, which includes representatives of employers, trade unions, and other interested groups from each member state.

■ The European Council

The European Council should not be confused with either the Council of Ministers or the Council of Europe. The latter is not an EU institution and is discussed briefly in Section 14.2.1 above. The European Council had no official status in the EU until the Single European Act 1986, but summit meetings between heads of government or heads of state and the President of the European Commission have been held on a regular basis for a number of years. The European Council now generally holds intergovernmental conferences (IGCs) every six months to discuss major policy issues which are outside the normal EU policy-making framework and also to promote the general development of the EU.

■ The European Commission

The European Commission consists of commissioners nominated by their respective governments. The larger countries each have two commissioners, the smaller countries have one. The President of the Commission is appointed by intergovernmental consensus for a five-year (renewable) term. The appointment of the president and the commissioners is now subject to the approval of the European Parliament. The Commission has four main functions: it acts as an official policy think-tank, making policy proposals for discussion by the Council of Ministers and Parliament; it is the EU's main administrative body and civil service, responsible for the day-to-day administration of EU policies; it is responsible for ensuring that EU laws and policies are implemented by the appropriate national authorities; and it has powers to investigate breaches of EU law and, if necessary, to impose fines on governments, companies, or individuals for non-compliance. These responsibilities represent a powerful combination of administrative, executive, and quasi-judicial functions. The work of the Commission is carried out by a number of Directorates-General and individual commissioners have responsibility for specific policy areas.

■ The European Parliament

Members of the European Parliament (MEPs) are directly elected by voters in their respective countries. The number of MEPs from each member country is proportional to its population. Although there are groupings of like-minded political parties, the party system is less important than in most national parliaments. Through its committees and in plenary session, the Parliament is active in making policy proposals, producing reports and amendments on draft legislation, debating important issues, and scrutinizing the work of the Commission. Until recently, however, its only significant powers were the power to approve or reject the EU budget and the power to dismiss commissioners. In practice, these powers are only used in extreme circumstances. Over the years the powers of the Parliament have gradually been extended, helping to reduce the so-called democratic deficit of the EU decision-making process. Under the co-decision procedure with the Council of Ministers, the Parliament is now likely to become more actively involved in decision-making, especially in the field of economic policy.

■ The European Court of Justice

The European Court of Justice is the highest legal authority in the EU and its decisions take precedence over national laws and courts on matters within EU jurisdiction. In areas such as employment and competition law, for example, the Court has established a number of important principles. Its decisions form part of the *acquis communautaire*—the whole body of laws, policies, procedures, and treaties of the EU. The Court has one judge from each member state, appointed by consensus. Some of its cases are now referred to the Court of First Instance in order to relieve its excessive workload. The European Court of Justice should not be confused with the European Court of Human Rights which was established by the Council of Europe and is not an EU institution.

■ The European Central Bank

The Maastricht Treaty's provisions on economic and monetary union set out the timetable for the introduction of the single currency. Under these provisions the European Central Bank (ECB) came into operation in 1998. The ECB coordinates the European System of Central Banks (ESCB, consisting of the ECB and the central banks of each member state), which in turn is responsible for financial supervision. The ECB's responsibilities include control over the issue of euro notes and coins, foreign exchange operations, and official reserves, and the conduct of monetary policy. Its primary monetary policy objective is the maintenance of price stability. All the central banks within the ECSC, including the ECB, are required to have operational independence from their respective governments and the EU institutions. In the case of the ECB, its independent authority is exercised by an Executive Board, consisting of the bank's president, vice-president, and four other members, and a Governing Council, comprising the Board and the governors of the national central banks. Its independence is counterbalanced by policy directions set out by Ecofin or by the newly established Euro-X group of eleven euro-zone finance ministers and by the scrutiny of the Commission and Parliament. The ECB will need to establish its credibility during its early years of operation and it will have to tread a fine line between rigid adherence to monetary stability and the political pressures that will inevitably be placed upon it.

14.2.4 Future developments in the European Union

Three major developments seem to be on the horizon for the EU. First, with the introduction of the single currency in 1999, economic and monetary union (EMU) is now becoming a reality. But EMU involves the coordination of economic policy beyond monetary union. The EMU stability pact already imposes a measure of budgetary discipline on participating governments. There have also been some attempts at the harmonization of taxation, especially in relation to value added tax and excise duties. Further measures are likely to follow, particularly in the area of corporate and capital taxation. Moreover, most observers agree that economic union inevitably brings a degree of political union. It is on this issue that the federalists and the functionalists are most divided.

The second major development is enlargement. During the first decade of the twenty-first century, as many as ten Eastern European countries may join the EU. In November 1998, entry negotiations were initiated with the Czech Republic, Estonia, Hungary, Poland, and Slovenia, together with Cyprus. Future members may also include Malta and the Eastern European states of Bulgaria, Latvia, Lithuania, Romania, and Slovakia. All these countries have applied for membership, as indeed have Turkey and Switzerland. This issue is discussed further in Chapter 17. Whatever the eventual size of the EU, the probable inclusion of the countries of Eastern Europe, with their legacy of communism and state planning, is likely to have profound implications for business and the people of Europe.

The third development is likely to be EU links with other economic groupings around the world. In particular, preliminary discussions have been held with NAFTA, on the creation of the so-called Transatlantic Marketplace, and with Mercosur in South America. These initiatives are intended to set up free trade agreements across the Atlantic. However, if the frequency of trade disputes between the USA, the EU, and Japan are a reliable indication, such ambitious trading areas are likely to prove problematic. The attainment of free trade is often thwarted by national attempts to protect vested interests and by a reluctance to relinquish trade policy sovereignty.

14.3 Major Policies of the European Union

IN order to implement its aims and objectives, the EU has developed a number of specific policies. Some of the major policies which have a direct impact on business are discussed below. Broader policy areas such as the single market, economic and monetary union, and the EU's external relations are considered at length in Chapters 15, 16, and 17. Many of the policies require some degree of EU funding, though in some cases the cost is shared with individual member states. The EU budget is funded through its 'own resources', a system which gives the EU control of its sources of revenue and also limits the overall size of the budget by agreement. 'Own resources' include revenue from customs duties (under the common external tariff), agricultural and sugar levies (on non-EU imports), a VAT levy (falling from a maximum rate of 1.4 per cent to 1 per cent by 1999) and an additional contribution related to each country's GNP. The current agreement allows for a small increase in the EU's 'own resources' to 1.27 per cent of EU GNP by 1999. On the expenditure side, the two largest items by far are the Common Agricultural Policy (CAP) and the structural funds. The structural funds include the European Social Fund, the European Regional Development Fund, the 'guidance' section of the European Agricultural Guidance and Guarantee Fund, and the Fisheries Guidance Instrument. These funds direct EU aid to the less developed regions within their respective policy areas.

The EU budget has been the subject of much controversy over the years. The main issues of concern have been the overall size of the budget, the amount spent on the CAP, the equity of net contributions between member states, and the potential cost of enlargement. The total EU budget in 1996 was ECU86.5 billion. Although this may sound large, it represented just under 1.2 per cent of EU GDP as compared with average EU national budgets of around 50 per cent of GDP. The CAP remains an expensive and controversial policy but its share of total EU expenditure has fallen from 68 per cent in 1985 to around 45 per cent in 1999. A country's net contribution depends not only on its revenue contributions but also on the extent to which it benefits from agricultural support and the structural funds in particular. Revenue contributions have tended to be higher for countries with large amounts of foreign trade and where consumer spending amounts to a large proportion of national income (hence large VAT levies). The general reduction in customs duties under GATT and an agreement to shift 'own resources' away from VAT towards GNP-related contributions should gradually reduce the imbalance between countries, though Germany's net contribution remains significantly higher than its relative economic strength would indicate. It is also likely that the issue of equity will be aggravated by the accession of poorer countries from Eastern Europe in the medium term.

14.3.1 From free trade to economic union

One of the original aims of the EU was to create a common market between its member states. Although it has taken most of the first forty years of the EU's existence to come close to completing this objective, it has nevertheless been a major achievement. During the first ten years internal tariffs were removed (a free trade area) and a common external tariff was set (a customs union). The common or single market has taken much longer to establish, but a single market is a huge step beyond a customs union. It requires not only the removal of customs and administrative barriers, but also measures to harmonize product and service standards and to facilitate the free movement of people and capital, among other things.

As the EU progresses down the integration road, one level of integration tends to lead to the next. For example, it could be argued that a single market requires a single currency, otherwise currency fluctuations and exchange transaction costs will form internal barriers. A single currency, in turn, involves monetary union. A similar argument could be made about tax harmonization in a single market. Tax harmonization is an example of economic policy coordination. Both monetary union and economic policy coordination are elements of an economic union. Thus, an economic union is in some ways a logical (though not inevitable) consequence of a single market. Since policy coordination, whether on monetary or fiscal policy, involves an element of political union, this too may be a logical progression. This process is now happening in the EU, though progress towards economic and political union will ultimately depend on the will of Europe's leaders and people.

The establishment of a customs union required the EU member states to adopt common tariff policies towards the outside world. This principle has also been applied to trade liberalization in general, export promotion, and anti-dumping measures. These policies are collectively known as the Common Commercial Policy. Under this policy the Commission has negotiated numerous trade or cooperation agreements with non-EU countries on behalf of the EU member states. These agreements include the association agreements or Europe Agreements with several countries in Central or Eastern Europe. The Commission also represents the member states at the World Trade Organization.

14.3.2 The Common Agricultural Policy

The Common Agricultural Policy (CAP) is one of the longest established and most highly developed EU policies. It has also been the most controversial. Its original objectives were to increase agricultural productivity, to ensure a fair standard of living for the agricultural community, to stabilize markets, to assure food supplies, and to make food available at reasonable prices.[2] With the exception of relatively high food prices, the policy has generally achieved these objectives, but at a high cost in terms of the EU budget and its distorting effects on agricultural production and trade.

Basically, the CAP operates a price support system for agricultural products. For example, each year a *target price* is agreed for wheat. This price is intended to provide a reasonable level of income for farmers throughout the EU and is therefore set above the market equilibrium price. This high price would allow imports to flood in at much lower world prices, so a *threshold price* is set for imports a little below the target price, allowing for transport and distribution costs from the port of entry. A *variable import levy* is then applied, increasing the price of imports from the world price to the threshold price. The setting of a high target price tends to encourage overproduction, but farmers' income is then protected through *intervention buying* by the EU authorities. The *intervention price* is normally 10 to 15 per cent below the target price, but it guarantees the farmer a price close to the target price. The authorities then end up with a surplus of wheat or some other product—the so-called 'food mountains' and 'wine lakes'. Farmers are also encouraged to export their surplus production with the help of an *export subsidy* which reduces their prices to the world price level. This policy forms the guarantee section of the European Agricultural Guidance and Guarantee Fund (EAGGF) and it accounts for about 90 per cent of the agriculture budget. The guidance section of the EAGGF is one of the structural funds and is used to improve the structure of agriculture in the less developed regions of the EU.

Although the EU is still a major importer of agricultural products, its import levies and export subsidies have been much criticized during successive GATT rounds and, in particular, by the USA and members of the Cairns Group of agricultural exporting nations.[3] Its wasteful production surpluses and the high cost of the CAP have also brought criticism at home. A further criticism is that the CAP tends to favour large intensive farms at the expense of smaller family farms and that these intensive production methods have an environmental cost. As a result of these criticisms, various changes have gradually been introduced. Between the late 1970s and the early 1990s, a number of piecemeal measures were taken to address the problem of overproduction; these included co-responsibility levies (sharing the cost of surpluses between producers and the EU), production quotas, agricultural stabilizers (price cuts for excessive overproduction), restricting access to intervention buying, the set-aside policy (where farmers are paid compensation to take land out of agricultural use), and an agreement to limit increases in CAP spending to between 70 and 80 per cent of increases in the total EU budget.

More radical reform, based on the McSharry proposals, was agreed in 1992. These reforms were partly in response to international pressure during the Uruguay Round. Significant reductions in the target prices for cereals and beef were introduced, bringing them closer to world prices. This measure should help to reduce the level of import levies, export subsidies, and intervention buying. Price support is now gradually being replaced by income support in the form of compensation for reduced production and set-aside land and aid to help farmers protect the environment. These measures represent a first step towards opening up agricultural production to international competition, whilst recognizing the need to provide some protection for farmers from the volatility and unpredictability of agricultural markets. Further, more far-reaching reform will be needed in the future in order to accommodate a doubling of the farm population when the countries of Eastern Europe join the EU. This process has now begun under the EU's Agenda 2000 in preparation for enlargement.

14.3.3 The Common Fisheries Policy

Fishing directly contributes less than 1 per cent of GDP in most member countries but its importance increased with the accession of Denmark, Ireland, and the UK in 1973 and especially with the accession of Spain and Portugal in 1986. In fact, it was not until 1983 that agreement was reached on a full Common Fisheries Policy (CFP). The basic objectives of the policy are to manage the EU's fish stocks in such a way that consumer demand is satisfied and fishing fleets have reasonable access to fishing grounds, whilst at the same time conserving fish stocks and the marine environment. Unfortunately, these objectives often conflict. Scientists and environmentalists tend to argue that over-fishing is causing a reduction in fish stocks and is harming the marine environment. The fishing industry and its small dependent communities see their livelihood being eroded by CFP restrictions and by foreign fishing fleets venturing into their traditional fishing grounds.

Under the CFP a 12-mile band around national shores is reserved for local fishermen and others who may have traditionally fished in these waters. Outside the 12-mile band access is in principle free to all EU fishing fleets, though in practice it is subject to a number of restrictions. Fishing permits limit the fishing effort of individual vessels as a means of managing the exploitation of fishing grounds. These restrictions are based on the concept of a 'total allowable catch' and quotas are allocated to member states with the intention of ensuring some degree of equity. In practice, the allocation of quotas has been controversial, as has the issue of 'quota-hopping' when fishermen sell their quotas to foreign fleets. Fishing effort is also controlled by a number of other measures such as restrictions on the minimum mesh size of fishing nets, the minimum size or weight of fish landed, the species of fish allowed to be caught, the number of days vessels are allowed to be at sea, and by structural measures aimed at reducing the size of fishing fleets. The result is a highly regulated EU fishing industry, overcomplicated by administrative procedures and checks, and the demise of many traditional fishing communities. The problems facing the industry are real, however.

14.3.4 Industry, research, and development

The EU has adopted a number of policy measures which come under the heading of industrial policy. The Maastricht Treaty defines industrial policy as measures designed to help industry adjust to structural change, to provide an environment conducive to business development, to encourage cooperation between businesses, and to encourage industrial innovation and research and development (R&D).[4] EU industrial policy was generally agreed on a piecemeal basis prior to the Maastricht Treaty and it was often difficult to achieve a common approach when each country had developed its own distinctive form of industrial policy. The present consensus has moved away from the more interventionist approaches of some member states towards a more market-based approach. The emphasis has now shifted towards deregulation and privatization as the route to international competitiveness. However, there has also been a move towards selective intervention to promote R&D and small and medium-sized enterprises (SMEs) in particular.

Many of the measures intended to open up the single market could be regarded as instruments of industrial policy, especially the harmonization or mutual recognition of standards. After initially favouring complete harmonization (often interpreted to mean unification) of standards, the EU now generally promotes the mutual recognition of national standards and voluntary agreement on EU-wide standards. These measures are designed to eliminate barriers to cross-border trade and to improve the international competitiveness of companies operating in the EU. The 1993 White Paper on Growth, Competitiveness and Employment emphasized the importance of intangible investment (on training, R&D, and other knowledge-based activities), industrial cooperation, the strengthening of competition, and the modernization of the role of public administration with regard to industrial policy.[5] EU industrial policy now encourages member governments to deregulate their often highly restricted energy and transport markets and to open up their public procurement to competitive tendering, though the public perception of EU policy is often one of regulation rather than deregulation.

Particular emphasis is now being placed on the encouragement of R&D. European countries have long been renowned for the inventiveness of their entrepreneurs and the quality of their academic and scientific research, but this effort has not always been translated into large-scale industrial innovation. While the EU spends about 2 per cent of its GDP on R&D, the USA and Japan spend about 3 per cent of GDP and EU companies generally lag behind in important sectors like computers and electronics. The EU operates a number of programmes designed to encourage R&D cooperation, involving companies, universities, and research laboratories, and the EU's Research and Technological Development framework programme had a budget of ECU13.1 billion between 1994 and 1998. One of its main R&D programmes is the European Strategic Programme for Research and Development in Information Technology (ESPRIT), which has been promoting research cooperation in microelectronics, information-processing, and related fields since 1983.

14.3.5 Competition policy

EU competition policy is well established and, with the exception of the merger regulation, the basic principles are set out in the Treaty of Rome. There are essentially four areas of competition policy: restrictive agreements, abuse of a dominant position, mergers, and state aids. The aim of the policy is to protect competition and thus to preserve the benefits of choice, price, quality, efficiency, innovation, and consumer satisfaction that should come from a competitive single market. Competition policy involving trade between member states is primarily the responsibility of the European Commission, though the Commission may delegate this power to the national authorities if the effects on competition are substantially in one country. The Commission carries out investigations into alleged anti-competitive behaviour (including unannounced 'dawn raids' if necessary) and may require 'undertakings' about future conduct or impose fines up to 10 per cent of a firm's annual turnover. It also investigates proposed mergers which fall within its jurisdiction and makes rulings on the acceptability of state aid. The Commission's decisions may be reviewed by the European Court of Justice or the Court of First Instance. It is also possible to take out a civil lawsuit to obtain damages for the loss suffered as a result of anti-competitive behaviour. Such an action would normally be taken in the national courts.

Box 14.1 EU Support for Small and Medium-Sized Enterprises

The EU's emerging enterprise policy attempts to coordinate a number of different measures which have been introduced to promote small and medium-sized enterprises (SMEs). The first real initiatives to form an enterprise policy were taken in the 1980s, in particular the European Council decision in 1985 to subject all EU proposals to an assessment of their impact on SMEs and to simplify the administrative, tax, and regulatory environment for SMEs. This was followed by the setting up of the SME Task Force in 1986 and the subsequent transfer of responsibility to Directorate-General XXIII in 1990. A specific legal basis for the enterprise policy is now provided by the Maastricht Treaty and in 1994 the Commission adopted the Integrated Programme in favour of SMEs and the Craft Sector. This programme is designed to bring together a variety of initiatives under a common framework. Further decisions have provided a budgetary basis for enterprise policy and have clarified the grounds for approving state aid to SMEs. The definition of SME for the purpose of EU policy is a firm with fewer than 250 employees and an annual turnover not exceeding ECU40 million or an annual balance sheet total not exceeding ECU27 million.[6]

A number of industrialized countries have adopted policies to help SMEs in recent years, but there are different views on what these policies should comprise. Some policies focus on providing financial support during the start-up period. Others concentrate on relieving the tax or administrative burden on SMEs. EU policy has two main emphases: first, to provide a supportive environment, minimizing the administrative, tax, and regulatory burdens on SMEs; and second, to coordinate the efforts of the various policies and agencies affecting SMEs. SMEs generally lack the specialist employees that large companies have to deal with the intricacies of company law, taxation, employment regulations, export procedures, and similar requirements. They also lack the resources to carry out systematic research and development. However, in many European countries SMEs are the main generators of new employment.

Restrictive agreements, or concerted practices which fall short of a formal agreement, are covered by Article 85 of the Treaty of Rome. Agreements 'which have as their object or effect the prevention, restriction or distortion of competition within the common market' are prohibited.[7] These typically include agreements to fix prices, share markets, or restrict supplies, often known as cartels. Agreements which provide benefits in terms of production, distribution, or technical progress may be exempted from the prohibition, provided they are indispensible to the achievement of these benefits, they share the benefits with the consumer, and they do not eliminate competition completely. Certain general types of agreement are exempted from the prohibition, such as subcontracting or agency agreements. The Commission also grants block exemptions for specific types of agreement, such as the motor industry's exclusive and restrictive distribution agreement on the sale of new motor vehicles. This agreement has been allowed on the grounds that motor vehicles are a technically complex product requiring trained and specialist personnel at the point of sale to protect consumer safety. There is growing criticism of the need for such block exemptions, especially with regard to exclusive dealerships. In general, however, the Commission's pursuit of firms engaged in price-fixing and similar agreements has been one of the more successful aspects of competition policy, as for example in the investigation into the market for cardboard packaging which resulted in substantial fines in 1994.

The abuse of a dominant position is covered by Article 86 of the Treaty of Rome. It should be noted that investigations under Article 86 require evidence of 'dominance' rather than monopoly or market share. Moreover, dominance alone is insufficient without evidence of 'abuse' of a dominant position. Dominance is determined by a firm's ability to act independently or indeed its ability to abuse its position in the market. Market share is only one of several factors which is taken into account, though in practice a 40 per cent market share is sometimes used as a guide in this respect. Commission investigations arise where the abuse of a dominant position affects trade between member states and where a firm or firms acting together have a dominant position in the common market as a whole or a substantial part of it. Examples of the abuse of a dominant position include the imposition of unfair prices or other trading conditions on customers or suppliers and refusal to supply or production restrictions which are to the detriment of consumers or competition.

It was not until the Merger Control Regulation of 1989, which came into force in September 1990, that the EU had a formal policy on mergers. Prior to that, Competition Commissioners had begun to use Article 86 to investigate mergers where there was the potential for the abuse of a dominant position or Article 85 to impose conditions on a proposed merger, arguing that it may be an agreement to restrict competition. However, neither of these approaches provided a clear path to the control of mergers. The desirability of transnational mergers in the EU is, in any case, the subject of much debate, but the Commission now has the power to investigate merger proposals where the companies involved have a combined worldwide annual turnover exceeding ECU5 billion, of which more than ECU250 million is generated within the EU by two or more of the companies involved (unless each of these companies derives more than two-thirds of its EU turnover within the same member state). The

Commission may refuse to allow a merger but, in practice, it is more common for it to allow a merger subject to certain restrictions. Strategic alliances between firms also pose difficult issues, such as the proposed alliance between British Airways and American Airlines which, at the time of writing, had still not been resolved after three years of deliberations by the competition authorities in the EU and the USA.

Competition policy also includes the investigation and approval of state aids to industry. These involve various forms of financial assistance from public funds to private or public enterprises in individual member states. State aids are basically covered by Articles 92 to 94 of the Treaty of Rome, or Article 90 in the case of state-owned enterprises, but it was not until the single market initiative that the Commission began to pursue this issue with vigour. The main test when considering state aid is whether the aid is likely to threaten competition within the EU. Allowable aid should generally promote sectoral or regional development which benefits the EU as a whole. The Commission also considers whether a project is entirely dependent on aid and whether the aid is proportional to the desired objectives. Whilst state aids are often allowed, especially where the amounts are small, the Commission has been concerned about the level of aid granted to major national airlines and other high-profile companies. Large aid packages to help struggling companies are in principle only allowed if they are time-limited and are accompanied by a restructuring programme. In practice, state aid is a sensitive issue as important companies and national pride are at stake and unaided competitors often claim unfair competition.

14.3.6 Regional, social, and employment policies

The structural funds account for about one-third of the EU budget. These funds are designed to promote the development of the disadvantaged regions of the EU. They include the European Regional Development Fund (ERDF) and the European Social Fund (ESF), two of the major components of the EU regional and social policies, as well as the agricultural and fisheries guidance funds. As the EU has developed, and especially since the single market project was launched, more emphasis has been placed on the balanced development of Europe's regions. More recently, employment has also become a dominant issue as observers increasingly see the high European unemployment rates as a structural rather than a cyclical problem.

Regional policy is primarily concerned with the allocation of funds from the ERDF for regional assistance in individual member states. The ERDF provides non-refundable grants under three headings: national programmes, community initiatives, and innovative measures. With the exception of innovative measures, which finance pilot projects and studies to encourage new policy approaches and account for only 1 per cent of the ERDF budget, all other ERDF funding involves co-financing by the national authorities. The national programmes account for 90 per cent of the budget and are negotiated between the Commission and national governments.

Disadvantaged regions are identified in each member state and national governments are normally expected to match ERDF spending—which is one reason why ERDF funds are not always fully utilized. The funds are actually deployed by the responsible regional or local authorities in each country. Community initiatives account for the remaining 9 per cent of ERDF funding and involve support for cross-border projects. The level of ERDF financing depends on the designation of each assisted region, those with Objective 1 status receiving the highest level of assistance. Objective 1 regions are classified as regions with income per capita which is below 75 per cent of the EU average. The Commission is currently proposing revisions to its designated regions, partly to reflect changing per capita income levels and partly to concentrate its regional aid budget on the most disadvantaged areas.

An addition to the regional budget was introduced in the form of the Cohesion Fund under the Maastricht Treaty. This fund targets EU aid for environment and transport infrastructure projects to the four member countries with per capita income below 90 per cent of the EU average: Greece, Ireland, Portugal, and Spain. This measure was designed to bring the EU's poorer nations more closely into line with the level of economic development in the richer nations. In the case of Ireland and, to a lesser extent, Spain, the Cohesion Fund and structural funds have had a significant effect on their development.

Social policy is implemented through a two-pronged approach. First, there is the European Social Fund (ESF) which provides financial assistance aimed at improving the labour market and employment prospects in disadvantaged regions. This is another key component of the EU's policy for economic and social cohesion. In particular, the ESF provides support for the long-term unemployed, young unemployed, education and training, the promotion of equal opportunities, and the creation of new jobs. The second prong is the so-called 'social chapter', which is in fact a protocol attached to the Maastricht Treaty. The social chapter is based on the 1989 Community Charter of Fundamental Social Rights of Workers—often known as the EU Social Charter, though not to be confused with the European Social Charter agreed by the Council of Europe in 1961 which entered into force in 1965. The social chapter provides the framework for subsequent agreement on matters relating to the working of labour markets, pay and employment, living and working conditions, trade union rights, gender equality, worker consultation, health and safety, and vocational training. The first two measures introduced under the social chapter were the European Works Council Directive, adopted in 1994, and the Directive on Parental Leave, adopted in 1996.

Although the regional and social policies generally help employment, either directly or indirectly, the emphasis on employment policy has been intensified during the 1990s. Measures under this heading could be said to include the single market project and the policy towards SMEs, but a more specific programme is being developed under the European Employment Action Plan and the use of the structural funds to foster job creation. The problem with action on employment is that governments and economists differ in their approach to the problem. While some focus on the general business environment and the flexibility of labour markets, others argue the case for public expenditure and aid targeted at job creation. The EU's emerging employment policy reflects these divergent approaches, though some of its critics inevitably demand more active intervention.

14.3.7 Transport and trans-European networks

Despite references to a common transport policy in the Treaty of Rome, it is only since the mid-1980s that real efforts have been made to develop such a policy. The current aims of the transport policy are to establish a single market for all forms of transport, allowing free access to the market in each member state, and the creation of an integrated transport system which is safe, reliable, and environmentally sustainable. Transport accounts for an estimated 6.5 per cent of the EU's GNP and employs over 6 million people. An efficient transport system is also vital for the free movement of goods and people.

The EU has now made considerable progress in establishing common safety standards and speed limits for commercial vehicles, though full freedom to operate road transport across frontiers (known as cabotage) has only been achieved from 1998. Liberalization of other forms of transport is also in progress. This has proved the most difficult aspect of transport policy. In the civil aviation market, for example, three successive deregulation packages agreed between 1987 and 1993 created the conditions for the opening up of competition in the European market. In particular, uniform criteria have been introduced for operating licences, full cabotage is now available, allowing airlines to fly and pick up passengers on any European route, and controls on fares (other than controls against excessive fares) have been removed. In practice, however, access to airport take-off and landing slots is often dominated by national 'flag-carriers' and competition is further distorted by subsidies to state-owned airlines and by the growing number of mergers and alliances in the airline industry.

The EU is now devoting a great deal of effort to the development of trans-European transport networks. Trans-European networks currently proposed would cost some ECU400 billion during the period up to 2010. Clearly, such ambitious proposals would require a large amount of private capital and many of them are unlikely to be realized. Several trans-European motorway and rail links are already under way, however. Perhaps an even more difficult challenge is the need to move freight transport from road to rail or, in a number of European countries, to the inland waterways. Road pricing systems are currently being investigated as a means of reducing road congestion and CO_2 emissions and steps have already been taken to encourage motor manufacturers to make vehicles cleaner and less noisy.

14.3.8 Consumers, education, and the environment

Consumer protection legislation is highly developed in most member states, but a number of EU directives have been adopted with the intention of providing minimum safety standards across the single market. Individual countries may impose higher standards provided they do not act as a barrier to competition. The legal basis of the consumer protection policy was strengthened by the Single European Act and Maastricht Treaty and the flow of directives has increased since then. Measures taken to date include directives on the labelling of foodstuffs, product liability, the provision of consumer credit, and the safety of toys, building materials, and gas appliances. It may be argued that the proliferation of legislation in this area imposes an administrative and cost burden on producers, but consumer protection may also be seen as a counterbalance to the freedom of producers to operate in a single market.

The development of cross-border business activity, as well the attainment of the EU's more ambitious political ideals, requires a greater understanding of Europe's diverse cultures and people. The EU attempts to foster this understanding through its cultural and education programmes. In the educational sphere, assistance is provided under the Socrates programme to facilitate student exchanges with universities in other EEA countries. This programme also promotes staff exchanges, the development of joint courses of study, and other links between partner universities. The Leonardo da Vinci programme provides similar opportunities for industrial training placements in other European countries. Another important feature of the EU's education policy has been the assistance it provides for the restructuring of higher education in Central and Eastern Europe under the TEMPUS programme. Although the immediate benefits of these programmes are normally experienced by small numbers of people, their indirect effects are potentially more far-reaching. Even university students who stay at home are exposed to cultural differences when foreign students join their classes. Developments in the higher education system in Eastern Europe will affect generations of students and companies in the future.

Environmental concerns have risen up the international agenda in recent years. It is therefore not surprising that the EU has adopted a number of regulations and directives on environmental protection since the 1970s. Some of its member states, especially the Scandinavian countries and Germany, already have strict standards in this field. The encouragement of business activity in the single market inevitably creates increased pressures on the environment. Moreover, pollution is no respecter of national borders. Concerted European action, as well as wider international action, is therefore required. EU measures have included the establishment of a European Environment Agency to monitor environmental problems and policies, environmental impact assessment of major projects, eco-labelling for environmentally friendly products, and numerous regulations and directives on water pollution, atmospheric pollution, noise, waste disposal, the manufacture and disposal of chemical products, and nature conservation. Gradually, the EU is also turning its attention to policy instruments such as pollution taxes, road pricing, and other market-based measures. These approaches are now receiving more widespread support though the EU has tended to rely on regulatory measures up to the present time.

14.4 The Significance of the European Union for Business Activity

MOST Western European countries conduct at least two-thirds of their trade within the European Economic Area, the wider single market between the EU and three members of EFTA. Several Eastern European countries are now diverting their trade towards the EU. Other countries such as Turkey also have strong trade links with the EU. The EU receives large amounts of foreign direct investment from the USA and Japan and many of its own companies invest in other EU countries. Some of the EU countries are also major outward investors, especially in the USA. These facts help to explain why the EU has become an important entity in international economic affairs. In the near future, the EU's single currency may become a leading currency for trade and investment around the world, though this will depend on the success of monetary union. In political terms, the EU has generally carried less weight in international affairs. Indeed, its efforts to resolve the situation in the former Yugoslavia have often been ineffective and overshadowed by United States diplomacy. Despite these weaknesses, the EU's influence in world affairs is unlikely to diminish in the foreseeable future. However, the primary aim of the EU has always been to promote peaceful cooperation between European nations, not to create a new world power.

Perhaps the most intriguing development for companies operating in the EU is the dynamic potential of the single market and economic and monetary union. This issue is discussed in Chapter 15, but in broad terms a large competitive market of this kind should act as a spur to efficiency and innovation, prompting the reorganization of companies, industries, and markets. There has already been a wave of merger activity and alliance forming in the EU since the late 1980s, reflecting not only global trends but also the restructuring of European industry. This process no doubt has some way to go. These changes have a bearing on the international competitiveness of European companies, not just on their competitiveness within the single market. A further dimension will be added to the dynamic single market when EU enlargement takes in the countries of Eastern Europe.

14.5 Summary

THE origins of the EU can be traced back to the early 1950s, but its principal founding treaty is the Treaty of Rome, 1957. The EU was intended to unite the peoples of Europe and to create a common market between its member states. Starting with six member states, the EU has gradually expanded to its present fifteen members. Further enlargement is planned, especially to encompass some of the former communist countries of Eastern Europe. Economic integration within the EU has led to the creation of the single European market and the introduction of a single currency. The main EU policy-making institutions are the European Council, which is an intergovernmental body, the Council of Ministers, European Parliament, and European Commission. Other important institutions include the European Court of Justice and the European Central Bank. The EU has a number of policies which affect the activities of business firms: these policies cover agriculture, competition, transport, regional and social policy, and a number of other areas. The development of the EU has considerable implications for business activity, both within its shores and beyond.

Review Questions

1 What are the main aims of the EU? To what extent have these aims changed since the EU was established in the 1950s?

2 What were the most significant developments in the EU during the 1990s?

3 What are the main roles of the Council of Ministers, European Parliament, and European Commission respectively?

4 Why is the Common Agricultural Policy so controversial? Why is it so difficult a policy to reform?

5 In what ways does EU policy promote industrial development and competition? Are these two policy areas compatible?

Study Topic: Will Enlargement Bankrupt the EU?

A major issue the EU is having to address before its enlargement to the east is the size and composition of its budget. Although the budget only represents around 1.2 per cent of the EU's combined GDP, the size and fairness of national contributions and the amount spent on particular policies have always been controversial. The amount spent on the Common Agricultural Policy, which still accounts for almost half the total budget, is the major area of concern, though the countries which benefit most from the structural funds and, in particular, the cohesion fund are also concerned that these funds may be a target for budget reform.

Eastern enlargement is focusing attention on these issues, but many of the underlying problems are not new. Whilst the CAP has provided a measure of protection for farmers and EU food supplies, its system of price support, export subsidies, import levies, and other forms of support has had a number of distorting effects, not only within the EU but also in the world food market. These problems will be exacerbated by the arrival of Eastern Europe's large agricultural countries, however. Farm prices set at German levels will simply not be feasible in Poland or Hungary. Considerable help and appropriate incentives will, of course, be needed to improve the productivity of Eastern European farmers. This will impose additional costs on the EU budget, as will the need to develop the transport and communication infrastructure and other aspects of their economies.

Having committed themselves to controlling the overall growth of the EU budget, the member states have little option but to reform the big spending policies. This has already met with resistance from the farm lobby, from the EU's lower-income countries which fear a reduction in funds for their economic development, and from the EU's larger economies which resent having to bear the lion's share of the budget contributions. Clearly, this is a difficult time of transition for the EU as well as for the countries of Eastern Europe. Failure to support economic regeneration in the east could be destabilizing for the EU as a whole. Major reform of the CAP is long overdue and some of the beneficiaries of the cohesion fund are perhaps now doing well enough to cope with a reduction in their share. The issue of greater equity in national budget contributions also needs to be resolved. Resolution of these tensions will require an unusually large dose of the spirit of compromise for which the EU is renowned.

Study Topic Questions

1 Given that the EU budget is small by comparison with its member states' national budgets, are the member states right to restrict its growth at a time of historic enlargement?

2 Is CAP reform an essential prerequisite to eastern enlargement? Is it fair to reduce the level of CAP subsidies and price support just before Eastern Europe's struggling agricultural producers enter the EU?

3 Is it essential for the EU to rebalance its regional development priorities in favour of the new entrants from Eastern Europe? If so, should this be a cause for concern for Greece, Ireland, Spain, and Portugal?

4 Would an increase in co-financing between the EU and individual member states be a partial solution to the EU budget problem?

5 If the budgetary problems are not resolved, could the EU go bankrupt? What would 'bankruptcy' mean in this context and how might the problem be resolved?

Notes

1 From the Preamble to the *European Economic Community Treaty* (Treaty of Rome), 1957.

2 Art. 39 of the *Treaty of Rome*.

3 The Cairns Group was formed during the GATT Uruguay Round (1986–93) and includes Argentina, Australia, Brazil, Canada, Chile, Colombia, Fiji, Indonesia, Malaysia, New Zealand, Paraguay, Philippines, South Africa, Thailand, and Uruguay.

4 Title XIII, Art. 130 of *The Treaty of Rome*, as amended by the *Treaty on European Union* (Maastricht Treaty), 1992.

5 European Commission, *White Paper on Growth, Competitiveness and Employment (COM(93)700 final, Brussels, 1993)*.

6 European Commission, *Community Guidelines on State Aid for Small and Medium-Sized Enterprises (96/C 213/04, Brussels, 1996)*.

7 Art. 85(1) of the *Treaty of Rome*.

Recommended Reading

- Bainbridge, T., *The Penguin Companion to European Union* (Penguin, 1995).

- El Agraa, A. M., *The European Union: History, Institutions, Economics and Policies* (Prentice-Hall, 1998).

- Hitiris, T., *European Community Economics* (Harvester Wheatsheaf, 1994).

- McDonald, F., and Dearden, S., *European Economic Integration* (Longman, 1999).

- Molle, W., *The Economics of European Integration: Theory, Practice, Policy* (Dartmouth, 1997)

- Nicoll, W., and Salmon, T. C., *Understanding the New European Community* (Harvester Wheatsheaf, 1994).

15

The Single European Market

Objectives

- to outline the aims and origins of the Single European Market
- to evaluate the impact of the single market
- to examine the reasons why the single market has not fully materialized
- to analyse the main single market measures to achieve the free movement of goods, services, people, and capital
- to discuss the implications of the single market for firms and industries

15.1 Introduction

THE creation of the Single European Market has undoubtedly been one of the main achievements of the European Union to date. The single market, or internal market as it is also known, builds upon the customs union that was established in the 1960s. But the single market goes much further than the removal of internal tariffs and the setting of a common external tariff. The single market project set about removing a wide range of non-tariff barriers which restrict the flow of goods, services, people, and capital between EU member states. Not all these barriers have yet been removed, but the European Council decision and subsequent White Paper in 1985 set in motion a vast flow of measures which have resulted in a much more barrier-free Europe. Some barriers will remain even when the single market project is completed: language, culture, and geography can act as barriers, as they sometimes do within individual countries. Some barriers will be removed as further measures are implemented, including the introduction of the single European currency. What is clear is that the single market is already having a significant effect on the level of competition, the structure of companies and industries, and on many other aspects of business activity.

15.2 Progress Towards the Single European Market

15.2.1 The aims and origins of the single market

The establishment of a common market has always been one of the primary aims of the EU, as stated in the Treaty of Rome. The customs union, Common Agricultural Policy, and other common policies were seen as stepping stones towards its achievement. It is doubtful, however, whether the full implications of the aim were understood at the outset. Reaching agreement on the removal of tariffs and some of the other more obvious trade barriers is relatively straightforward, but making it as easy to sell goods and services in a foreign country as it is in the home market is a much more difficult task. Inevitably, different countries have their own political and legal systems, their own practices and procedures, and their own industrial structure. As the EU has developed, national policies and economies have been converging, but this is a long and slow process.

Apart from the gradual adoption of common policies, a number of European Court decisions have also been establishing common market principles. The most important of these was the 1979 judgment in the *Cassis de Dijon* case.[1] The Court ruled that free trade could not be prevented by resorting to national food standards unless this was to protect the public health, the interests of the consumer, or the supervision of taxes. The German authorities had tried to prevent the importing of a French black-currant liqueur on the grounds that it did not satisfy the minimum alcoholic content for liqueurs allowed by German law. This decision established the principle of 'mutual recognition' which is now an important principle of the single market. Similar rulings were made against the German prohibition on foreign beers containing additives in 1987 and against the Italian prohibition on the sale of foreign pasta products not made from durum wheat in 1988.

Although some of the European Court's decisions have been influential in promoting the single market, by the mid-1980s it was felt that a more coordinated effort was required. Thus, in March 1985 the European Council made the momentous decision to initiate the single market project. This was followed by a detailed White Paper outlining around 300 measures which would be necessary to create the single market.[2] The passage of the Single European Act 1986, which came into force in July 1987, was also important in that it facilitated speedier decision-making on the basis of qualified majority voting and provided the legal framework for the White Paper's proposals. Lord Cockfield, the commissioner responsible for the White Paper, identified three types of trade barrier which needed to be removed: physical barriers (frontier controls), technical barriers (such as product standards), and fiscal barriers (differences in tax rates). The European Council's decision and the Cockfield White Paper set in motion what became known as the '1992 Project'. A target date of 31 December 1992 was set for the completion of the single market. This project, with a clear deadline and surrounded by publicity, created the impetus required to make the single market a reality. The term 'single market' was chosen to distinguish it from the 'common market' which had become the popular name for the European Economic Community. A single market implies one home market for the whole of the EU whereas a common market could exist in parallel to the separate national markets, though essentially the aim was always to create a single EU market.

15.2.2 The 'four freedoms'

It was recognized in the Treaty of Rome that 'four freedoms' underpin the creation of a common or single market. These freedoms are the free movement of goods, the freedom to provide services, the free movement of persons, and the free movement of capital. Many of the earlier policies of the EU focused on the free movement of goods, especially in relation to the removal of tariffs and quotas. This was understandable in that, for most European countries, foreign trade was predominantly in manufactured goods. Even with trade in goods, however, tariffs are by no means the only barrier. Increasingly, services are overtaking manufacturing in their share of GDP and, whilst this change is not yet fully reflected in most countries' balance of payments, trade in services is becoming more important. Tariffs do not generally apply to services, so the EU has had to turn its attention to the regulations and other restrictions which prevent cross-border trade in services. The free movement of persons applies not only to the general or business traveller but particularly to the free movement of workers. It also involves the freedom of establishment—the freedom to practise one's trade or profession in another country. Finally, the free movement of capital allows individuals and businesses to transfer funds and invest abroad without exchange controls and other restrictions on the nationality of the investor or the location of the investment. Without these freedoms a complete single market cannot be achieved, though some of the required measures involve complex changes in legislation and procedures.

15.2.3 The impact of the single market

The expected consequences of economic integration are discussed at length in Chapter 7. Here, we consider some of the specific effects of the Single European Market. Some of these effects are the cumulative outcome of EU integration over the years. The single market is, in any case, built upon the foundation of the customs union so it may be unnecessary to distinguish between the two. It is difficult to isolate the impact of the single market project, except where recent trends indicate new or changing patterns of activity. Even here, some of the effects of the single market may have an immediate impact, others may take longer to work through. However, whilst broad trends such as the level of intra-EU trade have been apparent for a number of years, changing patterns of merger and investment activity, among other things, seem to suggest that the single market project is having an identifiable impact.

The impact of the single market can be divided into static and dynamic effects. In outline, the static effects include trade creation and trade diversion, the effect of increased competition, the cost reductions resulting from technical harmonization and the removal of frontier controls, and efficiency improvements resulting from economies of scale and industrial restructuring. Static effects relate to the once-for-all benefits from trade, price reductions, and cost reductions. The dynamic effects are market forces which have a continual or repeated impact on efficiency, investment, research and development (R&D), and innovation, stimulating both micro- and macro-economic effects on firms, the structure of industries and markets, and the single market as a whole. The full impact of dynamic factors is difficult to measure as (a) their effect may be incomplete, (b) they may have numerous spillover effects on other firms or markets (such as the diffusion of innovation), and (c) some of their effects may be difficult to quantify (for example R&D expenditure does not necessarily equate to R&D output). For this reason, most studies have tended to concentrate on the static effects, though even here some effects may be difficult to quantify.

Probably the most comprehensive analysis of the expected consequences of the single market is a multi-volume study by the European Commission, which is summarized in the Cecchini Report.[3] The study estimates the expected welfare gains of the single market as between 4.25 and 6.5 per cent of EU GDP. Net welfare gains take account of changes in consumer and producer surpluses, government tariff revenues, deadweight losses, and similar factors resulting from the removal of tariffs and non-tariff barriers. The study also estimates the macroeconomic impact of the single market as a GDP increase of 4.5–7 per cent, an employment increase of 1.75–5 million and price reductions of 4.5–6 per cent. These estimates have been criticized as over-optimistic, especially as the Commission has a vested interest in the success of the single market project. Any estimates are, of course, dependent on the methodology used and even the European Commission study excluded some of the more dynamic and less easily quantifiable factors which result from technical progress and improved factor productivity.

If the Commission's estimates are at all valid, the single market should have a significant impact on the EU economy and the economic welfare of its citizens. Some of these benefits will also be experienced by foreign companies which operate in the EU. The competitive impact on EU firms should also improve their competitiveness in the world economy. Indeed, provided the EU remains open to international trade (see Chapter 17 on 'Fortress Europe'), even companies and countries outside the EU should benefit from increased exports to the growing EU market. The extent to which these effects materialize will, however, depend on several factors which are discussed in the next section.

15.2.4 Reasons why the single market has not fully materialized

The single market has had a significant impact on economic activity in the EU. Yet the more optimistic predictions of the 1988 European Commission study do not appear to have been justified.[4] Several explanations may be offered for the fact that the expected benefits of the single market have not yet fully materialized:

■ The failure to implement single market measures

By December 1992 about 260 of the original 282 single market measures had been agreed. However, not all of these had been incorporated into national law in each member state and, even where they had been, a number of them had not yet come into effect. In practice, while the Commission and other EU institutions moved quickly, some national authorities have been slower to implement the measures and enforcement has sometimes been ineffective. Failure to apply the principle of mutual recognition and differences in the interpretation of EU laws in each member state may also create uncertainty and act as a barrier to trade. In particular, the failure to remove restrictions on financial services and public procurement is making it difficult for foreign firms to enter these markets. Financial services markets are often highly regulated and organizations responsible for public procurement often favour preferred local suppliers. Despite this, the single market project was well under way, though not completed, by the end of 1992. Further measures have been agreed and implemented since then.

■ Some barriers are difficult to remove

Europe is a continent of many cultures and languages. It is also divided geographically by mountain ranges and seas. Whilst Alpine road and rail tunnels and the Channel tunnel have made travel between some of Europe's nations easier, physical and cultural barriers remain. The effect of cultural differences and geographical location should not be exaggerated but smaller, less experienced companies may be deterred by their perceptions of the difficulties involved. Other barriers have not yet been fully addressed by the EU—in particular, the lack of fiscal harmonization and restrictions on the free movement of people. Large tax differences between countries, particularly on goods, capital, and other highly mobile factors, are believed to encourage tax avoidance, trade distortions, and the misallocation of resources. The double taxation of companies operating in different member states also creates problems. The free movement of people raises concerns about criminals, drug traffickers, and illegal immigrants. These concerns have tended to limit progress in achieving this objective.

■ Monopolistic or fragmented national markets

A number of national markets are protected from competition by state ownership, market entry regulation, or preferential public procurement. These often include the public utility industries (electricity, gas, water, telecommunications), the defence industry, the postal service, and industries such as steel, shipbuilding, aircraft manufacture, and civil aviation. Restrictions on these markets allow them to remain monopolistic. Many of them are now in the process of being privatized, deregulated, or otherwise opened up to competition, but it is often a long and slow process. Other markets remain fragmented, with national or regional markets separated by their location or by the peculiarities of local customs and taste.

■ Economic recession and deflationary policies

The launch of the single market programme coincided with a period of economic growth during the mid- to late 1980s. This was a period of optimism and the single market's objectives seemed attainable. By 1993, when the single market was supposed to be fully operational, much of Western Europe was in recession. Some of the larger European economies have only experienced modest growth rates since then. Thus, the expected growth from the single market may have been held back by the downturn in the business cycle. This problem appears to have been exacerbated by the fact that several European governments were, at the same time, attempting to reduce their expenditure or raise taxes in order to reduce their budget deficits and public debt to meet the Maastricht convergence criteria for economic and monetary union (see Chapter 16). These deflationary policies would have caused downward pressure on aggregate demand, making the recession more severe and the recovery more sluggish.

■ Currency instability

The completion of the single market project was also accompanied by a period of turbulence in the currency markets, especially in 1992 when Italy and the UK left the Exchange Rate Mechanism and in 1993 when some of the other member currencies also came under speculative pressure. Although the period since then has been calmer in the foreign exchange markets, currency instability is generally bad for business. Firms trading abroad, borrowing or lending abroad, or making foreign investment decisions find currency instability disruptive and long-term planning more difficult. Even the lack of monetary union during most of the 1990s, and for some member countries beyond the 1990s, may have held back the completion of the single market. It is difficult to imagine a single market in which it is as easy to sell goods as in the home market but where each region of the market has a separate currency and a fluctuating exchange rate.

15.3 The Main Single Market Measures

15.3.1 The free movement of goods

The free movement of goods was initially tackled through the establishment of the customs union in the 1960s. Countries joining the EU subsequently have each removed tariffs and quotas with other members and adopted the common external tariff after a transition period. The movement of goods is also affected by a wide range of non-tariff barriers. One of the first barriers to be addressed under the 1992 programme was differences in the taxation of goods. The Commission initially proposed to harmonize national VAT rates within the following bands: between 14 and 20 per cent for the standard rate and 4 and 9 per cent for the lower rate applying to certain sensitive or essential goods. The term 'harmonize' is often used to describe single market measures and is sometimes understood to mean 'unify' or 'make the same', though in principle 'harmony' implies that rates or standards are compatible and fit well together. The term 'approximation' is also used to avoid this problem, especially with regard to taxation. In some cases the need for safety may mean that common standards are required, as for example with electrical wiring. In the case of taxes, however, comparisons with the USA suggest that cross-border trade is only affected if tax rates on goods vary by more than 5 or 6 per cent. Some degree of tax harmonization, or approximation, has been achieved, but political resistance has held back progress in this area. Although not within the bands originally proposed, VAT rates are now closer than before, but wide differences still exist between excise duties in different member states. This inevitably encourages a large cross-border trade in cigarettes, alcohol, and similar goods in order to avoid the higher excise duties.

Perhaps the most extensive barrier to the free movement of goods has been differences in product standards. Technical standards have often been developed in a piecemeal way over many years in each member country. Sometimes they are for safety or environmental reasons, sometimes for product compatibility, sometimes to accommodate national tastes and preferences. Sometimes they may have developed in a haphazard way and there is no longer a valid reason for their existence. It is also possible that some national authorities have devised standards which maximize the market entry barriers to foreign firms. Whether by intention or by accident, their effect is often to act as a barrier to trade. The EU's first approach to this problem was to attempt to harmonize vast numbers of individual national standards across a swathe of product categories. This approach proved almost impossible and largely unnecessary and met with resistance from people anxious to protect their distinctive

Figure 15.1 The Single European Market project

The Free Movement of Goods
customs union
tax harmonization or approximation
common standards (minimum standards for health and safety, etc.)
voluntary harmonization of standards
mutual recognition of standards
elimination of customs controls and documentation
harmonization of transport regulations
deregulation of transport and utility markets
liberalization of public procurement

The Freedom to Provide Services
freedom to operate across frontiers
mutual recognition of service regulations
adoption of common standards
mutual recognition of financial services
harmonization and deregulation of transport
privatization and deregulation of telecommunication

The Free Movement of Persons
right of workers to seek employment and reside abroad
freedom of establishment
right of citizens to move freely
reduction in border and passport controls
removal of passport controls under the Schengen Agreement
mutual recognition of qualifications

The Free Movement of Capital
removal of exchange controls
elimination of investment restrictions
free movement of capital under EMU

products. The *Cassis de Dijon* decision in 1979 opened up the way for the mutual recognition of standards and this approach was widely used in the single market programme. The EU now tends to restrict common standards to issues of health and safety and other core aspects of trade, though it also encourages national standards authorities to reach voluntary agreement on the harmonization of standards. Mutual recognition implies that standards which are acceptable in one member state should be accepted by all other member states. Certain minimum standards and common implementation of this approach are, of course, essential prerequisites for mutual recognition.

Symbolically, the most potent measure was probably the removal of physical barriers at border crossings. Some of the customs controls were in fact removed in dramatic fashion on 1st January 1993. This appeared to complete the opening of the single market. Certainly, the elimination of physical checks and procedures has helped to speed up the movement of goods and reduce the cost of border delays. Much of the customs documentation has also been removed or simplified. In some cases border posts are now barely in evidence, in others the role of customs officials is concentrated on security rather than customs matters.

The freedom to transport goods across frontiers is also important. The harmonization of transport regulations has played a part in this process, as has the deregulation of restricted national transport markets. Access to other member states was often limited by strict quotas in the road haulage industry and by entry regulation in the airline industry. Deregulation is now occurring in other industries such as energy and telecommunications. The supply of gas and electricity across national borders will therefore become easier in the future, helping to create a more competitive market for energy. Restrictions on public procurement represent a further obstacle to competition in the many markets where purchasing is dominated by local or national government, government agencies, or nationalized industries. Public bodies often favour preferred local suppliers and the market remains closed to foreign firms. Although competitive tendering for public services is becoming more common, political pressures tend to be more acute in the public sector and governments often seek to protect strategic local industries like defence. The Cecchini Report estimates that public procurement accounts for about one-sixth of the GDP of the EU, so the opening up of this sector will represent a significant step towards the completion of a single market.[5] Current merger proposals in the European defence industry suggest that some of the implications of more open European defence procurement are beginning to emerge.

15.3.2 The freedom to provide services

Understandably, the EU concentrated on the free movement of goods in the early years. At that time, goods dominated the international trade of most countries. Increasingly, services have become more important in international trade and services such as finance, insurance, transport, distribution, and a variety of manufacturing support services often accompany the movement of goods. The freedom to provide services has therefore risen up the EU's single market agenda. Essentially, this involves the freedom to operate across frontiers, regardless of where a business is established. The freedom to provide services is often restricted by rules on nationality, residence, and qualifications, or by procedures relating to the cross-border transfer of money to pay for services. In principle, most of these obstacles have now been removed, though measures to promote the mutual recognition of qualifications are still in progress. Certain services involving sensitive public policy are excluded from the provisions on the freedom to provide services.

Financial services have presented particular difficulties as markets for banking and insurance tend to be highly regulated. Regulations help to ensure the solvency of financial institutions and the safety of financial deposits and insurance funds, but the labyrinth of complex rules tends to deter foreign companies and protect mono-polistic national markets. At one level, bonds, loans, and currency deposits move freely in international markets, but for many companies and individuals financial services are still mainly provided by domestic institutions. Essentially, the issue is one of mutual recognition, together with the adoption of certain common standards. Credit institutions may now provide services and establish branches in another member state while remaining under home country control. In the insurance indus-try the issue is more complicated, as individual countries have quite different rules governing this sector. In view of the importance of financial services to the business sector as a whole, further progress in this area is crucial.

Transport and telecommunications are now becoming open, though restricted national monopolies still hold sway in the airline and telecommunications industries. Several national flag-carriers are still state-owned in the European airline industry and, despite deregulation, state aid and restricted access to major airports create an uneven playing field for smaller competitors. Telecommunications is also an important support service for business. Most European countries are in the process of deregulat-ing and privatizing this industry and progress is now being pushed by technological developments in the field. This is also the case with broadcasting and the EU is deve-loping agreed standards to facilitate the cross-border provision of television services.

15.3.3 The free movement of persons

Freedom to travel in Europe, for domestic or business purposes, has long been estab-lished. Indeed, the right of workers to seek employment and reside in other member states is also a well-founded principle, subject to certain restrictions relating to public policy, public security and public health, and employment in the public services. This right was later extended to students, retired people, and other citizens, provided they have sufficient income and sickness insurance to avoid being dependent on the host country's social security system. However, the free movement of workers, and the associated freedom of establishment—the right to practise one's trade or profes-sion—is in practice often hindered by border controls and the failure to recognize qualifications obtained in another member country. The single market programme aimed to tackle these two problems.

Border controls have now generally been reduced for EU passport holders and have been removed between countries which participate in the Schengen Agreement. Schengen was originally agreed between France, Germany, and the Benelux nations outside normal EU procedures. It entered into force in these countries in 1995 as well as in Portugal and Spain. Following the Amsterdam Treaty in 1997, the Schengen Agreement is being incorporated into the EU framework and thirteen EU countries now participate in the Schengen area, leaving only the UK and Ireland outside. Britain

Box 15.1 Duty-free Goods in the Single European Market

Travellers normally expect to find duty-free goods for sale on ships or aircraft and at ports, airports, and border crossings. This has included travel within the EU, though internal EU duty-free sales were abolished on 30 June 1999. Since there are no customs duties or tariffs between EU countries, 'duty-free' in this context means free of excise duty and other indirect taxes. Excise duty applies to goods such as alcoholic drinks and tobacco and applies whenever these goods are sold in a particular country, regardless of the country of origin. As some EU countries have large excise duties on these goods, however, duty-free sales may involve big tax savings.

There is little logic to justify the continuation of duty-free sales between EU countries in a border-free single market where consumers can shop around and bring large quantities of goods home for personal consumption without incurring further duty. If excise duties and other taxes were harmonized between member states and these taxes were levied in the country of origin (the 'origin principle' to which the EU is moving), the logic behind duty-free sales would be even weaker. Despite these arguments, there is a powerful lobby in favour of retaining the duty-free concession. Travellers see it as a perk which they are reluctant to lose. But the strongest opponents of abolition are the shipping companies, airlines, and operators of ports and airports. They often argue that a large proportion of their profit is made on duty-free sales and that this profit even subsidizes their other services. The abolition of duty-free sales will therefore not only create unemployment at airport terminals, for example, but will also increase the price of airline tickets.

One might expect the travelling public to be concerned about the claim that large profits are made on duty-free sales. This suggests that airport authorities and others may be taking advantage of their monopoly situation. In practice, travellers seem to be content to allow this to continue provided they avoid paying tax. Governments are sometimes persuaded by the risk of job losses as well as by the popularity of duty-free sales. It is unlikely, however, that even in the absence of the duty-free concession the companies involved will not continue to offer a selection of goods to tempt travellers with a little time (and money) on their hands. The goods may not be cheaper than elsewhere but at least their prices will be more transparent to the consumer. In a single market it is difficult to justify the continuation of a tax-free concession to a particular group of people—those who travel frequently across borders which have increasingly less significance. Duty-free sales also cause an element of distortion in patterns of consumer expenditure and may have an adverse effect on the sales of domestic retailers of these goods. On the other hand, whether they are retained or not, their impact on the single market is probably insufficient to warrant the degree of interest the issue seems to arouse in some member countries.

has reservations about the agreement in view of the ease with which criminals and illegal immigrants may move around the area. Ireland is constrained in this respect by its passport union with Britain. The success of the agreement depends on the ability of the EU to agree common policies on cross-border policing, intra-EU extradition, asylum, immigration at the EU's external borders, and related matters. Although individual member states have different approaches to these issues, some steps have been taken in these areas and external controls are becoming stricter. This in itself is a problem, however, as several member states have passport unions and other close links with neighbours outside the EU; this applies to members of the Nordic Council, two of whose members, Norway and Iceland, are outside the EU and will apply to some of the first Eastern European entrants when their relatively open borders with neighbours outside the EU become closed. Despite these difficulties, a number of EU countries have gone ahead with the removal of borders because of the benefits of free movement.

The mutual recognition of qualifications is proving a more difficult barrier. In a general sense, differences in academic qualifications are becoming better understood. Degree and diploma courses vary in length, structure, and content in different member countries, but employers often have a broad idea of the standard of education attained. The position with regard to vocational qualifications is altogether more complex. Not only is there a variety of levels and types of qualification but also, in some countries, qualifications are awarded by a variety of institutions. The regulation of professional conduct is also undertaken by a large number of professional bodies. At first, the EU strove to adopt common standards for each of the regulated professions but, as with harmonization in other areas, this proved problematic. A gradual programme to achieve mutual recognition is now in progress for all qualifications requiring a minimum of three years of higher education, together with appropriate professional training where applicable. The practical difficulties here are considerable.

15.3.4 The free movement of capital

The free movement of capital is necessary to allow companies and individuals to transfer funds and invest in other member states. The movement of capital is often restricted by exchange controls and by restrictions on the nationality of the investor or the location of the investment. Each EU country has its own planning and environmental regulations but these should apply equally to domestic and foreign investors. In practice, some countries have removed their capital restrictions more rapidly than others. With the exception of Greece, Ireland, Portugal, and Spain, member states were required to remove their capital controls by July 1990. All restrictions have now been removed. Whilst hidden barriers may sometimes apply to foreign investment, most EU countries encourage capital movements and capital moves freely, not only within the EU but in many cases beyond the EU's borders as well. The free movement of capital is now an integral part of the programme for economic and monetary union.

15.3.5 Measures to accompany the single market

The main emphasis of the 1992 project was the creation of a single market, but it was also recognized that free and fair competition needed to be protected and that some regions would lag behind in the competitive market. In order protect competition, the conduct of competition policy was extended in two areas: merger policy and the control of state aids. These policy areas are discussed in Chapter 14. Merger policy was essentially a new venture for the EU. The arrival of the single market has corresponded with an increase in the level of merger activity in the EU and it was during this period, in 1989, that the Merger Regulation was approved. Opinion is divided on the implications of trans-European mergers, but in practice the Commission has taken a reasonably cautious approach, only preventing mergers where there is likely to be a clear adverse impact on competition. Rules relating to state aids are included in the Treaty of Rome, but the Commission has used the single market project to set about tackling the issue more systematically.

The development of the EU's disadvantaged regions has also been given greater priority since the late 1980s. Substantial increases in the European Regional Development Fund were made during the periods 1989–93 and 1994–9. In fact, the structural funds as a whole were doubled during the latter period. Further measures to promote regional development included the following: the establishment of the Cohesion Fund to help the poorer EU countries; an additional temporary loan facility to help the European Investment Bank (EIB) finance infrastructure projects; and the setting up of a new European Investment Fund, involving both the EIB and private banks, to invest in trans-European networks and to provide support for small and medium-sized enterprises.

15.4 Doing Business in the Single Market

15.4.1 Opportunities and threats

The single European market is becoming arguably the second most competitive market in the world after the USA. Other markets around the world are competitive in terms of production costs and price but it is the combination of product quality, productivity, discerning consumers, and astute competitors that makes the US market, and increasingly the EU market, distinctive. Furthermore, Porter argues that national competitive advantage stems from four things: favourable factor conditions (skilled labour, efficient infrastructure, etc.); favourable demand conditions (including demanding and discerning consumers); the existence of related and supporting industries (including component suppliers and business support services); and firm strategy, structure, and rivalry (firms that are well organized and managed and exposed to healthy domestic competition).[6] Whilst some of these factors may be present in relatively closed economies like Japan or South Korea, Porter's 'Determinants of National Advantage' (known as 'Porter's Diamond') are more likely to be found in their entirety in a large competitive environment.

The single market therefore provides both a demanding competitive environment and the conditions for internationally competitive companies to develop. Its competitive environment provides opportunities for firms to venture beyond their national market and to make the European market their home market. For larger companies, this may be an opportunity to exploit economies of scale where they were previously constrained by their national market. For smaller firms, it is an opportunity to go international with fewer of the risks usually associated with doing business abroad. Of course, these same firms will also face increased competition from elsewhere in the single market, making their domestic market less secure. It is in these circumstances that firms with proactive strategies are likely to be more successful. Those which wait for the onslaught of competition are likely to struggle. The single market therefore increases the importance to a firm of seizing new opportunities and exploiting its strengths in a wider market.

One of the key benefits of the single market, often down-played or ignored, is its potential impact on the international competitiveness of firms operating in the European Economic Area. The very harshness of competition is the refining process that makes a firm do things better. Competition increases X-efficiency—the ability of an organization to maximize the potential of its labour and other resources. X-efficiency sharpens the focus of an organization and helps to unify the commitment of its workforce at all levels. In the long term, continual improvements in productivity are perhaps the surest way of enhancing international competitiveness. Productivity relates to a firm's ability to increase its output from a given set of inputs or to produce the same output with fewer inputs. It may also result from improvements in the quality of output derived from a given set of inputs. Productivity therefore involves adding value to resources and products. Thus, a firm may make a product which in some way is differentiated from its rivals or may produce a niche product. These benefits are not confined to large MNEs. Small firms are sometimes good at taking advantage of specialized markets. The single market provides an environment in which these challenges and opportunities are created, beyond as well as within Europe.

15.4.2 Company restructuring and industrial reorganization

In the single market, as in the global market place, competition is encouraging firms to restructure their operations in order to improve their effectiveness. Restructuring may involve relocation of production or distribution facilities, changes to organizational structure, refocusing of marketing effort, centralization of administrative or accounting functions, and similar reorganization. Where the market becomes the EU as a whole or a substantial part of it, marketing effort may be reorganized on a pan-European basis, with a unified sales force, coordinated advertising and a centralized budget. This may also have implications for the recruitment of sales personnel and a company's human resource management policy. Reorganization of other company activities and functions may well follow. Other processes are also at work, such as the pressure to cut costs and to improve management effectiveness. These processes may result in employee and management redundancies, company down-sizing, and even the closure of branches or entire companies. However, in this process company efficiency and productivity generally improve and competition brings down prices. Consumers therefore have more money to spend on the new products and services that competition promotes. Competition may thus be viewed as a dynamic process where existing firms either change and become stronger or fail to respond and are replaced by new firms producing new or improved products.

A particular feature of this restructuring process has been the wave of mergers and alliances which have taken place. Mergers not only alter company structure, they also affect industrial structure. In fact, large parts of major industries are being reorganized. This process is happening around the world and particularly in the USA, though whereas merger activity began to slow down during the latter half of 1998 in the USA, there was less sign of a slowdown in Europe. In fact, in the first nine months of 1998, six of the acquiring firms in the world's ten largest cross-border merger deals by value were European, including each of the top three.[7] Mergers and acquisitions have become an integral part of the reorganization and consolidation of European industry. Whilst it is difficult to find consistent evidence of post-merger efficiency gains, some writers argue that industrial consolidation is an inevitable consequence of the opening up of competition.[8] Thus, although internal company efficiency may not necessarily have improved, resources are allocated more efficiently by the industry as a whole or between different industries. This means that if barriers to competition áre really removed in the single market, industries and firms are likely to experience major changes in their structure and organization, in their products and in the way they do business.

15.5 Summary

THE creation of a Single European Market, or common market, was one of the original aims of the EU, though in practice only piecemeal progress beyond a customs union had been made until the single market project was launched in 1985. After the passage of the Single European Act, 1986, about 260 separate measures were agreed, though not all implemented, by the deadline set for completion of the single market: 31 December 1992. For a number of reasons, the single market has still not fully materialized, but considerable progress has been made in removing barriers to trade within the EU (and subsequently the European Economic Area). The single market is intended to allow the free movement of goods, the freedom to provide services, and the free movement of persons and capital. The measures implemented to date have gone some way towards achieving these objectives. The single market creates a number of opportunities for firms operating within its boundaries, opening up a large internal market, but the threat of increased competition keeps firms on their toes. Many firms and industries have already responded by reorganizing their activities to improve their effectiveness within the single market.

Review Questions

1 What progress had been made towards the creation of a common market before the single market initiative?

2 Why has the single market not yet fully materialized, despite agreement on a wide range of measures?

3 What kind of measures have contributed towards the free movement of goods and the freedom to provide services within the single market? To what extent have these objectives been achieved?

4 To what extent is there free movement of persons within the single market?

5 What are the opportunities and threats for firms operating in the single market?

Study Topic: Can SMEs Survive in the Single European Market?

The single market initiative set in motion a process of corporate and industrial reorganization. Firms have been repositioning themselves to take advantage of market opportunities and improve their competitiveness. Industries have undergone structural change in response to the wave of mergers, new market entrants, and business failures. Competition has increased but, with it, has come consolidation. Some analysts regard consolidation as an inevitable consequence of competition as the market adjusts to the removal of national trade barriers, resulting eventually in a more efficient industrial structure and allocation of resources. One industry after another is going through this consolidation process, depending on the speed with which an industry's markets are opening up to competition. Mergers and acquisitions are producing large European companies in the motor industry, banking, and a number of other industries.

In view of the scale economies and market power to be gained by these large companies, what role is there for SMEs? In Europe, as in other parts of the world, there is a large number of SMEs. These firms dominate Italy's textile and footwear industries, are common throughout Scandinavia and in the EU's less developed countries, and play an important role in all the EU economies. Are their days numbered in the single market? To answer this question, it is necessary to consider the type of goods and services these firms produce and to evaluate their strengths and weaknesses. Many SMEs are in the supply chains of larger companies or in industries which lack the high profile of the motor manufacturing and banking industries. They are frequently more adaptable and customer-oriented than their larger counterparts and are willing to supply custom-made products or services at short notice. In some cases, they specialize in niche markets where individuality is more important than mass production. In short, they often perform a different function from larger companies or sometimes coexist with larger competitors because they offer something their competitors are unable or unwilling to provide. The key question is: if faced with new competition from a large firm in the newly opened single market, how should a struggling SME respond?

Study Topic Questions

1 Do you agree that the processes of corporate reorganization and industrial consolidation are an inevitable consequence of increased competition in the single market?

2 What are the main advantages for those firms which have grown in size through expansion or merger in the single market?

3 What are the main threats to SMEs from these large European companies?

4 What are the main strengths of SMEs compared to their larger counterparts?

5 How should a struggling SME respond if faced with new competition from a large firm in the newly opened single market?

Notes

1 *Rewe-Zentrale AG v Bundesmonopolverwaltung für Branntwein*, Case 120/78.

2 European Commission, *White Paper on Completing the Internal Market*, (1985).

3 European Commission, 'The Economics of 1992', *European Economy*, 35, (Luxembourg, 1988), and European Commission, *Studies on the Economics of Integration*, i–iii, Research on the 'Cost of Non-Europe': Basic Findings, Document, (Luxembourg, 1988), which are summarized in P. Cecchini, *The European Challenge: 1992: The Benefit of a Single Market* (Wildwood House, Aldershot, 1988).

4 Ibid.

5 Ibid.

6 M. E. Porter, *The Competitive Advantage of Nations* (Macmillan, 1998).

7 *Financial Times* Survey: *Mergers and Acquisitions* (16 Oct. 1998). The three largest cross-border merger deals between January and September 1998 were British Petroleum's acquisition of Amoco (UK/US), Daimler-Benz's acquisition of Chrysler (German/US), and ABN Amro's agreed bid for Générale de Banque (Netherlands/Belgium) which was subsequently withdrawn.

8 See J. Kay, *The Business of Economics* (Oxford University Press, 1996).

Recommended Reading

■ El Agraa, A. M., *The European Union: History, Institutions, Economics and Policies* (Prentice-Hall, 1998).

■ McDonald, F., and Dearden, S., *European Economic Integration* (Longman, 1999).

■ Molle, W., *The Economics of European Integration: Theory, Practice, Policy* (Dartmouth, 1997)

■ Pelkmans, J., *European Integration: Methods and Economic Analysis* (Longman, 1997).

■ Swann, D., *The Economics of the Common Market: Integration in the European Union* (Penguin, 1995).

16

European Political and Economic Integration

Objectives

- to examine the process of enlargement and deeper integration in the European Union
- to outline the main provisions of the Treaty on European Union (Maastricht Treaty)
- to evaluate the advantages and disadvantages of European economic and monetary union (EMU)
- to discuss the implications of the single European currency for large and small firms
- to discuss the business implications of European political union

16.1 Introduction

THE pace of political and economic integration in the European Union appears to have quickened during the 1980s and 1990s, but the process of integration is not new. For over forty years the EU economies have gradually become more integrated and the member states have been working together in more and more policy areas. In itself, economic and monetary union (EMU) is a far-reaching measure, but it is built upon what has gone before: especially the European Monetary System and the Single European Market. Integration of this kind is sometimes known as deeper integration. Wider integration in the form of enlargement is also taking place. This again is not a new process as the EU has been enlarging since 1973 and it now has two and a half times its original membership. However, in terms of the number of countries from Eastern Europe which are likely to join during the early years of the twenty-first century, its current enlargement negotiations are of major historical significance.

The whole process of integration between Europe's nation states, whether wider or deeper integration, involves the pooling of sovereignty to some degree. Each country cedes an element of sovereignty when it joins the EU and every time it agrees to a common EU policy. The loss of national sovereignty resulting from EMU is therefore not a unique event but rather an important step along the road to European integration. Integration also has major implications for citizens, business firms, and other organizations in the EU and for the EU's relations with the rest of the world. In this chapter we focus mainly on the implications of integration for people and firms within the EU, though some aspects of the discussion will inevitably touch on the wider issues which are the subject of Chapter 17. In particular, we concentrate on the process of economic and political integration which was given legal effect by the Treaty on European Union (Maastricht Treaty). Given the immediate impact of the single currency, more attention is focused on EMU than on other aspects of integration.

16.2 Wider and Deeper Integration

16.2.1 EU enlargement

The EU is currently preparing the ground for the most extensive enlargement in its history. Table 16.1 indicates the current state of play with regard to countries which have applied for EU membership. Apart from the EU's Mediterranean neighbours, Cyprus and Malta, most of the next wave of entrants are likely to be from Eastern Europe. This will be a major step both for the EU and for the former communist countries of this region. Clearly, there will be economic challenges. The EU will have to adapt some of its policies and provide increased support for the region's development. The Eastern European economies will experience further painful adjustment to the Single European Market. In political terms, expansion to the east will be a historic development, all the more remarkable after forty–five years of Soviet domination. Some of these countries have been identified by the EU as having made sufficient progress in transforming their system of government and economies to be considered for entry negotiations starting in November 1998. These are the so-called 'first phase' applicants. Others have made less progress or, in the case of Slovakia, have been held back because of doubts over the government's democratic credentials.

Cyprus is also among the 'first phase' applicants. Cyprus would probably have had a relatively easy path to membership had it not been for the political division between the Greek and Turkish zones and their respective governments. Current membership negotiations are with the Greek Cypriot government which is responsible for two-thirds of the island and about four-fifths of its population. In fact, the Turkish Republic of Northern Cyprus, which declared unilateral independence in 1983, is not officially recognized either by the United Nations or the EU. Membership negotiations with Cyprus are therefore complicated. A further complication stems from the fact that Greece, an EU member, is keen that Cyprus should join whereas Turkey, whose membership application is on hold, is backing the Turkish Cypriot's claim for recognition. The EU, for its part, is not keen to admit a divided Cyprus. Malta also applied and was cleared for membership negotiations at the same time as Cyprus, but its application was withdrawn after a change of government. After a further change of government, it now seems likely that Malta's application will be renewed.

Switzerland, on the other hand, is surrounded by EU members and its companies trade and invest throughout the EU. If it were not for a long tradition of neutrality and its fiercely independent people, Switzerland would be a natural EU member. Having rejected membership of the European Economic Area in a referendum, however, it seems unlikely that the Swiss people would vote for full membership of the EU for the time being. Turkey is a different story. Only a small part of Turkey is attached to the European mainland, though Turkey has aspirations to become a fuller participant in Europe. Disputes with Greece, especially over the divided island of Cyprus, and doubts about Turkey's political situation make EU membership a contentious issue at present.

Table 16.1 Applicants for EU membership	
Applicant country	**Comments**
Turkey	Applied in 1967, received unfavourable Commission Opinion in 1969; unlikely to be admitted for the forseeable future because of question marks over its democratic credentials, economic suitability, and relationship with Greece; has a customs union with the EU.
Cyprus	Received favourable Commission Opinion in 1993; Greek Cypriot government started negotiations for entry in November 1998; problem of Greek/Turkish split.
Malta	Received favourable Commission Opinion in 1993; application withdrawn after change of government, now likely to be renewed after second change of government.
Switzerland	Officially still an applicant, but unlikely to join for the time being after rejecting membership of the European Economic Area in a referendum.
Czech Republic Estonia Hungary Poland Slovenia	'First phase' applicants from Eastern Europe; started entry negotiations in November 1998
Slovakia	Would probably have been a 'first phase' applicant except for internal political problems.
Bulgaria Latvia Lithuania Romania	Major economic problems, not yet ready for membership negotiations.

16.2.2 Steps towards a more integrated European economy

The degree of economic integration between the economies of Western Europe has generally been increasing since the EU was formed. This can be measured in terms of the growth rates of their gross domestic product (the business cycle), their inflation rates, their trade dependence on each other, the interdependence of their firms and industries, similarities in the structure of their economies, and several other factors. The process of integration follows many twists and turns and some of the economies on the periphery of Europe are less integrated into the European economy than those closer to the centre. However, two illustrations demonstrate the growing inability of European economies to act independently and the influence of major events in one country on the other European economies. First, when the French government tried unilaterally to reflate its economy in the early 1980s it soon became clear that they could not act without harming their balance of payments and severely weakening their currency. Then, in the early 1990s, Germany's high interest rates when it borrowed to finance the reconstruction of Eastern Germany forced other European countries to raise their interest rates in order to protect their currencies. Moreover, integration of the European economies appears to have been accelerating since the arrival of the single market and in the run up to the final stage of economic and monetary union (EMU).

The EMU project will, by design, lead to a more systematic type of integration as it removes exchange rate fluctuations and replaces national currencies with a single currency and single monetary policy. The first attempt at EMU was made following the 1970 Werner Report. This led to two brief periods of exchange rate management in the early 1970s (known as the 'Snake' and the 'Snake in the tunnel'), but the original intention of achieving a single currency by 1980 had to be abandoned in favour of more modest monetary cooperation. In 1979, the European Monetary System (EMS) came into operation. Its membership included all the EU member states at the time and its primary aims were twofold: to encourage closer cooperation on monetary policy and to stabilize exchange rates. In practice, the EMS's Exchange Rate Mechanism (ERM) has been the most prominent aspect of its activities, though not all member currencies have participated in the ERM. The UK only joined the ERM in 1990 and left it on 'Black Wednesday' during the currency turmoil of September 1992. Most countries which have joined the EU since 1979 have subsequently participated in the ERM, though Greece only entered the ERM in 1998 in preparation for joining the single currency in due course. Like the UK, Italy left the ERM in 1992 but later rejoined it.

The ERM is a target zone or crawling peg system of exchange rates. Until 1993, when there was further exchange rate turmoil, most member currencies were allowed to fluctuate 2.25 per cent above or below their bilateral central rates (the 'narrow band') with the other participating currencies, each of which in turn had a central rate with the European Currency Unit (ECU). If a currency approached its 'divergence indicator' (close to its agreed limits), national central banks were obliged to intervene in the currency markets or by altering interest rates to keep their currencies within the agreed limits. Some countries, including Italy (initially), the UK, Spain, and Portugal, were allowed to operate within a 'broad band' of 6 per cent. In practice, currencies were generally kept within their agreed limit in relation to the weakest currency in the ERM and the Deutsche Mark became the marker currency when a new currency entered the ERM. In some circumstances a currency was allowed to be realigned (revalued or devalued) to bring its central and bilateral rates closer to its market value. The currency crisis of 1992–3 almost led to the break-up of the ERM, but the introduction of a 15 per cent band in 1993 led to a return of exchange rate stability with little opportunity for destabilizing currency speculation. Germany and the Netherlands, with two of the more stable currencies, retained their 2.25 per cent band bilaterally. With the exception of 1992–3, the ERM has achieved a reasonable degree of stability between European exchange rates and against major world currencies.

Although the EMS and ERM were not primarily intended to be the forerunners of full EMU, they have in practice provided valuable lessons for the monetary authorities and, during 1997–8, gave a good indication of the bilateral exchange rates to be used for the single currency. The ERM effectively paved the way for the 1989 Delors Report on EMU, which subsequently became much of the substance of the Maastricht Treaty. Jacques Delors, then President of the European Commission, recommended a three-stage approach to EMU or, more particularly, to monetary union. The first stage involved the removal of exchange controls, the inclusion of all currencies within the narrow band of the ERM, and measures to achieve monetary convergence. The second stage involved the establishment of a European Monetary Institute to oversee the preparations for EMU and to pave the way for the European Central Bank. The third stage involved the 'irrevocable' fixing of exchange rates and the replacement of national currencies by a single European currency.[1]

These stages were incorporated into the Maastricht Treaty, together with a timetable for their implementation. At times the EMU project seemed as though it would be blown off course. Ratification of the Maastricht Treaty raised problems in several member states. Two countries, Denmark and the UK, negotiated opt-outs from EMU. Yet, in the end, monetary union went ahead in the eleven participating countries within its agreed timetable. Progress towards EMU, as with earlier developments like the single market, has often followed the upswings and downswings of the business cycle. Tsoukalis points out that steps towards major integration have tended to be taken during periods of Euro-optimism when the European economies are booming.[2] Thus, for example, the launch and early stages of the single market programme coincided with the economic growth of the late 1980s and the EMU project, based on the Delors Report, rode on the crest of this wave. However, by the time the single market came towards completion and the Maastricht Treaty came into effect, the European economies had gone into recession and Euro-pessimism had come to the fore.

16.2.3 Are wider and deeper integration compatible?

The EU is trying to achieve a difficult balance by enlarging the union at the same time as it is embarking on deeper economic and political integration. Deeper integration requires closer cooperation on policy-making whereas enlargement makes decision making more complex and increases the scope for disagreement. The latter problem has been partly anticipated by the extension of qualified majority voting in the Council of Ministers. But there are several key areas of policy where unanimity is still required (see Section 14.2.3). The requirement for new members to accept the entire *acquis communautaire*, including EMU, may also present problems for countries which have only recently introduced a market system.

Certainly, if the entire design for the EU had been planned in every detail at the outset, one would not have wanted countries to join at different stages, sometimes at the same time as major economic developments. On the other hand, both the deepening and the enlargement of the union are continuing strands in the EU's development. Having come so far towards economic union, it is doubtful whether EMU would be any easier to implement after rather than before enlargement. The failure to offer membership to the newly democratic countries of Eastern Europe at this crucial time in history would also seem to be a wasted opportunity. In any case, when Denmark, Ireland, and the UK became members in 1973, the customs union and Common Agricultural Policy were only recently established. By the time the first phase of Eastern European enlargement is completed, a similar period may have elapsed after the introduction of EMU. It is also possible that the accession of new members may proceed more slowly than originally envisaged to allow more time for membership preparations and that, as in the past with other policies, a lengthy phasing-in period for EMU will be allowed.

16.3 The Treaty on European Union (Maastricht Treaty): Key Measures

THE Treaty on European Union (TEU), commonly known as the Maastricht Treaty after the Dutch town where it was signed in 1992, was probably the most ambitious attempt at European integration since the founding Treaty of Rome in 1957. In some respects the Treaty tried to achieve too much, covering major areas of economic and political integration. For this reason, it was not only difficult to negotiate but several governments had difficulty in ratifying the Treaty through their legislative processes. The British government negotiated an opt-out from EMU and from the 'social chapter' but still achieved only a small parliamentary majority. Denmark failed to achieve the required parliamentary and public support and only ratified the Treaty after securing an opt-out from EMU and a second referendum. Ireland achieved the largest popular support with a 67 per cent majority, whereas a French referendum produced only a slender majority. The German government, which had supported EMU as a tangible step towards political union, had to persuade a sceptical public of the merits of abandoning the Deutsche Mark and was the last to ratify the Treaty in October 1993 after a failed legal challenge in the German Constitutional Court. The Maastricht Treaty finally came into effect on 1 November 1993. The key aspects of the Treaty concerning economic and political integration are outlined below.

16.3.1 Economic and Monetary Union

Economic and monetary union (EMU), sometimes described by the narrower term 'European monetary union', is probably the most significant and certainly the most controversial subject contained in the Maastricht Treaty. A timetable was attached to stages two and three of the Delors Report (see Section 16.2.2 above), indicating that the European Monetary Institute (EMI) would be established on 1 January 1994 and that the single currency would begin between 1 January 1997 and 1 January 1999. These deadlines were subsequently met, with the single currency arriving on the latter date in 1999. The EMI was set up to prepare the ground for the final stage of EMU and it was replaced by the European Central Bank, both located in Frankfurt, in 1998. Although the narrow ERM band was widened after the exchange rate turmoil of 1992–93, the Maastricht convergence criteria for countries preparing to participate in the single currency became a key aspect of EMU policy during the 1990s.

The convergence criteria were designed to ensure monetary stability in the run up to EMU. The government deficit and debt criteria are also included in the EMU stability pact which is intended to maintain budgetary discipline after the introduction of EMU. Price stability is not only seen as a prerequisite for economic growth but also as necessary to prevent tensions within the single currency area. A country with a high inflation rate would soon find that its goods were uncompetitive. With a single

Table 16.2 The convergence criteria for economic and monetary union

Inflation	not exceeding the average of the three best-performing countries by more than 1.5 percentage points.
Public sector deficit	not exceeding 3% of GDP in the year prior to entry.
Gross public debt	not exceeding 60% of GDP in the year prior to entry or, if above 60%, falling and approaching 60% at a satisfactory rate.
Exchange rates	within the 'normal fluctuation margins' of the ERM, without re-alignment, for at least two years prior to entry.
Long-term interest rates	not exceeding the average of the three best-performing countries (in terms of inflation) by more than 2 percentage points.

currency there would be no possibility of a country raising its interest rates independently or allowing its currency to depreciate in order to restore competitiveness. The onus would be on firms, workers, and trade unions to reduce production costs. This would be a painful and difficult process during the early years of EMU. The rationale for exchange rate stability follows similar lines. The risk of entering EMU at an unsustainable exchange rate would increase where a currency had been unstable. Tensions would inevitably follow if one country's goods were over- or under-valued. Interest rate convergence tends to occur naturally when capital controls are removed, but more so where the risks associated with different currencies are eliminated. Prior convergence is therefore likely to avoid the possibility of sudden capital movements or interest rate losses following EMU.

The reasons for the avoidance of excessive government deficits are perhaps less obvious. An annual budget deficit is the difference between government expenditure and tax revenue in a particular year. A large budget deficit creates a large borrowing requirement. This causes upward pressure on the money supply if 'printed' money is used or on interest rates if the debt is funded through government bond issues. Persistent annual deficits increase the gross public debt—the government's cumulative outstanding debt, sometimes known as the national debt. Higher taxes are needed to service this debt and governments owing large debts may have to pay a risk premium in the form of higher interest rates to attract additional funds. In a single currency area interest rates are determined centrally and there is less freedom to raise taxes unilaterally, so profligate governments may find it increasingly difficult to support a deficit and manage their debt repayments. This has led some sceptics to envisage the possibility of prudent governments being left to bail out imprudent ones. This fear has been raised during the debate on the provision of retirement pensions for Europe's large ageing population where most governments rely on unfunded state pension schemes paid for out of current tax revenue. The funding of retirement pensions is clearly an issue that needs to be addressed, but it is unlikely that an individual EU government would ignore the stability pact, peer pressure, and the discipline of the bond market by failing to contain excessive debts.

After persistent doubts about the ability of member governments to meet the convergence criteria, determined efforts and a good deal of budgetary discipline produced a surprising degree of convergence (see Box 16.1). The final stage of EMU, the introduction of the euro, began for eleven member states on 1 January 1999. The founder members of the single currency area are Austria, Belgium, Finland, France, Germany, Ireland, Italy, Luxembourg, the Netherlands, Portugal, and Spain. The euro will operate alongside the national currencies initially and euro notes and coins will not be introduced until 1 January 2002. The first six months of 2002 will then provide a transition period for cash transactions. This gradual introduction of the euro is intended to allow for the complexities of converting prices, wages, state benefits, accounting and payment systems, bank accounts, and numerous other records and transactions. It should not be assumed that the main impact of the single currency will be delayed until 2002, however, since the vast majority of financial transactions in Europe do not involve cash and many companies have adopted the euro from the beginning of 1999.

Box 16.1 EMU Convergence: Fact and Fiction

The sceptical European public had serious doubts that economic and monetary union would ever be achieved. Those who believed it would happen often spoke of a two-speed Europe with a hard core consisting of France, Germany, and a small number of other countries in the fast lane to EMU and a larger periphery in the slow lane. Many people were doubtful whether countries like Italy, Spain, and Portugal would be able to meet the convergence criteria (see Table 16.2), even if they wanted to. And when it became likely that no fewer than eleven countries may be joining, there was talk of governments 'fudging' the figures to qualify for EMU. So what were the facts?

First, it should be pointed out that most of the eleven countries, and indeed most of the remaining four, made much more progress towards EMU convergence than had been expected. Every country, with the exception of Greece, met the inflation criterion and the three best-performing countries had inflation rates of little more than 1 per cent. This was a remarkable achievement considering the general level of inflation at the beginning of the 1990s. A similar outcome was achieved with long-term interest rates. The only countries to fail the exchange rate criterion were Greece, Sweden, and the UK, all of which were outside the ERM and were either unwilling or, in the case of Greece, unprepared to participate in EMU. Ireland's punt was also revalued during 1998, though this was a technical correction to reflect its agreed market rate, not an indication of instability.

The budgetary criteria caused the main problems. With the exception of Greece, all countries achieved budget deficits of 3 per cent of GDP or under, though France, Germany, and Italy squeezed under the limit at the last minute. The last dash to qualify inevitably raised suspicions of 'fudging'; examples included Italy's refundable EMU tax, the transfer of state-owned France Telecom's pension fund assets to the French state budget, and Germany's abandoned proposal to record the paper profit from the revaluation of its gold reserves as government revenue. In terms of gross public debt, several countries qualified because their debt was falling at a satisfactory rate rather than because it was 60 per cent of GDP or under. Belgium's and Italy's debt, at just over 120 per cent of GDP were arguably too high, and Germany technically missed the target because its debt had crept above the 60 per cent limit and was still rising slightly. The cost of financing the reconstruction of Eastern Germany perhaps made Germany a justifiable exception, however, and EMU without Germany would in any case have been unthinkable.

Regardless of the interpretation of the deficit and debt criteria, these countries had made strenuous efforts to reduce their 'excessive deficits' and large public debts. Whatever else it may achieve, EMU has already spurred several EU governments into pruning their bloated budgets and adopting prudent macroeconomic management. The enthusiasm and tenacity which several European governments have shown in striving to qualify for EMU also caught many observers by surprise.

16.3.2 Intergovernmental decision-making

Although not worked out in the same detail as EMU, two other important policies were introduced by the Maastricht Treaty: the Common Foreign and Security Policy and cooperation in the fields of Justice and Home Affairs. European Political Cooperation, involving periodic meetings of the Conference of Foreign Ministers, had existed since 1970, but the Maastricht Treaty attempted to formalize the EU's approach to foreign policy and, for the first time, to work towards 'the eventual framing of a common defence policy' in cooperation with the Western European Union.[3] After failing to achieve effective foreign policy cooperation on issues such as the Gulf War and the conflict in the former Yugoslavia, the EU is now hoping to agree 'joint action' on foreign policy matters rather than simple 'cooperation'. In view of the divergent history of foreign policy among European nations and the complexities of their foreign relations, it may well take some time before a common foreign policy approach is achieved in practice.

Like foreign policy, some areas of cooperation had already been developed in the fields of justice and home affairs. This policy area has now been formalized by the Maastricht Treaty. Justice and home affairs include cooperation between the justice administrations of member states (on matters such as extradition or commercial law), cooperation between police forces through Europol, the European police office (on terrorism, drug trafficking, and other crime), and cooperation between customs authorities (especially on immigration and other matters at the EU's external borders). As the EU's internal border controls are removed, cooperation between the judicial authorities, police, and customs becomes much more important.

The Common Foreign and Security Policy and cooperation in the fields of Justice and Home Affairs are sometimes described as two 'pillars' of the EU. The EU is pictured as resting on three pillars: the first pillar represents the European Communities, made up of the European Community (formerly the EEC), ECSC, and EURATOM together with their collective institutions and policies. The second and third pillars are the foreign and security policy and the policy on justice and home affairs. The second and third pillars largely involve intergovernmental decision-making by the European Council, whereas the first pillar involves the full community decision-making procedures and institutions. The term 'European Union' was thus first introduced by the Maastricht Treaty to encompass each of the three pillars.

16.3.3 The 'social chapter'

A 'social chapter' was intended to be included in the Maastricht Treaty to amend the 'chapter' or title on social policy in the Treaty of Rome. However, the UK government refused to agree to its inclusion so, in order to expedite the Treaty, the other member states agreed to attach it as a separate protocol at the end of the Treaty. The 'social

Figure 16.1 The three 'pillars' of the European Union

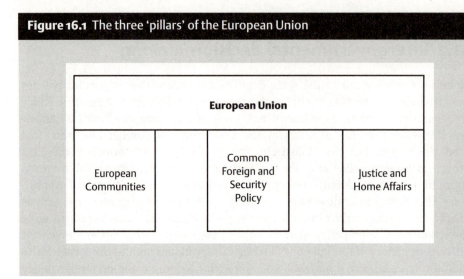

chapter', as it is still commonly known, provides a legal basis for the Charter on the Fundamental Social Rights of Workers (sometimes simply called the EU Social Charter) which was adopted by all member states except Britain in 1989. The social chapter provides the legal framework for subsequent directives on matters relating to employment, living and working conditions, social protection, industrial relations, training, and related issues (see Chapter 14). It also extends the principle of qualified majority voting to certain areas of social policy. Although a highly contentious issue in Britain, the social chapter was simply an extension of existing practice in several European countries. The new UK Labour Government in 1997 reversed its predecessor's 'opt-out' and the social chapter has now been brought within the main EU policy framework under the Amsterdam Treaty.

16.3.4 Other Maastricht measures

The Maastricht Treaty attempted to achieve a balance between economic union, political union, social and regional development, democratic accountability, and the rights and responsibilities of ordinary citizens. This was an almost impossible task and one of the reasons why it proved controversial. Whilst a great deal of space was dedicated to the details of EMU, the Treaty also provided for the establishment of the Cohesion Fund to promote infrastructure development in the poorer countries of the EU; it extended EU action in areas such as education, the environment, consumer protection, and trans-European networks; it introduced the co-decision procedure involving joint approval by the Council of Ministers and European Parliament and extended the powers of Parliament in other respects, along with the powers of the European Court of Justice and the Court of Auditors (see Chapter 14). It also created two new institutions: the Committee of the Regions, to advise on regional development, and the office of Ombudsman, who is empowered to consider complaints of maladministration.

Two further measures are worthy of mention: EU citizenship and the principle of subsidiarity. The Treaty introduced the concept of EU citizenship, whereby all nationals of EU member states are automatically citizens of the EU. Citizenship confers the right to move and reside freely, to vote and stand for election in municipal and European elections in a country in which he/she is resident, to receive the diplomatic protection of other member states, and other similar rights. Subsidiarity is the principle whereby political decisions should be made at the lowest appropriate level. Essentially, it is a principle of federalism, but during the Maastricht negotiations it was heralded by John Major, then British prime minister, as a means of limiting the centralization of power at the EU level. Subsidiarity is a general principle that can be applied to any matters in which the EU has exclusive competence. Although the Treaty contains only one paragraph on subsidiarity, it could potentially have significant implications for EU policy. As yet, there has been little tangible evidence of its effects.

16.4 The Implications of Economic and Political Union

16.4.1 The rationale for the single currency

The single European currency is an extreme case of monetary union. Monetary union could exist where there are permanently fixed exchange rates between separate currencies. Such a monetary union, however, would not capture all the advantages of a single currency as any exchange of currencies involves transaction costs which may act as a barrier to trade. A single currency has implications for individuals, companies, and markets as well as for the European economy as a whole. The main benefits of the European single currency may be summarized as follows:

■ Exchange rate stability and reduction in exchange 'exposure'

When exchange rates are stable for long periods of time, business people tend to have more confidence in making decisions involving cross-border transactions. This includes frequent decisions on the sale of goods or purchase of supplies as well as longer-term decisions such as the choice of supplier, a contract to supply goods or services over a period of time, or the location of a factory. A short-term transaction can be covered by a forward exchange contract, where the required amount of foreign currency is bought at a fixed price on an agreed date in the future. Forward exchange contracts are generally for relatively short periods, however, and they are not costless. Long-term contracts may require other forms of currency hedging but this process is more difficult to manage over a long period and the risk of loss is correspondingly greater. A company's 'exposure' to currency fluctuations is reduced by a single currency (or indeed by permanently fixed exchange rates) as far as its internal EU operations are concerned (see Chapter 4 on the various types of exchange exposure).

The merits of exchange rate stability are, in this respect, distinct from arguments about fixed versus flexible exchange rates or arguments about the 'correct' rate at which a currency should be converted to the single currency. Exchange rate stability, whether in a fixed or floating system, tends to promote business confidence and therefore to encourage cross border business activity, particularly for SMEs which are less well equipped to handle foreign exchange risks. Whilst an 'appropriate' rate of exchange is preferable, there is not always a uniquely appropriate rate. Stability still reduces uncertainty and unpredictability, which are the anathema of business confidence, and experience from Germany and Japan suggests that firms learn to live with high stable exchange rates by improving productivity and product quality.

■ Elimination of transaction costs

The exchange of currencies involves transaction costs. Transaction costs are the costs incurred when making a transaction over and above the price of a good. When buying a foreign currency the transaction costs include the dealer's commission charge and the difference between the market rate and the dealer's selling price. On small sums these charges may be quite substantial. Thus, for SME's or for larger businesses whose executives make small but relatively frequent foreign currency payments using their plastic cards, the transaction costs are significant. For large MNEs with their own foreign currency dealers, the transaction costs are considerably smaller. Even here, when companies deal in several currencies within a single business contract or where risk avoidance involves frequent switching between currencies, the transaction costs will begin to escalate. The elimination of currency transaction costs only arises where two or more countries use a single currency.

■ 'Completion' of the Single European Market

The existence of separate national currencies may be regarded as a barrier to trade within the Single European Market. A major part of this barrier are the transaction costs described above. These costs make foreign goods more expensive than they would otherwise be. The time, effort, and uncertainty involved in foreign currency transactions may also act as a barrier, either real or psychological, especially for smaller, less experienced firms. Perhaps more important are the dynamic effects which are likely to result from the arrival of the single currency. The removal of separate national currencies, more than any other single measure, seems to signify that the single market really is the 'home market' for companies and consumers throughout the union. Indeed, the activities of consumers as much as companies will help to create this effect. The more consumers are prepared to shop around, assisted by price transparency, the more quickly companies will have to treat the single market as a unified whole. Changes in companies' product innovation, marketing strategies, production and distribution methods, plant location, and other strategies will then follow. The single currency should therefore help to bring the single market closer to 'completion'.

■ Price transparency and increased competition

The ease with which consumers and firms can compare prices in different EU countries will increase dramatically with the single currency. No other measure could make prices immediately transparent in this way. Price differences are often hidden when quoted in different currencies. Even though a pocket calculator or computer program can easily make the conversion, currency fluctuations make it difficult to ensure consistent comparisons. Price transparency exposes monopolistic or isolated markets to competition. Restrictive practices which have long been protected from the rigours of competition will become increasingly difficult to defend. Pressure may even be brought to bear on governments to reduce taxes where they are significantly out of line with their neighbours. Europe's many protected markets will face pressures to become more open and flexible. Some industrialists believe that price transparency will be the most important effect of the single currency.

■ Low inflation, low interest rates, and macroeconomic stability

There are essentially two reasons why the single currency should help to keep inflation low: first from a public policy perspective, second because of the discipline imposed on firms, workers, and trade unions. Great care has been taken to ensure that the European Central Bank and the participating national central banks have operational independence and will operate monetary policy with the primary objective of controlling inflation. These requirements mirror the operation of the German Bundesbank and were agreed at German insistence. Although sometimes accused of being too single-minded and conservative, the Bundesbank's inflation record has been exemplary. The Maastricht convergence criteria have also strengthened the resolve of European governments to pursue monetary and budgetary stability. Budgetary discipline should subsequently be enforced by the EMU stability pact. The combined effect of stable monetary and budgetary policies should be to provide a climate of general macroeconomic stability which is conducive to business development.

Equally importantly, the single currency will force firms to keep their prices competitive. This, in turn, will require them to keep their costs down and will impose the same discipline on workers and trade unions. Failure to do so may result in the loss of markets to their more disciplined rivals. Thus, the actions of firms and their employees, together with the price consciousness of consumers, should help to reinforce the policy discipline of the European Central Bank and the EU member governments. Finally, the existence of transparent financial markets and the general expectation of low inflation should help to keep interest rates low. Low interest rates reduce the cost of borrowing and increase the profitability of capital investment. An increase in investment should help to stimulate economic growth.

16.4.2 The implications of the single currency for MNEs

MNEs are much more exposed to currency fluctuations than domestic firms. The extent to which this exposure will be reduced by the single currency will clearly depend on the proportion of their business which is within the single currency area. In some industries such as petroleum the US dollar is used as an international currency. This is also true for trade in general in certain parts of the world where the local currencies are not readily convertible. In these cases the arrival of the euro will have little immediate impact. It is possible in the future, however, that some of this business may be conducted in euros, especially where European companies are involved. This will, of course, depend on whether the euro becomes a strong, stable, and respected currency. In general, the single currency should simplify the operations of MNEs which do business in several EU countries.

In many ways large MNEs are better equipped to handle currency risks than smaller firms. They often have foreign currency departments and are well practised in currency hedging. They deal constantly in all the world's major currencies and hold deposits, take out loans, and issue bonds denominated in eurocurrencies—foreign currencies which are used outside their country of origin (originally but now not necessarily in Europe). In this sense, MNEs can manage quite well without the single currency. This is not to say that they will not benefit from the euro, however. It is not uncommon for an MNE to have its main production plant in one country (say Germany), obtain most of its supplies from another (say France), and sell most of its finished products in a third country (say Britain). This situation can cause major problems if currencies are fluctuating. For example, if the French franc appreciates against the German mark while the British pound depreciates against the mark, the company will find that its goods may be priced out of the market simply because of exchange rate movements. Bearing in mind that these transactions will occur in different time-periods, the situation may be even more complicated. If the company's operations are financed by a loan in a fourth currency whose initial low exchange rate later appreciates in value, the company will find that the loan repayments and interest have become more expensive than originally planned.

The introduction of the single currency will have a number of practical implications for companies operating across European borders. Their accounting procedures, pricing policy, information technology systems, and most of their management, administrative, and personnel systems will in some way be affected. Companies with subsidiaries in several countries will normally consolidate their accounts in the home country, bringing together accounting statements in a variety of currencies. The use of a single currency will make this task easier and will avoid the possibility of profit being devalued when the home currency appreciates against the currency in which the profit was made. Pricing policy may need to be reviewed when goods are sold in a single currency, especially where consumers are sensitive to price differences in other countries. Price differences may be less of a problem in traditional retailing as consumers generally shop locally. They may well cause problems in industrial goods markets, where goods are sold through catalogues or the Internet, or where expensive items like motor vehicles are involved. In most companies information technology systems will have to be adapted to accommodate the new single currency. During the transition period when the single currency is being introduced heavy costs will be incurred, but these are likely to be far outweighed by the cost savings from operating in one currency in the longer term.

16.4.3 The implications of the single currency for SMEs

SMEs generally have fewer international operations than their larger counterparts. This does not mean that they will be unaffected by the single currency. Many smaller firms export their products, sometimes a large proportion of them. Many of them are part of the supply chain of MNEs and may follow these companies abroad. Even if they are based outside the single currency area and supply only domestic customers, in Britain or Sweden for example, their larger customers may insist that prices are quoted and payment is made in euros as most of their other business will also be in euros. In small-scale retailing there may seem to be few long-term advantages to justify the short-term costs of changing over to the euro, but for many SMEs the single currency will open up new opportunities for selling abroad.

It is sometimes argued that SMEs in general will be the main beneficiaries of the single currency as they are the firms which face the highest transaction costs when exchanging currencies. SMEs are also less able to manage exchange risks and often have less experience in handling foreign currency transactions. Whereas many MNEs already treat the single market as their home market, many SMEs still have more limited horizons. The single currency may change this. It should also be remembered that, even when SMEs only sell to local customers, their supplies may come from abroad. For companies which find foreign currency transactions more of a hassle than a challenge, the single currency will be a boon to their business.

16.4.4 A critical evaluation of the single currency

There is clearly a question mark over the EMU project. No one knows at the outset how successful it will be. A single currency between fifteen independent countries, several of which are major trading nations, has never been attempted before. Inevitably there is a risk that policy failure, political disagreements, unforeseen circumstances, or technical difficulties will create problems. The worst-case scenario is that the single currency will collapse, leaving member countries to start afresh with their discarded currencies. Whatever the outcome, there will certainly be teething problems. It should be remembered, however, that EMU has not been pulled out of a magician's hat at the last minute. It is the culmination, perhaps even the logical conclusion, of a painstaking and systematic process of European integration. In any case, few things in the economic sphere are as irrevocable as they are sometimes portrayed. Experience suggests that the EU is tenacious in seeking solutions and at reaching compromises even to the most intractable problems.

We will now consider six of the more powerful criticisms of the single currency.

■ Flexible exchange rates are preferable to permanently fixed rates

Flexible exchange rates have an advantage over fixed rates in so far as they act as an automatic adjustment mechanism in correcting a balance of payments deficit. This is because a deficit tends to weaken the exchange rate and a low exchange rate makes exports cheaper and imports more expensive, thus helping to correct the deficit. Flexible rates also complement monetary policy in combating inflation because a rise in interest rates tends to reduce inflation and to raise the exchange rate, suppressing the price of imported goods. These policy weapons will be lost to individual EMU member countries. A more doubtful but popular argument is that floating rates allow national currencies to depreciate in order to cancel out the effect of domestic inflation. This, of course, is a false paradise as, if left unchecked, inflation will necessitate further currency depreciation in the future. Exchange rate depreciation is no substitute for a more coherent macroeconomic policy.[4]

■ The single currency requires flexible markets

Since the flexibility of national exchange rates is lost with a single currency, alternative adjustment mechanisms are required. The focus now turns to flexible markets. Capital, labour, and other factors of production need to be able to move freely throughout the single currency area to create efficient resource use and reallocate unemployed resources. Many resources already move freely, but labour markets are often inflexible, especially in Europe's social market economies (see Chapter 8). After all, the USA with its single currency and flexible labour markets persistently achieves lower unemployment than the European economies. Unfortunately, the debate is often limited to wage flexibility, the right of employers to hire and fire, and reductions in the influence of trade unions. Flexibility is also achieved when workers and managers are highly educated, have transferable skills and a flexible attitude to their job, and work cooperatively as a team, valuing each other's contributions.

■ One monetary policy for all

On entering the single currency, responsibility for monetary policy passes to the European Central Bank which coordinates the European System of Central Banks. Interest rate policy, the control of the euro money supply, and related monetary policy are determined centrally. Individual countries can no longer adapt monetary policy to suit their particular economic situation. Monetary policy will respond to the economic growth rate and inflationary pressures in the euro area as a whole. 'One monetary policy for all' may be too lax in areas of high economic growth and too tight in areas of slow growth, with corresponding effects on employment. Flexible markets may provide part of the solution to this problem (see above), though other EU policies may be needed to redistribute resources to the disadvantaged regions: regional, social, industrial, and enterprise policies, for example.

■ Insufficient 'real' convergence

Emphasis during the preparation for the single currency was focused mainly on monetary convergence criteria. What about the convergence of Europe's 'real' economies—the real growth cycles of gross domestic product, rates of unemployment, and the industrial structure of the European economies? Economic theory suggests that integration between countries is more likely to be successful if their economies are similar in terms of their stage of development, economic cycle, and economic objectives. This also applies to an optimum currency area or monetary union though research indicates that initial problems resulting from differences between economies can be corrected by coordinated policies over time.[5]

■ Jobs lost

If market flexibility, resource transfers, and other adjustment mechanisms prove insufficient to make up for the loss of exchange rate flexibility, unemployment may rise in some parts of the euro zone. Some observers argue that unemployment will therefore rise in the area as a whole, though this should be outweighed by the employment created as a result of the dynamic effects of removing currency barriers and completing the single market. On a more specific level, it is sometimes argued that jobs will be lost among currency dealers in the financial services sector. These short-term job losses should be balanced against the short-term jobs created by the wealth of consulting and other activities involved in preparing firms for the single currency, however.

■ Loss of sovereignty

The issue of policy sovereignty, in relation to monetary policy, is discussed above. The rules relating to budget deficits in the stability pact and moves towards to fiscal harmonization may eventually lead to a similar loss or pooling of sovereignty in the field of fiscal policy. For some people, however, sovereignty is a deeper issue of independence and national pride. Even the symbols to be used on euro notes and the loss of cherished national emblems become an issue of concern. This is essentially a political issue and will not be resolved simply by the merits of the economic arguments. The erosion of sovereignty has occurred gradually since the founding of the EU, though the single currency seems to symbolize a more significant step. Ultimately, it is a question of whether the voluntary pooling of sovereignty is justified by the benefits of a single currency or indeed the benefits of a more integrated Europe.

16.5 Political union and international business

ONE view on which there is a wide measure of agreement between those who are for and against EMU is that the single currency is as much a political as an economic project. Progress towards political union has also been advanced by the Common Foreign and Security Policy and by cooperation in the fields of Justice and Home Affairs. What then are the implications of political union for international business? Essentially, political union involves a high degree of policy coordination. Rules governing competition, the development of company and employment law, interest rates, taxation, accounting conventions, and numerous other aspects of business life are increasingly being determined by EU policy. This is creating a more level playing field and greater policy consistency across the EU. Political union also means that representation at bodies such as the World Trade Organization and increasingly at the IMF, World Bank, and United Nations will be at the EU level. Similarly, discussions with NAFTA, Mercosur, and APEC are generally now at this level. The interests of European companies should thus gain a stronger voice in these forums.

There is, of course, a tension within EU policy-making between the tendency to regulate and the encouragement of national governments and authorities to deregulate. This is often a concern of business. There is also a fear that closer political cooperation inevitably means a 'United States of Europe'. In the sense of a single unified state, this seems an unlikely possibility, given the safeguards of unanimous voting in key policy areas and the staunch defence of national interests by most of the EU states. From a business perspective, the danger of excessive bureaucracy in an over-centralized Europe is probably the main concern, but this is counterbalanced by the freedom to operate in a large single market and the spur to international competitiveness that this creates.

16.6 Summary

THE EU has been engaged in wider and deeper integration throughout much of its existence. Wider integration has involved successive enlargements, initially within Western Europe but now towards Eastern Europe. Deeper integration involves progress towards economic and monetary union (EMU) on the one hand and political union on the other. The most significant step towards deeper integration was taken with the signing of the Treaty on European Union (Maastricht Treaty) in 1992. The

Maastricht Treaty is particularly concerned with EMU, but it also contains sections on a Common Foreign and Security Policy, cooperation in the fields of Justice and Home Affairs, the 'social chapter', and several other policy areas. The key elements of EMU are the arrangements for the co-ordination of monetary policy through the European System of Central Banks and the introduction of a single European currency. The rationale for the single currency includes the benefits of exchange rate stability, the elimination of transaction costs, price transparency, and the creation of a low-inflation environment within a barrier-free single market. Most businesses will experience the effects of increased competition within the euro zone, but will also benefit from cost savings as they handle fewer currencies. SMEs, in particular will save on the transaction costs of exchanging currencies, though in some sectors the short-term change-over costs may be high. A number of doubts have emerged on the merits of the single currency. These include the loss of exchange rate flexibility or the lack of compensating flexibility in labour and other markets. Whether in the economic or political sphere, deeper integration has a number of implications for business firms.

Review Questions

1 Outline the successive enlargements the EU has undertaken since its inception. Which countries are currently waiting to join?

2 In what policy areas has the Maastricht Treaty extended EU cooperation?

3 What are the main advantages of the single European currency?

4 What are the costs and benefits of the single currency for business firms? Are these costs and benefits likely to be different for large MNEs and SMEs?

5 What are the main concerns about the single currency? Can these concerns be satisfactorily addressed?

Case Study: Honeywell Europe—A US Firm Embraces the Euro

Honeywell Europe is the European operation of Honeywell, a US company in the controls and building products industry. Its main competitors in the market for industrial and domestic controls are companies like Siebe (UK), Emerson and General Electric (US), Siemens (German), and ABB (Swedish/Swiss). Honeywell Europe has annual European sales of around $2.2 billion and employs 13,000 people, about 8,500 of whom are engaged in sales and service activities, with the remainder being involved in manufacturing. About a third of the company's revenue comes from standard products, but most now comes from customized products or services designed to meet individual customer requirements.

The president of Honeywell's European division, William Hjerpe, argues that the introduction of the euro will bring a number of benefits for the company. The company introduced structural changes to its European operations on 1 January 1999, organizing its activities around three business areas, each covering the whole EU market. This contrasts with the company's previous organization where regional teams operated in their own part of the European market. This pan-European organization should result in cost savings for the company. Mr Hjerpe also estimates that the reduction in currency hedging and in the transaction costs of changing currencies within the euro zone should lead to further cost savings of around $6 million a year.

One of the benefits of the single currency should be increased price transparency when goods are sold in different EU national markets. Mr Hjerpe sees this as a considerable benefit in relation to the company's suppliers. Price transparency and increased competition among suppliers could lead to estimated cost savings of $30 million a year, about 3 per cent of the company's current supply costs. Whilst there could be a similar effect on the prices of the company's finished product, Mr Hjerpe believes this is less likely to be the case as the majority of its activities involve high value-added service contracts and specialized manufacturing processes tailored to meet customers' specific needs. In providing these customized products and services, the company is exploiting its firm-specific assets and this specialist function enables it to secure higher profit margins than companies producing a more standardized product.

Mr Hjerpe's view of the benefits of the single currency may be unusually optimistic. Price transparency will sharpen competition in most European markets, no doubt including his own. Organizational cost savings should be unaffected by this, however, and can apply to any company which rationalizes its production, marketing, and other activities to take advantage of the wider European market. The other main point he makes is that companies which differentiate their product and provide a service that addresses a customer's specific problem, utilizing the companies' core competences, are more likely to gain from the single currency than companies which are less adaptable and responsive to the customer. *Source*: Adapted from P. Marsh, 'When transparency leads to added value', *Financial Times*, 28 Jan. 1999.

Case study questions

1 Honeywell Europe has introduced organizational changes to improve its marketing effectiveness and reduce costs. What are these organizational changes and what other changes could be made to take advantage of the single currency?

2 In what ways is price transparency likely to achieve savings in supply costs?

3 Do you agree with Mr Hjerpe that the company should be able to protect itself from the effects of price transparency in the markets for its finished products and services?

4 What are the firm-specific assets and core competences of a company like Honeywell Europe?

5 What are the lessons of this case for other companies seeking to make the most of the single European currency?

Notes

1   The Treaty on European Union refers to 'the irrevocable fixing of exchange rates leading to the introduction of a single currency' (amendment to Art. 3a of the EEC Treaty).

2   L. Tsoukalis, *The New European Economy Revisited* (Oxford University Press, 1997).

3   Treaty on European Union, Art. J4.

4   See R. Dornbusch, 'The effectiveness of exchange rate changes', *Oxford Review of Economic Policy* (1996), 12 (3): 26–38.

5   See T. Hitiris, *European Community Economics* (Harvester Wheatsheaf, 1994), 132–135.

Recommended Reading

■ Artis, M. J., and Lee, N. (ed.), *The Economics of the European Union* (Oxford University Press, 1997).

■ Gros, D., and Thygesen, N., *European Monetary Integration* (Longman, 1992).

■ Hansen, J. D., and Nielsen, J. U–M., *An Economic Analysis of the EU* (McGraw-Hill, 1997).

■ McDonald, F., and Dearden, S., *European Economic Integration* (Longman, 1999).

■ Molle, W., *The Economics of European Integration: Theory, Practice, Policy* (Dartmouth, 1997)

■ Tsoukalis, L., *The New European Economy Revisited* (Oxford University Press, 1997).

17

The European Union and International Business

Objectives

- to examine the claim that 'Fortress Europe' has become an obstacle to external trade with the European Union
- to examine the case for selective intervention to promote the EU's industrial development
- to outline the EU's relations with the rest of the world
- to discuss the competitive position of the EU vis-à-vis the other major trading nations and the role of EU policy in promoting international competitiveness

17.1 Introduction

HAVING considered the institutions, policies, and internal developments of the European Union in Chapters 14, 15, and 16, we now turn to the EU's role in promoting trade and international business. First, we evaluate the claim that 'Fortress Europe' is promoting its own business and exports at the expense of imports and free trade. Whilst free trade is often considered to be preferable in an ideal world, is there a case for protection in some circumstances? We discuss the arguments for intervention and draw on comparisons with other countries. Lessons from around the world send mixed messages as to the merits of supportive intervention in preference to free trade. Next, we examine the EU's relations with regional groupings around the world, both in the developing and the developed countries, and consider the implications of EU policy in this area. Finally, we discuss some of the ways in which the EU attempts to support business development and consider its successes and failures in this area.

17.2 'Fortress Europe': True or False?

17.2.1 The EU and external trade

Has the EU created a fortress, providing a protective base for its exporters but impregnable to imports? The label 'Fortress Europe' has been used by some of Europe's main trading partners to describe a rather protectionist European Union which erects high barriers to imports and subsidizes exports. This charge was made during the preparations for the single market, spurred on by the fear that external barriers would be strengthened as internal barriers were removed. It has also been made in relation to the Common Agricultural Policy. Frequent use has now almost made the phrase a truism. But is the EU really as protectionist as the term 'Fortress Europe' implies?

A large proportion of the trade of EU countries is with other member states but, even allowing for this, EU trade with the rest of the world accounts for about 15 per cent of world trade. Imports from the rest of the world account for a similar proportion. The EU as a whole has a larger share of world trade than either the USA or Japan. In this sense, it is certainly not a closed economy. Nor did the fears that the single market would prompt protectionist measures materialize. In some respects, however, EU policy does raise concerns. In principle, the Common Commercial Policy favours 'the progressive abolition of restrictions on international trade'[1] and the EU has been a strong supporter of GATT and the World Trade Organization. In practice, there have been times when the actions of individual member states or the EU authorities have suggested that the protection of domestic industries and the promotion of exports takes priority over free trade.

On the whole the EU acts as one on external trade matters, despite wide variations in the approach taken by individual countries. On occasion, member states have pursued their domestic interests too eagerly and either imposed their own restrictions on imports or threatened to disrupt a trade agreement. Even at the EU level, however, trade policy has at times given the impression that mercantilism prevails. This term describes the view that exports are paramount and imports are to be discouraged—a view that ignores the theory of comparative advantage and the merits of international trade in general (see Chapters 6 and 10). On the whole EU external tariffs have gradually been reduced and are now among the lowest in the world, though on certain sensitive products like textiles and consumer electronics tariffs are still quite high. Imports from the less developed countries receive preferential treatment, or in some cases are free from duty, under the Generalized System of Preferences or the Lomé Convention. The Europe Agreements also mean that imports from Eastern Europe are becoming tariff-free, but this does not apply to products like steel where the Eastern Europeans have a potential advantage. This leaves the impression that the EU favours free trade provided there is no threat to its own industries.

The EU is also at times rather quick to impose anti-dumping tariffs, especially on goods from Japan, China, and other Asian countries. Such measures are allowed in principle under World Trade Organization (WTO) rules, but they are clearly open to abuse. It is often difficult to be sure whether imported goods are being unfairly subsidized in their country of origin or whether they are simply produced at low cost. Subsidies are, in any case, so commonplace and so varied in type that it is almost impossible to be sure that they have not been used. Unfortunately, by responding to the demands of domestic producers to restrict low-priced imports, the EU sometimes becomes hostage to powerful interest groups. In the process, the interests of European consumers and industrial users of these products are often ignored. This is clearly not a straightforward issue, but import protection is sometimes used as a substitute for more considered policy action.

In a general sense, there have been moves to open the EU's external frontiers to competition in recent years. The Uruguay GATT agreement, although hard fought on agricultural products, led to significant EU tariff reductions and the European Commission has been at the forefront of WTO negotiations on the liberalization of services. Sometimes individual member states have attempted to retain trade barriers, however. There has been a tendency to replace import duties, over which individual countries no longer have control, with non-tariff barriers such as voluntary export restraints (VERs) or special import procedures. The VERs on imported motor vehicles from Japan are a classic example. These were later standardized across the EU and are to be removed in 1999. Japanese motor manufacturers have, in any case, circumvented these barriers by building car plants in Europe. Protective measures have a habit of provoking this kind of response.

In principle, the EU is in favour of free trade with countries beyond its borders, but in practice the picture is somewhat more complicated. Some of its policies are unmistakably protectionist. The Common Agricultural Policy is a prime example, with its import levies and export subsidies (see Chapter 14), though the direction of reform is broadly towards freer trade. In its dealings with Eastern Europe the EU has been bold in its vision of enlargement but timid in opening its markets—fearing the impact of competition on its higher-cost industries but, by erecting barriers, it has held back the rehabilitation of Eastern Europe's industries. The EU member states are also collectively and individually among the most generous aid donors to the developing world, but their trade policies with these countries have often been the subject of criticism. Whilst the EU has a number of preferential trading agreements with developing countries, they have tended to favour the exports of their former colonies, especially under the Lomé Convention (see below). These contradictory indications are perhaps the inevitable consequence of a trade policy which is pulled in various directions by its member states.

17.2.2 Is there a case for selective intervention?

Most governments intervene at some time by restricting imports, selectively approving inward investment, or promoting the development of a particular firm or industry. Here, we focus on intervention which is designed to promote industrial development. EU governments, acting cooperatively, have given their encouragement to several joint projects, especially in the aerospace industry. The Anglo-French Concorde, the European Airbus, and the Euro-fighter project are prime examples. Individual governments have also supported a variety of other industries through nationalization, subsidies, and special incentives. On the whole European government support has been much less intrusive than intervention in East Asia, however. Government targeting of industries identified for expansion is one of the key features of the so-called East Asian model (see Chapter 8). Whilst the type of intervention varies in different East Asian countries, it is common for governments to grant generous tax concessions, make finance available on preferential terms, encourage selective joint-ventures with foreign companies, and even to determine which companies are allowed to produce particular products.

Conventional wisdom has it that this kind of government intervention helped to create the East Asian 'economic miracle'. Certainly, many of the targeted industries had become the main engines of economic growth and the leading export industries in these countries up to the time of the Asian financial crisis. On the other hand, it may be that these very policies helped to bring about the resource misallocation which contributed to the crisis. Further, it has been suggested that the globalization of the world economy is making interventionist policies less meaningful. In a more open global economy, consumers play a greater role in determining resource allocation and governments will increasingly find that their attempts to manipulate resources are thwarted by the market place.[2]

There is still a legitimate debate about the role of government in promoting research and new technology, however. The EU has a number of schemes designed to foster research in universities and companies but, apart from the general direction of policy, they are supportive rather than directive. The extent to which the EU authorities should be involved in determining policy priorities is a more difficult question. When public funds are involved, accountability requires that money is spent wisely. Public decision making does not guarantee that public funds are used wisely, however, nor does it guarantee accountability. Perhaps a combination of public and private sector involvement is the answer, though this poses as many questions as it answers. Despite the growing doubts about the wisdom of public sector intervention in promoting industry 'winners', there are still those who feel that European governments have lost out to their Asian counterparts by not providing selective assistance to key industries.

17.3 The EU's Relations with the Rest of the World

17.3.1 The EU and the developing world

The EU and its member states contribute between 45 and 50 per cent of world public development aid. Much of this aid goes to sub-Saharan Africa, South America, and Southern Asia. It helps to provide food, medicine, and other humanitarian aid and also promotes agricultural and rural development projects. Much of the EU's development aid is channelled through the European Development Fund, which is made up of direct contributions from individual member states and is additional to the EU budget. In the early years EU development assistance was mainly used to help former colonies of EU member states, particularly the members of what has become the Lomé Convention. Increasingly, assistance is now given to developing countries in general, with less regard for political or strategic ties. Priority is given to countries which are engaged in economic and political reform, however, and EU companies benefit from contracts relating to project assistance.

The most extensive trade agreement which the EU has with developing countries is the Lomé Convention. The Convention was established in 1975 in Lomé, the capital of Togo, though it replaced earlier conventions dating back to 1963. Lomé IV covers the period 1990–2000 and is a preferential trading agreement allowing free access to exports of most industrial and agricultural products from about seventy African, Caribbean, and Pacific (ACP) countries. The Lomé Convention covers aid as well as trade and is supported by its own institutions. The agreement has recently been criticized for favouring some developing countries at the expense of others, especially in relation to the banana regime (see Chapter 6). In addition to Lomé there are numerous other association agreements of one type or another with developing countries. The EU also grants preferential access to exports of manufactured and semi-manufactured goods (but not agricultural products) from about 150 developing countries under its Generalized System of Preferences. These concessions, which were introduced on the recommendations of UNCTAD in 1971, have now become less attractive after successive rounds of GATT tariff reductions.

17.3.2 The EU's Mediterranean initiative

Much of the attention during the 1990s was focused on EU enlargement to the north and east and especially on policy towards Eastern Europe. This is understandable, given the momentous developments in that region, but in 1994 the EU decided to work towards closer cooperation with its southern neighbours around the Mediterranean. The EU has a number of trade and aid agreements with these countries, as it does with numerous other developing countries, but the 1994 decision recognizes the special position of the Mediterranean countries, both in terms of their geographical proximity and their links with France and Italy in particular. The EU is in fact a major export market for some of the Mediterranean countries. Whilst EU membership is not on offer, the proposal is to establish a Euro-Mediterranean partnership (sometimes dubbed 'Euro-Med') with the Maghreb countries (Algeria, Morocco, and Tunisia), the Mashreq countries (Egypt, Jordan, Lebanon, and Syria), and also Cyprus, Malta (both of which may join the EU), Israel, Libya, Turkey, and the ex-non-aligned communist states of Albania and the former Yugoslavia. The intention is to create a free trade area between the EU and these countries by 2010. This is an ambitious project as the southern and eastern shores of the Mediterranean include a diverse range of countries, only some of whom are natural bedfellows.

17.3.3 The EU and the Americas

Potentially the most ambitious development in trade between the industrialized countries is the proposed 'New Transatlantic Marketplace'—the proposal to create a free trade area between the EU and the USA. In one sense, transatlantic free trade has come closer in recent years because of the general reduction in tariffs under GATT. The USA and EU, in particular, made some of the largest tariff reductions following the Uruguay Round. These two economic powers have in fact become the main driving force behind the liberalization of world trade in general, attempting to prise open the Japanese and other restricted markets. Over a longer period, the USA has been the champion of free trade and its powerful economy has been a good advertisement for its cause. Of course, even the most avid supporters of free trade succumb to protective measures at times. The US import quota on Japanese cars in the early 1980s provides an example which supports the exception rather than the rule. Criticisms of EU protectionism, especially in agriculture, have been more frequent.

In general, there is a good measure of agreement on the merits of transatlantic free trade, but trade relations between the USA and the EU have at times been surprisingly fraught—usually over specific issues like the use of hormone treatment in cattle, rivalry between Boeing and Airbus, or the EU banana regime. Free trade in industrial goods is probably an achievable objective in the medium term, perhaps also the freedom to provide services. Free trade in agriculture, or in certain sensitive products like American television programmes in France, is likely to take longer. In political and military terms, the USA still dominates world affairs and the EU is still finding its feet. But in trade and investment, the two are on equal terms. The 'New Transatlantic Marketplace' therefore provides an opportunity for them to link the world's two largest economies if they can find enough common ground on the details of such an agreement.

The other main trade initiative involving the EU and the Americas is the proposed free trade area with Mercosur in Latin America. Mercosur is an ambitious trade grouping which has made significant progress towards achieving a customs union between its members, but it still has a high level of external tariffs. The will is there to create another transatlantic free market, but free trade in practice may take a little longer. The fact that these nations are keen to have free trade is itself a good sign for business relations with Latin America.

17.3.4 The EU and Asia

Although a number of European companies have business interests in Asia, trade between the EU and Asia is surprisingly modest. The main traders and investors in much of Asia, especially in South-East Asia, are the Americans and the Japanese. Europeans, of course, have historic links with the Indian subcontinent, Hong Kong, Vietnam, Indonesia, and one or two other parts of Asia, but while some of these links are still strong, others have now been dissolved. Cultural differences between Europe and Asia have sometimes made for uneasy relationships between the two.

The recent establishment of Asia Pacific Economic Cooperation (APEC), linking North (and South) America with the Asia Pacific region, now seems to have re-awakened European interest in Asia—perhaps fearing stronger American ties with China, Japan, and the newly industrializing countries of the region. Certainly, until the Asian financial crisis, Asia had been the most rapidly developing region. Economic growth slowed down during 1998, but there is still a good deal of potential for the region's future development. Europe–Asia summits, primarily involving the EU and ASEAN, are now on the EU's international agenda, though these have sometimes been soured by European sensitivities about some of Asia's political regimes. This was the case shortly after Burma was admitted to ASEAN in 1997 when European heads of government objected to Burma's military leaders being present at the summit. Although Burma's membership of ASEAN was controversial even within the region, ASEAN members tend not to interfere in each other's internal affairs. Similar problems arise when Western leaders criticize China for its human rights record. For Europeans, and Americans, trade and political issues are often interlinked. Thus, trade with China and South East Asia inevitably exposes a number of raw nerves when the two issues come together.

17.4 The EU's Role in Promoting International Business

IN this section we consider the extent to which EU policies help to promote international business. The promotion of business does not only involve active intervention. More often it means policies which provide a supportive environment for business. With one or two exceptions, EU policy is generally supportive rather than active, though it is sometimes also protective. In examining this issue, we will discuss the view that the EU could be more active in promoting business success.

17.4.1 The EU's competitive position

An interesting case which illustrates the debate on the EU's apparent economic shortcomings is the issue of international competitiveness. The term 'international competitiveness' should properly be applied to companies rather than countries, though countries may provide an environment which fosters competitiveness. Europe is sometimes perceived as a region which is internationally uncompetitive. This view stems from the fact that Western European labour and other production costs are high. In some cases, exchange rates are also strong against many of Europe's 'competitor' countries. Both these cost disadvantages apply to Germany, which has the highest hourly labour costs in the world and has also had one of the world's strongest currencies in recent years. Others claim that the inflexibility of Europe's labour markets and its complex environmental regulations are a barrier to competitiveness. Further arguments point to Europe's apparent inability to convert its research expertise into industrial innovation. Clearly, these factors do not apply equally to all European countries, but convincing evidence can be presented in each case.

However convincing, the above picture only presents a partial analysis of Europe's competitiveness. For, whereas Germany has the highest hourly labour costs, it also has one of the world's highest industrial productivity levels. Thus, its unit labour costs indicate a higher level of competitiveness than would otherwise appear to be the case. Competitiveness also depends on product quality, which is determined by design capabilities, technology, and the quality of the inputs used in production. Labour skills and technological know-how are crucially important. A firm's 'architecture', its structure and organization, its purchasing and marketing policies, its human resource management are all vital to its success in international markets. Even its responsiveness to change may be a determining factor in its competitiveness. European firms generally score well in these areas, though they still tend to lag behind the USA and Japan.

The distinctive contribution of the EU, as opposed to that of its firms or its member states, is its role in establishing the wider economic environment. Arguably, the single market has been its most important contribution not only to intra-EU competition and competitiveness, but also to the wider international competitiveness of its firms—indeed, of all firms operating within its borders. Measures to reduce border costs, harmonize technical standards, and liberalize public procurement expose firms to the rigours of competition. The arrival of the single currency will probably have a similar, if not more poignant, effect. Openness to external markets is also important. Industries such as telecommunications, which have been protected by state ownership and regulatory barriers, are only just beginning to respond to the new competitive environment. Industries like civil aviation have competed on world markets for many years, but their European operations have been protected by regulation and privileged access to airport slots. Airline deregulation is now chipping away at these national monopolies. Europe's motor industry also faces international competition, but in this case in its home market as well as abroad. Even here, however, import and distribution barriers have slowed down the adjustment process in Europe (see Box 17.1).

17.4.2 Intervention or market reforms?

Individual European governments have frequently intervened to support particular companies or industries. But, unlike Japan, which appears to have had more success in this area, Europeans seem to have picked more losers than winners. This is perhaps because they have tended to support declining industries like coal, steel, and shipbuilding, struggling inefficient companies like British Leyland in the 1970s and 1980s or several of Europe's national airlines, and technically advanced projects like nuclear power stations or the Concorde aircraft, whose economic and environmental viability are questionable. It is not just that Japan has been better at picking industries with a viable future, however, it is rather that they have chosen industries in which they have some potential competitive advantage. Japanese workers are good at producing technically intricate products to a high-quality specification: products such as cars, computers, and electronics. Japanese culture also fosters the practice of team-working and the networks of supporting companies (*keiretsu*) which have played a major part in the success of these industries.

If the Japanese experience is valid, does this mean that Europe should adopt similar policies? If so, this appears to contradict the current wisdom of market liberalism—the lesson from US experience and the 'Anglo-Saxon' model. The single market, for all the EU's bureaucratic intervention, is about removing barriers and opening up markets. Liberalization is the buzz word. Or perhaps there is a way to marry the two approaches. The Japanese have promoted their chosen industries in a variety of ways, some with more long-term benefits than others (see Chapters 8 and 9). Some of the more beneficial policies have included the encouragement of

Box 17.1 Competition and Change in the Motor Industry

Worldwide competition in the motor industry has prompted manufacturers to merge or form strategic alliances in recent years. A combination of over-capacity, low-priced Asian exports, and the need for even greater economies of scale is now increasing the pressure on the industry to consolidate through mergers and acquisitions. Several recent takeovers have involved marriages between prestige specialist firms and volume manufacturers. Examples include BMW's takeover of Rover, Volkswagen's takeover of Rolls-Royce (though not the long-term use of the Rolls-Royce name, which passes to BMW from 2003), the Daimler-Benz takeover of Chrysler, and Ford's takeover of Volvo. Volvo, a specialist manufacturer, was actively seeking to sell off or find a partner for its car division. The output of its car division is only one-tenth of Volkswagen's output, for example, and Volvo was finding that its sales volume is insufficient to cover the increasing cost of developing and marketing new models. It appears that modern car makers need large-scale production, a wide product range, and a widespread geographical coverage. From Ford's point of view, Volvo brings another prestige brand into its portfolio.

  Within the European market, restructuring in the motor industry has probably some way to go. The removal of barriers in the single market and global competitive pressures are now exposing the problem of over-capacity. At the same time, Japanese companies like Toyota have been continuing to expand production in Western Europe. Despite these pressures, the system of exclusive and selective distribution and the use of voluntary export restraints on Japanese cars have combined to provide a measure of protection for European car manufacturers. The gradual erosion of this protection has already brought job losses and plant closures, such as Renault's Vilvoorde factory in Belgium, but companies like Volkswagen and Renault are now emerging as stronger international competitors. Whether Renault and Peugeot-Citroen, two major manufacturers with a similar product range, will continue to survive as independent firms, remains to be seen. (*Main source:* H. Simonian, 'Fast and loose in Detroit', *Financial Times*, 8 Jan. 1999.)

cooperation between government and business, between lenders and borrowers, and between workers and managers. The emphasis on education and training has also been an important factor in their success. They have arguably been less successful in the long-run when governments have been too directive, creating barriers to competition and encouraging banks to lend with little regard to commercial viability.

  It is doubtful therefore whether European governments or the EU should try to emulate some of the more intrusive industrial policies of Japan or other East Asian countries. Even if there is merit in the idea that Europe should in some way support selected industries, it should learn from Japan's failures as well as its successes. Methods which work in one culture may, in any case, not work in another. Where then do Europe's potential competitive advantages lie? Some of these strengths may stem from European culture—a highly creative culture in terms of art, literature, music, exploration, and science. Some of its strengths will be country-specific such as the Italian flair for design, German engineering precision, or British exploitation of the English language. Specific industries or companies may have the competitive advantages to be successful in specialist markets.

The question is: how should Europe capitalize on these advantages and assets, if not by intrusive intervention? The argument has now come full circle: in some industries, the most effective thing governments and the EU can do is to open up markets which were previously closed to competition. Inert, inefficient, and unresponsive telecommunication providers will then turn themselves into internationally competitive companies. Financial institutions, arguably in one of Europe's potentially world-beating industries, will be strengthened by competing more fully in each other's markets. Europe's car manufacturers or airlines may consolidate to become major international competitors. Many companies will, of course, achieve success by specializing in what they do best, exploiting their core skills and making a good product. The provision of a supportive environment may also include the encouragement of industrial cooperation in research and development, an attitude of mutual trust between industry and higher education, and a greater emphasis on education and training, among other things. Whereas the German vocational training system is a significant competitive strength, some of Europe's workers, especially in jobs requiring intermediate level skills, have relatively low levels of education and training.[3]

17.5 The EU as a World Economic Leader

IT could be argued that, on the world stage, the EU is becoming an economic giant but remains a political pygmy. In the conventional sense of leadership in foreign affairs and defence, the EU is politically weak but it has often achieved political objectives through economic means. As an economic unit and a trading bloc, the EU is now on a par with the USA and NAFTA. As a unified regional grouping it is more highly integrated than NAFTA, both economically and politically, but in terms of world economic leadership the USA is still dominant. These conflicting indications leave the future role of the EU uncertain, though it is likely that the EU will play an increasing role in world economic affairs. Its currency, the euro, may eventually rival the US dollar as the world's major reserve currency. Its voice at the World Trade Organization and increasingly at the IMF, World Bank, and other international organizations will probably gain greater influence. This places a growing responsibility on the EU to be a voice for trade liberalization as well as to protect the interests of the weaker developing countries and to promote ethical and environmental causes. In some respects, the EU is held back by its cumbersome decision-making processes and by the lack of democratic accountability of some of its institutions. Arguably, the EU should use its influence in the economic sphere to minimize institutional interference in trade and investment, restricting the activities of international institutions to the laying of basic ground rules, arbitration in disputes, and the creation of a supportive business environment. A good deal of work remains to be done, however, to stream-line its procedures and strengthen its common policies in the field of international affairs.[4]

Box 17.2 Airbus—A lesson in European Collaboration

Probably the most prominent example of industrial collaboration in Europe is the Airbus project. Airbus Industrie, which manufactures the Airbus range of aircraft, is in fact a consortium of four European aircraft manufacturers: Aérospatiale of France, Daimler-Chrysler Aerospace of Germany, British Aerospace, and Casa of Spain. It was set up with the backing of their respective governments as a 'European economic interest grouping'. It is therefore an intergovernmental rather than an EU-sponsored project. The Airbus consortium was established in 1970 and the first Airbus aircraft flew in 1972. It was some years, however, before Airbus was seen as a major competitor to Boeing, the world's leading aircraft manufacturer.

Airbus was the subject of much criticism in its early years, partly because of its cumber-some decision-making structure and partly because of doubts about the wisdom of building an aircraft 'by committee'. However, in recent years, Airbus has achieved some success in establishing its reputation in world markets and its market share now rivals that of Boeing. Boeing, which had long regarded Airbus with scepticism, is now begin-ning to take its rival more seriously. The growing threat to its market share has led Boeing to complain about the level of subsidy Airbus receives from its backer governments. This is countered by the suspicion that Boeing also benefits from defence-related government support, especially since its purchase of McDonnell Douglas, the world's largest producer of military jets, in 1997. Rivalry between the two groups came to the fore when the European Commission challenged Boeing over the McDonnell Douglas takeover—appearing to be defending its European protégé against its mighty American rival.

Boeing's production facilities are generally less technologically advanced than Airbus's, perhaps because Boeing was slow to realize the competitive threat to its market dominance. Its sales have also been more seriously affected by the loss of orders during the Asian financial crisis than those of Airbus. Airbus, on the other hand, is still hampered by its committee management structure, though it plans to unify its activities under a single management as a profit-making entity towards the end of 1999. Perhaps there is a role for government-supported industrial collaboration after all. (*Main source:* M. Skapinker, 'Please wait in departure lounge', *Financial Times*, 3 Dec. 1998.)

17.6 Summary

Aᴏᴛᴇʀ the single market initiative was announced in 1985, US and other external commentators raised fears of a 'Fortress Europe'—a European Union with a barrier-free internal market but protectionist towards outsiders. The rhetoric of some European politicians gave substance to this view at the time. Whilst there is some reason for concern in relation to the Common Agricultural Policy and some of the EU's anti-dumping measures, EU external trade has not generally been subject to protectionist barriers. In fact, some observers argue that there is a case for selective intervention by the EU authorities to promote its industry more actively. The EU has numerous links with nations or groups of nations around the world; these include a preferential trading agreement with a number of developing countries under the Lomé Convention, an emerging trade agreement with several Mediterranean countries, and discussions on closer trade relations with the USA, Latin America, and Asia. Finally, the chapter discusses the competitive position of companies in the EU and the apparent tendency for European companies to lag behind their US and Japanese counterparts. There may be a case for more active intervention but it may be more important for the EU to provide a supportive business environment. On the world stage, the EU has a responsibility to provide economic leadership, though it may be some time before it assumes this role in the political arena.

Review questions

1 To what extent do you agree with the charge that the EU has become 'Fortress Europe'?

2 Outline the case for selective intervention by the EU authorities to promote business development.

3 What trade links does the EU have with developing countries? Are these generally beneficial to both the EU and the developing countries?

4 What type of trade links is the EU hoping to establish with the USA, Latin America, and Asia? What difficulties may lie on the road to these goals?

5 In what ways can the EU exercise world economic leadership?

Study Topic: The EU's lagging competitiveness

In a report produced for the European Commission, published in November 1998, it was argued that the EU lags behind the USA and Japan on most measures of international competitiveness. Gross domestic product per capita, sometimes used as an indicator of international competitiveness at the country level, was 33 per cent lower in the EU as a whole than in the USA and 13 per cent lower than in Japan. The EU's poor record in creating employment was singled out for particular criticism. As this appeared to apply across the board in most industrial sectors, it suggested that the EU's poor performance related to the business environment in general and, in particular, to the inflexibility of Europe's labour markets and excessive regulation in markets for goods and services. A shortage of risk capital for advanced technological development and the high cost and inefficiency of Europe's financial services were also highlighted by the report. For one reason or another, European industries generally lag behind in technology industries. If measured by the number of inventions patented in at least two countries, the USA is well ahead of most European countries, as well as Japan. Despite these shortcomings, the reports's authors focus attention on flexible markets, market liberalization, and the creation of a competitive business environment rather than on targeted intervention by the EU or national authorities.
Source: Adapted from E. Tucker, 'Competitiveness of European business lagging behind US', *Financial Times*, 16 Nov. 1998.

Study topic questions

1 Is gross domestic product per capita a useful indicator of international competitiveness in the EU?

2 Is it fair to point the blame for the EU's poor international competitiveness at inflexible labour markets, regulated goods and services markets, and a general lack of competition? What alternative explanations might be suggested?

3 What appears to be the problem with the EU's banking sector?

4 Is the number of patents registered a useful indicator of superior international competitiveness? Why do you think the USA does well in this area?

5 Should the EU consider more targeted intervention in the form of subsidies or strategic trade policy?

Notes

1 Article 110, *EEC Treaty* (Treaty of Rome), 1957.

2 See C. Lingle, *The Rise and Decline of the Asian Century* (Asia 2000, 1997).

3 An interesting discussion of these issues can be found in J. Kay, *The Business of Economics* (Oxford University Press, 1996), ch. 10, 69–80.

4 See L. Tsoukalis, *The New European Economy Revisited* (Oxford University Press, 1997), ch. 10, 223–76 for a fuller discussion of these issues.

Recommended Reading

- Dent, C. M., *The European Economy: The Global Context* (Routledge, 1997).

- El Agraa, A. M., *The European Union: History, Institutions, Economics and Policies* (Prentice-Hall, 1998).

- McDonald, F., and Dearden, S., *European Economic Integration* (Longman, 1999).

- Tsoukalis, L., *The New European Economy Revisited* (Oxford University Press, 1997).

Transition in Eastern Europe

Part V

Transition in Eastern Europe

18

Economic and political challenges for Eastern Europe in 1989

Objectives

- to identify the economic (and political) factors which led to the fall of communism in 1989
- to discuss the economic policy options available to the governments of Eastern Europe on the brink of economic transition (i.e. 'shock therapy' vs. gradualism)
- to identify the elements of the transition package known as the 'big bang' approach or 'shock therapy' and to understand the need for macroeconomic stabilization
- to discuss the limitations of the economic reform programme in Eastern Europe during the 1990s

18.1 Introduction

THE collapse of communism in Eastern Europe in 1989 occurred with dramatic spontaneity, the rise of Solidarity in Poland providing the spark that caused the sudden demise of political regimes which had managed to maintain themselves in power for half a century. This chapter aims to discuss the combination of economic, political, and social factors which were instrumental in providing the catalyst for the events of 1989. These countries faced severe economic and social problems caused by inherent faults in the central planning system itself. In addition, shifts in international alliances meant that the battleground in the cold war had shifted to the

Middle East with the Iran–Iraq War and into the heart of Africa with armed struggles occurring in Namibia and Angola. At the same time, the USSR was faced with its own Vietnam—a futile war fought in Afghanistan which never attracted much support at home.

However, an important impetus for change in the whole region was provided in 1985 when Mikail Gorbachev became General Secretary of the Communist Party of the USSR. There was no doubt that he clearly saw the writing on the wall—the Soviet economy was in desperate need of reform, but the 'Gorbachev factor' was unique in that it combined both political and economic reform in a way that had not been permitted by the Soviet leadership at any time in the past. As an initiator of *glasnost* in the USSR, Gorbachev actively encouraged a new era of open political discussion by opposition groups in Poland, Hungary, Czechoslovakia, and the German Democratic Republic (GDR). The option of sending tanks into Hungary in 1956 and Czechoslovakia in 1968 to put down a burgeoning political opposition was never a consideration for Gorbachev in 1989. Indeed, the main issue which arises in the present discussion is not simply why the end came so suddenly in 1989, but why did the communist regimes in the USSR and Eastern Europe last for so long? In other words, why had communism not collapsed before?

If the history of communism in the USSR is examined over a period of 70 years, it is possible to argue that there were a series of peaks and troughs representing periods of strength and weakness. Inevitably, the regime was at its weakest in the early years after seizing power in October 1917. After the end of World War I in Europe in 1918, the Western Allies concentrated their efforts on trying to remove the Bolsheviks from power. The ensuing civil war between the Whites (forces backed by the Western powers) and the Reds (the Bolsheviks) raged on until 1921. The USSR was at its most vulnerable during this period, the Bolsheviks could have been defeated and a system of capitalism and monarchy could have been restored.

Even during the period of the New Economic Mechanism after 1921, when a number of economic experiments were carried out using a mixture of state control and market mechanism, it was possible that the economy could have gone either way: more state control leading to socialism or an elimination of state control leading to capitalism. Indeed, the measures used under NEM were no more revolutionary than those economic policies advocated by the British Labour Party after its General Election victory in 1945.

If these were the troughs of communist power, why did the system survive in the USSR for so long? The simple answers are: the rise of Josef Stalin to power by 1926; and the inextricable link between the economic and political system provided by the Communist Party. As a result of Stalin's unique interpretation of Marxism-Leninism and the need to consolidate his own position by liquidating the opposition, a command economy was established with the First Five Year Plan in 1928. Stalin successfully used the First Five Year Plan and its successors to strengthen the economy and promote self-sufficiency in order to isolate the USSR from its enemies abroad. To achieve rapid rates of economic development, totalitarian methods of control were used to eliminate actual and potential elements of opposition. The existence, and even the legitimacy, of the communist system in the USSR from 1928 until the time of

Stalin's death in 1953 depended upon the maintenance of strong political control mechanisms, but also, upon strong public support for the economic successes achieved during this period.

18.2 Why Did Communism Fail?

T HE 1970s and 1980s saw a combination of economic and political factors provide the catalyst which eventually undermined the foundations of the communist systems in the USSR and Eastern Europe. The Soviet Union had managed to keep control of its own people and those of its satellites by a mixture of economic success, political coercion, and extreme nationalist ideology.

18.2.1 The post-1945 generation

The generation which could remember pre-revolutionary Russia had experienced substantial improvements in their living standards in the period following the First Five Year Plan. It was the younger generation, born after 1945, who were the post-revolutionary and post World War II generation, and who held different values and expressed different aspirations from their parents. It was this generation who became the strongest critics of the communist system. They objected to the practice of government nominees obtaining top positions in industry and the professions. The restrictions on entry into higher education meant that increasing numbers of young people were forced to enter the industrial labour force with few prospects of promotion. The dissident movement had previously been characterized as a minority movement, driven underground, but dominated by members of the intelligentsia. The new dissident movements of the 1980s saw an influx of support from among industrial workers, and, in the case of Solidarity in Poland, became a mass movement with the strength to challenge the political monopoly and control exercised by the Polish communist government.

18.2.2 Extensive vs. intensive growth

The post-1945 generation also objected to the economic problems facing the economies of Eastern Europe in the 1970s and 1980s, and the governments' apparent inability to introduce policies to alleviate them. The problems manifested themselves in reduced living standards, but were, in fact, inherent in all economies which had adopted the Soviet model of rapid industrialization involving high rates of economic growth being achieved by 'extensive' means.

The Soviet growth model was based on the rapid transfer of surplus labour and resources from a low productivity sector (agriculture) to a higher productivity sector (industry). In the USSR this process took the form of forced collectivization of agriculture from the late 1920s. In other words, agriculture provided labour for the new factories in the towns and, eventually, food supplies to feed the new industrial working class. The first stage of this model provides productivity gains by using more labour in the industrial sector until the transfer of resources from the agricultural sector dries up.

The consequences of the second stage of this model were particularly devastating on the economies of the USSR and Eastern Europe. Instead of attempting to achieve productivity increases through the introduction of new technology (intensive methods of development), countries of the region pursued an autarkic model of development, with the emphasis on high levels of investment in import-substituting industries. This means that heavy industries in steel production and the capital goods sector were developed at the expense of manufacturing industry. This policy produced a dramatic imbalance in the industrial structure which lasted for decades and which was forced upon the countries of Eastern Europe after 1945 when they found themselves under Soviet domination. Before 1939 countries like Czechoslovakia and Hungary had enjoyed successful manufacturing sectors with established patterns of international trade. These advantages rapidly disappeared with the introduction of the First Five Year Plans in the countries of Eastern Europe in 1950, after which their pattern of industrial development became subjugated to the economic and military needs of the USSR.

The autarkic approach to economic development was an important feature of the second stage of the Soviet model and the creation of the Council for Mutual Economic Assistance (CMEA) meant that a regional autarky could be established whereby import substitution could be achieved by the exchange of products between members throughout the region. However, it was not possible for the smaller countries of the region to achieve self sufficiency. Indeed, as 'extensive' sources of growth dried up, it became increasingly difficult to supply all product and technological needs from within the region. From the 1970s onwards, members of CMEA were forced to abandon import substitution and attempt to develop an export-oriented strategy which would allow them to obtain supplies of modern technology necessary to redress the structural imbalance.

18.2.3 Declining rates of economic growth

Any serious attempts to reform the ailing economies of Eastern Europe were effectively blocked by Soviet military intervention, especially in Czechoslovakia in response to the Prague Spring in August 1968 and the imposition of martial law in Poland in 1981 in the face of serious demands for economic and political reform from Solidarity. The economies of the region had lost all their previous advantages of rapid growth during the 'catching-up' process by the early 1970s. Angus Maddison estimates that between 1950 and 1973 the countries of Eastern Europe had enjoyed a growth rate of 3.9 per cent per capita GNP, compared with an average of 3.8 per cent for the core of the Western European countries and 3.7 per cent for the rapidly growing Asian economies during the same period.[1] However, between 1973 and 1987 annual economic growth rates for Eastern Europe fell dramatically from 3.9 per cent to 1.9 per cent, the same rate as the average for Western Europe, but well below the 3.7 per cent maintained in Asia.[2]

The oil crises which had so many far-reaching consequences for the world economy in 1973 and again in 1980, affected the economies of the region in two important ways. Firstly, as the price of oil rocketed, the USSR, the main supplier of oil to the countries of Eastern Europe, found itself with a trade surplus on its oil account, whereas its satellites, the main recipients of Soviet oil, found themselves facing increasing trade deficits. Secondly, state-owned industries in Eastern Europe could not produce goods for export which proved attractive to customers abroad and which could compete on equal terms with goods produced by Western companies. This meant that the increasing amount of Western technology which was imported by countries like Poland, Hungary, and Yugoslavia, in an attempt to modernize their industry, had to be paid for by obtaining loans and credits from Western financial institutions.

Ivan Berend estimates that by the late 1970s, Hungary, Poland, Romania, and Bulgaria had accumulated huge debts of between $6 billion and $18 billion each.[3] By 1990 net debt levels had reached $41.8 billion in Poland, $20.3 billion in Hungary, and $9.8 billion in Bulgaria.[4] Hungary remained the only country in the region which could sustain the level of repayments, while high debt burdens bankrupted Poland, Bulgaria, and Yugoslavia, all of which were forced to apply to their creditors for rescheduling. In this sense, a vicious circle became established where the countries of Eastern Europe were in desperate need of massive capital investment to achieve economic restructuring, but could not sustain higher levels of borrowing since all new credits obtained from international financial institutions were being used by their governments to finance existing debt.

18.2.4 Declining living standards

The economic problems discussed earlier stemmed from a failure to modify and reform the Soviet model and meant that living standards fell further behind those enjoyed by the citizens of Western Europe. Indeed, it became only too apparent to consumers in countries like Poland, Czechoslovakia, and the German Democratic Republic (GDR), situated on the fringes of Western Europe, just how wide the gap in living standards between East and West had become. West German television broadcasts to the East and the advent of satellite television meant that many Eastern European consumers were able to get a glimpse of Western consumer society for the first time. Given the earlier discussion on the attitudes of young people born after 1945, it was this group who aspired to the advantages of Western consumer society in the

1970s and 1980s. They were no longer satisfied with pairs of Levis smuggled in by Western tourists, but aspired to their view of a total Western capitalist lifestyle. Nevertheless, for many people this was a utopian view of capitalism—it did not contain the prospect of unemployment and the removal of the welfare safety net.

18.2.5 Rising levels of military expenditure

The continuing military build-up of the post-détente era of the early 1980s meant that increasing levels of Soviet government expenditure were being devoted to defence and the maintenance of the Warsaw Pact. It is estimated that Soviet defence expenditure amounted to approximately 16 per cent of GNP in the 1980s.[5] The USSR had embarked upon an expensive war in Afghanistan, which eventually dragged on for a decade, and which saw the legendary military prowess of the Red Army discredited on an international scale. The Afghan War also provided new recruits for the wider dissident movement from among the ranks of disgruntled servicemen, and especially from those who had been discharged disabled from the service. Many men in the latter category formed their own pressure groups which became very vociferous in the late 1980s towards the shortcomings of a government which had promised them everything as soldiers but which failed them when they left the service and became disabled civilians. Significantly, dissidents with military backgrounds joined with dissidents from the intelligentsia for the first time who, in turn, cooperated with dissidents from the industrial sector, providing a strong opposition which the government found very difficult to ignore.

In addition, the new Cold War era, heralded by the arrival of President Ronald Reagan in the White House in 1980 and the continuation of a series of mortally ailing general secretaries in the Kremlin until the appointment of Mikail Gorbachev in 1985, meant that the possibility of serious conflict between East and West was greater than at any time since the end of World War II. The development of the US STAR Wars programme meant that any potential conflict during the early 1980s would have forced both sides into testing their nuclear capability. In reality, these new developments in the US nuclear weapons programme forced the USSR into devoting resources into a military build-up which it could ill afford.

In 1985 Gorbachev realized that the current level of military expenditure could not be sustained if the Soviet government was to improve its citizens' standard of living by introducing economic reforms. The arms reduction agreements between the US and the USSR after 1985 would, in theory, give Gorbachev the opportunity to channel resources into redressing the imbalance of Soviet industry by developing a viable manufacturing sector and improving access to modern technology. In addition, the Chernobyl disaster and agitation by environmentalists about damage from endemic industrial pollution brought discussion of the need for the utilization of new technology and the implementation and monitoring of safety procedures into the public domain. It was no longer appropriate for environmental problems to be dealt with by national governments, the international community needed reassurance that the environmental and health catastrophe that was caused by Chernobyl would not be easily repeated in the future. It became the responsibility of Gorbachev to break the stalemate situation which characterized the Cold War and to sever the link between the defence and nuclear sectors to enable the nuclear industry to address neglected health and safety issues.

18.2.6 The 'Gorbachev factor'

The rise of Gorbachev to power meant that for the first time in seventy years economic reform went hand in hand with political reform. His encouragement of *glasnost*, which produced open political discussion and, by implication, dissent from the views expressed by the ruling party, meant that the policies pursued by the communist government came under attack. After 1985 the legitimacy of the Soviet Communist Party was very quickly called into question. The fact that the dissident movement had become more influential by that time and encompassed people who had no previous history of dissent meant that the old Soviet security machine was faced with an almost impossible task of control. However, it seems that the government under Gorbachev had no stomach to promote further repression and as the impetus for change came from Gorbachev himself, this encouraged other opposition groups to push for wide-ranging reform throughout Eastern Europe.

A view which was generally expressed by the press at the time was that Gorbachev actively encouraged the revolutions which overthrew the communists in Eastern Europe. In reality, even if Gorbachev's support was more passive than active, it must have been obvious to the communist governments and the dissident movements in Eastern Europe that the Soviet Union could no longer be relied upon to prop up these ailing regimes. Indeed, the USSR could no longer afford to do so, and had to look to redeploy its own resources in an attempt to redress its own economic problems. If such arguments are pursued to the limits, it may also be possible to suggest that the collapse of communism was inevitable, given the serious crisis it faced. The advantage of having a far-sighted and liberal politician in the Kremlin for the first time in seventy years meant that in most countries the collapse of communism proceeded peacefully with little evidence of resistance. The legacy of Gorbachev is that fewer lives were lost in 1989 than would have been the case if attempts at popular uprisings had occurred ten years previously. The fact that more countries than Yugoslavia failed to plunge into destructive civil wars waged between rival national groups was perhaps a tribute to the personalities involved in the leaderships of the new social democratic parties which came to power after the 1990 elections.

If *glasnost* encouraged more open political discussion, *perestroika* or, restructuring, implied that major economic reform would be introduced to sort out the economic legacy of central planning. From 1987 state enterprises were allowed greater control over their affairs, although private enterprise remained illegal. In 1988 the new law on cooperatives allowed small groups of individuals to establish enterprises, but these were confined to the service sector. At no point was there any attempt to dismantle the central planning mechanism and create a private sector by encouraging small firms and Joint Venture Agreements (JVAs), or through the process of privatization. The limited number of activities which could ostensibly be described as 'private enterprise' were confined to the service sector and individuals conducting illegal activities constituting the second economy had no real incentive to become legitimate. Indeed, the failure of the government to establish a private sector which was recognizable as such by market economists and which could be controlled by government legislation, meant that the new service sector was easily infiltrated by mafia groups and used to establish protection rackets and money-laundering facilities.

The limited number of economic reforms served merely to complicate the economic process in the USSR in the four years from 1985 to 1989. There was no real attempt to fundamentally reform or abandon the central planning process itself. Although *glasnost* allowed freedom of expression and criticism of the government to be aired in the media, the Communist Party still managed to hold on to its monopoly power until February 1990. Indeed, *glasnost* and *perestroika* did not in any circumstances represent an attempt to abandon socialism as an ideology or the political monopoly of the Communist Party, despite the eagerness with which Western economists awaited further developments. Although the 'Gorbachev factor' should not be underestimated in the encouragement it gave to opposition groups in the countries of Eastern Europe in the late 1980s, consideration should also be given to the fact that by 1989 the Soviet economy was in crisis and it was possible that the Communist Party was no longer interested in international political domination, given the seriousness of its mounting difficulties at home.

18.3 The Nature of the Economic Reform Programme

COUNTRIES whose governments were largely democratic before 1939 and whose economies were reasonably successful under market capitalism before the introduction of central planning after 1945, were the same countries which have achieved the most progress in the years following 1990. If the economic reforms in Poland, Hungary, and Czechoslovakia formed the blueprint for elsewhere in Eastern Europe, attempts by these countries to reform the central planning system, notably, with the New Economic Mechanism in Hungary in 1968, were doomed, since the systems themselves were unreformable.

The NEM constituted an attempt to make the central planning mechanism more flexible by gradually freeing up prices in the goods market, whilst at the same time retaining firm control over factor prices. This made a nonsense of the use of the price system as a signalling mechanism, factor prices failed to reflect real costs, and goods prices failed to reflect world price levels, but were determined by domestic costs. In addition, wages were kept artificially low and interest rates were not allowed to fulfil their market function in the allocation of investment funds. Although enterprises were given profit incentives under the 1968 reform in Hungary, they represented a marginal incentive since the government would never allow an enterprise to go bankrupt. The prospect of high unemployment led the government to continue with the practice of propping up inefficient enterprises by granting subsidies. It was only after 1990 that state enterprises in Eastern Europe faced the prospect of bankruptcy for the first time since before 1939. The NEM was based on microeconomic reform rather than the fundamental changes in the macroeconomy which were so desperately required. The government tried to use microeconomic regulators to solve the problem of inflation, while interest rates and the money supply did not enter the equation at all.

In contrast, the economic reform programme adopted by countries of the region after 1990 was characterized by wide-ranging political reform and also the need for Western governmental and institutional involvement in all aspects of the process. A fundamental issue relating to the reform process in all the countries concerned was for each government to establish its priorities and then decide on the sequencing of the reform process. Economic decisions relating to priorities can by no means be separated from the political decision-making process in which some governments may give emphasis to a particular set of policies whilst opposition parties may view the situation quite differently. These elements of debate and conflict which are quite natural within a democratic system have not been very easy for some governments throughout the early period of the reforms.

Problems arising from the implementation of the reforms vary from country to country, but the success of the programme introduced in Poland, Hungary, and Czechoslovakia rested largely on the fact that all of these countries had allowed some degree of private enterprise to exist in the final years of communism. In addition, these countries had also started to see some Western investment from companies forming partnerships with Eastern European state-owned enterprises (SOEs) through JVAs. Another important factor contributing to the success of the reforms was the existence of a largely honest and efficient bureaucracy which had become established, and which was capable of carrying through the complicated process of privatization and fiscal reform. These governments also received strong popular support for the reform programme, and this was particularly true in Czechoslovakia with the personal popularity enjoyed by the President, former dissident poet, Vaclav Havel, imprisoned by the former communist regime. President Havel managed to keep the nation together throughout the difficult period of early reform and also achieved the peaceful separation of Czechoslovakia into the two independent Czech and Slovak Republics in 1993.

The debates relating to the sequencing of economic reform programmes needed to be resolved. These not only involved discussions about the advantages, or otherwise, of the 'big bang' approach versus the gradualist approach, where the market reforms are phased in over a much longer time-period, but also questions about how quickly reforms were introduced within the framework of each overall approach. Although it was difficult to determine an optimal sequence in which the market reforms needed to be followed through, it was obvious that some policies like macroeconomic stabilization measures, privatization, and restructuring would be carried through over a long period of time, whilst the creation of a central bank and small-scale privatization could be implemented almost immediately. However, it should be recognized that all elements of the market reform package are closely interdependent. Reform cannot be achieved merely by price liberalization, since this alone, without macroeconomic stabilization, will produce hyperinflation. In turn, macroeconomic stabilization requires the support of a reformed fiscal and financial system. Although a general consensus among policy-makers was reached on the need for macroeconomic stabilization to precede structural transformation, in practice, however, structural reforms like privatization and deregulation were generally rushed through at the same time.

18.4 Macroeconomic Stabilization Policies

THE economic reform programmes adopted by the countries of Eastern Europe after 1990 generally consisted of a package of several measures.

18.4.1 Price liberalization

This is probably the most straightforward part of the entire reform package since all it involves is an announcement from the government indicating that from henceforth all prices will be determined by the market, that is, by buyers and sellers of goods and services. However, for full price liberalization to be achieved, the government itself needs to reduce its own intervention in the market by withdrawing subsidies from SOEs. The reluctance of some governments to do this has meant that many SOEs continue to face artificial prices and are being protected from potential bankruptcy which could occur if state subsidies are removed. In these circumstances SOEs (and some firms in the private sector) are unlikely to be exposed to competition which, in turn, would encourage restructuring. Persistently inefficient firms would face bankruptcy.

Given that the mechanism of price liberalization is in itself relatively straightforward, the countries of Eastern Europe seem to have had to contend with a number of severe problems arising from the liberalization process itself. For example, inequalities in the distribution of income can occur when some traders gain specialist knowledge about the availability of shortage goods and proceed to buy supplies of such goods at low prices in order to sell high later. It is recognized that no market will be able to function perfectly, but the scope for imperfections to occur is greater in countries which operated shortage economies before 1990 under the central planning system. The presence of monetary or inflationary overhang in the economy exacerbates this situation. This occurs where there is a high level of pent-up demand from consumers wishing to buy goods or services which are in short supply. High and accelerating rates of inflation occur causing additional problems with inequitable income distribution. After 1991 Russia and many of the newly independent states forming the CIS faced these problems after price liberalization, coupled with government enthusiasm for the printing presses, making monetary control impossible if, indeed, it had been attempted at all.

18.4.2 Monetary and fiscal stabilization (balancing the budget)

The use of tight fiscal and monetary policy has been an important feature of the reform packages in Eastern Europe. The successes and failures of such policies have largely determined the outcome of the reform packages themselves. Tight fiscal policies have been achieved by reducing expenditure on subsidies to SOEs, reforming the existing tax system, especially increasing tax rates and introducing VAT. New taxes and higher rates are never popular with the public, but governments were generally forced to place the emphasis on taxes since budget revenues declined as output fell. Fiscal imbalances have forced governments to cut back on social expenditures since there is little scope for increasing the tax burden further. Widespread tax evasion and corruption in the tax collection system (especially in Russia, but less so elsewhere), has led to governments being unable to pay wages to public sector workers. It could be argued that this was pursued as a deliberate policy in Russia following demand from the IMF to cut government expenditure and implement wage controls. In many cases, governments could increase the level of government expenditure by improving tax collection methods. Following an ultimatum received by the IMF, Russia has been forced to examine how its method of tax collection can be made more efficient. The main problem here is the high level of mafia involvement which has led to the complete disappearance of tax revenues in some parts of Russia and the killing of local tax collectors by mafia gunmen in order to obtain access to government monies.

The methods used by countries of the region to finance their budget deficits were generally inflationary. The pressing need to develop a viable financial sector became apparent when non-monetary instruments for deficit financing (i.e. borrowing on domestic financial markets and issuing government securities) were unavailable to most countries due to the lack of financial sector reform. However, Poland and Hungary did manage to meet their budget financing requirements by issuing government securities. In the case of Russia, when external financing was seen to be impossible due to the already high level of indebtedness and the poor international credit rating, the government resorted to borrowing from the central bank, which largely involved increasing the money supply by printing money. Subsequently, the money supply needed to be brought under control after 1994 and resulted in high interest rate policies which choked off investment and produced a flight of funds from savings accounts to safer havens abroad.

18.4.3 External liberalization

In many ways, trade liberalization is one element of external liberalization which should, in theory, be as relatively simple to achieve as the liberalization of prices. In other words, a decision could be taken by the government to eliminate all restrictions on imports and allow prices to be determined by those prevailing on world markets. However, there are two major problems associated with this policy: firstly, by eliminating tariffs the government would also deprive itself of a very useful source of revenue; and secondly, tariffs can be used as a simple policy to protect home industries against competition from abroad, preventing, in the case of the countries of Eastern Europe, wholesale bankruptcies of inefficient SOEs before the process of privatization and restructuring has time to improve the competitiveness of domestic industries. The wider issue of government intervention in the private sector will be discussed in some detail in Chapter 19, whilst the subject of tariffs and the relationship between Eastern Europe and the EU will be dealt with in Chapter 21. It is sufficient to consider here only the use of external tariffs as part of the macroeconomic stabilization process.

The second important element of external liberalization involves the introduction of convertible currencies and an exchange rate mechanism which can be used to determine the rate of exchange, that is, how many units of a domestic currency will be required to purchase one unit of a foreign currency. In order to retain some degree of credibility, a government will endeavour to keep its exchange rate stable. The countries of Eastern Europe have encountered some serious problems in their attempts to introduce currency convertibility and exchange rate stabilization, notably, with no recent history of external liberalization, the sudden exposure of currencies and exports to the vagaries of the markets has meant that most countries in the region have suffered from overvalued currencies, with consequent overpriced exports causing current account deficits. However, it is difficult to determine whether a currency is over- or under-valued in these circumstances as full convertibility has not yet been achieved (except in the Czech Republic in 1995 when full convertibility for capital transactions was introduced). Additional difficulties arise from the underdevelopment of the financial markets and the absence of large stocks of gold and foreign currency reserves which can be used to stabilize currencies under a fixed or pegged exchange rate mechanism. From 1997 financial assistance has been available from the IMF to create a type of Exchange Equalization Account for Bulgaria, Russia, and Ukraine to draw upon when exchange rate stability is threatened.

18.4.4 The creation of the private sector

In order to allow price liberalization to work effectively, state control of production activities had to be relaxed or relinquished altogether. Since 1990 the creation of a viable private sector in the economies of Eastern Europe has been a fundamental part of the reform process in which large-scale privatization has taken place, incentives have been available to allow entrepreneurs to set up SMEs, and governments have encouraged the removal of restrictions on the importation of foreign investment by Western companies intending to establish JVAs with Eastern European firms. Activities by companies operating in the private sector need to be fully supported by a well-developed banking and financial services sector, with both the facility for firms to obtain investment capital and to allow the purchase and disposal of shares through a stock exchange.

In addition, the activities of companies and those of the financial services sector require legal protection, whilst the rights of shareholders and consumers need full legal protection through the introduction of new laws on to the statute book. As it was difficult to initiate the complicated process of developing forms of statutory protection in the early years of the reforms, most countries embarked upon a massive programme of privatization before both essential legal regulations and frameworks for financial markets had been developed. The subject of privatization will be discussed in detail in Chapter 19.

18.5 Problems Facing the Economic Reform Programme

IT is difficult to assess the effectiveness of the economic reforms in Eastern Europe after so short a time-period. In many respects, the reforms are ongoing and some aspects, like fiscal, legal, and currency reform will evolve as the economies develop, possibly over a period as long as two decades. This means that the governments of the region have to draw a fine line between delivering economic success in the short term and so retaining the support of the electorate, and planning the long-term development of the economy to ensure that living standards will rise in the future. Early problems with severe recessions and falling living standards meant that the former communists did well in the 1993 elections in Poland and Bulgaria, whilst difficulties with actually formulating a realistic programme of reform meant that countries like Romania and Bulgaria failed to enjoy dramatic political reform after 1990. In other words, the pendulum has swung between radical economic reform, accompanied by political reform leading to democracy, and the re-election of former communist parties in response to the economic hardships caused by the reforms, signalling a slowdown of the reforms themselves. Despite this 'stop–start' process, there is no doubt that most countries have now made substantial progress and some, like Poland, Hungary, and the Czech Republic, are front-line contenders for full EU membership early in the twenty-first century. Indeed, the former Eastern bloc's old enemies in the West have already indicated their approval of the reform process by their willingness to accept Poland, Hungary, and the Czech Republic into NATO, a development which has demolished any aspirations cherished by Russia to continue in the role as the provider of defence for the East.

In general, macroeconomic stabilization has been successful, with several countries achieving decelerating inflation rates and some, like Hungary, Poland, and the Czech Republic, managing inflation rates which are even respectable by Western standards. In countries where the reform process has been slow, then success with implementing macroeconomic stabilization measures has been very mixed. Although hyperinflation has not been a serious or longer-term problem in the region, rapidly accelerating rates of inflation were experienced by Russia in 1992–93 and also by some of the newly independent states. The fact that such difficulties are being overcome is a tribute to the fact that countries in the region are keen to embrace the idea of economic reform. In addition, privatization has also caused the rapid expansion of the private sector and has led to thousands of SMEs being established, many of which produce goods conferring the advantages of import substitution. Countries which have enjoyed the most economic success have also been able to attract an increasing amount of foreign investment, largely originating from the USA and Japan, with the remainder from mainland Europe.

Countries which continue to face difficulties with the reform process, like Bulgaria, Romania, and the former Soviet Union, have encountered strong resistance towards both political and economic change. People have been opposed to the prospect of change which may mean falling living standards and have shown a deep suspicion of the private sector—a feeling which is often justified given the high level of mafia activity in some countries of the region. In these countries, the wholesale dismantling of the central planning system has left a large void when no feasible alternative has been put in its place. The ensuing economic chaos caused by a lack of macroeconomic control has produced high inflation, declining or negative rates of economic growth, rapidly rising unemployment, increasing levels of poverty, and social inequality where the needs of people are not being met by a weak social welfare system.

If this appears to be an overly pessimistic view of the problems encountered by some countries of the region, there is, in fact, strong support for this view from Jonathan Steele and Richard Layard, who argue that, in the case of Russia, Western governments have been too optimistic about the progress of reform.[6] They claim that Russia is being treated with increasing complacency, on the assumption that the reform process is well under way. The authors point out that the only 'reform' that has met with any degree of success is that which has allowed inflation to fall to single figures per month—a situation which was originally created by the government itself in 1992–93. In addition, privatization has not produced further investment, corruption is rife, and the economy is heavily indebted by foreign loans. Steele and Layard argue that 'Russia today is a political and economic disaster, with one major difference from the Soviet period. At that time, the West bore little responsibility for what was going wrong. Since 1991 the Russia show has been Western-inspired, and Western governments bear a large part of the blame.'[7]

18.6 Summary

Iᴛ has been seen that the economies of the USSR and Eastern Europe were in crisis by the 1980s. The willingness of the leadership of the USSR to turn a blind eye to demands for political reform throughout the region by the late 1980s meant that feasible programmes for reform could be considered for the first time in more than half a century. But in Eastern Europe economic reform was a subject which could not be considered without political reform and this gave impetus to the collapse of the political monopoly of the communist parties in Eastern Europe.

The most successful countries in implementing economic reform, like Poland, Hungary, and the Czech Republic, adopted 'shock therapy' and have made significant progress in reducing the budget deficit and national debt. However, these countries still need to reduce inflation and interest rates, and make serious attempts at industrial restructuring and increasing the pace of privatization. Additional pressure to continue the momentum of reform has recently come from the EU, which will require the countries of Eastern Europe to implement further wide-ranging reforms prior to accession in the early part of the twenty-first century.

Countries which have been less economically successful have tended to pursue a reform programme based on gradualism, but progress has been slow with half-hearted attempts to undertake privatization coupled with little enthusiasm for industrial restructuring. In addition, the foundations for the economic success demonstrated by Poland and Hungary were laid during the 1970s and 1980s when both countries attempted to reform the central planning mechanism. Countries like Bulgaria, Romania, and the former Soviet Union remained unreformed, did little to attract foreign investment, and consequently have made slow economic progress in the 1990s.

Review Questions

1 Was the fall of communism inevitable in Eastern Europe in 1989?

2 For what reasons did some countries in Eastern Europe adopt the 'big bang' 'shock therapy' approach to economic reform whilst others in the region adopted a 'gradualist' approach?

3 Why was it important for the countries of Eastern Europe to adopt a policy of macroeconomic stabilization after 1990?

4 Why have some countries (e.g. Russia) experienced more difficulties with implementing economic reform after 1990 than have other countries in the region?

5 What has been the role of the international financial institutions in the economic reform process in Eastern Europe after 1990?

Group Activity: Reforming a State-owned enterprise

In 1995, Zil, a Russian manufacturer of fridges, trucks, and 'battleship-style' limousines formerly used by Eastern European heads of state, was in need of a Western management and marketing team to revitalize its operations. At one time the company had produced 180,000 trucks a year with a workforce of 186,000, but by 1995 output had declined to 30,000 trucks a year with 25,000 workers. By Russian standards the company's plant was reasonably modern and its workforce had strong technical capabilities, with skilled engineers earning about $1 an hour. Much of the company's market, in the former CMEA area, however, had disappeared. Now privatized through a management and employee buy-out, free of debt but with little capital, few customers, and growing competition from cheap second-hand vehicles in a market suffering from overcapacity, Zil was in desperate need of a new start. Despite having a 600-acre site only a few kilometres from Moscow and considerable technical expertise, the company's designs were twenty years out of date and it had no capital to do anything about it. Adapted from S. Caulkin, 'Zil and the art of motorcar maintenance', *Observer*, 29 Oct. 1995.

Working in groups of three or four in the role of a Western consultant to Zil, each group should now undertake *one* of the following tasks:

1 Investigate the possibility of Zil being able to attract a foreign partner or buyer. What form might such FDI take and what factors would a foreign investor have to take into account before making such a commitment?

2 What difficulties might a foreign investor have to overcome in relation to the general management, human resource management, and internal administration of the company?

3 How might a foreign owner set about developing new products and new markets for the company?

4 Despite the best efforts of the foreign investor and the company's own staff, the political and economic situation in Russia will militate against efficient Western business practices. What sort of problems are they likely to encounter and how might these problems be resolved?

Notes

1 A. Maddison, 'Measuring European growth: the core and the periphery', a paper presented at the *International Economic History Congress, Leuven, Belgium*, 1990.

2 I. T. Berend, 'The collapse of state socialism: causes and consequences', in D. F. Good, *Economic Transformations in East and Central Europe: Legacies from the Past and Policies for the Future* (Routledge, 1994), 79.

3 Ibid. 78.

4 Ibid. 79.

5 M. Lavigne, *The Economics of Transition: From Socialist Economy to Market Economy* (Macmillan, 1995), 92.

6 J. Steele, and R. Layard, 'Russia: boom or bust?', *Observer* (29 Dec.1996).

7 Ibid.

Recommended Reading

■ Buckley, P. J., and Ghauri, P. N., *The Economics of Change in East and Central Europe: its Impact on International Business* (Academic Press, 1994).

■ Gregory, P., and Stuart, R., *Soviet Economic Structure and Performance* (Harper & Row, 1990).

■ Gros, D., and Steinherr, A., *Winds of Change: Economic Transition in Central and Eastern Europe* (Longman, 1995).

■ Nove., A., *An Economic History of the USSR 1917–1991* (Penguin, 1994).

■ Swain, G., and Swain, N., *Eastern Europe Since 1945* (Macmillan, 1993).

19

Privatization in Eastern Europe

Objectives

- to outline the importance and role of privatization in the economic reform process in Eastern Europe after 1990
- to discuss the difficulties encountered by the countries of Eastern Europe when pursuing a policy of rapid privatization
- to identify the different methods of disposing of state-owned enterprises (SOEs) used by the countries of Eastern Europe and their effectiveness

19.1 Introduction

THE history of property ownership had been based on private property relationships before the communist takeovers after 1945. The main feature of the communist system was the emergence of economies where property ownership was the responsibility of the state—private companies were nationalized and turned into administrative units of the state. Apart from a determination to see the political objectives of communism fulfilled (with the emphasis on public ownership not private wealth), wide-scale public ownership was essential to allow the imposition of state control over resource allocation and production through the central planning mechanism.

The rigidly centralized economies in Eastern Europe after 1945 rapidly proved to be inoperable, and as early as the 1950s the communist governments began to introduce a series of economic reforms in an attempt to improve economic performance. The reforms attempted to break down the layers of bureaucracy which had developed in response to the governments' need to exercise control over all aspects of production and over the activities of the enterprises themselves to ensure that they successfully fulfilled national planning targets. Until the 1960s such attempts at reform concentrated mainly on improving central control over the administrative structure at local level responsible for the control of individual enterprise units. The objective was to ensure that centralized control was tightened by removing power from local administrative bodies enabling channels of communication between central bodies and enterprises to become established.

However, the reforms of the late 1960s, notably, the New Economic Mechanism in Hungary in 1968, heralded a movement away from the traditional central planning mechanism of communist economies. The NEM replaced the system of rigid administrative controls over enterprises with indirect controls based on financial indicators and incentives. This was not an attempt by the government to introduce a market-based allocation mechanism at this time, but rather an attempt to bring in a *socialist* market system, giving enterprises incentives but stopping short of radically reforming the existing system of property relationships. The result of the NEM was to strengthen the position of enterprise managers relative to the higher echelons of state bureaucracy. This was reinforced with the introduction of 'Enterprise Councils' in Hungary in 1984 when a large group of enterprises were granted the right of 'self-management'. These 'self-managing' enterprises were members of an Enterprise Council and their managers wielded a great deal of influence over decisions taken by the Councils. By the late 1980s the Hungarian government found it increasingly difficult to cope with the increasing economic difficulties facing the country and, consequently, more and more decision-making powers were devolved to individual enterprises. The 1988 Company Law was the first stage towards creating private property relationships by allowing the creation of subsidiaries within existing enterprises using state-owned assets. In fact, as if by coincidence, the conditions for creating full-scale privatization after 1989 had already been established by the last communist government, whose members were losing control of the central planning mechanism. By permitting the creation of subsidiaries in 1988, the government had already established the pattern which would be taken by the privatization process in Hungary after 1989.

In contrast, the situation in Czechoslovakia was determined by the Soviet-led invasion of 1968 which put an end to any plans held by the government to introduce economic reforms on the same lines as those in Hungary. The economy of Czechoslovakia remained highly centralized in the wake of the Soviet invasion. The Czechs had made the mistake of mixing economic reform with a call for radical political change in the Prague Spring of 1968, providing a strong challenge to the political monopoly of the Communist Party, and therefore, of the Soviet Empire. Whilst many managers of state enterprises in Hungary were able to provide the impetus for privatization in 1990, the situation was reversed in Czechoslovakia, where the impetus came from the new government, often with the result that Czech managers lost power rather than gained it as their powerful Hungarian counterparts had done.

The situation in Poland in the 1980s was characterized by the imposition of martial law in 1981 in an attempt by the communist authorities to retain control in a situation where the powerful workers' movement, Solidarity, continually presented their demands for political and economic change. Despite the imposition of military rule, the communist government gave in to many of the demands of the Solidarity leadership and allowed them substantial concessions. During the 1980s, control over Polish state enterprises not only shifted from state organizations to the enterprises themselves, but was vested in employee councils organized by the workers in a unique experiment in worker participation.

19.2 Why Privatize?

IF privatization is defined as the transfer of more than 50 per cent of the ownership of a business from the public sector to the private sector, the question is what were the governments attempting to achieve by undertaking this process in Eastern Europe after 1990?

19.2.1 Pressures from international financial institutions

Privatization came to be seen as a 'quick-fix' method of creating a private sector in economies where all enterprises had traditionally been in the hands of the state. It could be argued that generally there was no real debate about the advantages and disadvantages of pursuing a policy of rapid privatization throughout the region. Many governments launched into mass privatization irrespective of the difficulties of attracting genuine shareholders with savings to invest and the problems arising from the inability of newly privatized firms to cope with exposure to foreign competition for the first time. Although privatization can be viewed as a method of promoting efficiency in a market economy, private ownership can also be a means of achieving the separation of political and economic decisions. It is argued that it is this separation which can achieve increased efficiency.

The arguments used to promote privatization in Eastern Europe have been supported by international financial institutions like the World Bank and International Monetary Fund (IMF). These are similar to those put forward by the Conservative Government in the UK to justify its extensive, and often controversial, policy of privatization in the 1980s. However, it is difficult to superimpose this free market philosophy on the economies of Eastern Europe where there had been little evidence of legitimate forms of private enterprise before 1989. If privatization was to bring increased efficiency, then greater accountability to shareholders would also bring pressure to restructure, possibly resulting in high levels of unemployment. In 1990, the prospect of mass unemployment was regarded as an inevitable result of a policy which would radically alter the ownership of production. Many state-owned enterprises (SOEs) had been subject to subsidies from government and this had removed any incentive to improve efficiency by removing excessively labour-intensive forms of production and to introduce new technology to improve production methods. The monopolization of production under communism had removed any incentive for firms to seek to achieve productive efficiency. It was the role of SOEs to fulfil their production plans and also maintain full employment by whatever means was necessary. In this way the political and economic objectives of the communist regimes were inextricably linked.

19.2.2 To achieve a reduction in the budget deficit (PSBR)

The scale on which privatization has been undertaken has been massive, although the process itself has been frequently criticized as being too slow. For example, in the 1980s, the UK government took about ten years to privatize approximately 7 per cent of its national output, but Poland, Hungary, and the Czech Republic, on the other hand, tried to transfer about 50 per cent of their output into the private sector within a period of three years. The enormity of the task faced by Eastern European governments was phenomenal. In the UK, the government effectively achieved reductions in the budget deficit (and indeed created a budget surplus) as a result of the revenues from privatization sales. However, in Eastern Europe the same objectives could not be fulfilled due to the massive amount of government expenditure required for restructuring and for maintaining a minimum level of welfare benefits in the face of rising unemployment accompanied by pressures to cut central government expenditure from the IMF.

19.2.3 Promoting and widening share ownership

How far was the drive to promote rapid privatization in Eastern Europe more to do with fulfilling the governments' political objectives as defined by the major international financial institutions than with promoting the economic objectives of improved efficiency and the creation of market incentives? If it is true that Eastern European governments blindly embarked upon a programme of privatization under the auspices of the World Bank and the IMF, then a similar criticism could be levelled at the UK government's privatization programme in the 1980s in that privatization was seen as a means of fulfilling a free market philosophy which meant less intervention in the public sector. The objectives of increasing competition, promoting efficiency, and widening share ownership cannot be fulfilled when a substantial proportion of the public sector subject to privatization is represented by the public utilities.

The problems which faced the privatized utilities in the UK have been similar to those encountered by many former SOEs in Eastern Europe, although the gas, electricity, and water industries in the UK were subject to restructuring before privatization. Nevertheless, difficulties relating to efficiency arising from the monopolization of industry under communism have been seen to continue in a free market. In any case, the tendency of newly privatized shares to be sold at a quick profit by first-time shareholders in the UK and then purchased by large institutional shareholders has been replicated in Eastern Europe, although some countries like the Czech Republic distributed some shares free in the first instance. In Eastern Europe privatization was regarded by reformers as an opportunity to redress the balance of society by promoting more egalitarian methods of property ownership. This was the case in the Czech Republic where the free distribution of shares was seen to be a great success. Members of the public generally felt that they could take an active part in the reform process by exercising their right to exchange their share vouchers for real shares in privatized companies. However, the Russian experience indicates that the opposite is true. Share vouchers which had been distributed free in 1992 with a face value of 10,000 roubles were subsequently seen to be circulating on the black market with a face value of only 4,000 roubles. It should be noted that a British football supporter would be unlikely to obtain a Wembley FA Cup Final ticket on the black market for *less* than the price advertised by the football club, but would expect to have to pay many times more than this! This example serves to demonstrate that the government's privatization programme was generally unpopular in Russia.

In the UK, Lord Stockton, the former Conservative Prime Minister Harold Macmillan, noted in the House of Lords that privatization of UK national assets was similar to the situation faced by the landed gentry when selling off the family silver. In other words, once such a transaction has taken place, it is unlikely that the state will be able to return that company to the public sector in the future. Indeed, this was a sentiment with which many people in Russia could feel sympathy—the prevailing view was that since SOEs were communally owned, the practice of selling them to the public was pointless as the public already owned these assets which were held in trust by the state. However, the public possessed neither the cash nor the enthusiasm to undertake share ownership. In Russia, there was no attempt by the government to carry the public along with the tide of reform as had been achieved so successfully with the free share distributions in the Czech Republic. The shortage of willing shareholders in Russia meant that shares of newly privatized companies fell into the hands of the *nomenklatura* (former communists who continue to hold high government office), organized crime, or were bought by large foreign institutional investors or foreign companies. The utopian view put forward by political commentators on the Right in the UK that privatization could act as a form of social engineering by reorientating the balance of society, has also been unable to achieve credibility in Russia.

19.3 Method and Form of Privatization: Differences in Approach

19.3.1 Hungary

By the late 1980s, state control of industry in Hungary was being eroded after the Company Law of 1988 permitted SOEs to create subsidiaries with part of their assets. Although this meant that only a small proportion of their assets were genuinely held by private shareholders, the process was extended in 1989 with the enacting of the Transformation Law by which Enterprise Councils were allowed to transform SOEs as a whole into private companies. Although this process has been called 'spontaneous privatization', it did not actually represent anything as far-reaching, given that ownership usually remained in the hands of state institutions, albeit state banks, other SOEs, or similar corporate entities created as a result of 'spontaneous privatization'.

Nevertheless, the process did achieve a significant loss of influence by the state over the activities of the newly privatized SOEs. In order to establish overall control and

Table 19.1 Methods of privatization in Russia and Eastern Europe

Method	Country							
	PL	H	CZ	SK	R	BG	ROM	SL
Mass privatization (mainly free vouchers)			✓	✓	✓		✓	
Sectoral privatization (sale of whole industry)	✓	✓				✓		
Auctions (small firms, e.g. shops, restaurants)	✓	✓	✓	✓	✓	✓	✓	✓
MBOs/EBOs	✓	✓			✓			
Restitution/compensation (to former owners) (none in CIS countries)		✓	✓	✓	✓[a]	✓		
Direct sales to foreign investors or through existing JVAs	✓	✓[b]	✓	✓	✓	✓	✓	✓

[a] Restitution in kind for land only in Russia.
[b] Although assets have been sold to foreign investors in all countries, this method has been practised almost exclusively in Hungary.

Key: PL = Poland; H = Hungary; CZ = Czech Republic; SK = Slovakia; R = Russia; BG = Bulgaria; ROM = Romania; SL = Slovenia.

scrutiny of privatization practice the State Property Agency (SPA) was set up by the government in 1990. In reality, the SPA was seen to exercise merely a supervisory role and did not manage to significantly influence the pattern of privatization in Hungary in the 1990s. Indeed, it could be argued that far from avoiding the issue of instituting a mass privatization programme in the early 1990s, the government played safe and delivered a programme which was actually thought to be more palatable to the general public who may have resented a process where ownership fell into the hands of a small number of large private investors. Although methods of privatization involving the free distribution of shares were not favoured by the government, other methods involving discounts on share purchases by existing workers and managers did generate some support for privatization from the general public.

Despite this, assets of privatized companies tend to be grossly undervalued and criticism arose when it was seen that foreign investors were being encouraged to acquire substantial stakes in privatizing Hungarian companies. In 1990 about 200 companies were privatized by closed tender and sold to established partners, foreign companies, and other organizations offering a more secure future than if firms had been offered solely to Western investors. The SPA did exercise some control over the resulting activities of companies involved in privatization, like asset-stripping and attachment of liabilities to other SOEs. Nevertheless, a public outcry ensued over what was perceived as evidence of corrupt practices and much of the criticism was not only levelled at the government but also at the foreign investors themselves. However, this did not prevent an increase in foreign investment and, ultimately, foreign ownership occurring during the early 1990s.

About four-fifths of the first 200 SOEs to be privatized were purchased by foreign investors, who were particularly attracted by the prospect of acquiring shares in consumer goods companies in order to increase their existing market share. By the end of 1992 it was estimated that more that 15 per cent of state property had been privatized, but not all of it successfully.[1] However, by 1993 it had started to become apparent that the enthusiasm previously shown by foreign investors had become dampened by the prevalence of high interest rates, so that many large private investors and foreign multinationals had switched their allegiances to Poland and the Czech Republic where new investment opportunities were becoming available.

In order to appease the growing public disquiet over the foreign ownership of traditional Hungarian companies, the government has recently undertaken more stock exchange privatizations and introduced methods of payment by instalments to attract small, domestic investors. In addition, a compensation scheme was introduced to assist those who had suffered confiscation of assets when the communists nationalized private companies after seizing power in 1945. The benefits of private ownership were further extended when small businesses like grocery shops and restaurants were sold to their existing tenants.

19.3.2 Czechoslovakia

The problem of attracting purchasers of shares in privatized companies has dogged the governments of the countries of Eastern Europe in their bid to implement rapid privatization programmes in the 1990s. This was overcome effectively in Czechoslovakia by distributing the majority of shares free to the population by issuing vouchers under the scheme devised by Vaclav Klaus. In a situation where an enterprise employed more that 500 people, a proportion of the share equity was exchanged for vouchers and the remainder was sold through auctions or direct sales. In practice, many people placed their vouchers at the disposal of investment fund managers who then acquired a portfolio of assets on their clients' behalf. Inevitably, this has placed investment funds in a very powerful position in the economy, despite the fact that the banking institutions have been restricted to ownership of one-tenth of privatized property.[2]

In contrast to Hungary, economic reforms had been very limited in Czechoslovakia after the Soviet crackdown in 1968. In other words, the control of SOEs remained centralized, with little or no power vested in the hands of enterprise managers, as had been the case in Hungary after 1968. It was not possible for Czechoslovak managers to easily acquire assets in SOEs, as in the case of the process of 'spontaneous privatization' which took place in Hungary in the late 1980s. It could be argued that the unreformed Czechoslovak economy actually ensured a more equitable process of privatization than was the case in Hungary. In effect, Czechoslovak managers were in no position to ensure that they received preferential treatment from the process itself. However, privatization of small firms has generally been carried out through auctions, although restitution and compensation has been awarded to the former owners (or their descendants) of businesses seized by the communists after 1945.

After the completion of the 'velvet divorce' and the creation of two separate republics in 1993, the Czech Republic continued with its programme of privatization whilst the new government in Slovakia orchestrated a slowdown in the speed of privatization there. The Slovakian government claimed that it needed to give priority to employment and that jobs could be better protected by retaining control of enterprises by the state. The combination of the slowing down of the reform programme, suspicion of Western investment, recent political scandals reaching the highest echelons of government, and the display of a xenophobic attitude towards Slovakia's minority community of Hungarians has not helped to foster good relationships with the international community, though a new, more pro-Western government was elected in October 1998.

Although privatization in the Czech Republic has been more rapid and was sustained by a second wave of privatization taking place in 1994, in the early years SOEs were sold off before a stock exchange could be established. In addition, privatization has occurred without substantial restructuring in the majority of industries. The reason that high rates of unemployment failed to occur as had been predicted was due mainly to continued subsidization by the government and the delay of substantive restructuring. However, it is also true that many people left their employment with SOEs to start their own businesses.

Modernization and restructuring has been led by foreign firms which may have initially entered the market to establish Joint-Venture Agreements (JVAs) with Czech SOEs, but then acquired a substantive shareholding on privatization. In former SOEs where foreign investors or Western multinationals hold the majority of assets, the average level of wages and labour productivity levels are higher than in similar industries where foreign involvement is absent. However, the general lack of extensive restructuring has meant that privatization has not produced efficiency gains for the companies involved. Some foreign investors have been seen to abuse their power in the market in the absence of anti-competition law, by exploiting the monopolistic nature of industry in the Czech Republic (and elsewhere in Eastern Europe). As a result, there has been no shortage of foreign investment, and the government has not seen the need to provide financial incentives to attract foreign capital, especially with the continued interest shown by German investors and also with the increasing number of North American multinationals entering the market.

19.3.3 Poland

In Poland, the Privatization Law of 1990 laid down two methods of privatization, both demonstrating that the balance of power in SOEs which had shifted in favour of employees was maintained even throughout the period of martial law during the 1980s. The Privatization Law was the driving force which influenced the form privatization would take in the 1990s. The first method of privatization allowed an SOE to become a joint-stock or limited liability corporation which could then undergo privatization with shares being offered for sale to the public or directly to large domestic or foreign investors (usually institutions or MNEs). This process became known as 'corporatization', but also meant that little or no restructuring of the SOE had taken place prior to sale. However, the 1990 Law required the consent of the majority of the workforce, which gave them the opportunity to block the privatization process. In reality, the government had the power under the Law to veto or overrule any attempt by the workforce to hamper the privatization process by withdrawing their consent. There has been, as yet, no attempt by the government to intervene in the privatization process in this way, and it is unlikely that it will do so in the future. In effect, the progress of privatization has remained very slow through the corporatization method and has not been popular with workers' representatives in SOEs.

The second method of privatization is initiated by employees and management and has involved the sale of assets of SOEs to newly created corporations. The shares are offered for sale at preferential rates to existing workers and managers with the provision to allow shares to be acquired over a period of time, thereby eliminating the need to raise capital quickly. Of course, some workers' and managers' groups have successfully raised capital in partnership with the financial institutions. All SOEs privatized in this way have generally been sold at rates which are well below market valuation. However, it has been difficult to ascertain accurate and true company valuations in economies which have little experience of exposure to market forces until recently. Consequently, it appears that most company valuations in Poland were kept low in order to achieve rapid privatization.

Problems relating to valuation have, perhaps, been more clearly seen in the privatization of small retail units where the incumbent tenant or manager has generally been successful in acquiring the business at an extremely preferential rate. This practice has become known as 'insider privatization'. It can be argued that local authorities responsible for the disposal of small SOEs in Poland have actually contributed to restricting competition in the SME sector by preventing new entrepreneurs from entering the market and bidding for small business units. The pressure of demand from this group of entrepreneurs could well have bid up the market price of small firms sold through auctions, and consequently, it could be argued that a substantial source of revenue for local authorities has been lost.

Despite successes gained with the privatization of small businesses, the overall privatization process was slow in the period up to 1994 due to the shortage of capital available for the purchase of shares in the private sector. The failure of quoted stock exchange companies to announce dividends in 1992 did not fill potential investors with enthusiasm, while many SOEs on the list for privatization were so unprofitable and their practices so rigidly entrenched in the past, the state actually had difficulties giving shares away to potential investors. Since 1994, the government has attempted to move towards a policy of mass privatization involving the sale of shares at full price to private investors and investment funds. Although one-fifth of shares in larger SOEs have been offered to employees at discounted rates, the government has rejected the idea of free share distributions in Poland, popular elsewhere in the region, since it takes the view that it is difficult to establish and foster values of ownership and responsibility among new shareholders using this method. This process has been slowed down as a result of the opposition from the trade unions towards the general process of privatization in recent years. Trade unions have expressed the view that employees have lost out during the reform process due to falling wages, also eroded by high inflation and rising unemployment.

In 1995 the government permitted five privately managed National Investment Funds (NIFs) to be established to deal with the privatization of 512 SMEs. But by mid-1997 there was criticism of the slow pace of privatization since there were still 3,700 companies left in state hands. The Poles plan to extend the NIF concept of privatizing companies through independent funds to the remaining SOEs. However, it is essential to ensure that the government passes legislation to specify that the fund managers' role is to restructure companies, not just be passive investors, and that fund management needs to be depoliticized as soon as possible, by including foreigners among fund managers. By mid-1997 all NIFs had made a loss in the first year as it became apparent that companies could not avoid direct restructuring—accounting has to be sorted out, technology caught up with and, more importantly, direction imposed on companies. Although at present the fund managers' chief concern is to reshape companies' business and marketing strategy, there is little evidence of the serious work of restructuring taking place in terms of raising capital for investment and sorting out the problem of overmanning of about 20–40 per cent of the labour force. However, the NIF programme was not only concerned with privatization and restructuring but it was also a political move to make privatization popular.

19.3.4 Romania

The case of Romania in its attempts to introduce privatization will be discussed here since its experience provides an interesting contrast to that of other countries in the region. Before 1990 Romania was governed by a rigidly totalitarian government which effectively strangled any attempts to introduce measures designed to reform the central planning mechanism on the same lines as those introduced in Poland, Czechoslovakia, and Hungary from the 1970s. Strict central control was maintained by the state over all aspects of economic and political life. The sinister and corrupt leader, Nicolae Ceaucescu, maintained this system of rigid central control through an elaborate network of security police informers and terror tactics employed by the security police itself. In other words, after the televised execution of the hated Ceaucescu and his wife in late 1989, Romania was left with an unreformed centrally planned economy which, in theory, meant that privatization could be implemented without the presence of any real opposition from employees' organizations and other interest groups. In reality, it was the ensuing political instability which caused delays with the implementation of economic reforms during the 1990s.

After the introduction of the Privatization Law in 1991, about 70 per cent of shares in SOEs were transferred to the State Ownership Fund (SOF), modelled on Germany's Treuhand, while the remaining 30 per cent were allocated to five Private Ownership Funds (POFs), the latter being owned by Romanian citizens through their 'Certificates of Ownership' distributed to members of the public in an attempt to allocate free shares in privatizing companies.[3] The main features of this system were a mixture of free share allocation and public share issues. Under the Privatization Law 1991, the SOF was charged with selling off one-seventh of its holdings of shares every year, with the result that all holdings by the state would be disposed of within seven years. The retention of a substantial stake in privatized SOEs by the government agency has caused problems of excessive bureaucratization in an economy where few people have experience or knowledge of the working of market-based institutions. However, it is difficult to know what the alternative could have been in Romania—with a shortage of private investors, exacerbated by the continuing political and economic uncertainties which have beset the country after 1990, the government probably had little choice but to adopt a method of privatization which would avoid a short-term flooding of the market for shares for which there continued to be a chronic shortage of purchasers. But continued government involvement at a high level also invites the criticism of unnecessary government intervention after privatization has taken place. The use of subsidies and other artificial methods of support have meant that some firms have failed to improve efficiency and would probably have been candidates for bankruptcy without state intervention.

Despite the shortage of willing investors and the free distribution of vouchers to the public through POFs, an enthusiastic black market became established, with books of vouchers reaching 100,000 times their original value in some regions of Romania. Apart from speculative activity surrounding the price of voucher books, the pace of privatization was deliberately slowed down by the vested political interests of the *nomenklatura*. However, it is possible that in some parts of government there was real concern about the fate of state dinosaurs being privatized quickly and then bankrupted with even greater rapidity.

In 1995–1996 the pace of privatization in Romania was accelerated when the government introduced a scheme to distribute non-transferable vouchers to the public amounting to 60 per cent of the equity available for allocation. Although more than 70 per cent of citizens invested their vouchers, the companies themselves remained stagnant, unprofitable, and in desperate need of comprehensive restructuring. In addition, the state remained the majority shareholder in most privatized companies. Although shares in SOEs have been offered to foreign firms, there has been little interest shown compared to elsewhere in the region. Romania's continuing economic and political difficulties have meant that foreign investors have taken opportunities elsewhere in the region where risks are lower and the reform programme is more established, especially in Poland, Hungary, and the Czech Republic. The government was to have completed its privatization programme by 1998 in order to keep to the seven-year target set in 1991. The privatization agency, the SOF, increased the pace of privatization in 1997 by increasing the number of privatizing companies by 40 per cent on the list from the previous year.

19.3.5 The former German Democratic Republic

The introduction of monetary, economic, and social union in August 1990 meant that complete reunification could be undertaken by the end of the same year. Of course, reunification had major implications for the economic development of a region in which former GDR firms faced competition from established West German or foreign multinationals almost overnight. In addition, the exchange rate of the Ostmark against the Deutsche Mark underwent substantial revaluation with the currency reform which converted Ostmarks into DM at 1:1 with large holdings (over 4,000) being exchanged at 2:1. This massive appreciation of the Ostmark by over 300 per cent meant that goods produced by former GDR SOEs suddenly became more expensive and difficult to sell. This was exacerbated by the steady influx of West German goods into the Eastern market where the demand for 'Western' goods had become insatiable in a market which had been deprived of a wide selection of good-quality products for so long. The difficulties associated with reunification caused economic problems symptomatic of recession, a phenomenon which was experienced by West Germany for the first time since the completion of reconstruction after the end of World War II. Notably, the rate of unemployment had risen to 17.2 per cent by 1993 despite the introduction of numerous government-supported education and training programmes.[4]

The privatization process was assisted by the creation of an agency, the Treuhand-anstalt, set up by the government of the GDR in early 1990, whose role was to take over the assets of SOEs targeted for privatization and to identify those which could be sold off quickly without the need for prior restructuring. SOEs accounted for 88 per cent of net output in 1988, with cooperatives accounting for a further 8.4 per cent.[5] The Treuhand was also charged with the task of dismantling the institutions of the former regime in the GDR, including properties belonging to the secret police and the armed forces. Some conglomerates were too large and unwieldy to attract potential purchasers, so these were broken up into smaller units, although examples of SOEs attracting heavy government subsidies were a constant problem. Many companies in this situation did not survive long after privatization and became subjects for bankruptcy. In many cases, the Treuhand identified possible purchasers from among firms producing similar products in West Germany or in other parts of Western Europe. This was one way of increasing foreign investment into the region, but it also effectively destroyed competition and encouraged monopolization in the industries concerned.

The Treuhand had supervised the privatization of as many as 3,400 enterprises by the summer of 1991. By 1994 its role had come to an end with only 350 enterprises left to privatize. The Treuhand was disbanded and the remaining enterprises passed to the supervision of the Ministry of Finance. Small enterprises in the service sector nationalized in 1972 were privatized by returning them to their former owners, or by paying compensation where a small business had been absorbed into a large enterprise. However, the process has been complicated by numerous claims from dispossessed owners of properties seized by the communists after 1949. The main difficulty arises from property disputes involving confiscation under the Nazi regime prior to 1945. It is recognized that it may take until the early part of the 21st century to achieve a satisfactory solution to this problem. Indeed, the privatization process has actually been suspended in cases where there are ongoing disputes over ownership rights.

19.3.6 The former Soviet Union

In Russia and the newly independent states of the former Soviet Union, the chaotic political and economic conditions have meant that any attempts to follow a normal privatization programme, similar to that introduced by the countries of Eastern Europe, has not been successful. Difficulties arising from the economic transition process relating to the inability of many new governments to establish viable reform programmes has meant that the economic conditions have not been conducive to the creation of new enterprises in Russia and the former Soviet republics. This has meant that the process of privatization has been characterized not necessarily by the mass sale of state assets and the creation of many SMEs from small SOEs in the service sector, but by the retention of state control in many 'privatized' enterprises by introducing a leasing arrangement from state agencies. Retention of some control by the state tends to discourage efficiency and competition—both of these objectives are generally best served by a system of ownership where 100 per cent of the firm's assets are in private hands.

Early attempts to introduce limited privatization in the Soviet Union began in 1987 when the Law on State Enterprises was introduced by the new General Secretary of the Communist Party, Mikail Gorbachev, appointed in 1985. This permitted employees working in state enterprises in the service sector (small shops, restaurants, etc.) to form workers' collectives or cooperatives consisting of two or more members. In effect, this also constituted an attempt by the state to legalize the 'second economy'—consisting of numerous semi-legal private enterprises in the service sector which had already been operating on a substantial scale. This was not an attempt to introduce full-scale privatization in a centrally planned economy, although it has been argued that this was the first stage of privatization in the Soviet Union. However, it seems likely that Gorbachev envisaged the possibility of radically reforming the centrally planned economy by introducing a marketized sector. This did not constitute an attempt to abandon socialism and socialist forms of ownership, but rather, it represented a desire to introduce a system of incentives into the economy aimed to increase the productivity of workers and managers. Indeed, these reforms actually stopped short of bringing in more radical methods of property ownership which characterized capitalism and which amounted to the wholesale transfer of assets from the state to the private sector.

The Decree on Leasing and Lease Relations introduced in 1989 was the second important legislative development during *perestroika* which permitted the establishment of 'leased enterprises'. These were SOEs whose assets were 'leased' from the state usually by existing insider managers and occasionally by existing workers. Whilst cooperatives were generally relatively small, averaging about twenty five workers, leased enterprises were typically much bigger, averaging about 700 workers each, and their activities were not confined to the service sector.

In the latter period of *perestroika* until the disintegration of the Soviet Union in 1991, no formal programme of privatization was established despite rhetorical calls for one in the doomed '500 Day Plan' put forward by the economists, Stanislav Shatalin and Grigor Yavlinsky in late 1990. The three significant events relating to privatization which occurred up to the time of the failed coup attempt against Soviet President Gorbachev in August 1991 were, firstly, the conversion of a large number of cooperatives into small private firms, although some new firms were established by individual entrepreneurs. Secondly, as a result of the Soviet Law on Ownership in 1990, managers and workers of a number of leased enterprises were permitted to buy out their leased assets at prices below current valuation. Thirdly, a phenomenon known as '*nomenklatura* privatization' achieved increasing popularity during 1991. This consisted of the conversion of SOEs into private enterprises in which the major shareholders were former managers or public officials or agencies. The period from 1990–1 saw an increase in the number of leased enterprises of about 6 per cent but the number of private enterprises increased by only 1 per cent in the same period.[6]

The new administration under President Boris Yeltsin started to speed up the process of privatization in late 1991 by increasing the sale of small enterprises and buying back large enterprises which had previously undergone *nomenklatura* privatization, so that the latter could be prepared for full privatization by public share issue. However, the main problems relating to the issue of privatization in Russia in recent years have been the disputes inherent in the government. Privatization has become a political football, although it seems that all sides are agreed about the policy in principle, but bitter disputes have been fought by opposing groups in government over the form and pace which the privatization process should take. However, the privatization programme adopted by the Yeltsin administration in June 1992 represented a compromise between radical reformers and those members of the government who wanted a more gradual approach to be adopted.

In the case of small enterprises with up to 200 employees and a book value of capital of less than 10 million roubles (at January 1992 prices) these were to be privatized through open auctions in which insiders (managers and workers) as well as the general public would be willing to place bids. The plan was to privatize 50 per cent of the 200,000 small enterprises from the service sector by the end of 1992. In the case of medium to large enterprises with employees of between 1,000 and 10,000 or a book value of capital from 50 to 150 million roubles (at January 1992 prices) these were converted into joint-stock companies before the public sale of shares was undertaken. A slightly different approach was adopted for about 6,000 enterprises comprising SOEs largely in the industrial sector. For these companies, once joint-stock status had been reached, employees were allowed to make a choice between three different privatization options. Firstly, a minority non-voting share ownership of 25 per cent for insiders distributed free of charge, with the remainder being offered for sale to workers, and foreign and domestic investors. Secondly, an option for insiders to purchase voting shares of up to 51 per cent of the total authorized capital at a concessional rate, with the remainder of the shares being sold through public auctions. The third option was the formation of a one-year agreement with insiders to restructure the enterprise in order to avoid bankruptcy. If successful, they would gain the right to purchase 20 per cent of the shares at a concessional rate.

Other large firms were classified as 'strategic enterprises' or were those with over 10,000 employees, and could only be privatized, if at all, with the direct permission of the government. 'Strategic enterprises' were likely to be in the extractive, energy generation, space, or nuclear industries. It was possible for these industries to undergo corporatization, but only on condition that the state retained a controlling share in the company and that foreign investors were excluded from share ownership.

In order to encourage Russian citizens to participate in the privatization process, they were issued with free share vouchers with a face value of 10,000 roubles. The total value of the vouchers distributed free amounted to approximately 35 per cent of the book value of 600 medium and large-scale enterprises which were due to be privatized by the end of 1993. Russian citizens could use their vouchers to purchase shares in joint-stock companies due to be privatized or bid for enterprises sold through auctions, or deposit them in investment trusts or sell them for cash to a private buyer. However, in 1993 vouchers were fetching only 50 per cent of their face value on the secondary market as many people quickly exchanged them for cash.

The evidence suggests that until 1993 the pace of privatization was more rapid in the service sector where enterprises were generally small and therefore could be presented as more affordable to shareholders. Estimates suggest that out of 218,000 SOEs due to be privatized in 1992–3 about 60,000 had been sold by the first quarter of 1993.[7] By the middle of 1993 voucher privatization was more or less complete—over 80 per cent of Russian industry had been sold.[8] Despite this, the revenue received by government from privatized assets remained below target. At January 1992 prices, privatization proceeds amounted to about 15 billion roubles, only 16 per cent of the targeted revenue total of 92 billion roubles.[9]

Although privatization in the former Soviet Union has been largely dominated by insider control (with the attendant problems of poor incentives to ensure improved efficiency) there was evidence that by the end of 1993 privatization was attracting interest from potential large institutional investors like the newly established commercial banks. In general, it is the underdeveloped state of the financial markets in the region which has undermined the process of privatization and the possibility of insider knowledge has meant that large blocks of shares have fallen into the hands of the *nomenklatura*. The success of privatization in the former Soviet Union will depend on the continued development of an independent financial sector, the implementation of Western-style accounting and regulatory procedures to reduce the incidence of further corruption. Privatization will need to ensure that increased competition can be achieved, greater availability of incentives to managers and workers, and also methods of attracting and retaining increasing levels of foreign investment need to be explored. Although privatization in the former Soviet Union has been subject to much valid criticism, it is generally thought that Russia's rapid privatization programme now needs to go through a period of consolidation so that those companies which can function efficiently in a commercial environment can be identified.

19.4 Privatization and Regulation of Utilities

IN centrally planned economies public utilities, railways, telecommunications, and energy industries were relatively weak because of the low investment priorities of the governments of Eastern Europe and the Soviet Union. Their lack of modern infrastructure and use of obsolete technology meant that they lagged far behind similar industries in market economies. On the other hand, low prices led to excess demand and the tendency to misuse scarce energy resources at a time when producers and consumers in Western economies were being urged to conserve energy resources and also try to reduce the associated problem of pollution.

Inevitably, as a result of the methods of organizing production under central planning, industries in Eastern Europe have shown a tendency towards monopolization, a phenomenon which Western governments endeavour to control through regulatory frameworks. The solution for Eastern Europe would seem to be the introduction of increased competition by breaking up industries into smaller production units, or by encouraging competition by allowing the entry of other firms into the industry. However, it has been argued that in the case of energy and water suppliers, the service can often be provided more cheaply by one single firm serving a particular area. This does not imply that the industry necessarily must remain monopolistic, but that some parts of it must remain so (the distribution networks in the energy supply industries), while other parts could attract competition (energy generation and supply can be potentially competitive as in the case of the electricity and gas industries in the UK during the 1990s).

The Eastern European countries face four main problems when deciding how to manage the utilities: who should own the utilities (the state or private investors, foreign or domestic investors); the nature of the regulatory structure; the desirability of allowing entry and competition; and how to determine procedures for fixing price structures. The ownership of the utilities is an important issue in Eastern Europe. Although governments have naturally tended towards maintaining control by the state, in practice, good arguments can be distinguished for allowing some element of private ownership and so attracting an influx of new investment into the industry. The process of economic transition has placed an increasingly heavy burden on government finances and has prevented governments from being able to afford to provide new investment themselves. In addition, other sources of new capital from the World Bank and the European Bank for Reconstruction and Development (EBRD), may be more inclined to contribute if they can see that substantial private investment is already involved.

Important decisions also have to be made about the regulatory function in the utility industries. In general, the Western view has been to separate the regulatory function from those running the business, and in the case of the UK and the USA, regulation has normally been undertaken by an independent agency. An important advantage of this would be that an independent regulatory agency would be removed from the political process and a regulator may intervene to promote competition or increase/decrease prices with less opposition than would be faced by a government. However, there is also a view that regulation should be the responsibility of the government and should not be removed from political control.

19.5 Summary

THE transfer of public property into the private sector is a fundamental policy underpinning the economic (and political) transition process in the former Soviet Union and Eastern Europe. Privatization is the single element of transition policy which straddles both the economic and political spheres. In the economy, privatization is part of the process necessary to create a private sector with the associated objectives of increasing efficiency and promoting competition. In the political environment, privatization can achieve the transfer of power from the hands of the political élite (or *nomenklatura*) into the hands of ordinary citizens with the widening of share ownership and the benefits which arise from less interference in the activities of enterprises by the state once they transfer into the private sector. But how far have the experiences of countries in the region demonstrated the truth of these arguments?

There is no doubt that privatization cannot succeed in circumstances where there is no attempt to restructure enterprises prior to the sale. At best, such firms will limp along for a short time in the private sector, and then, in the absence of state subsidies or a rescue bid by a foreign investor, bankruptcy will result. A full programme of restructuring constitutes a complete overhaul of all current practices adopted by the enterprise, especially in relation to management and labour practices, use of technology, the introduction of Western methods of accounting and financial control, and the implementation of modern sales and marketing techniques. Poland has been largely successful in this respect as a result of the use of the NIFs to ensure that restructuring takes place since investment managers can usually be relied upon to operate through self-interest to increase the value of their fund holdings. If NIFs are completely independent from the state this reduces the amount of political interference in an often painful restructuring process. However, there have been plenty of examples in Poland of SOEs delaying restructuring through political influence. The classic case is the Lenin Shipyard in Gdansk, Lech Walesa's former workplace, a company which avoided restructuring for years, with the inevitable result of bankruptcy.

It could be argued that since the Poles were late-starters at privatization they learned from the mistakes of the Czechs who were early starters with their comprehensive programme of voucher privatization. Most Czech enterprises have now been privatized with about 75 per cent of the economy in private hands. This method of voucher privatization was uniquely original resulting in one of the highest percentages of small shareholders in the world. However, it has been argued by Milos Zeman, leader of the opposition Czech Social Democratic Party, that the Marxists had the same idea: ownership of property by the people with all citizens becoming symbolic co-owners of the national wealth.[10] The question is: did privatization after 1990 really alter this situation? Zeman argues that to have millions of owners each holding only a few shares is the same as having no real owners. He claims that most small shareholders have invested their shares in investment funds which now own the majority of enterprises. The funds themselves are largely owned by the banks and the majority of the banks are still in the hands of the state. Indeed, twelve out of a total of sixty Czech banks have themselves collapsed since the reforms began. Corporate governance and restructuring are determined by the short-term view taken by the banks in the absence of private owners of enterprises who are capable of restructuring the enterprise and who possess sufficient sources of independent capital.

In any case, there has been criticism in most countries in the region of the nature of the ownership which privatization often produces. For example, in Russia, scandals in high government circles have emerged during the course of 1997 concerning the concentration of privatized firms in the hands of a few powerful individuals with close government connections. The establishment of 'hard core' shareholders has led to disputes among politicians who have claimed that the ministers in government in charge of privatization have favoured their friends. The actual managers of newly privatized companies are often the former ones owing to the difficulties of finding able managers willing to do the job. The problem remains for all countries in the region that privatization has largely resulted in either corporate governance by insiders (former managers or workers or both) or control by intermediaries (investment funds, banks, etc.) which are, in many cases, in the hands of foreign investors.

Review Questions

1 What methods of privatization were used by Russia and the countries of Eastern Europe after 1990?

2 How did the privatization process adopted in Russia and Eastern Europe in the 1990s differ from the methods adopted by the Thatcher Government in the UK during the 1980s?

3 Was mass privatization the optimum solution for Russia and Eastern Europe after 1990 and how far did they achieve their objectives?

4 How far did the process of privatization in the former GDR differ from elsewhere in Russia and Eastern Europe?

5 What are the factors which need to be taken into account by the governments of Russia and Eastern Europe when undertaking the privatization of the public utilities?

Study Topic: Privatization in Poland

In August 1998, the Polish government announced its intention to accelerate the privatization of several important sectors, including steel, telecommunications, and sugar. Despite a number of similar announcements in the past, privatization of these sectors has been slow to materialize. State-owned enterprises, numbering well over 3,000, still employed 45 per cent of Poland's industrial workforce in 1998. These companies are generally less competitive, less profitable, and invest less than private sector companies. An OECD report claims that SOEs are investing only about the same as they did in the early 1990s, whereas investment in the private sector increased by 50 per cent.

The sugar industry is a sensitive sector whose future is bound up with the reform of Poland's large agricultural sector, but government control has kept the sugar industry fragmented, outdated, and inefficient. An estimated $2 billion investment in new plant is needed to modernize the industry. Whilst this level of investment may not be immediately available in the private sector, state ownership has delayed the necessary restructuring of the sugar-refining industry, based as it is on small-scale, scattered production units in a similar way to Poland's farms. Similar problems exist in Poland's telecommunication industry. TPSA, the state telecommunications operator, has been held back from privatization in an attempt to secure a better price for this important asset, whereas other countries in the region have attracted strategic foreign partners. The result is that Poland's telecommunications system remains poor.

Poland's generally favourable economic performance has obscured its patchy record on privatization. Fortunately, the country is one of the more attractive locations for foreign investors, but delays in the privatization programme have left some of Poland's key sectors unreconstructed. (Adapted from *Business Central Europe*, (Sept. 1998, Editorial, 5.)

Study Topic Questions

1 What was the role of privatization in the economic transition process in Eastern Europe after 1990?

2 What was Poland's approach to privatization and how did this differ from the experience of Russia?

3 Why has Poland been slower to privatize than some of its neighbours, despite a reputation for fast-track reform?

4 In what ways is privatization likely to benefit industries like sugar, telecommunications, and steel in Poland?

5 In what ways can privatization contribute to attracting and retaining FDI in Poland?

Notes

1 J. Karsai and M. Wright, 'Accountability, governance and finance in Hungarian buy-outs', *Europe-Asia Studies*, 46 (1994): 997–1016.

2 D. Turnock, *The East European Economy in Context: Communism and Transition* (Routledge, 1997), 179.

3 J. S. Earle, R. Frydman, and A. Rapaczynski, *Privatization in the Transition to a Market Economy* (Pinter, 1993), 10.

4 Turnock, *The East European Economy in Context*, 188

5 G. Pugh, 'Problems of Economic Transformation in Eastern Germany: An Overview', *British Review of Economic Issues*, 15 (37): 122.

6 *Ekonomika I Zhizn'*, 43 (1991): 7.

7 *Ekonomika I Zhizn'*, 45 (1993): 4.

8 J. Parker, and R. Layard, 'A Strange Dichotomy', *Business Central Europe: The Annual* (Dec. 1996), 20.

9 *Ekonomika I Zhizn'*, 45 (1993): 4.

10 *Business Central Europe: The Annual* (1996–7), 11.

Recommended Reading

■ Earle, J., Frydman, R., and Rapaczynski, A. (eds.), *Privatization in the Transition to a Market Economy: Studies of Preconditions and Policies in Eastern Europe* (Central European University Press, 1993).

■ —— —— —— and Turkewitz, J. (eds.), *Small Privatization: The Transformation of Retail Trade and Consumer Services* (Central European University Press, 1994).

■ Estrin, S., *Privatization in Central and Eastern Europe* (Longman, 1994).

■ Gros, D., and Steinherr, A., *Winds of Change: Economic Transition in Central and Eastern Europe* (Longman, 1995).

■ Koves, A. *et al.*, (eds.), *Privatization Experiences in Eastern Europe* (UNCTAD: Geneva, 1995).

■ Lavigne, M., *The Economics of Transition: From Socialist Economy to Market Economy* (Macmillan, 1995).

■ Sachs, J., 'Privatization in Russia: Lessons from Eastern Europe', *American Economic Review*, 82(2): 43–8.

20

Foreign Direct Investment in Eastern Europe

Objectives

- to examine the role of FDI in the economic transition process in Eastern Europe after 1990
- to identify the forms of FDI being attracted to Eastern Europe in the 1990s
- to highlight the example of the motor vehicle industry as an important source of FDI and the long-term benefits which may accrue from these activities
- to discuss why the experience of some firms has been more successful than others and the difficulties which Western firms have encountered when attempting to enter Eastern European markets in the 1990s

20.1 Introduction

THIS chapter will discuss the implications for the countries of Eastern Europe of successfully attracting and retaining a wide variety of foreign investors. Whilst it is acknowledged that many companies are increasingly becoming integrated into the global economy—indeed, it has become difficult to avoid it, there are also many companies which have internationalized their activities for the first time. This chapter will briefly discuss the factors which influence firms to undertake commercial activities abroad, and especially those firms that have chosen to expand their activities into Eastern Europe in recent years. The discussion will be restricted to the three main forms of FDI in Eastern Europe—Joint-Venture Agreements (JVAs), acquisitions, and greenfield investments. Portfolio equity investment will be ignored here in order to concentrate on the activities of companies as investors.

In many cases, companies do not make a strategic decision to internationalize their activities, but may do so as a result of an informal enquiry. In the experience of the author, a small firm operating in the UK (but with connections in the Middle East) decided to form a JVA to export secondhand trucks and spares to Poland in 1994 as a result of a conversation with a fellow passenger on a train travelling between Warsaw and Krakow. The market in Eastern Europe after 1990 has been seen by many firms as one representing great risk but also potentially high rewards, but not in the immediate future. Firms must not expect high short-term profits but must be prepared to subsidize operations in Eastern Europe from international activities elsewhere. The entrepreneur who began selling secondhand trucks in Poland in 1994 subsidized his new activities from his more profitable operation in the Middle East. Indeed, he took the long-term view that he may need to switch his interests to Eastern Europe in the future given the political instabilities prevalent throughout the Middle East.

It could be argued that the factors motivating this entrepreneur were spontaneity and defensive factors in that he was also reacting to difficulties experienced in other markets. Although demand for the product throughout the Middle East was far from becoming saturated, this entrepreneur saw an opening in a developing market for products which had come to the end of their natural life cycle at home. In addition, the entrepreneur entered the Eastern European market at a time when there was virtually no competition present and when acquisition of spare parts for trucks operated by firms in Poland was extremely difficult. This example serves to illustrate some of the motives for a firm wishing to internationalize its activities. Other factors may include the benefits of economies of scale which a larger operation may bring, combined with the advantages to be gained from the local situation with an abundance of cheap labour and raw materials. Indeed, lower production costs have undoubtedly been important for foreign companies choosing to locate their operations in Eastern Europe. However, these benefits need to be tempered with the problem of lower labour productivity levels and the application of backward and obsolete technology by indigenous Eastern European firms.

20.2 The Role of Economic Reform

Aɴ important component of the economic reform programme pursued by the countries of Eastern Europe in recent years has been the need to create and formalize a private sector. Under communism, and in the early years of the transition, private sector activities were largely undertaken by individuals or groups operating in the second economy. An advantage of formalizing these activities meant that legitimate business activities would become subject to income and corporate taxation. However, it is recognized that in many countries of the region a substantial number of business activities remain outside the formal private sector.[1] The problem of organized crime and the inability of the authorities to control mafia activities has meant that these activities remain outside government control (especially in Russia) and also increase the risks faced by firms undertaking legitimate business activities.

The role of privatization in the creation of a private sector in the economies of Eastern Europe has already been discussed in Chapter 19. The problem of restructuring privatized firms continues to pose a subject for discussion in the present chapter since, as a result of JVAs and/or acquisitions by Western companies, the burden of restructuring often falls to the Western partner. It is the Western companies which hold the keys to restructuring—Western managers know what it takes to survive and make profits in a market economy, where the only alternative to success is bankruptcy. It has largely fallen to Western firms (usually MNEs) to provide the knowledge and expertise (with an injection of investment capital) necessary to enable former SOEs to operate successfully in the private sector. Failure to restructure and the inability to cope with the prospect of competition from other firms in the market (usually foreign) should lead to bankruptcy. However, in practice, many governments in Eastern Europe have deliberately continued to subsidize former SOEs in order to dissuade them from shedding labour and so adding to the already high level of unemployment in these economies. The continuing level of government interference in some economies in the region (especially in Russia) has discouraged some Western companies from attempting to enter the market, and, coupled with the high crime rate, this often makes the total risk unacceptably high.

Problems with achieving currency convertibility and stability have also presented difficulties for Western investors. In the early years of the reform process, several important foreign investors (notably, Ford), pulled out of Russia in the face of difficulties in acquiring supplies of hard currencies to import parts and other materials, and also to repatriate profits to pay dividends to shareholders abroad. These problems persisted for some time despite a declaration of intent by Eastern European governments to liberalize foreign trade practices. In reality, fears of causing domestic currency instability meant that many governments continued to maintain close control of their hard currency supplies. The dilemma which was caused by pursuance of this policy in foreign trade relations has only been recently resolved with some domestic currencies being pegged to a major international currency like the US$ or the Deutsche Mark. In general, countries of the former Soviet Union have looked towards the US$ as a means of currency stabilization, with Russia pegging the rouble to the dollar with a 'corridor' of flexibility around which the rouble has been allowed to fluctuate. Other countries like Poland, Hungary, and the Czech Republic have looked towards the Deutsche Mark to provide a marker for currency stability. This is especially appropriate for countries of the region with strong aspirations to become full members of the European Union early in the 21st century.

The difficulties of achieving full currency convertibility and subsequent stabilization of the domestic currency by the countries of the region also highlighted the need for the creation of a domestic banking system along Western lines, coupled with the development of a legal system capable of protecting the interests of both shareholders and consumers. However, it is necessary to discuss the development of the banking system within the context of the financial services sector as a whole to ensure the adequate provision of a share flotation and dealing service through stock exchanges, the availability of capital for investment by firms, and the facility to enable borrowing by government. The drive to undertake privatization as rapidly as possible meant that some countries found themselves in the difficult position of having sold or distributed free shares to the public without providing them with the means for exchanging their shareholdings for cash. In addition, there has been a chronic shortage of investment funds in the region, due partly to a general shortage caused by the world recession in the early 1990s, but also by the inability of Eastern European banks to provide adequate funds to lend to investors. Persistently high interest rates pursued by many governments of the region have choked off enthusiasm for domestic borrowing by foreign investors.

20.3 The Nature and Availability of FDI

THE three major methods of FDI in Eastern Europe have been in the form of JVAs, acquisitions, and greenfield sites. It has been estimated by John Howell of Ernst and Young that whilst the number of deals completed in these three areas have been fairly evenly distributed (with the exception of Russia), the value of the investments made have varied considerably.[2] For example, acquisitions have generally proved to be very expensive for foreign investors and is not a method favoured by those looking for a cheap deal. Although JVAs should be regarded as a more risky form of investment and such agreements tend to be unstable over a long period of time, they are useful in the short term to facilitate entry of Western firms into a relatively inaccessible market. It may be the case that other forms of FDI are too risky in countries where the current economic and political situation is unstable. This situation has occurred in the case of Russia where the risks are high for investors and there is a prevalence of FDI in the form of JVAs. In these cases, Western firms can pull out of the agreement quickly should the need arise.

However, an increasingly popular form of FDI in all countries of the region (apart from the former Soviet Union) is greenfield investment. Given the increasing availability of low-cost greenfield sites in prime locations earmarked for Western MNEs by central and local governments in the region, this type of FDI will see further increases in popularity in the future. This form of investment received encouragement by governments of the region only after 1994. Initially, greenfield site investment was viewed with suspicion by many local authorities because of the possibility of large Western MNEs providing competition and squeezing out local firms from established markets. Before 1994 greenfield investment was largely confined to areas with high structural unemployment.

In 1996 a major greenfield investment was made by General Motors near Katowice in southern Poland. Initially, GM had planned to acquire the Polish car manufacturer, FSO, but were overtaken by the South Korean car manufacturer, Daewoo, which submitted a higher offer. This forced GM into developing a new car production plant on a greenfield site. This change of plan may have long-term benefits as the company has been able to take the opportunity of installing modern technology from the start, rather than have to make additional investments to modernize an existing Eastern European car plant using low-level production line technology. Greenfield investments allow Western firms to install up-to-date technology which allows them to produce a high-quality product which can meet the standards of Western customers. Local people have continued to be suspicious of Western MNEs and this has led to foreign investors adopting methods of subterfuge in order to acquire greenfield sites to allow them to become established in a particular market. It seems likely that by gradually establishing a presence in a region by building up trust and goodwill among the locals, Western investors will face less opposition from local people and from local firms.

Since restrictions were lifted on foreign investment in the region, shares acquired by Western companies in Eastern European firms have increased, with many firms taking a 100 per cent share in their Eastern European partners after privatization. Governments had to be prepared to allow foreign firms to acquire controlling shareholdings in former SOEs with which many had previously operated JVAs in order to retain their continued participation in the newly acquired company. In countries like Poland, Hungary, and the Czech Republic, Western companies were reluctant to continue operating JVAs in which they did not have a controlling interest and in which they found it increasingly necessary to risk substantial investment by becoming involved in the process of restructuring.

It seems likely that the governments of Eastern Europe expected a flood of Western investment into the region once the restrictions imposed by the former regimes were removed. Indeed, it is not unreasonable to suppose that the new governments expected Western MNEs to provide the entire capital requirements necessary to restructure the ailing industries of the region. In retrospect, it is obvious that there were few realistic expectations of the level of investment (capital, technology, and expertise) available given that the countries of the region were emerging markets in just one area of the world where the competition for investment from emerging economies in other regions was extremely intense. Although Dawes estimates that between 1990 and 1993 total private capital flows to the non-OECD world almost quadrupled, the countries of Eastern Europe only managed to attract a 3 per cent share of worldwide investment flows in 1993.[3] China attracted over three times the amount of FDI going to all the countries of Eastern Europe, and other countries like Argentina, Mexico, Malaysia, and Indonesia have also experienced substantial increases in FDI. The finite total of available investment has meant that the expansion seen in South America and the Far East has been mirrored in the loss of potential investment to Eastern Europe. It seems likely that investment in Eastern Europe posed a far greater risk to investors than did the more stable political and economic situation presented by countries elsewhere.

A further problem arose as the liberalization in Eastern Europe occurred at the same time as the industrialized countries in the West, which represented the largest potential investors into the region, were entering a deep recession. A contraction of investment funds available for new projects occurred, both as a result of Western firms revising their international expansion plans and also, from the large international financial institutions which had been forced to offer support elsewhere. Indeed, by the time Western Europe had begun to emerge from recession, Western investors had been attracted by the emerging markets of countries like China and Vietnam, which seemed to present a more stable economic and political environment for long-term investment than did the countries of Eastern Europe. By 1993 it became apparent that opportunities for investment had become regionalized on a worldwide scale and that Western investors were looking more readily to the Far East in the expectation of higher returns. This was exacerbated by the governments of the region placing too much reliance on Western investment and their inability to explore the possibilities of sourcing capital from the development of local industry. Inevitably, a proportion of the returns arising from Western investment will be repatriated to the home country and opportunities for re-investment at local level will be lost. In addition, the development of some economies can be distorted by a number of large investments which are constrained by Western companies in different regions. This may not be a deliberate action by Western companies but rather a response to the existing situation with local SOEs continuing to receive state subsidies in an attempt to protect the employment opportunities of the region. This may mean that SOEs are at an unfair advantage when competing with Western firms or where the Western investor is unable to establish a network of local suppliers because they are subject to continued state intervention. The situation would necessitate a Western firm bringing in its own supplies of parts and other raw materials for local assembly.

20.4 How Can FDI Contribute to the Development of the Economies of Eastern Europe?

IN addition to satisfying the much needed capital requirements of the emerging economies discussed earlier, FDI can also make important contributions in the areas of technology transfer, management skills, export promotion, new product development, and direct employment. However, it is questionable whether smaller investments can actually achieve these benefits and whether they can be evenly distributed throughout the economy given the lower than expected levels of investment realized. Probably the greatest benefit brought by Western companies is the ability to develop local sectors of industry as suppliers of raw materials through which the country can develop a competitive advantage. In many cases, the countries of Eastern Europe possessed few competitive advantages since industry was subject to the dictates of central planning requirements rather than the need to exploit their competitive advantage. The governments have reinforced these problems by continuing to offer subsidies to former SOEs simply because bankruptcy is not on the agenda due to the high levels of unemployment which would result.

However, a number of early-reforming governments, especially Poland, have tended to embark upon a longer-term strategy designed to address the uneven distribution of domestic industry. A policy based on the idea of 'picking winners' has been adopted, that is, selecting those domestic industries which can contribute to the long-term development of the economy, especially in the areas of exports and sustainable employment. This requires a certain level of government intervention. Obviously, there is a difficult balance to be reached between the need to support industries identified as 'winners' and the continuing practice of some countries to subsidize industries because they are losers, and the inability of governments to face up to the consequences of this. However, the former strategy of 'picking winners' involves considerable political courage and the ability of the government to integrate its industrial policy into the overall reform programme, including encouraging export companies and formulating targeted inward investment programmes. In other words, FDI should bring in Western firms which can develop the activities of existing Eastern European firms by providing capital investment, management expertise, and technology transfer. Eastern European governments have few material incentives to offer Western firms apart from the recent proliferation of greenfield sites available at low cost. Some governments have conferred less tangible benefits to encourage Western firms by 'ring-fencing' the market for a particular product so that other foreign companies are effectively excluded from the market while the first company develops the market for its own product. In effect, some countries have actually promoted the creation and development of monopolies by Western companies in order to encourage them to assist with the restructuring of former SOEs. The bulk of FDI has been seen in the oil and gas industries and in the motor vehicle industry, although in other sectors investment has been more evenly distributed. The case of the motor vehicle industry will be discussed in more detail in the next section of this chapter.

It is difficult to assess the specific contribution made by FDI in the development of the economies of Eastern Europe. There is no doubt that a significant contribution to exports has been made by the major Western MNEs in the oil, gas, and motor vehicle industries. Other Western companies have also assisted with the restructuring of local industries in food-processing, beverages, chemicals, electronics, etc. These firms have helped to produce consumer goods which have been able to satisfy demand in local markets, especially in countries like Poland, Hungary, and the Czech Republic where wages are rising and consumers are demanding increasingly sophisticated products. In countries where consumers were faced with poor-quality goods and little choice before 1990, the same consumers are now demanding high-quality Western products and are refusing to be 'fobbed off' with cheap substitutes. They are now willing to enter into credit agreements to obtain cars and other larger consumer products. It is Western companies which must take the lead by providing the right products at the right price to satisfy consumer demand. On the other hand, by doing so, Western firms can also contribute to redressing the imbalance in the balance of payments of countries of the region and achieve substantial import substitution.

However, John Howell of Ernst and Young has questioned whether FDI has made any significant contribution to the economies of the region. He argues that the real test is whether FDI has achieved any cultural benefits by actually producing any real changes in the mentality of the government, managers, and workers to accept restructuring and redundancy.[4] In addition, the question remains whether FDI has helped to liberate entrepreneurship to create an expanding private sector containing newly established SMEs, probably in the service sector. There has been significant progress made in both the Czech Republic and Poland to achieve major cultural change and entrepreneurial advances, but in many other countries, especially Russia, FDI has had little influence on the way domestic firms operate, and enthusiasm by governments to subsidize loss-making former SOEs has persisted unchecked.

20.5 The case of the Motor Vehicle Industry

A N important motivation of Western firms taking the decision to invest in Eastern Europe has been the desire to achieve competitive advantage over rival firms operating in the same industry, usually with their operations based in the EU. There is no doubt that the countries of Eastern Europe offer a number of significant benefits, not least of which is low wages, which should, in normal circumstances, confer competitive advantage. However, the benefits which foreign firms can accrue depends largely on the speed with which they take advantage of the opportunities offered by the emerging market. In Eastern Europe after 1990 there seems to be a correlation between opportunities for Western investors and the speed with which the privatization process has been carried out. In many cases, Western firms entering the market using the JVA mode of entry, have benefited from privatization by being able to partially or completely acquire former SOEs when they are transferred to the private sector. On the other hand, the managers of former SOEs have been keen to enter into JVAs or other arrangements with Western firms in order to improve the efficiency of the existing enterprise and also, more realistically, provide themselves with an escape route should the stream of state subsidies dry up. It is for these reasons, therefore, that the importance of privatization should not be underestimated in creating opportunities for existing firms entering the private sector and also for encouraging more investment from abroad.

John Howell has identified the average size of investments made in the region as a whole as being about US$10 million, although larger investments have been made amounting to over US$100 million by Western motor vehicle manufacturers.[5] However, if US$10 million represents the average size of an investment, then this figure overstates the numerous niche opportunities found by firms making up the remaining investments. Western car manufacturers have seen unrivalled opportunities for investing in the motor vehicle industry in Eastern Europe. A major commitment has been necessary to undertake all three forms of FDI identified in this chapter. Initially, Western MNEs forming JVAs have often seen such associations transformed into acquisitions on privatization, notably, in the case of Volkswagen of Germany and Skoda of the Czech Republic. Other firms like General Motors have undertaken high-profile greenfield investment in order to capture the competitive advantages of the emerging market. The main areas for investment by Western firms in the motor vehicle industry have been in Poland and the Czech Republic, thought to be the largest combined market for new vehicle purchase in the world in the future (outside China). For example, in 1990 the countries of the region had about 120 cars per thousand of the population whereas in Western Europe the comparable figure was around 360 cars per thousand people.[6] The motor vehicle industry has accounted for about 20 per cent of total investment made by just 8 per cent of investing companies.[7]

The countries represented by this large market traditionally contained few indigenous car manufacturers—FSM and FSO in the case of Poland, and Skoda in Czechoslovakia. Although the Western MNEs were confident that increased investment and restructuring could improve the efficiency of domestic firms, all were generally reluctant to perpetuate JVAs where influence of Western firms over long-term product development would remain limited. It was essential that Western firms adopted a long-term strategy to take advantage of a market amounting to an estimated 9 per cent of new car sales by 2010.[8] It was insufficient to use the excess production capacity of domestic firms to produce Western designed cars. The output of cars needed to be increased dramatically, so in the long term it was essential that Western investors abandoned JVAs in favour of acquisitions or greenfield investment as much more favourable alternatives. The motor vehicle industry in Eastern Europe already possessed a highly skilled workforce, albeit with lower labour productivity levels than their Western counterparts. If this factor is balanced with the advantage of low-cost labour, the benefits of competitive advantage become apparent. However, this situation cannot remain static forever. The Western motor vehicle manufacturers are confident that the existing highly skilled labour force in Eastern Europe can be persuaded to produce a high-quality product comparable to Western standards. In order to ensure that improvements in productivity occur, Western firms will have to offer incentives to their workers in the form of higher wages. If the present competitive advantage enjoyed by Western firms disappears in the future, this may be offset by the benefits of having established themselves in an expanding consumer market where rising wages become translated into increased demand for luxury goods.

The motor vehicle industry in Eastern Europe was already benefiting from various cooperative deals with Western MNEs which commenced before 1990. The earliest agreement was formed in 1976 between Fiat and FSM, the Polish car manufacturer. This was an arrangement to allow FSM to produce the small Fiat 126 model under licence from the Italian car manufacturer. This allowed Polish consumers access to a small, economical car of Western design and permitted Fiat to extend the life cycle of a product which was already being squeezed out of Western markets by more up-to-date competition. Experience obtained from early entry to the market by Fiat, and also by Citroën and Renault, benefited other firms wishing to invest in the Eastern European car industry after 1990.

Although car production in Eastern Europe before 1990 was small by Western standards, output from factories in Poland and the Czech Republic did feature in international production data for the industry. In Czechoslovakia, Skoda had tried to look towards the Western car market by developing the new model 'Favorit' for Western customers. Despite these efforts, car manufacturers in Eastern Europe could not manage to produce a model which could compete with Western cars manufactured to higher-quality standards, although it was possible for Skoda to capture a small percentage of the market with its 'Favorit'. Indeed, in 1993 motor journalists from Western Europe voted the Skoda Favorit winner of the *What Car? Magazine* 'East European Car of the Year' competition, with the Opel Astra and Fiat Cinquecento placed second and third respectively. It seems likely that improvements to the product made by the involvement of VW had become apparent at this stage. The decision of VW to take advantage of cheap labour has also influenced the decision to move production plants to regions of the former GDR. In 1992, VW took over the Trabant factory and converted it to manufacture the 'Golf'. Similarly, BMW and Opel have taken over the former Wartburg plant at Eisenach to produce an estimated 150,000 cars per annum. The German car manufacturers have been attracted by the engineering skills of the workforce in Poland and the Czech Republic, despite low productivity levels.

There can be no doubt that Poland can now be regarded as the centre for motor vehicle production in Eastern Europe. In 1995 Daewoo came on the scene with a major investment proposal for both FSO and FSL (a state car and lorry plant manufacturer near Lublin). This meant that the government required both firms to withdraw from agreements made separately with GM and Peugeot in 1993. The major advantage of Daewoo over GM and Peugeot for the Polish factories was that the South Korean company intended to retain the whole workforce to create a production base with an output of 220,000 to 300,000 cars per annum. This was nearly four times the target given by GM whose operations were largely confined to vehicle assembly. By September 1997 Daewoo had captured nearly 27 per cent of the market for new cars in Poland where consumers had bought 371,000 new cars in the first nine months, an increase of nearly 30 per cent from 1996.[9] However, Fiat still dominates the Polish market with a 35 per cent share, with GM trailing behind in third place with a 10 per cent market share.

The market is dominated by Daewoo and Fiat because these firms bought into the existing Polish car manufacturers and have invested heavily with Fiat spending over US$1 billion and Daewoo nearly US$500 million. They have tended to concentrate on producing small, low-cost cars suited to the Polish market. Until recently, there has been little evidence of strong competition from rival Western car manufacturers. Daewoo is not happy about the prospect of large numbers of GM cars coming off the production line at its new greenfield development near Katowice in southern Poland, and Daewoo is even more alarmed by the prospect of direct competition from a rival South Korean car manufacturer, Hyundai, which also has a new car plant under construction. In 1996 Daewoo thought that it could prevent new investments by its rivals when the government, led by the former communists, announced a ban on any further 'hit-and-run' assemblers who had been importing components duty-free into the country. Instead of Hyundai being forced to abandon its plans, it formed an association with the car dealership, SZC, which already assembled Mercedes cars. The outgoing government agreed to let this new venture go ahead and gave permission to allow duty-free components to be imported into the country. The new Solidarity-led government has confirmed that it supports this decision despite the continuing threat by Daewoo to cut 12,000 jobs among the 20,000 workers at its Warsaw plant and to limit further investment into the country. The new government has also received complaints from Fiat and from VW which assembles vans and Czech-made Skodas in Poland. It is obvious that the objective of this behaviour by large Western MNEs is to maintain and increase their monopoly power in a market where there are few restrictions on the behaviour of firms in the private sector. However, it is extremely unlikely that companies like Daewoo will try to force the government's hand by actually withdrawing from this market. The future of the Eastern European car market is too lucrative to be deserted at such a crucial stage of its development.

In fact, Daewoo is now facing difficulties with selling its cars which it hardly anticipated when it entered the market in 1995. Indeed, it is likely that the company will have problems with maintaining sales in the near future. It has been argued that it simply makes too many cars in its plants in Poland, Romania, Ukraine, and Russia which are beyond the capacity of these markets to absorb.[10] In Romania, for example, consumers prefer cheap runabouts produced by the domestic car manufacturer, Dacia, to the more expensive models made by Daewoo. Actually, many Western car manufacturers erroneously believed that Eastern European car buyers would be prepared to make do with old models which have reached the end of their life cycle in Western markets. A salutary lesson should have been learned from the experience of Rover in Bulgaria after it became impossible to sell its 'Maestro' model in any significant numbers. Daewoo has made the same mistake and consumers have soon realized that some 'new' Daewoos are in fact old Opel designs from the 1980s, and in Romania alone Daewoo have difficulty in selling 10,000 cars a year. Eastern European customers would rather purchase secondhand models of Western cars than spend more on a new car based on an old design. If Daewoo fails to improve the design and quality of its product, it will find itself stuck in a low-price niche, competing with the likes of Lada on price alone.

Russia is also seen as an important region for FDI by Western motor vehicle manufacturers as it is set to become an important car market in the same league as Poland, although with a larger number of potential customers. Fiat has recently entered into a JVA with Avtogaz, manufacturer of the notorious Volga cars, investing US$850 million with an additional substantial investment made by the EBRD. In the past few years Fiat has undertaken several large new investments with Russian and Eastern European car manufacturers in a desperate attempt to achieve economies of scale and reverse the losses it made in its operations in 1996. A mark of the success enjoyed by Fiat, in contrast to the strategy pursued by Daewoo, is the popularity of its new model, the 'Palio', a car specifically developed for the emerging markets of Russia and Eastern Europe, and for South America. This is an important part of the strategy to attempt to meet the challenge known as globalization and GM, through its German car manufacturer Opel, is similarly planning to enter emerging markets. In 1997 GM formed a JVA with the other Russian car manufacturer, Avtovaz, by investing US$30–50 million in the first part of a three-phase project with the objective of producing 25,000 to 50,000 old-style Opel Astras in the early part of the 21st century. However, the second phase of the JVA plans to produce a larger engine in the range of 1.8 to 2.2 litres for a car which will be jointly developed with Avtovaz with a projected production of 150,000 units a year.

In order to overcome the continuing opposition to foreign firms operating in Russia, GM have promised to allow Avtovaz a role in the development of the new model. Despite the notoriety attached to Ladas in the West, GM recognized that Avtovaz possesses an enormous pool of specialist knowledge necessary for producing cars which can operate under difficult climatic and road conditions. Obviously, both Fiat and GM plan to transfer Western technology in their bid to contribute to the restructuring of the Russian car industry over the next few years. However, a new report published by the Economist Intelligence Unit suggests that if Russian companies do not gain access to modern Western technology very quickly, they will not survive beyond the year 2005.[11] Within a very short time, the old-fashioned and low-quality products traditionally produced by the Russian car industry will be in direct competition with the more advanced Western cars produced in Russia costing the consumer about the same price. Russian car buyers of the future are bound to opt for Western-designed cars and this will mean the complete collapse of the domestic producers when it becomes impossible to sell low-quality products in these markets. FDI in the motor vehicle industry in Russia has been curtailed by the financial crisis of August 1998 when consumer confidence fell as a result of the collapse of the financial sector. However, the car industry did enjoy a temporary respite with the 'mini boom' caused by those consumers who could afford to purchase new cars before 1 January 1999 in order to beat a new law being introduced by the Russian government from that date. All consumers making a single purchase over US$4,000 will be compelled to register that transaction which will then become subject to additional purchase tax.

20.6 Successes and Failures of FDI

IT has already been stated that the expected level of FDI to countries of the region did not materialize after 1990 due to the world recession hitting potential investor countries. In addition, the regional nature of FDI generally favours Asia and Latin America. This has meant that FDI in Eastern Europe has been left largely to MNEs already operating in EU countries with relatively low levels of Japanese investment and US companies concentrating on developing activities in the former Soviet Union. Although it is true that investment from the Far East was slow to take off up to 1993,

South Korean companies like Daewoo have made substantial investment commitments, notably in Poland, since that time. Even within the EU itself, further geographical bias has been apparent with the majority of FDI coming from MNEs operating in Germany, Austria, and Italy. Some large European MNEs have been reluctant to take the risk of the uncertain economic and political situation in emerging Eastern European markets.

Since 1993 Poland and the Czech Republic have become the centre for the Eastern European motor vehicle industry and have attracted investment from all the major players in the industry. GM, VW, Fiat, and Daewoo have made a substantial investment in the region, but they have generally confined their activities to countries likely to be the first to join the EU in the very near future. These countries are the most stable economically and politically and now enjoy stable rates of economic growth. It could be expected that the other major South Korean companies would follow Daewoo and Hyundai's example in Eastern Europe in the future, but in the aftermath of the financial crash experienced by the South-East Asian economies in late 1997 and early 1998, it is not yet clear what will be the outcome and how far these events will affect FDI in the future. Hyundai and Samsung have already stated their intention to delay major investments which were planned for Western Europe and this is also going to affect their decision to invest elsewhere.

Investment decisions are also affected by the way in which privatization proceeds are being utilized by the governments of Eastern Europe. Inevitably, a conflict arises between the long-term investment needs of the business enterprise itself and the needs of the government requiring additional revenue for the exchequer in order to meet IMF targets, debt repayments, etc. Foreign firms see privatization proceeds largely as a contribution to the costs of restructuring, in effect, a subsidy which would reduce the costs of FDI. A further difficulty has arisen from the attitude of Western governments and official investment agencies themselves. In some cases, advice received by firms from government agencies has deterred potential investors from undertaking a basic feasibility study. In addition, tariffs imposed by Western governments or by the EU for its member countries, have simply reinforced the prejudices of many Western firms against the prospect of competition from products manufactured by firms in Eastern Europe. This policy has not only inhibited investment and damaged relations between East and West causing some countries seriously to question their chances for early EU membership, but it has also held back the development of Eastern European companies by preventing them from seeking competition in foreign markets.

20.6.1 Poland

Poland has seen a steady growth of FDI since 1990 and this is expected to continue in the future. The highest gains have been seen in the motor vehicle industry but recent plans for a US$1 billion greenfield investment from Hyundai may be delayed due to the problems in the financial markets of South-East Asia. Discussions between

Poland and the EU started in November 1998 in order to negotiate Poland's entry into the EU shortly after the year 2000. In view of this, investment is expected to continue to pour into Poland since investors see it as a gateway to the EU. In 1997 the US multinational, Heinz, acquired a majority stake in Pudliszki, a food-processing company, and Electricité de France has paid US$80 million for a 55 per cent stake in a Krakow power station. ING Barings estimated that FDI worth up to US$6 billion could flow in during 1998, compared with just US$1.1 million three years earlier in 1995.[12]

20.6.2 Hungary

Similarly, FDI continues to be attracted to Hungary but investors are now having to look beyond the golden triangle of Budapest–Szekesfehervar–Gyor which has attracted 75 per cent of FDI so far. However, the level of FDI of US$4.5 billion achieved in 1995 has not been repeated since that time and the forecast was for the level to fall in 1998 to US$1.5 billion.[13] The reason for this is that the larger investors from the Western car manufacturers have virtually bypassed Hungary in favour of Poland and the benefits to be obtained from establishing JVAs with the indigenous car manufacturers there. In addition, lax and constantly changing legislation has posed threats to foreign firms. A recent attempt by the government to introduce anti-monopoly legislation was abandoned when several large Western MNEs pointed out that they would have to review their positions if their activities were investigated by an anti-monopoly committee. Nevertheless, the government has recently introduced a system of tax breaks to encourage investors to locate in other regions away from the capital in an attempt to redress the regional imbalance of FDI which has arisen.

Problems in the Hungarian banking system arising from a lack of capital have largely been eliminated with the acquisition of banks by foreign investors, culminating in the sale of Mezobank and K&H Bank in 1997. This should have a beneficial effect on the whole business sector with increased competition producing improved services at lower prices, interest rates, and bank charges.

20.6.3 Czech Republic

The prospects for FDI in the Czech Republic remain poor with levels falling from US$2.52 billion in 1995 to US$900 million in 1997.[14] The main problem has been the crisis in the economy which has been building up recently with growth declining from 5.9 per cent in 1995 to 1.2 per cent in 1997.[15] The floods which devastated the industrial areas of Moravia during the summer of 1997 were partly responsible for the poor economic performance, but the Czech economy has been going through a sluggish period for some time. The government and business must press ahead with full-scale corporate restructuring if greater efficiencies are to be achieved. Inevitably, this will mean that unemployment starts to rise above the unnaturally low levels enjoyed by the Czech Republic in comparison to its neighbours in recent years. The government intended to sell off its stake in the partially privatized banking system in 1998, and it has already sold its share in the most troubled bank, IPB, to the Japanese investment bank, Nomura. Although the increased activity at this level from foreign firms may cause public concern in the country about the crown jewels being sold off to foreign investors, it is hoped that it will bring in much needed changes in management and attitudes into the business community.

20.6.4 Slovakia

The level of FDI in Slovakia has remained low as a result of potential foreign investors remaining sceptical of the government's ability to maintain its democratic credentials. Slovakia's economic prospects are also bleak with a US$1.2 billion foreign debt repayment due in 1998. The central bank's tight monetary policy has presented severe problems for the business community. Earnings have remained flat as companies have struggled to maintain their interest payments on debts, but the government has announced that Sk70 billion (about US$1.9 billion) will be made available in the form of a revitalization package to support troubled exporters. Financial assistance which helps out firms facing current problems means that attempts to undertake wide-ranging restructuring will probably have to be postponed. By the end of 1997 FDI stock had reached just US$1 billion. Nevertheless, some of Slovakia's best domestic companies surged ahead pursuing their own investment opportunities. Slovakia's largest steel producer, VSZ, which accounts for 12 per cent of the country's exports signed a JVA with US Steel and tried to buy out Hungary's DAM steelmill. There are also the first signs of owner-managers seeking know-how and capital from foreign investors with the most significant example being Matador, the tyre maker, becoming linked to Bridgestone of Japan.

20.6.5 Russia

Despite Russia's substantial resource base and growing market potential per capita FDI of US$57 million is much lower than in Eastern Europe. Recently, the large tobacco multinational, Philip Morris, and confectionery manufacturer, Mars, have been acquiring greenfield sites, while others like Fiat have formed JVAs with local companies. FDI flows reached US$2 billion in 1997 and were estimated to grow to US$3.5 billion in 1998.[16] This level of FDI is still too low given the potential of the economy, although Western investors now seem less worried about the prospect of political instability rather than the fact that the Russian government continues to pursue its reform programme half-heartedly. It appears that, at the time of writing, the financial crisis in August 1998 has had little impact on investments already undertaken by Western MNEs. It is not clear to what extent predictions for future FDI levels have now been adversely affected by the financial crisis and the subsequent collapse of the financial sector.

Indeed, the reluctance of new Western MNEs to invest in Russia in the short-to medium-term may have absolutely nothing to do with the financial crisis at all. Previous companies have faced years of negotiations with Russian enterprises to establish JVAs and other commercial relationships. In addition, the general lack of industrial restructuring of newly privatized firms has meant that most Western partners can expect to face massive bills for capital investment with little possibility of seeing profits coming on stream in the near future. In the event, Western firms see countries like Poland, Hungary, and the Czech Republic as safer havens for long-term investment with the obvious possibility of using these bases to export finished goods to the more economically and politically unstable areas of Russia and the CIS. Accession of the first wave of Eastern European countries to the EU early in the twenty-first century will further underline the benefits of this arrangement to Western firms.

A serious problem has arisen in the aftermath of the mass privatization programme undertaken in 1995 when a 'loans-for-shares auction' sold a huge amount of state assets to large banks creating an economic oligarchy in Russia. The result is that the seven major financial industrial groups (FIGS) control over 40 per cent of the economy. On the one hand, it may be possible for the FIGS to attract the requisite capital for restructuring, but on the other, there is increasing concern being expressed by economists over the growth of the FIGS encouraging the criminalization of Russian society. This grey market accounts for over 40 per cent of GDP, and factors like confusing tax laws, high lending rates, and rampant corruption only serve to severely distort the already fragile business environment.

In addition, there is evidence that a recentralization of the economy was occurring in 1999 under an increasingly ageing and ineffectual leadership. Increased state intervention means that industries will be heavily subsidized to protect employment and a recent Presidential Decree will permit the nationalization of most loss-making industries or, alternatively, these industries will be integrated into the monopoly structures of the FIGS, providing them with guaranteed markets. It is also envisaged that stricter controls will be placed on capital flows (and prices to a certain extent), with high tariff barriers to protect Russian industries from foreign competition by discouraging imports. The sharp devaluation of the rouble has contributed to this already, so Western firms will find that importing raw materials and parts into Russia becomes prohibitively expensive in the near future. The long-term results of such policies will be effectively to kill off competition in Russia altogether and, indeed, the very existence of the fragile private sector itself is under threat, as the state persists in supporting large monopolies in the guise of FIGS, unrestructured and not amenable to competition from Western firms.

20.7 Summary

THE immense importance of FDI to the countries of Eastern Europe should not be underestimated. Foreign investment is inextricably linked to the economic reform process and to privatization. The success of the reforms largely depends upon countries being able to attract foreign firms in sufficient numbers to provide investment resources which will make an impact on the restructuring process. In other words, foreign investment must be regarded as part of government economic policy and also as an important factor determining the size and structure of the private sector. However, FDI and privatization should not be regarded as the twin saviours of the economies of Eastern Europe, but should be fully integrated with the governments' policy objectives, especially with respect to economic growth and the imperative need to maintain political stability. In countries like Russia where too much reliance has been placed on attracting foreign investors, without a high rate of success, the government itself has failed to recognize the need for the implementation of a consistent reform programme. It is easy to see that the cycle being described here is no other than a Catch-22 situation where the level of FDI entering a country is dependent on the success of the economic reforms and the maintenance of political stability, whereas the future of the reform programme is itself dependent on the scale of foreign investment entering the country. However, it is recognized that foreign firms are willing to take risks in order to internationalize their activities and meet the challenges of globalization.

In their attempts to concentrate on FDI as a means of achieving import substitution, governments of the region must avoid falling into the trap of returning to the production-led policies pursued under communism. Recently, it has been recognized that it is not practical to encourage Western investors to expand domestic production when there are not enough customers with sufficiently high-income levels to be able to afford to purchase the goods. The result is a return to the stockpile situations facing firms during the communist era. The efforts of governments must now concentrate on implementing policies to promote exports rather than continually increasing production destined for the domestic market, and this may mean discouraging some potential investors in the future who fail to fulfil exporting criteria.

The main difficulty with this has been the reluctance of countries in the EU to lift controls on Eastern European exports coming on to the Western European market. The EU's desire to promote greater integration in Europe with the proposed accession of the more advanced countries in Eastern Europe to the EU early in the twenty-first century is negated by the continuing practice of imposing controls on Eastern European exports, enabling the EU to run a trade surplus with countries from the region. The issue of EU membership and integration of the countries of Eastern Europe into the wider European polity is discussed in Chapter 21. However, it is important to state here that in order to prepare the countries of Eastern Europe for EU membership it will be necessary for existing EU member countries to offer support of a more concrete nature for restructuring of industry (and agriculture) in Eastern Europe through the existing PHARE programme. An input of expertise from companies from EU member countries, and especially those with operations already located in Eastern Europe, can ensure that funds are targeted towards priority needs.

A more balanced relationship needs to be established by Western companies in order to avoid accusations of 'hit-and-run' tactics which have been levelled at some MNEs with activities in Eastern Europe. The move towards EU membership may involve less reliance on major FDI from outside the European area, and this process may have just started to occur as a result of the recent financial crisis faced by investors from the Far East. However, it could be argued that the recent crisis affecting the 'tiger economies' will also have repercussions in Western Europe with losses incurred by Western banks causing a long-term shortage in funds available for investment. The countries of Eastern Europe may not only lose investment opportunities presented by the likes of Hyundai and Samsung, but may also suffer from the consequences of capital shortages among Western banks.

Review Questions

1 What has been the role of Western MNEs in the economic transformation process in Russia and Eastern Europe?

2 What methods of entry into the Russian and Eastern European market have been adopted by Western firms?

3 What role, if any, have the activities of Western firms played in fostering a culture of 'entrepreneurship' in Russia and Eastern Europe?

4 In what ways will the accession of the first wave of countries from Eastern Europe into the EU be likely to affect the level of FDI in these countries?

5 How has the Asian financial crisis affected the decision to invest in Russia and Eastern Europe?

Case Study: Skoda's New Model

The Czech car manufacturer, Skoda, which is 70 per cent owned by Volkswagen, accounts for 5.5 per cent of the Czech Republic's GDP and about 10 per cent of Czech exports. Skoda employs about 22,000 people in the Czech Republic, including about 3,000 Polish 'guest workers'. Components are sourced in the neighbouring countries of Slovakia, Poland, and Hungary, but Czech-based companies also provide 60 per cent of the company's supplies. A number of these suppliers have followed Volkswagen from Western Europe, locating greenfield plants and engaging in joint ventures close to Skoda's plant in Mlada Boleslav. Local supply arrangements help the company to avoid import barriers and reduce assembly costs. The company is currently investigating the possibility of extending its supply network to Russia and Ukraine. It also has an assembly plant at Poznan in Poland and may set up similar plants in Russia and Belarus.

In 1997 Skoda's main plant produced 357,400 cars and the company planned to increase annual production to 500,000 by the year 2000. Most of this increase in production will come from productivity improvements. Between 1998 and 2002 Volkswagen intends to invest $1.3 billion in its plant at Mlada Boleslav. This investment will come from the proceeds of the company's growing sales, which rose by 29 per cent in 1997 and an expected 15 per cent in 1998. The investment will include improvements in Skoda's skills base. For example, its design and development centre at Mlada Boleslav has increased its workforce from 600 to 1,100. The design centre is now working on a third, upmarket model, using the same chassis as the Audi A4 and Volkswagen Passat, as well as a successor to the existing Felicia model.

In some respects, Volkswagen is following the example of other major car manufacturers which have invested in Russia and Eastern Europe, producing or assembling vehicles close to these increasingly competitive emerging markets. Its Skoda operations have become the company's main development arm in the region, enjoying the advantage of low costs and a flexible workforce, unlike Volkswagen's highly unionized home base in Germany. In other ways, its investment in Skoda represents a model of successful FDI in the region, combining capital injection, technology and skills transfer, new product development, and local sourcing and assembly, at the same time as the company is spear-heading a flow of high-quality FDI from Western to Eastern Europe. (Adapted from *Business Central Europe*, Apr. 1998, 36.)

Case Study Questions

1 What do you consider were the factors that influenced VW when deciding to invest in Czechoslovakia in 1991?

2 What have been the major contributions made by VW to the economic development of the region during the 1990s?

3 What other forms of FDI have been undertaken by Western car manufacturers in Russia and Eastern Europe during the 1990s and why have some forms been more successful than others?

4 In what ways might VW have assisted the privatization process in the Czech Republic by maintaining and increasing its investment in Skoda?

5 How far do you think that the financial crisis in Russia in August 1998 may have affected VW's decision (and those taken by other Western MNEs) to invest in the future? How will current FDI in Russia be affected by the financial crisis of 1998?

Notes

1   Some estimates of the size of the hidden economy in Eastern Europe and the former Soviet Union, including both criminal and informal activities, put it as high as 50% of official GDP, especially in the former Soviet Union: Oto Hudec, 'The informal economy in the Slovak Republic and its implications for economic statistics', a paper given at the Conference on the 'Slovak Economy in a United Europe', Technical University of Košice, 1/2 Oct. 1998 (published in proceedings).

2   J. Howell, *Understanding Eastern Europe: The Context of Change* (Ernst & Young, 1994), 108.

3   B. Dawes, *International Business. A European Perspective* (Stanley Thornes, 1995), 227.

4   Ibid. 116.

5   Ibid. 119.

6   D. Turnock, *The East European Economy in Context* (Routledge, 1997), 311.

7   J. Howell, *Understanding Eastern Europe*, 128.

8   Ibid. 129.

9   M. Kapoor, 'Changing gear', *Business Central Europe*, 13.

10   Ibid. 13.

11   Ibid. 13.

12   *Business Central Europe: The Annual* (1997–8), 26.

13   Ibid. 24.

14   Ibid. 23.

15   Ibid. 23.

16   Ibid. 32.

Recommended Reading

- Buckley, P. J., and Ghauri, P. N., *The Economics of Change in East and Central Europe: Its Impact on International Business* (Academic Press, 1994).

- Dawes, B., *International Business: A European Perspective* (Stanley Thornes, 1995).

- Gros, D., and Steinherr, A., *Winds of Change: Economic Transition in Central and Eastern Europe* (Longman, 1995).

- Lavigne, M., *The Economics of Transition: From Socialist Economy to Market Economy* (Macmillan, 1995).

- G. Pugh, 'Problems of Economic Transformation in Eastern Germany', *British Review of Economic Issues* (Oct. 1993), 15–37.

- Turnock, D., *The East European Economy in Context* (Routledge, 1997). *Business Central Europe*, various issues. *Central European Economic Review*, various issues.

21

The Relationship between the European Union and Eastern Europe

Objectives

- to discuss the reasons why the countries of Eastern Europe have vigorously pursued their applications for EU membership since the early 1990s
- to identify the areas of reform and conditions which will be applicable to countries from Eastern Europe prior to their being granted full EU membership
- to identify the costs (and benefits) to existing EU members from further enlargement
- to discuss the implications of EU enlargement in the twenty-first century

21.1 Introduction

THE issues to be discussed in this chapter are current and ongoing. Formal discussions between the EU and Hungary, Poland, the Czech Republic, Slovenia, and Estonia, the principal countries forming the next wave of new entrants (along with Cyprus) round about the year 2002, began in November 1998. The new raft of entrants must demonstrate credible democratic and economic credentials. There is no doubt that all five of the candidates from Eastern Europe can show full commitment to both political and economic reform and that substantial progress has been made since the beginning of the transition process in 1990. This chapter will not only discuss the benefits which may arise from EU membership, but will also explore whether the countries of Eastern Europe will be able to fulfil the economic and monetary strictures laid down by EU members in the Maastricht Treaty. In other words, how far can new members accrue a full range of benefits for themselves from EU membership and how far will they constitute a burden to richer countries, especially in the modernization of agriculture and the reform and stabilization of their currencies and financial markets?

The second stage of development for the advanced economies of Eastern Europe should perhaps be termed the 'Westernization' of their economies. This process involves the implementation of economic policy measures which result in a greater integration of their economies with those of the countries of Western Europe. Inevitably, the burden will fall on the existing members of the EU to support, both financially and with relevant expertise, the transformation of the financial services sector, the legal system, and the social welfare system of the countries concerned, both prior to and also in the period following EU entry. This process of transformation and development will undoubtedly benefit new members but it is not known how far this will constitute a burden to existing members who were already facing restrictions on their domestic economies in the years preceding the introduction of monetary union. There is also the issue of further EU enlargement. The current fifteen member countries could easily become twenty-five members in ten years time, but expansion could be a disaster for the EU if it were allowed to proceed unchecked and richer members found themselves increasingly having to shoulder the financial burden required to support poorer countries entering late. The rush of Eastern European countries to 'Westernize' their economies and to disengage themselves both economically and politically from the perceived old enemies of the former Soviet Union may force them into alliances which are difficult to sustain in the future.

21.2 The Changing International Political Environment

THE events which caused or contributed to the break-up of the Soviet bloc in 1989 have already been discussed in Chapter 18. However, the changing nature of international relations came about as a result of the disintegration of the Eastern bloc caused by Mikail Gorbachev entering the political stage in 1985, and also from the enthusiasm for greater economic and political integration demonstrated by the countries of Western Europe in the years preceding the creation of the Single European Market in 1992. It may be tempting to try to identify a causal link between the events leading to the creation of a free internal European market with the 1992 initiative and the breakdown of the traditional control mechanisms of the communist regimes in Eastern Europe. Perhaps there is no definable link between the dramatic changes which have been taking place in the East and the West recently. Nevertheless, the changes have produced revolutionary consequences for the countries taking part in the new developments. The failure to introduce economic and political reform into the declining Soviet system would have meant an inevitable collapse of the Soviet Empire in the future due to its inability to survive economically. *Perestroika* was a response to the reduced power position of the USSR within the international system. The reform process throughout Eastern Europe illustrated the need for all countries to adjust to the new circumstances in order to maintain or improve their positions within the new international environment. Similarly, the policies behind the 1992 programme were an attempt to respond to the rapidly changing circumstances of international relations.

After 1945 Western Europe became dependent upon the USA for the maintenance of its military defence mechanism and the development of a nuclear deterrent, whilst the countries of Eastern Europe were dependent upon the Soviet military machine for the maintenance of their national security, albeit in some cases reluctantly, as demonstrated by the popular uprisings in Hungary and Poland during the 1950s. In other words, the balance of power formed after 1945 created a bipolar world dominated by the two superpowers, the USA and the USSR, and for the most part international relations were conducted in an atmosphere of secrecy and distrust based on the race for military hegemony which became known as the 'Cold War'. In the 1970s and 1980s the Cold War was being fought by the two superpowers in the Third World, with the opposing sides of popular conflicts in Angola, Namibia, and Somalia being supported financially by the USA or by the USSR.

In addition, the shift of economic dominance in the West away from the USA and towards the countries of the Pacific, notably Japan (with its monopoly on sophisticated computer technology), meant that Western European countries were forced to establish new relationships in the international arena for the first time since the end of World War II. The events after 1989 destroyed this idea of a 'bipolar world' with the countries of Eastern Europe in revolt against the power of the Soviet bloc, whilst at the same time, EU member countries were actually moving closer towards the creation of a federal European state with the advent of the Single European Market and plans for the implementation of full economic and monetary union in the early part of the twenty-first century. In addition to these changes came pressures for the reform and reorganization of the existing international monetary and financial institutions, since these had been, by and large, established to deal with the bipolar world. The World Bank, IMF, EBRD, and the EU itself, had to be willing to adapt to demands placed upon them by the reforming countries of Eastern Europe and the former Soviet Union.

In other words, two 'revolutions' can be identified—1989 and 1992—both of which can be said to have changed the balance of power on the world stage, with the changes in Eastern Europe heralded by the events of 1989 perhaps being marginally more far reaching. The 'revolution' in the East was prompted by *perestroika* and *glasnost* and the process reached its climax with the reunification of Germany in 1990, whilst the 'revolution' in the West was represented by the 1992 initiative resulting in a reworking of the 'European idea' as well as a reorientation of Europe's role in the world at large. However, the proximity of the two ideals, albeit of 'disintegration' and 'integration', can be seen in the promotion of the idea of a 'Common European Home' launched by Mikail Gorbachev in 1988, who spoke of a new united Europe stretching from the Atlantic to the Urals.

It is not clear whether Gorbachev was insinuating that he viewed the European Community merely as a glorified free trade area which could be employed as such by the many potential new participants from Eastern Europe. However, this does not explain why the area east of the Urals was excluded from the idea and therefore the future of the Asian region of Russia remained unclear. However, it is possible that cynics would argue that the idea of the 'Common European Home' was simply another attempt by the Soviet Union to disengage Western Europe from its traditional alliance with the USA. If the USA did indeed become excluded from the 'Common Home' it was not clear to what extent the operation of NATO could continue to function as a defensive organization protecting countries which had been previously members of the Warsaw Pact. It is unlikely that Gorbachev in 1988 envisaged the importance, both strategically and psychologically, for the countries of Eastern Europe to obtain NATO membership and so underline the extent and success of their 'Westernization' process. The rush to join NATO is largely symbolic for the countries of Eastern Europe: it represents a break with the past and indicates that friendships have been formed with their old enemies in the West. In other words, for Eastern Europe, NATO membership (and EU membership) represents the final chapter in the break with the former Soviet empire which commenced in 1989.

An alternative view held by George Soros, the Hungarian-American financier, attacks the idea of European integration as a means of achieving a more open society and claims that the idea of Europe as an open society that would attract others and reinforce democracy has failed, with the opportunities being afforded by the events of 1989 being ignored.[1] Soros argues that the Schengen Treaty, for example, which was supposed to open up borders within Europe has actually ended up controlling the borders of Eastern Europe. It could be argued that in the years since 1989 Europe has moved more in the direction of a fortress haunted by its fears of the economic and social costs of admitting new members to the EU. Soros claims that by adopting this attitude the countries of Western Europe have abandoned the ideals of an open society since they no longer have to actively pursue the idea because, with the collapse of communism (the archetypal closed society), all opposition to the open society was removed.

Indeed, Soros argues that it was this opposition to communism which formed the common ground to hold Europe together. Before 1989 the common goal of achieving an open society in opposition to a closed society created by communism meant that power in Europe was more evenly balanced with each of the countries in a minority. After 1989 reunification shifted the balance of power towards Germany and member states started to behave in their national interests by playing the power game once again. Soros argues that in order to achieve an open society the countries of Western Europe need to be driven by collective interests rather than national interests. The idea of the open society needs to be redefined in terms of the drive towards EU integration and future enlargement. Soros questions whether integration can ever be successfully achieved since individual member countries continue to be driven by national concerns rather than by the collective interests of the EU as a whole. If this cannot be achieved, how far can further EU enlargement be successful if existing members continue to pursue national interests (tariffs and quotas on agricultural and other goods) by putting up barriers to discourage the countries of Eastern Europe from obtaining early entry.

It seems that Soros ignores the *costs* of achieving an open society if this is indeed defined by the need to pursue EU enlargement more vigorously to allow the countries of Eastern Europe easy entry. Perhaps the real crime which has been committed by the members of the EU since 1989 is to have closed ranks against early entry by the countries of Eastern Europe in order to protect their own economies and the EU budget from the drain which will occur when the entry of Hungary, Poland, the Czech Republic, Slovenia, and Estonia is finally permitted. Perhaps it is right to make countries delay their entry until the economic transition has been more or less completed and so avoid the EU having to shoulder the financial burden of wholly supporting the transition process. Although the EU has contributed both financial support and know-how to facilitate the transition process, it has been recognized that the cost of supporting the restructuring of agriculture and industry is too high for the EU at a time when member countries face domestic financial and monetary restrictions to meet the criteria for EMU. In other words, the question which arises here is whether the prospect of further EU enlargement is actually compatible with the move towards European integration heralded by the advent of the Single European Market in 1992.

21.3 Eastern Europe: the Rush for EU Membership?

AFTER 1989, with the break-up of the Soviet bloc and the elimination of both the military and economic institutions which supported it, the countries of Eastern Europe naturally cast about for alternative alliances, and those situated towards the west of the former Soviet Union gravitated towards the EU. Despite initial hopes, it was not possible to allow countries of the region immediate membership, but the EU did establish an important trade development in December 1991 when the former Czechoslovakia, Poland, and Hungary signed 'Europe Agreements' (EAs), with Bulgaria and Romania becoming signatories by the end of the following year. Although the EAs heralded closer economic cooperation between the EU and the Visegrad countries (as the EA signatory countries became known), and the Commission opened serious negotiations with the first wave of potential new members in November 1998, the issues relating to membership are extremely complex and not every Eastern

European country will eventually become a member. The EU is already a great deal more than a free trade area and plans to become a fully integrated single market with free movement of capital and labour, supported by a monetary union with a central bank and a common regulatory framework. The issue which will be discussed later in this chapter is how far and at what cost will the countries of Eastern Europe be able to fulfil these criteria?

Generally, the establishment of EAs was viewed positively as it underlined the fact that signatories would eventually gain full EU membership. The agreement also established a commitment by members of the EU to provide assistance and cooperation to move towards harmonization of regulatory legislation, to establish joint partnerships in science and technology, and also provide financial and technical support in the economic transition process. In addition, the EU signed 'Partnership and Cooperation Agreements' with Russia and most western CIS countries, but these did not go as far as the EAs and most certainly did not anticipate possible EU entry in the future. Indeed, these agreements failed to go much beyond the granting of 'most favoured nation' status and did not produce significant liberalization of trade.

Nevertheless, the EAs have had their critics especially over the protectionist attitude taken by the EU towards so-called sensitive goods produced by the countries of Eastern Europe. The categories of goods include agricultural, steel, textile, and leather products which remain protected in the EU. Since 1995 trade restrictions on these goods have been reduced but much criticism has been received on both sides since the countries of Eastern Europe are very competitive in the production of these goods. Trade restrictions damage the ability of Eastern Europe to compete and sell their products, but trade liberalization also reduces the incomes of EU producers from the sale of their own goods.

Since EAs can only be obtained by those countries who will eventually join the EU, not all countries, therefore, can benefit from the advantages of EAs. However, work undertaken by Brenton and Kendall, published in 1993, indicates that trade between the EU and the countries of Eastern Europe is about 23 per cent larger than would otherwise be expected when the factors of geography and GDP alone are taken into account.[2] Other results show that trade between EU members is about 60 per cent larger than normally expected on the basis of distance and income, but that in 1992 trade between the EU and the EFTA countries was about normal. Some EU member countries have received greater benefits than others by fostering trade relations with Eastern Europe after 1989. Germany is itself in a unique geographical position and data compiled by Brenton and Kendall demonstrate that trade between Germany and Eastern Europe is about 100 per cent higher than would have been expected when income and geographical position is taken into account. It is not surprising that Germany has promoted greater cooperation between the EU and Eastern Europe. However, the fact that a higher than average volume of trade is taking place indicates that there is little foundation in the criticism levelled at the EU for the protectionist policies its members are supposed to have pursued. Even the fact that the EU has been running a trade surplus with Eastern Europe can be explained by the need of EU members to transfer aid to assist the economic transformation process. This process is facilitated by the EU maintaining a trade surplus.

If the countries of Eastern Europe are already receiving benefits from increased trading opportunities within the EU without the benefits of EU membership, why then are Poland, Hungary, the Czech Republic, Estonia, and Slovenia, lining up to be admitted to full membership at the earliest possible opportunity? The most immediate benefit for new members would be access to the markets of the world's leading rich nations. The EU accounts for 80–90 per cent of all trade with the rich part of the world and 60–70 per cent of overall trade.[3] Of course, membership of the EU offers far more than access to a free trade area. Additional benefits which may initially impose financial costs on new members include free movement of labour and capital, and eventual economic and monetary union. Some of the costs of membership can be offset by access to EU structural other funds which offer financial aid and support for agriculture, scientific development, and industrial restructuring.

There is no doubt that the rush for EU membership will mean that a new group of 'haves' and 'have-nots' will be established among the countries of Eastern Europe. In other words, those countries which do obtain full membership will gain access to the support afforded by the structural funds and CAP as well as being able to operate in a large free trade area, but those who are not admitted to membership will continue to operate on the periphery of Europe and will seek to establish their economic and political alliances elsewhere. Inevitably, it is the countries which conform most closely to the European ideal, in both economic and political terms, which will be successful in entering the EU. It is not surprising that the EU is well disposed towards taking Poland, Hungary, the Czech Republic, Estonia, and Slovenia at an early stage, and that countries like Belarus, with its difficulties in achieving democracy and its government's reluctance to implement effective economic reform, have little chance of being admitted to the EU, even in the long term. Potential new members need to be able to demonstrate that they are able to achieve integration with the EU by showing that the requisite economic, political, and social reform is being implemented.

The important issue here is whether the existing EU member countries can actually afford to support new members and whether the drain on the CAP and other structural funds will be too great to allow EU enlargement to proceed as rapidly as has been anticipated. The CAP will need to be substantially reformed to allow the policy to sustain the demands made upon it by new entrants. If agriculture in Eastern Europe fails to respond to the higher prices under the CAP, then there will be little benefit obtained by farmers who largely operate small-scale and subsistence units. However, it is perhaps more likely that farmers in Eastern Europe would respond to the higher prices offered under the CAP by attempting to increase yields. It has been estimated that the entry of Hungary, Poland, and the Czech Republic to the EU could increase the cost of the CAP by 60 per cent of the current levels of support.[4]

In addition, new members from Eastern Europe would be eligible for substantial support from the EU structural funds. If it is assumed that per capita transfers to new members from these funds would be similar to the amount already received by the EU's poorer members like Greece and Portugal, then Hungary, Poland, and the Czech Republic would easily receive in excess of 12 per cent of their GDP.[5] Despite this, such transfers from the structural funds would have little effect on the total EU budget, amounting to about 0.3 per cent of EU GDP.[6] In effect, by admitting the first wave of new entrants the cost to the EU would be around 15 billion euros per annum.[7] This may seem a substantial burden given that the total EU annual budget amounts to around 90 billion euros, but the additional cost would represent only about 0.25 per cent of the total GDP of the EU. The benefits obtained by new members receiving transfers from the structural funds in particular would be substantial since these would represent a significant proportion of GDP for poorer countries. The main benefit would be to enable new members to raise the standard of living within their countries towards the level enjoyed by established members. They would be able to afford to import more goods from abroad without the need to match them with exports. Since exports into the EU from Eastern Europe are at present negligible, manufacturers in the EU would have everything to gain by being able to export to a new and rapidly developing market.

21.4 EU Membership: How Do Eastern European Applicants Shape Up?

IT is necessary to discuss EU expansion within the context of the enlargement of NATO, since the combined effect of these two events is likely to produce an ineradicable dividing line between East and West and also within the former Eastern bloc itself. As far as NATO goes, the have-nots will be offered closer cooperation but no firm guarantees will be given of membership in the future. The primary aim of NATO is to create stability across the region, so it was always unlikely that more than three countries would be accepted for membership during the first round, although more countries may become eligible early in the twentieth-first century. It is argued that those countries who have been excluded from early NATO membership will also be at an economic disadvantage since FDI will naturally gravitate towards the new members. This economic gap will worsen once countries start joining the EU. Candidates for EU membership will be judged on their political readiness, economic criteria, laws, and administration. Hungary is widely regarded as top of the list, but all candidate countries still have a great deal of work to do in order to demonstrate that they are operating a market economy with the transition process completed.

The Czech Republic must deregulate its banking industry, tackle its environmental problems, and strengthen its regional government. Although Poland probably holds the trump card of location which will guarantee its membership (it forms a buffer between Germany and the volatile states of Belarus, Ukraine, and Russia), there is still cause for concern that privatization has been moving at a snail's pace with nearly half of the economy remaining in state hands. Price controls continue to be largely responsible for petrol and electricity prices running at half the level of those in Western Europe. Another crucial indicator, income per head, is also much lower in Poland than in any previous country at the time of EU admission. Poland needs to undertake substantial restructuring in key areas like steel, telecommunications, defence, shipping, coal, and the financial services sector.

In addition, Poland suffers from the usual range of environmental problems caused by the central planning mechanism before 1990. The World Bank accepts that all the necessary environmental legislation is in place but that it will cost US$21 billion for industry to comply with it. However, by far the biggest problem for EU negotiators to contend with is agriculture. For example, if Poland was eligible for funds at the present time under the CAP, it would cost the EU US$30 billion a year or 40 per cent of the CAP's total budget.[8] In addition, all new member countries from Eastern Europe will have to conform to the core of the new *acquis communautaire*, a 320,000-page statement of EU law. All of these problems point to the fact that no one is likely to gain entry to the EU until the year 2005, despite claims that some countries were to be admitted by 2000. It took over five years for Austria, Sweden, and Finland to progress from application to full membership. The next wave of negotiations are likely to take much longer. Apart from the problems posed by agriculture, industry, and the environment already discussed, the poorer members of the EU are not enthusiastic at the prospect of Eastern European countries clamouring for hand-outs from Brussels. For new countries to join, all fifteen member governments must ratify an accession treaty.

Countries like Slovakia who do not achieve EU membership in the first wave will face external tariffs not covered by their EAs in addition to a range of more subtle trade barriers from border delays to certification. Since the Visegrad countries accounted for 41 per cent of Slovakia's exports in 1996–7, it is perhaps not surprising that the former Prime Minister, Vladimir Meciar, regarded Russia as Slovakia's most 'prospective' trading partner.[9]

The only way that the excluded Eastern European countries can hope to be considered in the second wave of membership is to quicken up the economic reform process and implement monetary and fiscal measures accompanied by a privatization programme which includes substantial restructuring and industrial reform. Bulgaria and Romania are both in this category at the present time, having been badly served by governments which have dragged their feet over reform. If they do show a commitment towards the transition to capitalism this may be rewarded by accession to the EU at a later stage, but if they fail to implement economic reform they may find that EU membership ceases to become a possibility and they are simply dropped from the list.

Despite this, there is no room for complacency among those countries which expect early EU entry. There is the danger that the dividing line between East and West could stay exactly where it is at present—between the former communist countries and their wealthy Western neighbours. It is questionable whether the countries of Eastern Europe will ever be able to achieve the same economic performance levels already enjoyed by Western countries. It has been estimated that the Polish economy would have to grow by 6 per cent a year for twenty years just to catch up with where Greece, the poorest country, is today.[10] The fear is that the countries of Eastern Europe will remain low-wage areas even after accession to the EU. This will not only depend upon the conditions of entry, but also on the performance of the economies of

Western Europe over the next few years. The prospect of high unemployment persisting among existing EU members may cause restrictions to be placed on new members enjoying the facility of free labour movement. Indeed, the EU could exclude new members from many of the EU's benefits for the foreseeable future. But some prospective members already have other ideas. In a statement released on 26 February 1998 the Polish Ministry of Labour insisted that Polish citizens should be allowed to work in other EU countries as soon as Poland becomes a member of the EU.[11] This statement seems to have been a response to that of the German Ambassador to the EU, Dietrich von Kyaw who said that free movement of labour for Poland would be 'unthinkable' immediately upon entering the EU. Germany already has more than 12 per cent of its workforce unemployed so a large influx of migrant workers would undoubtedly increase unemployment beyond its present level.

A report on the costs and benefits of entry which suggests that EU enlargement will generate US$30 billion in investment and trade to new member countries also speculates on the impact which the EU's body of law may have on Eastern European growth and unemployment rates.[12] The authors suggest that because EU rules were designed for wealthy social democracies with extensive welfare networks, they may be inappropriate for poorer Eastern European countries with high growth rates. By being forced to adopt Social Charter rules and EU environmental standards, the countries of Eastern Europe could well end up with structures that hamper their attempts to catch up. The experience of Spain, Portugal, and Greece may have parallels here. In the case of Spain and Portugal the huge surge in investment was caused largely by their willingness to implement far-reaching reforms, but Greece did not, and remains the EU's charity case. Greece's experience suggests that new members must force through painful reforms rather than avoid them. This is the reason why some Eastern European aspirant members want a longer transition period after membership, to allow the gradual restructuring of core, but decrepit industry, in an attempt to protect themselves against high unemployment. Delay in implementing a far-reaching and effective restructuring programme makes the social costs of reform higher in the future. This is particularly important for those countries excluded from membership in the first wave and who will need to increase their efforts to gain acceptability to the West. In the end, it matters little who joins NATO or the EU, the real dividing line across Europe will be between rich or poor countries. It is the role of the governments of Eastern Europe to ensure that their countries end up on the right side of the economic divide.

21.5 Eastern Europe and EMU

THE discussion relating to the implications of a single currency on governments, banks, and companies in the EU area has failed to recognize or consider the problems facing the countries of Eastern Europe with membership ambitions. However, the prospect of monetary union will not have immediate implications for new members since EMU and ERM II, a new exchange rate mechanism for non-participants, will have been in operation for some years prior to the accession of the first new members. Initially, their main tasks will be to work with the new currency by redenominating contracts, deciding on the weight of the euro in currency baskets, coordinating with the European Central Bank, etc. The most pressing issue which needs to be resolved immediately (and certainly, well in advance of entry to the EU) is whether Eastern Europe should accept that it will have to remain outside the mechanism for the foreseeable future. Indeed, this boils down to the question of whether it really makes sense for the region to pursue the monetary and fiscal convergence criteria laid down by the Maastricht Treaty. Some Eastern European countries have pointed to their successes in reducing budget deficits and debt levels, believing that this puts them into the same economic performance category as the rest of the EU. However, this ignores their less than perfect record on reducing high inflation levels and non-existent long-term interest rates mean that convergence is still years away.

The real issue is not whether any of the countries of Eastern Europe can meet the convergence criteria, but whether they can realistically sustain them. The issue here is whether EU membership for Eastern Europe should be inextricably linked to the fulfilment of the Maastricht criteria. However, it could be argued that fulfilment of the convergence criteria was never intended to be a precondition of membership. Their purpose is to ensure sufficient similarity among members' economies, in terms of levels of development, to ensure stability within EMU. If Eastern European countries place too much emphasis on reaching convergence targets and ignoring the more pressing need to restructure their economies, then this would be against the overriding aim of Maastricht. In addition, when countries become members of EMU then this removes the use of exchange rates as an instrument of macroeconomic policy, and forces monetary and economic policy into line with that of the EU. For the countries of Eastern Europe this would be a very difficult situation as it would tie the hands of governments in their attempts to reduce inflationary pressures in the face of appreciating exchange rates resulting from large capital inflows. The problem is compounded for Eastern Europe with its weak central banks and underdeveloped capital markets. It is also against the EU's interests to force new members into a potentially unsustainable fixed exchange rate to the euro. A period of transition within the ERM II would give Eastern European members an opportunity to adjust towards a stable exchange rate gradually.

The issue which currently needs to be addressed by the EU is what will be the consequences for countries which are left out of EMU for many years and what impact will this have on the EU? The divisions between wealthy and poor members may well be perpetuated and exaggerated in the future, especially if a second division of members remain outside of EMU because membership can never be sustained. This problem needs to be resolved at the formal accession discussions which began in November 1998 since the implications for the long-term development of the EU are immense. It may well be that if most of the new members of the EU remain outside EMU, the division between the richer and poorer nations will shift in the future and become defined by participation or non-participation in EMU.

21.6 The Role of Western Assistance in the Transition

SINCE 1990 the EU has played an important role in assisting the countries of Eastern Europe to transform their economies into market systems underpinned by the introduction of parliamentary democracy. Obviously, EU involvement has seen mixed success and the effectiveness of such assistance has been reduced in the face of political instability suffered by countries like Romania and Bulgaria. The EU has played an important role as an intermediary in coordinating aid from the West to the East. The break-up of the Eastern bloc in 1989 undermined the traditional bipolarity in international relations, and this has enabled the EU as a 'civilian' or 'economic' power to take a more independent part in European politics. The EU has generally been thought to have acquitted itself well and this has resulted in its ability to form a major influence on the design of post-Cold War Europe.

In July 1989 at the summit of the G7 countries in Paris, it was decided that the European Commission should act in a coordinating capacity to ensure that the assistance provided by the OECD countries reached its targets. The coordinating role of the EC was also thought to provide a mechanism to limit Germany's potential economic influence in the East. Financial assistance was provided by a new economic aid programme called PHARE (Poland and Hungary: Assistance for Restructuring Economies), initially restricted to Poland and Hungary but later extended to all the transition countries except the CIS where a specific programme known as TACIS was established (Technical Assistance for the Commonwealth of Independent States). The largest contributors to PHARE have been EU member countries, followed by the USA and Japan. In reality, the USA was apparently overwhelmed by the demands from the East for financial assistance and decided to limit its own involvement due to domestic budgetary problems. As a result, for the first time since the end of World War II, the USA left the EU in control of this important foreign policy issue. The PHARE programme was based on five major objectives:

(1) supplying immediate food aid;
(2) facilitating Eastern European access to EU markets (the EAs signed in 1992 were discussed earlier);
(3) giving Poland and Hungary access to funds available from the EIB and other EU financial institutions;
(4) transfer of 'know-how' by the provision of special training particularly in order to allow Eastern Europe to establish market-oriented management; and
(5) providing special assistance in environmental matters.

The provision of assistance under PHARE was conditional upon the adherence of Eastern European countries to extensive economic and political reform programmes. Although Poland and Hungary have taken the lion's share of PHARE funds actually allocated (34 per cent and 26 per cent respectively), the schemes have tended to fund basic infrastructure projects like the construction of sewage disposal plants, road repairs, etc. However, the programme has acquired a much harder political edge with the onset of the membership accession talks in November 1998. The EU has stated that PHARE will become accession-driven with a clear targeting of money towards accession-related projects. In other words, it seems that PHARE is turning into an incentive scheme. A failure by countries to meet specific, timetable-bound objectives could mean that the EU decides to cut off aid and give the funding to more deserving candidates. Ultimately, PHARE's new 'carrot-and-stick' approach has to work despite doubts relating to the ability of notoriously factional governments to carry out fundamental reforms. If applicants do not accelerate EU-related reform—especially the adoption and enforcement of at least 80,000 pages of EU legislation—then their negotiating power will disappear.

The founding of the European Bank for Reconstruction and Development (EBRD) was a major development of the 1990s as this was the first important international financial institution to see the light of day at the end of the Cold War. The EBRD has fifty-eight shareholder states representing both donors and recipients and included developing countries like Mexico, Morocco, and Egypt, as well as the EU and EIB as institutional shareholders. The aims of the EBRD were to promote the transition to democracy and market economies by investing and lending to both private sector enterprises and SOEs involved in privatization. Since 1996 the emphasis of the EBRD lending policy has shifted towards the private sector with an emphasis on forging paths for commercial banks to follow. The success of the EBRD rests on having reinvented itself as a transition-aided investment bank rather than a classic development institution.

In the next stage of its development, the EBRD is trying to adopt a policy of 'graduation'—the process of moving business eastwards away from Visegrad countries and forcing it to look harder for more exotic opportunities in countries of the former Soviet Union. The problem with this is finding realistic investment opportunities in countries like Belarus and Armenia. It would also be wrong to assume that the EBRD's work in the Visegrad countries is over, but its work could be made more relevant if it turned away from investment projects involving Western partners and became involved in:

- providing long-term finance for the restructuring of privatized or privatizing heavy industry;
- the financing of important infrastructure projects like road construction, telecommunications, and utility schemes; commercial banks cannot hope to fund these seriously underinvested areas of the economy alone; and
- targeting long-term loan capital firms which often find it difficult to acquire funds from traditional sources. For example, the EBRD could offer loans for five or six years to medium-sized companies but it must ensure that this capital is additional to that available from the banking institutions: some Czech banks have been complaining that the EBRD is crowding them out.

The international financial institutions have also played a major role in facilitating the economic transition in Eastern Europe. By 1992, all Eastern European countries, the Baltic States, and the other countries of the former Soviet Union had become members of the World Bank and the IMF. Assistance from the latter has been made conditional upon the implementation of macroeconomic stabilization programmes. Approval of such measures by the IMF has produced assistance with balance of payments financing (including debt write-offs and rescheduling), and establishing a stabilization fund to facilitate the move towards currency convertibility, etc. Inevitably, private investment flows are inextricably linked to aid flows because private finance can be increased by the implementation of specific aid measures from the EU and other international organizations. Similarly, the overall confidence in the market potential of a country can be enhanced by the approval it receives from the IMF.

21.7 Summary

ACCESSION of the five Eastern European candidate countries currently with applications to join the EU is essential. By offering Poland, Hungary, the Czech Republic, Slovenia, and Estonia full membership this will ensure that the second stage of economic transition can be undertaken. In other words, the 'Westernization' of the economies of the countries of Eastern Europe is assured. This will also safeguard the political reforms in countries where former political élites often place pressure on reformist governments to reverse or slow down the important changes which have already taken place. However, it may be erroneous to regard the talks which began in November 1998 with the five leading candidates for membership as accession negotiations. Endre Juhasz, the Hungarian Ambassador to the EU has said that 'these will not be negotiations between partners of equal weight . . . we are applying for membership so we have to adjust to the system.'[13]

Applicants will have to pursue accession in two broad areas. Firstly, they must meet reform targets contained in the EU's 'accession partnership' documents which give details of the objectives which each country must achieve by the end of 1998, and also what is expected of them in the medium-term (see the Appendix to this chapter). If these targets are not met, then applicants may find themselves permanently out of the running for membership. The second area of reform facing applicants from Eastern Europe is the adoption of the EU's *acquis communautaire*, and this is the area which will be monitored most closely by EU representatives from 1998. It is likely that once the five candidates have demonstrated their commitment, the real negotiations on the real issues will begin in 1999. In effect, this next stage of negotiations will constitute reaching agreement on transition periods for new members entering the EU.

All Eastern European countries can expect to have some transition periods granted by the EU in order to allow them time to carry out far-reaching reforms in agriculture, transport, the environment, and in the deregulation of financial markets. However, it may be that ultimately the EU is not prepared to countenance long transition periods when new members join as this may be seen to constitute an opt-out. On the other hand, if some Eastern European countries refuse to accept transition periods on farming or the free movement of labour, this may well put the EU on the spot as it would have to admit that some of its current members require protection and would not be prepared to allow new members into the EU or free movement from day one. For example, Germany and Austria are extremely worried about the effects on their economies of large numbers of immigrant workers arriving from the East. However, the issue of labour emigration may well have been exaggerated and initially fuelled by evidence of the strong migration drive in 1989 which was used by the Western media as evidence that many more millions of Eastern Europeans were preparing to emigrate. There is no doubt that emigration would make sense due to the disparity in wages between East and West, but this also in itself limits permanent migration, given that it is usually enough to improve one's situation to work for a few weeks in the West as a 'tourist'. In addition, the high rates of unemployment which were predicted for Eastern Europe have not materialized, so this has removed the incentive for people to find work outside the region. Despite this, the EU is demanding that the countries of Eastern Europe strengthen their border management schemes—it seems that Eastern Europe must learn the hard lesson that economic liberalization stops where labour movements are concerned. The potential cost for Western Europe from labour emigration could be high.

In parallel to the accession talks, the EU itself must restructure its own institutions in preparation for the entry of its new members. This is necessary in order to meet the costs of enlargement and also to reassure its current members that a larger EU will not drastically curtail their own access to funds. The EU is proposing to freeze spending on regional aid in real terms between 2000 and 2006. This will mean that Eastern Europe will get 44 billion euro of regional assistance but may mean that the EU's current poorer members like Spain, Portugal, Greece, and Ireland, may lose out. Consequently, the five new applicants from Eastern Europe will not get in until these issues are settled—enlargement requires ratification by all fifteen national parliaments.

Nevertheless, it is essential that the five candidate countries from Eastern Europe should be admitted to the EU at the same time at a date to be determined based on their willingness to implement the accession criteria which must be firm and not subject to renegotiation or revision. The Commission itself will be faced with the task of monitoring the fulfilment of the criteria and also it will make its structural funds, PHARE, and other programmes available to assist with the economic adjustments which will need to take place in the candidate countries. Once granted, membership of the EU must be full and not partial, but cannot be linked with EMU membership in the early stages. Some countries may be unable to fulfil the conditions for EMU, but those countries which can, notably the Czech Republic, should have this option made available to them.

Review Questions

1 What do you understand by the term 'Westernization' of the economies of Eastern Europe and, in general terms, what changes will this process produce?

2 How far do you think that the 'two revolutions' of 1989 and 1992 defined the pattern of European integration in the 1990s?

3 Did the Europe Agreements signed between the EU and the Visegrad countries in 1992 achieve any of their objectives?

4 In what ways will it be necessary to reform the CAP prior to the accession of new members to the EU and how will this affect both EU farmers and farmers in the countries of Eastern Europe?

5 How far have Western financial institutions contributed to the economic transition of Eastern Europe during the 1990s?

Study Topic: Is EMU Good for Eastern Europe?

A recent report from the IMF suggests that, if the euro is successfully introduced within the EU, monetary union should also benefit the countries of Eastern Europe, especially those closest to the EU which are preparing for EU membership, often known as the Visegrad countries. This is because increased transparency and the removal of exchange risks should bring about efficiency and competition in goods and financial markets between EMU countries and increase their collective GDP. The IMF estimates that every 1 per cent increase in Europe's GDP may boost Eastern Europe's exports by 1.5 per cent. This, in turn, may lead to a 0.9 per cent increase in the Eastern European countries' GDP.

These estimates depend on how things develop in the euro zone. If, as seems to be happening, interest rates tend to converge around the lower rates in the EU, portfolio investors may move some of their funds out of the EU, especially from the formerly higher-rate countries of southern Europe. The more actively reforming countries of Eastern Europe may be the beneficiaries of these investment movements, offering higher interest rates in the region's more stable emerging markets. On the other hand, the Eastern European countries may also benefit as borrowers in the EU's lower-rate and more liquid securities markets. These benefits could disappear, however, if EMU interest rates rise in order to protect a weak euro, increasing the servicing costs of Eastern Europe's heavy debt burden. The estimated improvement in the EU's economic growth rate may also fail to materialize if the labour market reforms needed to achieve euro-zone adjustment mechanisms are not achieved. The countries of Eastern Europe therefore appear to have a strong vested interest in the euro's success, even before they become active participants in monetary union themselves. (Adapted from 'Flying EMUs: If the euro is good for the EU, it'll be good for Central Europeans too', *Business Central Europe*, Dec. 1998/Jan. 1999, 39.)

Study Topic Questions

1   In what ways might the advent of the euro benefit some countries in Eastern Europe more than others in the region?

2   On what kind of factors is the success of the euro likely to depend?

3   What economic/political/legal reforms will be required by the first wave of entrants from Eastern Europe prior to their joining EMU in the future?

4   What are the prospects for the countries of Eastern Europe fulfilling the conditions of the Maastricht Treaty and entering the euro zone?

5   What might be the implications for the euro if the countries of Eastern Europe eventually adopt the single currency?

Appendix

The EU has set the following reform tasks for the five Eastern European applicants which must be 'completed or taken forward in 1998':

Czech Republic
- improve corporate governance
- accelerate bank restructuring
- enforce stock market supervision
- improve bank supervision
- set up structures for regional policy
- develop effective border management

Estonia
- improve integration of non-citizens, including stateless children
- enhance Estonian language training for ethnic Russians
- accelerate land reform
- begin pension reform
- develop civil service training
- adopt competition law
- take concrete steps to combat corruption and organized crime
- develop effective border management

Hungary
- advance structural reform, particularly of health care
- enforce intellectual property rights

- implement refugee laws consistent with the Geneva Convention
- develop effective border management

Poland
- accelerate privatization
- accelerate development of the financial sector
- adopt and start steel restructuring programme by 30 June 1998
- liberalize capital movements
- establish a coherent rural development policy
- upgrade dairies and meat processing plants
- develop effective border management, in particular with Belarus and Ukraine

Slovenia
- promote market driven restructuring in enterprise, banking, and finance sectors
- prepare pension reform
- introduce a civil service law
- adopt VAT law
- liberalize capital movement
- adopt anti-trust law
- clarify property laws

Source: 'Not negotiable', *Business Central Europe* (March 1998), 19.

Notes

1 G. Soros, 'Lost Opportunity', *Business Central Europe: The Annual* (Dec. 1995), 24.

2 P. Brenton and T. Kendall, 'Back to Earth with the Gravity Model: Further Estimates for Eastern European Countries', *Centre for European Policy Studies* (Dec. 1993).

3 D. Gros and A. Steinherr, Winds of Change: Economic Transition in Central and *Eastern Europe* (Longman, 1995), 491.

4 Ibid. 505.

5 Ibid. 504.

6 Ibid.

7 Ibid. 505.

8 R. Lyons and P. Simpson, 'Of Hype and Halos' (A Survey of Poland), *Business Central Europe* (Feb. 1997), 40.

9 J. Cook, 'The New Wall?', *Business Central Europe* (July/Aug. 1997), 12.

10 Ibid. 12.

11 Reported by *RFE/RL Newsline*, 2(40): pt. II (27 Feb. 1998).

12 R. Baldwin, J. Francois, and R. Portes, 'The Costs and Benefits of EU Enlargement', *Economic Policy*, 24.

13 J. Cook, 'Talking it Over', *Business Central Europe* (Mar. 1998), 18.

Recommended Reading

■ Dobrinsky, R., and Landesmann, M., *Transforming Economies and European Integration* (Edward Elgar, 1995).

■ Gros, D., and Steinherr, A., *Winds of Change: Economic Transition in Central and Eastern Europe* (Longman, 1995).

■ Lavigne, M., *The Economics of Transition: From Socialist Economy to Market Economy* (Macmillan, 1995).

■ Van Ham, P., *The European Community, Eastern Europe and European Unity: Discord, Collaboration and Integration since 1947* (Pinter, 1993).

22

Doing Business in Eastern Europe

Objectives

- to identify the successes and failures of the economic reform process since 1990
- to discuss the ongoing problems facing Eastern Europe at the end of the 1990s in implementing and sustaining economic reform
- to identify the challenges faced by Western firms operating in the region in the future
- to identify policy changes which are required by governments to enable FDI to be promoted in the future

22.1 Introduction

THIS chapter discusses the success of the economic transformation process in Eastern Europe and whether the development of an entrepreneurial business culture has been an effective tool in promoting private sector business activity. A successful economic transition should be based on policies which will transform a centrally planned economy (characterized by the political monopoly of the communist party, a predominance of public ownership, a direct command managerial structure, economies of shortage, a negligible role for monetary policy, and external imbalances), to a market economy demonstrating import liberalization, market clearing of prices, a unified exchange rate and current account convertibility, the elimination of direct and indirect state subsidies, rapid privatization, and a competitive banking system subject to close supervision.[1] The risks to the success of the economic reforms have largely been of a political nature. The rapidly changing nature of some governments in the region has meant that elections result in the appearance of former communists posing as social-democrat politicians. In many cases, this has led to a slowing down of the reform process, especially with respect to privatization with the resulting effects on efficiency, profitability, and the ability of SOEs to compete with companies already operating in the private sector.

It has been argued that the only real change which has occurred is the abolition of the monopoly of the Communist Party since serious economic problems continue to beset governments of the region, principally unemployment, inflation, poverty, and a failure to control corruption and mafia activity.[2] One measure of how far there has been real change in the economies of the region since 1990 is the extent to which macroeconomic stabilization has been successful. The answer is not clear although attempts have been made to introduce currency convertibility, reduce the barriers to trade, and maintain restrictive monetary and fiscal policies. However, it is not sufficient to look at macroeconomic stabilization policies alone since another important measure of real change is how far the private sector has undergone transformation in its management practices, accounting techniques, and culture as a result of privatization and activity by foreign investors. In other words, this chapter discusses the extent of the 'Westernization' of the economies of Eastern Europe and how the business cultures spawned under central planning have had to adapt to the new challenges. Western investors have played an important role in the development of the private sector and in the growing awareness of the need to adopt a Western entrepreneurial business culture if countries of the region are to take their place in the global economy in the future.

22.2 The Successes and Failures of the Transformation Process in Eastern Europe since 1990

THE economic reform programmes implemented by the countries of Eastern Europe after 1990 were received with high expectations. It was thought that policies which would enable the economies to transfer from decades of central planning causing economic stagnation to fully operational market economies would produce astonishing results within a very short period of time. In addition, there were no doubts in the minds of policy-makers that such reforms would receive unqualified support from the countries' electorates, since having themselves been faced with decades of poor living standards, the prosperity that would come with capitalism would be welcomed by everyone. The reality was very different: no one could have predicted that within two years of the start of the transition, the economies of

Eastern Europe would be plunged into a deep recession causing living standards to decline further.

All countries of the region were hit by recession and those countries facing difficulties with maintaining the momentum of reform (perhaps due to problems with political instability) are still struggling to lift themselves out of recession. On the other hand, countries which have taken a more robust approach to reform (Poland, Hungary, and the Czech Republic) have seen major progress being made in increasing economic growth, reducing inflation, and in preventing unemployment rising to the levels which had been predicted in 1990. The causes of the recession in Eastern Europe in the early 1990s can be attributed to internal and external factors.

22.2.1 Internal factors: 'shock therapy' vs 'gradualism'

One factor which can be attributed to the results of the reform process itself relates to the speed with which countries dismantled the intensely bureaucratic mechanism of central planning replacing it with structures designed to allow free market competition. The early approaches to reform taken by Poland and Czechoslovakia can be described as 'big bang' or 'shock therapy' whereby all the major changes necessary for transition to a market economy were implemented within a very short period of time. The first country to adopt 'shock therapy' was Poland in early 1990, where reductions in public spending, virtual elimination of all subsidies, a strict incomes policy, an immediate devaluation to encourage exports, and a removal of foreign trade restrictions, meant that GDP fell by more than 18 per cent in just two years from 1990–1. Although Czechoslovakia claimed to be in the 'shock therapy' camp, the degree of government intervention and the delays in implementing some of the reform measures means that this is highly debatable. Hungary was generally considered to be a 'gradualist' reforming economy since the principal reform measures were implemented over a two-year period and could be said to be a continuation of the New Economic Mechanism, a package of reforms which started in the late 1960s. In some ways Hungary's industrial and competition policy conformed to the 'shock' approach as it became increasingly harsh with enforced bankruptcies, reductions in state subsidies, and rapid trade liberalization. Russia and Kazakhstan also started out as supporters of 'shock therapy' in 1991 but industrial policy became more 'gradualist' when the governments realized that a reduction of subsidies to enterprises to force them to cut costs would mean high and escalating unemployment.

Recently, Slovenia and Croatia have applied 'shock therapy' in the implementation of monetary policy in order to control accelerating inflation resulting from the collapse of Yugoslavia. Slovenia has taken a far more 'gradualist' approach to industrial reform with policies designed to restructure the enterprise sector being undertaken over a longer period of time in order to avoid high rates of unemployment. The inability of countries of the region to effectively restructure their industrial enterprises apparently has not been confined to those adopting a 'gradualist' approach to reform. The gap in unemployment rates between the former GDR and other countries in Eastern Europe indicates that the West German government forced enterprises in the former East Germany to undertake extensive restructuring with the setting up of the privatization agency, the Treuhand, to oversee restructuring prior to privatization. In other countries, privatization generally occurred prior to restructuring in order to avoid the high rates of unemployment which would arise from improvements in efficiency. Rising rates of unemployment in recent years have indicated that some countries, notably the Czech Republic, are starting to adopt a more serious attitude towards enterprise restructuring.

It is probably true to say that the ensuing blame for the severe recession of the early 1990s can be placed at the door of the rapid process of change undertaken by all economies irrespective of whether the government was adopting 'shock therapy' or a 'gradualist' approach. The three main policies which produced the most damaging effects on enterprises were: liberalization of prices; a payments crisis faced by enterprises; and the dismantling of the planning system itself.

■ Liberalization of prices

Price liberalization led to hyperinflationary conditions nearly everywhere in the region and was accompanied by a fall in real wages. This produced a rapid reduction in consumer spending forcing many enterprises into bankruptcy.

■ A payments crisis

Firms found themselves unable to pay for the rising costs of raw materials and many enterprises started demanding payment from customers even before delivery. In view of the lack of assistance from government, enterprises either cut production because payment in advance was not forthcoming, cut production because raw materials were not available, or the rate of investment fell dramatically due to enterprises diverting capital to pay wages.

■ The rapid dismantling of the central planning system

The central planning system had meant that many enterprises neither knew who their suppliers were nor who were their customers. In addition, trade liberalization meant that the sudden influx of Western competitors took advantage of the confusion of domestic firms to establish a foothold in the market.

22.2.2 External factors

A portion of the blame for the severe recession suffered by the countries of Eastern Europe can be attributed to external factors, principally, the collapse of the communist trading bloc, the Council for Mutual Economic Assistance (CMEA) in 1991, and the introduction of hard currency payments for exports by the Soviet Union during the same year. The CMEA had effectively been a Soviet invention to enable a monopoly on trade to be exerted over its Eastern European satellites. By 1990 the countries of Eastern Europe were looking for new trading partners, notably in the EU, and the collapse of intra-enterprise trade and countertrade between CMEA members led to the rapid demise of the CMEA itself. But the legacy of nearly fifty years of Soviet control over trade was that the structure of industry in Eastern Europe became dominated by extractive and military goods producers and capital investment in manufacturing was neglected. Countries like Hungary, Poland, and Czechoslovakia were able to recover more quickly than the former Soviet republics since they had turned towards Western Europe and signed Association Agreements with the EU by the end of 1992. The former Soviet republics suffered a severe decline in trade, especially in raw materials and energy supplies, which had often been subject to extensive subsidies forming a vital lifeline of support and, when removed, meant that the newly independent states found themselves devoid of both trade and aid. At the same time, this situation was exacerbated by the Gulf War in 1991, which effectively closed export markets in regions which had formerly provided the Soviet Union and Eastern Europe with lucrative trade.

During the early years of the economic reform process most Western industrialized countries were going through a recession. It is not surprising, therefore, that as the economies of Eastern Europe became subject to the external influences from the world economy, their own economic situation should be affected by recessionary forces. Perhaps the most notable effect was the shortage of investment funds available for developing the transition economies. The amount of investment funds from foreign companies and international organizations never reached the expectations of the countries of the region. However, it should be noted that the amount of investment funds is finite and shortages become acute as investors are deterred in a recession. Also, foreign investment tends to be geographically biased with the US concentrating on South America and the Japanese traditionally looking for investment opportunities in the Far East and South-East Asia. In other words, the countries of Eastern Europe have tended to become dependent upon investment capital from Western Europe, although in recent years MNEs from the USA and Japan have taken advantage of opportunities in the region.

The successes and failures of the transition policies and the effects of the recession in Eastern Europe during the early to mid-1990s can be discussed in terms of the problems of unemployment and of inflation and economic growth.

22.2.3 Unemployment

The fear of rising unemployment resulting from the economic reform programme did hit all Eastern European countries in the period up to 1995, and the average rate of unemployment in 1998 still stood at 12 per cent. During the transition process governments had no real choice but to liberalize labour markets and radically restructure industry with the aim of creating real long-term jobs rather than a continuation of the problem of overemployment prevalent in the Soviet Union and Eastern Europe before 1989. However, the temptation remains in Eastern Europe to postpone industrial restructuring and so delay the spectre of unemployment which normally arises. There is evidence to suggest that even in the late 1990s most countries had only recently attempted to implement industrial restructuring, with the exception of the former GDR where the West German government bit the bullet in the early 1990s and enforced a comprehensive restructuring programme through the Treuhand prior to the commencement of privatization. In the united Germany the social costs of the transition have probably been more apparent than elsewhere with the rising voice of protest by the unemployed and the increase in the activities of right-wing racist groups. The prospects for social unrest are immense, especially since to ignore unemployment will create an underclass with large numbers of young people, older workers, the unskilled, and ethnic minorities tending to be the hardest hit by unemployment.

In addition, geographical blackspots exist indicating the regional imbalance in unemployment. For example, the regional economy of northern Poland is dominated by agriculture, and unemployment has reached about 20 per cent compared to 5 per cent in Warsaw. Another problem relates to the heavy reliance on 'one company towns' in Eastern Europe where all workers in an area are dependent for their employment on one large company—the effect of the company withdrawing would be disastrous. Before 1989 companies hoarded labour regardless of efficiency in order to increase their status and income, but increasing efficiency involves sacking large numbers of workers. In other words, a true market economy cannot exist in these circumstances; the reality is that a dual economy prevails with market and non-market sectors. Non-market sectors pay people for being employed, but not for working, so a basic step towards creating a market economy is to lay these workers off. Hence suspicions have been expressed over the Czech Republic's ability to keep unemployment down below 4 per cent by simply avoiding, rather than paying, the costs of reform. The problem could stem from Czech voucher privatization which did nothing to force firms to restructure, whereas in Hungary sales of shares by tender to strategic investors forced more ruthless rationalization and resulted in higher unemployment. Unfortunately, voucher privatization has also meant continued state influence over the private sector. Investment funds controlling privatized companies are run by banks, which are ultimately answerable to government. On the other hand, new jobs are being created in the rapidly growing Czech service sector which has been developed much more rapidly than elsewhere. The Czechs have also avoided the dangers of an over-generous welfare benefit system, keeping benefits low in order to force people into low productivity (and low-paid) jobs. Benefits are only provided for six months, compared with one year elsewhere in the region, with unemployment benefits amounting to only 24 per cent of average wages.[3]

In the future, Eastern European governments need to concentrate on building flexibility into labour markets by introducing legislation to encourage flexible working hours, part-time work, and even performance-related pay. However, labour market liberalization is not enough by itself. In the past, economic growth has been seen to be the main engine of job creation in the 'tiger economies' of South-East Asia, but this cannot be relied upon in Eastern Europe to the same extent. Undoubtedly, governments should provide mechanisms to protect against the shock of the transition, whether by carefully planning the downsizing of obsolete industry or by providing adequate welfare systems. But true employment opportunities will only increase by allowing the market to create jobs and not by insulating industry from market forces in order to achieve short-term political gains. In reality, the market may be dominated by the activities of Western MNEs and they will take an important role in shaping the industrial structure of Eastern Europe in the future.

22.2.4 Inflation vs growth

All reforming economies in Eastern Europe suffered from high inflation and dramatic falls in GDP during the early 1990s. For the early reformers, Poland, Hungary, and Czechoslovakia, positive growth rates were achieved in 1992 for Poland and in 1994 for the other two countries. At the other end of the scale, countries like Russia and Kazakhstan may not have achieved positive growth rates until the end of the century. It has been argued that low inflation lays the foundation for high growth.[4] The high inflation rates suffered by the economies of Eastern Europe since 1990 were an inevitable result of the restructuring of industry and the welfare system, along with price and trade liberalization. Inflation can be contained in the short run by high interest rates or an appreciating exchange rate. Such policies should also be accompanied by far-reaching industrial restructuring and deregulation, but until 1995 countries like Hungary and the Czech Republic both failed to introduce microeconomic reform early enough.

Orthodox economic theory predicts that tight monetary policy will cause a fall in investment if interest rates remain high and a deterioration in the balance of trade will occur if the domestic currency remains high. However, such conclusions relating to the sensitivity of investment to interest rates need to be redrawn in the case of the economies of Eastern Europe. Spare capacity arising from unused reserves of machinery, buildings, infrastructure, and skilled labour mean that the return on any given investment will be higher. Since the level of investment is rising faster than GDP in all Visegrad countries, this will increase capacity and reduce inflation and so reduce the potential damage which can arise from high interest rates. In addition, appreciating domestic exchange rates may actually produce benefits for the transition economies. Firstly, an exchange rate which appreciates gradually will reduce the prices of imports of consumer goods thereby forcing domestic companies to reduce their own prices to become competitive or go out of business, and also by making the imports of capital goods cheaper, improving the efficiency of local production. Secondly, it is perhaps surprising that controlled exchange rate appreciations in the region seem to have had very little impact on exports. The main reason for this is that the growth in productivity has more than compensated for the erosion of price competitiveness. However, many countries of the region are continuing to labour with an unbalanced industrial structure, a legacy of communism, which will require fundamental restructuring, backed by government industrial policy and foreign investment. The fact remains that the industrial structure in Eastern Europe will have to undergo a fundamental shift away from emphasis on heavy industries towards the development of manufacturing industry.

Involvement of foreign investors is inevitable and so too is that of the state through the implementation of policies which may be appropriately termed 'picking winners'. In order to take their place in the global economy in the future the governments of Eastern Europe may be advised to identify those industries which can be expected to contribute to exports and economic growth. In other words, how far can the countries of Eastern Europe expect that growth will be 'export-led' in the next few years and is this a realistic proposition at all? There is evidence that there has been significant increases in exports to the EU in the cases of Poland, Hungary, and the Czech Republic, with over 50 per cent of the exports from Eastern Europe going to the EU, an increase from only 10–20 per cent prior to the collapse of the CMEA.[5] Although these countries undoubtedly benefited from the Europe Agreements signed with the EU in 1992 to facilitate the gradual introduction of Eastern European products on to the EU market, trade has not increased as rapidly as was expected due to the recession in Western Europe and also the reluctance of EU countries to allow far-reaching trade concessions for the countries of Eastern Europe.

In addition, imbalances in the industrial structures of Eastern European economies have led to excessive reliance on exports of low-value-added goods and raw materials, and an increasing dependence upon imported technology and consumer goods. This problem is multiplied tenfold when the situation of the former Soviet Union is considered. This market was entirely unprepared for the massive influx of consumer goods after 1991 and for the collapse of its own export market to neighbouring economies, particularly in the supply of raw materials and energy. However, the future for the former Soviet Union is bright given the tremendous potential to re-establish and develop energy supply chains to Eastern Europe and to the West although there is undoubtedly a danger of creating an overdependence on raw material exports. Trade revenues from raw materials and energy exports can be directed into investment and into the restructuring and development of the existing manufacturing base. Other countries in Eastern Europe may not be able to enjoy this luxury. These countries need to address problems with their industrial imbalances now rather than delaying until after entry into the EU. Delays in restructuring will result in an inability to compete with companies based in Western Europe after full membership of the EU has been granted.

At present, the capacity to achieve export-led growth through the manufactured goods sector is absent in Eastern Europe and the former Soviet Union, and the area is in danger of becoming a region of subsidiaries. Heavy dependence on foreign investors, particularly MNEs, and the fact that domestic markets have already been more or less captured by foreign companies, means that local manufacturers will find it difficult to establish for themselves a significant market share, thereby taking advantage of economies of scale. The worst-case scenario, therefore, is that local companies will either fail to survive or will become subsumed by large Western MNEs (or possibly by those of South-East Asian origin) entering the market to take advantage of the benefits of economies of scale in the increasingly global economy of the future.

22.3 The Development of Western Business Culture: The Role of Entrepreneurship

A N important part of the economic reform process for the countries of the former Soviet Union and Eastern Europe is the successful transfer from the bureaucratic-administrative business culture to a Western entrepreneurial business culture. This process will be a long one but is vitally important as it underpins the whole reform programme and is essential for both the microeconomic and macroeconomic reforms to succeed. The bureaucratic-administrative business culture was a legacy of the communist system, an inevitable result of the unwieldy central planning structures in which local administrators and enterprise administrators had to work together to fulfil the targets in the plans they had been given by central government. In centrally planned economies there was no room for either administrators or enterprise managers to be diverted from the main task in hand—plan fulfilment; there was no need to consider the problems of flexibility, change, and the application of new technology. SOEs were monopolies, there was no competition (either foreign or domestic) and their output was determined not by them (and certainly not by the market), but by the decisions taken by bureaucrats in a division of the central planning authority. This was 'producer sovereignty' at its worst—fulfilment of the plan was so important since the payment of workers' bonuses depended upon it, so issues relating to quality, new product development, the environment, and health and safety were largely ignored.

However, this is not to say that the bureaucratic-administrative business culture was not immensely effective during the early years of communism. The period of rapid industrialization required the concentration of resources into heavy industry, for which central planning methods were eminently suitable. However, these methods became increasingly redundant from the 1970s onwards and the economic and technological gulf between East and West began to grow more rapidly. This change occurred largely as a result of two important developments:

(1) The new electronics and computer industries—the 'sunrise' industries—which were emerging in the West led the drive for developing new products and new technologies.
(2) In the West, consumers' incomes continued to rise resulting in increasing demands from consumers for improved products using new technologies.

These developments could only be contained by the use of flexible production methods and responsive entrepreneurial management.

The problems arising from falling living standards and the economic gulf between East and West have already been discussed in Chapter 18. It has been suggested that these could be important factors contributing to the fall of communism in 1989, accompanied by the government's inability to introduce more flexible production and management systems. Indeed, the bureaucratic-administrative culture had become a barrier to internal progress as well as effectively preventing integration of countries from the region into the world economy.

For the economic reform process in Eastern Europe to be a success it is essential that the business culture also makes the transition. In the bureaucratic-administrative business culture, it was the state which assumed the role of the entrepreneur. But in an entrepreneurial business culture it is the individual who is the key player in the start-up of any business and she/he must be solely responsible for allocating resources and applying a successful strategy for realizing market opportunities. It is therefore essential that the governments of the region should take into account how the conditions can be created to enable entrepreneurial activities to take place. It can be argued that policy-makers should concentrate on four main areas in the reform programme.

22.3.1 Establishing the private sector

Private sector activities are seen as fundamental to underpin the new entrepreneurial business culture in Eastern Europe. In the early years of the reform programme, privatization was seen as the most important factor which could contribute to the development of the private sector. It is now recognized that a combination of private sector activities needs to be established in order to encourage the transfer to an entrepreneurial business culture. This includes creating an economic environment which is conducive to FDI, either in the form of 'greenfield' investment or by the creation of JVAs. The countries of Eastern Europe have been heavily dependent upon outside support from foreign companies and international organizations like the IMF and the EU.

There is also the need to consider how far the state should intervene in the private sector as it develops and also in the future. After the onset of the deep recession in the early 1990s suffered by countries in the early stages of reform, some governments in the region, notably Poland and Hungary, decided to adopt a more openly interventionist policy involving providing incentives to local firms regarded as important potential contributors to employment, exports, and growth in the future. Interventionist industrial policy of this type has been described earlier in this chapter as 'picking winners' and has perhaps been responsible for Poland's success in becoming the motor vehicle manufacturing centre in Eastern Europe. Foreign investors have also been encouraged by tax incentives, low-cost greenfield sites, and assistance with cutting red tape with the local planning authorities. Of course, a policy involving 'picking winners' may also involve 'ditching the losers' and enforced bankruptcy of firms who cannot compete in the new entrepreneurial environment may well be an inevitable result. It is hoped that as the private sector develops, labour which is displaced in this way can be accommodated by new firms, especially those which are now becoming established in the SME sector.

22.3.2 Business law reform

An effective legal framework needs to be established which not only defines the obligations of companies and provides protection to shareholders and consumers, but also provides effective anti-monopoly regulations and bankruptcy laws. There is a continuing feeling of hostility towards many activities undertaken by the private sector, since in some countries, especially Russia, it has been plagued by corruption and monopolization, and is associated with the mafia in the minds of many people. This hostility should subside and confidence should develop in Eastern Europe as the private sector becomes more established and real competition exists between firms. The introduction of new laws to support the private sector is a vital factor which will ensure that, over time, an entrepreneurial business culture can develop.

22.3.3 Financial sector reform

A comprehensive reform of the financial sector is necessary to enable support structures to be established to assist firms operating in the private sector. Where there is a genuine two-tier banking system established along Western lines, commercial banks need to make it clear to firms that the old system of subsidies cannot continue and it will only be the most efficient enterprises which can expect to gain access to loans. In order to eliminate the continuous transfer of funds from the banks to support ailing SOEs, as was the case under the communist system, it is necessary to ensure that the banks are themselves privatized and cease to be subject to pressure from governments to effect the payment of subsidies.

22.3.4 Education and training programmes

A comprehensive education programme in business and management training is required to bring Eastern European managers closer to the standards of the West by training them in strategic planning techniques, marketing, quality control, and financial management. This has been possible through the establishment of business schools in Eastern Europe teaching MBAs supported by Western universities through the EU's TEMPUS funding or the British Council's 'Know-how Fund'. There is no doubt that much practical management expertise can be transferred directly by Western firms themselves operating in Eastern Europe. In addition, Western companies have provided training programmes for workers in an attempt to raise their productivity levels closer to those of their Western counterparts. This is one of the major benefits of being employed by the large Western MNEs since, in most cases, workers are given a programme of continuous training to assist them in adapting to new production processes using up-to-date Western technology. On-the-job training was rarely available to workers under communism, indeed, there was no real need to upgrade skills when the system itself discouraged the introduction of new technology to upgrade the specification and quality of the product.

22.4 Limitations to the Development of Entrepreneurship

IT has been argued already in this chapter that the success of the whole economic reform programme in Eastern Europe is dependent upon the development of a Western entrepreneurial business culture. The transition from central planning to a market economy is a very complicated process, but despite this, entrepreneurs in Eastern Europe have already achieved a great deal. Most countries have undertaken a far-reaching privatization programme and some have also started restructuring SOEs (although in most countries it has become the responsibility of the new owners after privatization). In addition, major changes in the industrial structure are currently underway and the creation of a new sector dominated by SMEs has meant that the shift away from heavy industry (steel production, coal mining, chemicals, etc.) towards developing manufacturing and service sectors has now begun. However, many problems remain, especially those born out of an extremely fragile business environment and which relate to the incidence of corruption in business and the presence of organized crime continuing to exist on the peripheries of the private sector.

22.4.1 Corruption and 'white-collar crime'

The high incidence of 'white-collar crime' poses a serious threat to entrepreneurship and the future of legitimate business activities in Eastern Europe. Activities which can be defined under this heading include fraud, bribery, corruption, influence-peddling, political patronage, and unethical business practices. In 1995 the Czech Interior Ministry estimated that more than 17,000 cases of white-collar crime were recorded during that year, an increase of 350 per cent on 1989.[6] In the same year, Hungary's Business Protection Coordination Secretariat (BPCS) recorded more than 32,000 cases of financial crime, up 162 per cent on 1990.[7] During the first nine months of 1996 the Polish police recorded more than 40,000 cases of economic crime, up 34 per cent on the same period in 1994.[8] Reported cases of corruption in business are probably just the tip of the iceberg since most financial crime is invisible. Apart from the inevitable lost tax revenue to government and the immediate costs to companies, such activities also carry more serious, long-term costs. Corruption effectively puts the brakes on free competition by rewarding vested interests to the extent that corruption itself is detrimental to the building of a democratic society and can undermine confidence in public institutions.

There is no doubt that corruption in the private sector undermines the development of an entrepreneurial business culture. However, the situation is also complicated in Eastern Europe because of the close relationship between business and politics in each country, a legacy of communism where the state was the all-pervading influence in society. It is hoped that as the power of the state recedes from the private sector, the relationship between state sector companies and their controllers in the ministries will be severed. Nevertheless, at present the power to facilitate the development of entrepreneurial activity in the economies of Eastern Europe lies in the hands of the state which remains in charge of selling import quotas and the granting of licences, as well as encouraging and facilitating the activities of foreign investors.

Obviously, the elimination of corruption will only be possible over a period of time. This was recognized in 1992 by the OECD when its Centre for Cooperation with the Economies in Transition established SIGMA (Support for Improvement in Governance and Management in Central and Eastern Europe) to assist the reform of public administration in the countries of the region. SIGMA works closely with governments to help countries eliminate corruption by analysing laws, legal procedures, and the recruitment and remuneration of civil servants. In 1996 an organization called Transparency International (TI) was established in Berlin with the aim of curbing corruption and encouraging governments to establish and implement effective laws. Although TI aims to be a non-profit-making and non-governmental body, it is funded by Western governments and multilateral institutions. It has received funding from the EU's PHARE programme and has established missions in Albania, the Czech Republic, Hungary, Poland, Romania, and Slovakia. Another possible solution to the problems caused by corruption in the region is to raise awareness of managers operating in the private sector by establishing business ethics courses through university business schools and the chambers of commerce.

22.4.2 Mafia activities and organized crime

After the demise of communism in 1989 and the dismantling of the central planning mechanism, there were many opportunities for individuals to establish dubious business practices in the chaos which followed. In the event, there were often high profits to be made from legitimate business activities so seeds of suspicion were often sown in the minds of the public and a certain degree of mistrust of private sector activities remains in many countries in the region. Although in the aftermath of the events of 1989–90 mafia activity was identified in all Eastern European countries, organized crime in Russia has proved to be the most difficult to control by the authorities. Such activities have also infiltrated into other countries in the region where Russian gangs have become dominant over indigenous criminals in countries like the Czech Republic, Hungary, and Bulgaria.

Perhaps the most important feature of mafia activity in Russia which sets it apart from its activities elsewhere is that the Russian mafia has managed to gain large stakes in legitimate business acquired during the government's mass privatization programme. However, such acquisitions are normally used as a means of siphoning off cash to ship abroad to avoid tax, or as a vehicle through which to launder money acquired from criminal activities involving drugs, prostitution, and arms trafficking. It was estimated that by 1997 the mafia controlled more than 40 per cent of the Russian economy.[9] The main problem is that profits from mafia activities are being exported from Russia and estimates indicate that the amount of capital shifted over-seas since 1991 ranges from US $50 billion to US $150 billion (of which mafia capital is estimated at about 40 per cent), and this dwarfs the level of FDI which amounted to US $6.5 billion over the same period.[10] The export of mafia capital on this scale produces far more difficulties for the Russian economy than the activities of the Colombian drugs barons or the Italian Mafia godfathers, who at least invest some of their ill-gotten gains at home.

The activities of organized crime in Russia are undermining the reform process and the transition to an entrepreneurial business environment. IMF pressures to ensure that tax revenues increased by improving the efficiency of the tax collection system has been seriously thwarted by the mafia not paying their own taxes and by taking tax arrears from companies which should have been paid to the inland revenue. Many tax inspectors collude with mafia bosses by allowing them access to com-panies' tax records. Criminals can then either impersonate tax collectors or extract bribes from companies to ensure that unpaid taxes are overlooked. In early 1998 there were some reports by the Radio Free Europe/Radio Liberty News Service of accounts of four contract killings of tax inspectors in Russia who refused to cooperate with mafia activity in their tax areas.

The police authorities continue to demonstrate an inability to cope in the face of the increasingly sophisticated nature of organized criminal activities. The police are underpaid, underequipped, and are unable to make any significant headway in the pursuit of such criminals. Indeed, many policemen have left the service in recent years to start up or take up posts in the many private security companies which are currently flourishing in post-communist Russia. Anecdotal evidence gathered by the author from senior personnel of two large US MNEs operating in Russia and Eastern Europe indicates that some of the Mafia bosses in Russia are themselves former employees of the state security service, the KGB. This indicates a possible uncomfort-able link between the criminal organizations and the state, and one which has become increasingly difficult to sever.

How far has the criminalization of business activities restricted the emergence of the entrepreneurial business culture? One author argues that it may not be as serious as it appears and that it may be an inevitable stage of business development.[11] Bateman points to the difficulties arising from mafia activity in Chicago in the 1930s where large fortunes were made from criminal activities involving violence and corruption. Over a period of time the prevailing business culture became more sophisticated and ethical, developing in parallel to the changes which took place in American society. Moreover, this argument can be applied to the case of the countries of Eastern Europe where developments like chambers of commerce, university business schools, MNEs, and Western consultancies are showing a lead for indigenous entrepreneurs to follow.

22.4.3 What went wrong in Russia? The financial crisis of August 1998

A recent critic of the reform programme in Russia, Boris Fyodorov, former Deputy Prime Minister and Finance Minister, argues that after years of reform, the Russian government has produced nothing more than 'pseudo-reform'.[12] The privatization process was overshadowed by corruption with large industries being auctioned off to form the FIGs. Free share vouchers were acquired on the black market by mafia organizations and these were later exchanged for shares in legitimate companies on privatization. Privatization in Russia has failed to create a private sector which is competitive and in which firms are free from state control. However, Fyodorov blames the financial crisis of August 1998 on the increased level of Russian indebtedness with the West accumulated during the course of the 1990s. He argues that US$50 billion of Western debt proved to be of very little benefit to the reform programme, whilst about 99 per cent of the US$57 million of US technical assistance channelled through the Harvard Institute of International Development was misspent.

By mid-1998 both internal and external debt levels had become unmanageable as a result of the government's inability to collect taxes and meet interest payments. The intitial response of the Moscow Central Bank was to print money to meet its obligations, but by August 1998, the situation had become more serious with the government taking the decision to devalue the rouble by 50 per cent in an attempt to reduce the value of the country's external debt. Russian banks found themselves on the verge of bankruptcy while citizens rushed to withdraw savings from rouble accounts, the value of which had fallen dramatically. In an attempt to prevent further pressure on the rouble, the Moscow Central Bank raised interest rates to a level of 150 per cent. These measures had the effect of killing off Western imports, especially those of luxury consumer goods.

The effect of the financial crisis on FDI is discussed in Chapter 20, where it is concluded that the situation is unlikely to have forced large Western MNEs to pull out of Russia in the short term, but there is no doubt that Western small and medium-sized investors have tended to think twice about making investment plans to enter the Russian market in the near future. In addition, the creation of the FIGs and the increasing monopolization of Russian industry will further reduce competition and deter Western firms.

An important aspect of the financial crisis is that the consolidation of the FIGs has developed in parallel with a massive recentralization of the economy during early 1999, led by a resurgence of elderly Soviet era bureaucrats. Increased state intervention means that industries will be heavily subsidized to protect employment, with plans to nationalize loss-making industries or integrate them into the FIGs with guaranteed markets. A new structure of tariffs on imports is designed to further protect Russian industries from foreign competition.

What could be the probable results of these policies over the next few years? Although the government thinks that it can contain the financial crisis by recentralizing the economy and supporting Russian industry, many Western economists think that the new policy direction since late 1998 will be disastrous. Russia's corrupt, incompetent bureaucracy is not up to running the economy, and the fall-out from this may be the even greater criminalization of economic activity. A further problem arises from the government's plans to invest without the help of foreign lenders, indicating that this cannot be done without printing money. Further cash will be required to reflate the economy and rescue the ailing banks, but this could lead to new difficulties with hyperinflation.

However, Western economists also argue that the more disastrous the results of these policies, then Russia may have no choice but to get back on to the road to reform by early in the twenty-first century. The defining event may be the presidential elections in 2000 when a new president may take up office and the erratic behaviour of an often-absent Boris Yeltsin becomes a thing of the past. However, at the time of writing, Russia still has some months to go before it can say goodbye to Mr Yeltsin, who is still trying to demonstrate that he retains a firm grip at the helm, as evidenced by the dismissal of Prime Minister Yevgeny Primakov and the government in May 1999. Such actions allow the communists in government to gain popular support—and then who knows what will happen after the elections in 2000?

22.5 Summary

To ensure the continual evolution of entrepreneurial activity in Eastern Europe all governments will need to move away from the tradition of large industrial monopolies towards the further development of the SME sector. This will be difficult to achieve in Russia where the large Financial Industrial Groups (FIGs) are continuing to grow in power and influence in the private sector with the maintenance of the link between entrepreneurs and the state bureaucracy which was a common feature under central planning. The combination of the government's unwillingness to curb the power of the FIGs through anti-monopoly legislation and its inability to control the activities of organized crime means that the development of legitimate SMEs in the private sector in Russia will prove very difficult to sustain in the foreseeable future. On the other hand, in countries like Poland, the Czech Republic, Hungary, and Slovenia, the SME sector, largely dominated by service providers, is showing signs of growth.

Despite this, political and economic power remains in the hands of the large industrial monopolies even in the countries where progress is being made, but privatization has gone some way to undermine the dominance of these industrial giants. As in all Western countries, the SME sector has been vulnerable in the face of turbulent economic conditions, but in Eastern Europe small firms find themselves in a very weak position during a recession. This means that the SME sector will see significant development only in countries where economic stability can be achieved.

The transition from central planning to a market-based economy is a very complicated process and has been an uncomfortable experience for all countries in the region. There seems to have been a combination of the two approaches to economic reform—'shock therapy' and 'gradualism'—favoured by the governments concerned. In other words, 'shock therapy' has been the approach adopted to try to solve serious monetary problems and accelerating inflation rates, but a 'gradualist' approach has been favoured as a less radical method of dealing with the problems of privatization, restructuring, and overmanning. Over the next few years it will be necessary for all governments of the region to turn their backs on the institutions of central planning whilst, at the same time, constructing and developing market institutions and processes which can effectively support the growing private sector and, in particular, SMEs. For example, there is more room for improvement in the development of the banking sector where privatization and restructuring have been slow, with many banks remaining state-owned and the government continuing to influence the activities of the private sector. The problem of capital shortages faced by many banks has led to small firms being unable to access adequate supplies of investment capital. The fact that many banks can be defined as technically bankrupt themselves serves to further underline the precarious nature of the developing private sector in Eastern Europe.

It has been argued in this chapter that the transition from a bureaucratic-administrative business culture to an entrepreneurial-oriented one is of crucial importance for the success of the economic and political reform programme itself. However, entrepreneurs in Eastern Europe have already managed to achieve considerable success. In addition to the process of privatization and restructuring, the creation of SMEs and the reorientation of the whole industrial structure are important reforms which are currently taking place throughout the region. However, major work relating to transition has yet to be completed and it is the task of entrepreneurs to ensure that the private sector continues to grow and develop. It would certainly be erroneous to assume that economic intervention and economic planning can have no role in the market economies of the future given the experience of most successful Western economies in the post-1945 period where government intervention has represented support for the market as opposed to the old form of intervention which strove to destroy and replace the market system itself.

Review Questions

1 What are the principal economic problems facing the economies of Russia and Eastern Europe at the end of the 1990s?

2 What are the consequences of the collapse of the CMEA for the development of Russian and Eastern European trade?

3 What changes will need to take place to allow Eastern European firms to shed the legacy of a bureaucratic-administrative business culture?

4 Why have the activities of organized crime been more prevalent in the Russian economy and what have been the consequences of this?

5 Why might it be necessary for governments in Eastern Europe to introduce formal industrial policies for some time into the future?

Case Study: Western Management Techniques at Tyumen Oil

In February 1998, Semyon Kukes became president and chief executive of Tyumen Oil Company (TNK), Russia's sixth biggest petroleum producer. TNK had been privatized but only partly restructured, and the Russian government still owned 49 per cent of the company, allowing it to retain two seats on the board. Kukes had spent fifteen years working for Amoco in the USA and was appointed to introduce Western management techniques at TNK.

The company was typical of many large Russian oil enterprises: a disorganized collection of oilfield operations in Western Siberia, a Moscow refinery, and distribution companies in Southern and Central Russia. One of Kukes's first actions was to centralize control of the company's operations from its Moscow headquarters. This led to a 20 per cent reduction in staff to 40,000. He then set about changing the emphasis of the company's activities from a fixation with technology and the skills of its scientists and engineers to the development of highly motivated and varied teams, regular staff rotation, and similar human resource strategies. Economic and business forecasting also became an important activity, enabling the company to anticipate market trends and potential cash-flow problems. The company's top-heavy management, typical of large Russian companies, is being slimmed down and Kukes's two deputies manage cost-control and planning and day-to-day operations respectively. TNK now has a six-man supervisory board and a seven-man external board to represent shareholders' interests.

New cost-control techniques have led to the introduction of competitive tendering for all major purchases and have brought about a 60 per cent reduction in the company's procurement costs, helping to eradicate an inherited mountain of debt. Responsibility for TNK's 'social assets', such as housing, schools, and hospitals for its workforce, has been handed over to the government. Wages are now paid only one month in arrears, compared with the company's previous practice of paying five months in arrears and a current industry average of three months. Despite the shedding of former responsibilities, Kukes still retains a belief in the role of government in protecting employment and redistributing corporate wealth—a view which remains prevalent in Russia and Eastern Europe.

The Russian financial crisis of mid-1998 and generally weak oil prices have accentuated the need for cost-cutting and other efficiency improvements. It is these risk factors which a company like TNK can do least about. In fact, Kukes admits that, unless there is a recovery in crude oil prices, real tax reform in Russia, and a further depreciation of the rouble, TNK will struggle to survive. Certainly, the Russian financial crisis has been a major setback. However, Kukes has at least begun to tackle the problems over which the company has some control and a well-managed company is more likely to survive the current economic conditions than an unrestructured former state enterprise. (Adapted from 'The third way: Semyon Kukes of Tyumen Oil is trying to apply Western management techniques to Russia', *Business Central Europe*, Nov. 1998, 31.)

Study topic questions

1 How far has Semyon Kukes managed to introduce a Western entrepreneurial style of management at TNK since February 1998?

2 What problems is Kukes likely to have encountered when introducing Western management methods?

3 What are the main elements of industrial restructuring which Russia and the countries of Eastern Europe have tended to neglect in companies like TNK?

4 What difficulties are likely to have been faced by TNK as a result of the Russian financial crisis and Russia's economic problems generally?

5 Why has it proved difficult for Russia to separate the activities of the state from those of the private sector during the economic reform process in the 1990s? To what extent is this likely to be a problem for a company like TNK and how might the company address this problem if it arises?

Notes

1 I. Zloch-Christy, 'Industrial Policy: Does Eastern Europe Need One?' in I. Zloch-Christy (ed.), *Eastern Europe and the World Economy: Challenges of Transition and Globalization* (Edward Elgar, 1998), 182.

2 Ibid. 183.

3 R. Lyons, 'Labour pains', *Business Central Europe* (Dec. 1996/Jan. 1997), 10.

4 R.Lyons, 'Burnout mechanism', *Business Central Europe* (Sept. 1996), 26.

5 M. Bateman, *Business Cultures in Central and Eastern Europe* (Butterworth Heinemann, 1997), 209.

6 J. Cook, 'Sleaze under the collar', *Business Central Europe* (December 1995/Jan. 1996), 9.

7 Ibid.

8 Ibid.

9 R. Lyons, 'Bandit class', *Business Central Europe* (May 1997), 24.

10 Ibid.

11 Bateman, *Business Cultures*, 229.

12 S. Pirani, 'Russian reforms were "complete failure"', *Observer* (21 Mar. 1999).

Recommended Reading

- Bateman, M., *Business Cultures in Central and Eastern Europe* (Butterworth Heinemann, 1997).

- Gros, D., and Steinherr, A., *Winds of Change: Economic Transition in Central and Eastern Europe* (Longman, 1995).

- Lavigne, M., *The Economics of Transition: From Socialist Economy to Market Economy* (Macmillan, 1995).

- Sharma, S. (Ed.), *Restructuring Eastern Europe: The Microeconomics of the Transition Process* (Edward Elgar, 1997).

- Turnock, D., *The East European Economy in Context: Communism and Transition* (Routledge, 1997).

- Zloch-Christy, I. (Ed.), *Eastern Europe and the World Economy : Challenges of Transition and Globalization* (Edward Elgar, 1998).

Glossary

Absolute advantage A country with an absolute advantage is more efficient than another country in the production of a particular good.

Acculturation A process of learning how to live and work in a culture other than one's own through adjustment and adaptation.

Acquis communautaire The entire body of laws, policies, procedures, and treaties of the EU.

Anglo-Saxon model A description applied to free market economies, especially the USA and UK, where government economic intervention is confined largely to cautious fiscal and monetary policy and where individual freedoms take priority over collective action.

Arbitrage The process by which financial assets are bought at a lower price or borrowed at a lower interest rate in one market and sold at a higher price or loaned at a higher interest rate in another market. The effect of arbitrage is to equalize prices or interest rates between markets, provided there is completely free movement of capital.

Architecture (of a firm) Architecture describes the culture of an organization, a unifying corporate ethos which underpins all its activities and relationships. It incorporates its procedures and knowledge base, its cooperative ethic, its commitment to quality, its organizational relationships, and its sense of purpose as an organization.

Austrian School of Economics A free market view of economics which emphasizes the dynamic nature of competition and the importance of entrepreneurial discovery. Members of this school of thought tend to combine a belief in individual freedom and liberalism with a belief in the supremacy of free markets.

'Austrian' economists include Ludwig von Mises, Joseph Schumpeter, and F. A. Hayek.

Autarky National economic self-sufficiency.

Balance of payments The official record of all transactions between residents of one country and residents of the rest of the world over a given period of time, usually a year. A balance of payments surplus (deficit) on current account should normally be matched by a capital and financial account deficit (surplus), after allowing for adjustments in official financing.

Brand DNA The essential characteristics of a brand which help to distinguish it from its rivals.

Capital and financial account The section of the balance of payments which records transactions in financial assets between a country and the rest of the world, including both real assets (property, plant, and equipment, etc.) and paper assets (shares, government bonds, etc.).

Chaebol A South Korean conglomerate—one of a number of diversified groups of companies which dominate the South Korean economy.

Co-determination (*Mitbestimmung*) The German system of industrial relations whereby workers participate formally in company decision-making.

Common market A regional economic grouping which combines a customs union with the removal of internal non-tariff barriers, allowing goods, services, people, and capital to move freely across internal frontiers.

Comparative advantage A country has a comparative advantage in the production of a good which it can produce comparatively (relatively) more efficiently, i.e. where its absolute advantage over another country is greatest or absolute disadvantage least.

Consumer surplus The difference between what consumers are willing and able to pay (represented by their demand curve) and the market price. The consumer surplus is therefore a welfare gain enjoyed by consumers.

Contestable markets theory A contestable market is one where established firms are subject to the constant threat of entry from firms outside the market. Contestability exists where there are no sunk costs (costs incurred on entry which are irrecoverable on leaving a market) or regulations preventing entry. The theory claims that such markets achieve welfare maximization regardless of the number of firms in the market and without the other restrictive assumptions of perfect competition.

Corporatization The creation of a corporate legal entity (i.e. a joint-stock or limited liability company) from a former state-owned enterprise prior to privatization.

Countertrade The international exchange of goods for goods as a means of payment for international trade.

Created assets Assets which a country has developed through human endeavour or the supportive actions of firms, governments, and other organizations over a period of time. They include *tangible assets*, such as industrial infrastructure or distribution networks, and *intangible assets*, such as skills, technological knowledge, the capacity for innovation, the stock of intellectual property, and relationships between governments, companies, universities, and other organizations.

Currency convertibility The ability to exchange a currency for foreign currencies, especially hard currencies, on the open market.

Current account The section of the balance of payments which records flows of goods, services, and transfer payments between a country and the rest of the world, including both *visible trade* and *invisibles*. Visible trade includes exports and imports of goods, whereas invisibles include exports and imports of services, and transfer payments (including interest, profit, and dividends).

Customs union A regional economic grouping which combines a free trade area with a common external tariff.

Deadweight loss This term describes the loss of consumer surplus and/or producer surplus which results from an increase in prices, taxes, or tariffs, etc. and the corresponding reduction in supply.

Debt capital That part of the capital of a business which comprises loans, bonds, and other interest-bearing securities.

Deregulation The opening of markets to competition by removing regulations which restrict entry or otherwise hinder the operation of market forces.

Derivative A financial contract which is 'derived' from an underlying asset such as a currency, commodity, or equity. Examples include a forward exchange contract, a futures contract, or a share option. These contracts, and numerous similar variants, provide one of the parties with insurance or a 'hedge' against fluctuations in the price of the asset; the other party bears the risk in return for a 'premium' on the asset price.

Direct exporting/importing The exporting and importing of goods from one country to another without the services of an intermediary.

Dirigisme A form of indicative economic planning involving close cooperation between government and industry, primarily associated with post-war economic development in France. The term is sometimes used more generally to describe any active form of industrial policy.

Diversification The process whereby a firm branches out into a varied range of business activities (*product-based diversification*) or a varied range of geographical locations (*geographical diversification*). Large firms with a diversified product range are sometimes known as *conglomerates.*

Drawing rights Members of the IMF have drawing rights which allow them to borrow foreign currencies from the fund to help finance a balance of payments deficit.

Dumping Exports sold at prices below their cost of production or (less commonly) the practice of charging different prices in separate markets where the price variations do not reflect differences.

East Asian model A description applied to Japan, South Korea, and some of the other East Asian countries which represents an authoritarian, close-knit, and highly regulated view of society where the collective good supersedes individual freedom and where selected industrial development and exports are actively promoted by government.

Economic exposure An exchange rate risk resulting from currency fluctuations which bring about changes in the price of a product, labour and raw material costs, or the cost of a foreign investment when a firm operates internationally.

Economic union A regional economic grouping which combines a common market with the harmonization of national economic policies, especially monetary and fiscal policies.

Economic and monetary union (EMU) The name given to the EU project, agreed under the Treaty on European Union (Maastricht Treaty), which culminated in the establishment of a European Central Bank and a single European currency. Strictly speaking, economic union also requires further measures to harmonize fiscal and other economic policies.

Economies of scale This term is commonly applied to *internal economies of scale,* i.e. falling unit costs which can be achieved when a firm or plant expands to its minimum efficient scale. Large-scale operation can lead to reductions in production, purchasing, marketing, transport, administrative, and other costs, either at the level of the plant (*plant economies*) or the firm as a whole (*firm economies*). *External economies of scale* exist where a group of related firms at a particular location gain mutual benefits through shared access to supplies, markets, facilities, support services, and infrastructure.

Economies of scope Falling unit costs which result from an increase in the variety of goods produced from a given set of inputs.

Effective exchange rate A measure of a national currency's international value in terms of a given basket of other national currencies.

Elasticity of demand and supply A measure of the responsiveness of (a) demand or (b) supply to a change in the price of a product, usually calculated as the percentage change in the quantity demanded or supplied divided by the percentage change in price.

Electronic commerce (e-commerce) The conduct of business by electronic means via computers and the Internet. There are two basic types of e-commerce: (a) transactions where the Internet is used to advertise, place orders, and make payments, but goods are delivered by conventional means; and (b) transactions where the goods are delivered or the service is provided 'on-line' and then downloaded by the purchaser.

Emerging economy A country which is experiencing rapid economic development, a term used especially to describe the newly industrializing countries of Asia and Latin America and the Eastern European countries in transition to market economies.

Enculturation The process by which individuals are introduced to and inculcated into a particular culture, learning how to do 'things' in the correct and appropriate manner.

Endogenous growth theory A theory of economic development which attaches importance to internal factors within an economy. It is argued that long-term growth is created not only by the existence of free market forces, but also by investment in the infrastructure and in knowledge-intensive activities such as education, research and development, and new technologies.

Entrepreneur Someone who invests capital and runs a business, a decision-maker and risk-taker whose reward is profit.

Equity capital The ordinary share capital of a company.

Eurocurrency Originally, a foreign currency held in a European country, though the term now has more widespread use. Thus, a US dollar deposit at a European or other non-US bank is known as a eurodollar deposit. Eurocurrencies are also used to denominate loans, bonds, and other financial products.

Europe Agreements Association agreements between the EU and several Eastern European countries, intended to prepare these countries for full EU membership.

European model A description applied to Europe's *social market economies*, especially Germany, France, Austria, Switzerland, Belgium, the Netherlands, and the Scandinavian countries. These social market economies are characterized by high levels of taxation to pay for extensive public services and by a desire for social consensus.

Exchange Rate Mechanism (ERM) The target zone within which most of the EU member currencies operated between 1979 and the introduction of the euro in 1999. For most of this period the majority of currencies were allowed to fluctuate within a 2.25 per cent band above or below their agreed rate though, after the currency crisis of 1992–3, the normal band was increased to 15 per cent.

Extensive growth A method of industrial development used in the former Soviet Union whereby labour resources were transferred from a low productivity sector (agriculture) to a higher productivity sector (industry).

Externalities The external consequences of economic activity. The term is commonly applied to negative externalities such as pollution when the cost is borne by society

rather than by the producers and consumers directly involved.

Factor productivity The number of units produced using a given factor of production such as labour or capital, e.g. the quality of skilled labour in a particular location will affect a firm's labour productivity.

Federalism A system of government where some political decisions are made centrally whilst others are delegated to regional authorities. In the context of the EU, federalism relates to the organized division of responsibilities between EU institutions and individual member states and is sometimes contrasted with functionalism.

Firm-specific assets (FSAs) Those assets, both tangible and intangible, which give a firm a distinctive advantage when entering a new market. FSAs include technological know-how, marketing techniques, intellectual property, innovative ability, and management skills developed over a period of time.

First-mover advantage A strategic gain which a firm achieves by entering a market ahead of its rivals, e.g. the establishment of an industry standard which favours the firm's own product or the building of a large production plant which monopolizes existing economies of scale.

Fixed exchange rate A rate of exchange for a national currency which is fixed against another currency as a matter of policy. The central bank is required to maintain the currency's value at or close to the fixed rate either by buying or selling the currency or by raising or lowering interest rates. If a fixed rate becomes indefensible, the currency will normally be *revalued* or *devalued*.

Flexible (or floating) exchange rate A rate of exchange for a national currency which is allowed to fluctuate against other currencies according to market forces. In such circumstances the currency will *appreciate* or *depreciate* automatically (a *clean float*), though the authorities sometimes find it difficult to resist intervening in the foreign exchange market completely (a *dirty float*).

Foreign direct investment The establishment or acquisition of income-generating assets in a foreign country over which the investing firm has some degree of control, e.g. the building of a factory abroad, the takeover of a foreign firm, or a foreign joint-venture agreement.

Forward exchange contract A contract for the purchase of currency at an agreed price on a future date.

Franchising A form of licensing arrangement whereby the *franchiser* agrees to allow the *franchisee* to use the franchiser's intellectual property, such as a trademark, brand name, marketing technique, or particular business system, to undertake a business activity in a prescribed manner in return for a fee. The franchiser also agrees to provide support services such as staff training, marketing and management techniques, quality control, and other forms of logistics support.

Free trade area A regional economic grouping where all internal tariff (and similar) barriers have been removed.

Functionalism In the context of the EU, a theory of political development in which progress towards political integration is achieved through pragmatic economic and social cooperation between member states. Functionalism is sometimes contrasted with federalism.

Futures contract A contract for the purchase of a commodity at an agreed price on a future date.

Glasnost A policy of 'openness' introduced by President Gorbachev in the former Soviet Union in 1985, under which open political discussion was encouraged and which had the effect of encouraging dissent from the views of the ruling party.

Global governance Co-ordinated international oversight of world affairs through organizations such as the UN, IMF, or WTO.

Globalization The increasing interdependence of the world's economies and business activity. Events in one country increasingly have 'global' implications, and 'global' firms sell their products in 'global' product markets and acquire their resources in 'global' resource markets.

Gradualism An approach to reform adopted by some of the countries of Eastern Europe, notably Hungary, whereby policies designed to restructure the enterprise sector have been undertaken over a lengthy period of time in order to avoid high rates of unemployment.

Hard currency A major convertible currency, such as the US dollar or Deutsche Mark, which is readily convertible on the foreign exchange market. Hard currencies are held by many countries as *reserve currencies* and are often used in international trade in preference to currencies which are less widely accepted.

Hecksher–Ohlin theory A development of the traditional theory of international trade which emphasizes the role of factor endowments in determining a country's comparative advantage. Also known as factor proportions theory, it helps to explain why a country may take advantage of a resource which is plentiful, and therefore relatively cheap, by specializing in industries which make intensive use of this resource.

Hedging A method of insuring against fluctuations in exchange rates (a forward exchange contract) or fluctuations in the price of goods or commodities (a futures contract).

Horizontal integration A takeover or merger between firms at the same stage of production.

Import substitution The development of domestic industries whose output replaces the need for imports.

Indirect exporting/importing The exporting and importing of goods from one country to another via the services of an intermediary, such as an export/import agent or specialist exporter/importer.

'Information age' A description sometimes applied to the present-day situation where information is readily available in most parts of the world through computers, the Internet, and related technological means.

Insider privatization The privatization of state-owned enterprises in Eastern Europe through low-priced sales to workers and managers within the enterprise.

Intellectual property rights Legal rights arising from the ownership of patents, copyrights, trade marks, etc.

Intensive growth A method of industrial development whereby productivity increases are achieved through the introduction of new technology.

Intergovernmentalism In the context of the EU, the term describes the deliberations of heads of government in the European Council outside the normal EU policy-making process. In particular, the two 'pillars' of the common foreign and security policy and policy in the field of justice and home affairs are being developed at an intergovernmental level.

Internalization The process of bringing or maintaining activities within a firm in order to keep control of the firm's operations or to mimimize the transaction costs of dealing with external organizations. One of the main motives of a multinational enterprise in going international, especially when engaging in foreign direct investment, is to internalize production, purchasing, marketing, and other activities within the firm.

International competitiveness The ability of a firm or industry to compete against foreign firms or industries, usually measured by market share or some other performance indicator. The term is sometimes also used to describe the ability of a country to increase the size of its economy, share of world trade, or national

wealth (income per capita), though it is probably more accurate to speak of a country's ability to provide a favourable business environment or favourable real exchange rate.

Invisibles Exports and imports of services (e.g. tourism, shipping, banking, and professional services) and transfer payments between countries (interest, profit, dividends, compensation of employees, and government grants, aid, and other contributions).

Joint-venture agreement (JVA) An agreement where two or more firms hold equity capital in a venture over which they each have some degree of control. The venture may be a separate operation set up by the shareholding companies or one of the companies may hold shares in the other(s).

Just-in-time system A stock control system initiated by Japanese companies, whereby materials and components are delivered as and when they are needed for production in order to avoid the costs of holding large amounts of stock.

Kaizen The policy of 'continuous improvement' practised by Japanese companies in all aspects of their operations, subsequently adapted by Western companies as *total quality management*.

Keiretsu The term given to a group of companies in Japan which operate a mutual support network, including interlocking directorates. A *horizontal keiretsu* contains a group of companies in a variety of industries, usually headed by a bank. A *vertical keiretsu* consists of a major manufacturing company and its network of suppliers and supporting firms.

Keynesian The term used to describe interventionist macroeconomic policy where governments attempt to manage the level of aggregate demand and hence the major macroeconomic variables (inflation, economic growth, employment, and the balance of payments) in an economy.

Laissez-faire The term used, especially

during the nineteenth century, to describe a policy of free trade between nations. The term is also used to refer to free market policies in general.

Liberalism A political philosophy which advocates open democratic government and maintains that individual freedom should take priority over collective action.

Liberalization The opening of domestic markets or external trade to competition by removing regulations, laws, restrictive practices, and other obstacles to the operation of market forces. Liberalization is a broader term than deregulation.

Licensing An arrangement whereby a *licenser* agrees to sell to a *licensee* the right to use the licenser's intellectual property, including technical know-how, brand names, and patents, for a specified period of time in return for an agreed fee or royalty.

Logistics The process of managing the flow of materials into and out of an organization and controlling the movement of goods at all stages of manufacture and distribution.

Macroeconomic stabilization Government policies which maintain *fiscal stability* (something approaching a balanced budget, efficient tax collection, and manageable public debt) and *monetary stability* (price and exchange rate stability, and control of the money supply), generally regarded as a prerequisite to balanced economic growth.

Managed exchange rate A rate of exchange for a national currency which essentially floats against other currencies but which the authorities maintain close to an agreed rate either by buying or selling the currency or by raising or lowering interest rates.

Management contract A type of licensing agreement between one firm and another, whereby the contracting firm makes available its managerial expertise and some of its management personnel in training local managers for the efficient operation of a project for a specified period in return for an agreed fee.

Marketing mix The combination of factors which need to be considered when forming an effective marketing strategy. Conventional analysis of the marketing mix focuses on the 'four Ps': *product*, *price*, *promotion*, and *place*.

Mass privatization The sale or transfer of large numbers of state-owned enterprises to the private sector over a short period of time, a form of privatization used in Russia, the Czech Republic, and other countries in Eastern Europe.

Mercantilism An early view of international trade, still surprisingly prevalent in a variety of guises today, which holds that exports should be promoted and imports discouraged. This should be contrasted with the theory of comparative advantage which holds that all international trade is beneficial, both exports and imports, provided countries specialize according to their comparative efficiencies.

Monetarist The term used to describe government policy which combines a belief in free markets with a belief in the importance of controlling the money supply in order to maintain low inflation.

Monopolistic competition A market where large numbers of competing firms, with freedom to enter or leave the market, produce differentiated products, allowing each firm to vary its price to some extent.

Monopoly A pure monopoly is a market with a sole producer, protected by considerable entry barriers and with considerable influence over price. In practice, the term is also used where a small number of firms individually or collectively have a substantial market share.

Moral hazard In the context of international finance, moral hazard describes the problem which arises when governments become less careful in the stewardship of their economies or the regulation of financial markets when experience suggests that the international lending organizations will bail them out if things go wrong.

Most-favoured nation principle The GATT principle which means that member countries agree to treat all members in the same way as they treat their most-favoured trading partner—the principle of non-discrimination.

Multinational enterprise (MNE) Whilst precise definitions vary, in this book we define a MNE as an enterprise which extends its business activities into more than two countries with the aim of responding to worldwide opportunities for the most efficient employment of its firm-specific assets in pursuit of clearly defined aims and objectives.

Multiplier effect The 'ripple' effect of an increase in aggregate demand, such as an increase in investment or government expenditure, on the national or regional economy, which generates further income and demand each time it is spent by the recipient. The resulting effect on national income is a multiple of the original increase in aggregate demand. The higher the proportion of additional income which is spent (the *marginal propensity to consume*), the larger is the value of the multiplier.

Nomenklatura The name given to the political élite—public officials, managers of SOEs, and other senior party members—in the former Soviet Union and countries of Eastern Europe during the communist years. Whilst the situation in this region has now changed, some former members of the *nomenklatura* still hold important positions.

Nomenklatura privatization A form of privatization undertaken in Russia whereby SOEs were converted into private enterprises in which the major shareholders were former managers or public officials or agencies (members of the so-called *nomenklatura*).

Nominal exchange rate A measure of a national currency's international value in terms of another currency at a particular time.

Nuisance cost A cost incurred as a result of bureaucracy, corruption, or organized criminal activity when doing business in certain countries, which may have the effect of discouraging foreign direct investment.

Official financing The section of the capital and financial account of the balance of payments which records increases or decreases in a country's official foreign currency reserves or in its official foreign debts.

Oligopoly A market with significant entry barriers, dominated by a few large, interdependent firms each with a differentiated product.

Opportunity cost The cost of an activity measured in terms of the alternatives forgone.

Optimum currency area A group of countries operating a fixed exchange system which are highly integrated in terms of cross-border trade and where the factors of production move freely between them.

Perestroika The policy of 'restructuring', adopted by President Gorbachev in the former Soviet Union during the late 1980s, intended to introduce major economic reform to sort out the economic legacy of central planning but, in practice, the reforms were modest.

Perfect competition A textbook theory describing the ideal welfare-maximizing form of market structure, where consumers and producers have perfect knowledge and large numbers of competing firms producing a homogeneous product have complete freedom to enter or leave the market. Under such conditions, resources would be allocated and used efficiently, prices would reflect costs of production, and only 'normal profit' would be made, i.e. just sufficient to keep firms in the market.

'Picking winners' A term used to describe an interventionist industrial policy where a government supports a firm or industry which it thinks is likely to be a commercial success in the future.

Political union In its fullest sense, political union involves the unification of previously separate nations. A limited form of political union may also exist where two or more countries share common decision-making bodies and have common policies.

Portfolio investment The acquisition of stocks and shares, financial deposits, and other financial assets in order to earn a return on surplus funds.

Preferential trading agreement A loose form of economic integration allowing preferential access for the exports of specified countries—typically reduced tariffs or special quotas granted to developing countries.

Privatization The most common use of the term describes the sale of state-owned companies and other assets to the private sector, usually through the transfer of shares. The term is sometimes also used to describe (a) the removal of state regulations and restrictions (more commonly known as deregulation) and (b) the contracting out of 'public' services to the private sector.

Producer surplus The difference between the marginal cost of production and the market price. The producer surplus is therefore a welfare gain enjoyed by producers.

Purchasing power parity The valuation of foreign exchange rates on the basis of the amount of income or currency required to purchase a given 'basket' of goods in different countries, allowing an effective international comparison of GNP or GNP per capita.

Quota A quantitative restriction on the value or volume of imports allowed to enter a country.

Real exchange rate A measure of a national currency's international value in terms of another currency after taking account of the relative inflation rates in the two countries. The real exchange rate is sometimes used as a measure of international competitiveness.

Reciprocity principle The GATT principle which means that reductions in trade barriers should be made equally by all participating countries—a balanced move towards free trade.

Regional economic grouping A group of countries which have voluntarily come together to form a trading area or *trade bloc*.

Relationship marketing An approach to marketing which is concerned with the building up of long-term, mutually beneficial customer relationships. The seller hopes to gain repeat orders and effective feedback from the customer, while the customer feels more valued and can influence the development of the product.

Restructuring The process of overhauling the practices of SOEs or former SOEs in Russia and Eastern Europe, especially in relation to management and labour practices, the use of technology, the introduction of Western methods of accounting and financial control, and the use of modern sales and marketing techniques.

Segmentation The division of a market into groups of potential consumers with particular characteristics. These characteristics may include geographical location, age group, gender, income level, social group, occupation, education, and a number of other factors.

Share option A contract which provides an option to sell an amount of shares at a fixed price within a specified time.

Shock therapy ('big bang') An approach to reform adopted by some of the countries of Eastern Europe, notably Poland, whereby the reforms necessary for transition to a market economy were implemented within a very short period of time.

Single European Market The project initiated by the EU in 1985, and substantially completed by the end of 1992, which has created something approaching a common market between the countries of the European Economic Area (the EU and three of the EFTA countries).

Small-scale privatization The sale of state-owned shops, restaurants, and other small businesses to the private sector.

Social dumping The practice employed by some MNEs of closing a plant in a high-cost country and transferring their investment to a low-cost country, leaving unemployed workers behind.

Special drawing rights Additional drawing rights periodically allocated to members of the IMF which provide an extended credit facility allowing them to borrow additional amounts of foreign currency from the fund.

Special economic zone One of a number of regions in eastern and south-eastern China officially designated as areas of economic development.

Spontaneous privatization The gradual erosion of state control of industry in Hungary after the Company Law of 1988 and the Transformation Law of 1989, which permitted SOEs to create subsidiaries and allowed entire SOEs to transform into private companies respectively. In practice, ownership usually remained in the hands of state institutions, however.

Spot market A market where currencies or commodities are bought and sold for immediate delivery and payment.

STEP factor analysis An evaluation of the *sociocultural*, *technological*, *economic*, and *political* environments facing a firm.

Strategic alliance A non-equity co-operation agreement between two or more firms which is intended to promote their joint competitive advantage. Strategic alliances generally involve co-operation in one or more of three areas: production, research and development, and marketing.

Strategic trade policy A government policy aimed at protecting a domestic industry from imports or promoting its exports.

Structural adjustment programme An IMF aid package where the aid is conditional upon the recipient country undertaking specified structural economic reforms.

Structural funds EU funds designed to promote the development of Europe's disadvantaged regions. The structural funds include the European Regional Development Fund, European Social Fund, and the agricultural and fisheries guidance funds.

Sustainable development A term usually understood to mean economic growth which is consistent with the protection of the environment.

SWOT analysis An evaluation of a company's *strengths* and *weaknesses* and the *opportunities* and *threats* it faces in the external environment.

Synergy Joint effort or combined action which achieve more than the sum of their individual components.

Target zone A modified version of a flexible exchange rate system in which the central bank intervenes in the foreign exchange market to maintain the exchange rate within an agreed target zone or band, with clearly indicated upper and lower limits (such as the EU Exchange Rate Mechanism). A target zone is sometimes known as a *crawling peg* or *adjustable peg* exchange rate system.

Tariff An import or customs duty added to the value of goods imported into a country, usually calculated on a percentage basis.

Terms of trade The quantity of imports which can be purchased with a given quantity of exports.

Trade creation An increase in trade between the members of a regional economic grouping, where no trade previously took place, as a result of the removal of internal tariffs and other trade barriers.

Trade diversion Trade which is diverted from countries outside a regional economic grouping to countries inside as a result of the removal of internal tariffs and other trade barriers.

Trade suppression Trade which occurred before the establishment of a regional economic grouping but which has now ceased because the external tariff is higher than before and there is no exporter within the trading area who is efficient enough to replace an efficient external producer.

Transaction cost A cost incurred when making a transaction over and above the price of the goods or currency being bought. Examples of transaction costs include legal costs, search costs, and commission charges.

Transactions exposure An exchange rate risk resulting from currency fluctuations when a sales or purchase transaction has been undertaken in a foreign currency.

Transactions marketing An approach to marketing which views customers as one-off consumers of a product where the marketer's task is to persuade people to make a transaction on the basis of the product's features, price, and attractiveness at a particular place and time.

Transfer pricing The system of internal pricing used for transactions between one subsidiary or department of a company and another.

Translation exposure An exchange rate risk resulting from currency fluctuations when converting foreign currency financial statements into the currency of a parent company.

Treuhandanstalt The Treuhand, as it was commonly known, was set up by the government of the GDR in early 1990 to take over the assets of SOEs targeted for privatization and to identify possible purchasers. The Treuhand continued in this role after the unification of East and West Germany until 1994.

Triad or trade triangle The term sometimes used to describe the three groups of leading industrial nations: North America (especially the USA), the EU, and Japan, now sometimes known as the *quad* nations to include the USA and Canada separately.

Trilateralism The term used to describe international cooperation between the Triad nations to promote a stable world economic order.

Turnkey project An agreement under which a firm or consortium of firms undertake to design, build, equip, and train personnel to operate an entire production or service facility before turning it over (that is, handing over 'the key') to its owner, which may be a private company or the government of the host country.

Vertical integration A takeover or merger between firms at different stages of production.

Visible trade Exports and imports of goods.

Voluntary export restraint A type of import quota imposed with the agreement of the exporting country.

Voucher privatization A form of mass privatization, pioneered by the Czech government, where citizens receive an allocation of vouchers which can be exchanged for shares in companies being privatized.

Washington consensus The prevalent view of the major international financial institutions, notably the IMF, that economic development is best achieved through free trade and market liberalization, following the example of the industrialized countries.

Welfare gain/loss The net gain or loss to society as a whole (including both producers and consumers) after taking into account changes in the consumer surplus, producer surplus, and deadweight loss resulting from an increase or decrease in prices, taxes, or tariffs, etc.

X-efficiency The use of a resource, especially labour, to its maximum potential. In the absence of competition, X-efficiency is less likely to be achieved as workers may be motivated by the desire for a quiet life or the pursuit of leisure.

Zaibatsu Conglomerate companies, many of them family-owned and some large and powerful, which were dominant in Japan before World War II.

Index

A

ABB 34
absolute advantage 218, 219, 229
acculturation 103
acquis communautaire 343
ACP group of countries 145–6, 149
African Development Bank 139
Airbus 363, 365, 371
Alfa Laval AB 30
Algeria 110, 111
Amazon (bookseller) 134
American Standard 280
Andean Pact 162–3
Anglo-Saxon model 174–5, 181–2,
    183, 257, 258, 283, 368
Apple Computers 38
'architecture' 281–2
Argentina 193, 198, 202, 204
Asia Pacific Economic Cooperation
    (APEC) 158, 164–5, 366
Asian Development Bank 139
Asian financial crisis (1997–8) 84–5,
    138, 139, 192, 204–7, 251, 257
Association of South-East Asian
    Nations (ASEAN) 85, 124, 125, 149,
    151, 164, 192, 366
Atlanta Airport Authority 19
attitudes 111–13
Australia 165
Austria 13, 254
Austrian School of Economics 130,
    201–2
Avis car rental 18

B

balance of payments 48, 49, 226–8
Bayer 34
Belarus 89
Belgium and Luxembourg 13, 173,
    184
Benetton 41

'big bang' 385–6, 456–7
    see also 'shock therapy'
Body Shop 18
Boeing 115, 174, 229, 288, 365, 371
bonds 69–70
BMW 188, 266, 369
BP 31, 175
brand 'DNA' 279
Brazil 86, 193, 202, 254
bribery and corruption 120–1
Bridgestone 429
British Airports Authority (BAA)
    19
British Airways 288
British Leyland 288, 368
British Steel (Corus) 32
Brunei 165
Budget car rental 18
Bulgaria 443
Burger King 18, 279
Burma (Myanmar) 125, 164

C

Cadbury Schweppes 35
Cambodia 164
Canada 162, 165, 173, 199
Canon 230
capital 67–8, 69–70, 71
capital account 226, 227–8
capital arbitrage theory 263
Caricom 163
cash flow 67–8, 71
Cassis de Dijon case, 321
Caterpillar 32, 52, 280
Cecchini Report 156, 157, 323, 328
Central American Common Market
    152, 163
Central European Free Trade Area
    161, 193
centrally planned economies 87

CFA Franc Zone 166
chaebol 203, 205, 206, 207
Chile 113, 165, 193, 198, 202, 204
China 9–10, 23, 28, 88, 99, 129, 165,
    173, 174, 180, 192, 194, 204, 252,
    254, 255, 265–6, 280, 366
Chorion 20
Christian Aid 123
Coca-Cola 16, 27, 38, 105, 115, 142,
    174, 279
codetermination (*Mitbestimmung*)
    67, 184
Cold War 382–3, 438
collectivism 119
common external tariff 151, 155,
    160, 320
common market 152–3, 306
Common Market for East and
    Southern Africa (COMESA) 166
Commonwealth of Independent
    States (CIS) 88, 89, 161
communism, collapse of 377–84
company evaluation 57–8
company mission 56, 57
comparative advantage 44, 102, 131,
    218, 219–21, 224, 229, 262–3
competition 8, 58, 60, 121–2, 130,
    156, 333
competitive advantage 21, 22, 33,
    38–40, 41, 58, 72, 81, 181, 279, 281,
    282, 286, 288
Concorde 363, 368
contestable markets theory 201–2
contract 96
core competences 58, 59, 278, 279
corporate restructuring 401–2
corporate strategy 56, 59
corporatization 402–3
Council for Mutual Economic
    Assistance (CMEA) 88, 160–1,
    457–8

Council of Europe 141, 159, 296, 313
Council of the European Union
    (Council of Ministers) 301–2
countertrade 19, 87–8
Crédit Lyonnais 288
Cuba 135
culture 6, 7, 63, 101–20, 182, 200,
    257, 275, 283–4
    cross-cultural literacy 106
    cultural adjustment 114–17
    cultural assessment 118–20
    cultural awareness 102, 114
    cultural sensitivity 102, 114
currency convertibility/
    stabilization 388
currency appreciation 237, 241
currency depreciation 237, 241,
    277
current account 226–8
Curry's 280
customs 114
customs union 151–2, 306
cyber currency 5
Cyprus 339–40
Czech Republic (and former
    Czechoslovakia) 64, 88, 195
    EU accession 442
    FDI 428–9, 430
    motor vehicle industry 422–5,
        427
    privatization 401–2

D

Daewoo 179, 427
Daimler-Chrysler (Daimler-Benz) 31,
    34, 188, 288, 369
debt problem 208–9
degree of openness 12–13, 226
Denmark 13
dependency theory 197
derivatives 250
devaluation 287
diseconomies of scale 43
Disney Corporation 41, 281
diversified MNE 35, 40
Dixons 25
documentation 73
dumping 62, 92, 94, 132–3
Dunning's eclectic paradigm 44–7,
    264

duty-free goods 330
dynamic effects of integration 158,
    323
Dyson 40, 41

E

EASDAQ 70
East Africa Cooperation (EAC) 166
East Asian model 177, 200, 283
economic and monetary union
    (EMU) 68, 245, 299, 300, 341, 342,
    343, 344–6
    convergence criteria 344, 346
    accession of Eastern Europe
        444–5
Economic Community of West
    African States (ECOWAS) 166
economic growth, extensive vs.
    intensive 379–80
economic union 153, 306
economies of scale 24, 35, 38, 39, 43,
    156–7, 222, 224–5
economies of scope 35, 43
education 108
Egypt 110
Electricité de France 428
Electrolux 40
electronic commerce 128, 133–4
Elf Aquitaine 34
emerging economies 90–1, 191–213
employment strategy 65–6
enculturation 103
endogenous growth theory 198–9
environmental protection 132, 135,
    143–4
entry barriers 39–40, 42, 49
equity 70
Estonia 195
ethics 120–2
ethnocentric MNE 33
ethnocentrism 117, 122
Euratom 297
euro — see single European
    currency
eurocurrency 69, 352
Euro-fighter project 363
Euro-Mediterranean Agreement
    165, 364–5
Europe Agreements 84, 160, 439–40
European Bank for Reconstruction

and Development (EBRD) 128,
    138–9, 447
European Coal and Steel
    Community (ECSC) 297
European Central Bank 245, 303–4
European Commission 302–3
European Council 302
European Court of Justice 93, 303
European Economic Area 160, 298
European Free Trade Association
    (EFTA) 151, 160, 298
European model 176, 183–4, 283
European monetary union — see
    economic and monetary union
European Parliament 303
European political union 356
European Union 22, 81, 148–9, 151,
    152, 153, 155, 158, 159, 160, 175–6,
    284, 295–374
    budget 305
    citizenship 349
    cohesion fund 313, 348
    Common Agricultural Policy
        (CAP) 299, 306–8, 362, 441
    Common Fisheries Policy (CFP)
        308
    Common Foreign and Security
        Policy 347, 348
    competition policy 309–12, 332
    consumer affairs 315
    development aid 364
    directives 300
    education 107, 315
    employment policy 313–4
    enlargement 304, 317–8, 339–40,
        435–49
    environment 315–6
    extension of powers 348–9
    external relations 364–6
    external trade 361–2
    financial assistance (PHARE,
        TEMPUS, TACIS) 446–7, 466,
        468
    history and development
        298–300
    industrial policy 308–9
    institutions 300–4
    justice and home affairs 347, 348
    origins and aims 296–8
    regional policy 312–3, 332
    regulations 300

research and development policy 309

subsidiarity 349

SME policy 310

social policy 313

sovereignty 339, 355

structural funds 312-3

transport policy 314

exchange exposure 68-9

Exchange Rate Mechanism (ERM) 244, 247, 325, 341-2

exchange rate systems 241-5

adjustable peg exchange rate system — see target zone

crawling peg exchange rate system — see target zone

flexible (or floating) exchange rate system 241-2

fixed exchange rate system 242-3

managed exchange rate system 243

target zone 243-4

Exxon 31, 34

export financing 70

exports/exporting 4-5, 12-13, 42-3, 61, 173

F

factor endowments 7, 45, 199-200, 225, 262-3, 285-6

factor productivity 157

federalism 154, 349

femininity 119

Fiat 31, 34, 427

financial management 67-9

Finland 13

firm-specific assets (FSAs) 22, 28, 30, 32, 33, 38-9, 40-4, 45, 58, 102, 278-9, 281

Ford 24, 34, 44, 115, 174, 188, 369

foreign direct investment (FDI) 4-5, 13-15, 39, 40, 42-3, 45-6, 47, 49, 61, 180, 181, 182, 193, 195, 200-1, 249-64, 268

determinants 255-62

global trends 253-4

government policy 257-8

impact 254-5

meaning 251

measurement 251-2

theoretical explanations 262-4

foreign direct investment (FDI) in Eastern Europe 415-34

acquisitions 416

contribution to economic development 420-2

effect of Russia's financial crisis 468-9

greenfield investment 418-19

joint venture agreements 389, 418

mafia activity 466-8

motives for 415-16

motor vehicle industry 418-20, 422-6

nature and availability 418-20

need to establish a private sector 463-4

problems 455-62

role of EBRD 447-8

role of entrepreneurship 462-4, 465-8

role of privatization 400-1, 406, 422

foreign exchange market 239-40

spot market 240

forward market 240

foreign exchange rates 67, 68, 206, 232-40

effective exchange rates 233-4

nominal exchange rates 233, 234-7

real exchange rates 234

'Fortress Europe' 92, 93, 155, 361-3

forward exchange contract 250

four 'Ps' – see marketing mix

France 13, 14, 173, 184-5, 253, 254, 257

free movement of:

capital 152, 322, 326, 331

goods 152, 322, 326-8

persons 152, 322, 326, 329-31

services 152, 322, 326, 328-9

free trade 128-31, 143, 197-8, 218

free trade area 149-51, 306

Free Trade Area of the Americas (FTAA) 164

franchising 17-18, 61, 115

Fuji 176, 189

futures contract 250

Fuyo 178, 189

functionalism 154

G

G7/G8 86, 141, 175, 177, 179, 181

General Agreement on Tariffs and Trade (GATT) 4, 39, 85, 92, 128, 131, 134, 136, 137, 139-40, 167, 362, 364, 365

General Agreement on Trade in Services (GATS) 140

General Electric 30, 34

General Motors 34, 265, 427

geocentic MNE 33, 50

Generalized System of Preferences 361, 364

German Democratic Republic (GDR) privatization 405-6

Treuhand 406

Germany 13, 14, 67, 71, 83, 88, 154, 173, 174, 184, 229, 253, 254, 261, 283, 367, 370

Gillette 27

glasnost 88, 383-4

Glaxo-Welcome 288

global economy 91-2

global governance 135-6, 144

global MNE/firm 50

globalization xvii-xix, 10, 14, 50, 127, 135, 166-7, 253

'Gorbachev factor' 378, 383-4

government intervention 363, 368-70

in East Asia 203-4

gradualism 384-6, 456-7 (Slovenia and Croatia)

Greece 13

H

harmonization 93, 153, 327, 328

Heckscher-Ohlin theory 131, 218, 221, 224, 262-3

hedging 240

Heinz 279, 428

Hilton Hotels 18, 37

Hitachi 41

Hoechst 34

Hofstede on culture 103, 118

Honda 178

Honeywell Europe 357-8

Hong Kong 47, 165, 173, 177–8, 192, 194, 199, 203, 254
Hoover 40
horizontal integration 35, 40, 43–4, 264
Hospitality Inns 18
human resource management 63–7
Hungary 87–8, 195, 200
  privatization 399–400
  FDI 428
Hyundai 179, 203, 288, 427

I

IBM 34, 230
ICI 32
import substitution 48, 193, 203
imports/importing 12–13, 173
income similarities theory 224
India 178, 195, 202, 284
individualism 118
Indonesia 124, 125, 165, 178, 192, 194, 204
inflation
  Eastern Europe 390
  versus growth 460–2
information age 133
ING Barings 428
innovation 63, 281
intellectual property 15–17, 41, 95
Inter-American Development Bank 139
Intercontinental Hotels 18
inter-governmental decision making 347
internalization 21–2, 25, 36, 38, 40–4, 262, 264
international accounting 71–2
international competitiveness 234, 272–91, 333
  determinants 278–88
  in European Union 367–8, 373
  meaning 273–5
  measurement 275–7
  national characteristics 283–8
  role of government 287–8
International Court of Justice 136
International Development Association 138, 210

International Finance Corporation 138
International Labour Organization 122
International Monetary Fund 10, 28, 85–6, 128, 134, 137–8, 158, 175, 197, 198, 201, 205, 208, 210
  aid for economic transition 448
  on privatization 396–7
  support for currency convertibility 388
international taxation 71–2
international trade theory 131, 218–26
Internet 63, 95, 128, 133
intra-industry trade 224–5
invisible trade 227–8
Iraq 135
Ireland 13, 260
Israel 111, 204
Italy 13, 83, 110, 173, 185, 286, 370

J

Jaguar 224
Japan 13, 14, 67, 71, 81, 92, 93, 102, 132, 165, 174, 175, 176–7, 186–7, 199, 200, 203, 204, 206, 207, 223, 229, 253, 254, 259, 283, 284, 286, 296, 368–9
Japanese management practices 9, 61–2, 66–7, 177
Japanese model — see East Asian model
JCB 52–3
joint venture (agreement) 61, 265–6, 389
  development of motor vehicle industry 422–6
  see also foreign direct investment

K

Keynesian 202–3
keiretsu 132, 175, 178, 188–9, 200, 203, 207, 282, 368
Kellogg 279
Kimberley-Clark 280
Kodak 41
Komatsu 52

Kuwait 283

L

labour relations 66–7
labour standards 67, 121–2, 132, 135, 142–3
language 107–8
Latin American Free Trade Area (LAFTA) 162
Latin American Integration Association (LAIA) 162
least developed countries (LDCs) 207, 210
legal environment 7, 92–8
legal systems 92–3
Lego 41
Levi 27, 105, 115, 122, 132
licensing 15–17, 40, 42–3, 61
loans 69
logistics 56, 62, 72–4
Lomé Agreement 133, 149, 361, 362, 364

M

Maastricht Treaty 86, 153, 260, 299, 342, 343–9
macroeconomic stabilization 202–3, 260, 287, 386–9
  creation of a private sector 389
  external liberalization 388, 456–7, 460–1
  inflation 460–2
  institutional reform 464–5
  monetary and fiscal liberalization 387–8, 456–7
  price liberalization 386–7, 456–7
  problems 389–91
  role of entrepreneurship 462–3
  Russia's financial crisis 468–9
  successes and failures 389–91
  unemployment 458–60
mafia and corruption 390–1, 465–8
Malaysia 124, 125, 165, 178, 192, 194, 204
Malta 340
management contract 18–19, 61
Manchester United Football Club 281
manners 113

maquiladora industries 162
market economies 87
market imperfections 37–40
market screening and selection 57, 59
market segmentation 60–1
marketing mix 56, 61, 62
marketing strategy 56, 57, 61–3
Marks and Spencer 25, 35, 282
Mars 429
masculinity 119
McDonalds 7, 17, 18, 42, 49, 106, 174, 279
McDonnell Douglas 371
mercantilism 129, 218, 274
Mercedes 224
Mercosur 132, 151, 152, 155, 163, 366
mergers and acquisitions 14–15, 49, 61, 334
Mexico 138, 162, 165, 193, 204, 254
Microsoft 27, 41, 115, 174, 229, 279
Mitsubishi 34, 176, 188–9
Mobil 31, 34
mode of entry 61
monetarism/monetarist 82, 202–3
monetary union 153, 160
  see also economic and monetary union
monopolistic competition 36–7
monopoly 36, 47, 48
moral hazard 205
motor vehicle industry (in Eastern Europe) 422–30
multinational enterprise 10–11, 27–54, 142, 143, 144, 249, 254, 352–3
mutual recognition 321, 331, 327, 328, 329

N

North American Free Trade Agreement (NAFTA) 4, 85, 151, 158, 162, 182, 284
NASDAQ 70
national champions 288
neoclassical growth theory 197–8
Nestlé 34, 62, 288
net present value 71
Netherlands 13, 173, 184, 225, 254
networking 31–2

New Economic Mechanism
  USSR (post 1921) 377–9
  Hungary (1968) 384–5
New Transatlantic Marketplace 164
New Zealand 165, 174, 202
Nigeria 199, 254
Nike 9, 16, 27, 122
Nissan 34, 46, 81, 157, 178, 188–9, 288
Nokia 288
Nomura 429
non-tariff barriers 131–3, 152, 156, 262
  see also trade barriers
Nordic Council 331
North Atlantic Treaty Organization (NATO) 135, 141, 390, 438, 442–4
Northern Ireland 111, 257
Norway 199, 254
nuisance costs 257

O

Odebrecht 32
Organization for Economic Cooperation and Development (OECD) 28, 140, 177
Organization for European Economic Cooperation (OEEC) 159, 161
official financing 228
oligopoly 36–7, 40, 47
Oneworld Alliance 267
OPEC 141, 195
opportunity cost 220

P

Pakistan 110
Papua New Guinea 165
PepsiCo (Pepsi Cola) 37, 38, 115, 210, 279
perestroika 88, 383–4, 407, 437–8
perfect competition 36, 38, 130
Peru 193, 198
Peugeot-Citroën 280, 369
PHARE - see European Union
Philippines 124, 125, 165, 194, 204
Philip Morris 429
Philips 34, 41, 289–90

'picking winners' 287–8, 368–70, 463
Pilkington Glass Company 40
Pizza Hut 18, 279
Poland 87–8, 89, 193, 195, 202
  EU accession 442–3
  FDI 426–30
  motor vehicle industry 422–6
  privatization 402–4
  unemployment 443–4
political union 153–4
polycentric MNE 33
Porter's determinants of national advantage ('Porter's Diamond') 225–6, 285–7, 333
portfolio investment 33, 250–1
Portugal 13, 257
power distance 118
'Prague Spring' (1968) 395
Preferential Trade Area (PTA) 166
preferential trading agreement 149, 150
prices 155–6
pricing 62
privatization 4, 9, 48, 82, 83, 89, 193, 198, 266
  Czechoslovakia 401–2
  Eastern Europe 394–412
  GDR 405–6, 457
  Hungary 399–400
  Poland 402–4
  Romania 404–5
  USSR (Russia) 406–9
  'insider privatization' 408
  role of EBRD 447
  utilities in Eastern Europe 409–10
proactive firm 21–2
product differentiation 36–40
product liability 96–7
product life-cycle theory 222–4, 263–4
product standards 327
protectionism 31, 39, 92, 128, 195, 218, 365
purchasing power parity 238–9, 277

Q

quotas 129–30, 131–2, 149, 262, 365
  see also trade barriers

R

reactive firm 21–2
recruitment and selection 64–5
regional economic grouping 148, 158, 159–67
regional integration 10, 135–6, 148–70
relationship marketing 62–3, 261
religion 110–11
Renault 188, 288, 369
reputation 279–80
risk insurance 85
Rolex 115
Rolls Royce 15, 266, 369
Rolls Royce Aerospace 266
Romania
    EU accession 443
    privatization 404–5
Rostow's 'stages of economic development' 196–7
Rover 264, 369
rules of origin 94, 132
Russia 86, 89, 90, 161, 174, 205, 257
    FDI 429–30
    financial crisis (August 1998) 468–9
    mafia 466–8
    motor vehicle industry 425–6
    privatization 406–9

S

Safeway 123
Sainsbury 123
Samsung 179, 427
Saudi Arabia 102, 110, 283
savings and investment 200–1
Scandinavian model 184
Schengen Agreement 329
SEAT 83
share option 250
Shell 31, 34, 43, 175, 210
'shock therapy' 89, 202, 391, 456–7
    see also 'big bang'
Siemens 175, 252
silent trade 4
Singapore 124, 165, 177–8, 192, 194, 200, 203, 284
Single European Act 300, 322

single European currency 68, 160, 244–5, 247, 345, 349–55, 357–8, 444–5
    see also economic and monetary union
Single European Market 8–9, 23, 39, 79, 80, 91, 95, 152–3, 156–7, 160, 320–37
    main measures 326–31
SKF 31
Skoda 266, 288
Slovakia (see also Czechoslovakia) 195
    EU accession 443
    FDI 429
Slovenia 195
small and medium-sized enterprises (SMEs) 185, 261, 335–6, 353, 389
Social Charter/Social Chapter 97, 313, 347–8
social market economy 184
social systems 111
'Solidarity' 395–6
Sony 16, 32, 41, 176, 288
Soros, George 438–9
South Africa 254
South Korea 47, 165, 173, 179, 192, 194, 200, 203, 204, 205, 261, 284
Southern African Customs Union (SACU) 166
Soviet model of growth 379–80
Soviet Union (USSR) 88, 154, 161, 174
    Cold War 382–3, 437
    communism, collapse of 377–84
    'Gorbachev factor' 377–8, 383–4
    motor vehicle industry 425–6
    privatization 406–9
    see also Russia
Spain 13, 83, 185–6, 199, 257, 269
standardization 8, 62
Star Alliance 267
state-owned enterprises 385, 386, 387, 397, 398, 399, 400
static effects of integration 156–7, 323
STEP factor (PEST) analysis 58, 80
strategic alliance 38, 46, 266–7, 268
strategic trade policy 133

sub-Saharan Africa 207
Sumitomo 52
sustainable development 136
Sweden 13, 175
Switzerland 71, 175, 229, 254, 283, 340
SWOT analysis 24, 57

T

TACIS 446
Taiwan 47, 165, 192, 194, 200, 201, 203–4, 255
tariffs 149–52, 128–31, 154–5, 156, 262, 320
    see also trade barriers
technology transfer 47, 49, 94–5
TESCO 123
Thailand 124, 139, 165, 192, 194, 204, 205, 206
'tiger economies' 191–3, 197, 198, 199, 200, 202, 204, 206–7
Toyota 34, 69, 176, 178, 188, 262, 265, 288, 369
trade balance 226
trade barriers 93–5, 128, 129, 131–3, 157, 262
trade bloc - see regional economic grouping
trade creation 154–5
trade diversion 154–5
trade liberalization 4, 9–10, 14, 23, 39, 48, 50, 128, 129, 134, 138, 152, 160, 193, 198, 201–2, 253, 284
Trade-Related Aspects of Intellectual Property Rights (TRIPS) 140
trade suppression 155
training 65, 370
Trans-European Networks 314
transaction costs 42, 43, 102, 262, 264, 350, 353
transaction marketing 62
transfer price 62
transnational corporation 29
transport and distribution 72–3
Travelodge 18
triad nations 13, 85, 91, 173–4, 181
Turkey 19, 102, 105, 110, 151, 195, 199, 340

turnkey project 19–20

U

Uganda 198, 210
Ukraine 89, 199
uncertainty avoidance 119
unemployment (in Eastern Europe)
    458–60
Unilever 31, 34, 175, 210
United Kingdom 13, 14, 71, 98, 155,
    173, 174, 202, 227, 253, 254, 257,
    284, 370
United Nations 10, 29, 128, 134, 135,
    136–7, 143, 175, 197
    UNCTAD 136, 197, 208, 209, 364
    UNESCO 109, 136
    UNHCR 136
Uruguay 193, 204
USA 14, 71, 91, 93, 162, 165, 173,
    174–5, 182, 199, 223, 229, 252,
    253–4, 257, 283, 296
US-Canada Free Trade Agreement
    161–2

V

value creation 274
values 111
venture capital 70
vertical integration 35, 40, 43–4,
    49, 264
Vietnam 125, 164
Visegrad Agreement 161
visible trade 226
Volkswagen 15, 34, 64, 83, 175, 266,
    288, 369, 427
Volvo 288, 369
VSZ (Slovakia) 429

W

Washington consensus 208–9
welfare loss 129–30
Western European Union (WEU)
    296
Whirlpool 280
Wings Alliance 267
World Bank 85–6, 134, 137–8, 175,
    197, 198, 201, 205, 210
World Health Organization 136
World Trade Organization 4, 9–10,
    39, 85, 86, 122, 128, 129, 132, 134,
    136, 139–40, 143, 145–6, 158, 175,
    181, 198, 201, 284, 362

Y

Yamaha 176